SCREENTIME

ALSO BY JERRY SCOTT AND JIM BORGMAN

Zits: Sketchbook 1
Growth Spurt: Zits Sketchbook 2
Don't Roll Your Eyes at Me, Young Man!: Zits Sketchbook 3
Are We an "Us"?: Zits Sketchbook 4
Zits Unzipped: Zits Sketchbook 5
Busted!: Zits Sketchbook 6
Road Trip: Zits Sketchbook 7
Teenage Tales: Zits Sketchbook No. 8
Thrashed: Zits Sketchbook No. 9
Pimp My Lunch: Zits Sketchbook No. 10
Are We Out of the Driveway Yet?: Zits Sketchbook No. 11
Rude, Crude, and Tattooed: Zits Sketchbook No. 12
Jeremy and Mom
Pierced
Lust and Other Uses for Spare Hormones
Jeremy & Dad
You're Making That Face Again
Drive!
Triple Shot, Double Pump, No Whip Zits
Zits en Concert
Peace, Love, and Wi-Fi
Zits Apocalypse
Extra Cheesy Zits
Dance Like Everybody's Watching!
Not Sparking Joy

TREASURIES

Humongous Zits
Big Honkin' Zits
Zits: Supersized
Random Zits
Crack of Noon
Alternative Zits
My Bad
Sunday Brunch
What Was That All About?: 20 Years of Strips and Stories

GIFT BOOK

A Zits Guide to Living with Your Teenager

SCREENTIME

A ZITS® Treasury by Jerry Scott and Jim Borgman

Andrews McMeel
PUBLISHING®

For Attikus and Lucien

—JB

To Cady Lane Scott, high school graduate

—JS

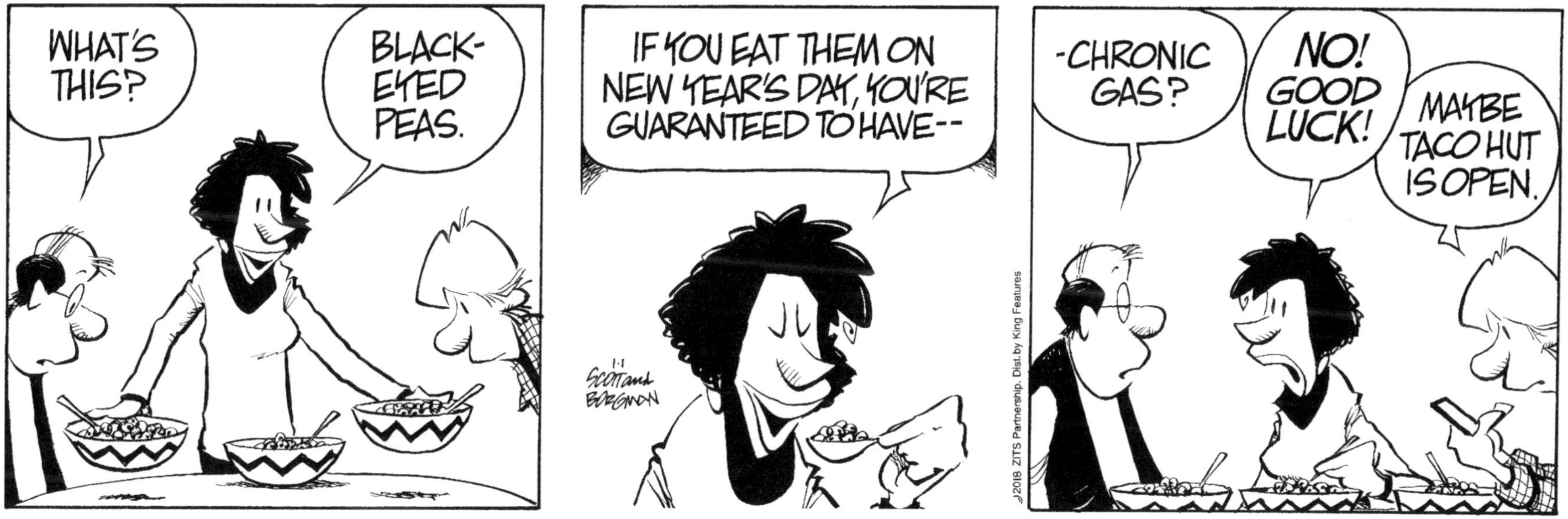
WHAT'S THIS?
BLACK-EYED PEAS.
IF YOU EAT THEM ON NEW YEAR'S DAY, YOU'RE GUARANTEED TO HAVE--
1·1 SCOTT and BORGMAN
©2018 ZITS Partnership. Dist. by King Features
-CHRONIC GAS?
NO! GOOD LUCK!
MAYBE TACO HUT IS OPEN.

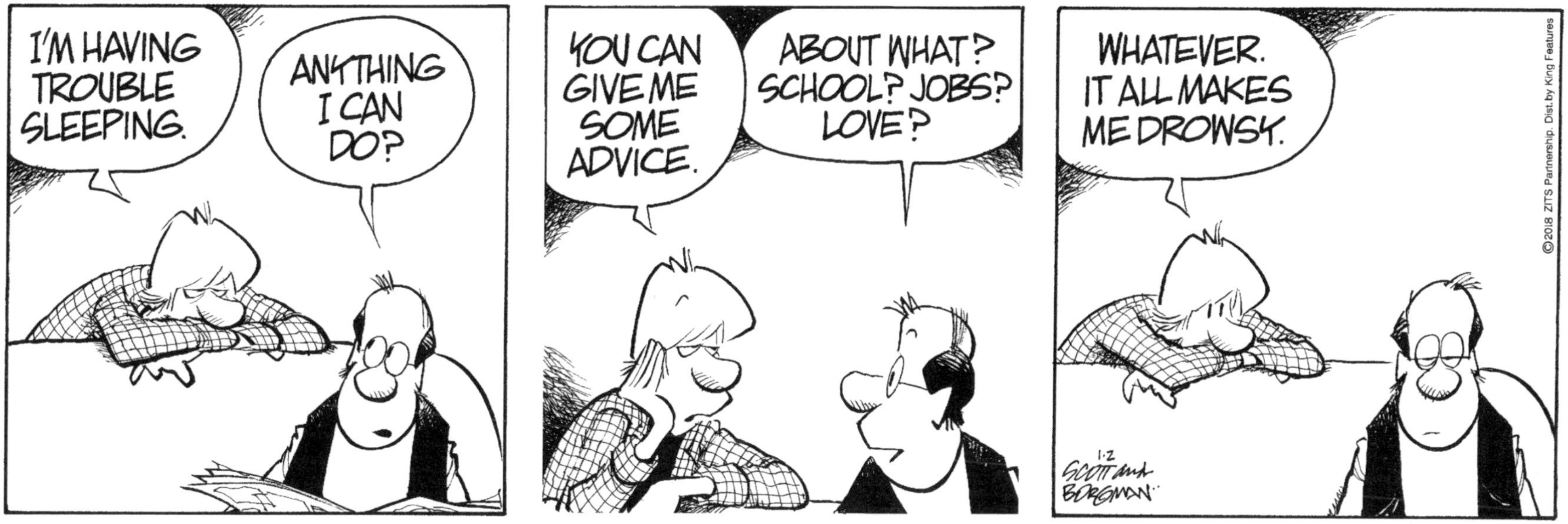
I'M HAVING TROUBLE SLEEPING.
ANYTHING I CAN DO?
YOU CAN GIVE ME SOME ADVICE.
ABOUT WHAT? SCHOOL? JOBS? LOVE?
WHATEVER. IT ALL MAKES ME DROWSY.
©2018 ZITS Partnership. Dist. by King Features
1·2 SCOTT and BORGMAN

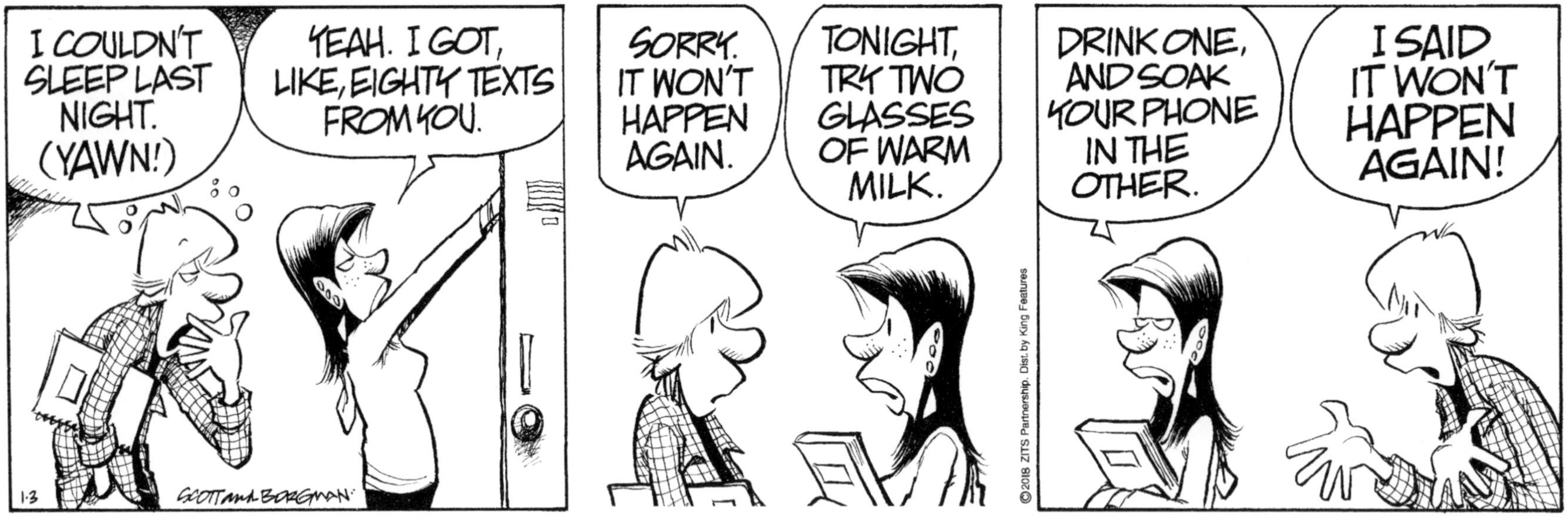
I COULDN'T SLEEP LAST NIGHT. (YAWN!)
YEAH. I GOT, LIKE, EIGHTY TEXTS FROM YOU.
1·3
SCOTT and BORGMAN
SORRY. IT WON'T HAPPEN AGAIN.
TONIGHT, TRY TWO GLASSES OF WARM MILK.
© 2018 ZITS Partnership. Dist. by King Features
DRINK ONE, AND SOAK YOUR PHONE IN THE OTHER.
I SAID IT WON'T HAPPEN AGAIN!

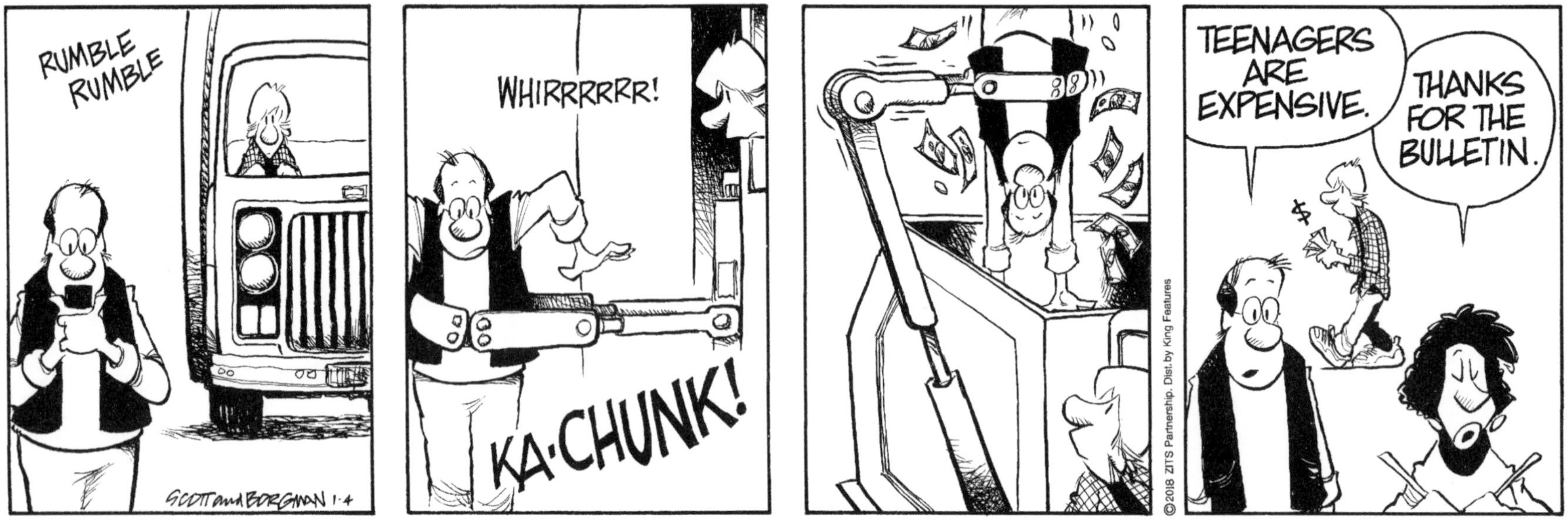
RUMBLE RUMBLE
SCOTT and BORGMAN 1·4
WHIRRRRRR!
KA·CHUNK!
©2018 ZITS Partnership. Dist. by King Features
TEENAGERS ARE EXPENSIVE.
THANKS FOR THE BULLETIN.

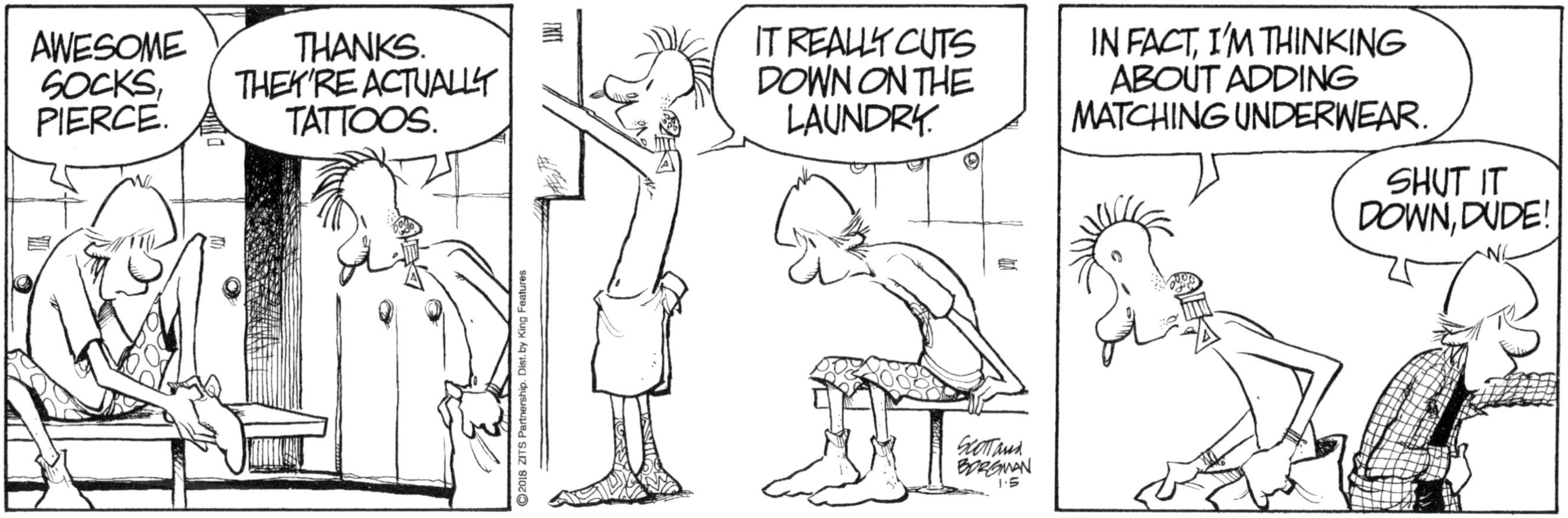
AWESOME SOCKS, PIERCE.
THANKS. THEY'RE ACTUALLY TATTOOS.
©2018 ZITS Partnership. Dist. by King Features
IT REALLY CUTS DOWN ON THE LAUNDRY.
SCOTT and BORGMAN 1·5
IN FACT, I'M THINKING ABOUT ADDING MATCHING UNDERWEAR.
SHUT IT DOWN, DUDE!

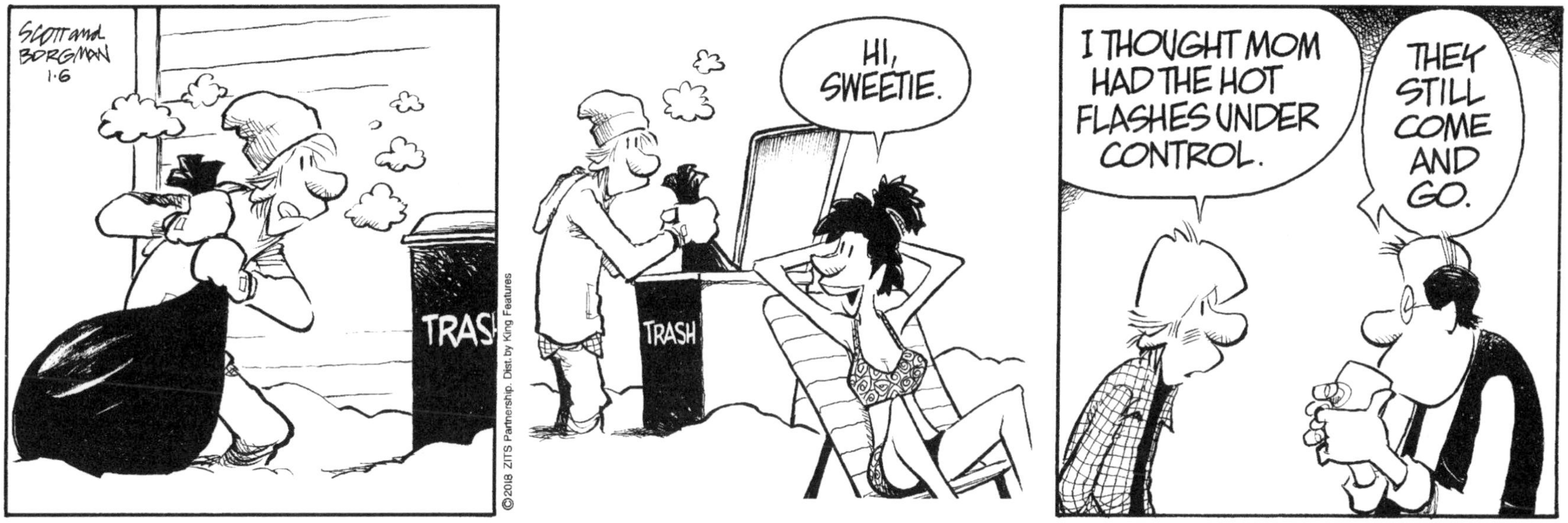
SCOTT and BORGMAN 1·6
TRASH
©2018 ZITS Partnership. Dist. by King Features
TRASH
HI, SWEETIE.
I THOUGHT MOM HAD THE HOT FLASHES UNDER CONTROL.
THEY STILL COME AND GO.

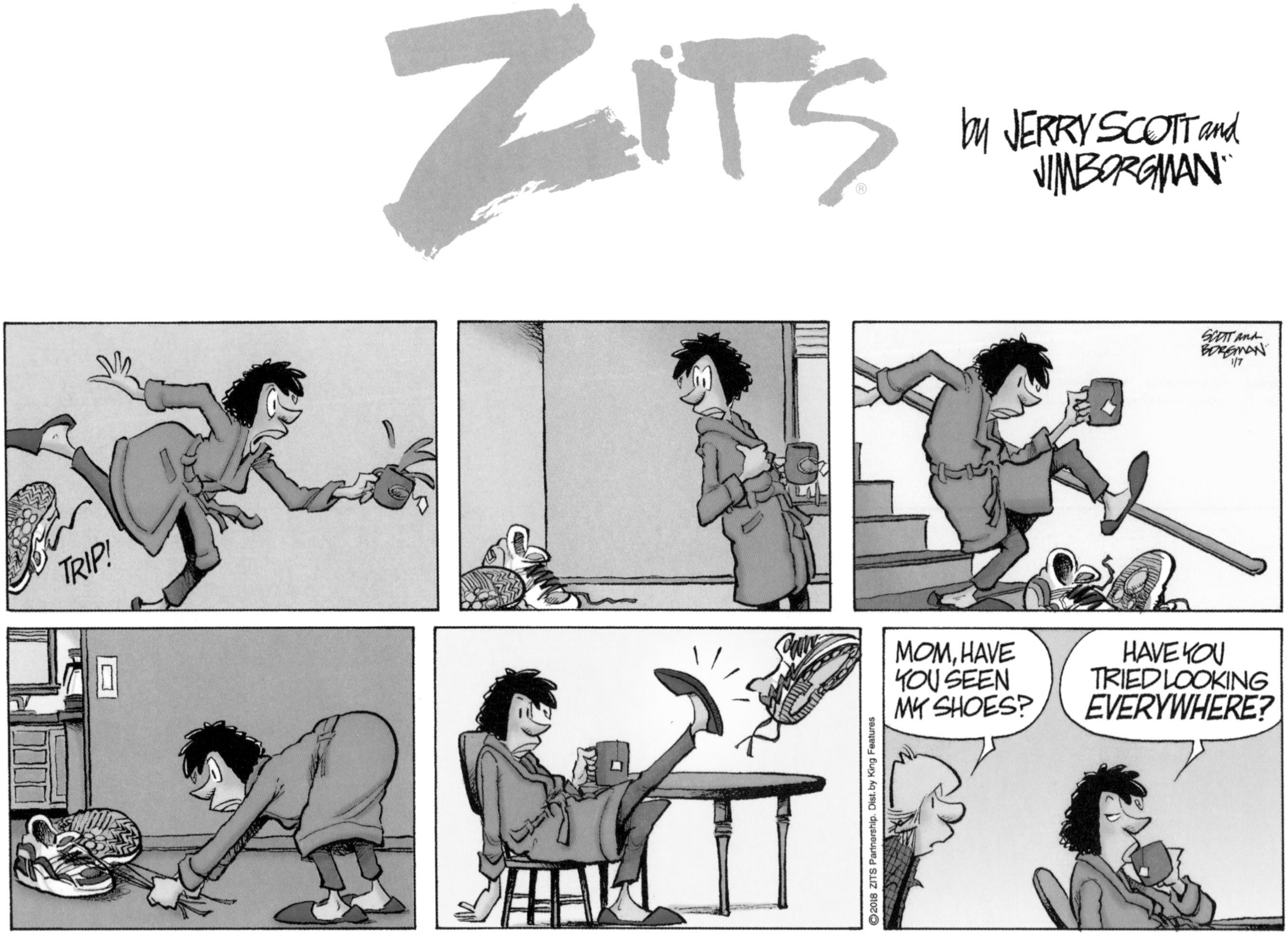
ZITS
by JERRY SCOTT and JIM BORGMAN
TRIP!
SCOTT and BORGMAN 1/7
©2018 ZITS Partnership. Dist. by King Features
MOM, HAVE YOU SEEN MY SHOES?
HAVE YOU TRIED LOOKING EVERYWHERE?

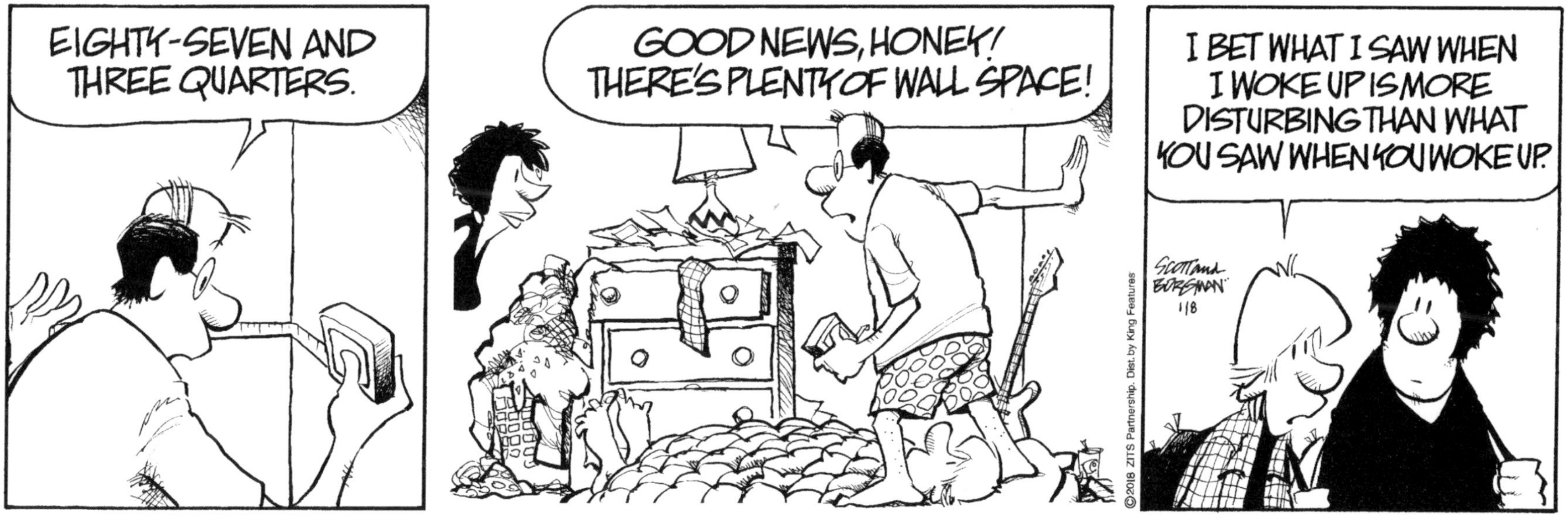
EIGHTY-SEVEN AND THREE QUARTERS.
GOOD NEWS, HONEY! THERE'S PLENTY OF WALL SPACE!
I BET WHAT I SAW WHEN I WOKE UP IS MORE DISTURBING THAN WHAT YOU SAW WHEN YOU WOKE UP.
SCOTT and BORGMAN 1/8
©2018 ZITS Partnership. Dist. by King Features

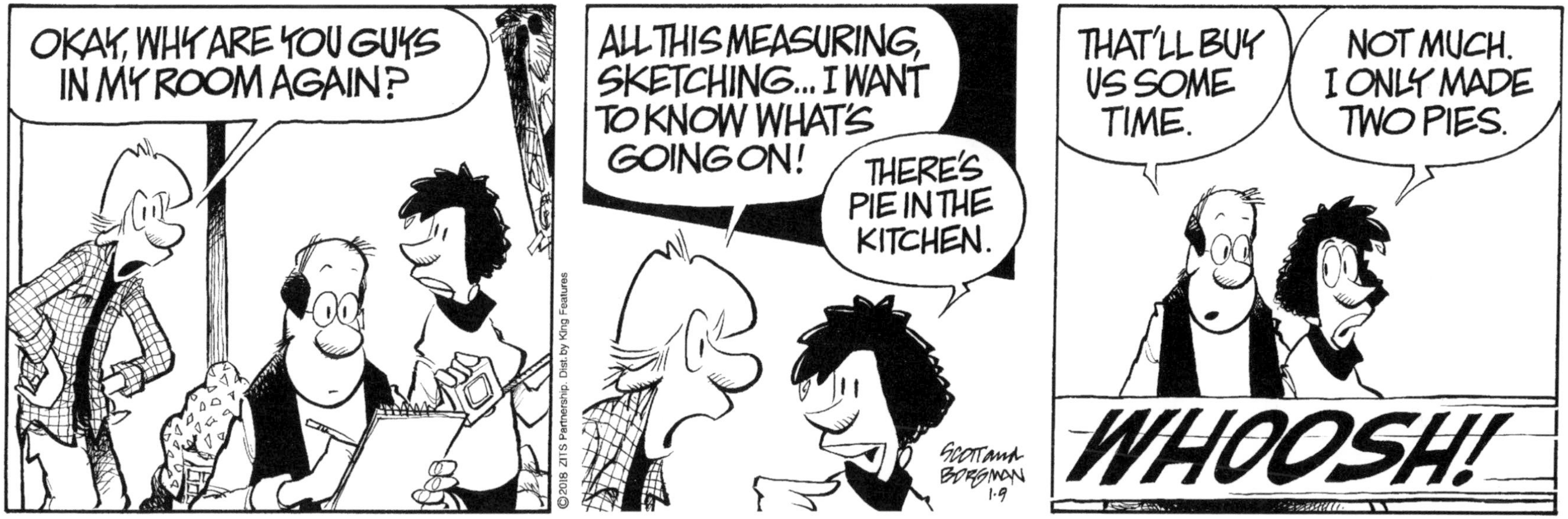
OKAY, WHY ARE YOU GUYS IN MY ROOM AGAIN?
©2018 ZITS Partnership. Dist. by King Features
ALL THIS MEASURING, SKETCHING... I WANT TO KNOW WHAT'S GOING ON!
THERE'S PIE IN THE KITCHEN.
SCOTT and BORGMAN 1-9
THAT'LL BUY US SOME TIME.
NOT MUCH. I ONLY MADE TWO PIES.
WHOOSH!

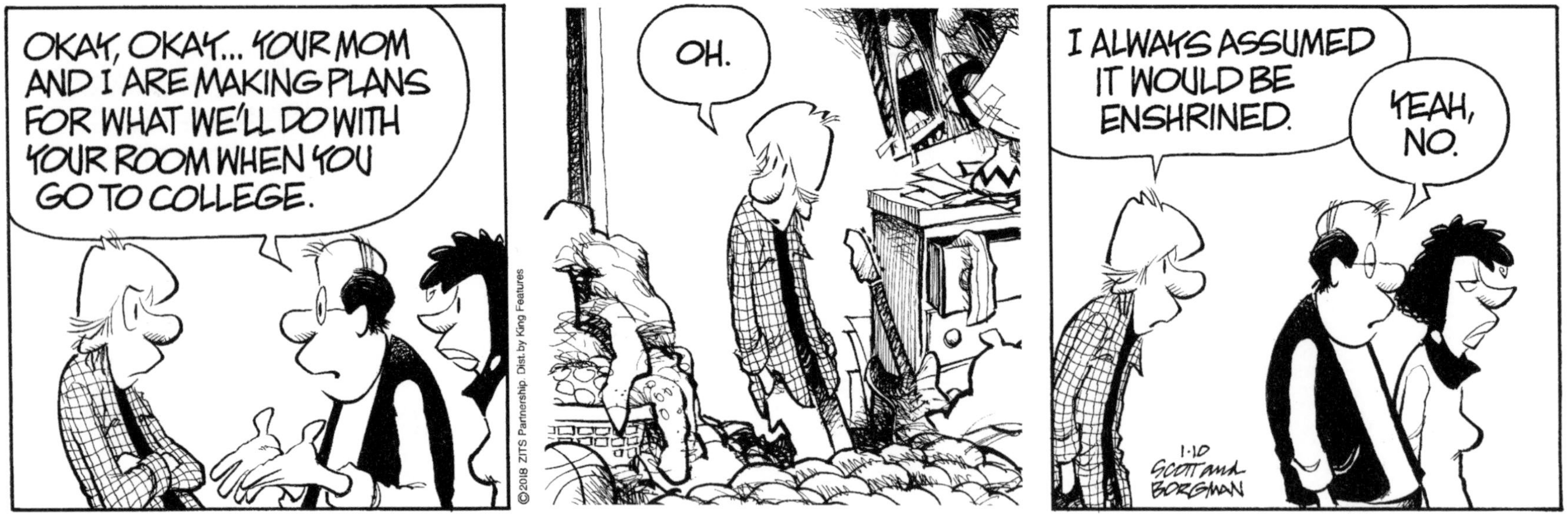
OKAY, OKAY... YOUR MOM AND I ARE MAKING PLANS FOR WHAT WE'LL DO WITH YOUR ROOM WHEN YOU GO TO COLLEGE.
© 2018 ZITS Partnership. Dist. by King Features
OH.
I ALWAYS ASSUMED IT WOULD BE ENSHRINED.
YEAH, NO.
1·10 SCOTT and BORGMAN

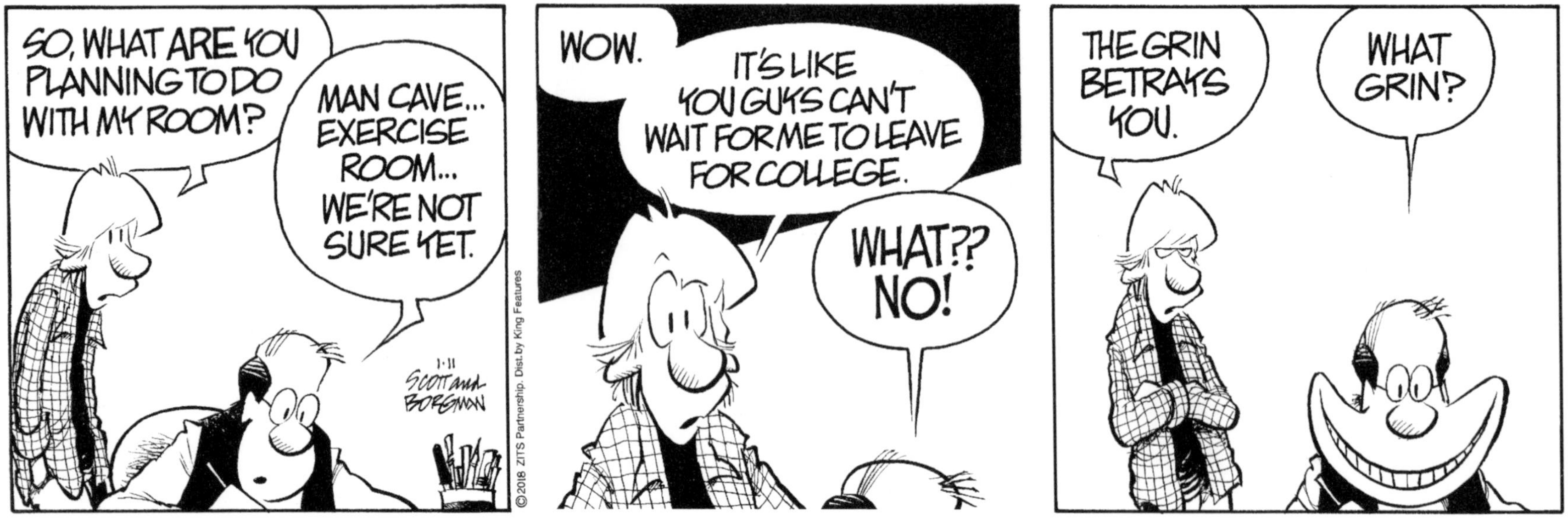
SO, WHAT ARE YOU PLANNING TO DO WITH MY ROOM?
MAN CAVE... EXERCISE ROOM... WE'RE NOT SURE YET.
1·11 SCOTT and BORGMAN
© 2018 ZITS Partnership. Dist. by King Features
WOW.
IT'S LIKE YOU GUYS CAN'T WAIT FOR ME TO LEAVE FOR COLLEGE.
WHAT?? NO!
THE GRIN BETRAYS YOU.
WHAT GRIN?

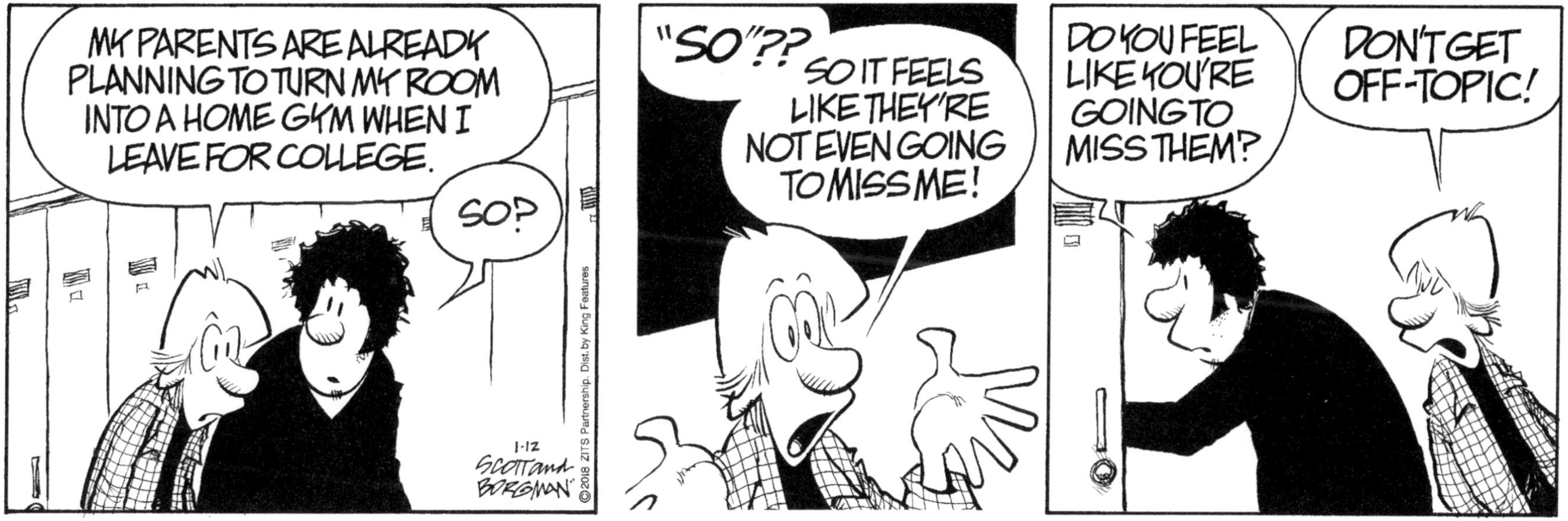
MY PARENTS ARE ALREADY PLANNING TO TURN MY ROOM INTO A HOME GYM WHEN I LEAVE FOR COLLEGE.
SO?
"SO"??
SO IT FEELS LIKE THEY'RE NOT EVEN GOING TO MISS ME!
DO YOU FEEL LIKE YOU'RE GOING TO MISS THEM?
DON'T GET OFF-TOPIC!
1-12 SCOTT and BORGMAN
© 2018 ZITS Partnership. Dist. by King Features

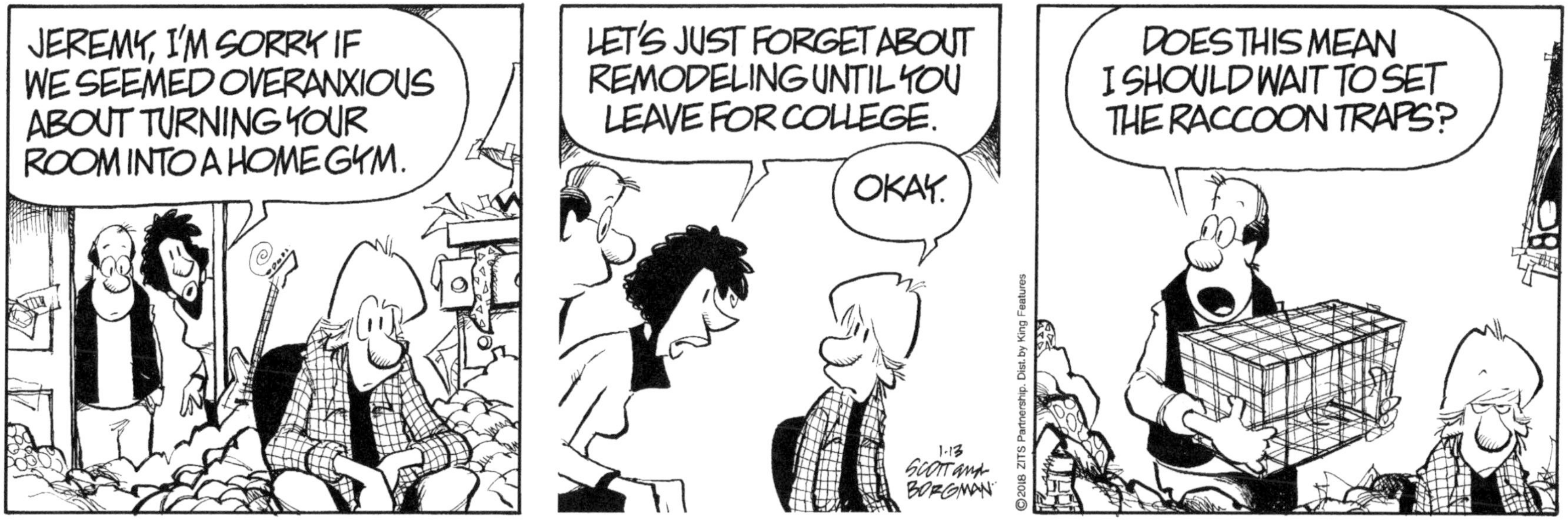
JEREMY, I'M SORRY IF WE SEEMED OVERANXIOUS ABOUT TURNING YOUR ROOM INTO A HOME GYM.
LET'S JUST FORGET ABOUT REMODELING UNTIL YOU LEAVE FOR COLLEGE.
OKAY.
DOES THIS MEAN I SHOULD WAIT TO SET THE RACCOON TRAPS?
1-13 SCOTT and BORGMAN
© 2018 ZITS Partnership. Dist. by King Features

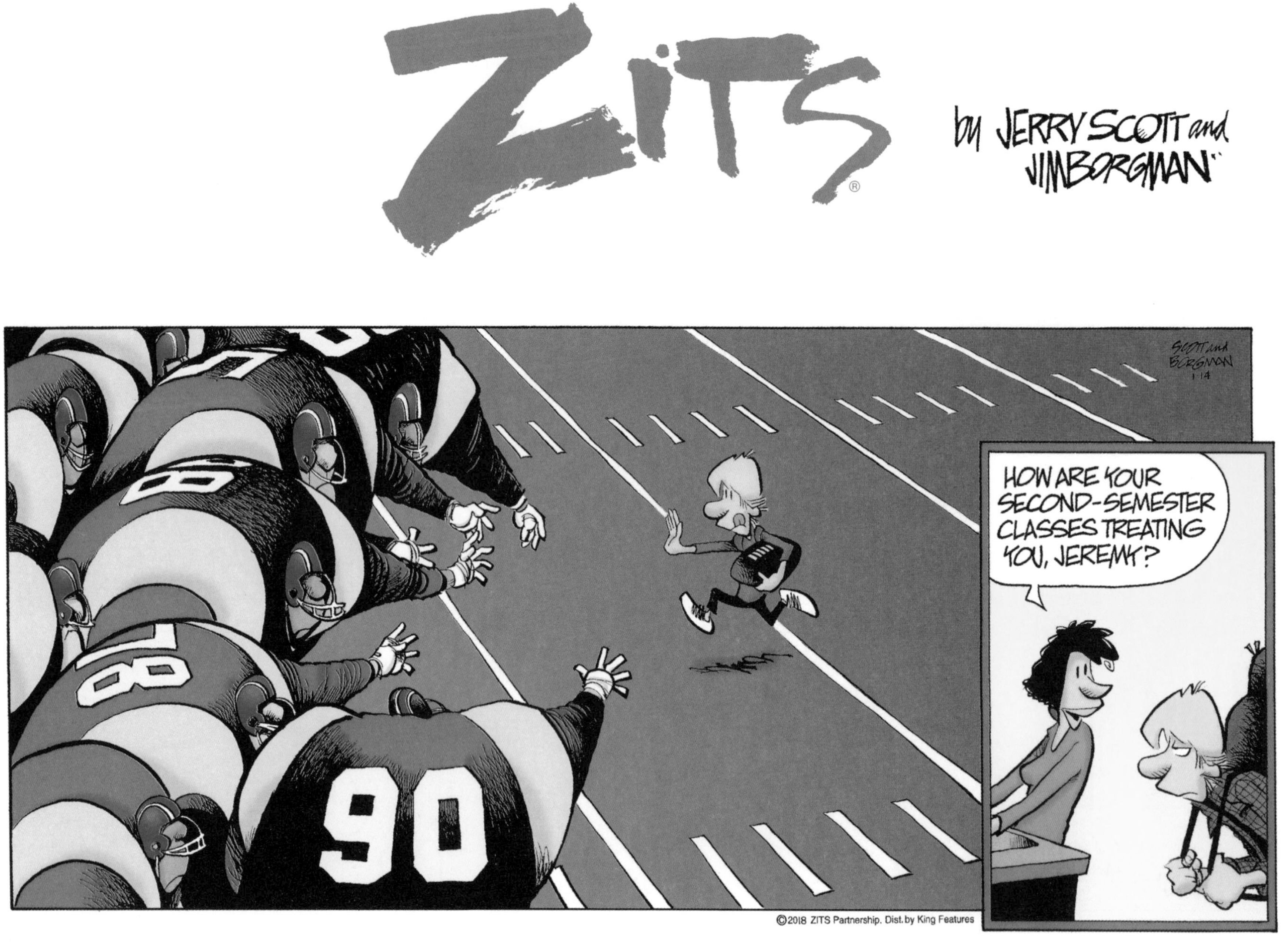
ZITS
by JERRY SCOTT and JIM BORGMAN
SCOTT and BORGMAN 1-14
90
HOW ARE YOUR SECOND-SEMESTER CLASSES TREATING YOU, JEREMY?
©2018 ZITS Partnership. Dist. by King Features

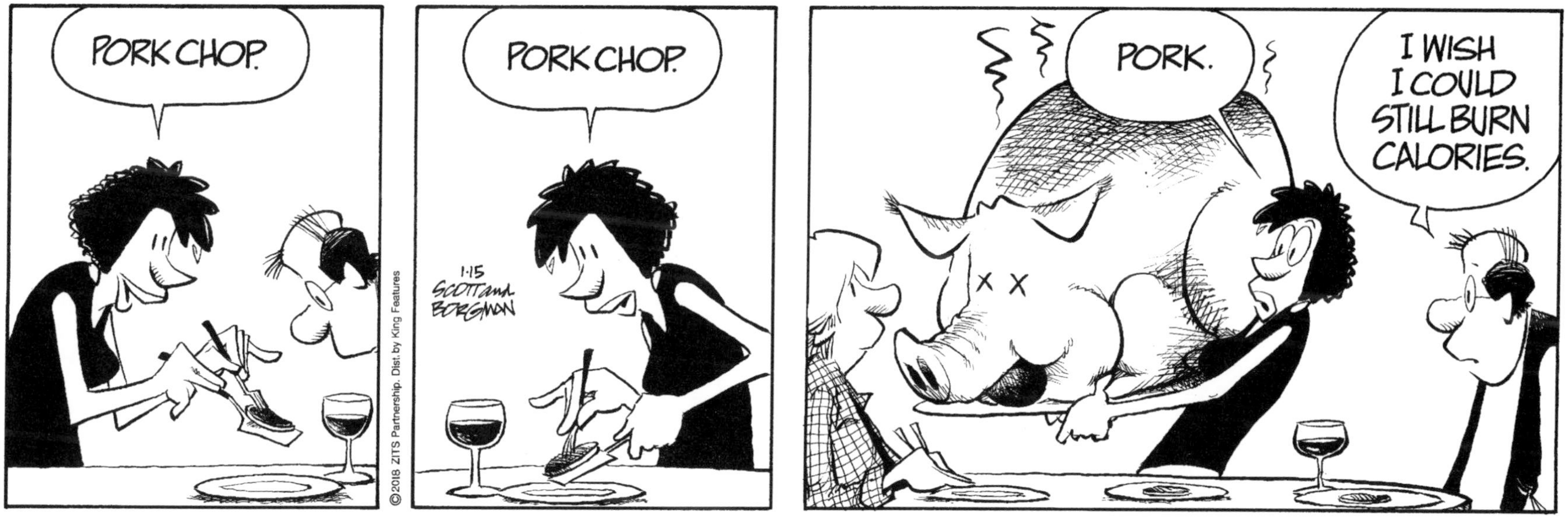
PORK CHOP.
PORK CHOP.
1·15 SCOTT and BORGMAN
PORK.
I WISH I COULD STILL BURN CALORIES.
©2018 ZITS Partnership. Dist. by King Features

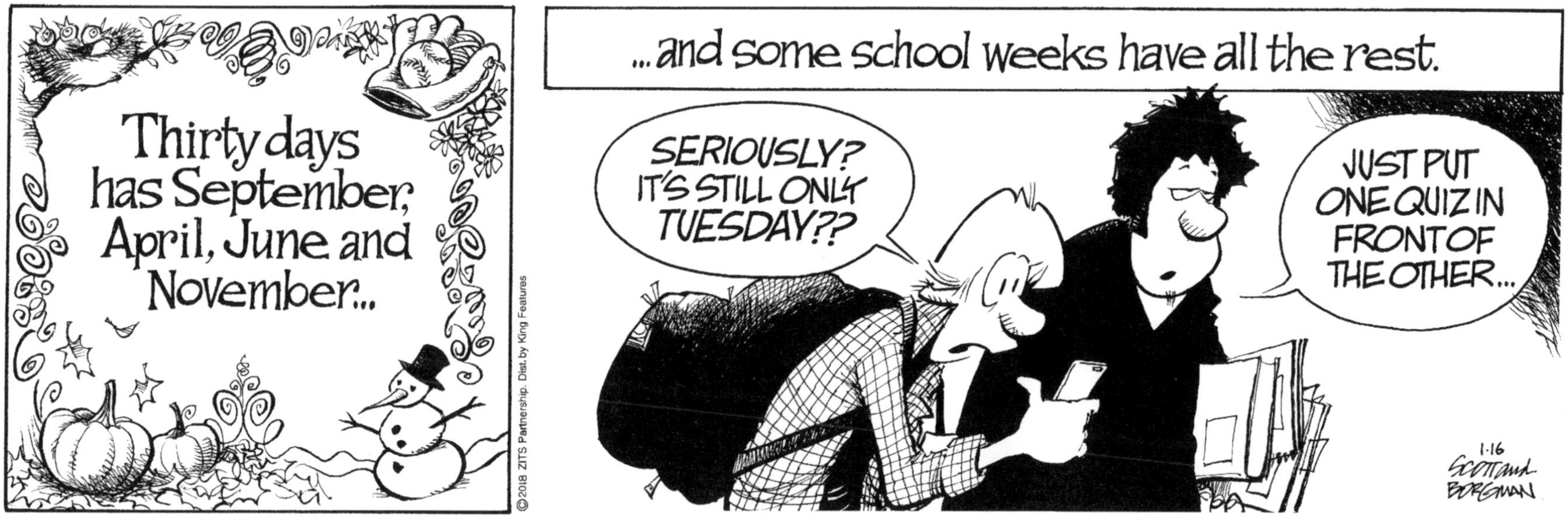
Thirty days has September, April, June and November...
...and some school weeks have all the rest.
SERIOUSLY? IT'S STILL ONLY TUESDAY??
JUST PUT ONE QUIZ IN FRONT OF THE OTHER...
1·16 SCOTT and BORGMAN
©2018 ZITS Partnership. Dist. by King Features

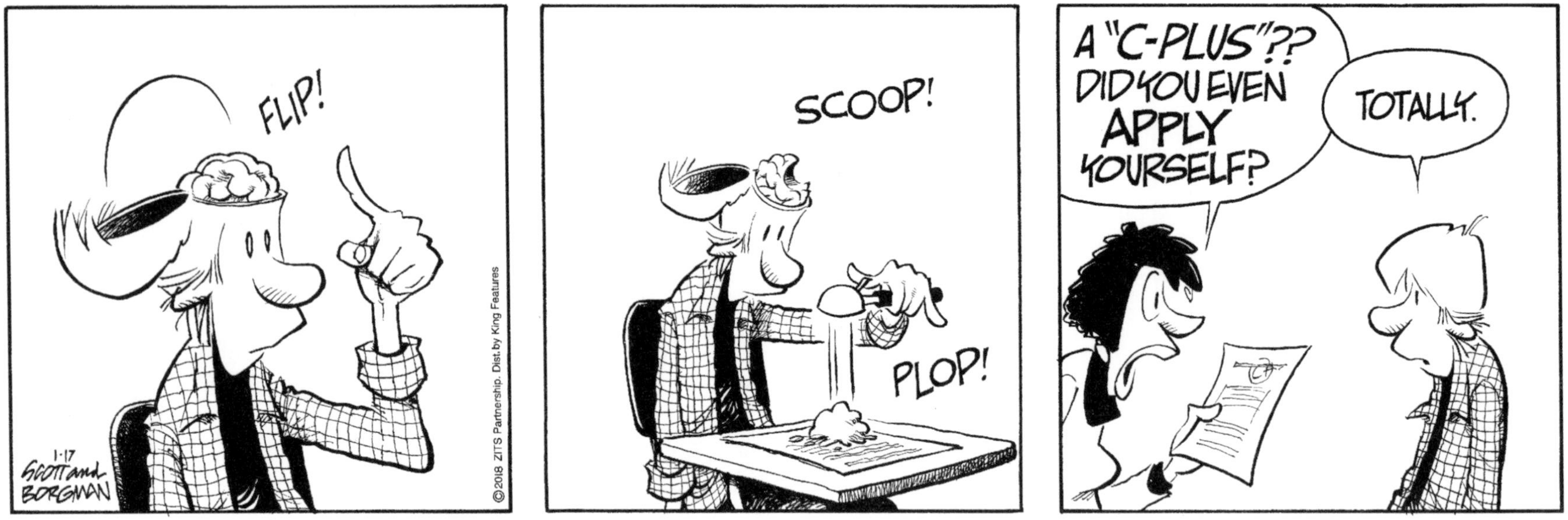
FLIP!
SCOOP!
PLOP!
A "C-PLUS"?? DID YOU EVEN APPLY YOURSELF?
TOTALLY.
1-17
SCOTT and BORGMAN
© 2018 ZITS Partnership. Dist. by King Features

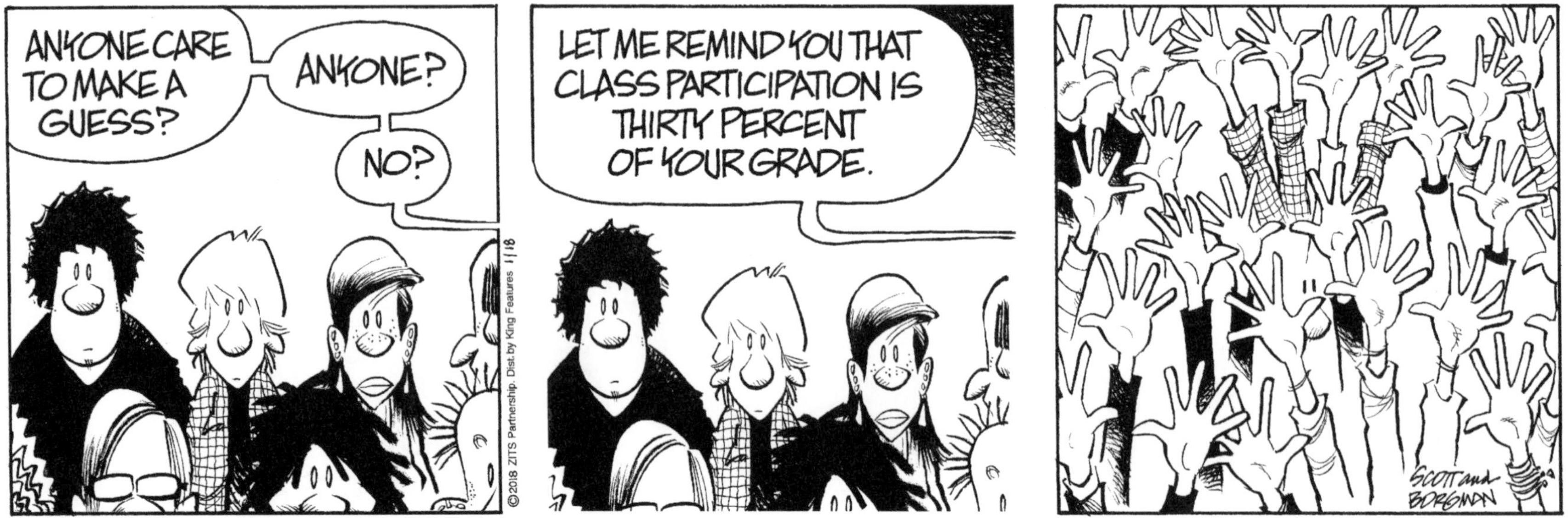
ANYONE CARE TO MAKE A GUESS?
ANYONE?
NO?
LET ME REMIND YOU THAT CLASS PARTICIPATION IS THIRTY PERCENT OF YOUR GRADE.
1/18
© 2018 ZITS Partnership. Dist. by King Features
SCOTT and BORGMAN

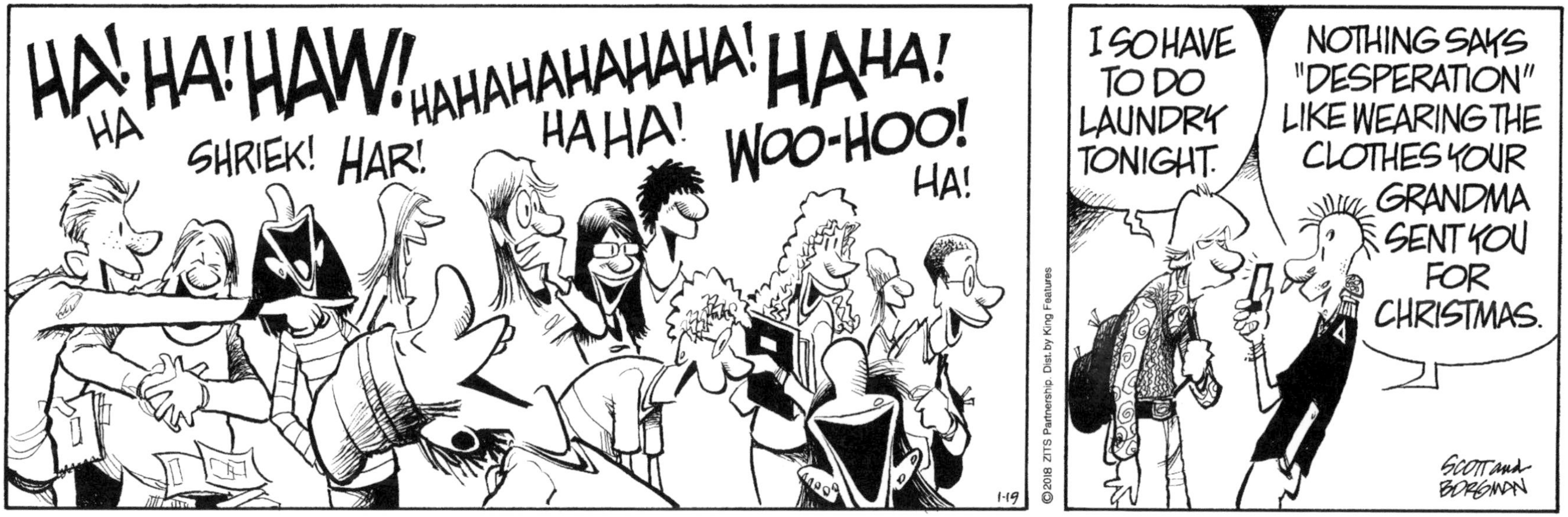
HA! HA! HAW! HAHAHAHAHAHA! HAHA!
HA
SHRIEK! HAR!
HA HA!
WOO-HOO!
HA!
1·19
© 2018 ZITS Partnership. Dist. by King Features
I SO HAVE TO DO LAUNDRY TONIGHT.
NOTHING SAYS "DESPERATION" LIKE WEARING THE CLOTHES YOUR GRANDMA SENT YOU FOR CHRISTMAS.
SCOTT and BORGMAN

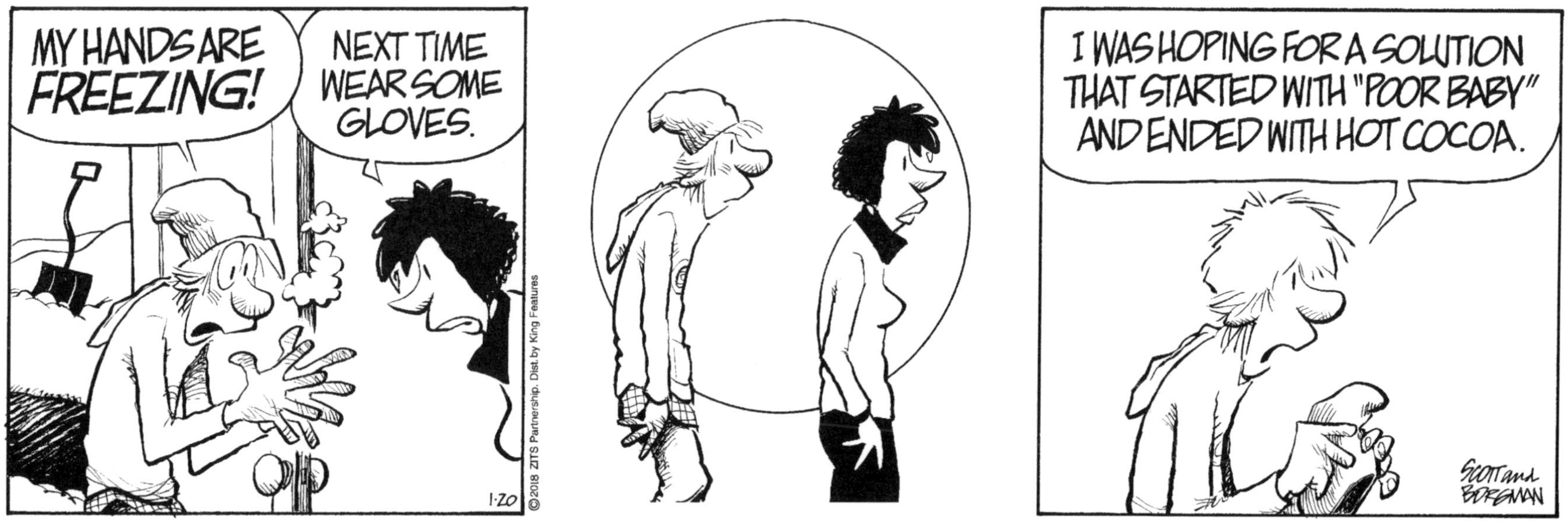
MY HANDS ARE FREEZING!
NEXT TIME WEAR SOME GLOVES.
1·20
© 2018 ZITS Partnership. Dist. by King Features
I WAS HOPING FOR A SOLUTION THAT STARTED WITH "POOR BABY" AND ENDED WITH HOT COCOA.
SCOTT and BORGMAN

ZITS

by JERRY SCOTT and JIMBORGMAN

HEY, SARA. 'SUP?

NOT MUCH. WHAT ARE YOU UP TO?

I AM LITERALLY DOING NOTHING WHILE I GET MY CHRISTMAS THANK-YOU CARDS WRITTEN.

WAIT— WHAT?

JEREMY, YOU CAN'T "LITERALLY" BE DOING NOTHING AND WRITING THANK-YOU CARDS AT THE SAME TIME.

1·21
SCOTT AND BORGMAN

YOU UNDERESTIMATE ME.

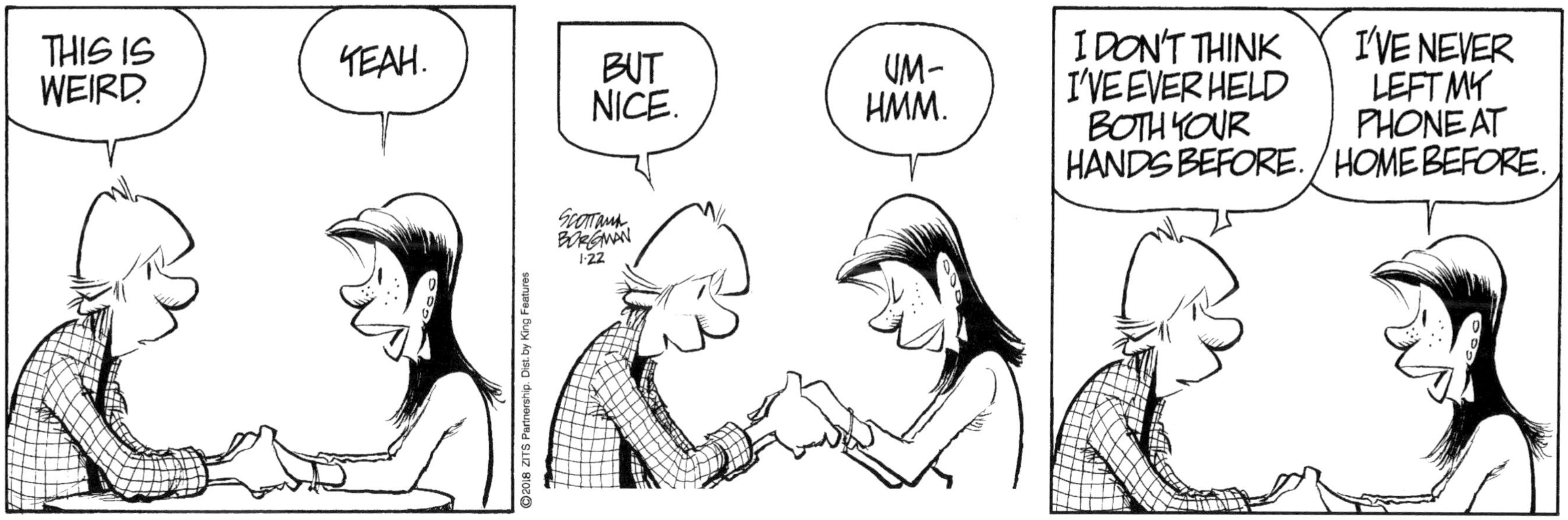
THIS IS WEIRD.
YEAH.
BUT NICE.
UM-HMM.
SCOTT and BORGMAN 1·22
©2018 ZITS Partnership. Dist. by King Features
I DON'T THINK I'VE EVER HELD BOTH YOUR HANDS BEFORE.
I'VE NEVER LEFT MY PHONE AT HOME BEFORE.

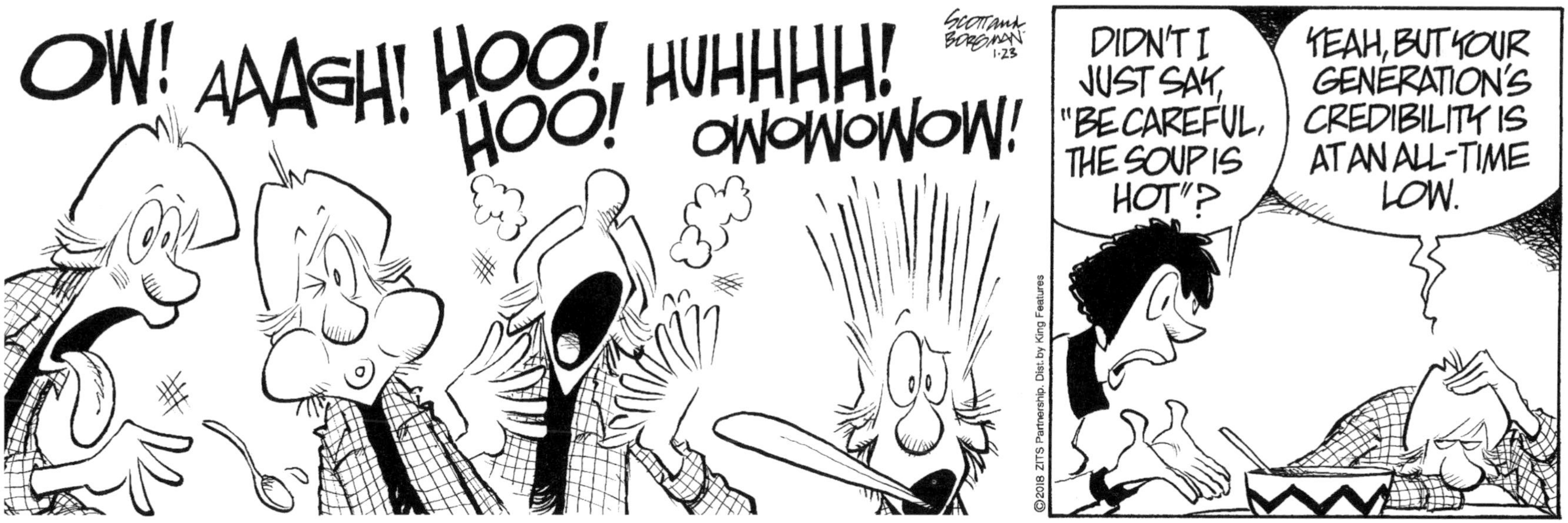
SCOTT and BORGMAN 1·23
OW!
AAAGH!
HOO! HOO!
HUHHHH!
OWOWOWOW!
©2018 ZITS Partnership. Dist. by King Features
DIDN'T I JUST SAY, "BE CAREFUL, THE SOUP IS HOT"?
YEAH, BUT YOUR GENERATION'S CREDIBILITY IS AT AN ALL-TIME LOW.

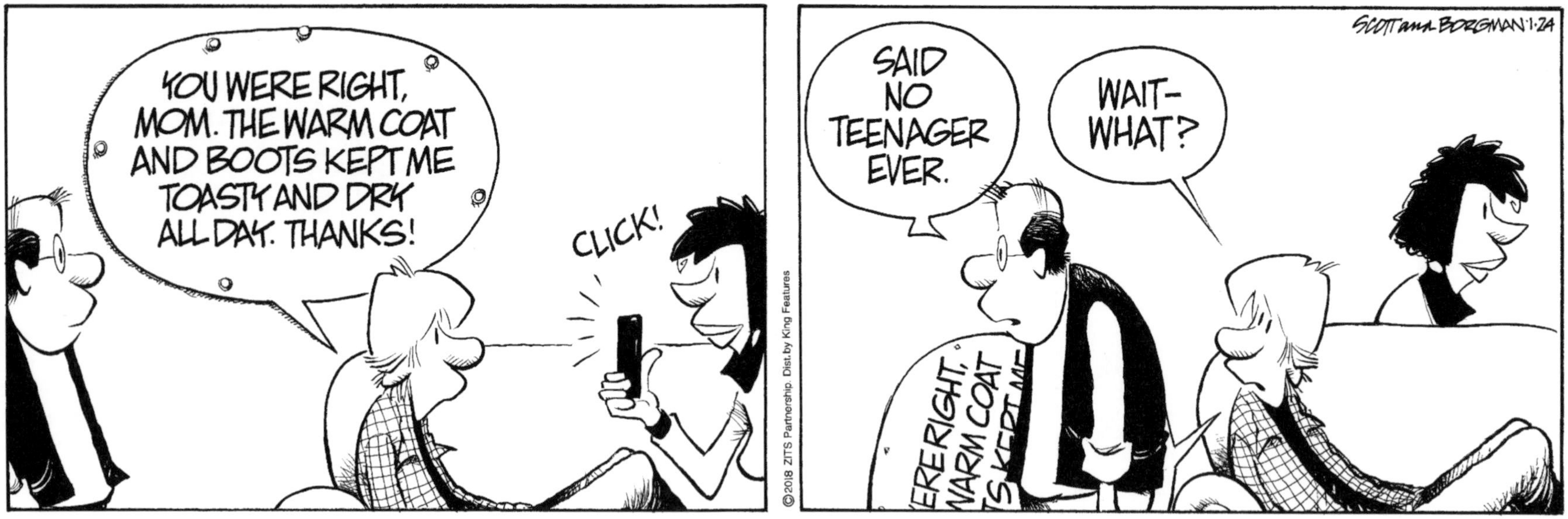
YOU WERE RIGHT, MOM. THE WARM COAT AND BOOTS KEPT ME TOASTY AND DRY ALL DAY. THANKS!
CLICK!
SCOTT and BORGMAN 1·24
SAID NO TEENAGER EVER.
WAIT- WHAT?

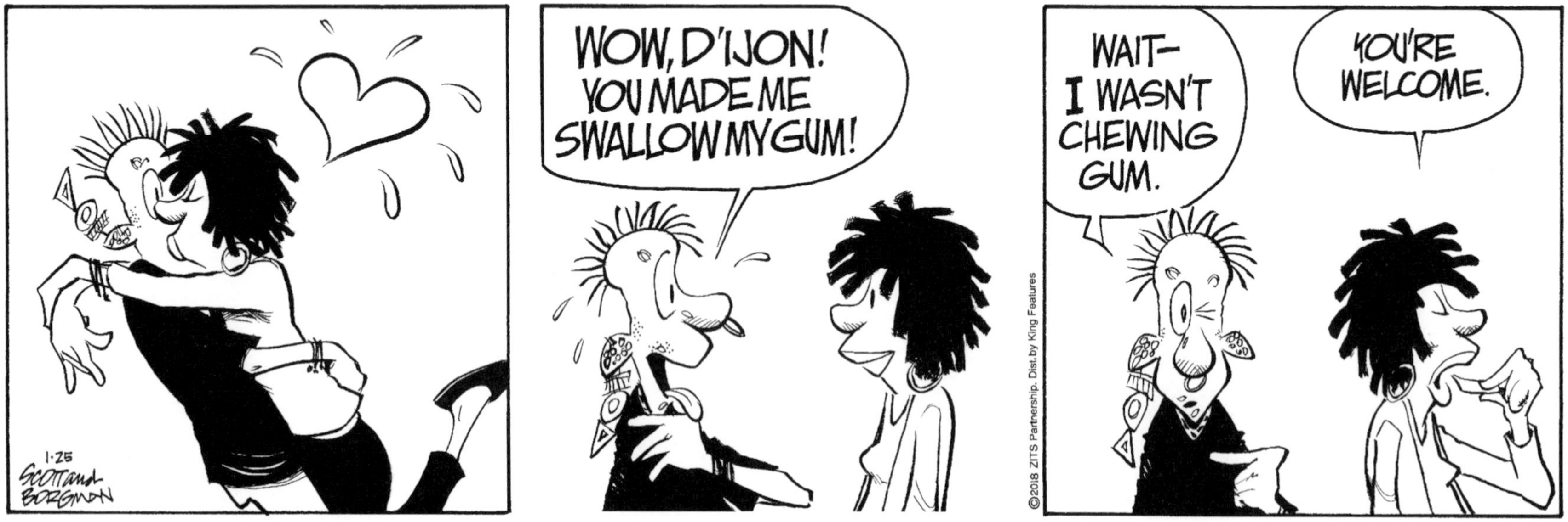
1·25 SCOTT and BORGMAN
WOW, D'IJON! YOU MADE ME SWALLOW MY GUM!
WAIT- I WASN'T CHEWING GUM.
YOU'RE WELCOME.

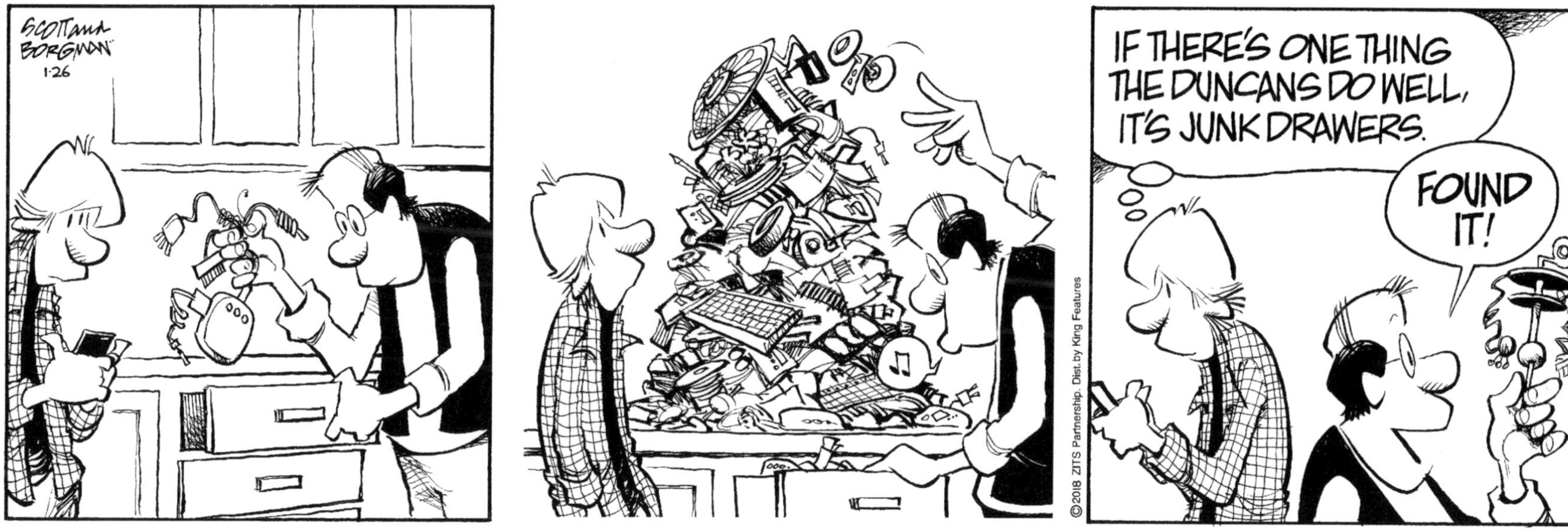
SCOTT and BORGMAN 1·26
©2018 ZITS Partnership. Dist. by King Features
IF THERE'S ONE THING THE DUNCANS DO WELL, IT'S JUNK DRAWERS.
FOUND IT!

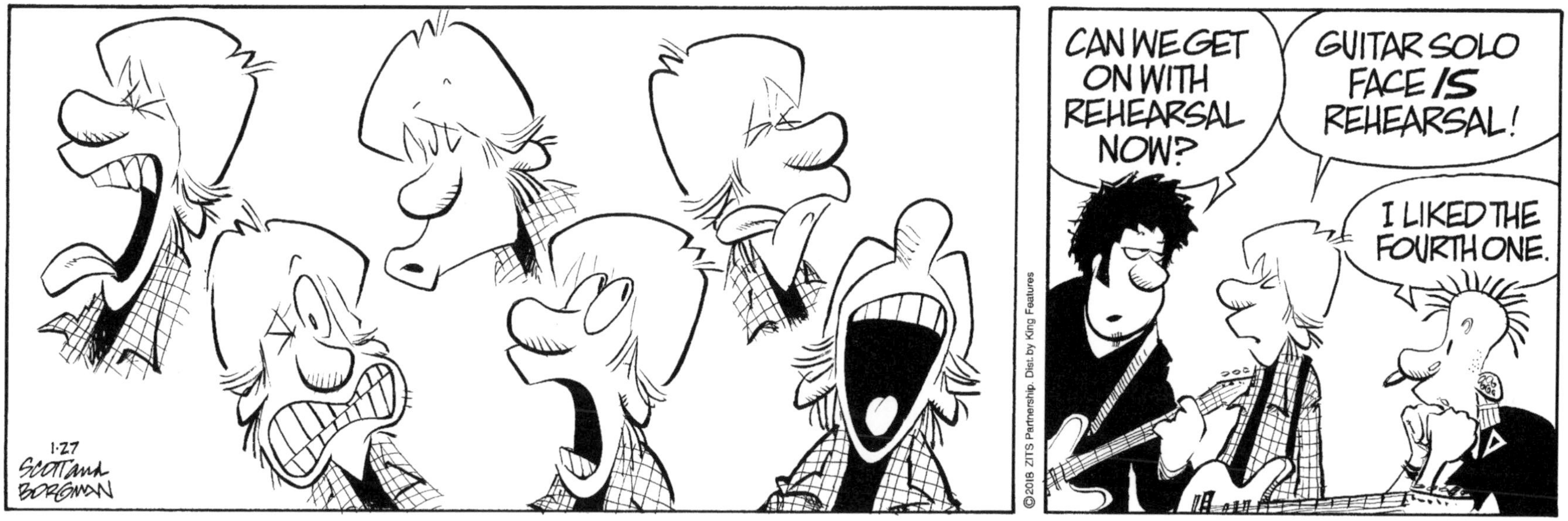
1·27 SCOTT and BORGMAN
©2018 ZITS Partnership. Dist. by King Features
CAN WE GET ON WITH REHEARSAL NOW?
GUITAR SOLO FACE *IS* REHEARSAL!
I LIKED THE FOURTH ONE.

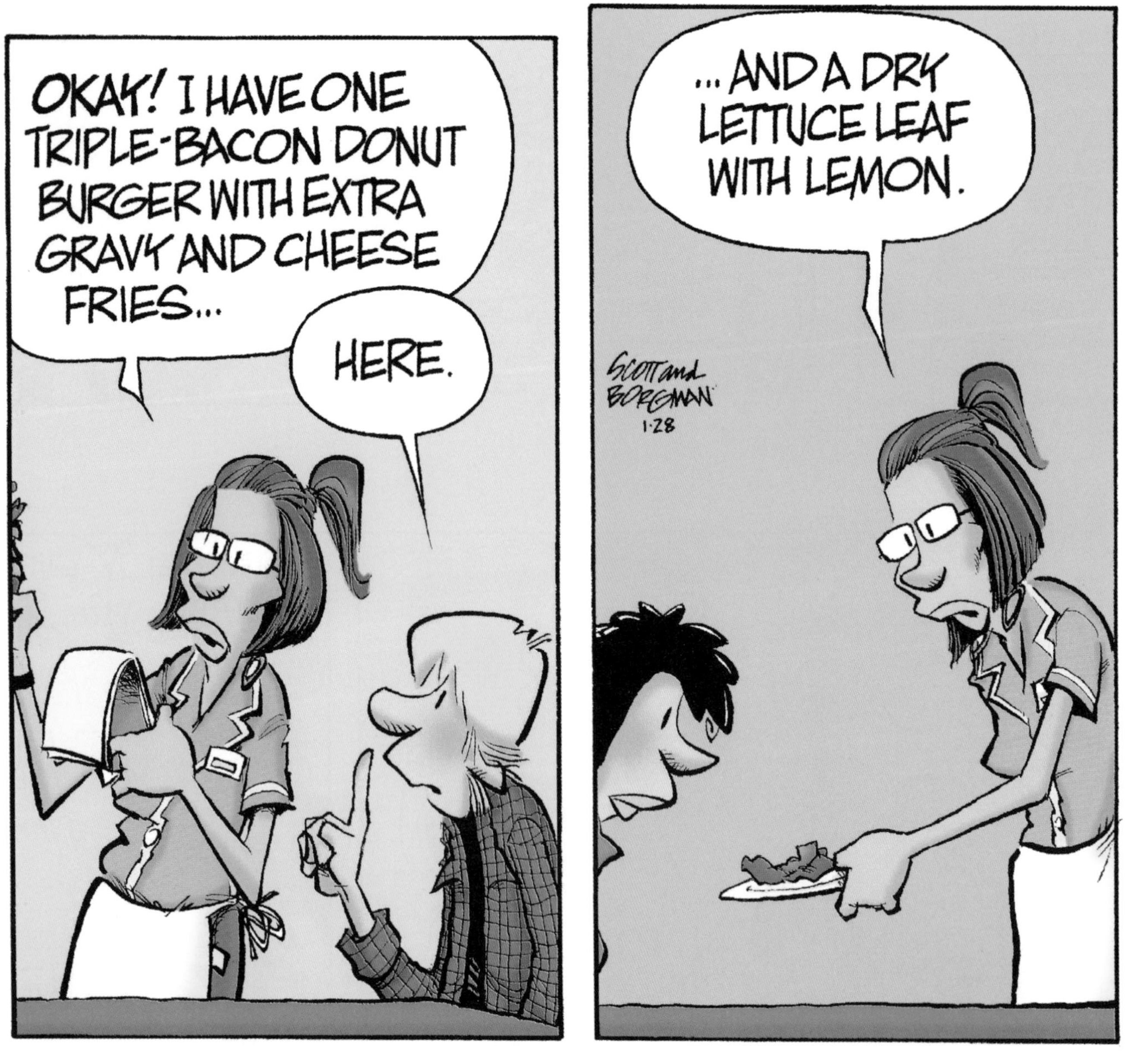
OKAY! I HAVE ONE TRIPLE-BACON DONUT BURGER WITH EXTRA GRAVY AND CHEESE FRIES...
HERE.
...AND A DRY LETTUCE LEAF WITH LEMON.
SCOTT and BORGMAN 1·28

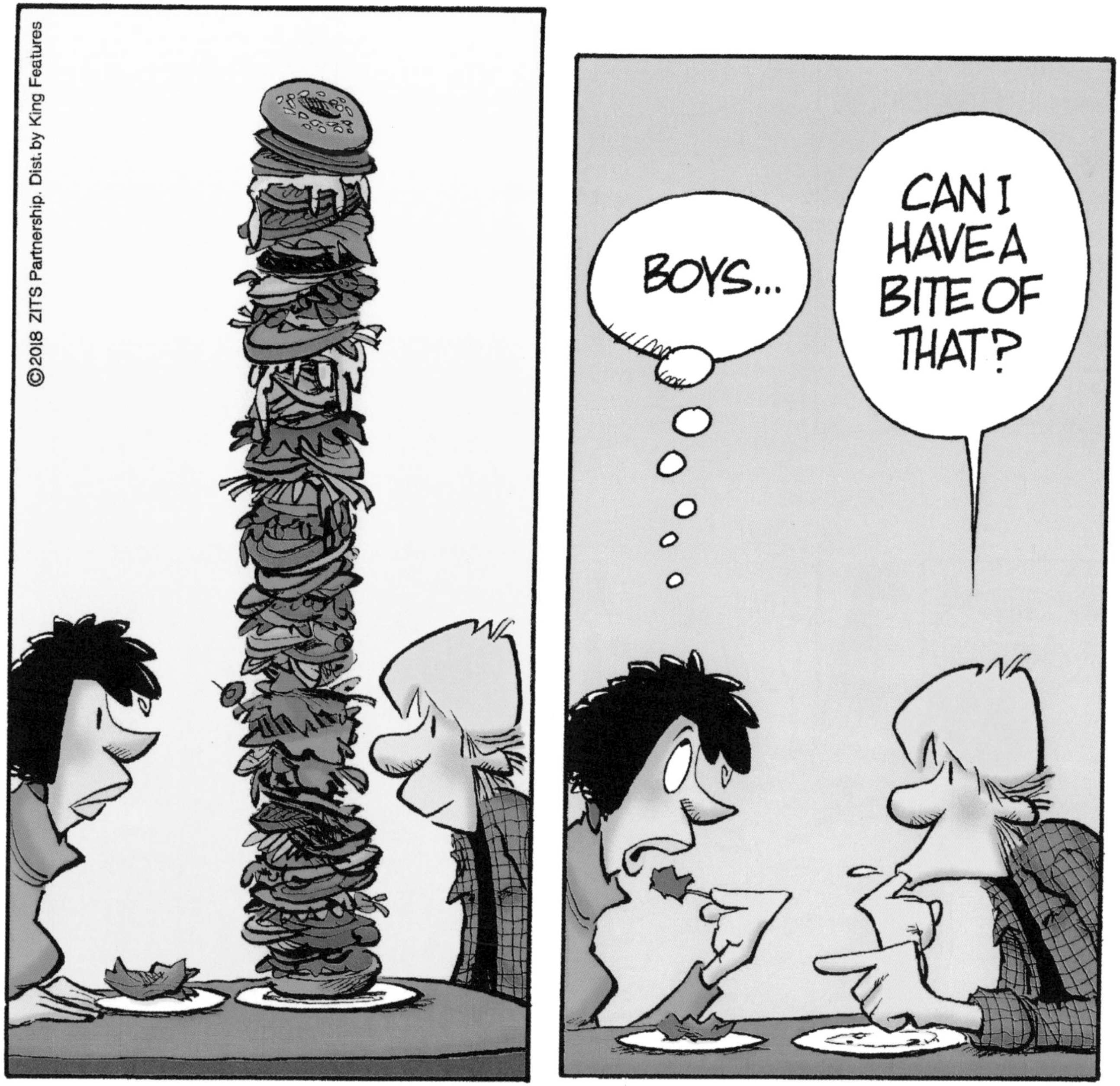
©2018 ZITS Partnership. Dist. by King Features
BOYS...
CAN I HAVE A BITE OF THAT?

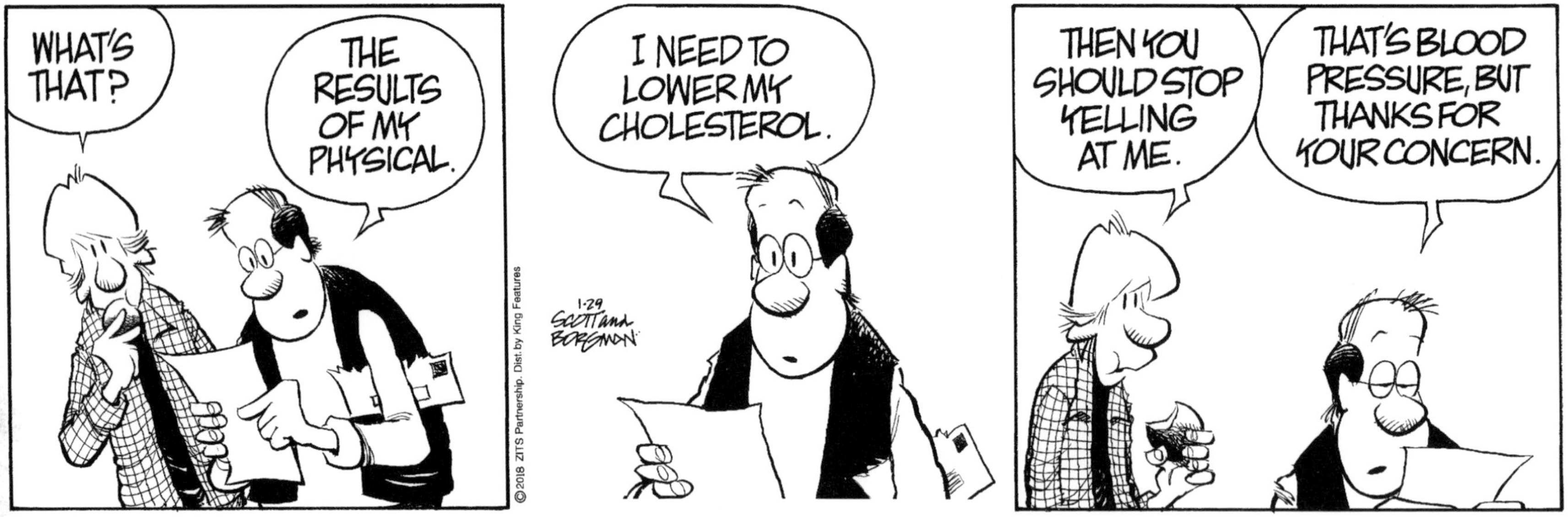
WHAT'S THAT?
THE RESULTS OF MY PHYSICAL.
© 2018 ZITS Partnership. Dist. by King Features
I NEED TO LOWER MY CHOLESTEROL.
THEN YOU SHOULD STOP YELLING AT ME.
THAT'S BLOOD PRESSURE, BUT THANKS FOR YOUR CONCERN.

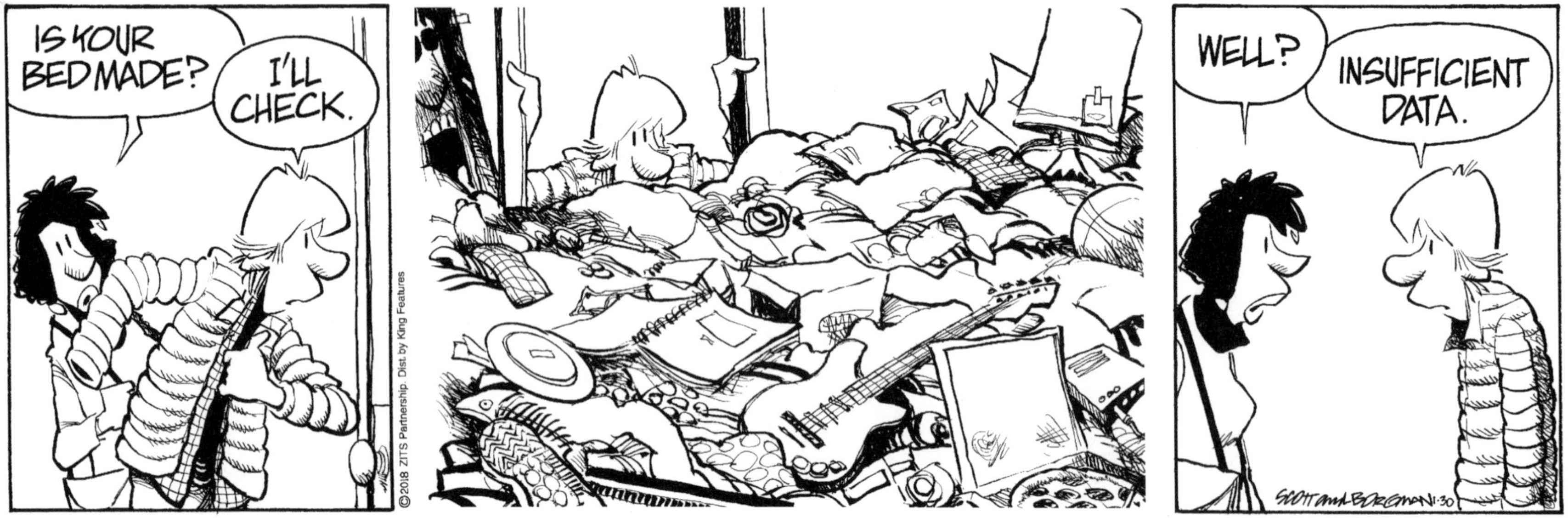
IS YOUR BED MADE?
I'LL CHECK.
© 2018 ZITS Partnership. Dist. by King Features
WELL?
INSUFFICIENT DATA.

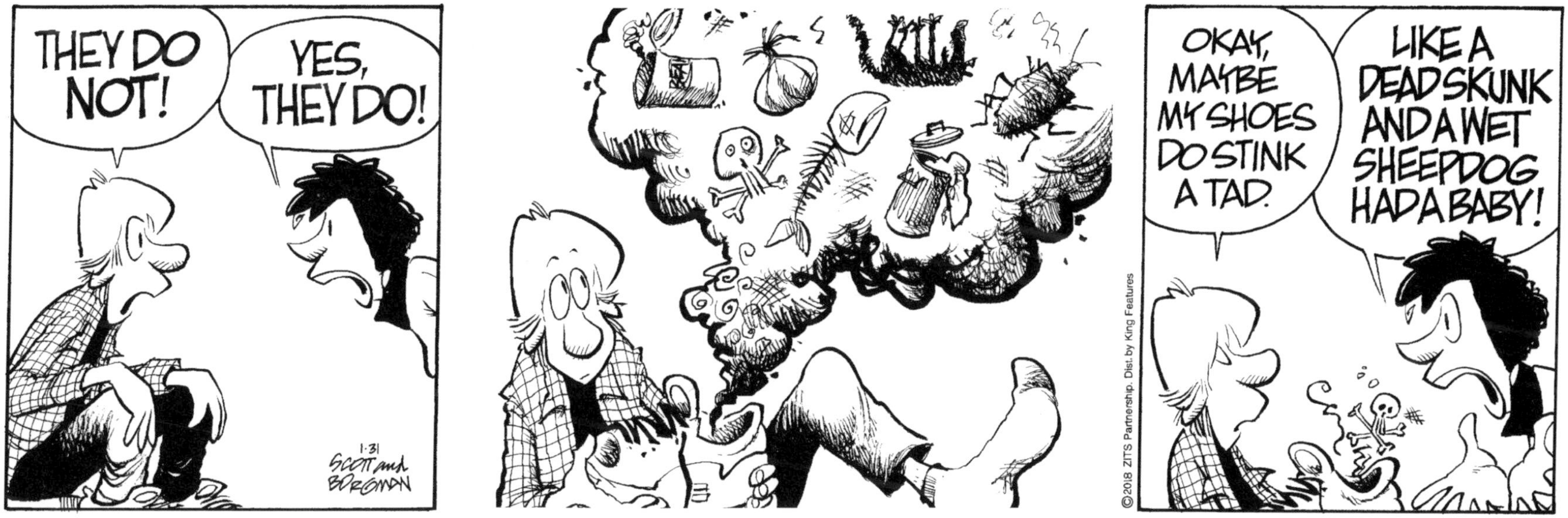
THEY DO NOT!
YES, THEY DO!
1·31 SCOTT and BORGMAN
OKAY, MAYBE MY SHOES DO STINK A TAD.
LIKE A DEAD SKUNK AND A WET SHEEPDOG HAD A BABY!
© 2018 ZITS Partnership. Dist. by King Features

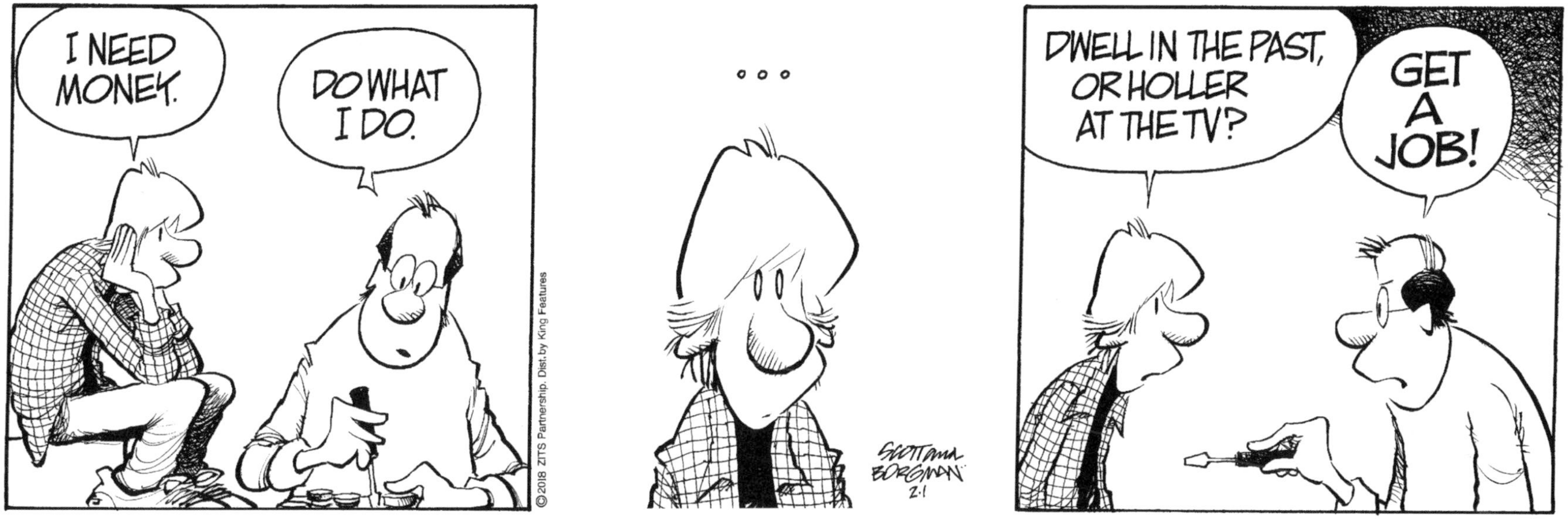
I NEED MONEY.
DO WHAT I DO.
© 2018 ZITS Partnership. Dist. by King Features
...
SCOTT and BORGMAN 2·1
DWELL IN THE PAST, OR HOLLER AT THE TV?
GET A JOB!

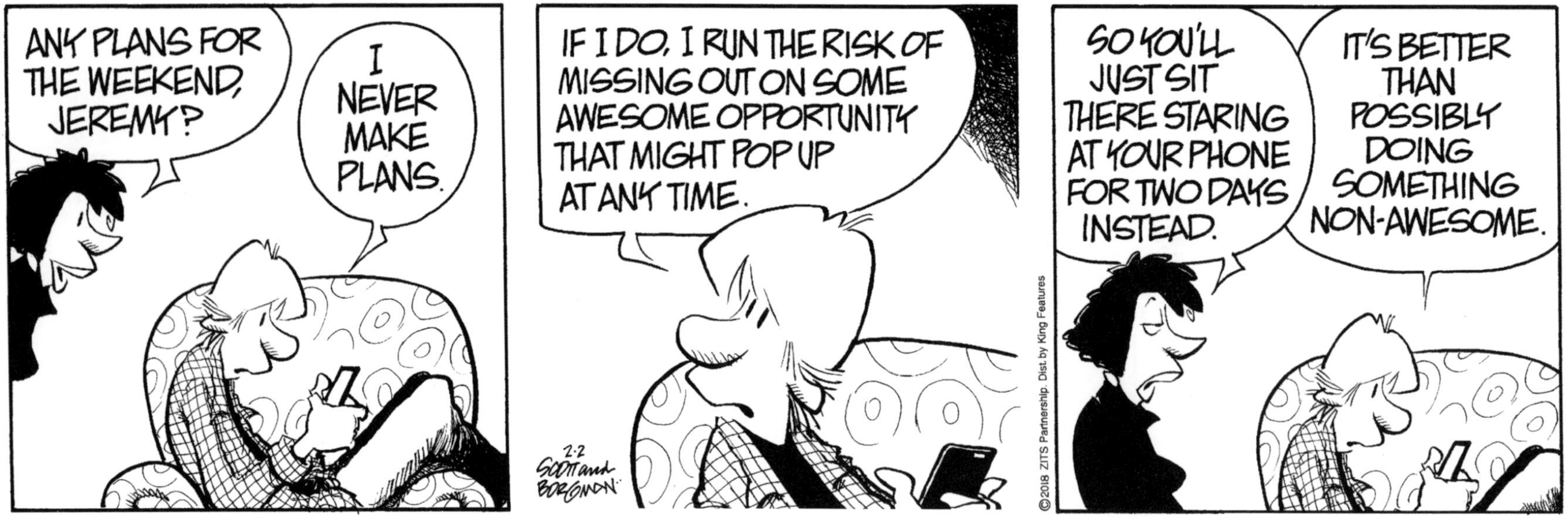
ANY PLANS FOR THE WEEKEND, JEREMY?
I NEVER MAKE PLANS.
IF I DO, I RUN THE RISK OF MISSING OUT ON SOME AWESOME OPPORTUNITY THAT MIGHT POP UP AT ANY TIME.
SO YOU'LL JUST SIT THERE STARING AT YOUR PHONE FOR TWO DAYS INSTEAD.
IT'S BETTER THAN POSSIBLY DOING SOMETHING NON-AWESOME.
©2018 ZITS Partnership. Dist. by King Features

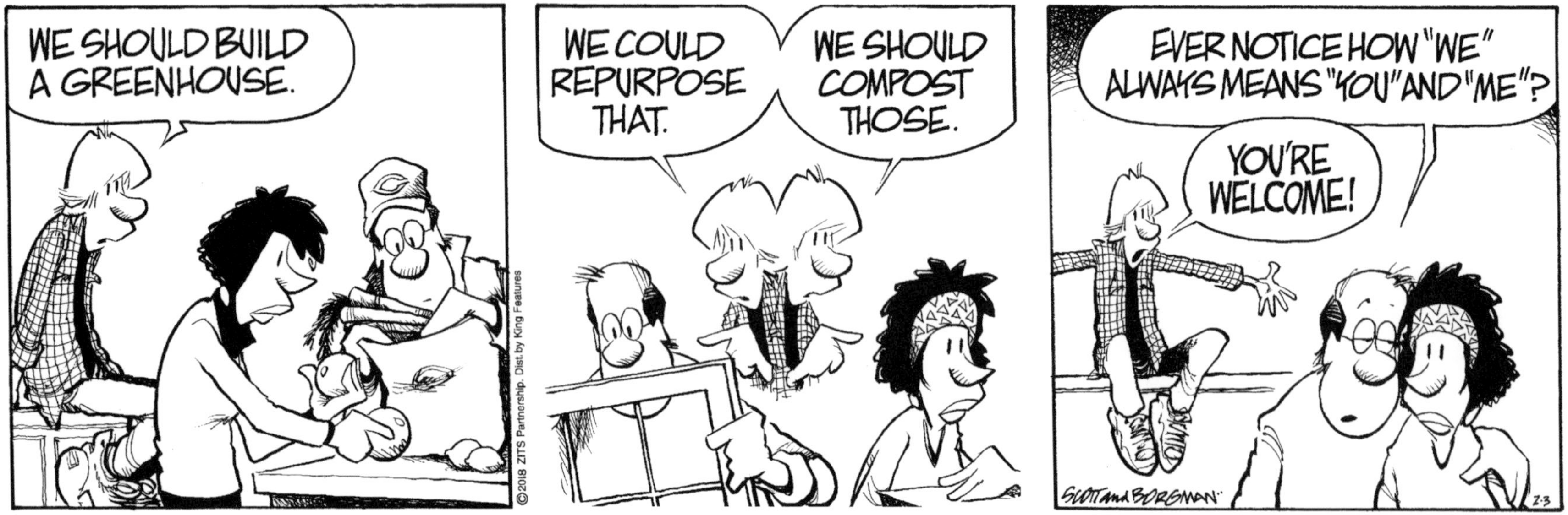
WE SHOULD BUILD A GREENHOUSE.
©2018 ZITS Partnership. Dist. by King Features
WE COULD REPURPOSE THAT.
WE SHOULD COMPOST THOSE.
EVER NOTICE HOW "WE" ALWAYS MEANS "YOU" AND "ME"?
YOU'RE WELCOME!

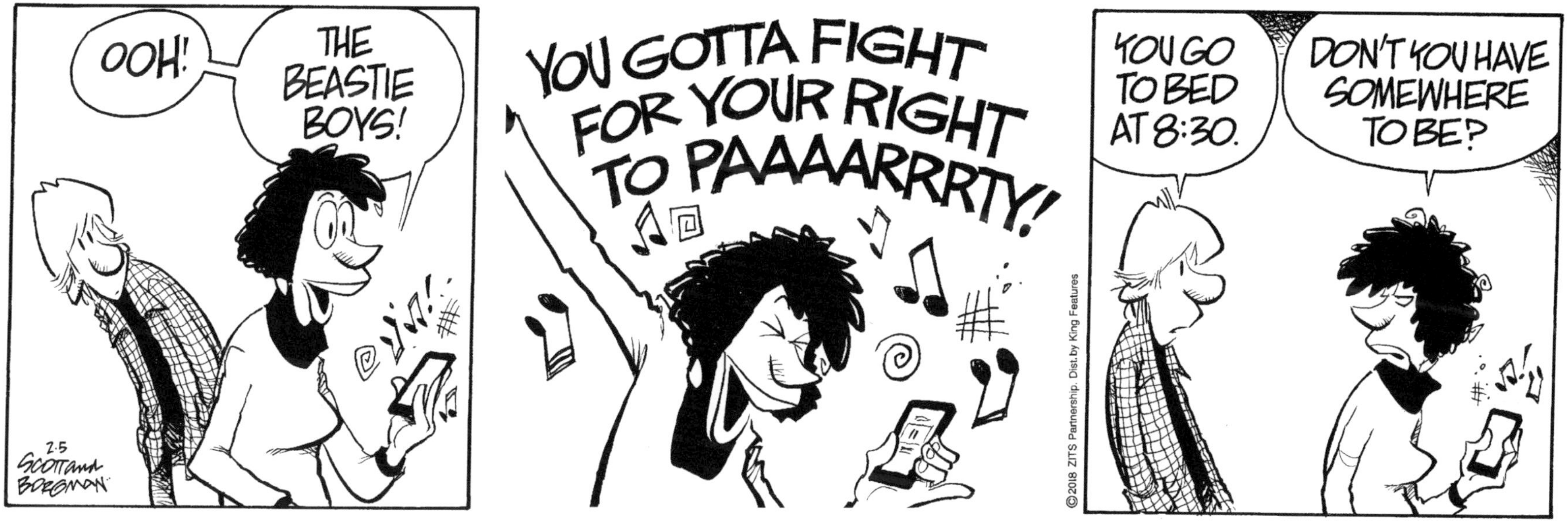
OOH!
THE BEASTIE BOYS!
2-5 SCOTT and BORGMAN
YOU GOTTA FIGHT FOR YOUR RIGHT TO PAAAARRRTY!
© 2018 ZITS Partnership. Dist. by King Features
YOU GO TO BED AT 8:30.
DON'T YOU HAVE SOMEWHERE TO BE?

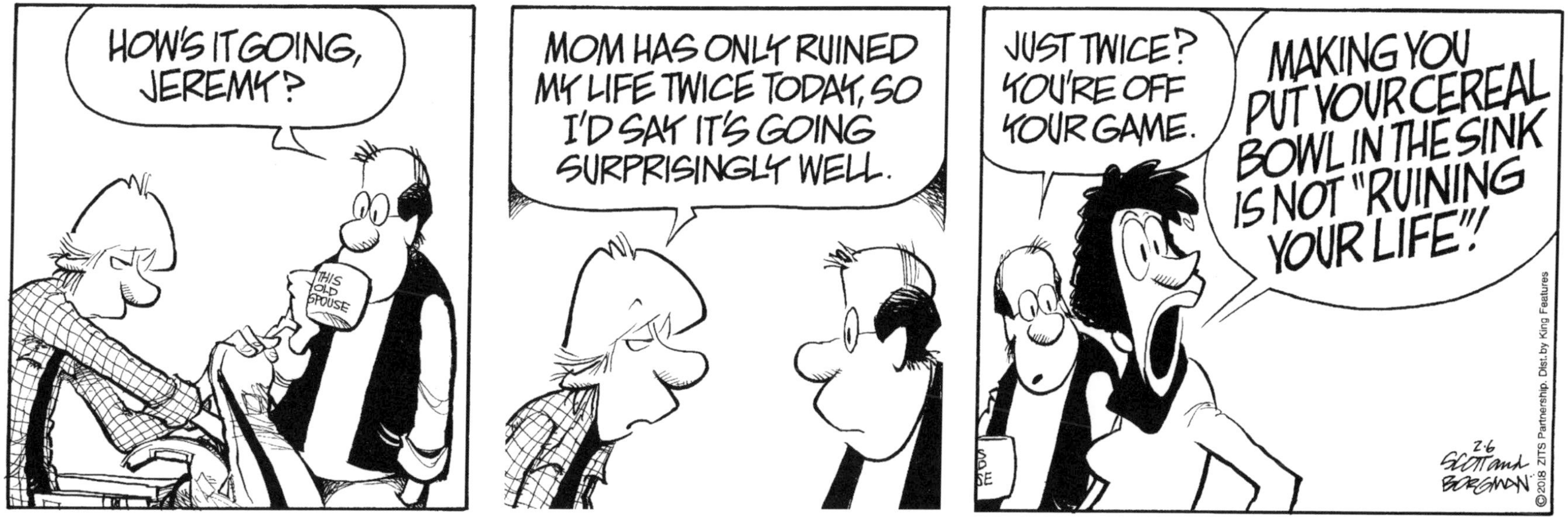
HOW'S IT GOING, JEREMY?
THIS OLD SPOUSE
MOM HAS ONLY RUINED MY LIFE TWICE TODAY, SO I'D SAY IT'S GOING SURPRISINGLY WELL.
JUST TWICE? YOU'RE OFF YOUR GAME.
MAKING YOU PUT YOUR CEREAL BOWL IN THE SINK IS NOT "RUINING YOUR LIFE"!
2-6 SCOTT and BORGMAN
© 2018 ZITS Partnership. Dist. by King Features

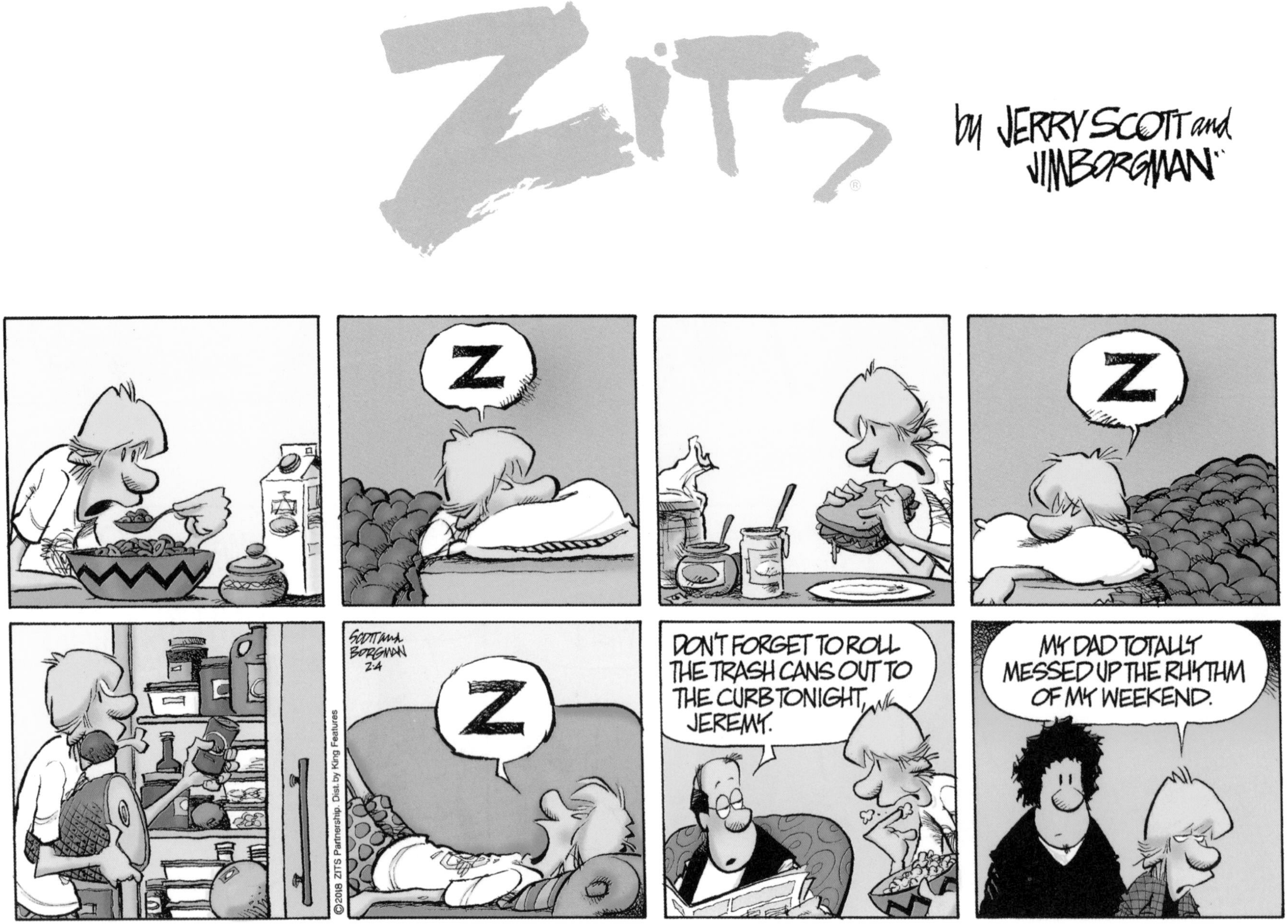
ZITS
by JERRY SCOTT and JIM BORGMAN
Z
Z
Z
SCOTT and BORGMAN 2-4
©2018 ZITS Partnership. Dist. by King Features
DON'T FORGET TO ROLL THE TRASH CANS OUT TO THE CURB TONIGHT, JEREMY.
MY DAD TOTALLY MESSED UP THE RHYTHM OF MY WEEKEND.

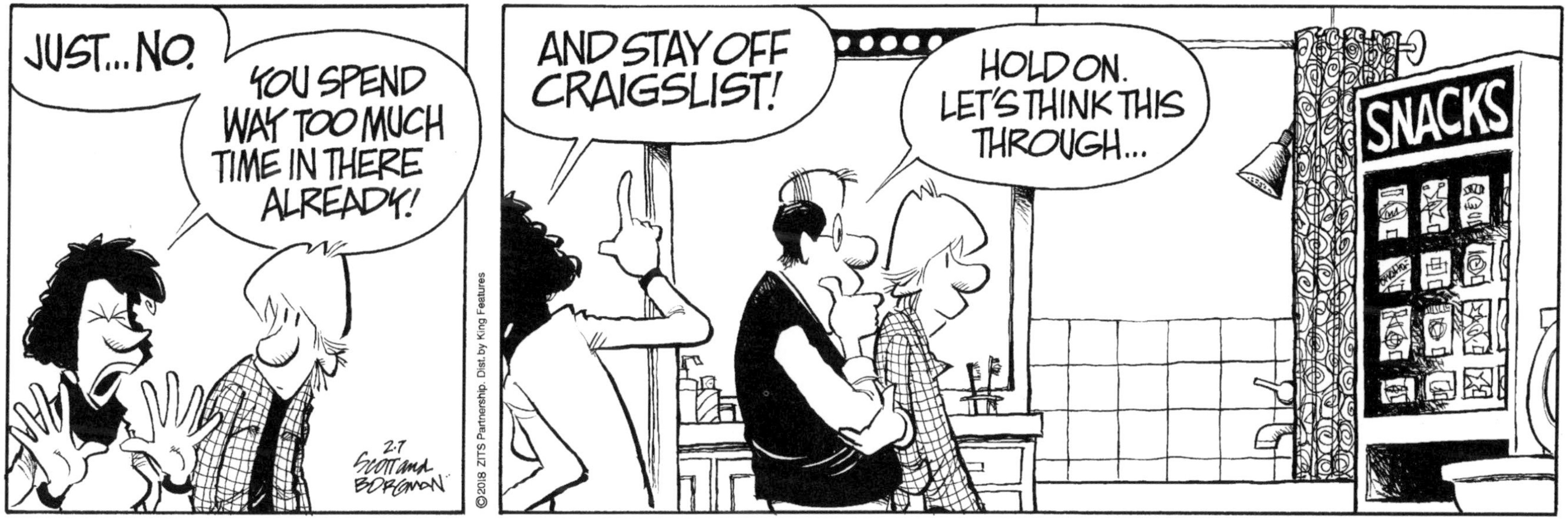
JUST... NO.
YOU SPEND WAY TOO MUCH TIME IN THERE ALREADY!
2·7 SCOTT and BORGMAN
© 2018 ZITS Partnership. Dist. by King Features
AND STAY OFF CRAIGSLIST!
HOLD ON. LET'S THINK THIS THROUGH...
SNACKS

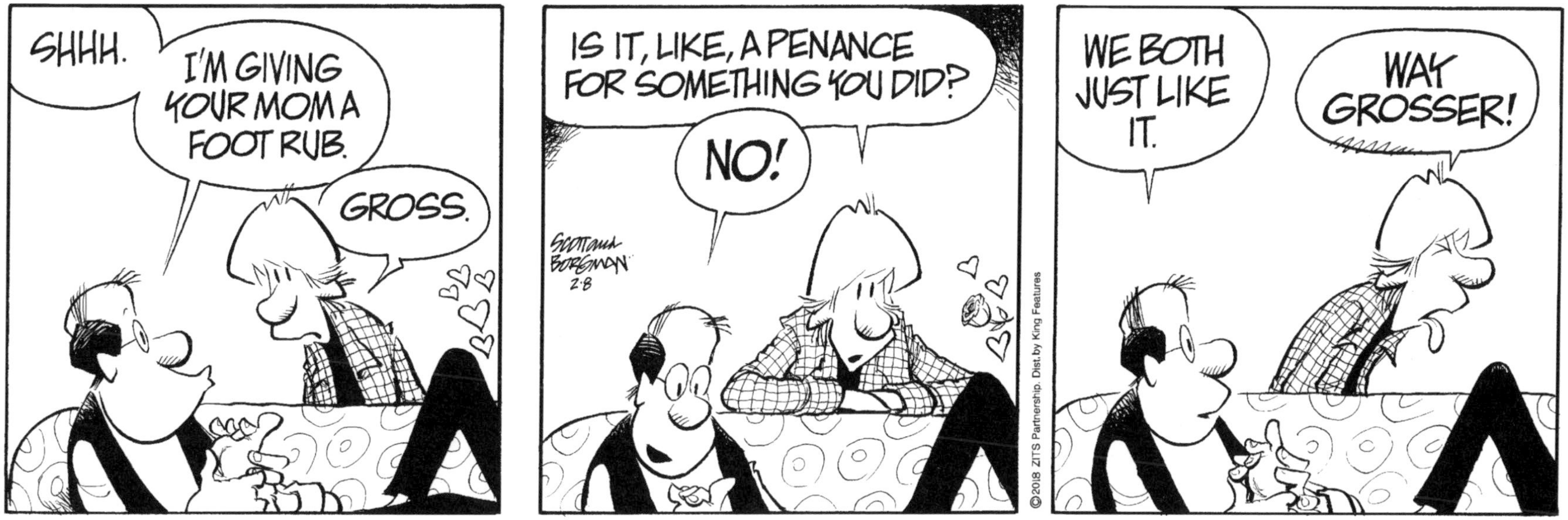
SHHH.
I'M GIVING YOUR MOM A FOOT RUB.
GROSS.
IS IT, LIKE, A PENANCE FOR SOMETHING YOU DID?
NO!
SCOTT and BORGMAN 2·8
© 2018 ZITS Partnership. Dist. by King Features
WE BOTH JUST LIKE IT.
WAY GROSSER!

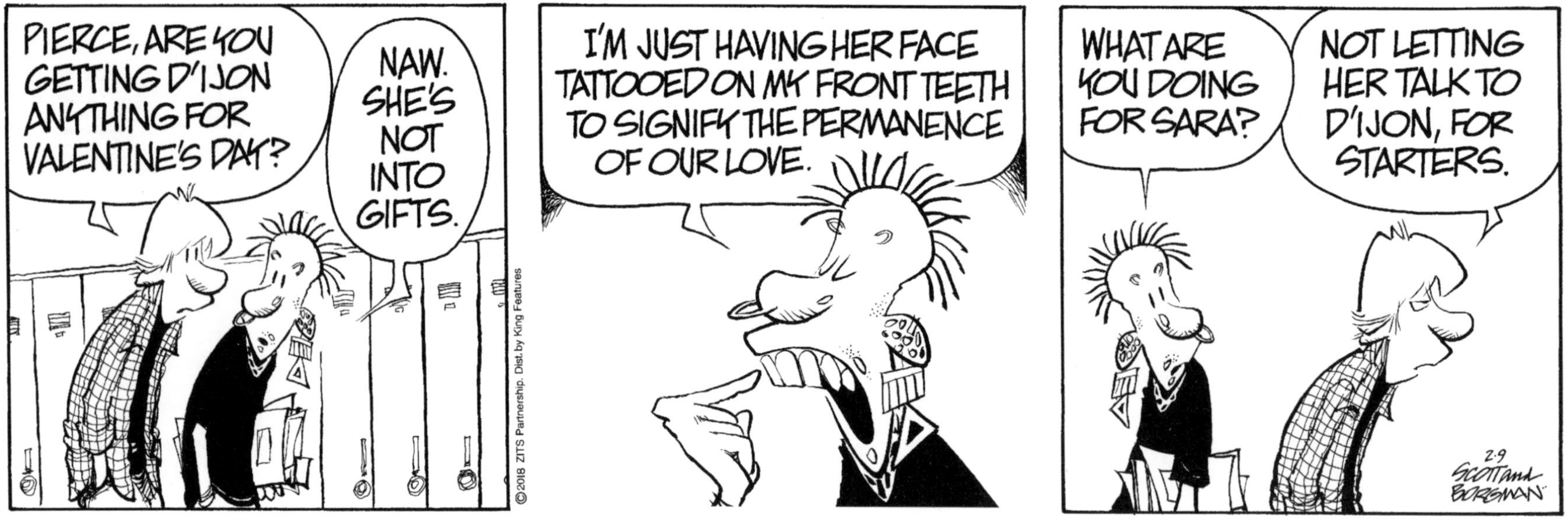
PIERCE, ARE YOU GETTING D'IJON ANYTHING FOR VALENTINE'S DAY?
NAW. SHE'S NOT INTO GIFTS.
I'M JUST HAVING HER FACE TATTOOED ON MY FRONT TEETH TO SIGNIFY THE PERMANENCE OF OUR LOVE.
WHAT ARE YOU DOING FOR SARA?
NOT LETTING HER TALK TO D'IJON, FOR STARTERS.
© 2018 ZITS Partnership. Dist. by King Features
2·9 SCOTT and BORGMAN

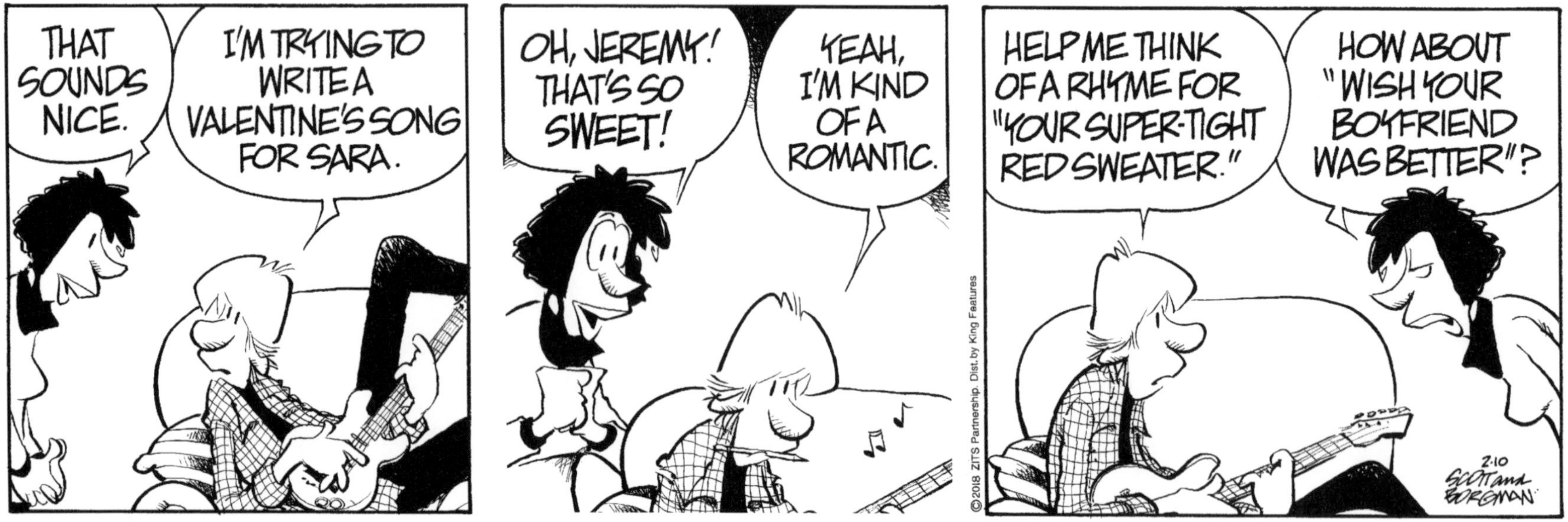
THAT SOUNDS NICE.
I'M TRYING TO WRITE A VALENTINE'S SONG FOR SARA.
OH, JEREMY! THAT'S SO SWEET!
YEAH, I'M KIND OF A ROMANTIC.
HELP ME THINK OF A RHYME FOR "YOUR SUPER-TIGHT RED SWEATER."
HOW ABOUT "WISH YOUR BOYFRIEND WAS BETTER"?
© 2018 ZITS Partnership. Dist. by King Features
2·10 SCOTT and BORGMAN

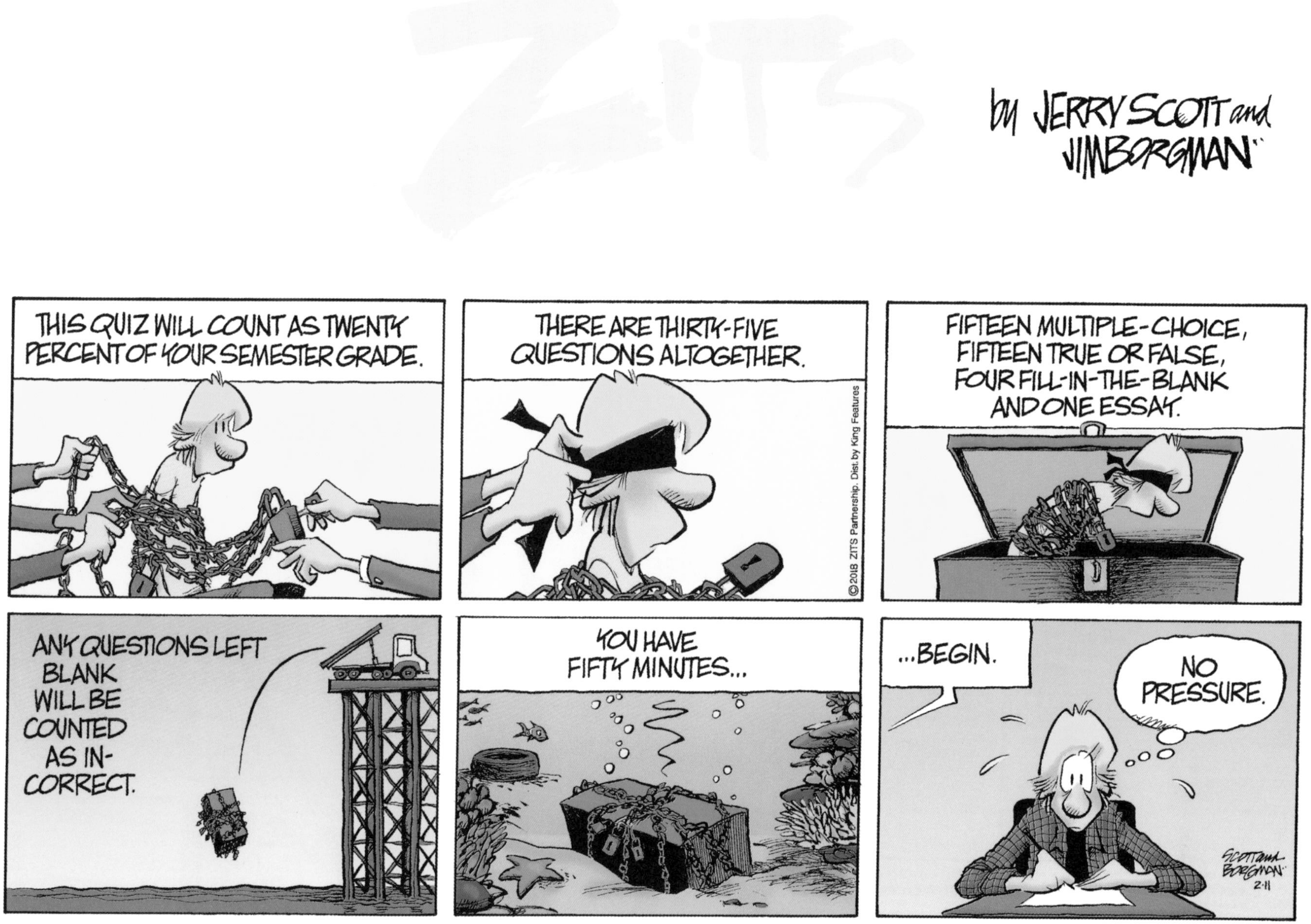
ZITS
by JERRY SCOTT and JIM BORGMAN
THIS QUIZ WILL COUNT AS TWENTY PERCENT OF YOUR SEMESTER GRADE.
THERE ARE THIRTY-FIVE QUESTIONS ALTOGETHER.
© 2018 ZITS Partnership. Dist. by King Features
FIFTEEN MULTIPLE-CHOICE, FIFTEEN TRUE OR FALSE, FOUR FILL-IN-THE-BLANK AND ONE ESSAY.
ANY QUESTIONS LEFT BLANK WILL BE COUNTED AS IN-CORRECT.
YOU HAVE FIFTY MINUTES...
...BEGIN.
NO PRESSURE.
SCOTT and BORGMAN 2·11

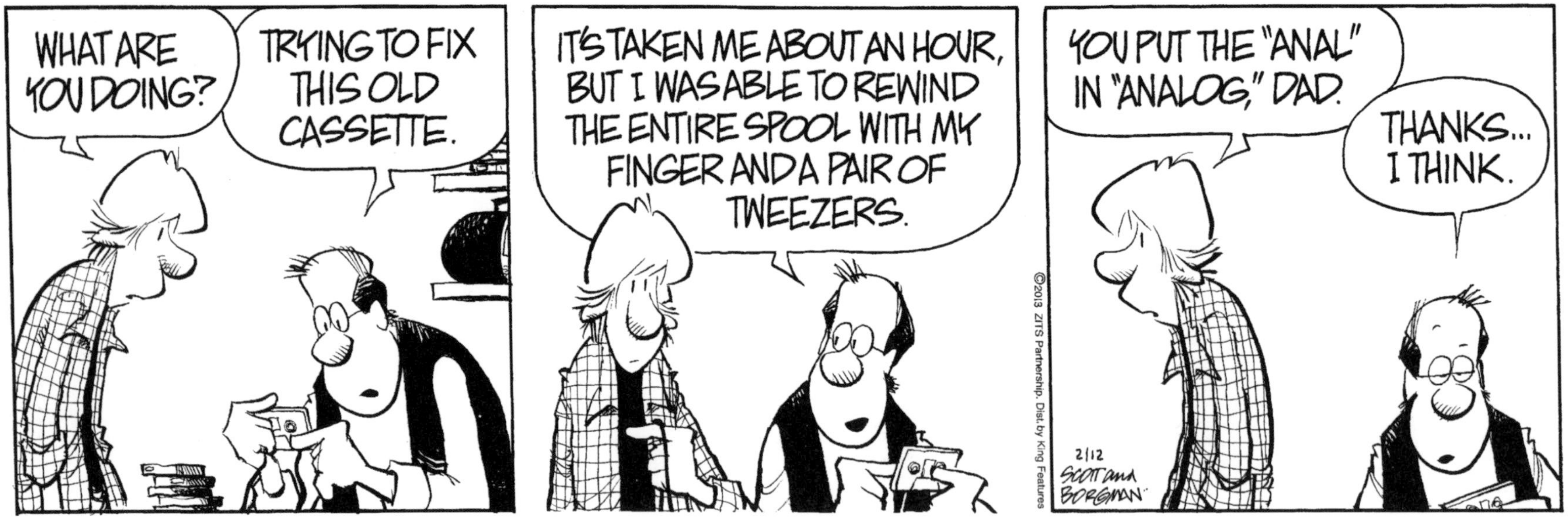
WHAT ARE YOU DOING?
TRYING TO FIX THIS OLD CASSETTE.
IT'S TAKEN ME ABOUT AN HOUR, BUT I WAS ABLE TO REWIND THE ENTIRE SPOOL WITH MY FINGER AND A PAIR OF TWEEZERS.
©2013 ZITS Partnership. Dist. by King Features
2/12 SCOTT AND BORGMAN
YOU PUT THE "ANAL" IN "ANALOG," DAD.
THANKS... I THINK.

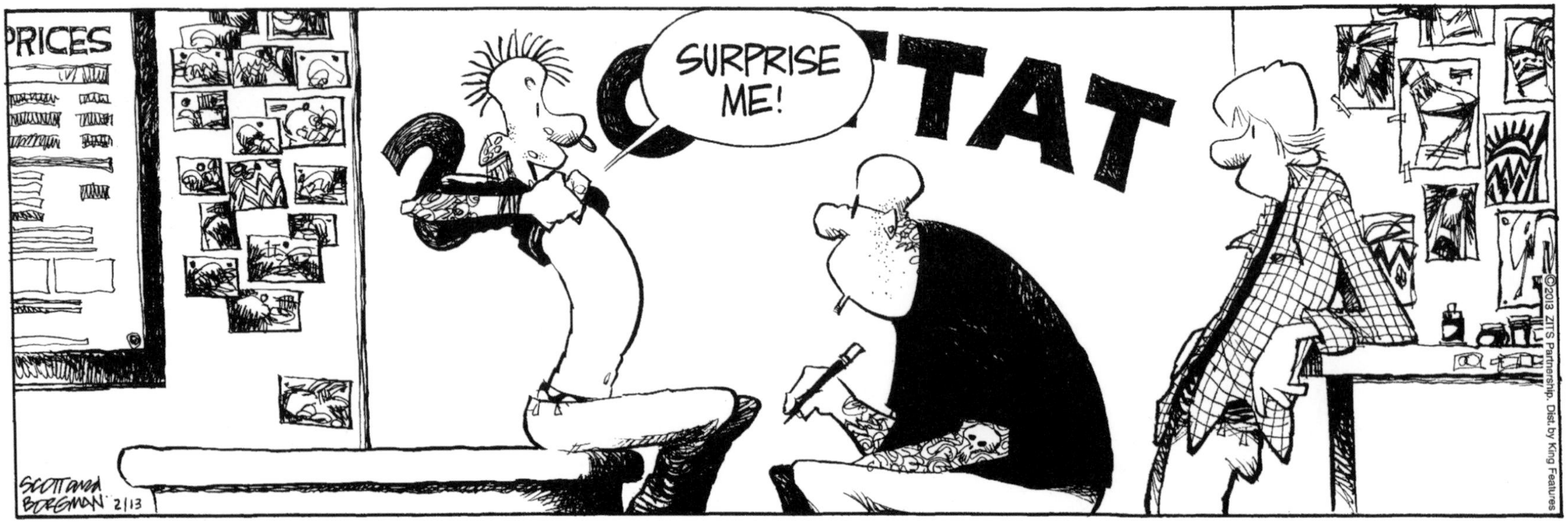
PRICES
TAT
SURPRISE ME!
SCOTT AND BORGMAN 2/13
©2013 ZITS Partnership. Dist. by King Features

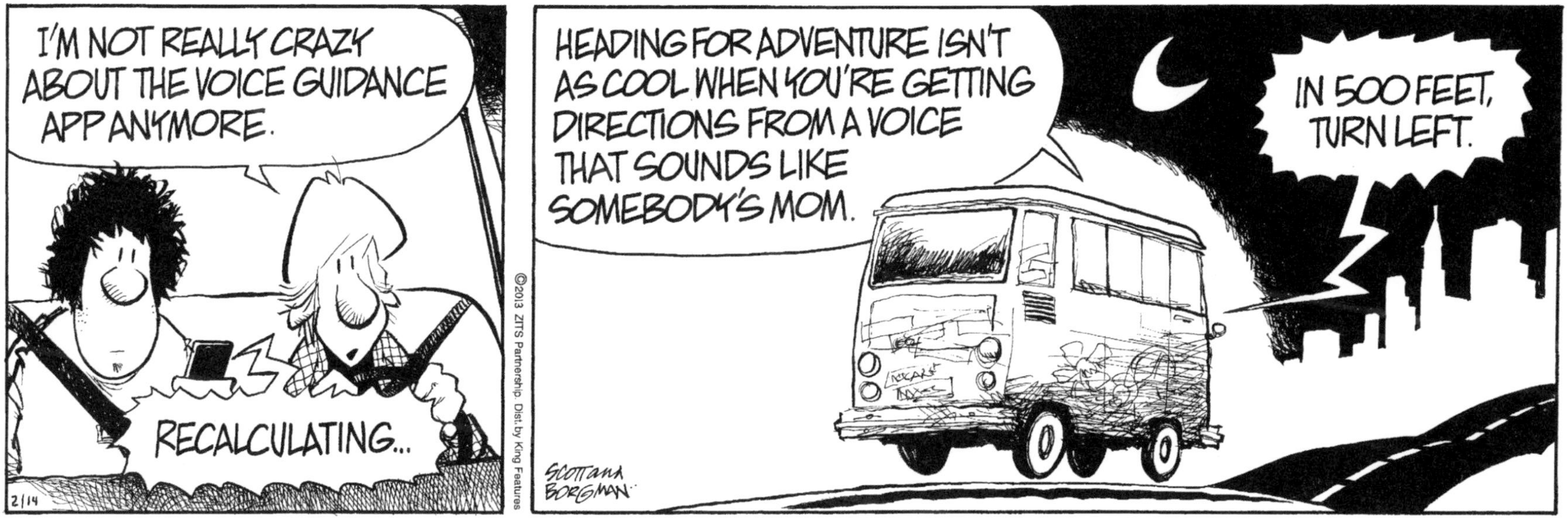
I'M NOT REALLY CRAZY ABOUT THE VOICE GUIDANCE APP ANYMORE.
RECALCULATING...
HEADING FOR ADVENTURE ISN'T AS COOL WHEN YOU'RE GETTING DIRECTIONS FROM A VOICE THAT SOUNDS LIKE SOMEBODY'S MOM.
IN 500 FEET, TURN LEFT.
2/14
©2013 ZITS Partnership. Dist. by King Features
SCOTT AND BORGMAN

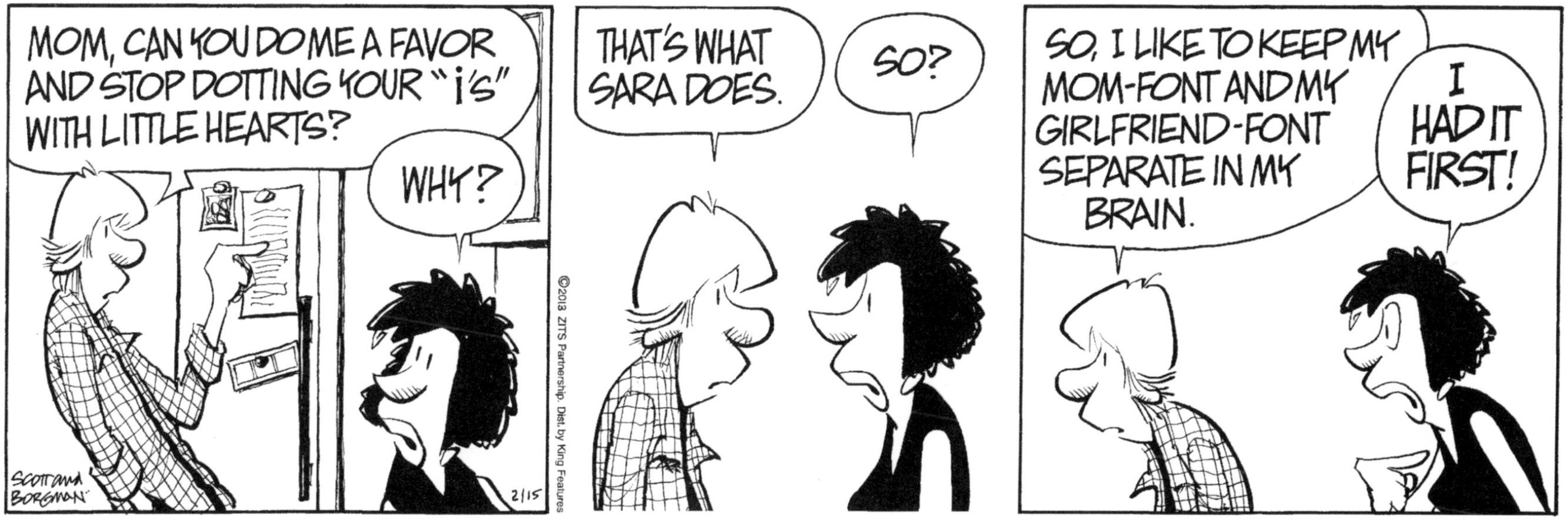
MOM, CAN YOU DO ME A FAVOR AND STOP DOTTING YOUR "i's" WITH LITTLE HEARTS?
WHY?
THAT'S WHAT SARA DOES.
SO?
SO, I LIKE TO KEEP MY MOM-FONT AND MY GIRLFRIEND-FONT SEPARATE IN MY BRAIN.
I HAD IT FIRST!
SCOTT AND BORGMAN
2/15
©2013 ZITS Partnership. Dist. by King Features

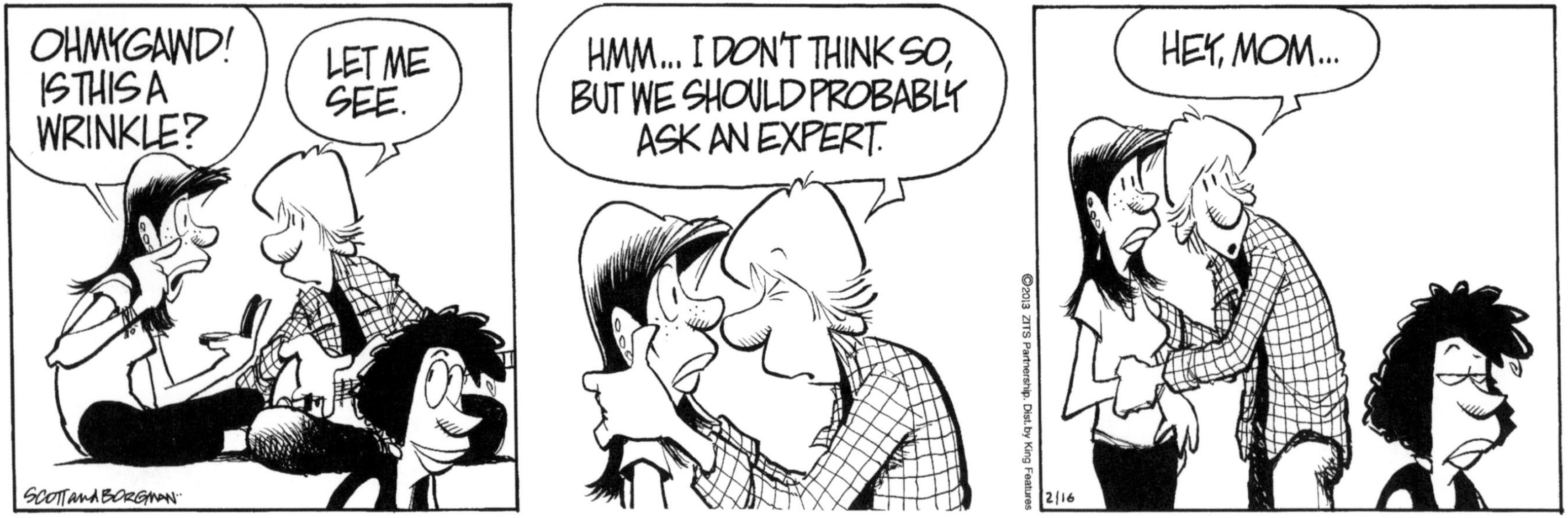
OHMYGAWD! IS THIS A WRINKLE?
LET ME SEE.
SCOTT AND BORGMAN
HMM... I DON'T THINK SO, BUT WE SHOULD PROBABLY ASK AN EXPERT.
©2013 ZITS Partnership. Dist. by King Features
HEY, MOM...
2/16

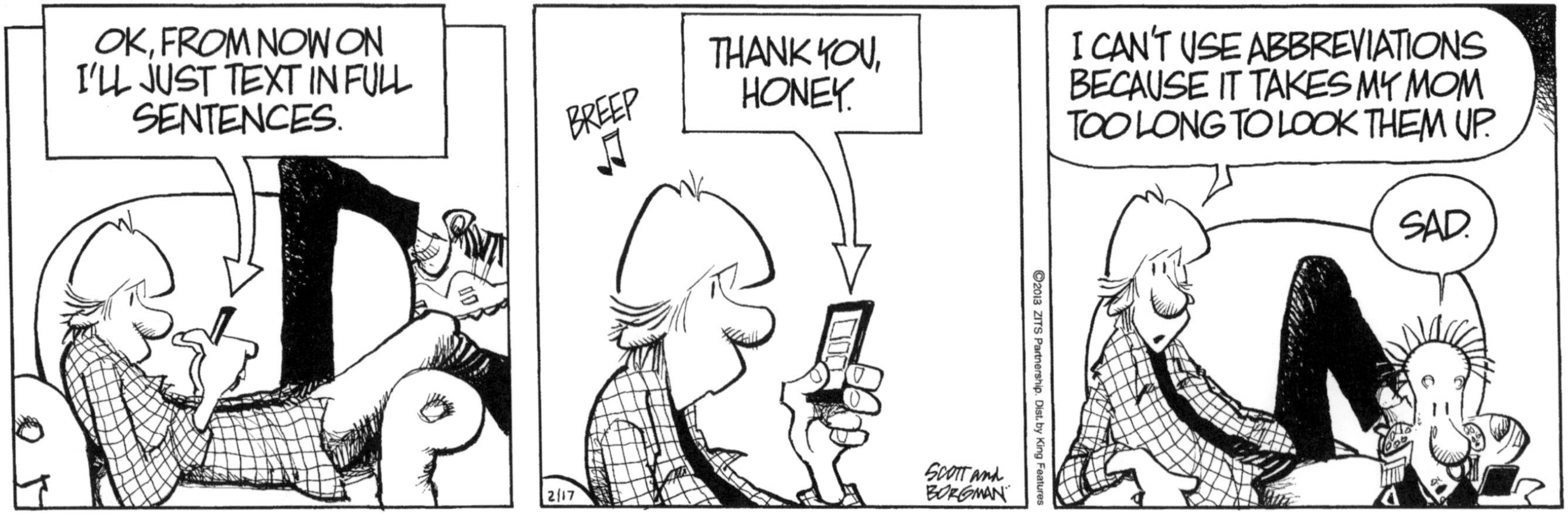
OK, FROM NOW ON I'LL JUST TEXT IN FULL SENTENCES.
BREEP
THANK YOU, HONEY.
2/17
SCOTT AND BORGMAN
©2013 ZITS Partnership. Dist. by King Features
I CAN'T USE ABBREVIATIONS BECAUSE IT TAKES MY MOM TOO LONG TO LOOK THEM UP.
SAD.

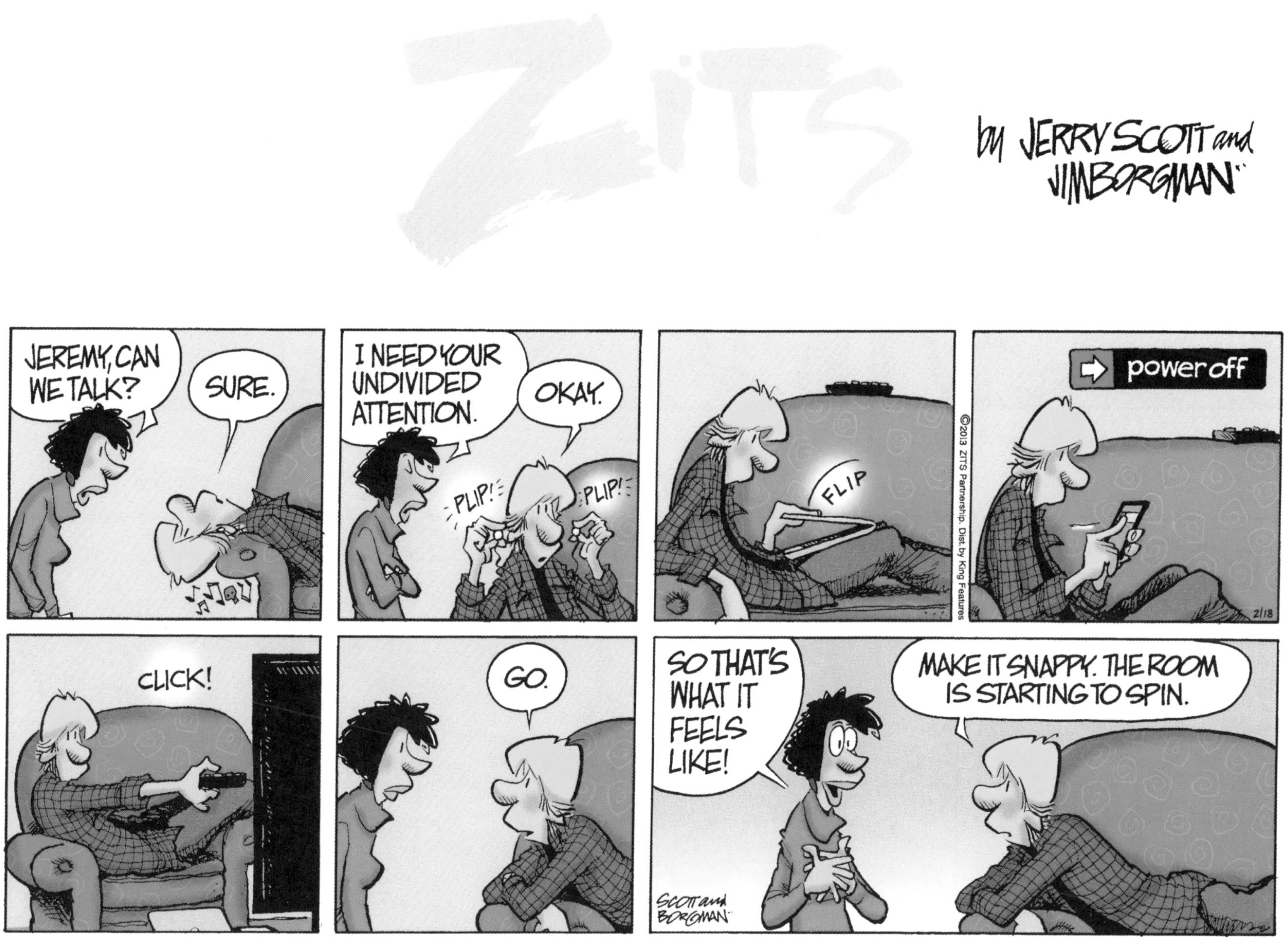
ZITS
by JERRY SCOTT and JIM BORGMAN
JEREMY, CAN WE TALK?
SURE.
I NEED YOUR UNDIVIDED ATTENTION.
OKAY.
PLIP!
PLIP!
FLIP
©2013 ZITS Partnership. Dist. by King Features
power off
2/18
CLICK!
GO.
SO THAT'S WHAT IT FEELS LIKE!
MAKE IT SNAPPY. THE ROOM IS STARTING TO SPIN.
SCOTT and BORGMAN

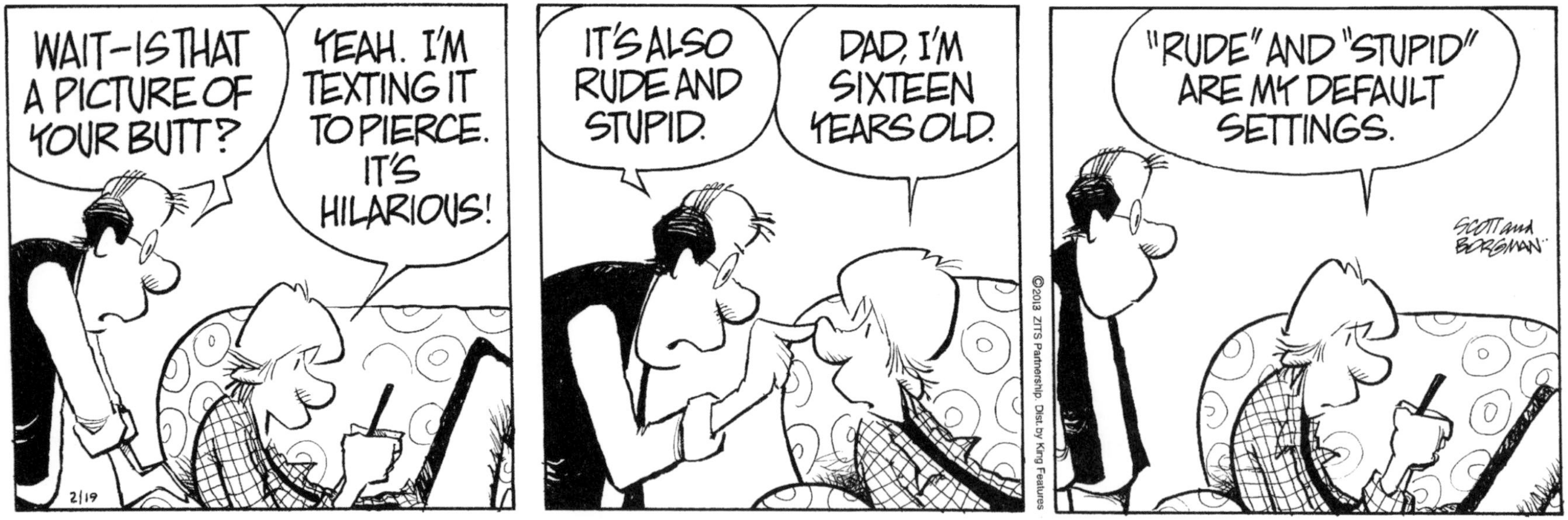
WAIT–IS THAT A PICTURE OF YOUR BUTT?
YEAH. I'M TEXTING IT TO PIERCE. IT'S HILARIOUS!
2/19
IT'S ALSO RUDE AND STUPID.
DAD, I'M SIXTEEN YEARS OLD.
©2013 ZITS Partnership. Dist. by King Features
"RUDE" AND "STUPID" ARE MY DEFAULT SETTINGS.
SCOTT and BORGMAN

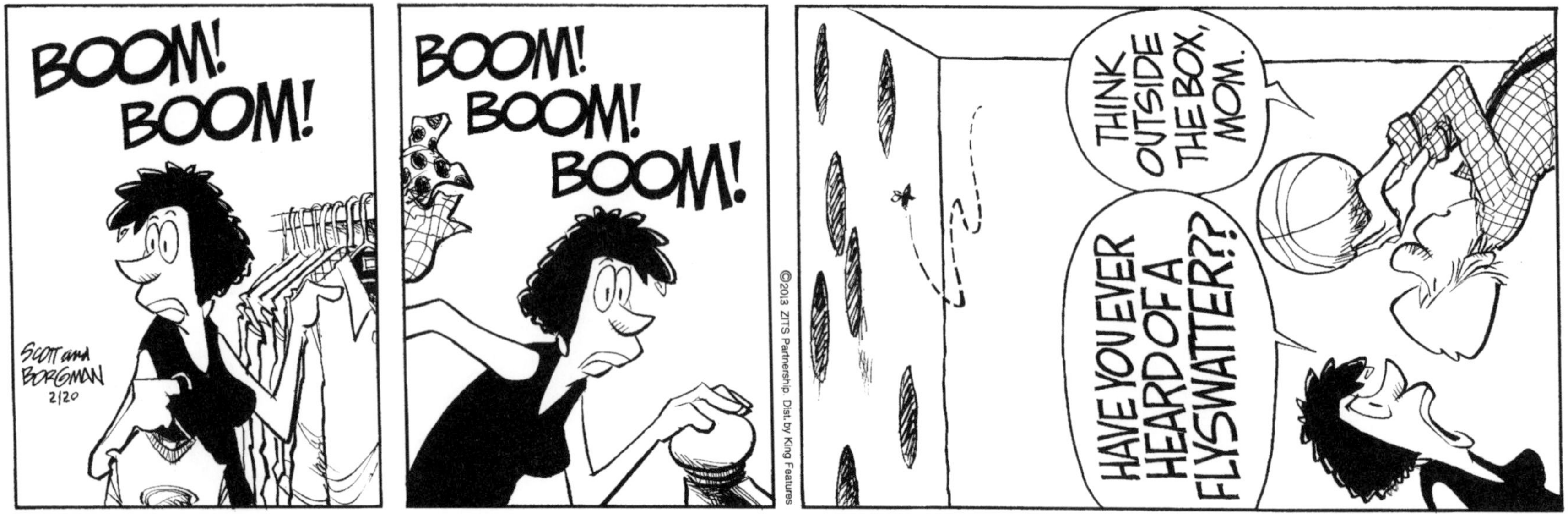
BOOM! BOOM!
SCOTT and BORGMAN 2/20
BOOM! BOOM! BOOM!
©2013 ZITS Partnership. Dist. by King Features
HAVE YOU EVER HEARD OF A FLYSWATTER!?
THINK OUTSIDE THE BOX, MOM.

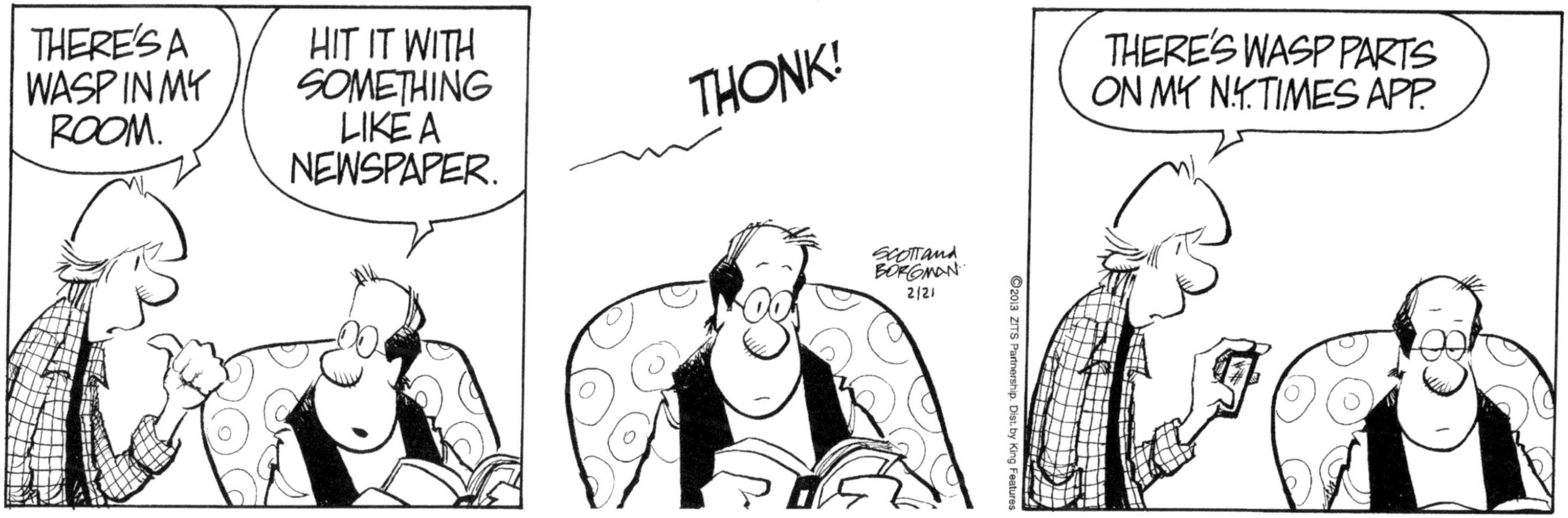
THERE'S A WASP IN MY ROOM.
HIT IT WITH SOMETHING LIKE A NEWSPAPER.
THONK!
SCOTT and BORGMAN 2/21
©2013 ZITS Partnership. Dist. by King Features
THERE'S WASP PARTS ON MY N.Y. TIMES APP.

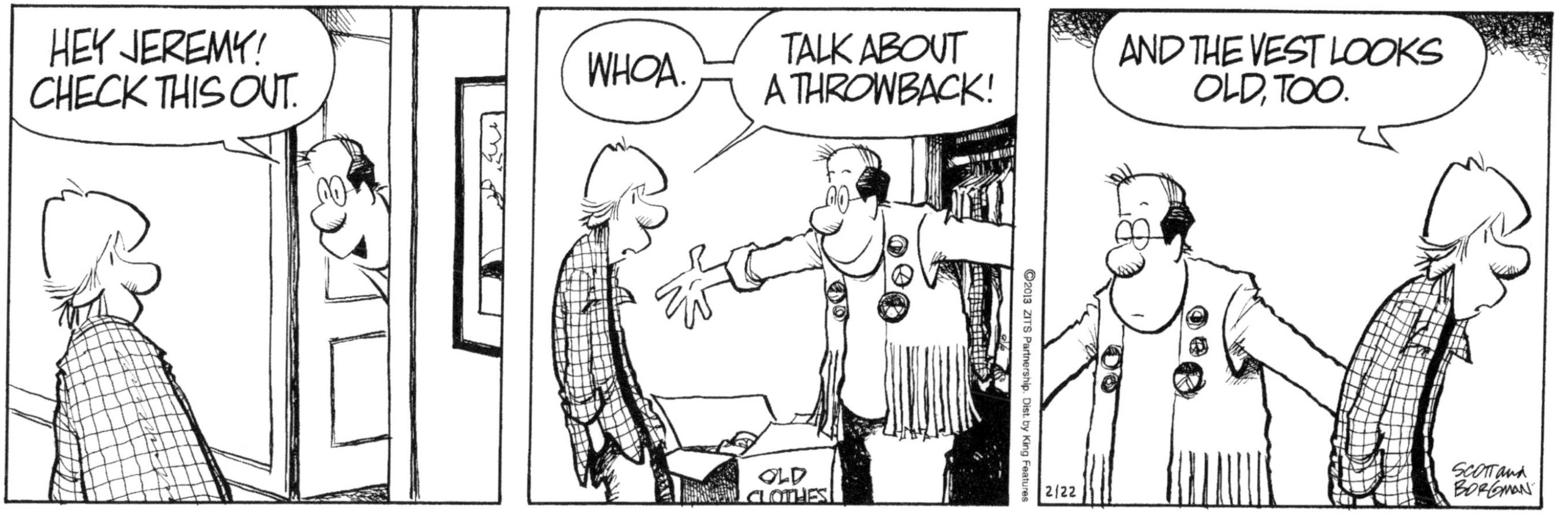
HEY JEREMY! CHECK THIS OUT.
WHOA.
TALK ABOUT A THROWBACK!
OLD CLOTHES
©2013 ZITS Partnership. Dist. by King Features
AND THE VEST LOOKS OLD, TOO.
2/22
SCOTT and BORGMAN

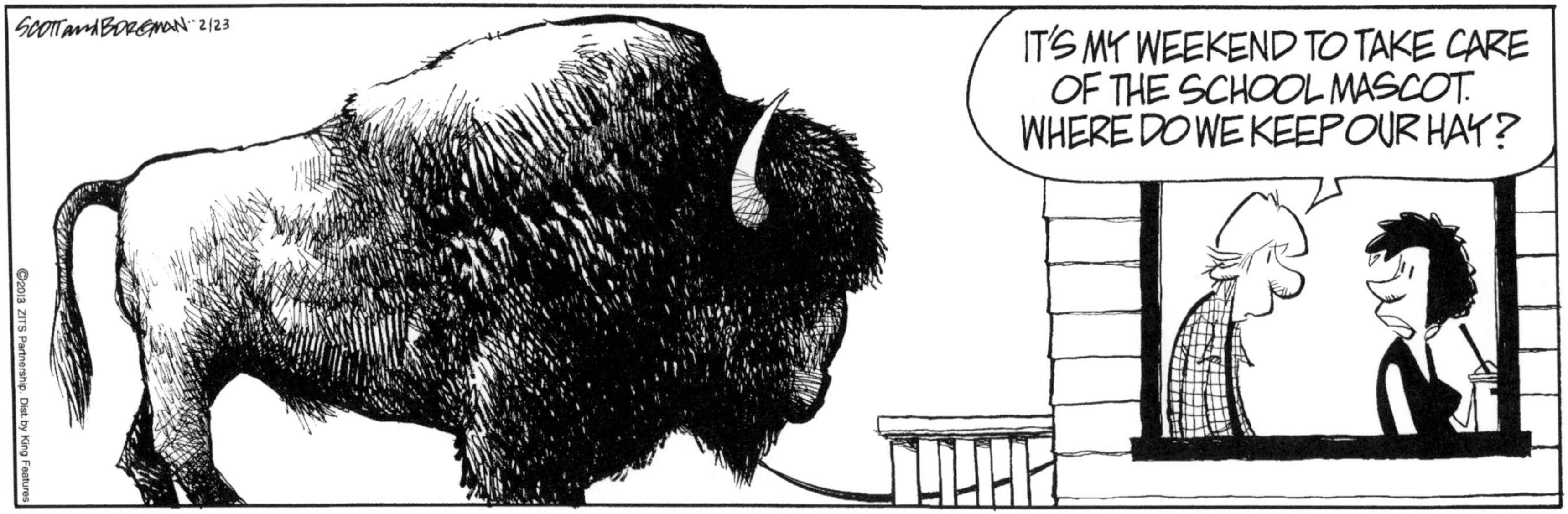
SCOTT and BORGMAN 2/23
©2013 ZITS Partnership. Dist. by King Features
IT'S MY WEEKEND TO TAKE CARE OF THE SCHOOL MASCOT. WHERE DO WE KEEP OUR HAY?

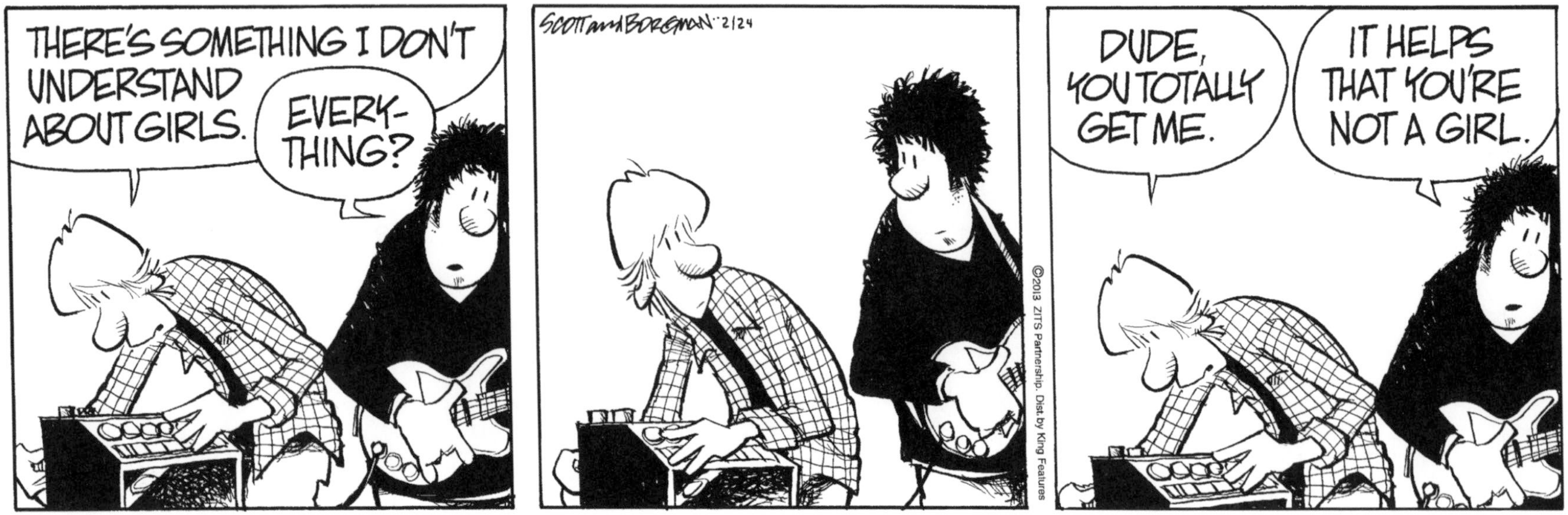
SCOTT and BORGMAN 2/24
THERE'S SOMETHING I DON'T UNDERSTAND ABOUT GIRLS.
EVERY-THING?
©2013 ZITS Partnership. Dist. by King Features
DUDE, YOU TOTALLY GET ME.
IT HELPS THAT YOU'RE NOT A GIRL.

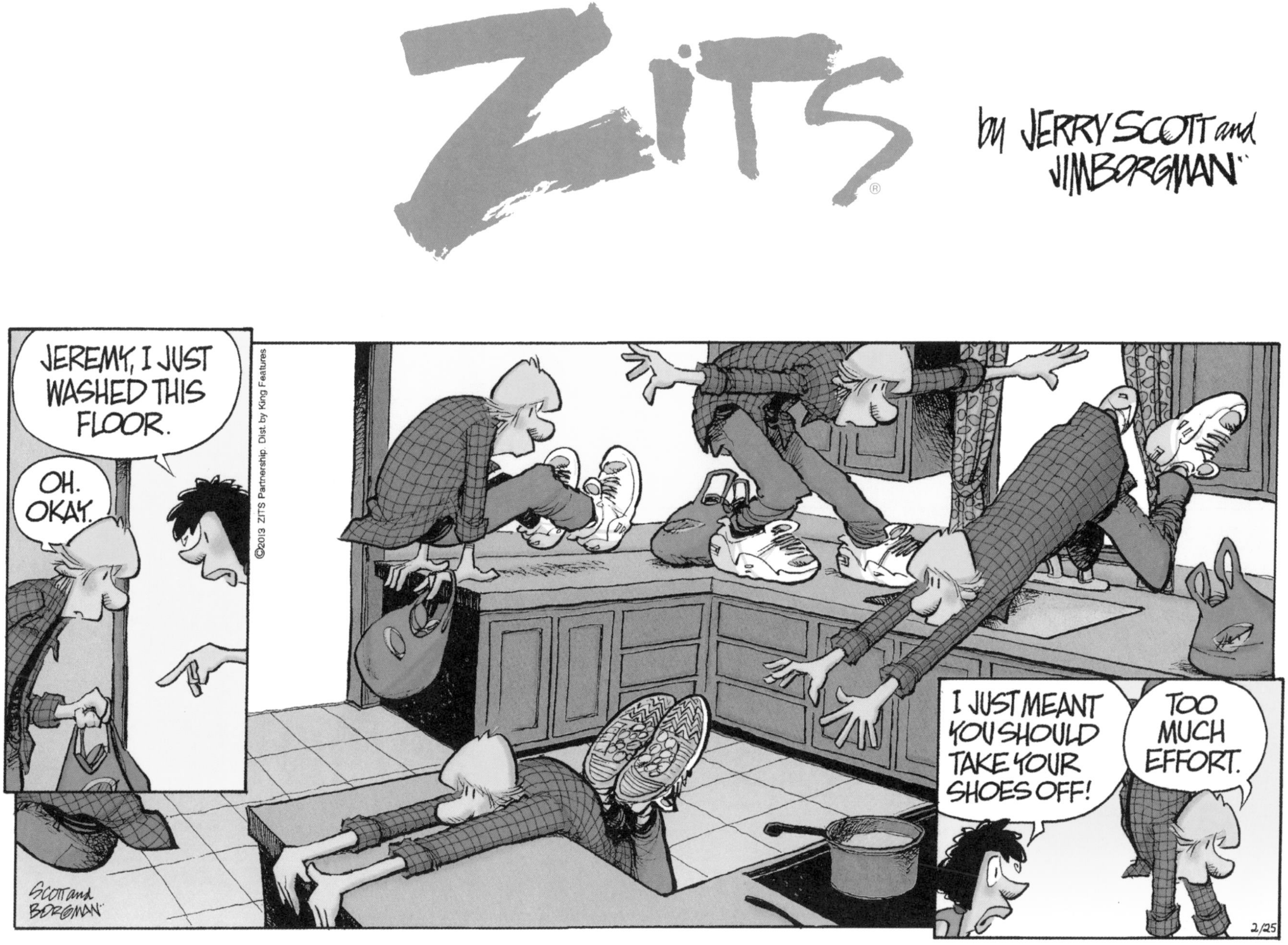
ZITS
by JERRY SCOTT and JIM BORGMAN
JEREMY, I JUST WASHED THIS FLOOR.
OH. OKAY.
©2013 ZITS Partnership. Dist. by King Features
I JUST MEANT YOU SHOULD TAKE YOUR SHOES OFF!
TOO MUCH EFFORT.
SCOTT and BORGMAN
2/25

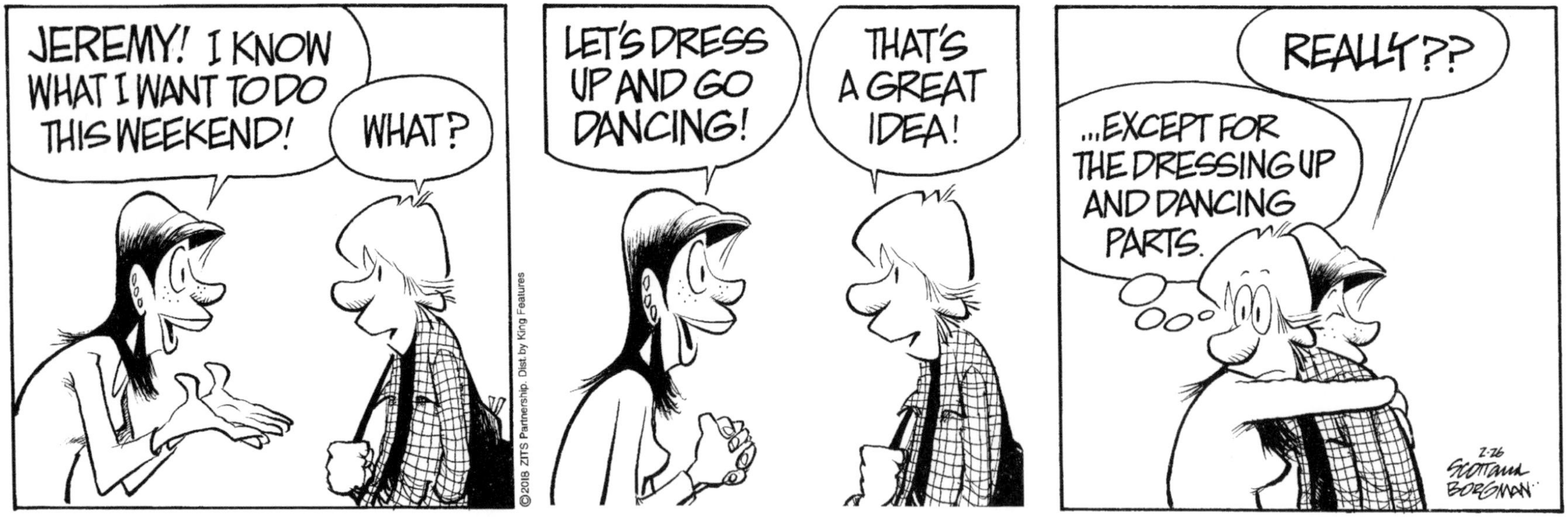
JEREMY! I KNOW WHAT I WANT TO DO THIS WEEKEND!
WHAT?
LET'S DRESS UP AND GO DANCING!
THAT'S A GREAT IDEA!
REALLY??
...EXCEPT FOR THE DRESSING UP AND DANCING PARTS.
©2018 ZITS Partnership. Dist. by King Features
2-26 SCOTT and BORGMAN

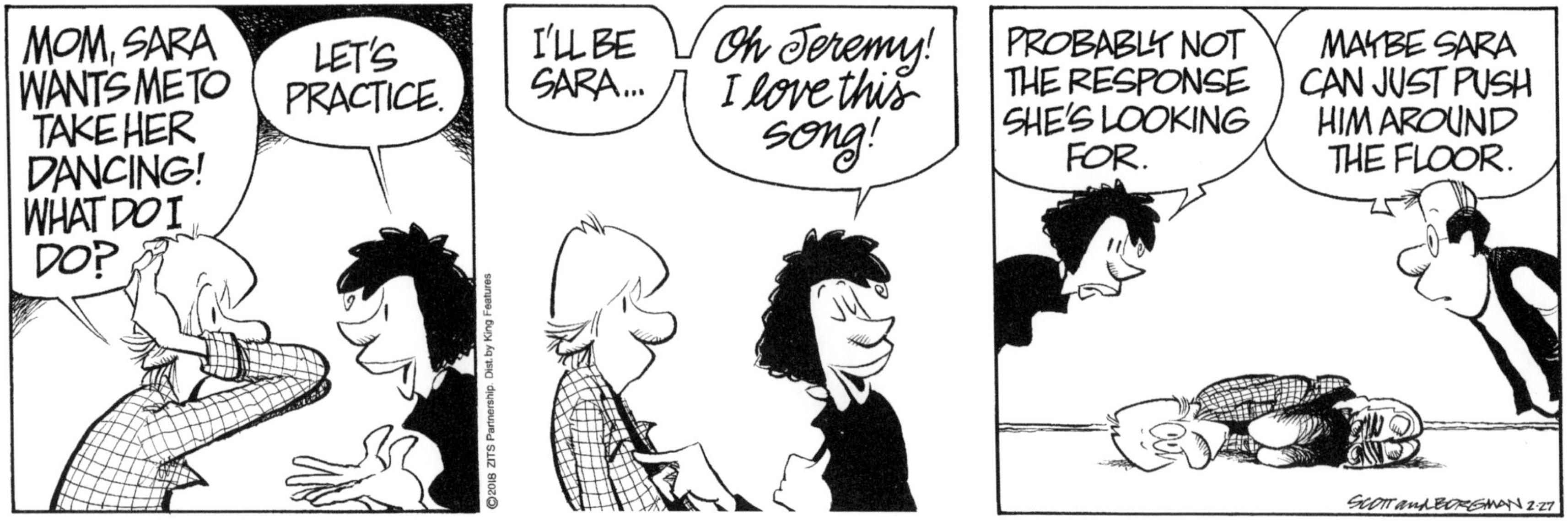
MOM, SARA WANTS ME TO TAKE HER DANCING! WHAT DO I DO?
LET'S PRACTICE.
I'LL BE SARA...
Oh Jeremy! I love this song!
PROBABLY NOT THE RESPONSE SHE'S LOOKING FOR.
MAYBE SARA CAN JUST PUSH HIM AROUND THE FLOOR.
©2018 ZITS Partnership. Dist. by King Features
SCOTT and BORGMAN 2-27

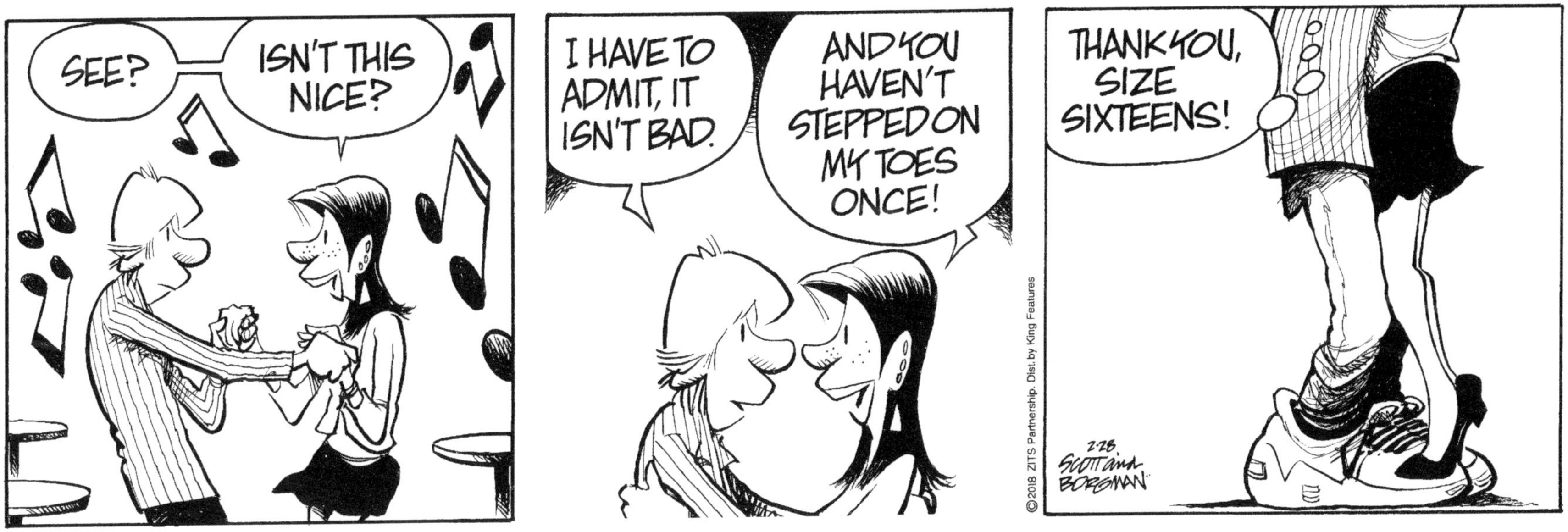
SEE?
ISN'T THIS NICE?
I HAVE TO ADMIT, IT ISN'T BAD.
AND YOU HAVEN'T STEPPED ON MY TOES ONCE!
THANK YOU, SIZE SIXTEENS!
©2018 ZITS Partnership. Dist. by King Features
2-28 SCOTT and BORGMAN

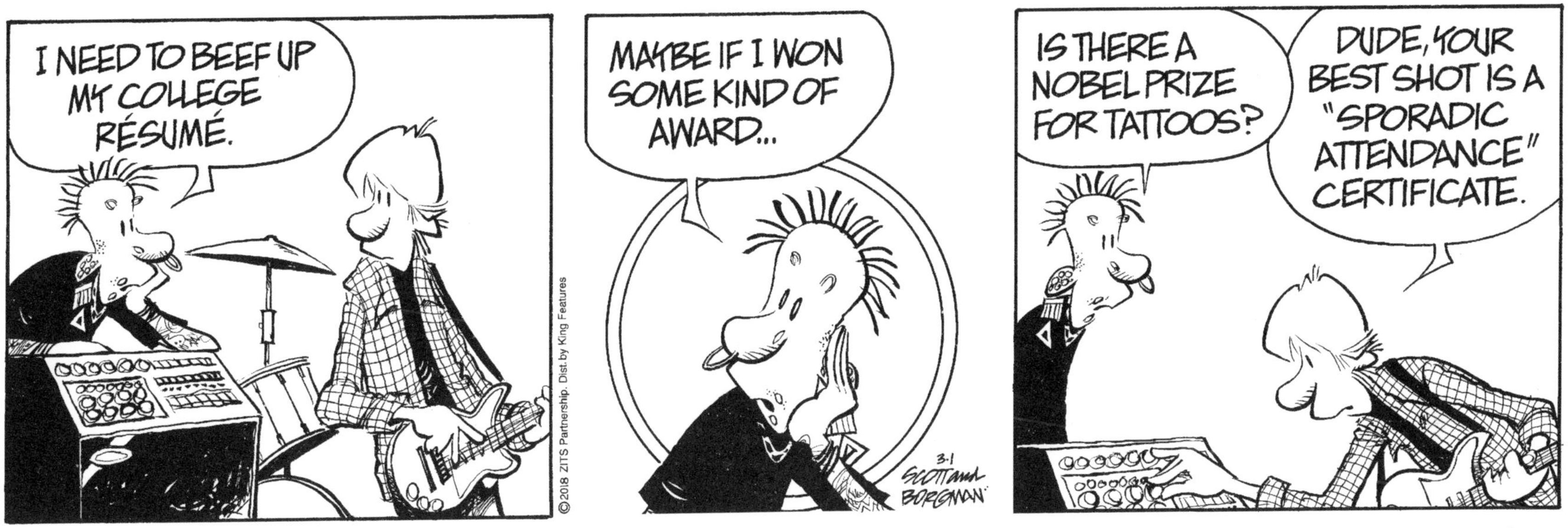
I NEED TO BEEF UP MY COLLEGE RÉSUMÉ.
©2018 ZITS Partnership. Dist. by King Features
MAYBE IF I WON SOME KIND OF AWARD...
3-1 SCOTT and BORGMAN
IS THERE A NOBEL PRIZE FOR TATTOOS?
DUDE, YOUR BEST SHOT IS A "SPORADIC ATTENDANCE" CERTIFICATE.

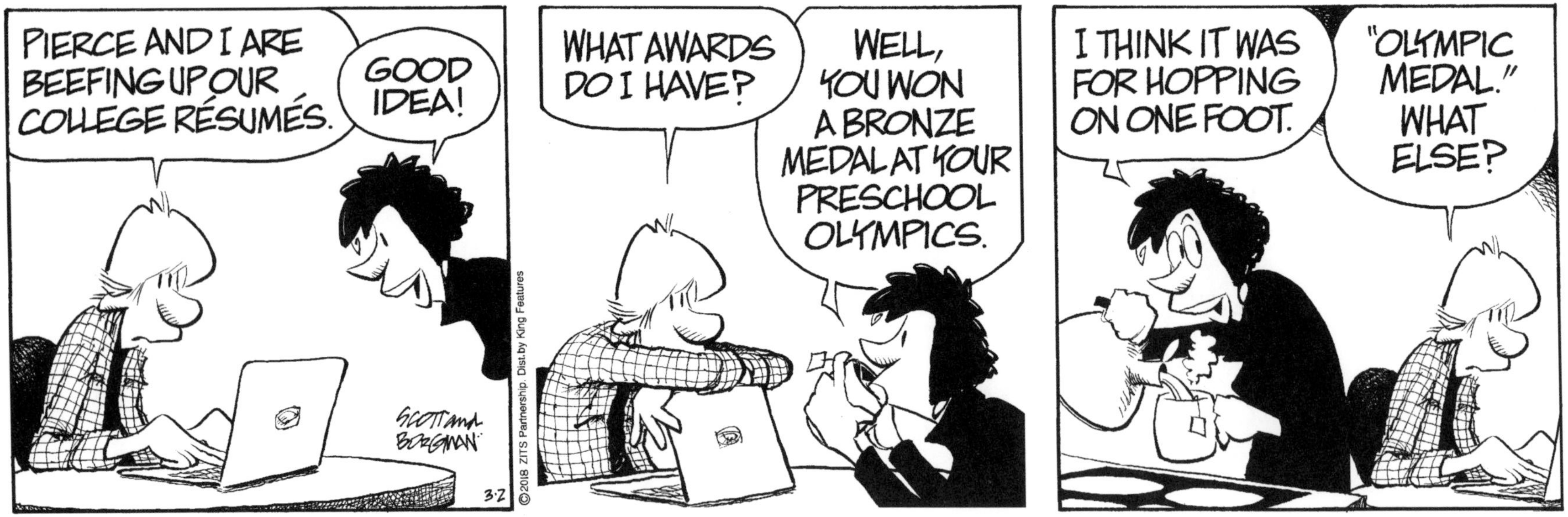
PIERCE AND I ARE BEEFING UP OUR COLLEGE RÉSUMÉS.
GOOD IDEA!
WHAT AWARDS DO I HAVE?
WELL, YOU WON A BRONZE MEDAL AT YOUR PRESCHOOL OLYMPICS.
I THINK IT WAS FOR HOPPING ON ONE FOOT.
"OLYMPIC MEDAL." WHAT ELSE?
SCOTT AND BORGMAN
3·2
©2018 ZITS Partnership. Dist. by King Features

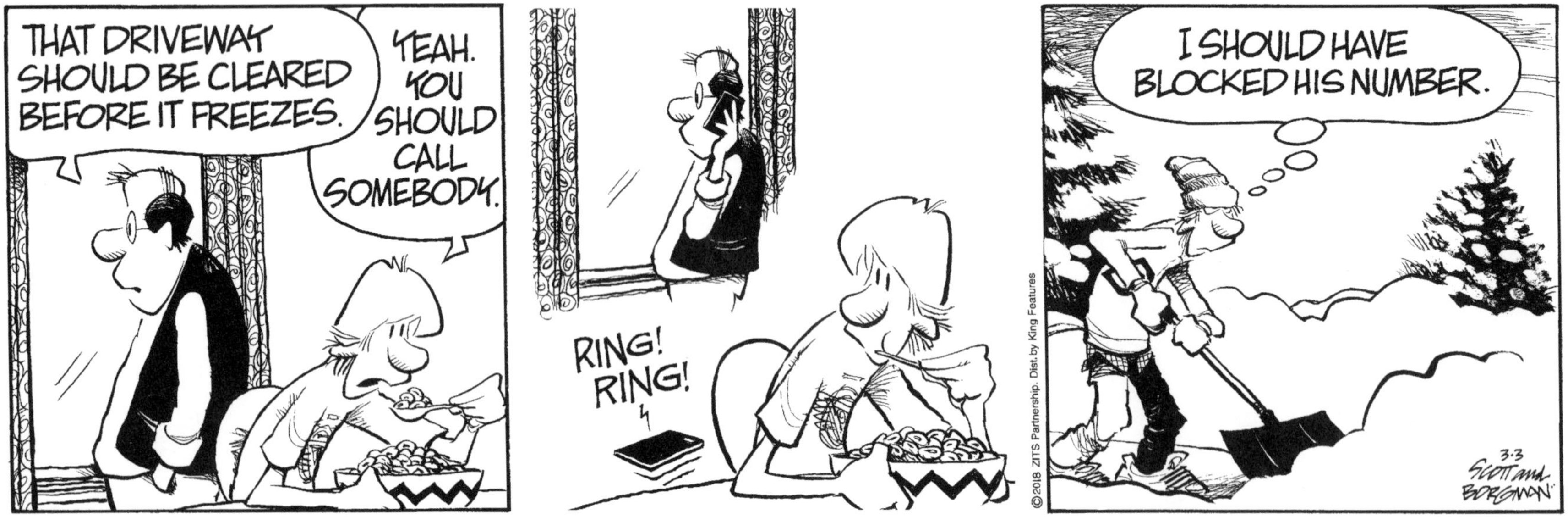
THAT DRIVEWAY SHOULD BE CLEARED BEFORE IT FREEZES.
YEAH. YOU SHOULD CALL SOMEBODY.
RING! RING!
I SHOULD HAVE BLOCKED HIS NUMBER.
3·3
SCOTT AND BORGMAN
©2018 ZITS Partnership. Dist. by King Features

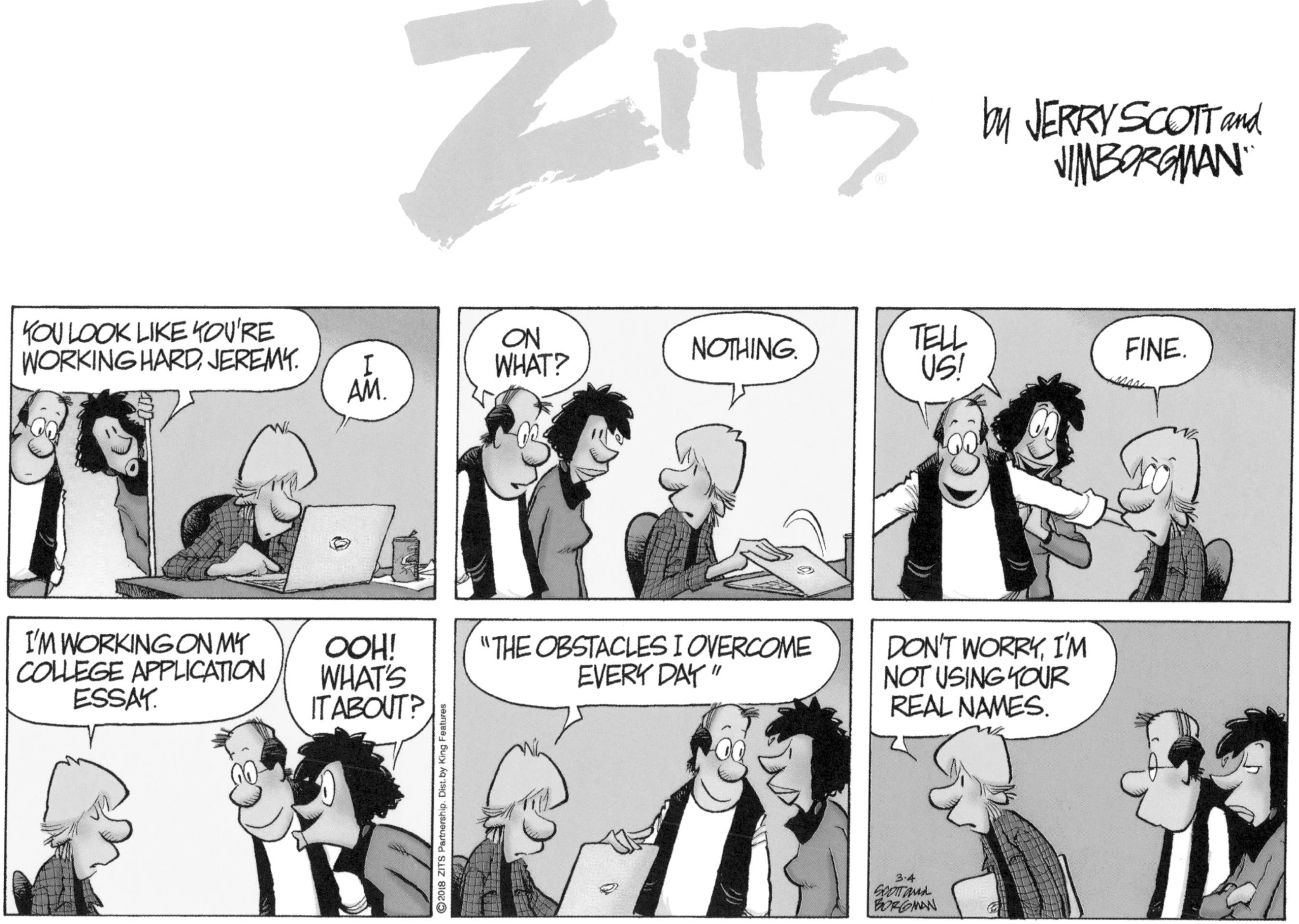
ZITS
by JERRY SCOTT and JIM BORGMAN
YOU LOOK LIKE YOU'RE WORKING HARD, JEREMY.
I AM.
ON WHAT?
NOTHING.
TELL US!
FINE.
I'M WORKING ON MY COLLEGE APPLICATION ESSAY.
OOH! WHAT'S IT ABOUT?
©2018 ZITS Partnership. Dist. by King Features
"THE OBSTACLES I OVERCOME EVERY DAY"
DON'T WORRY, I'M NOT USING YOUR REAL NAMES.
3-4 SCOTT and BORGMAN

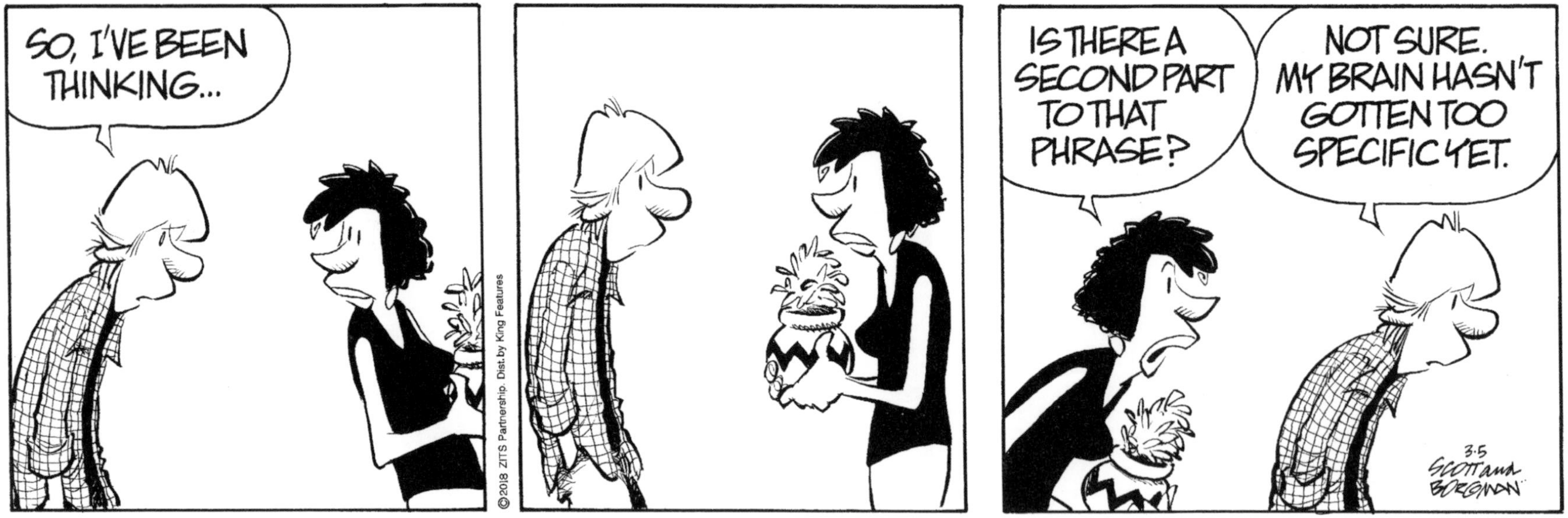
SO, I'VE BEEN THINKING...
©2018 ZITS Partnership. Dist. by King Features
IS THERE A SECOND PART TO THAT PHRASE?
NOT SURE. MY BRAIN HASN'T GOTTEN TOO SPECIFIC YET.
3·5 SCOTT and BORGMAN

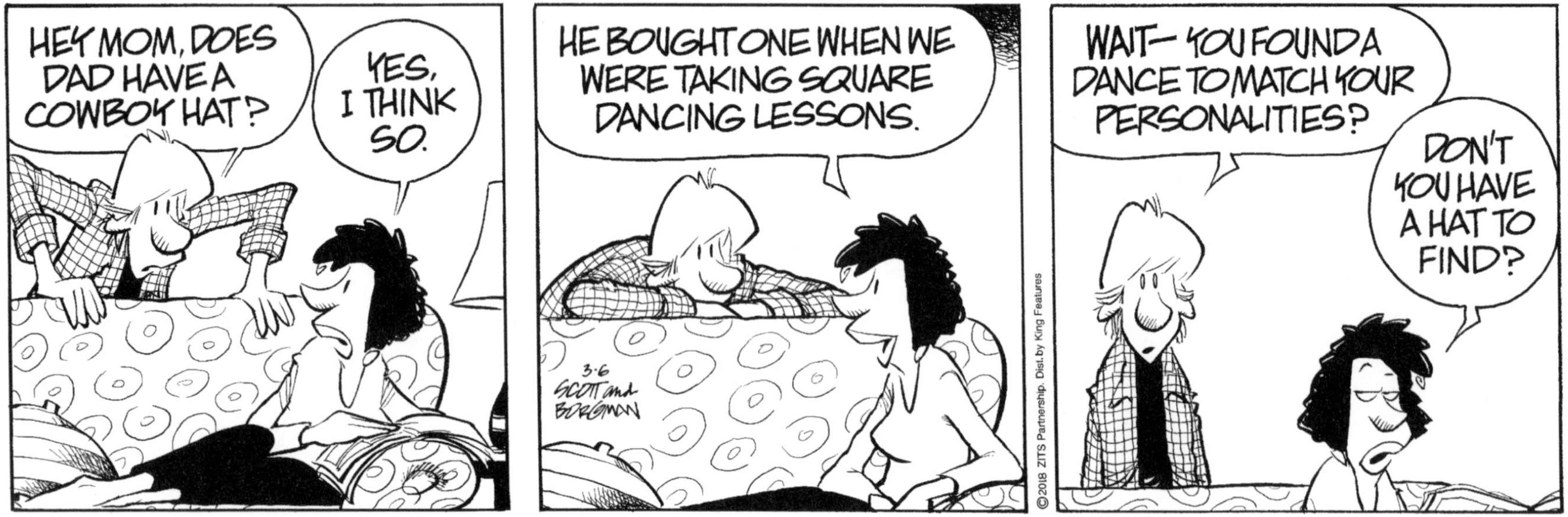
HEY MOM, DOES DAD HAVE A COWBOY HAT?
YES, I THINK SO.
3·6 SCOTT and BORGMAN
HE BOUGHT ONE WHEN WE WERE TAKING SQUARE DANCING LESSONS.
©2018 ZITS Partnership. Dist. by King Features
WAIT— YOU FOUND A DANCE TO MATCH YOUR PERSONALITIES?
DON'T YOU HAVE A HAT TO FIND?

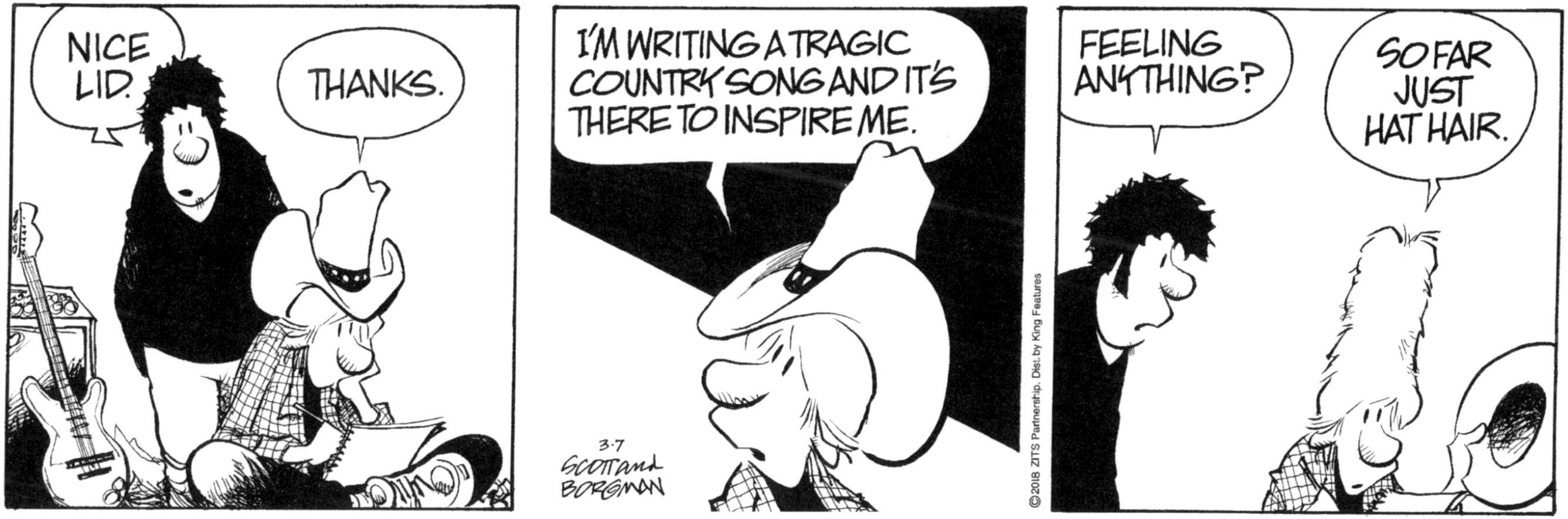
NICE LID.
THANKS.
I'M WRITING A TRAGIC COUNTRY SONG AND IT'S THERE TO INSPIRE ME.
3·7
SCOTT and BORGMAN
FEELING ANYTHING?
SO FAR JUST HAT HAIR.
©2018 ZITS Partnership. Dist. by King Features

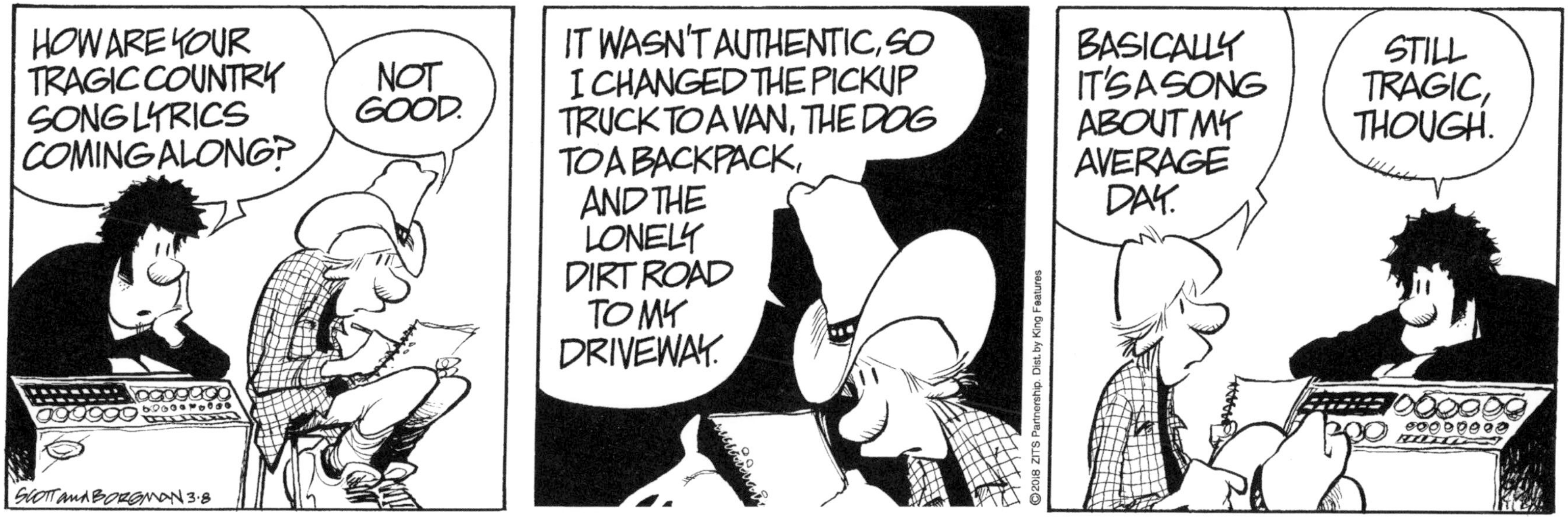
HOW ARE YOUR TRAGIC COUNTRY SONG LYRICS COMING ALONG?
NOT GOOD.
SCOTT and BORGMAN 3·8
IT WASN'T AUTHENTIC, SO I CHANGED THE PICKUP TRUCK TO A VAN, THE DOG TO A BACKPACK, AND THE LONELY DIRT ROAD TO MY DRIVEWAY.
©2018 ZITS Partnership. Dist. by King Features
BASICALLY IT'S A SONG ABOUT MY AVERAGE DAY.
STILL TRAGIC, THOUGH.

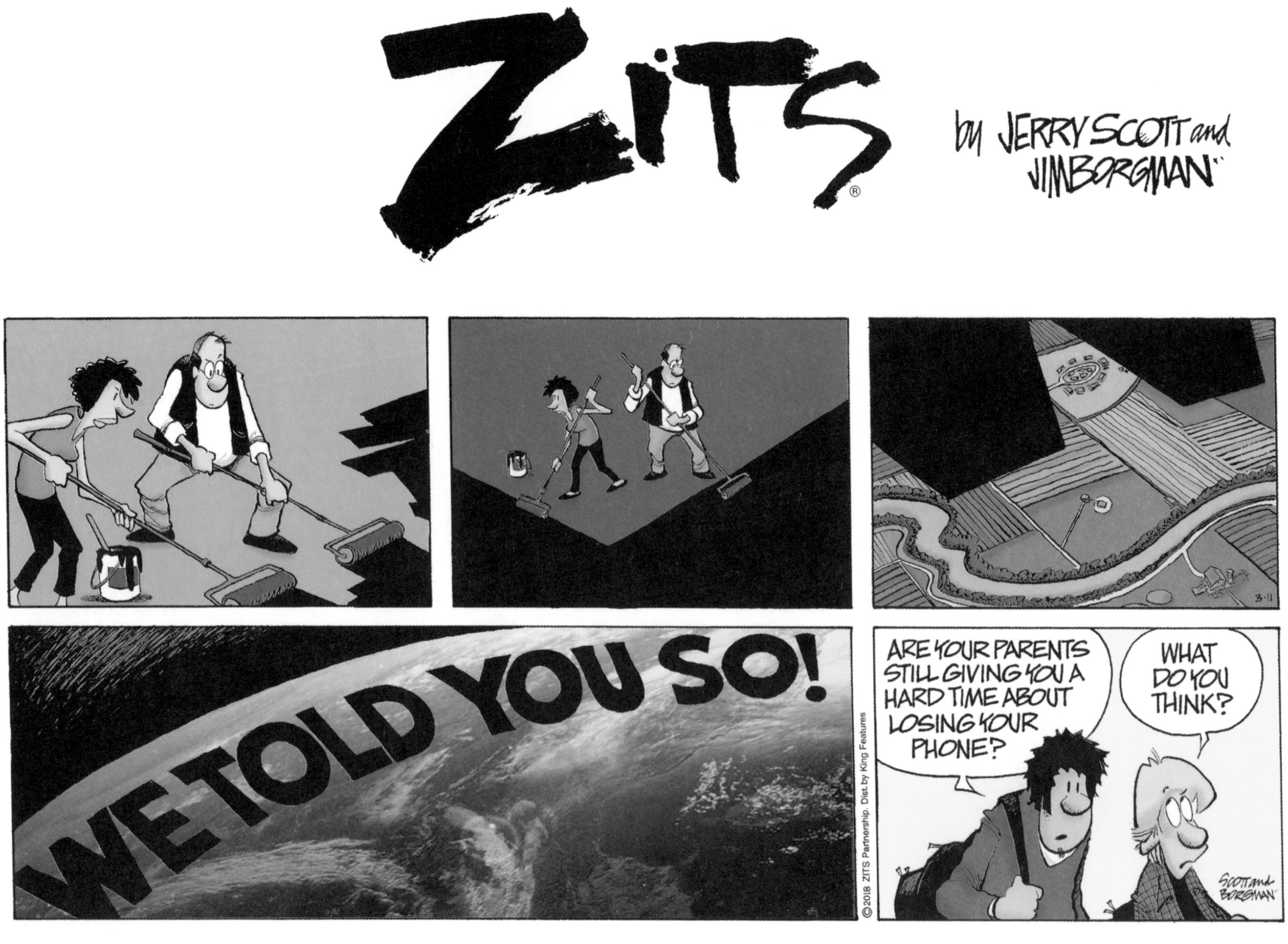
ZITS
by JERRY SCOTT and JIM BORGMAN
3-11
WE TOLD YOU SO!
©2018 ZITS Partnership. Dist. by King Features
ARE YOUR PARENTS STILL GIVING YOU A HARD TIME ABOUT LOSING YOUR PHONE?
WHAT DO YOU THINK?
SCOTT and BORGMAN

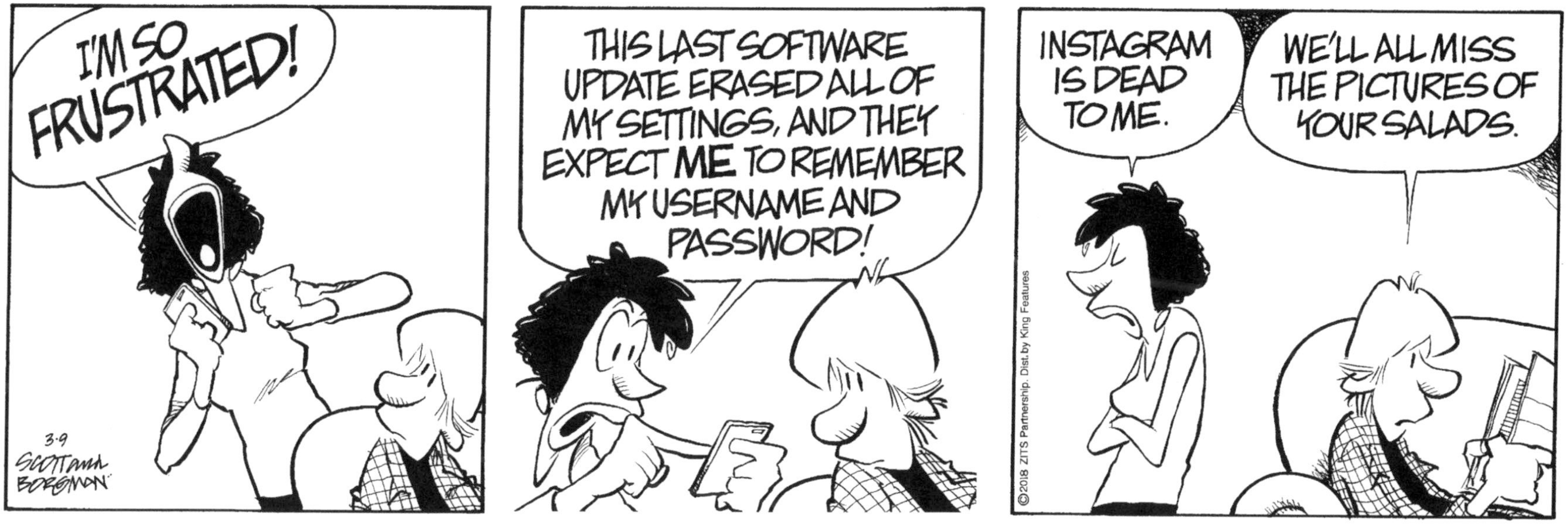
I'M SO FRUSTRATED!
3·9 SCOTT and BORGMAN
THIS LAST SOFTWARE UPDATE ERASED ALL OF MY SETTINGS, AND THEY EXPECT ME TO REMEMBER MY USERNAME AND PASSWORD!
©2018 ZITS Partnership. Dist. by King Features
INSTAGRAM IS DEAD TO ME.
WE'LL ALL MISS THE PICTURES OF YOUR SALADS.

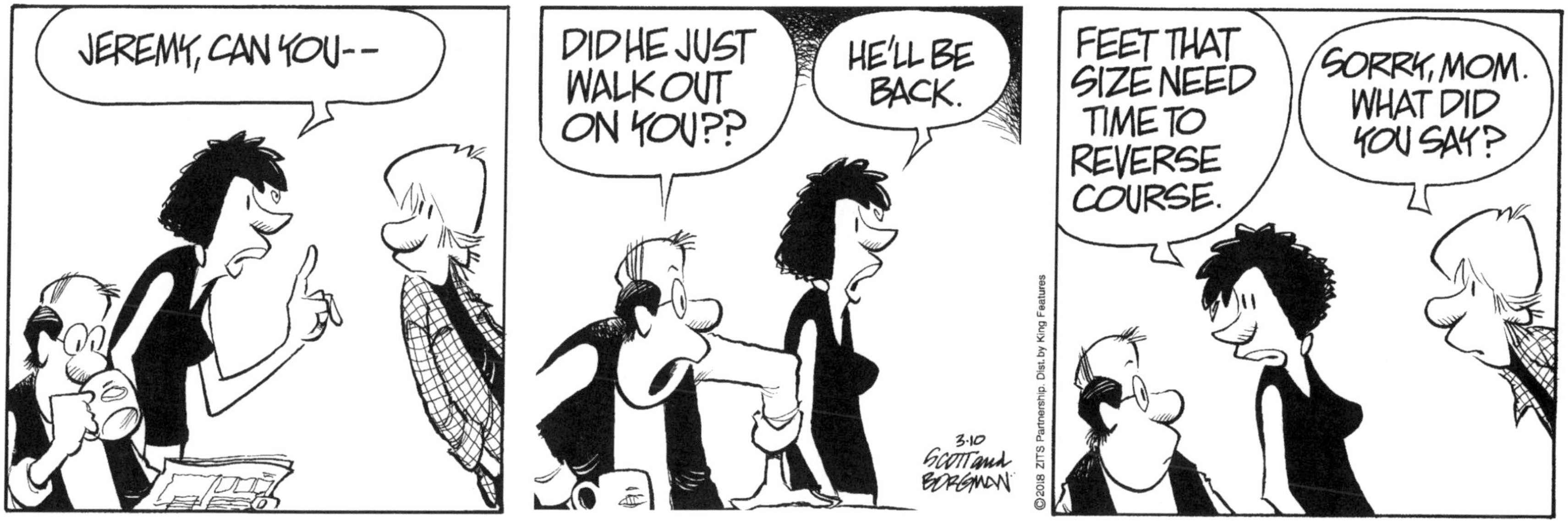
JEREMY, CAN YOU--
DID HE JUST WALK OUT ON YOU??
HE'LL BE BACK.
3·10 SCOTT and BORGMAN
©2018 ZITS Partnership. Dist. by King Features
FEET THAT SIZE NEED TIME TO REVERSE COURSE.
SORRY, MOM. WHAT DID YOU SAY?

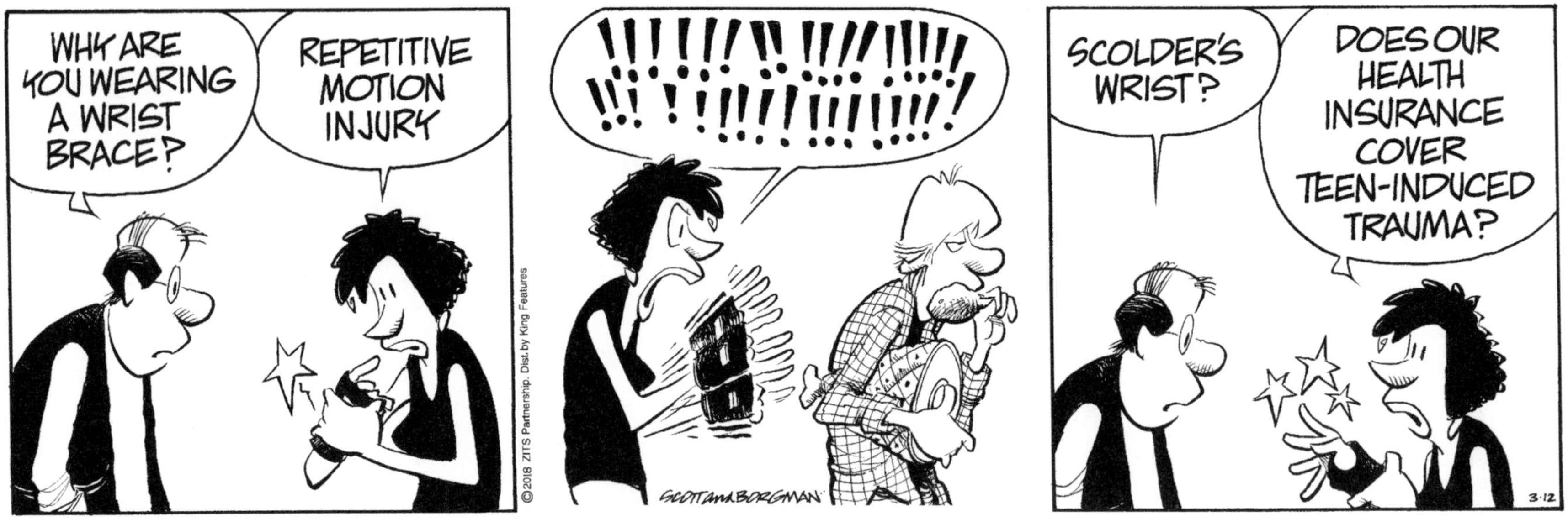
WHY ARE YOU WEARING A WRIST BRACE?
REPETITIVE MOTION INJURY
©2018 ZITS Partnership. Dist. by King Features
!!
SCOTT and BORGMAN
SCOLDER'S WRIST?
DOES OUR HEALTH INSURANCE COVER TEEN-INDUCED TRAUMA?
3.12

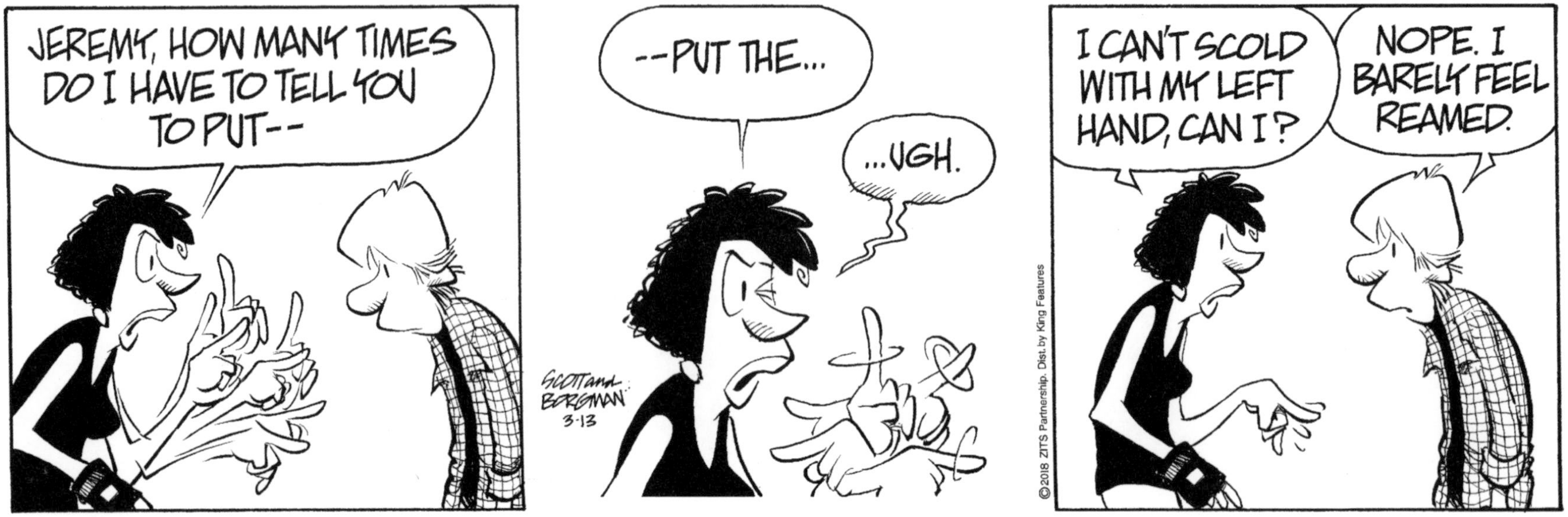
JEREMY, HOW MANY TIMES DO I HAVE TO TELL YOU TO PUT--
--PUT THE...
...UGH.
SCOTT and BORGMAN 3.13
©2018 ZITS Partnership. Dist. by King Features
I CAN'T SCOLD WITH MY LEFT HAND, CAN I?
NOPE. I BARELY FEEL REAMED.

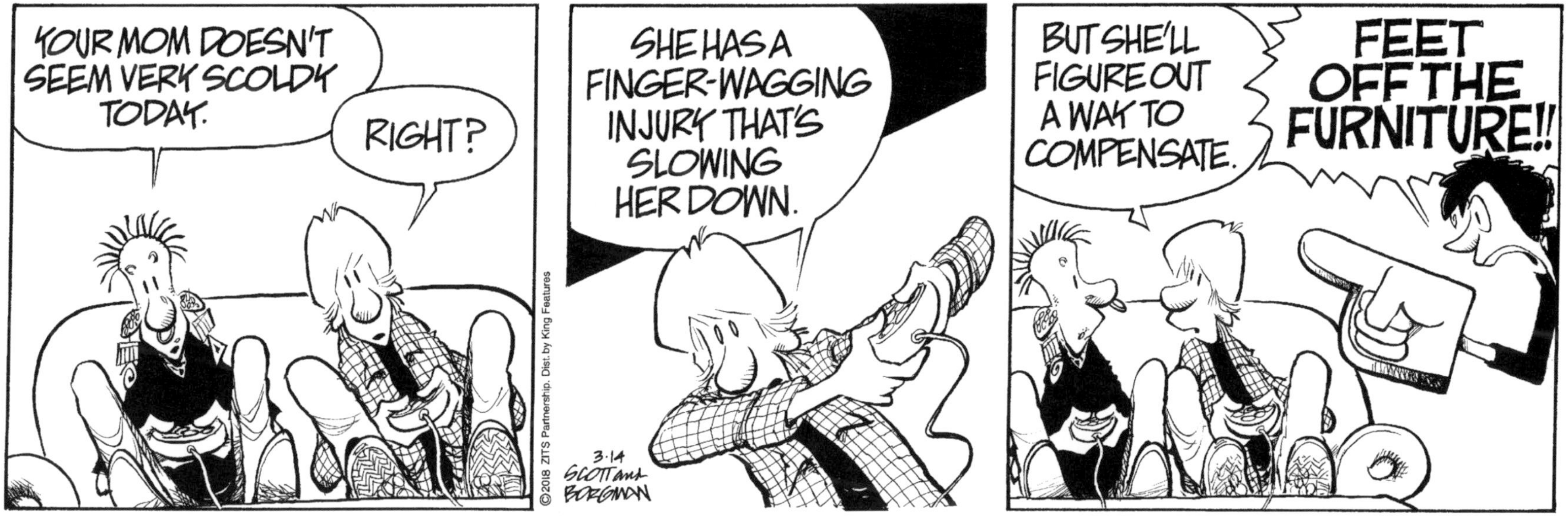
YOUR MOM DOESN'T SEEM VERY SCOLDY TODAY.
RIGHT?
SHE HAS A FINGER-WAGGING INJURY THAT'S SLOWING HER DOWN.
©2018 ZITS Partnership. Dist. by King Features
3.14 SCOTT and BORGMAN
BUT SHE'LL FIGURE OUT A WAY TO COMPENSATE.
FEET OFF THE FURNITURE!!

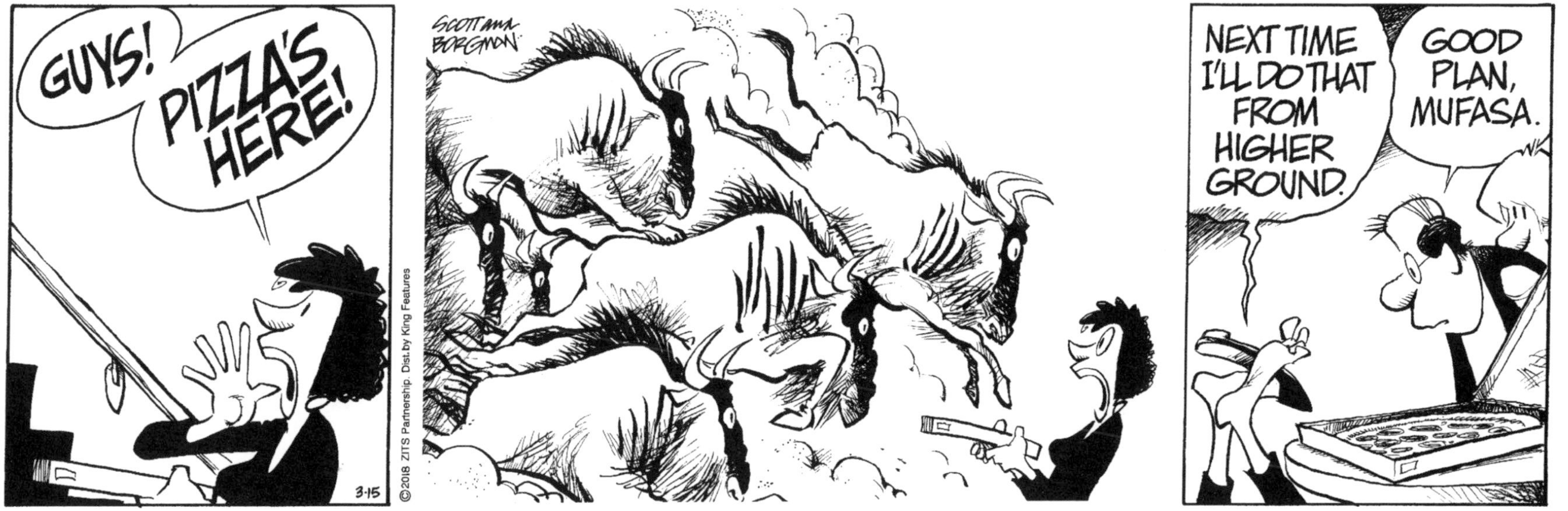
GUYS!
PIZZA'S HERE!
3.15
©2018 ZITS Partnership. Dist. by King Features
SCOTT and BORGMAN
NEXT TIME I'LL DO THAT FROM HIGHER GROUND.
GOOD PLAN, MUFASA.

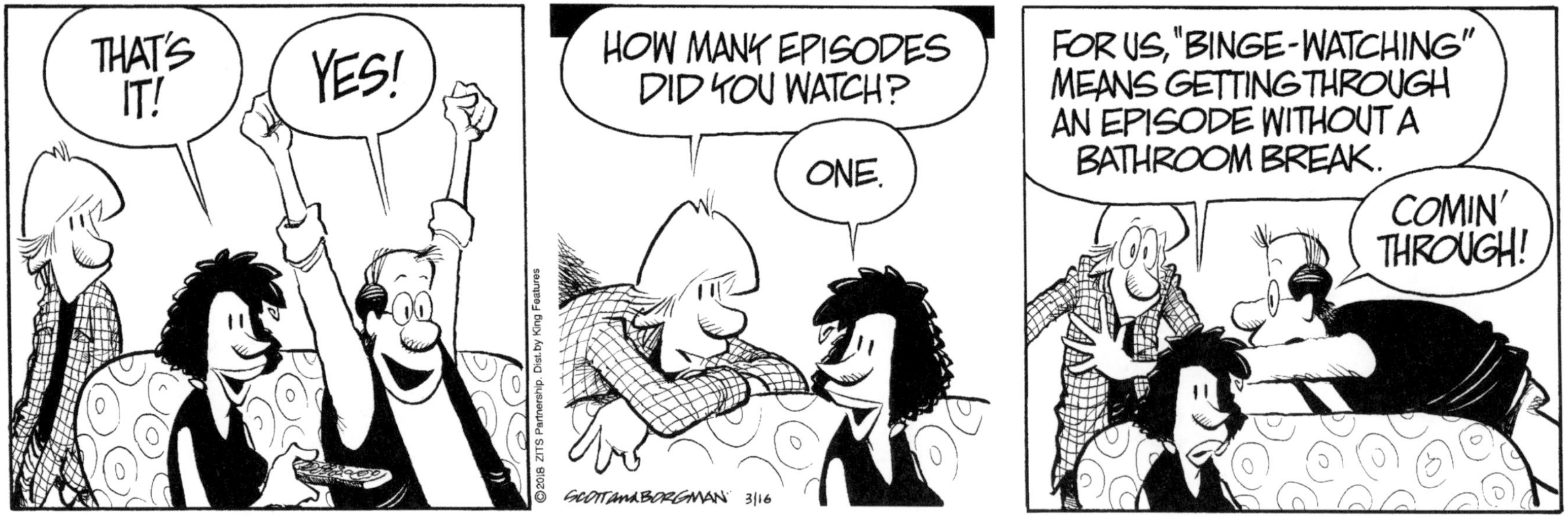
THAT'S IT!
YES!
© 2018 ZITS Partnership. Dist. by King Features
HOW MANY EPISODES DID YOU WATCH?
ONE.
SCOTT and BORGMAN 3/16
FOR US, "BINGE-WATCHING" MEANS GETTING THROUGH AN EPISODE WITHOUT A BATHROOM BREAK.
COMIN' THROUGH!

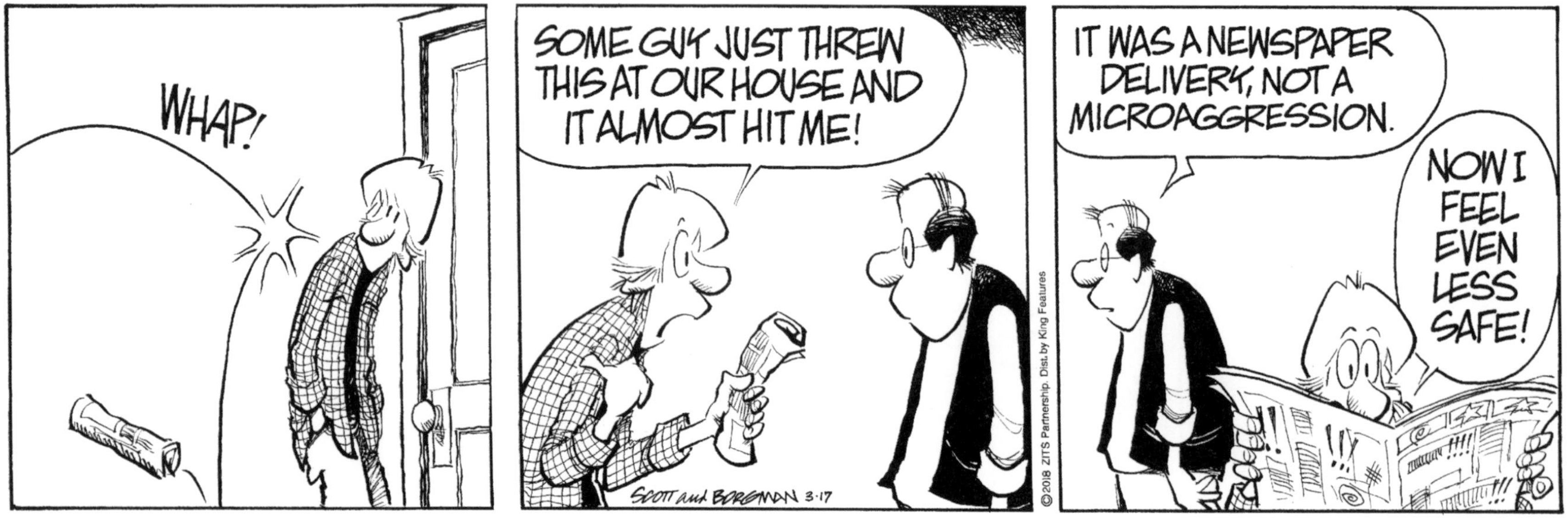
WHAP!
SOME GUY JUST THREW THIS AT OUR HOUSE AND IT ALMOST HIT ME!
SCOTT and BORGMAN 3·17
© 2018 ZITS Partnership. Dist. by King Features
IT WAS A NEWSPAPER DELIVERY, NOT A MICROAGGRESSION.
NOW I FEEL EVEN LESS SAFE!

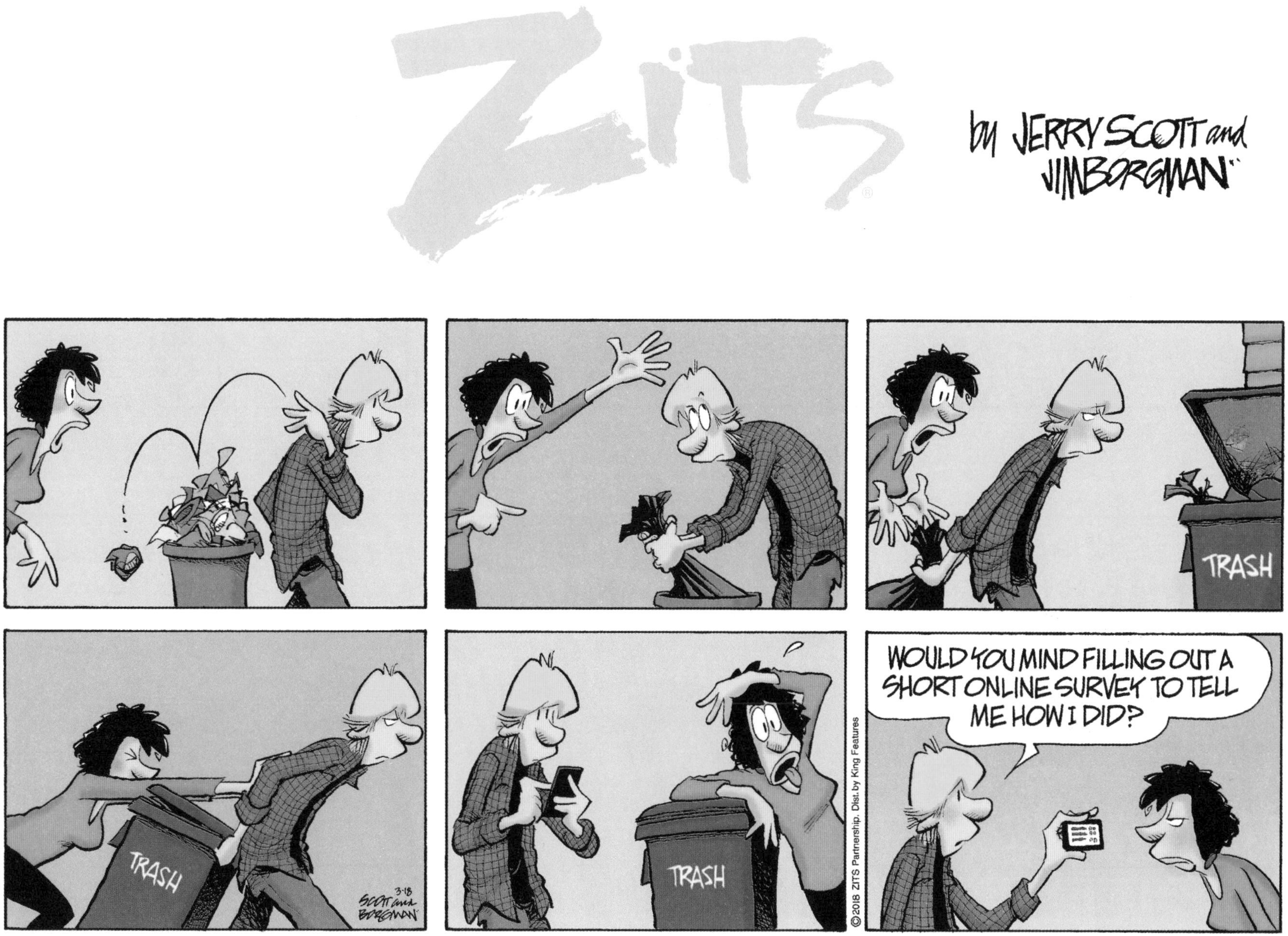
ZITS
by JERRY SCOTT and JIM BORGMAN
TRASH
TRASH
3-18 SCOTT and BORGMAN
TRASH
©2018 ZITS Partnership. Dist. by King Features
WOULD YOU MIND FILLING OUT A SHORT ONLINE SURVEY TO TELL ME HOW I DID?

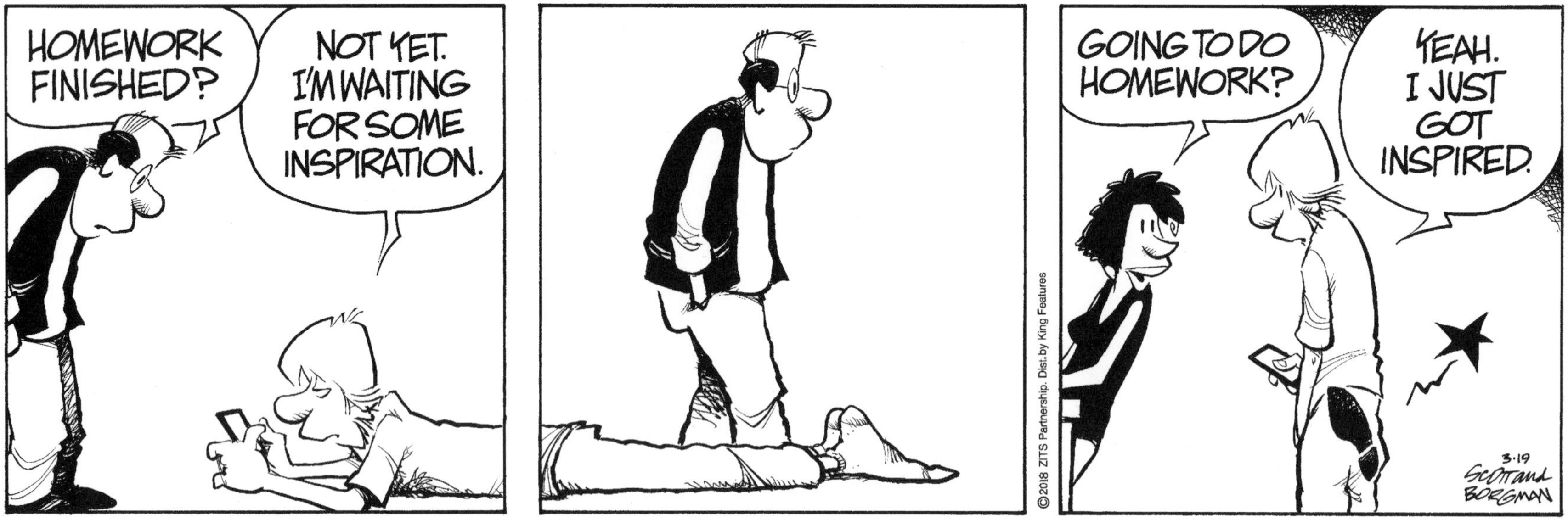
HOMEWORK FINISHED?
NOT YET. I'M WAITING FOR SOME INSPIRATION.
GOING TO DO HOMEWORK?
YEAH. I JUST GOT INSPIRED.
©2018 ZITS Partnership. Dist. by King Features
3·19 SCOTT and BORGMAN

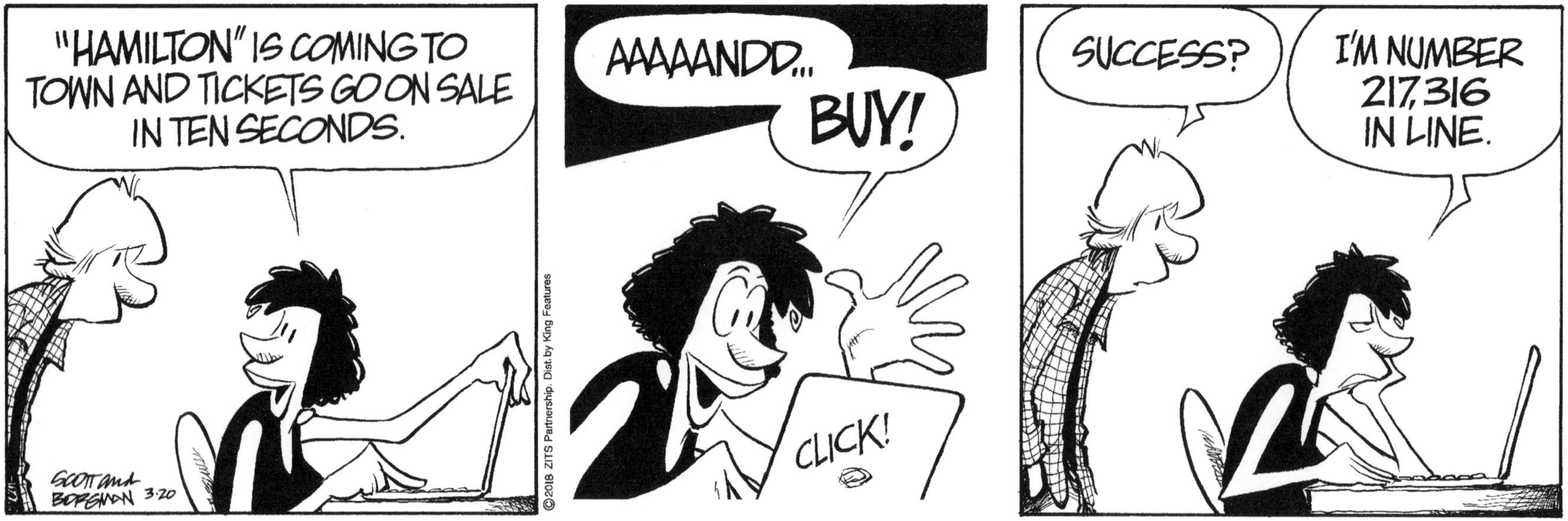
"HAMILTON" IS COMING TO TOWN AND TICKETS GO ON SALE IN TEN SECONDS.
SCOTT and BORGMAN 3·20
©2018 ZITS Partnership. Dist. by King Features
AAAAANDD...
BUY!
CLICK!
SUCCESS?
I'M NUMBER 217,316 IN LINE.

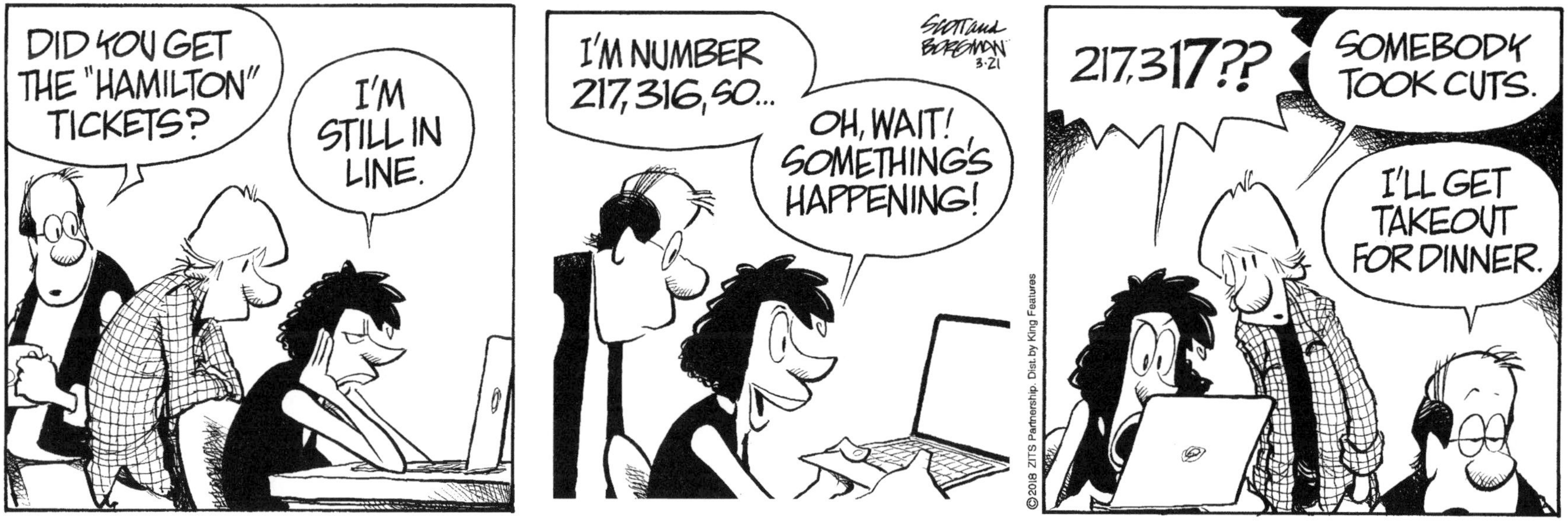
DID YOU GET THE "HAMILTON" TICKETS?
I'M STILL IN LINE.
SCOTT and BORGMAN 3·21
I'M NUMBER 217,316, SO...
OH, WAIT! SOMETHING'S HAPPENING!
©2018 ZITS Partnership. Dist. by King Features
217,317??
SOMEBODY TOOK CUTS.
I'LL GET TAKEOUT FOR DINNER.

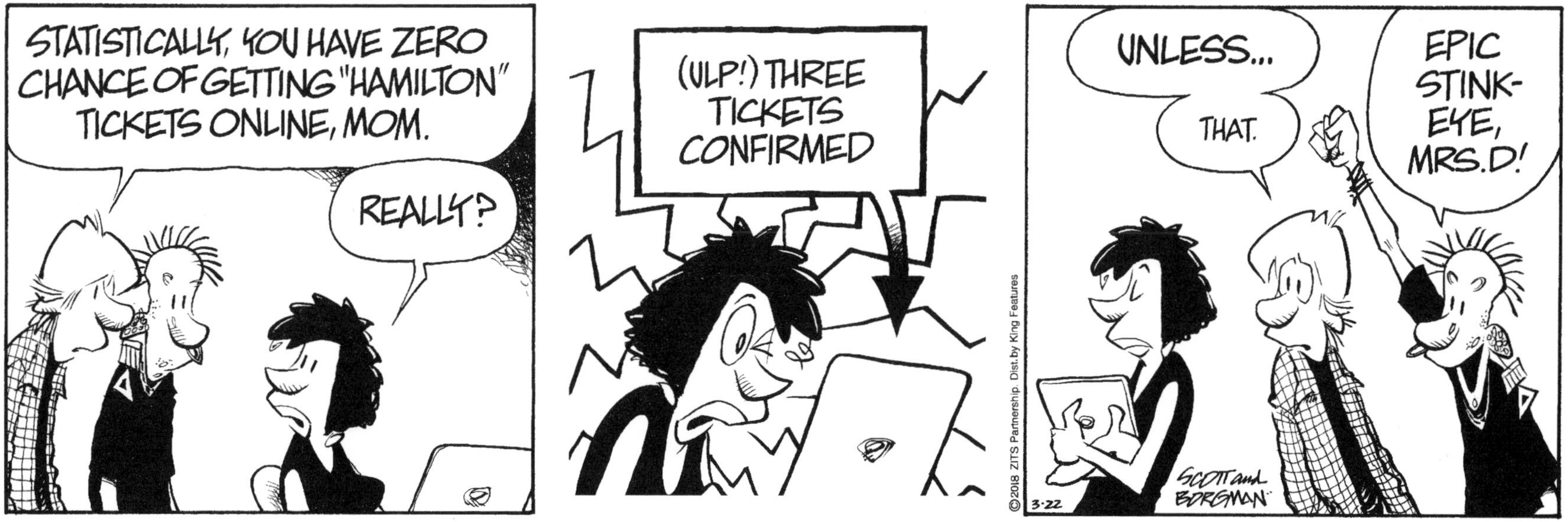
STATISTICALLY, YOU HAVE ZERO CHANCE OF GETTING "HAMILTON" TICKETS ONLINE, MOM.
REALLY?
(ULP!) THREE TICKETS CONFIRMED
©2018 ZITS Partnership. Dist. by King Features
UNLESS...
THAT.
EPIC STINK-EYE, MRS. D!
3·22
SCOTT and BORGMAN

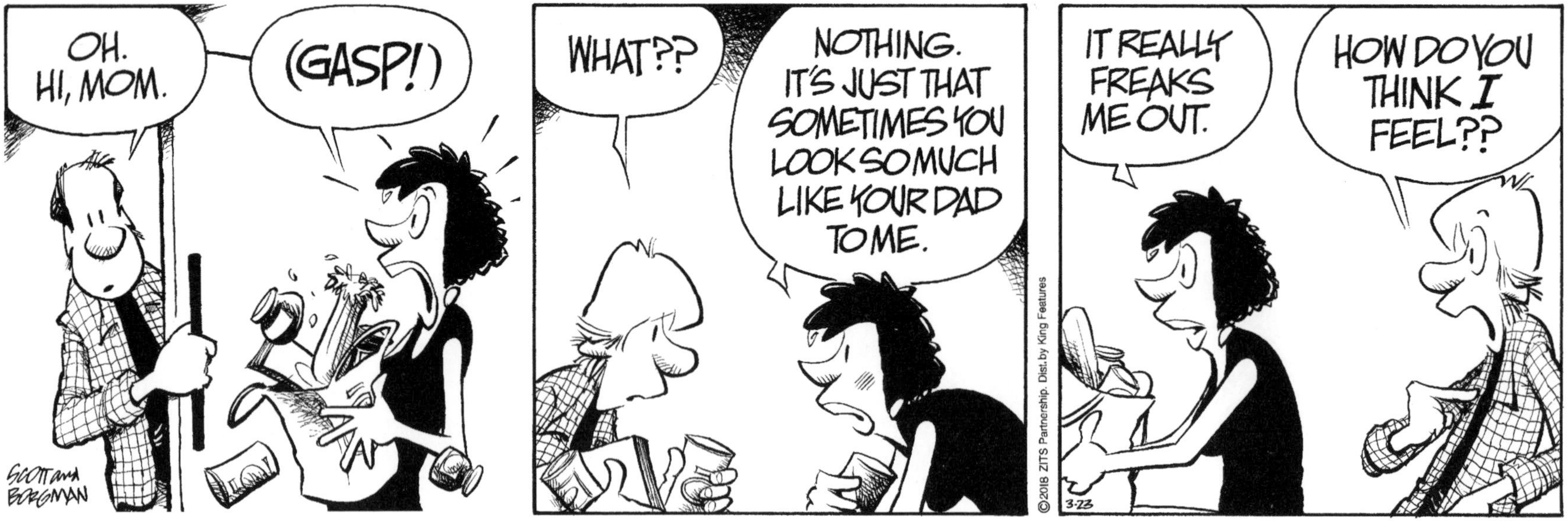
OH. HI, MOM.
(GASP!)
WHAT??
NOTHING. IT'S JUST THAT SOMETIMES YOU LOOK SO MUCH LIKE YOUR DAD TO ME.
IT REALLY FREAKS ME OUT.
HOW DO YOU THINK I FEEL??
SCOTT AND BORGMAN
©2018 ZITS Partnership. Dist. by King Features
3-23

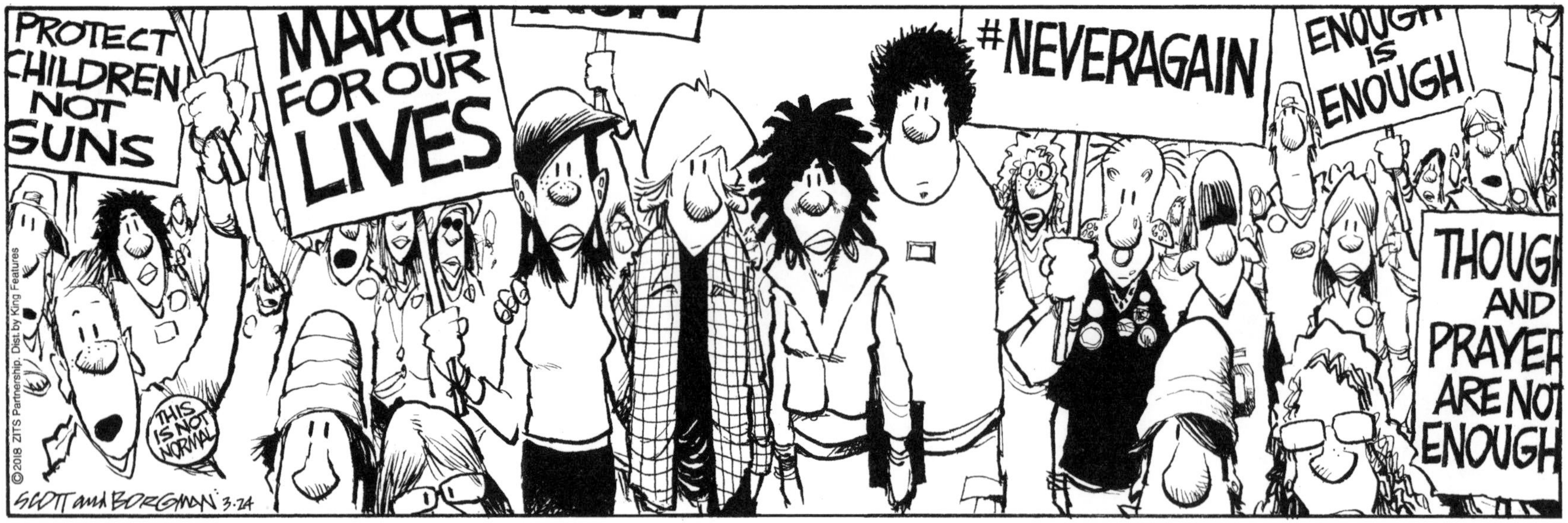
PROTECT CHILDREN NOT GUNS
MARCH FOR OUR LIVES
#NEVERAGAIN
ENOUGH IS ENOUGH
THIS IS NOT NORMAL
©2018 ZITS Partnership. Dist. by King Features
SCOTT AND BORGMAN 3-24

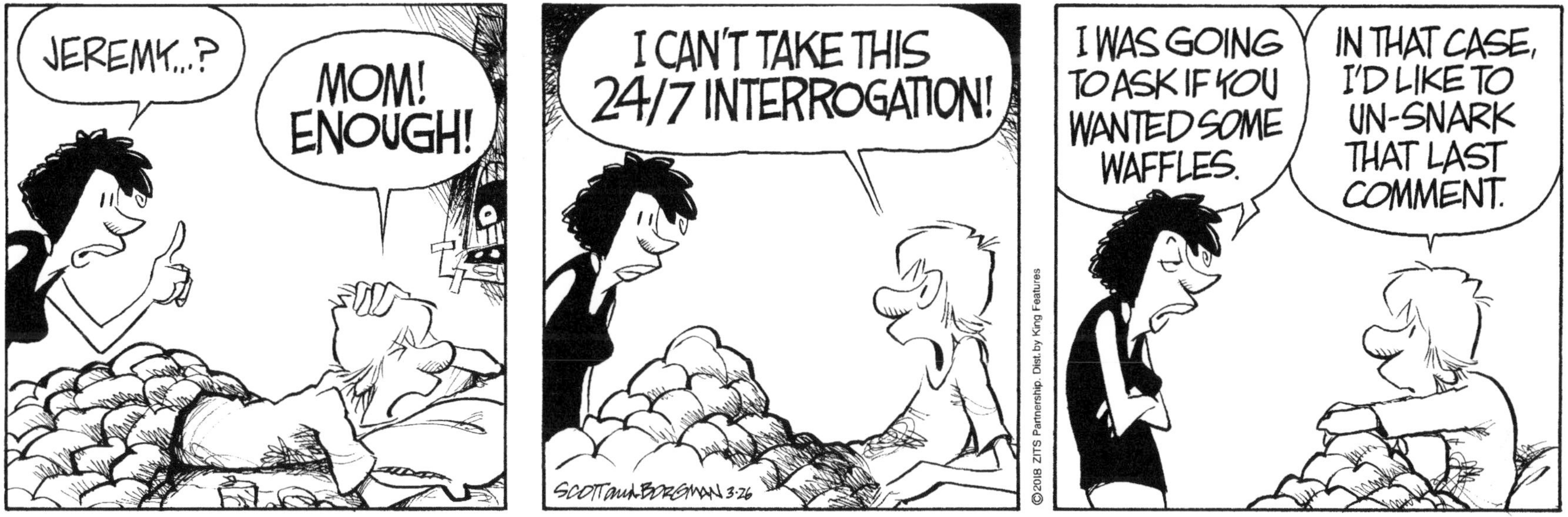
JEREMY...?
MOM! ENOUGH!
I CAN'T TAKE THIS 24/7 INTERROGATION!
SCOTT AND BORGMAN 3·26
©2018 ZITS Partnership. Dist. by King Features
I WAS GOING TO ASK IF YOU WANTED SOME WAFFLES.
IN THAT CASE, I'D LIKE TO UN-SNARK THAT LAST COMMENT.

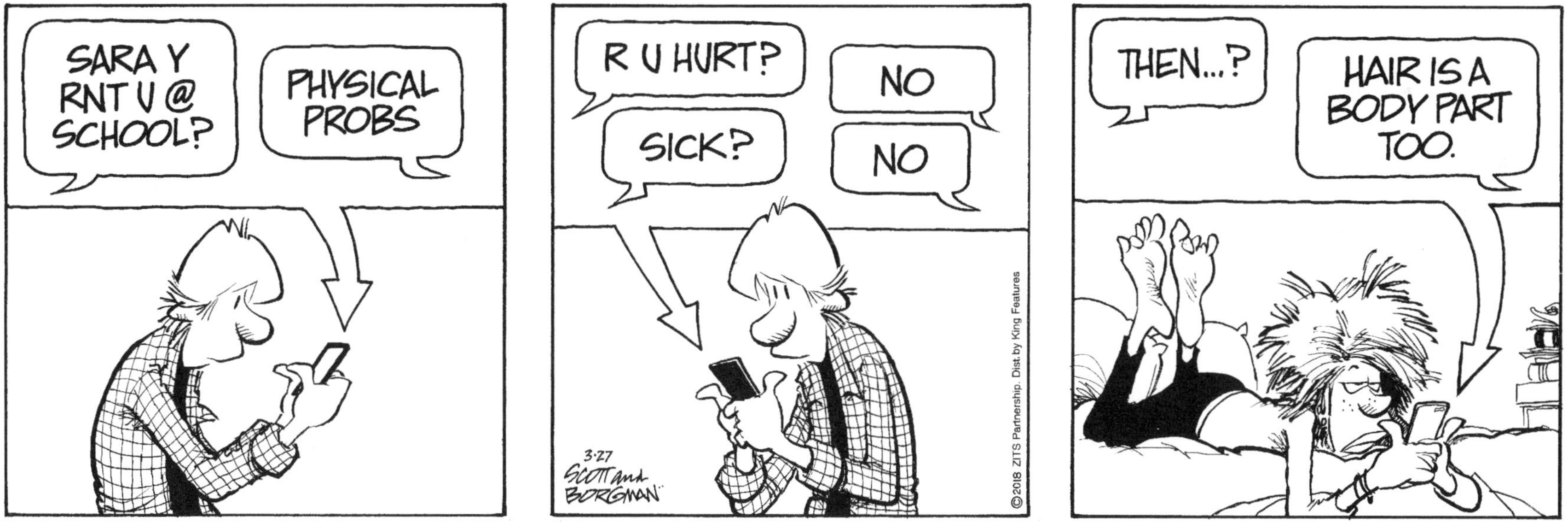
SARA Y RNT U @ SCHOOL?
PHYSICAL PROBS
R U HURT?
NO
SICK?
NO
3·27 SCOTT AND BORGMAN
©2018 ZITS Partnership. Dist. by King Features
THEN...?
HAIR IS A BODY PART TOO.

STARGAZING?
YEAH. HAVE A SEAT, DAD.
3-25
SCOTT and BORGMAN
WHEN YOU WERE LITTLE WE USED TO DO THIS ALL THE TIME.
I STILL REMEMBER THE NAMES OF THE CONSTELLATIONS YOU TAUGHT ME.

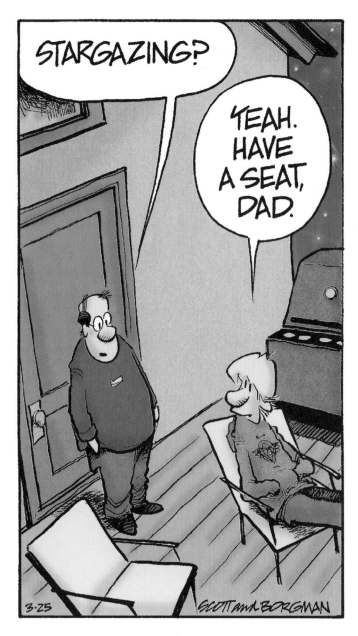

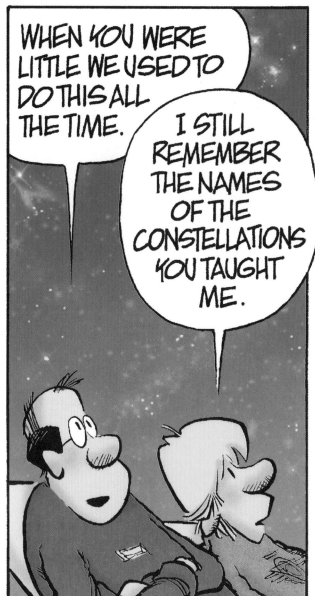

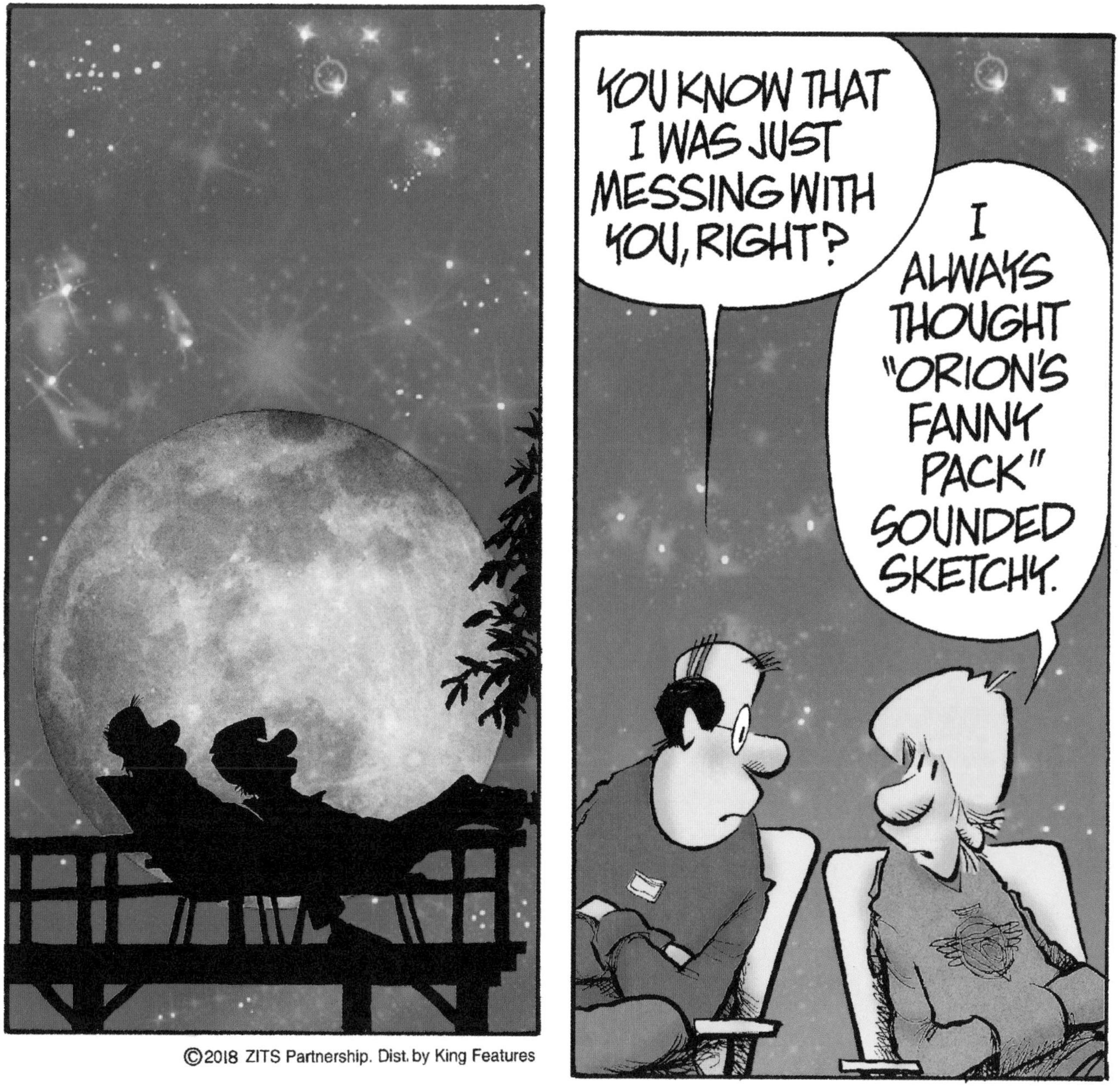
YOU KNOW THAT I WAS JUST MESSING WITH YOU, RIGHT?
I ALWAYS THOUGHT "ORION'S FANNY PACK" SOUNDED SKETCHY.

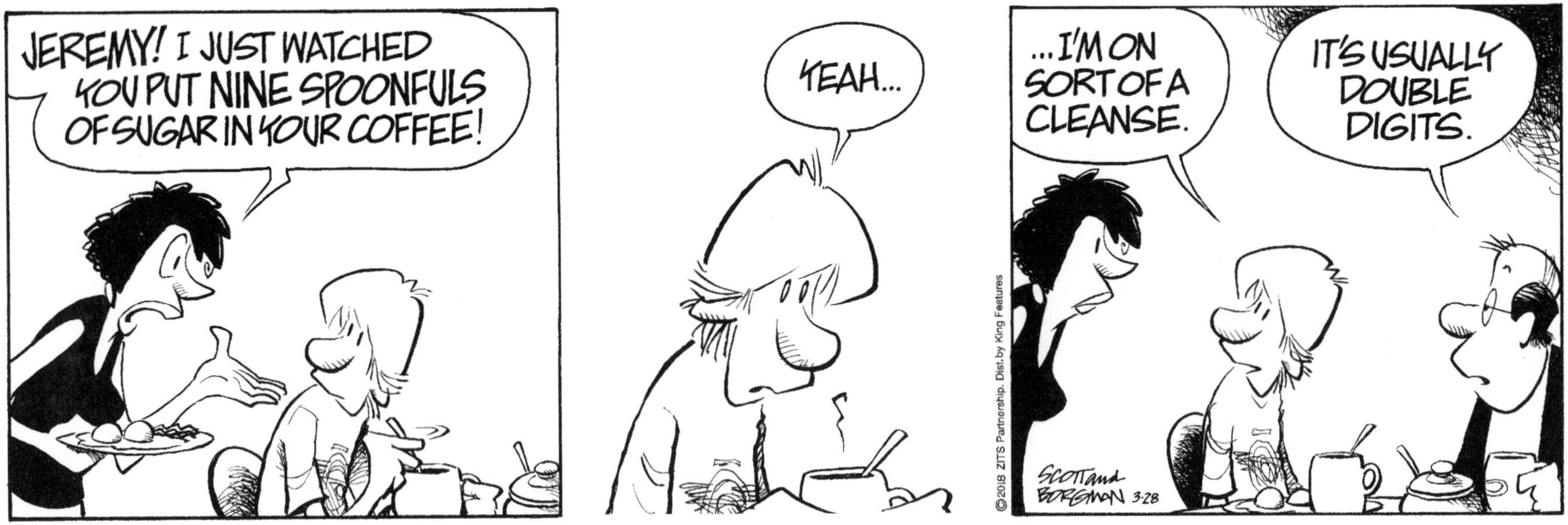
JEREMY! I JUST WATCHED YOU PUT NINE SPOONFULS OF SUGAR IN YOUR COFFEE!
YEAH...
...I'M ON SORT OF A CLEANSE.
IT'S USUALLY DOUBLE DIGITS.
SCOTT and BORGMAN 3·28
©2018 ZITS Partnership. Dist. by King Features

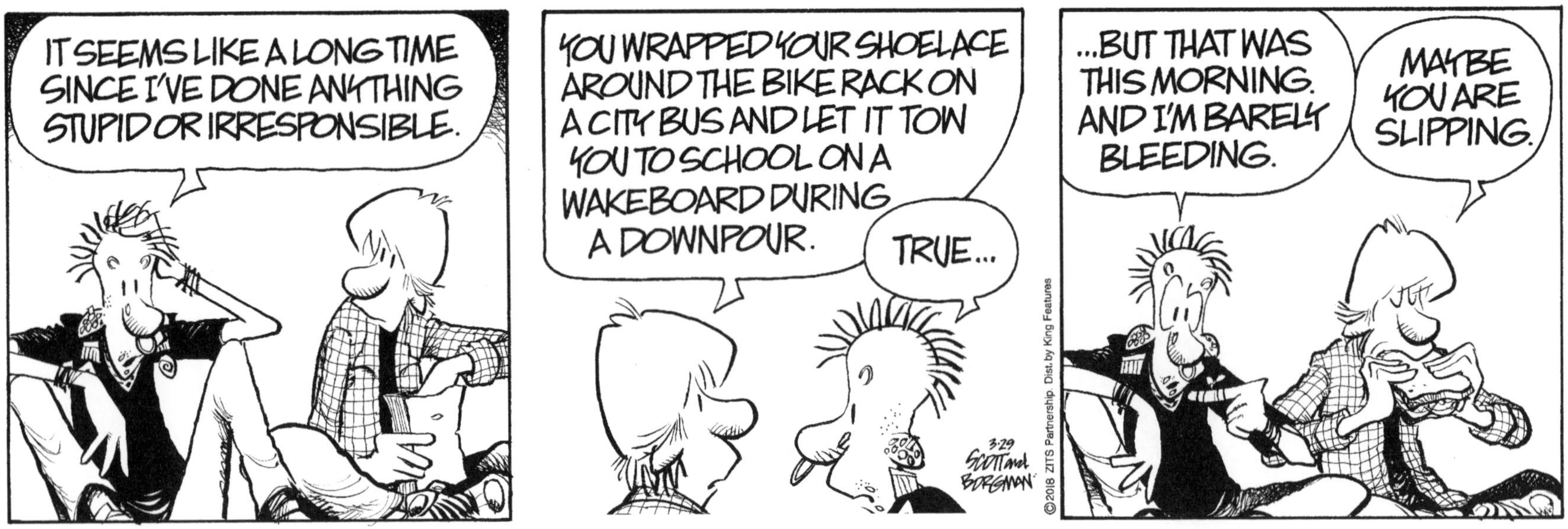
IT SEEMS LIKE A LONG TIME SINCE I'VE DONE ANYTHING STUPID OR IRRESPONSIBLE.
YOU WRAPPED YOUR SHOELACE AROUND THE BIKE RACK ON A CITY BUS AND LET IT TOW YOU TO SCHOOL ON A WAKEBOARD DURING A DOWNPOUR.
TRUE...
3·29 SCOTT and BORGMAN
©2018 ZITS Partnership. Dist. by King Features
...BUT THAT WAS THIS MORNING. AND I'M BARELY BLEEDING.
MAYBE YOU ARE SLIPPING.

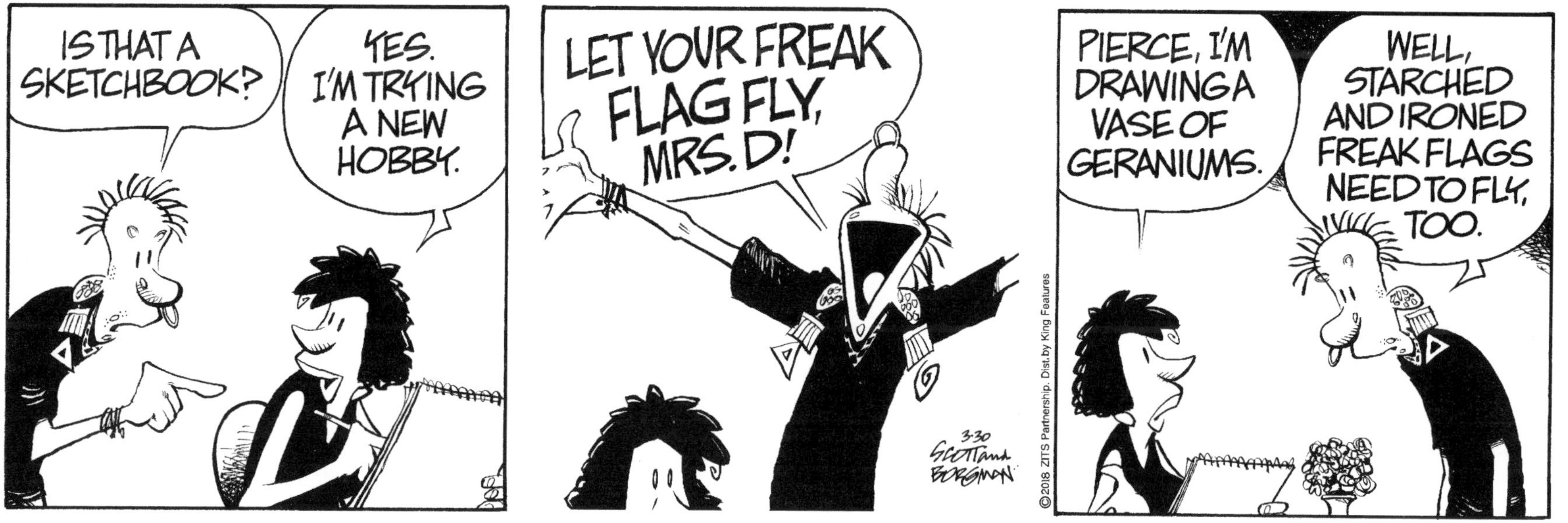
IS THAT A SKETCHBOOK?
YES. I'M TRYING A NEW HOBBY.
LET YOUR FREAK FLAG FLY, MRS. D!
3-30
SCOTT and BORGMAN
©2018 ZITS Partnership. Dist. by King Features
PIERCE, I'M DRAWING A VASE OF GERANIUMS.
WELL, STARCHED AND IRONED FREAK FLAGS NEED TO FLY, TOO.

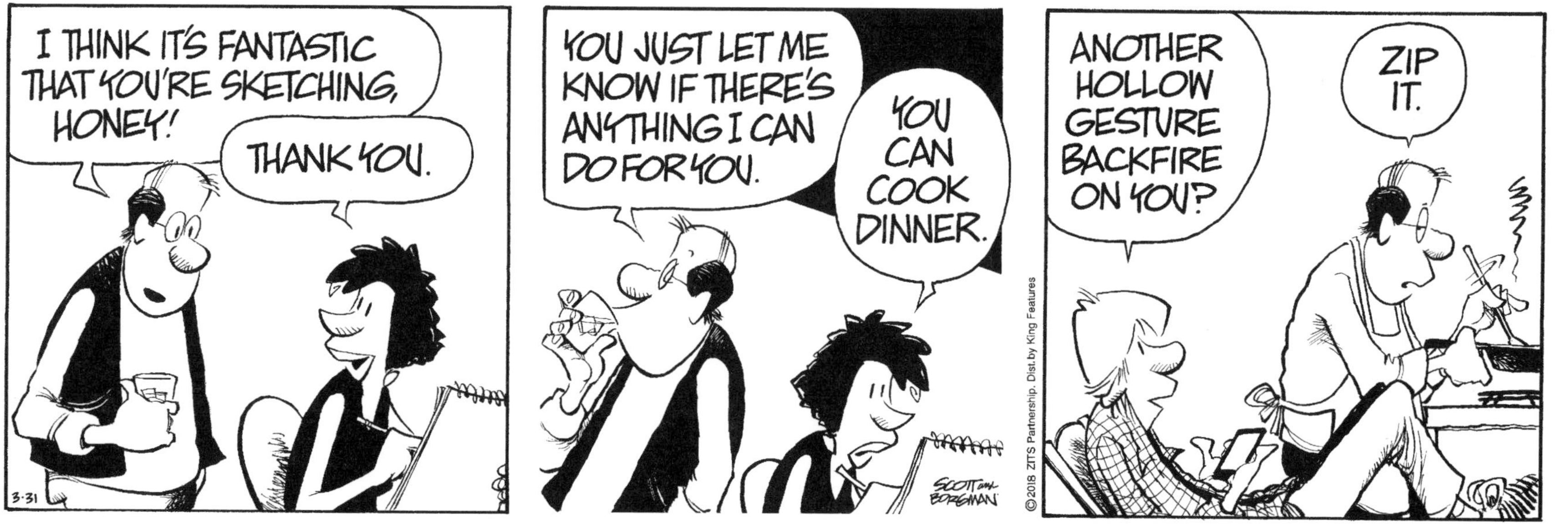
I THINK IT'S FANTASTIC THAT YOU'RE SKETCHING, HONEY!
THANK YOU.
3-31
YOU JUST LET ME KNOW IF THERE'S ANYTHING I CAN DO FOR YOU.
YOU CAN COOK DINNER.
SCOTT and BORGMAN
©2018 ZITS Partnership. Dist. by King Features
ANOTHER HOLLOW GESTURE BACKFIRE ON YOU?
ZIP IT.

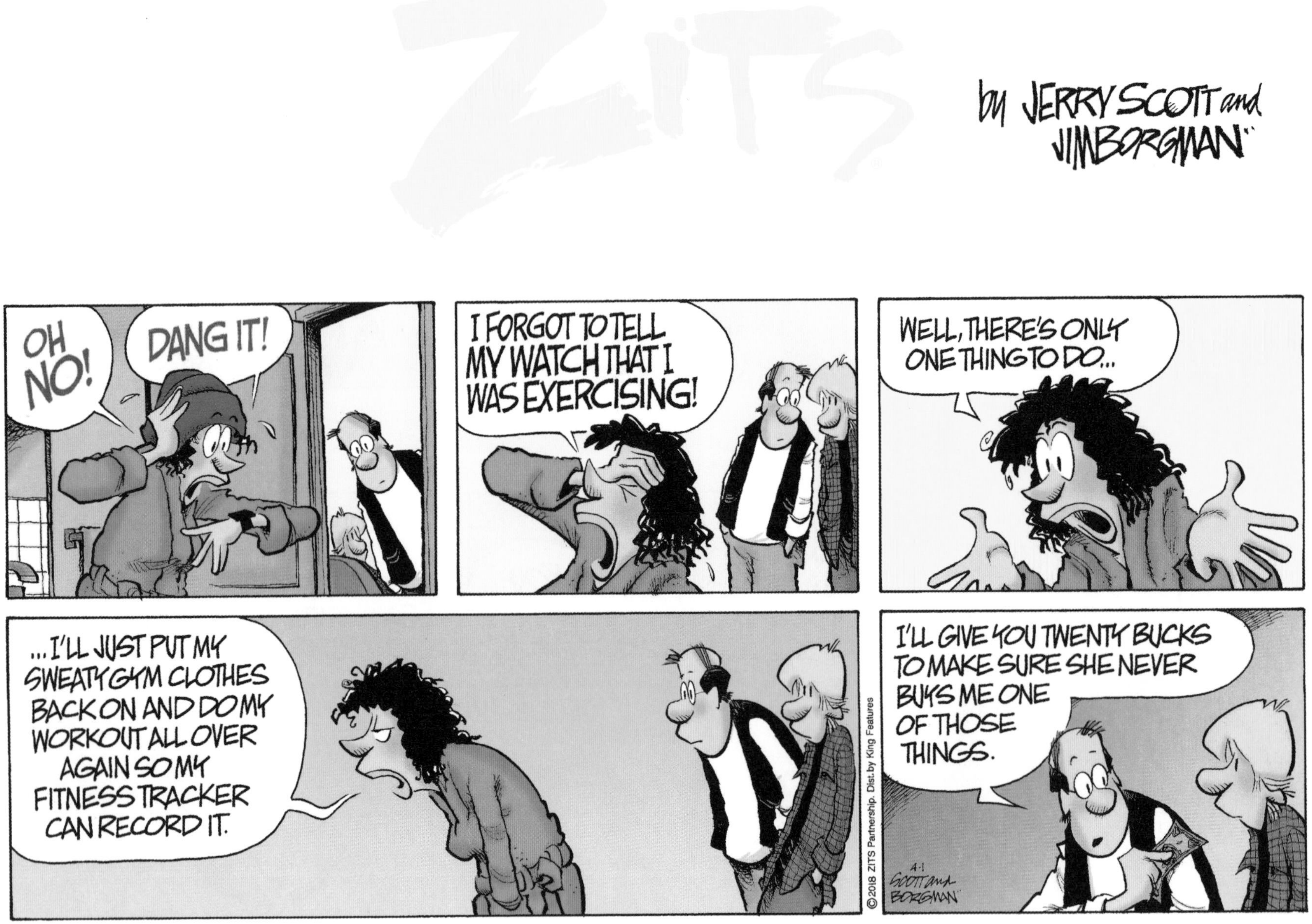
ZITS
by JERRY SCOTT and JIM BORGMAN
OH NO!
DANG IT!
I FORGOT TO TELL MY WATCH THAT I WAS EXERCISING!
WELL, THERE'S ONLY ONE THING TO DO...
...I'LL JUST PUT MY SWEATY GYM CLOTHES BACK ON AND DO MY WORKOUT ALL OVER AGAIN SO MY FITNESS TRACKER CAN RECORD IT.
©2018 ZITS Partnership. Dist. by King Features
I'LL GIVE YOU TWENTY BUCKS TO MAKE SURE SHE NEVER BUYS ME ONE OF THOSE THINGS.
4-1 SCOTT and BORGMAN

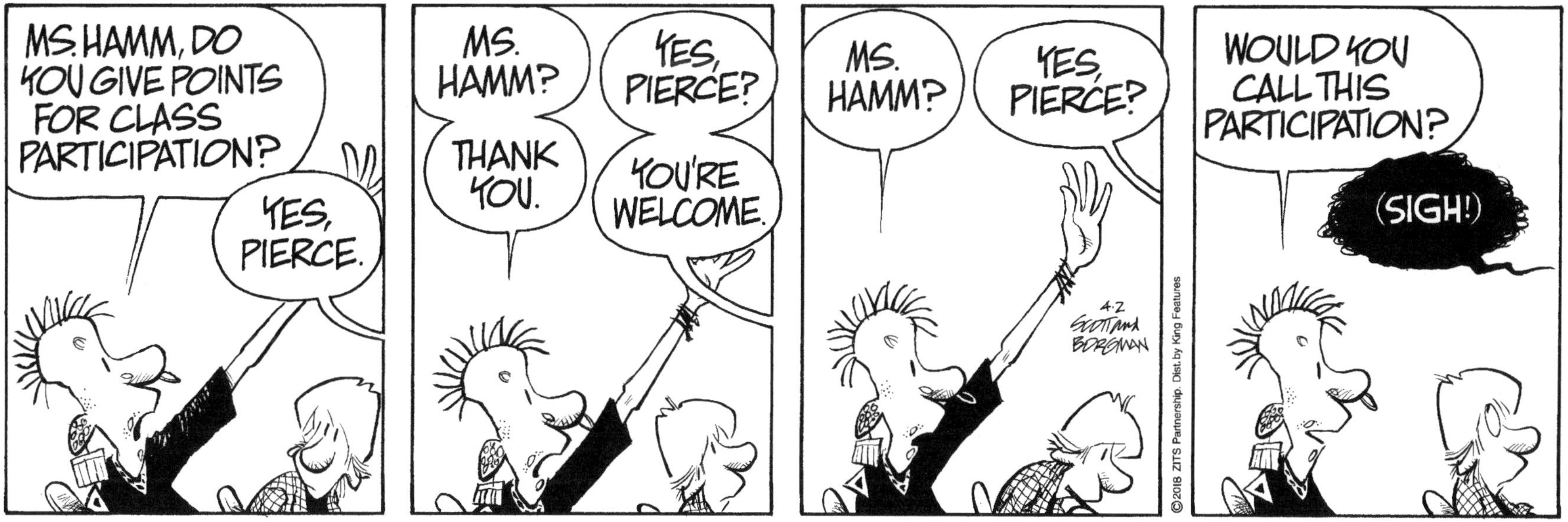
MS. HAMM, DO YOU GIVE POINTS FOR CLASS PARTICIPATION?
YES, PIERCE.
MS. HAMM?
YES, PIERCE?
THANK YOU.
YOU'RE WELCOME.
MS. HAMM?
YES, PIERCE?
4-2 SCOTT AND BORGMAN
©2018 ZITS Partnership. Dist. by King Features
WOULD YOU CALL THIS PARTICIPATION?
(SIGH!)

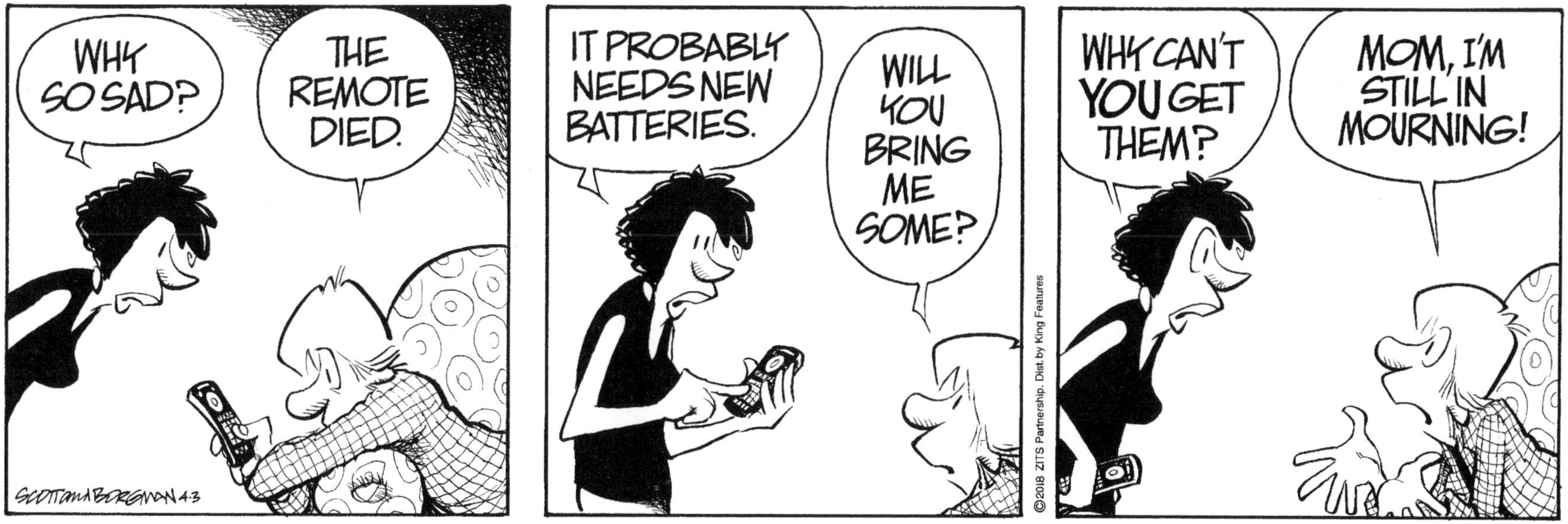
WHY SO SAD?
THE REMOTE DIED.
SCOTT AND BORGMAN 4-3
IT PROBABLY NEEDS NEW BATTERIES.
WILL YOU BRING ME SOME?
©2018 ZITS Partnership. Dist. by King Features
WHY CAN'T YOU GET THEM?
MOM, I'M STILL IN MOURNING!

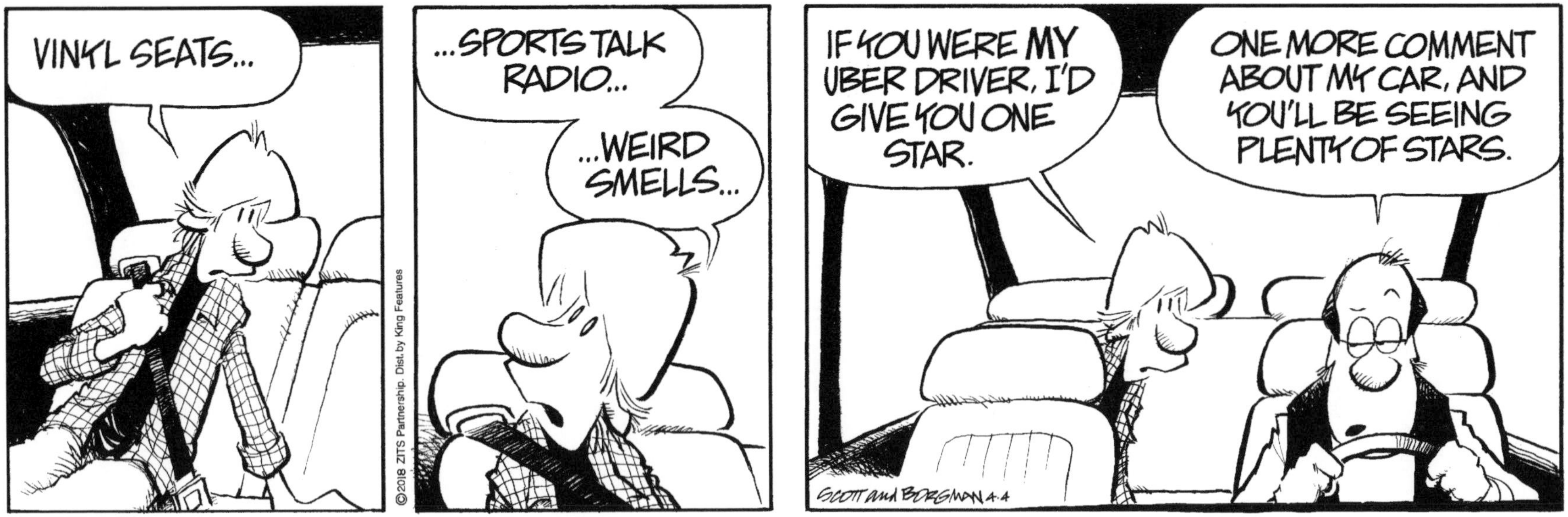
VINYL SEATS...
...SPORTS TALK RADIO...
...WEIRD SMELLS...
IF YOU WERE MY UBER DRIVER, I'D GIVE YOU ONE STAR.
ONE MORE COMMENT ABOUT MY CAR, AND YOU'LL BE SEEING PLENTY OF STARS.
SCOTT and BORGMAN 4.4
©2018 ZITS Partnership. Dist. by King Features

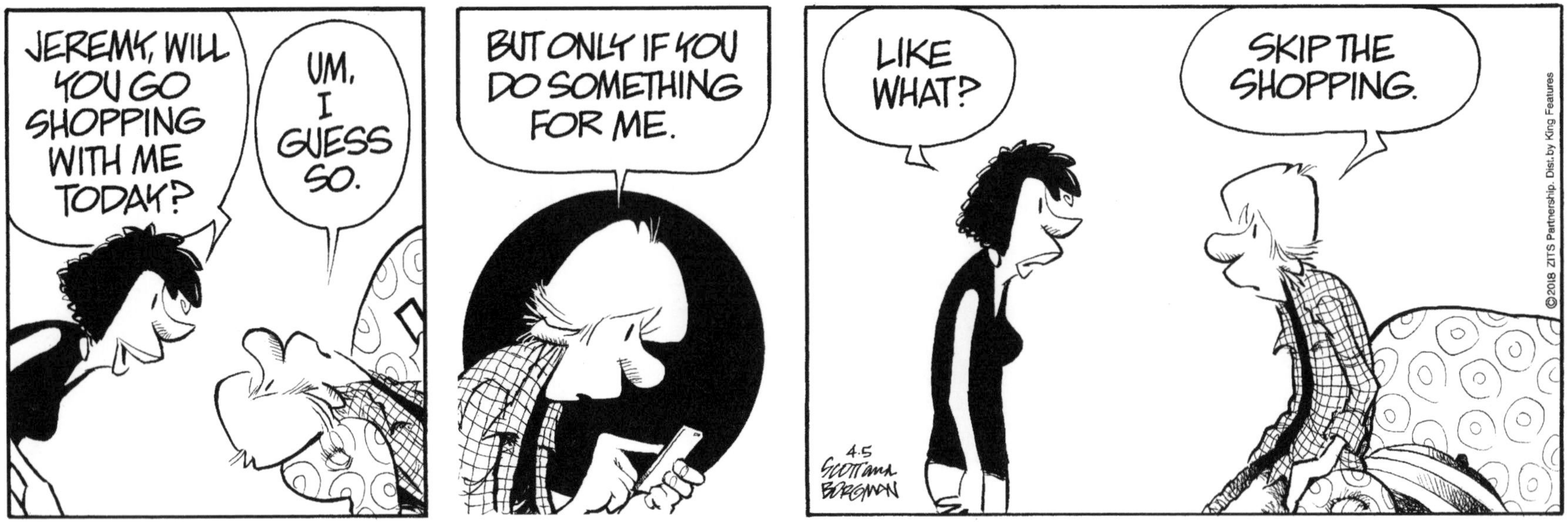
JEREMY, WILL YOU GO SHOPPING WITH ME TODAY?
UM, I GUESS SO.
BUT ONLY IF YOU DO SOMETHING FOR ME.
LIKE WHAT?
SKIP THE SHOPPING.
4.5 SCOTT and BORGMAN
©2018 ZITS Partnership. Dist. by King Features

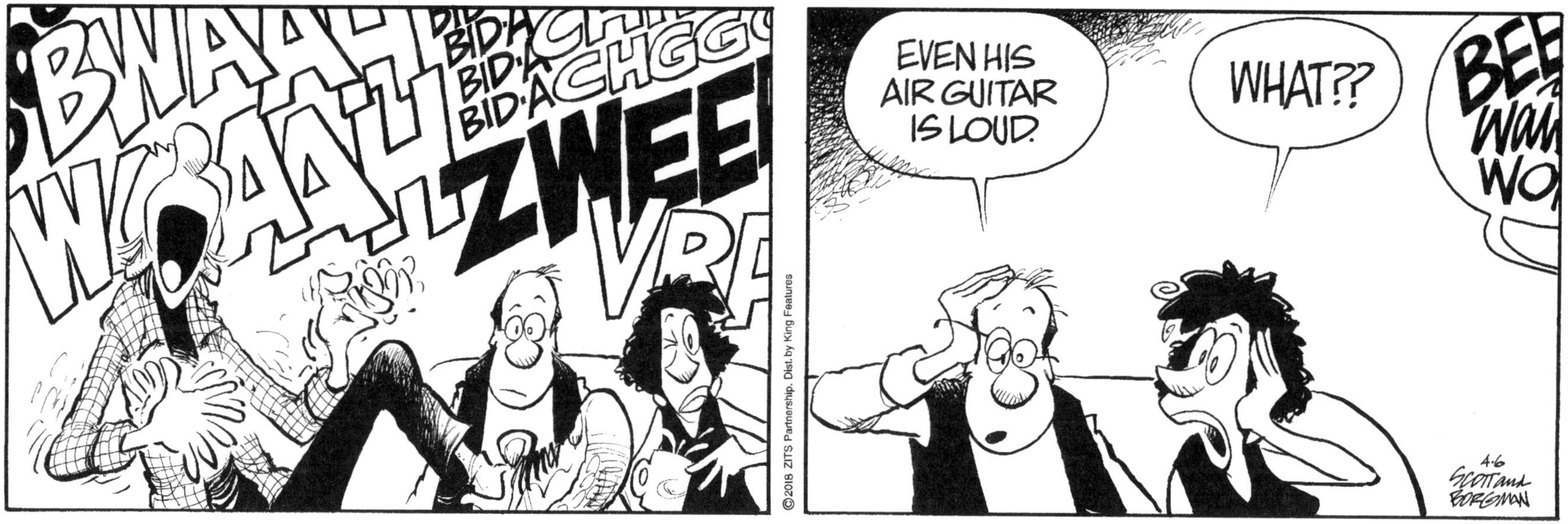
BID·A
BID·A
BID·ACHGGG
©2018 ZITS Partnership. Dist. by King Features
EVEN HIS AIR GUITAR IS LOUD.
WHAT??
4·6 SCOTT and BORGMAN

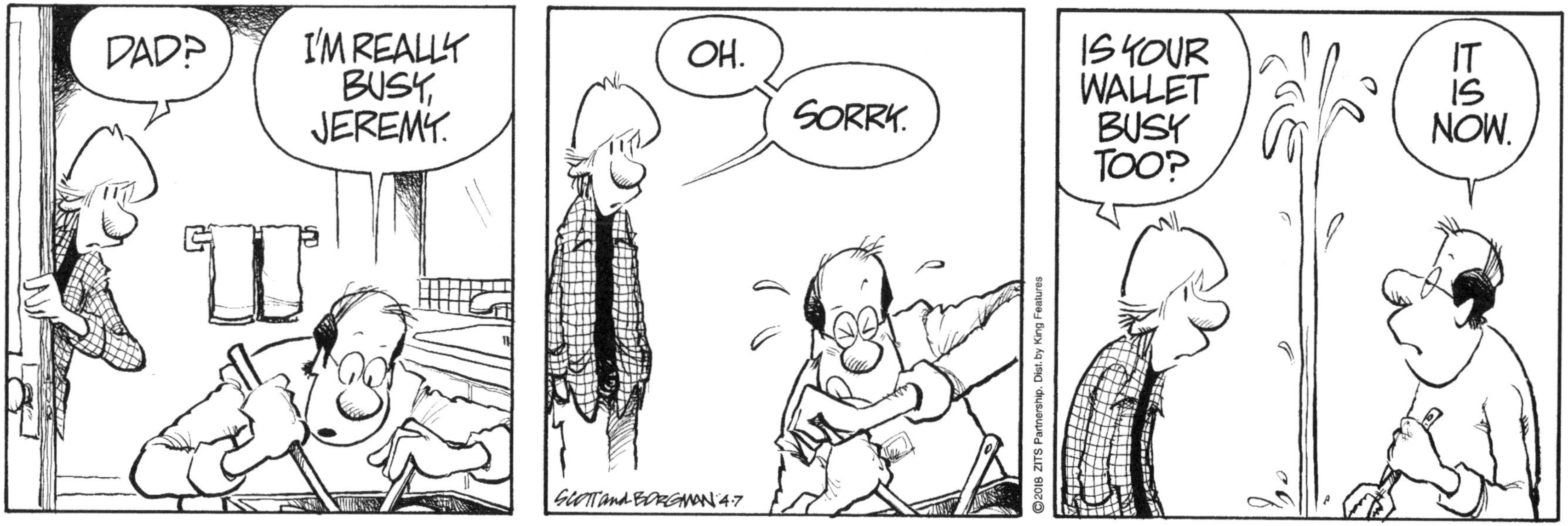
DAD?
I'M REALLY BUSY, JEREMY.
OH.
SORRY.
SCOTT and BORGMAN 4·7
©2018 ZITS Partnership. Dist. by King Features
IS YOUR WALLET BUSY TOO?
IT IS NOW.

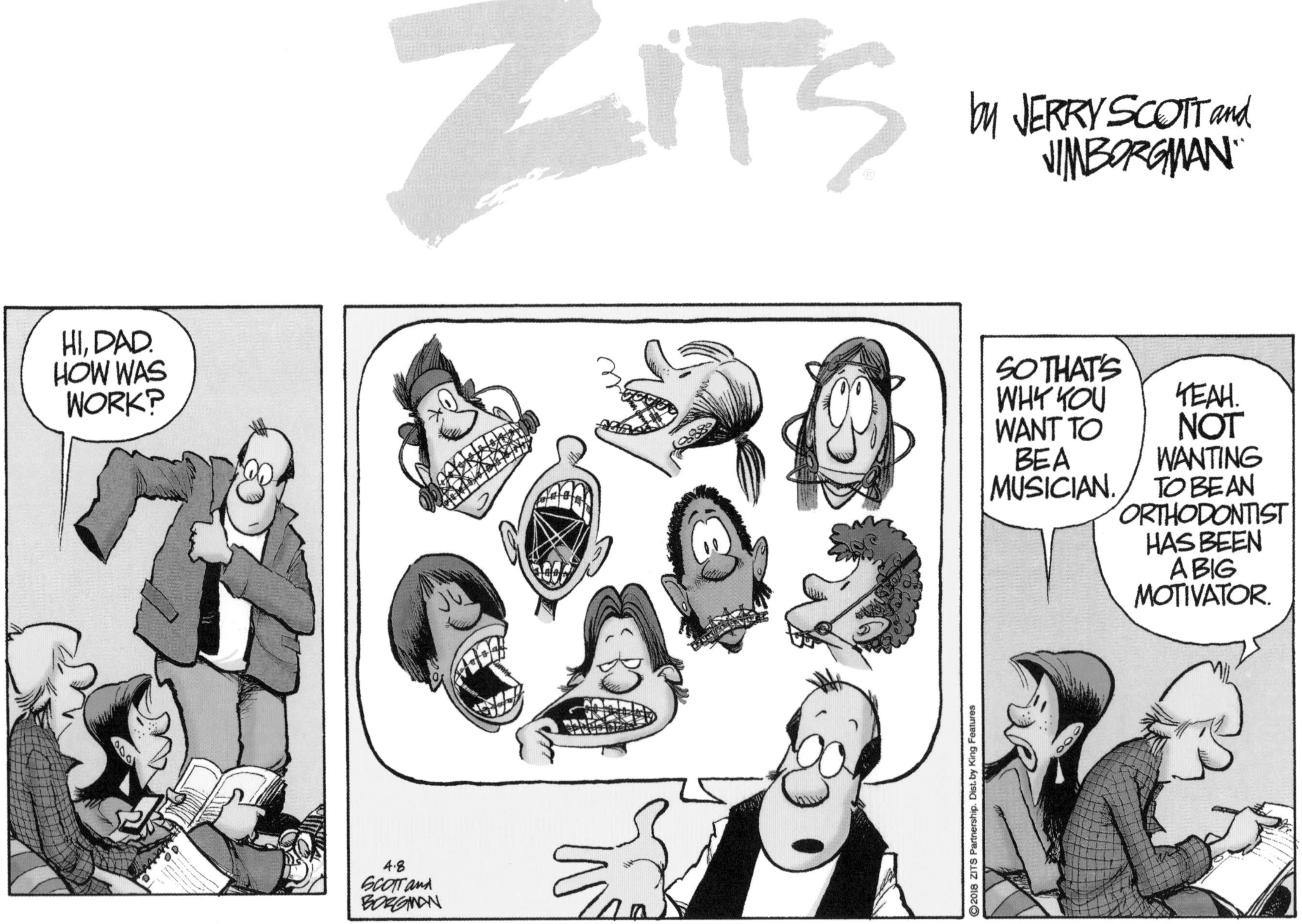
ZITS
by JERRY SCOTT and JIM BORGMAN
HI, DAD. HOW WAS WORK?
4·8 SCOTT and BORGMAN
SO THAT'S WHY YOU WANT TO BE A MUSICIAN.
YEAH. NOT WANTING TO BE AN ORTHODONTIST HAS BEEN A BIG MOTIVATOR.
© 2018 ZITS Partnership. Dist. by King Features

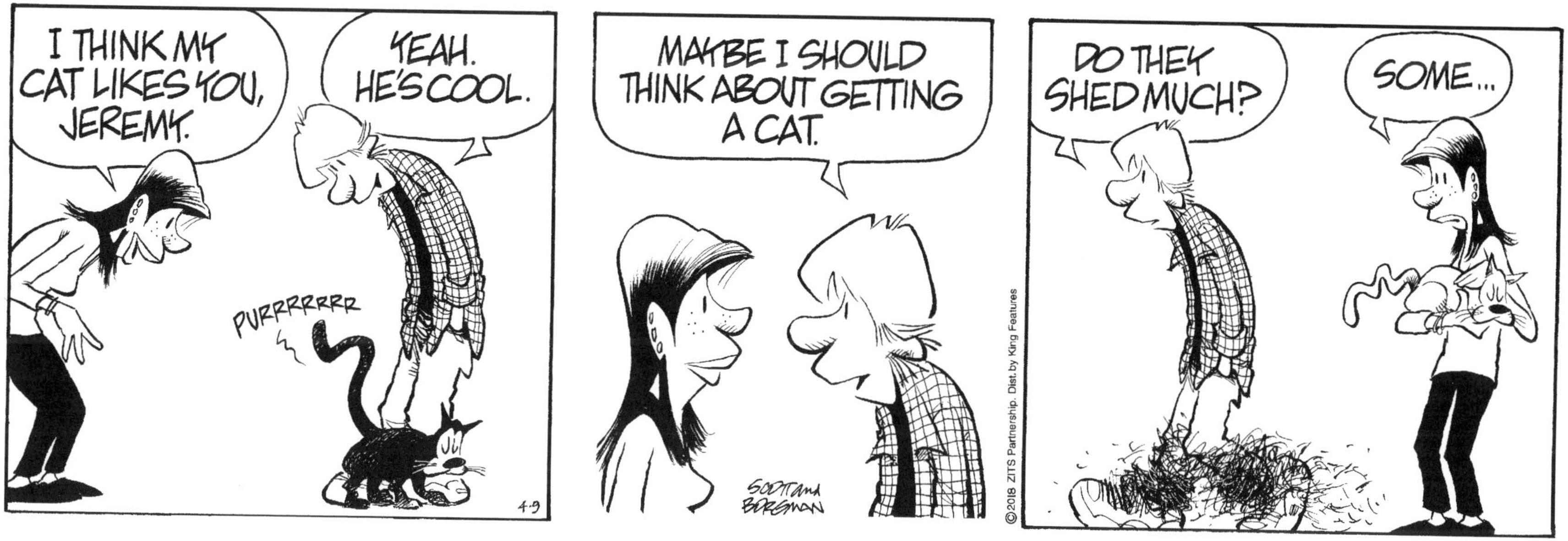
I THINK MY CAT LIKES YOU, JEREMY.
YEAH. HE'S COOL.
PURRRRRRR
MAYBE I SHOULD THINK ABOUT GETTING A CAT.
SCOTT and BORGMAN
©2018 ZITS Partnership. Dist. by King Features
DO THEY SHED MUCH?
SOME...

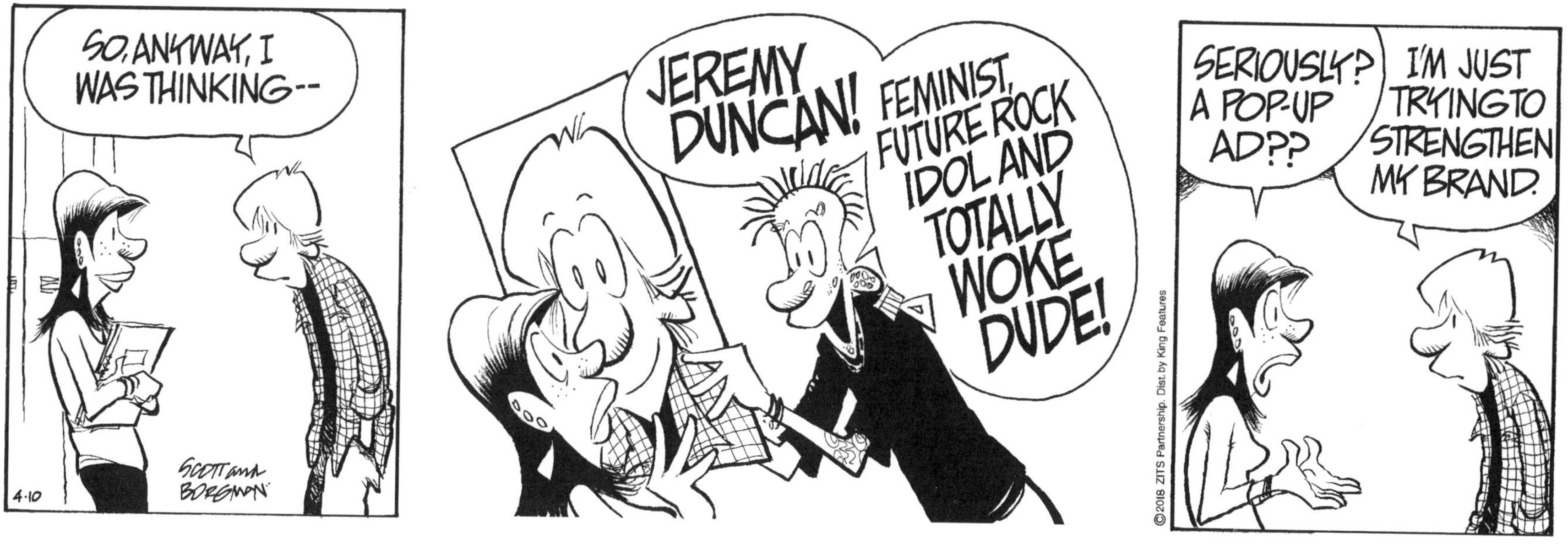
SO, ANYWAY, I WAS THINKING--
SCOTT and BORGMAN
JEREMY DUNCAN!
FEMINIST, FUTURE ROCK IDOL AND TOTALLY WOKE DUDE!
©2018 ZITS Partnership. Dist. by King Features
SERIOUSLY? A POP-UP AD??
I'M JUST TRYING TO STRENGTHEN MY BRAND.

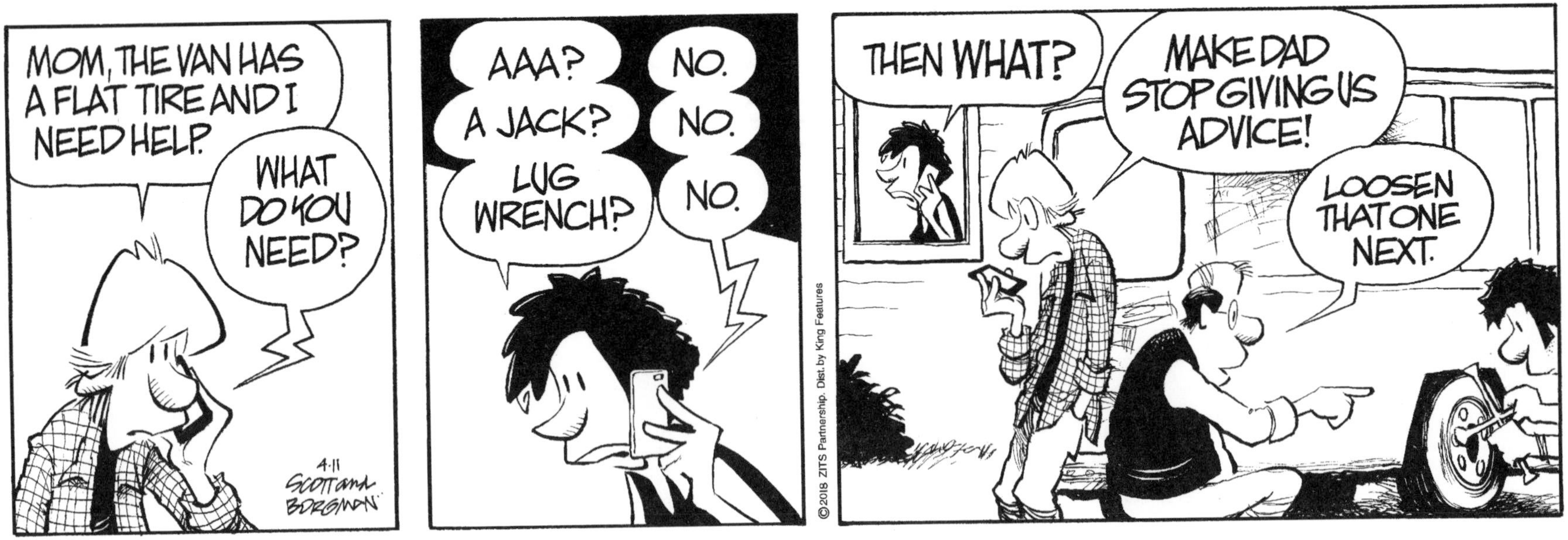
MOM, THE VAN HAS A FLAT TIRE AND I NEED HELP.
WHAT DO YOU NEED?
AAA?
NO.
A JACK?
NO.
LUG WRENCH?
NO.
THEN WHAT?
MAKE DAD STOP GIVING US ADVICE!
LOOSEN THAT ONE NEXT.
4·11
SCOTT and BORGMAN
©2018 ZITS Partnership. Dist. by King Features

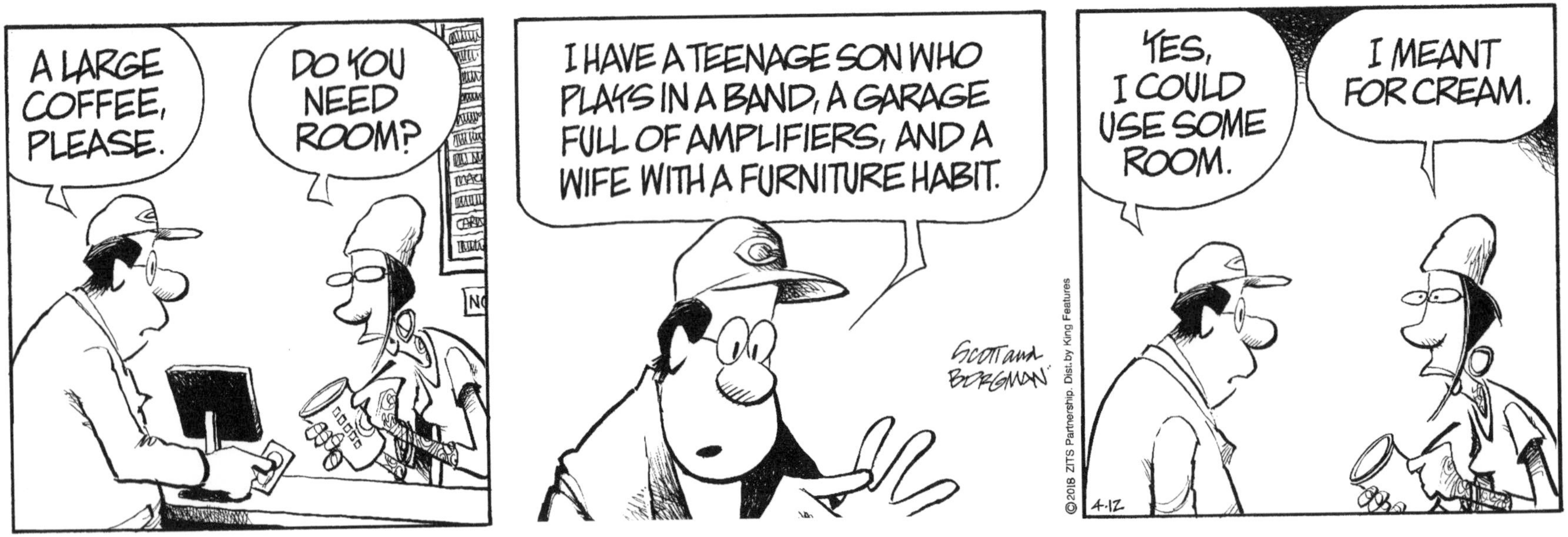
A LARGE COFFEE, PLEASE.
DO YOU NEED ROOM?
I HAVE A TEENAGE SON WHO PLAYS IN A BAND, A GARAGE FULL OF AMPLIFIERS, AND A WIFE WITH A FURNITURE HABIT.
SCOTT and BORGMAN
YES, I COULD USE SOME ROOM.
I MEANT FOR CREAM.
©2018 ZITS Partnership. Dist. by King Features
4·12

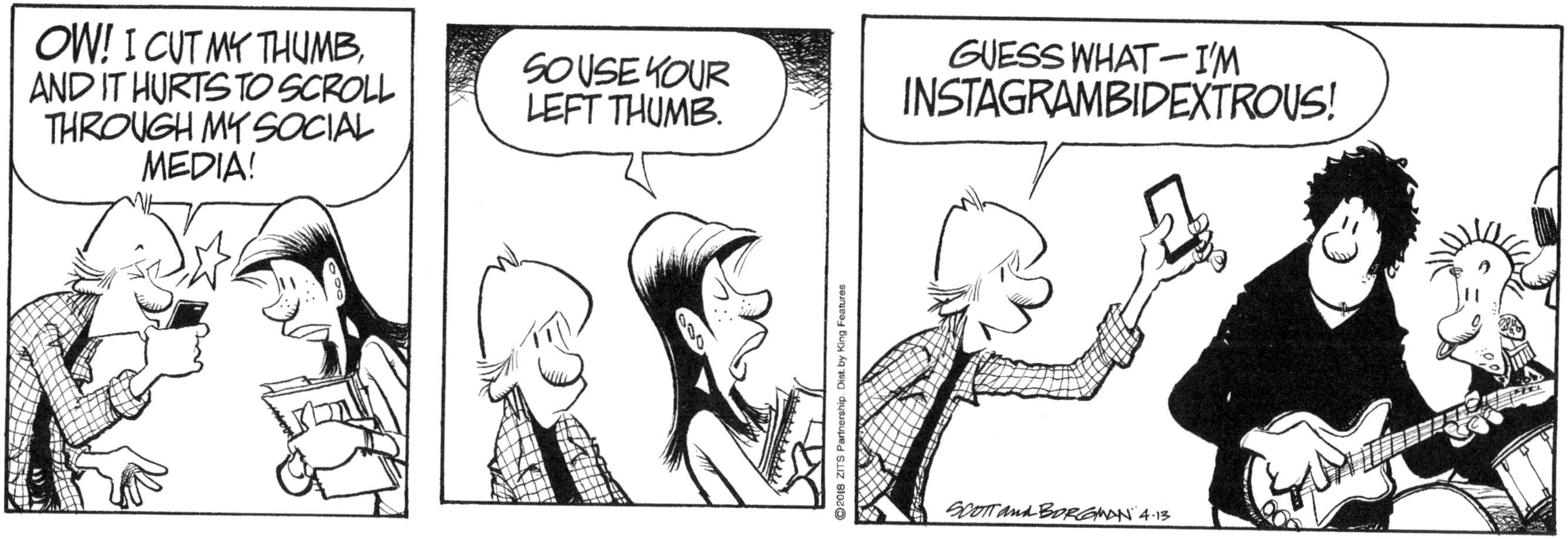
OW! I CUT MY THUMB, AND IT HURTS TO SCROLL THROUGH MY SOCIAL MEDIA!
SO USE YOUR LEFT THUMB.
GUESS WHAT—I'M INSTAGRAMBIDEXTROUS!
© 2018 ZITS Partnership. Dist. by King Features
SCOTT and BORGMAN 4·13

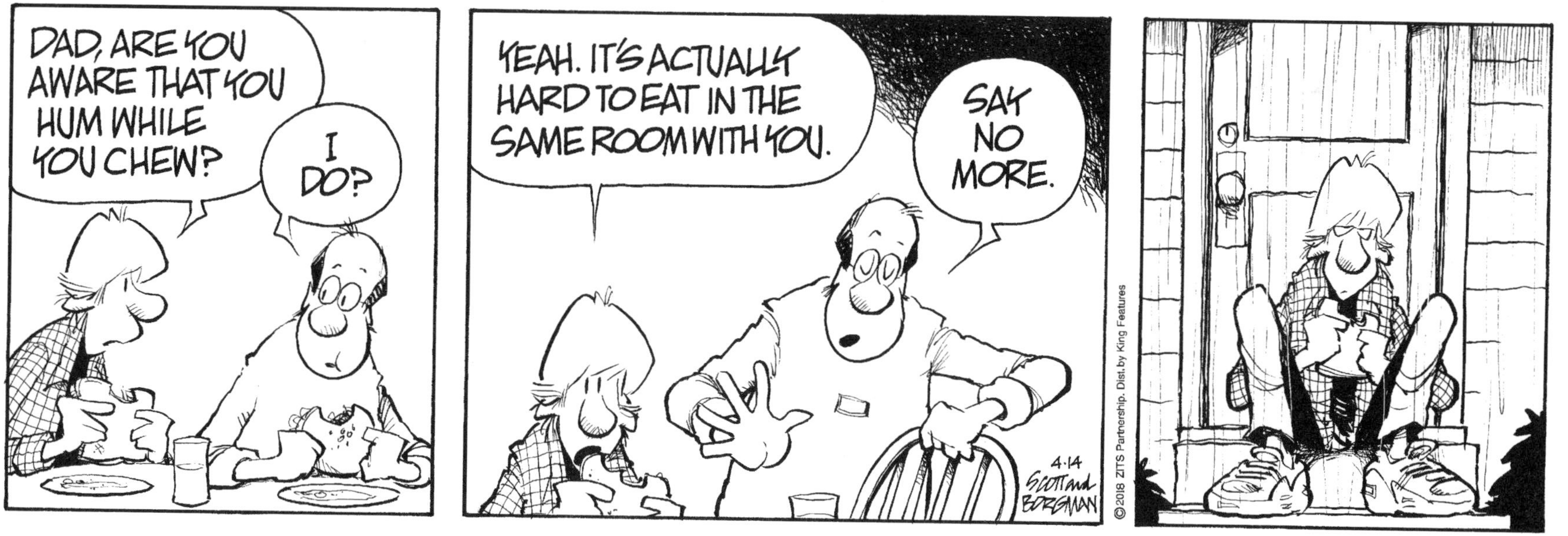
DAD, ARE YOU AWARE THAT YOU HUM WHILE YOU CHEW?
I DO?
YEAH. IT'S ACTUALLY HARD TO EAT IN THE SAME ROOM WITH YOU.
SAY NO MORE.
4·14 SCOTT and BORGMAN
© 2018 ZITS Partnership. Dist. by King Features

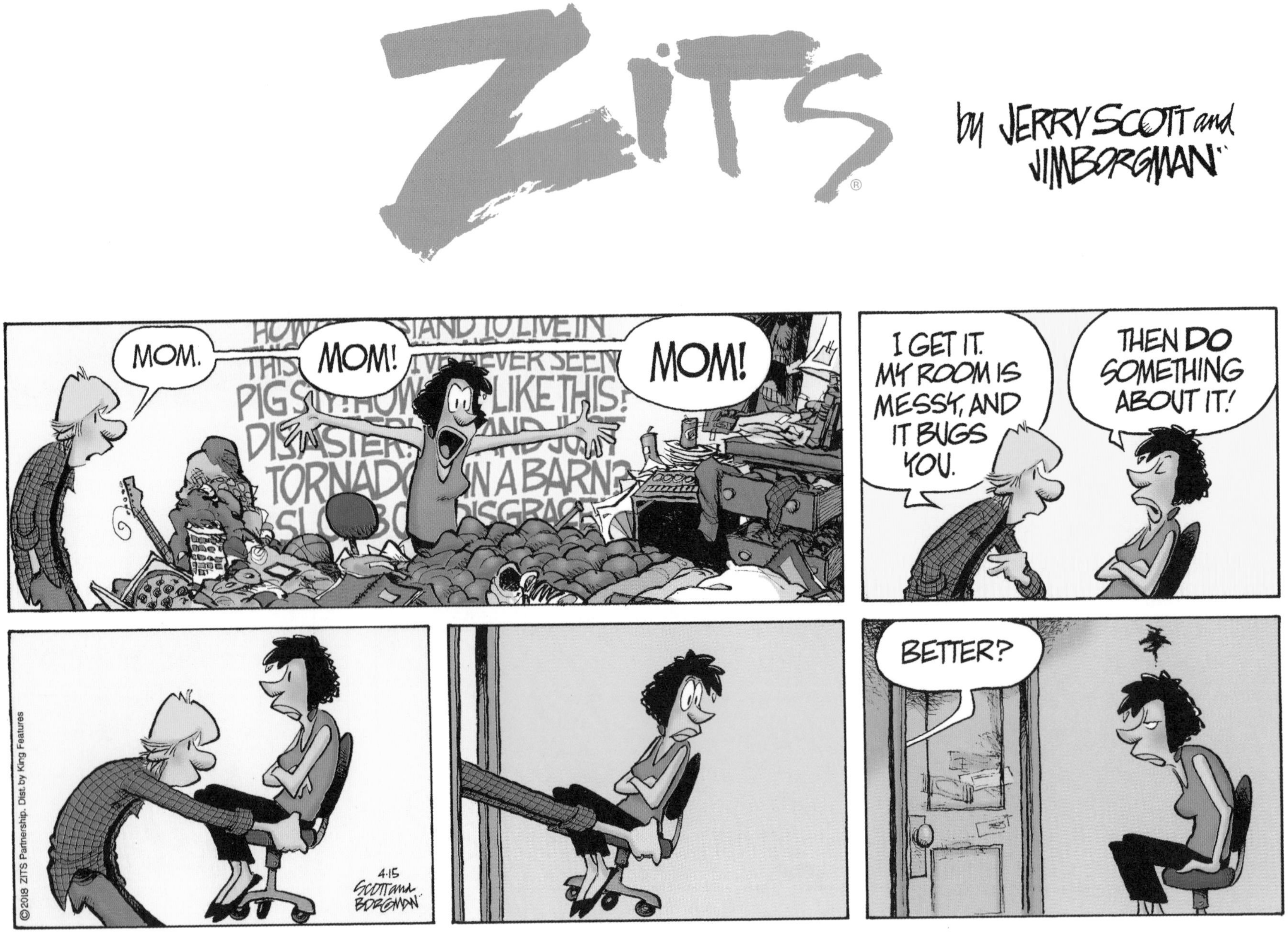
ZITS
by JERRY SCOTT and JIM BORGMAN
MOM.
MOM!
MOM!
I GET IT. MY ROOM IS MESSY, AND IT BUGS YOU.
THEN DO SOMETHING ABOUT IT!
©2018 ZITS Partnership. Dist. by King Features
4-15 SCOTTand BORGMAN
BETTER?

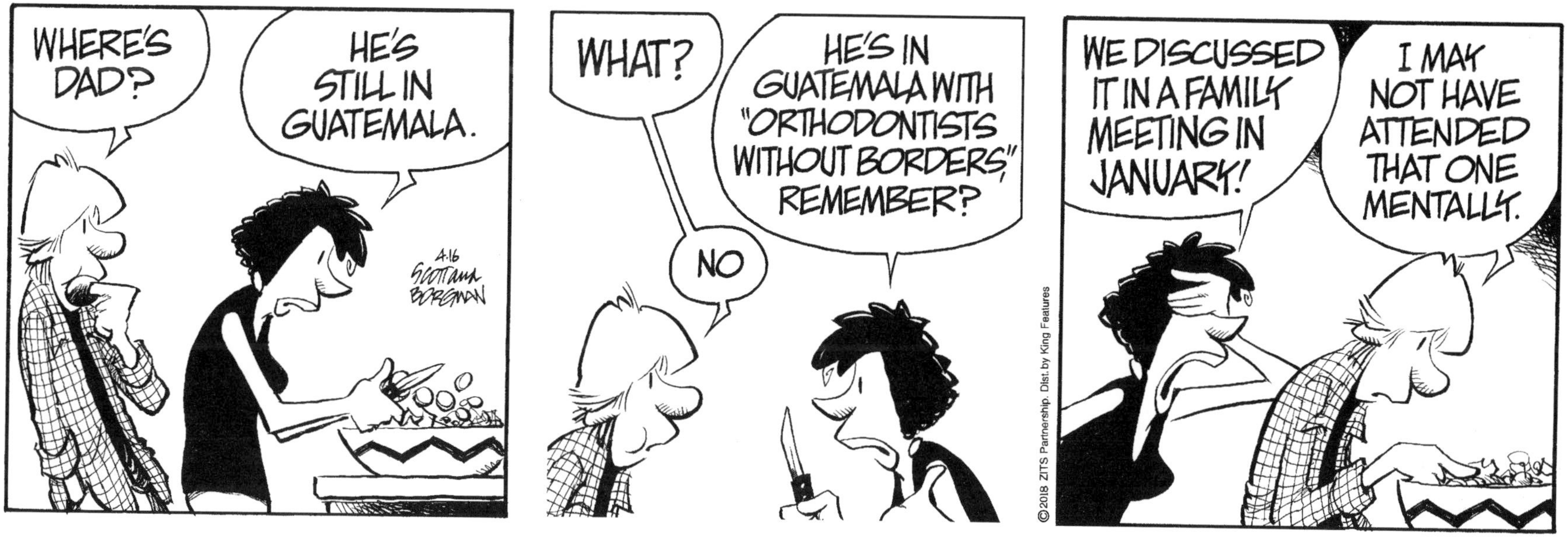
WHERE'S DAD?
HE'S STILL IN GUATEMALA.
WHAT?
NO
HE'S IN GUATEMALA WITH "ORTHODONTISTS WITHOUT BORDERS," REMEMBER?
WE DISCUSSED IT IN A FAMILY MEETING IN JANUARY!
I MAY NOT HAVE ATTENDED THAT ONE MENTALLY.

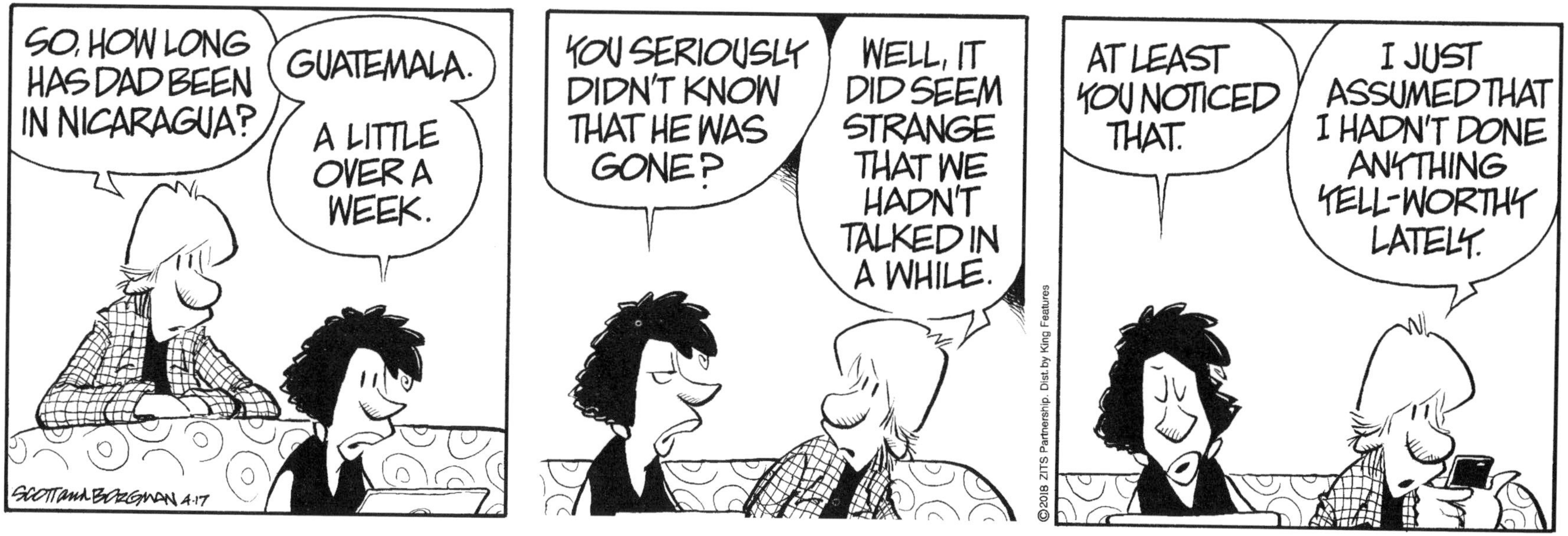
SO, HOW LONG HAS DAD BEEN IN NICARAGUA?
GUATEMALA.
A LITTLE OVER A WEEK.
YOU SERIOUSLY DIDN'T KNOW THAT HE WAS GONE?
WELL, IT DID SEEM STRANGE THAT WE HADN'T TALKED IN A WHILE.
AT LEAST YOU NOTICED THAT.
I JUST ASSUMED THAT I HADN'T DONE ANYTHING YELL-WORTHY LATELY.

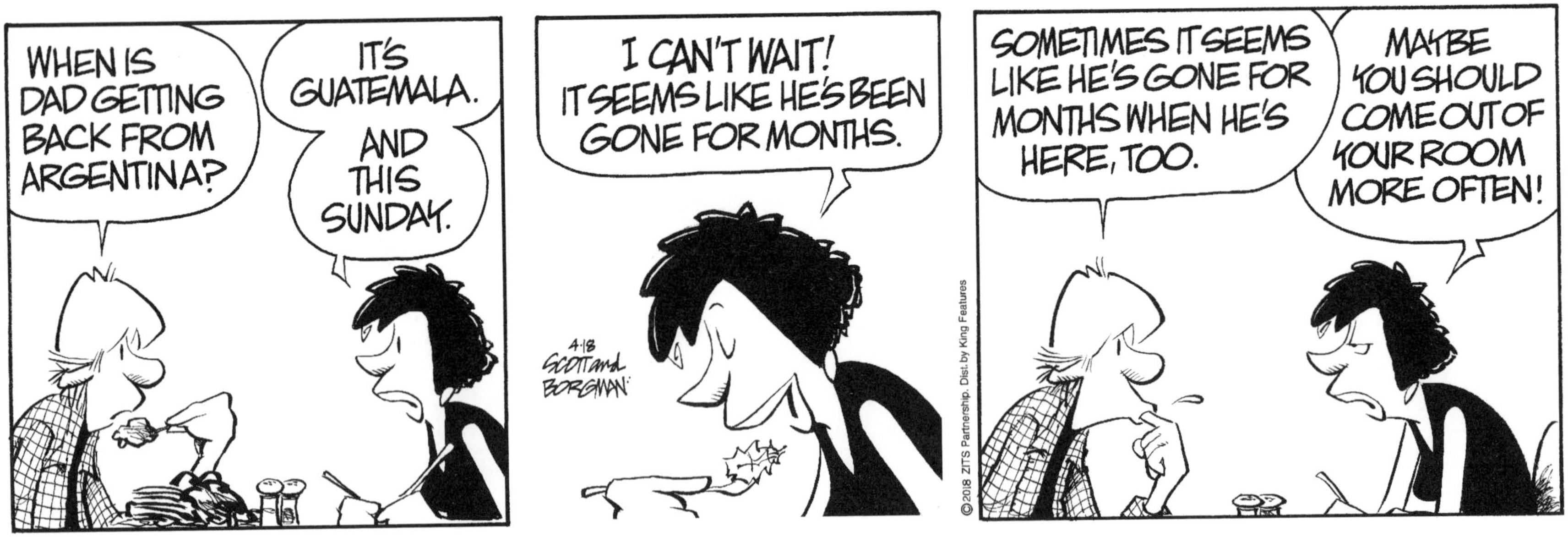
WHEN IS DAD GETTING BACK FROM ARGENTINA?
IT'S GUATEMALA.
AND THIS SUNDAY.
I CAN'T WAIT! IT SEEMS LIKE HE'S BEEN GONE FOR MONTHS.
4·18 SCOTT and BORGMAN
SOMETIMES IT SEEMS LIKE HE'S GONE FOR MONTHS WHEN HE'S HERE, TOO.
MAYBE YOU SHOULD COME OUT OF YOUR ROOM MORE OFTEN!
©2018 ZITS Partnership. Dist. by King Features

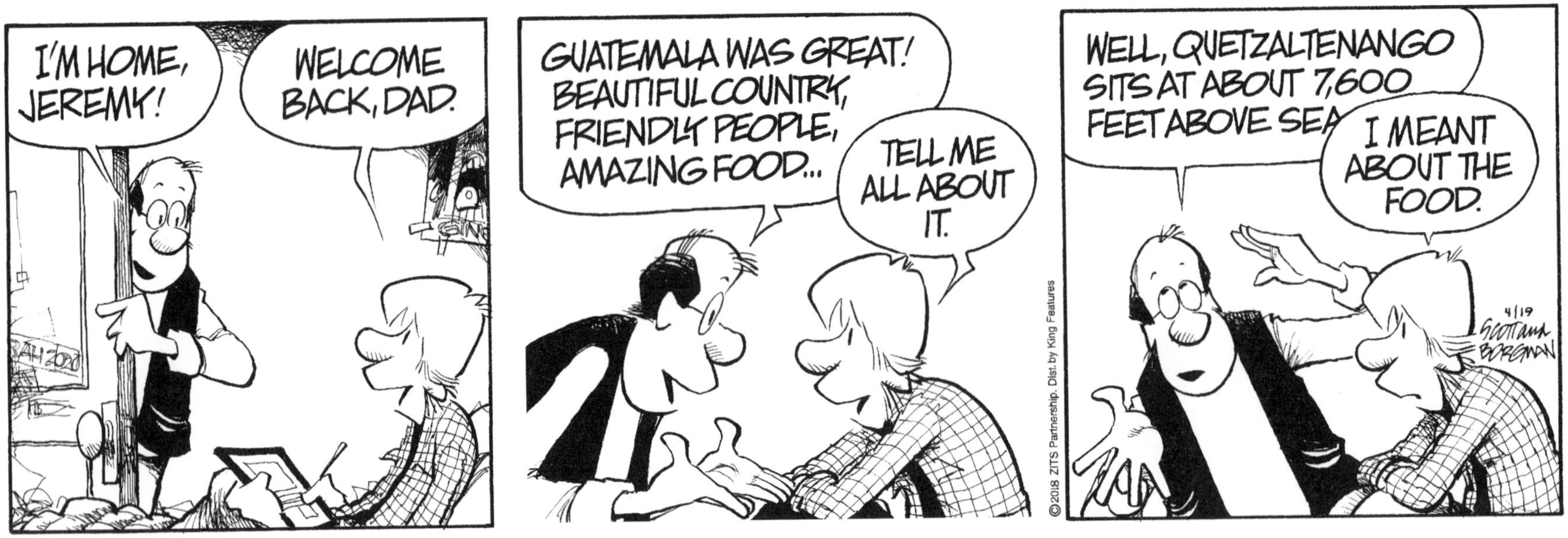
I'M HOME, JEREMY!
WELCOME BACK, DAD.
GUATEMALA WAS GREAT! BEAUTIFUL COUNTRY, FRIENDLY PEOPLE, AMAZING FOOD...
TELL ME ALL ABOUT IT.
©2018 ZITS Partnership. Dist. by King Features
WELL, QUETZALTENANGO SITS AT ABOUT 7,600 FEET ABOVE SEA
I MEANT ABOUT THE FOOD.
4/19 SCOTT and BORGMAN

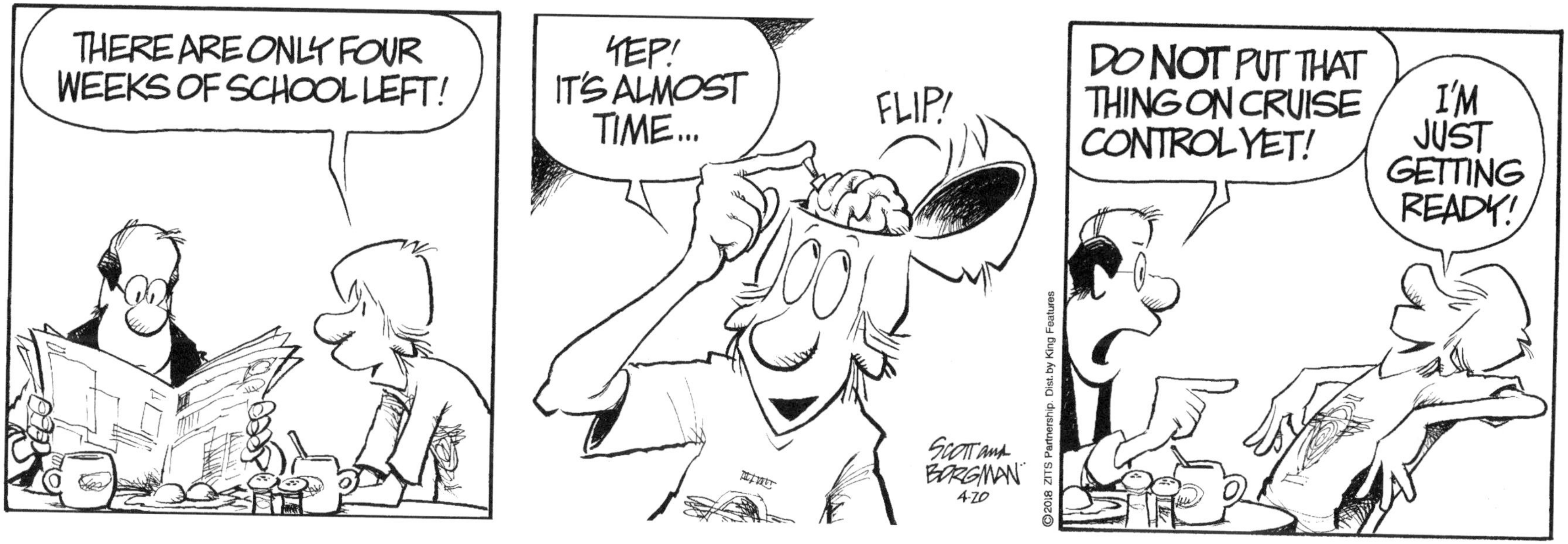
THERE ARE ONLY FOUR WEEKS OF SCHOOL LEFT!
YEP! IT'S ALMOST TIME...
FLIP!
SCOTT and BORGMAN 4-20
DO NOT PUT THAT THING ON CRUISE CONTROL YET!
I'M JUST GETTING READY!
©2018 ZITS Partnership. Dist. by King Features

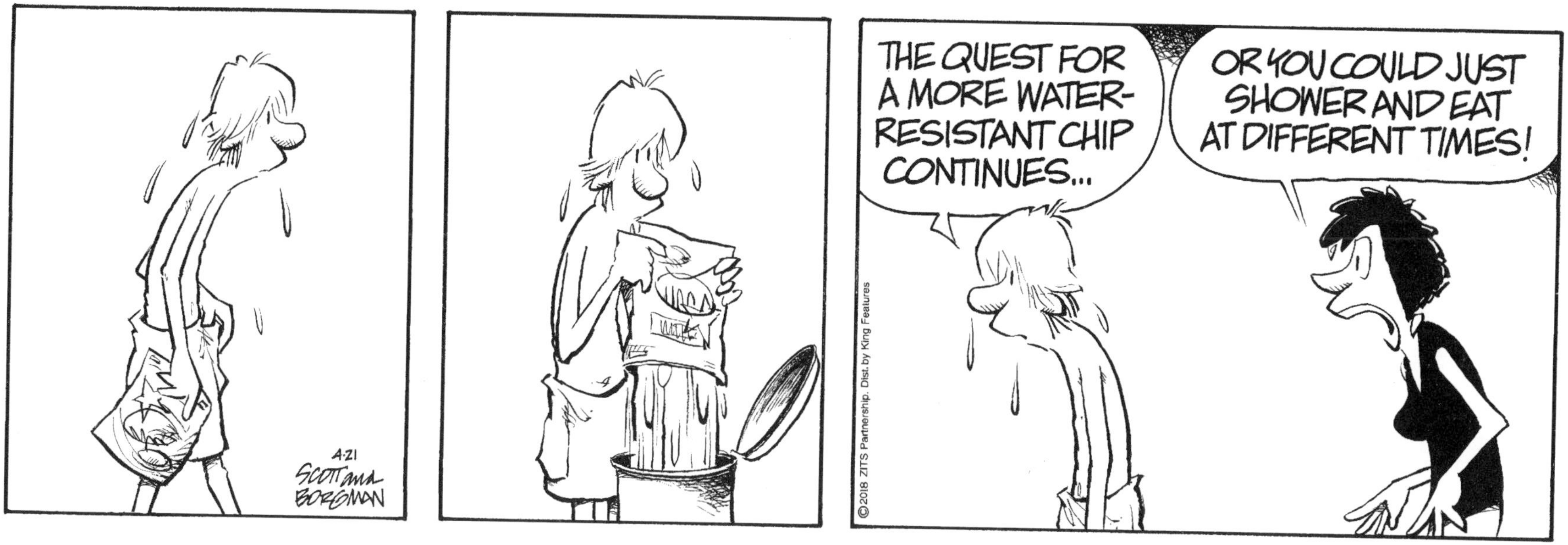
4-21 SCOTT and BORGMAN
©2018 ZITS Partnership. Dist. by King Features
THE QUEST FOR A MORE WATER-RESISTANT CHIP CONTINUES...
OR YOU COULD JUST SHOWER AND EAT AT DIFFERENT TIMES!

ZITS

by JERRY SCOTT and JIM BORGMAN

6:00 7:00 8:00 9:00 10:00 11:00 12:00 1:00 2:00 3:00 4:00 5:00 6:00
IF SCHOOL DAYS HAD EKGs
SCOTT AND BORGMAN 4-22
©2018 ZITS Partnership. Dist. by King Features

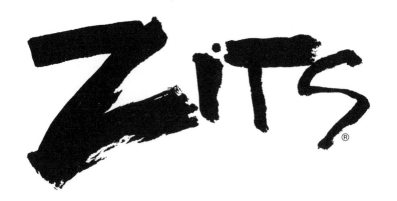

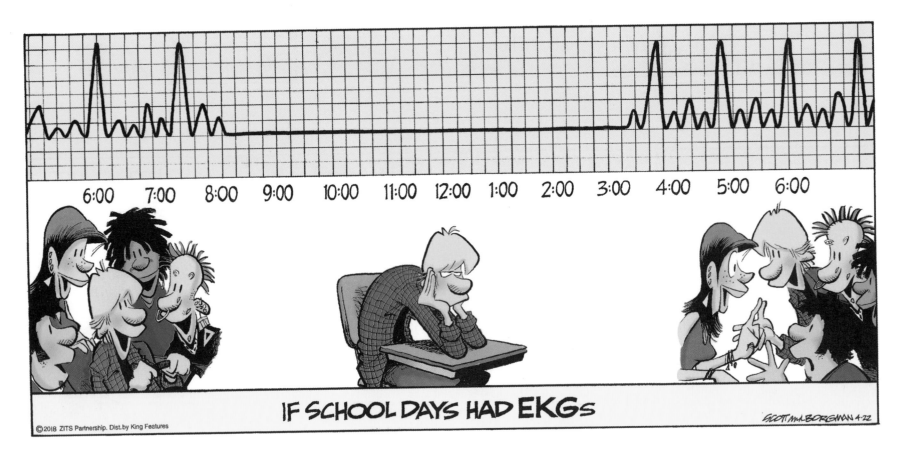

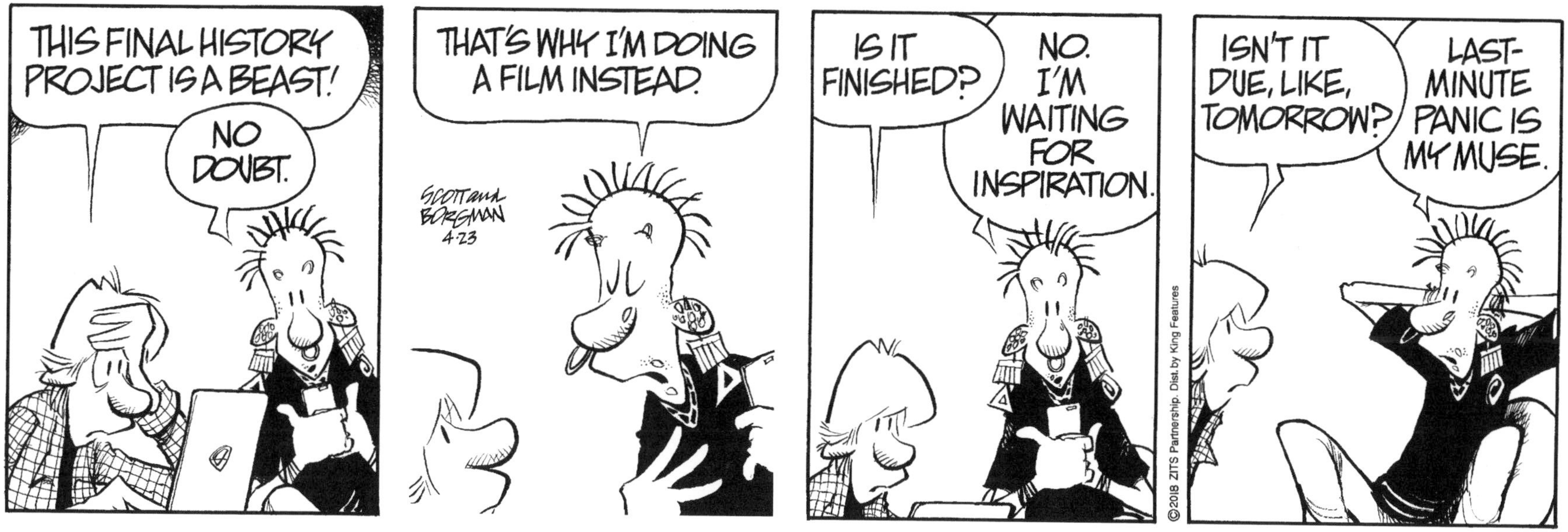
THIS FINAL HISTORY PROJECT IS A BEAST!
NO DOUBT.
THAT'S WHY I'M DOING A FILM INSTEAD.
SCOTT and BORGMAN 4-23
IS IT FINISHED?
NO. I'M WAITING FOR INSPIRATION.
©2018 ZITS Partnership. Dist. by King Features
ISN'T IT DUE, LIKE, TOMORROW?
LAST-MINUTE PANIC IS MY MUSE.

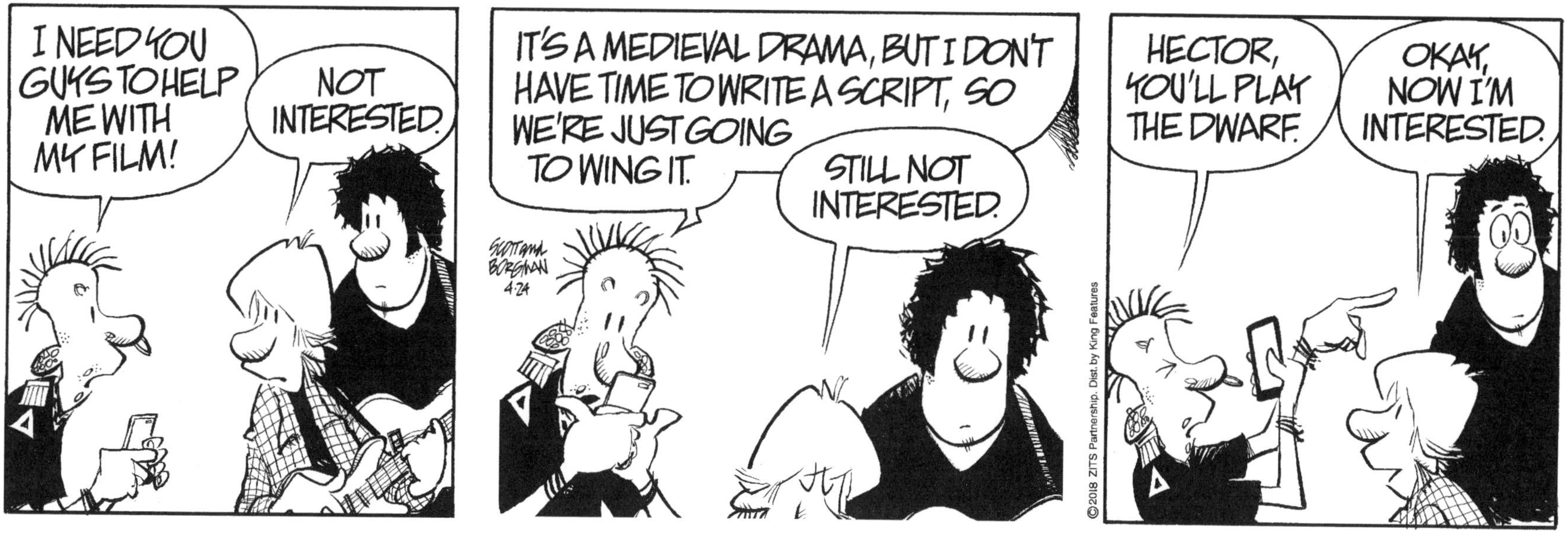
I NEED YOU GUYS TO HELP ME WITH MY FILM!
NOT INTERESTED.
IT'S A MEDIEVAL DRAMA, BUT I DON'T HAVE TIME TO WRITE A SCRIPT, SO WE'RE JUST GOING TO WING IT.
STILL NOT INTERESTED.
SCOTT and BORGMAN 4-24
©2018 ZITS Partnership. Dist. by King Features
HECTOR, YOU'LL PLAY THE DWARF.
OKAY, NOW I'M INTERESTED.

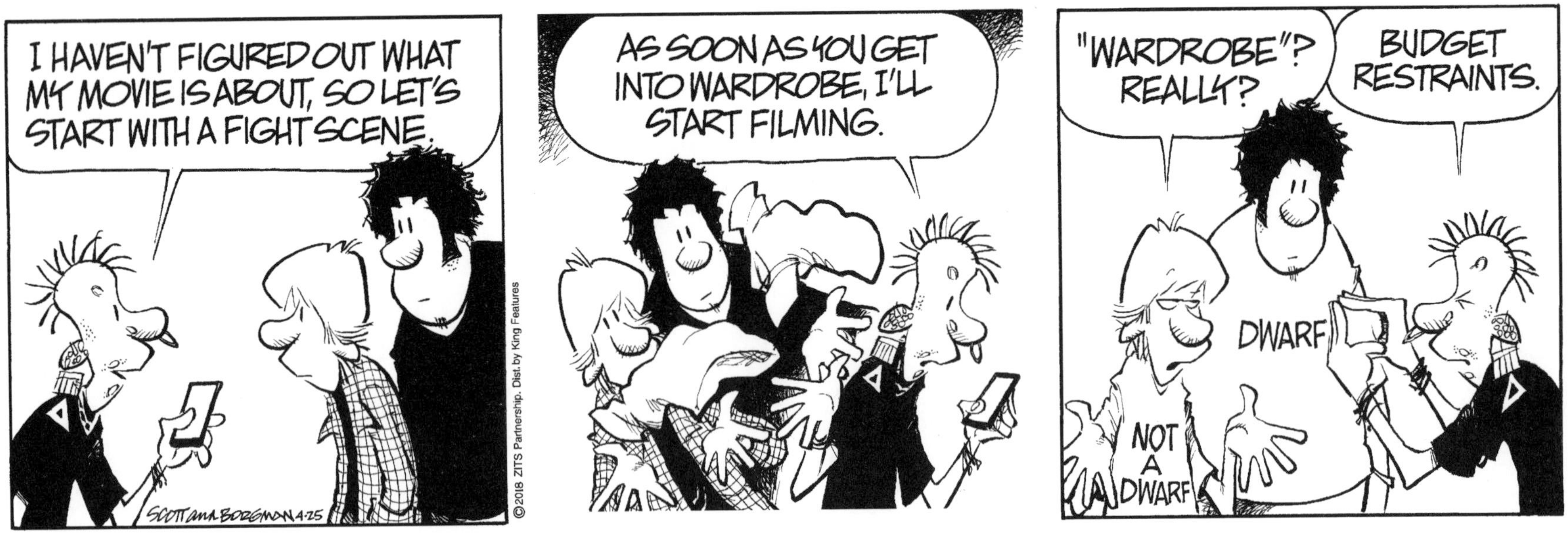
I HAVEN'T FIGURED OUT WHAT MY MOVIE IS ABOUT, SO LET'S START WITH A FIGHT SCENE.
SCOTT and BORGMAN 4-25
©2018 ZITS Partnership. Dist. by King Features
AS SOON AS YOU GET INTO WARDROBE, I'LL START FILMING.
"WARDROBE"? REALLY?
BUDGET RESTRAINTS.
NOT A DWARF
DWARF

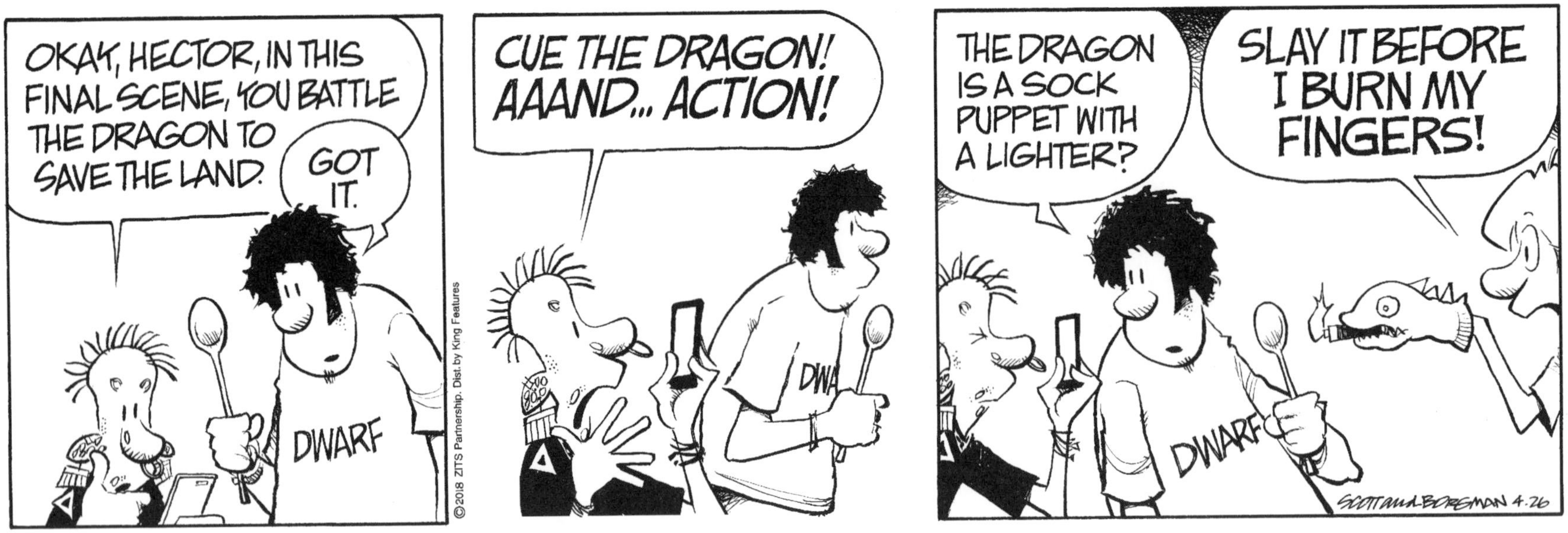
OKAY, HECTOR, IN THIS FINAL SCENE, YOU BATTLE THE DRAGON TO SAVE THE LAND.
GOT IT.
DWARF
©2018 ZITS Partnership. Dist. by King Features
CUE THE DRAGON! AAAND... ACTION!
THE DRAGON IS A SOCK PUPPET WITH A LIGHTER?
SLAY IT BEFORE I BURN MY FINGERS!
DWARF
SCOTT and BORGMAN 4-26

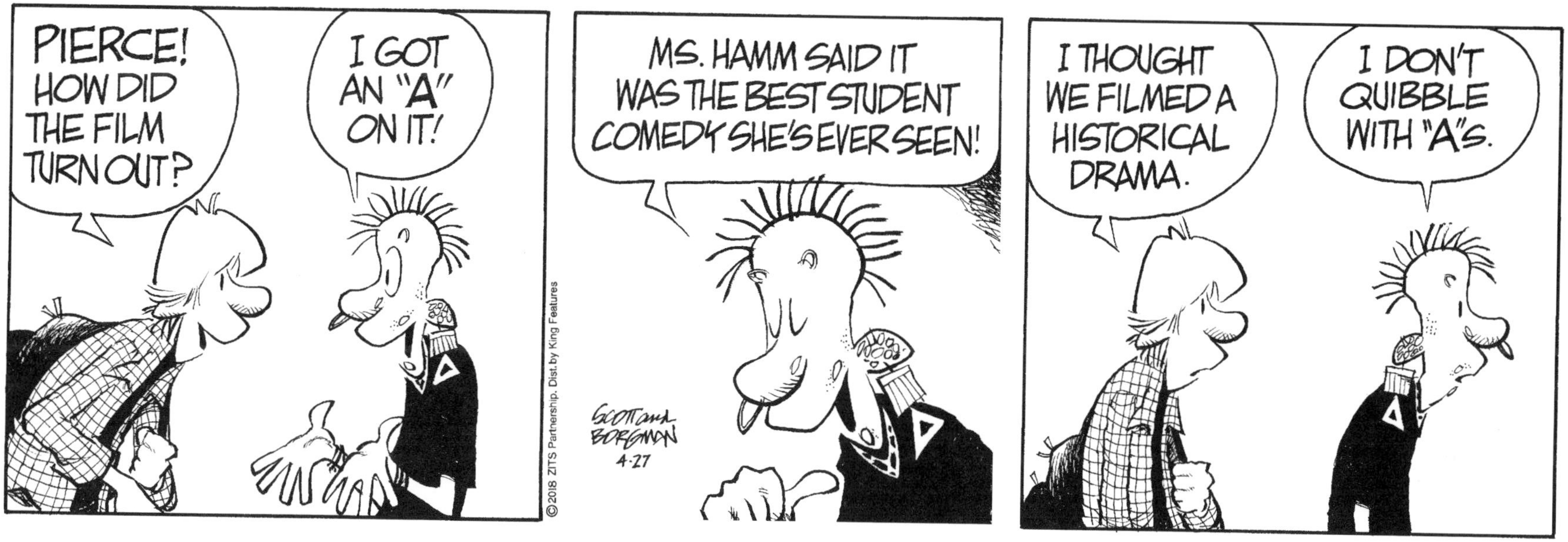
PIERCE! HOW DID THE FILM TURN OUT?
I GOT AN "A" ON IT!
MS. HAMM SAID IT WAS THE BEST STUDENT COMEDY SHE'S EVER SEEN!
I THOUGHT WE FILMED A HISTORICAL DRAMA.
I DON'T QUIBBLE WITH "A"S.
SCOTT and BORGMAN 4-27
©2018 ZITS Partnership. Dist. by King Features

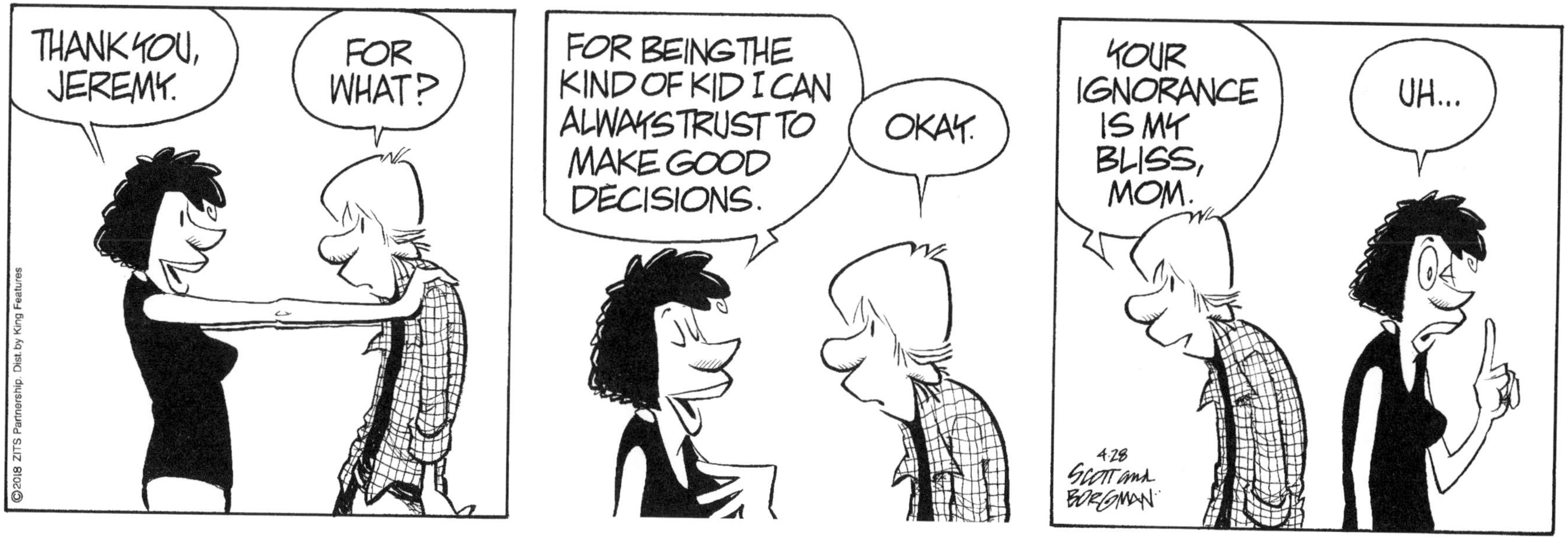
THANK YOU, JEREMY.
FOR WHAT?
FOR BEING THE KIND OF KID I CAN ALWAYS TRUST TO MAKE GOOD DECISIONS.
OKAY.
YOUR IGNORANCE IS MY BLISS, MOM.
UH...
4-28 SCOTT and BORGMAN
©2018 ZITS Partnership. Dist. by King Features

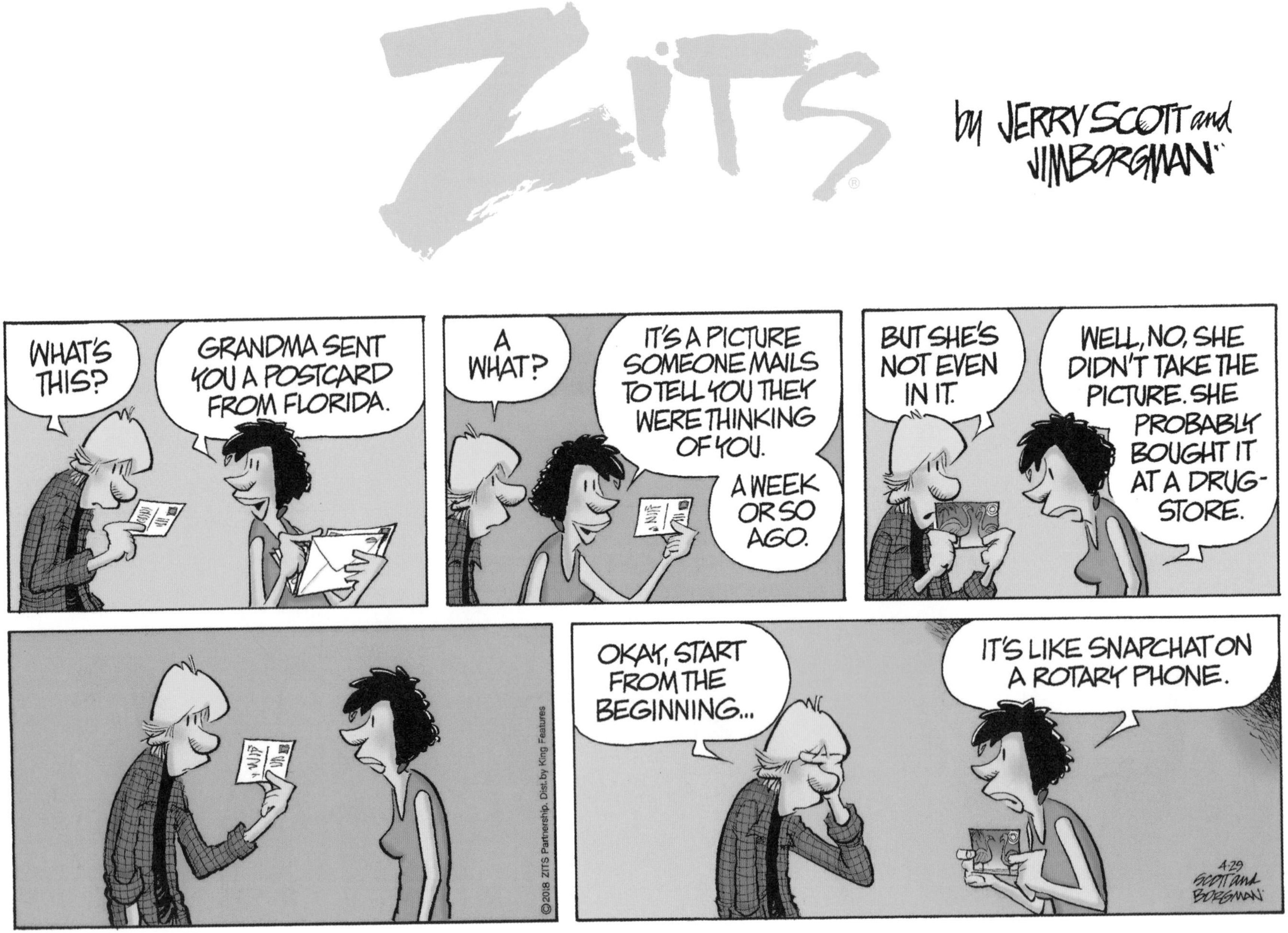
ZITS
by JERRY SCOTT and JIM BORGMAN
WHAT'S THIS?
GRANDMA SENT YOU A POSTCARD FROM FLORIDA.
A WHAT?
IT'S A PICTURE SOMEONE MAILS TO TELL YOU THEY WERE THINKING OF YOU.
A WEEK OR SO AGO.
BUT SHE'S NOT EVEN IN IT.
WELL, NO, SHE DIDN'T TAKE THE PICTURE. SHE PROBABLY BOUGHT IT AT A DRUG-STORE.
© 2018 ZITS Partnership. Dist. by King Features
OKAY, START FROM THE BEGINNING...
IT'S LIKE SNAPCHAT ON A ROTARY PHONE.
4-29 SCOTT and BORGMAN

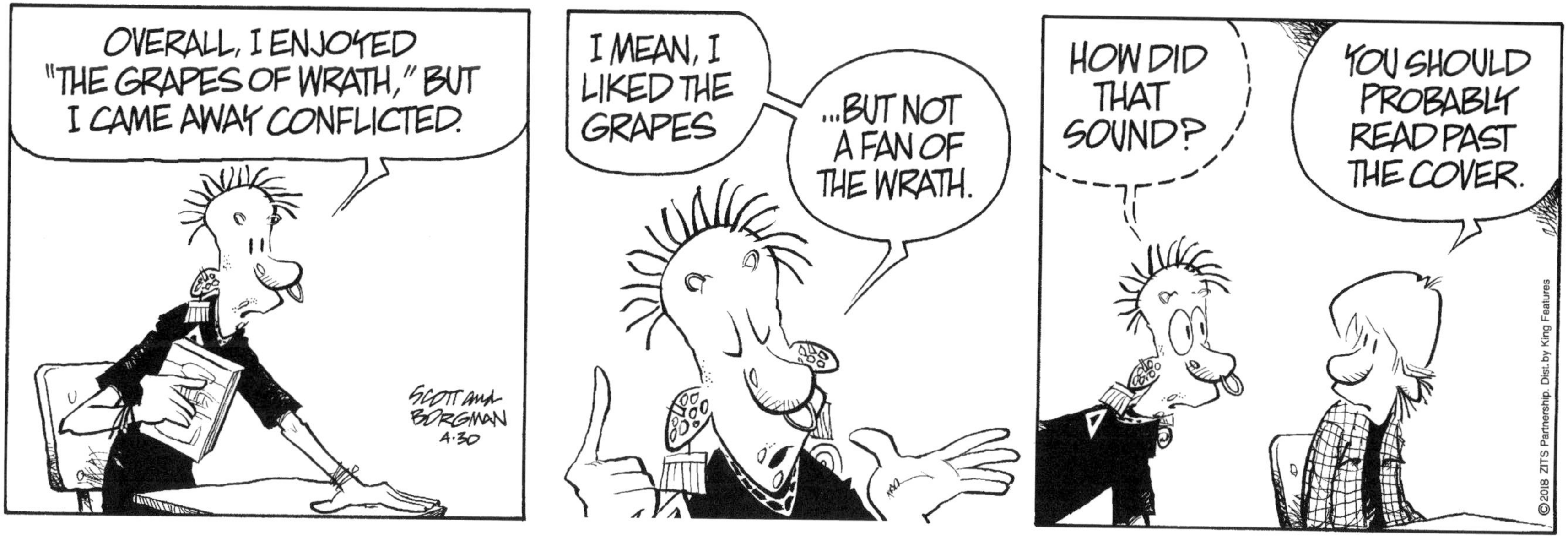
OVERALL, I ENJOYED "THE GRAPES OF WRATH," BUT I CAME AWAY CONFLICTED.
SCOTT AND BORGMAN 4·30
I MEAN, I LIKED THE GRAPES
...BUT NOT A FAN OF THE WRATH.
HOW DID THAT SOUND?
YOU SHOULD PROBABLY READ PAST THE COVER.
©2018 ZITS Partnership. Dist. by King Features

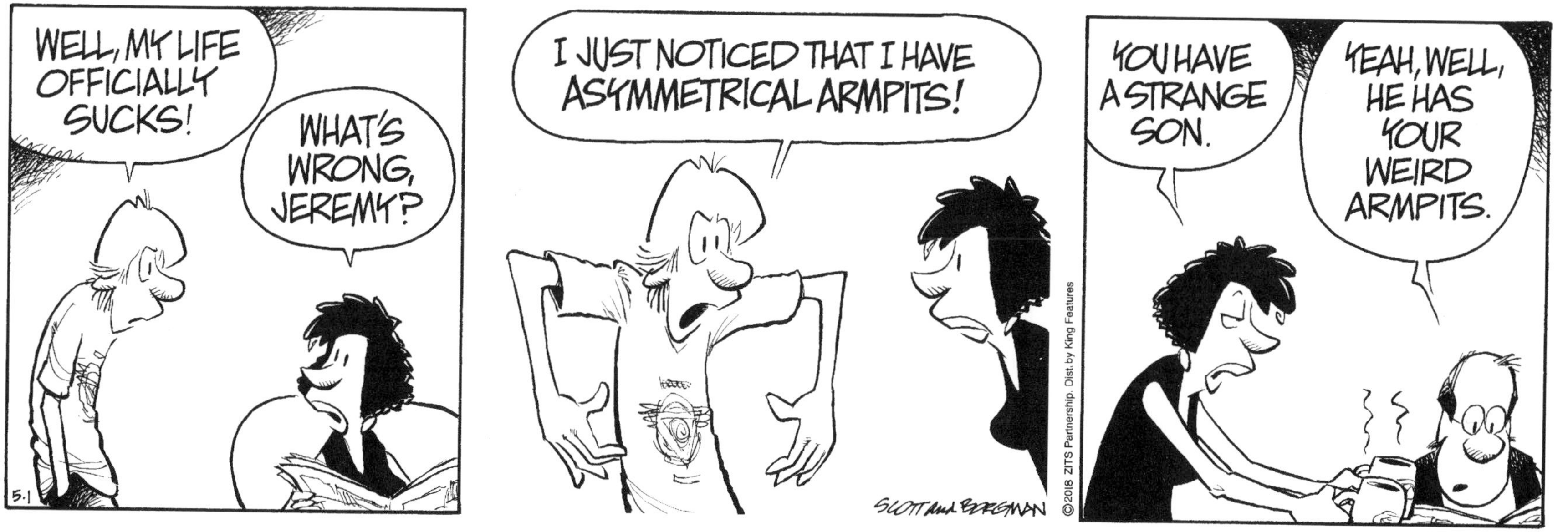
WELL, MY LIFE OFFICIALLY SUCKS!
WHAT'S WRONG, JEREMY?
5·1
I JUST NOTICED THAT I HAVE ASYMMETRICAL ARMPITS!
SCOTT AND BORGMAN
©2018 ZITS Partnership. Dist. by King Features
YOU HAVE A STRANGE SON.
YEAH, WELL, HE HAS YOUR WEIRD ARMPITS.

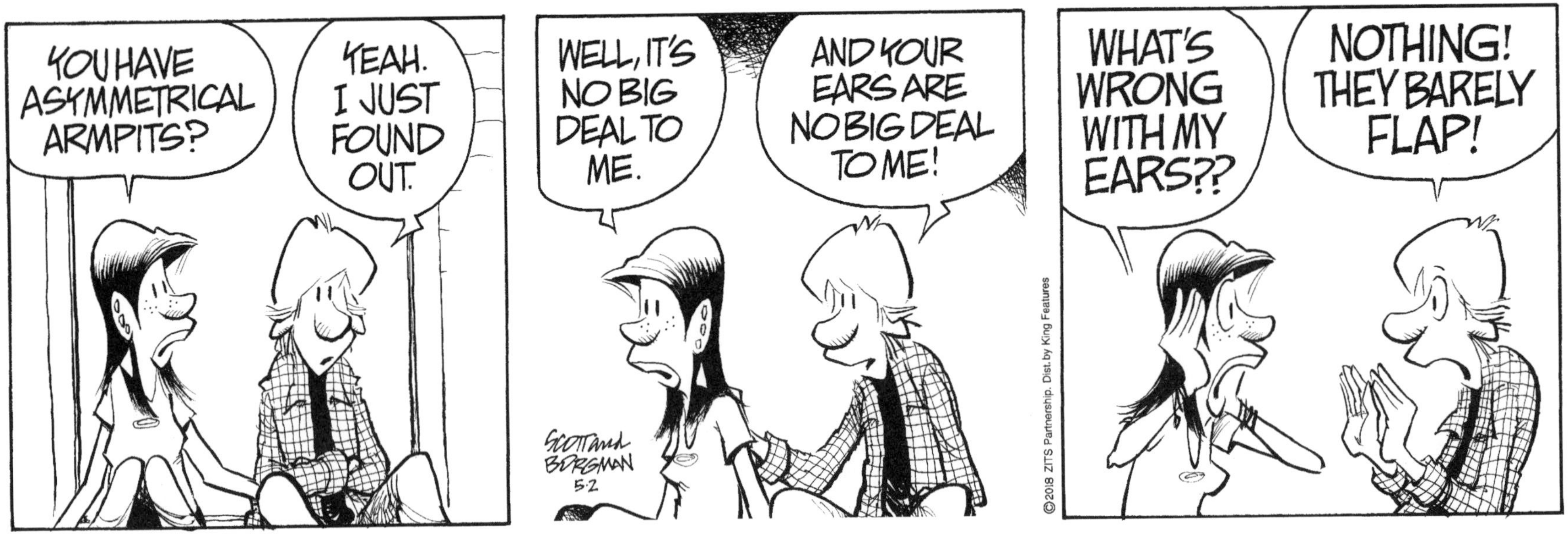
YOU HAVE ASYMMETRICAL ARMPITS?
YEAH. I JUST FOUND OUT.
WELL, IT'S NO BIG DEAL TO ME.
AND YOUR EARS ARE NO BIG DEAL TO ME!
SCOTT and BORGMAN 5·2
WHAT'S WRONG WITH MY EARS??
NOTHING! THEY BARELY FLAP!
©2018 ZITS Partnership. Dist. by King Features

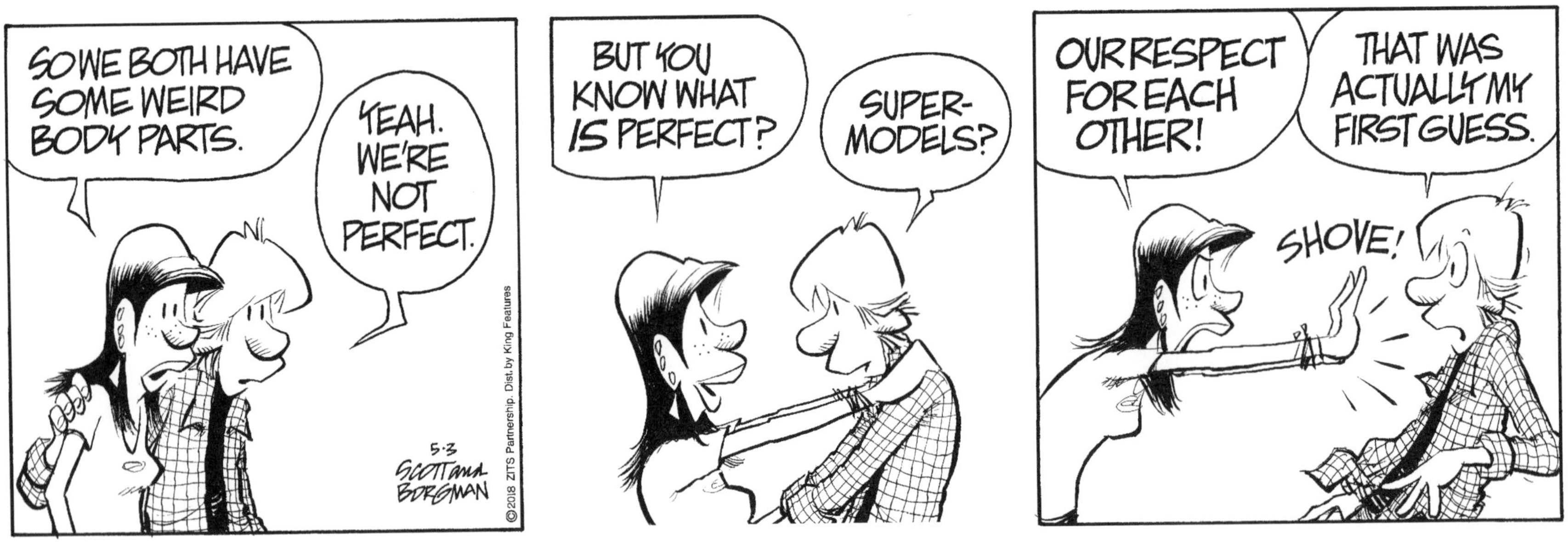
SO WE BOTH HAVE SOME WEIRD BODY PARTS.
YEAH. WE'RE NOT PERFECT.
5·3 SCOTT and BORGMAN
©2018 ZITS Partnership. Dist. by King Features
BUT YOU KNOW WHAT IS PERFECT?
SUPER-MODELS?
OUR RESPECT FOR EACH OTHER!
THAT WAS ACTUALLY MY FIRST GUESS.
SHOVE!

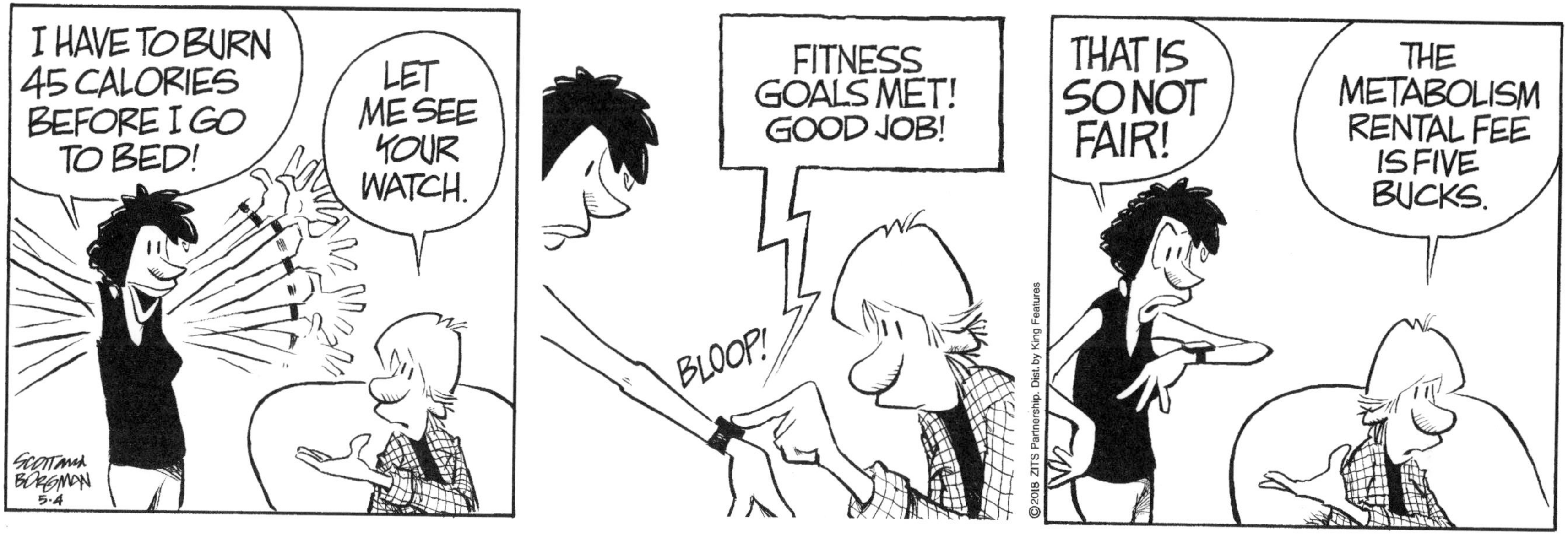
I HAVE TO BURN 45 CALORIES BEFORE I GO TO BED!
LET ME SEE YOUR WATCH.
SCOTT AND BORGMAN 5·4
BLOOP!
FITNESS GOALS MET! GOOD JOB!
©2018 ZITS Partnership. Dist. by King Features
THAT IS SO NOT FAIR!
THE METABOLISM RENTAL FEE IS FIVE BUCKS.

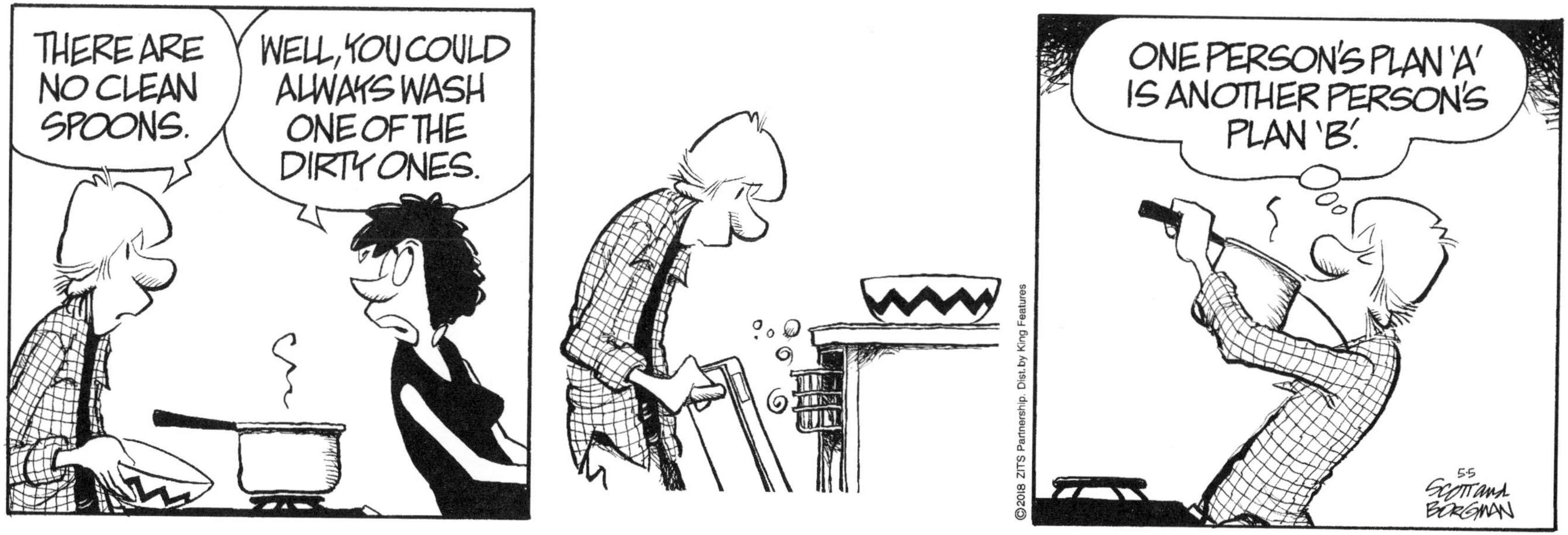
THERE ARE NO CLEAN SPOONS.
WELL, YOU COULD ALWAYS WASH ONE OF THE DIRTY ONES.
©2018 ZITS Partnership. Dist. by King Features
ONE PERSON'S PLAN 'A' IS ANOTHER PERSON'S PLAN 'B'.
5·5 SCOTT AND BORGMAN

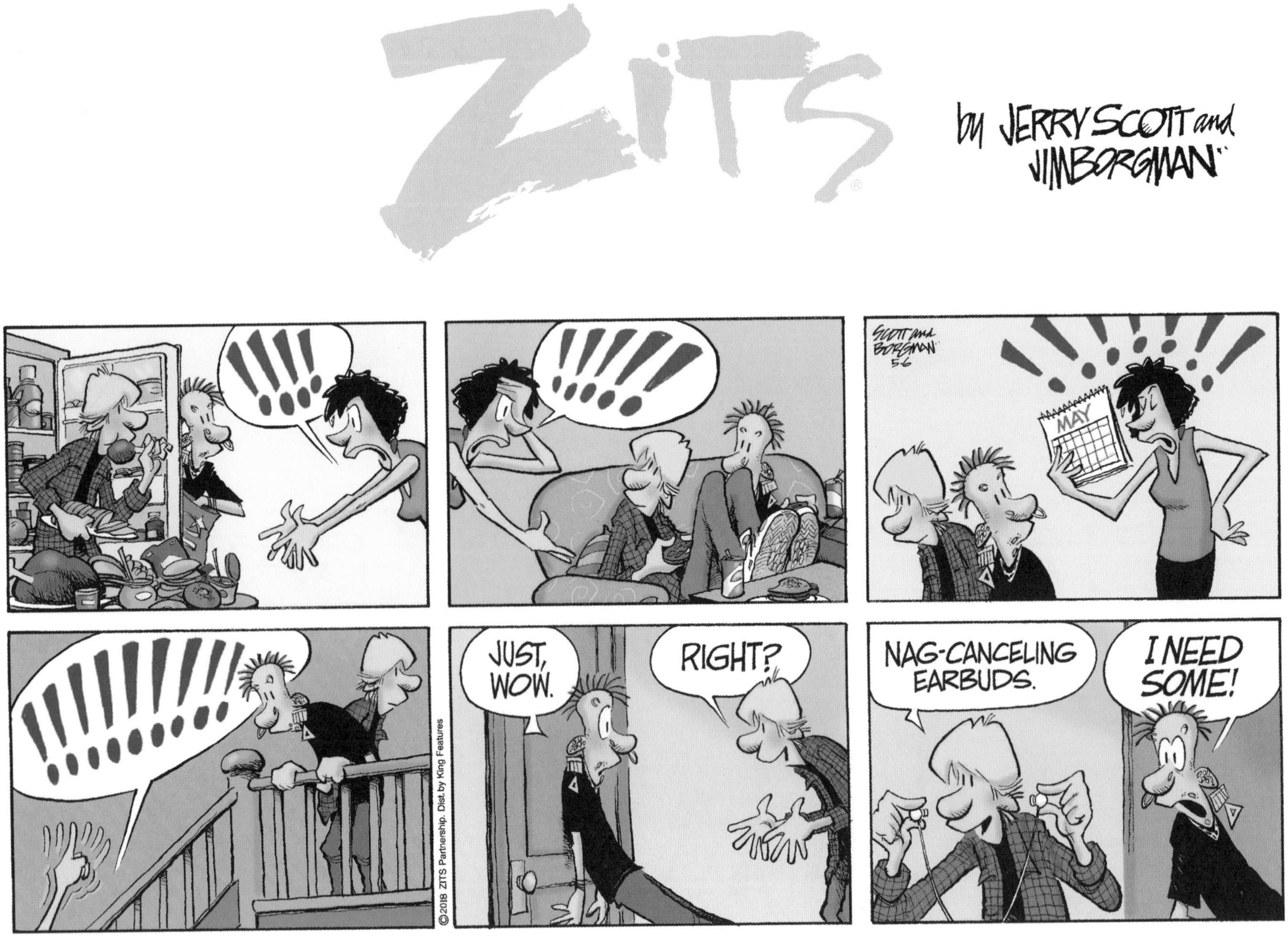
ZITS®
by JERRY SCOTT and JIM BORGMAN
SCOTT and BORGMAN 5-6
MAY
© 2018 ZITS Partnership. Dist. by King Features
JUST, WOW.
RIGHT?
NAG-CANCELING EARBUDS.
I NEED SOME!

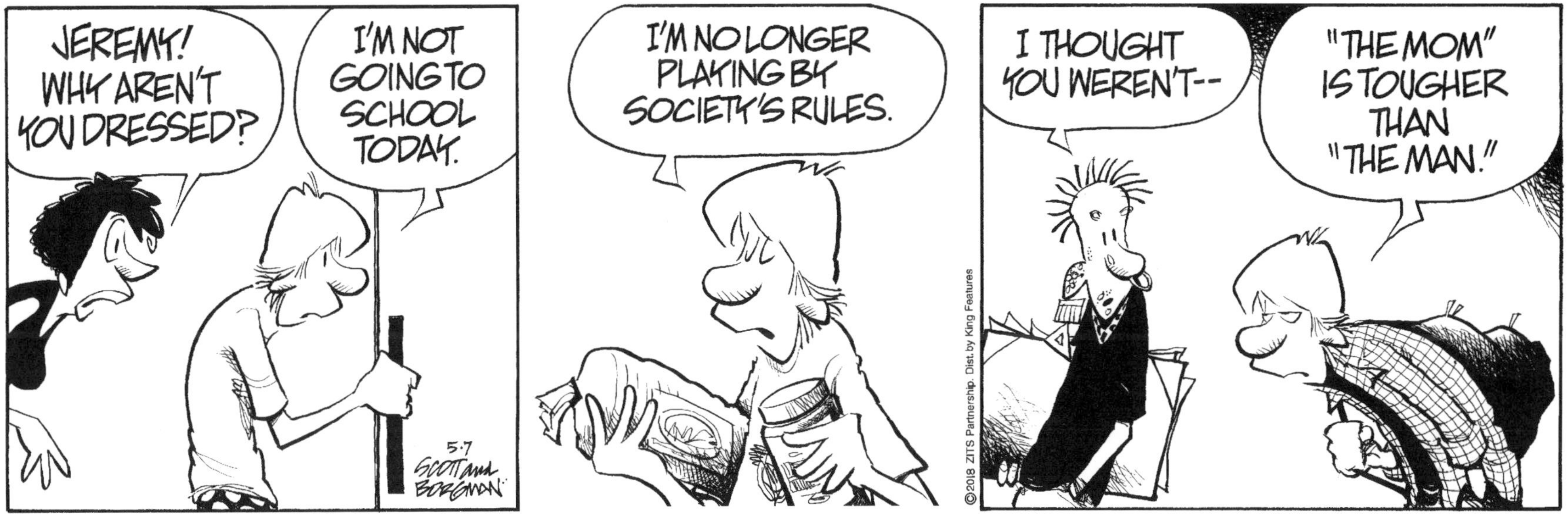
JEREMY! WHY AREN'T YOU DRESSED?
I'M NOT GOING TO SCHOOL TODAY.
I'M NO LONGER PLAYING BY SOCIETY'S RULES.
I THOUGHT YOU WEREN'T--
"THE MOM" IS TOUGHER THAN "THE MAN."
©2018 ZITS Partnership. Dist. by King Features

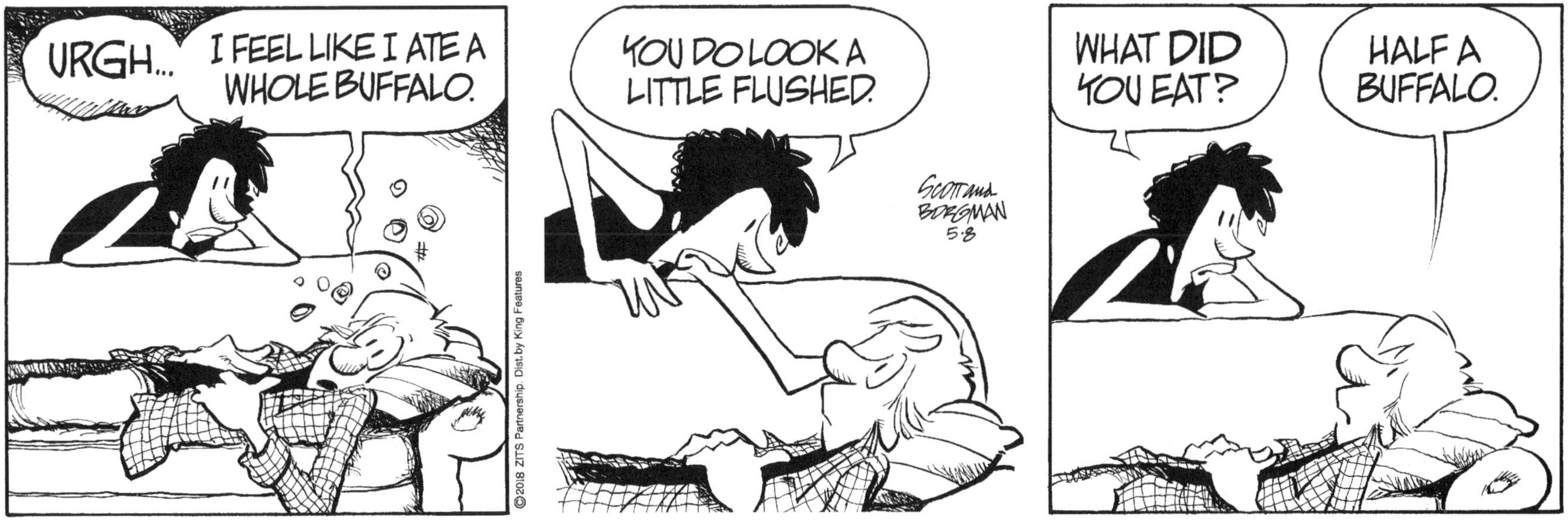
URGH...
I FEEL LIKE I ATE A WHOLE BUFFALO.
YOU DO LOOK A LITTLE FLUSHED.
WHAT DID YOU EAT?
HALF A BUFFALO.
©2018 ZITS Partnership. Dist. by King Features

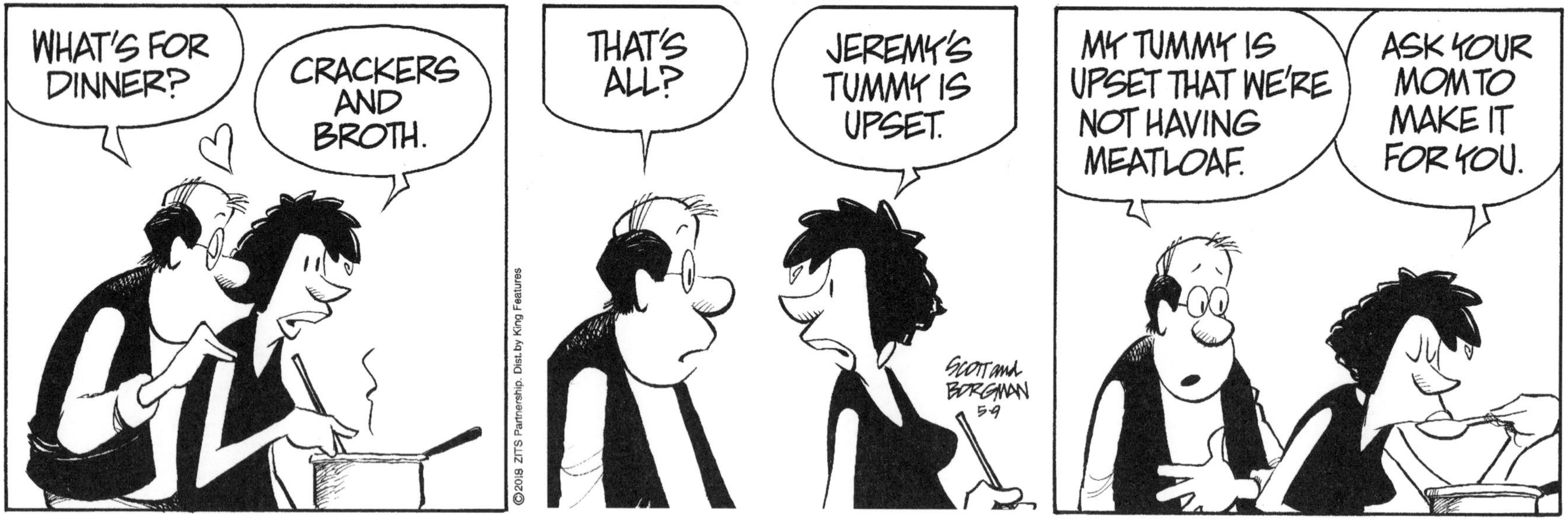
WHAT'S FOR DINNER?
CRACKERS AND BROTH.
©2018 ZITS Partnership. Dist. by King Features
THAT'S ALL?
JEREMY'S TUMMY IS UPSET.
SCOTT and BORGMAN 5-9
MY TUMMY IS UPSET THAT WE'RE NOT HAVING MEATLOAF.
ASK YOUR MOM TO MAKE IT FOR YOU.

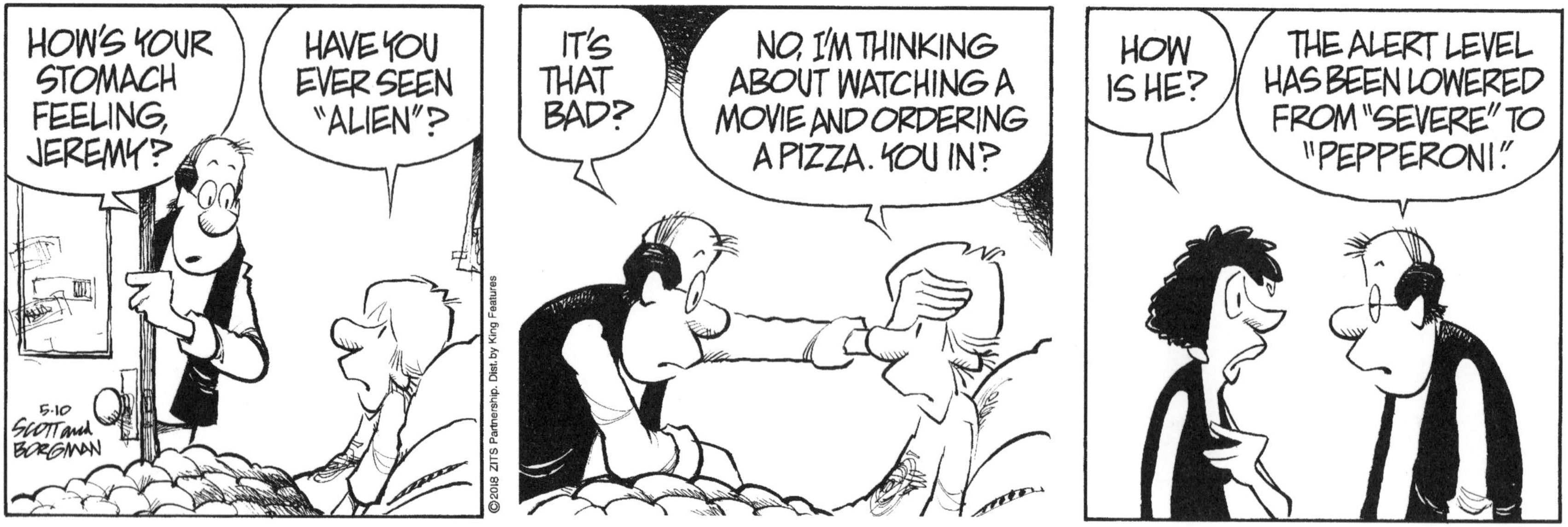
HOW'S YOUR STOMACH FEELING, JEREMY?
HAVE YOU EVER SEEN "ALIEN"?
5-10 SCOTT and BORGMAN
©2018 ZITS Partnership. Dist. by King Features
IT'S THAT BAD?
NO, I'M THINKING ABOUT WATCHING A MOVIE AND ORDERING A PIZZA. YOU IN?
HOW IS HE?
THE ALERT LEVEL HAS BEEN LOWERED FROM "SEVERE" TO "PEPPERONI."

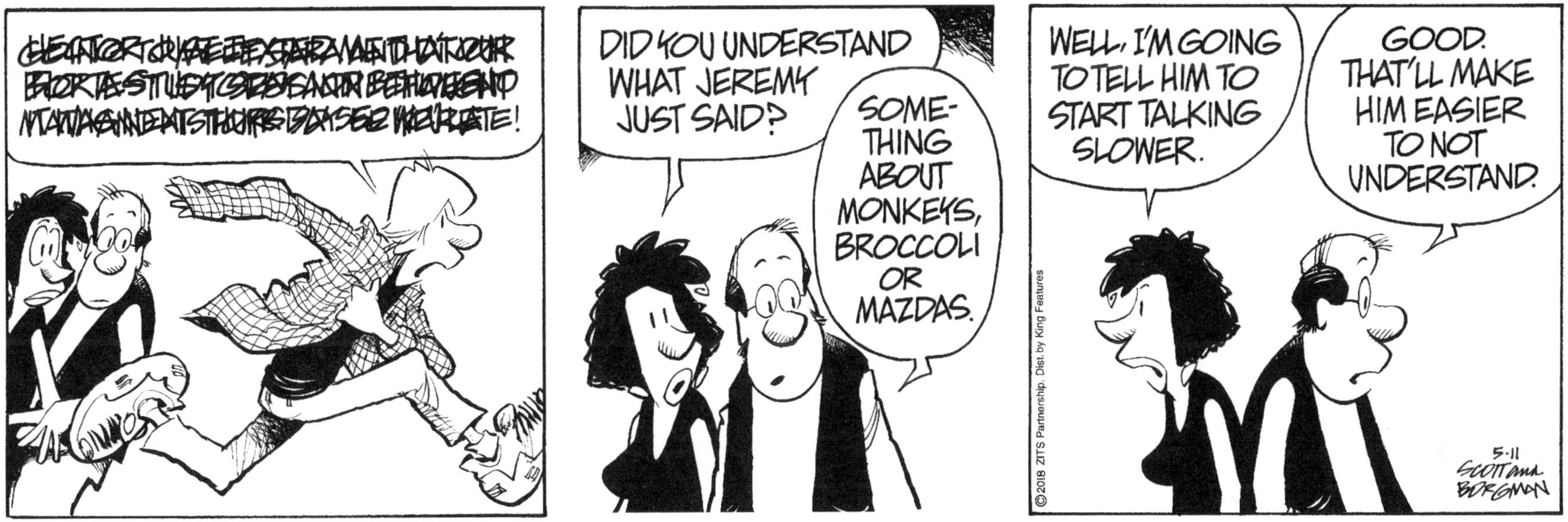
DID YOU UNDERSTAND WHAT JEREMY JUST SAID?
SOME-THING ABOUT MONKEYS, BROCCOLI OR MAZDAS.
WELL, I'M GOING TO TELL HIM TO START TALKING SLOWER.
GOOD. THAT'LL MAKE HIM EASIER TO NOT UNDERSTAND.
©2018 ZITS Partnership. Dist. by King Features
5-11
SCOTT and BORGMAN

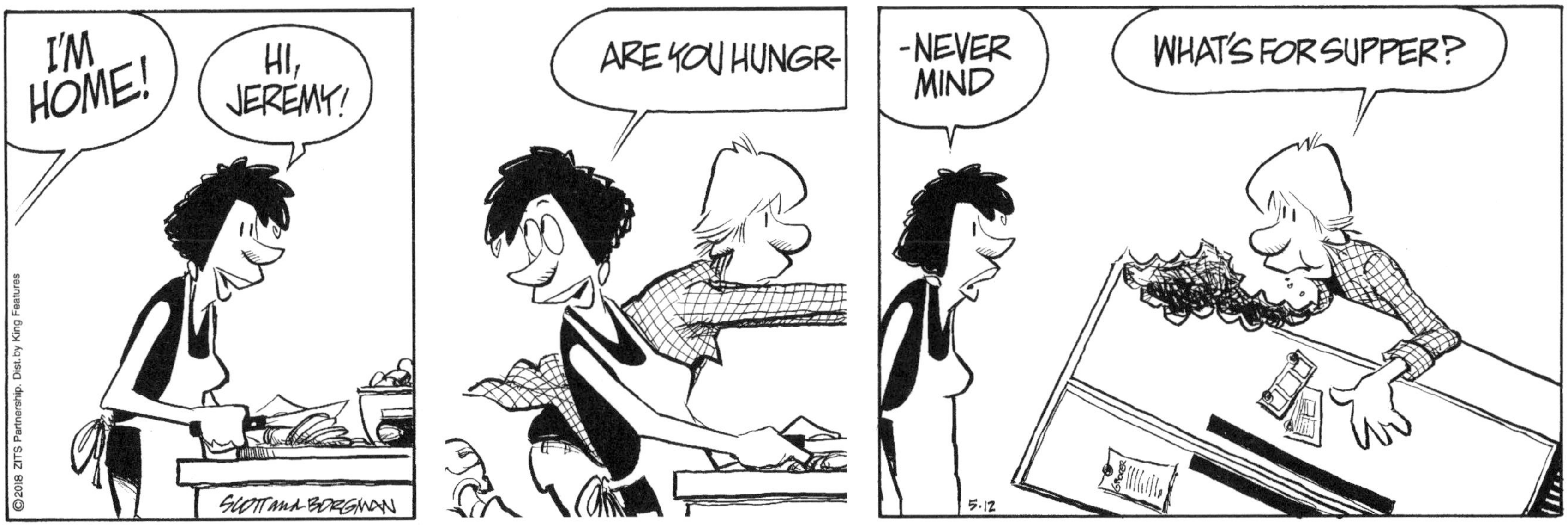
I'M HOME!
HI, JEREMY!
©2018 ZITS Partnership. Dist. by King Features
SCOTT and BORGMAN
ARE YOU HUNGR-
-NEVER MIND
WHAT'S FOR SUPPER?
5-12

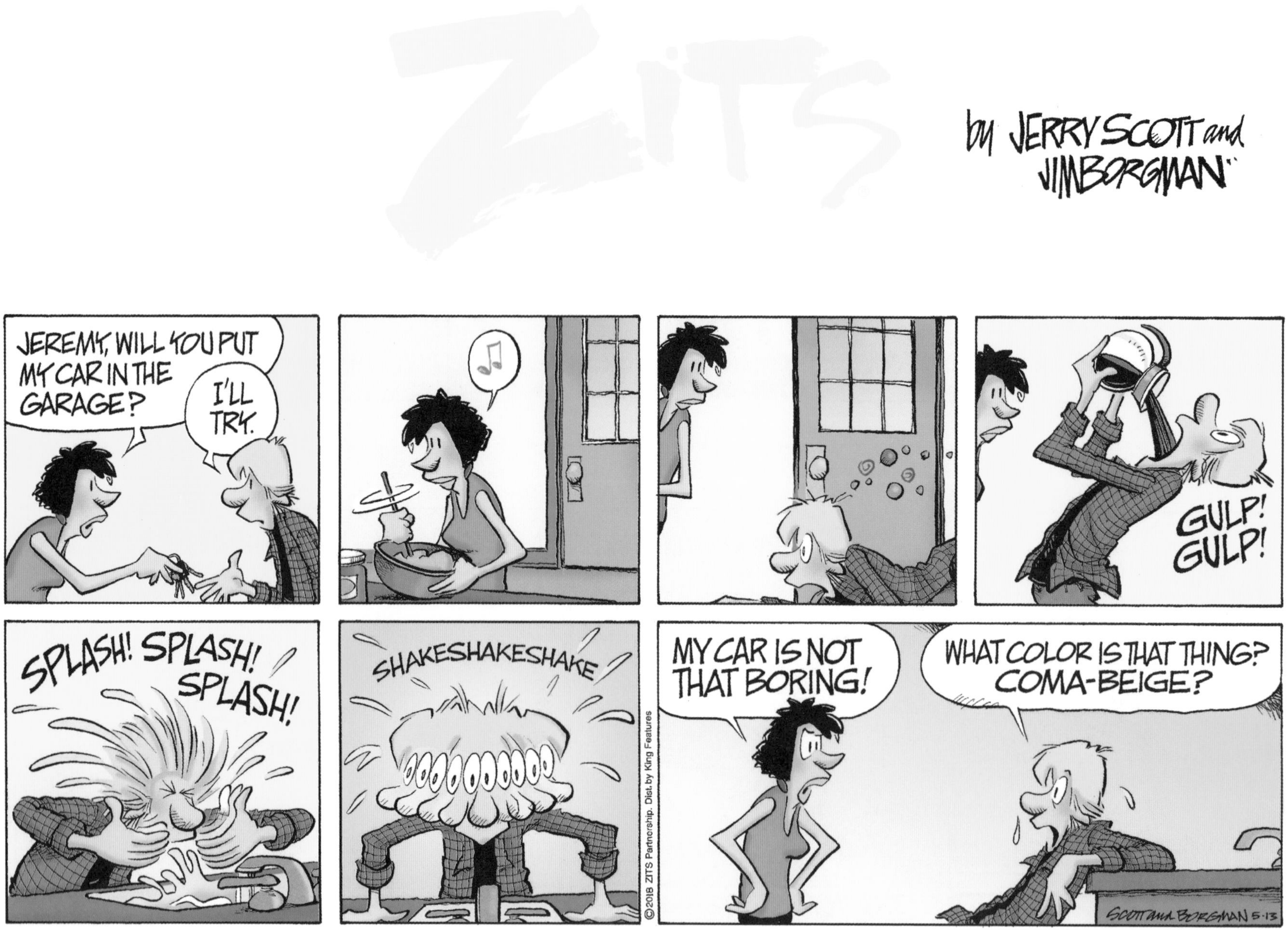
ZITS
by JERRY SCOTT and JIM BORGMAN
JEREMY, WILL YOU PUT MY CAR IN THE GARAGE?
I'LL TRY.
GULP! GULP!
SPLASH! SPLASH! SPLASH!
SHAKESHAKESHAKE
©2018 ZITS Partnership. Dist. by King Features
MY CAR IS NOT THAT BORING!
WHAT COLOR IS THAT THING? COMA-BEIGE?
SCOTT AND BORGMAN 5-13

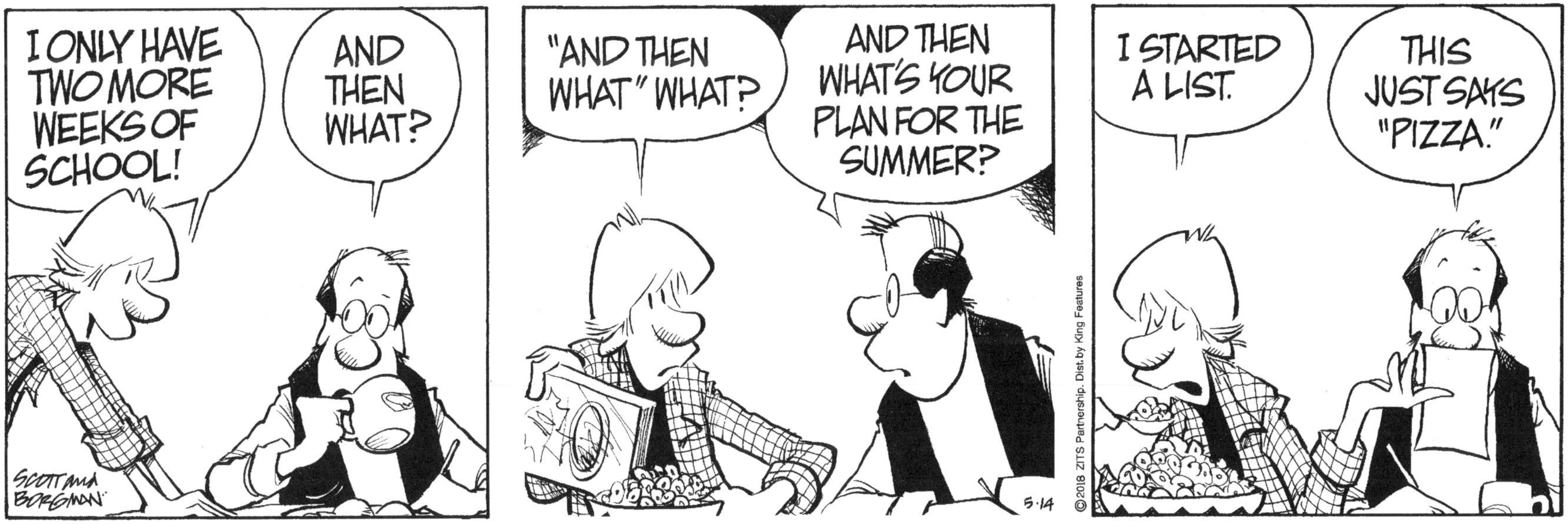
I ONLY HAVE TWO MORE WEEKS OF SCHOOL!
AND THEN WHAT?
SCOTT and BORGMAN
"AND THEN WHAT" WHAT?
AND THEN WHAT'S YOUR PLAN FOR THE SUMMER?
5·14
©2018 ZITS Partnership. Dist. by King Features
I STARTED A LIST.
THIS JUST SAYS "PIZZA."

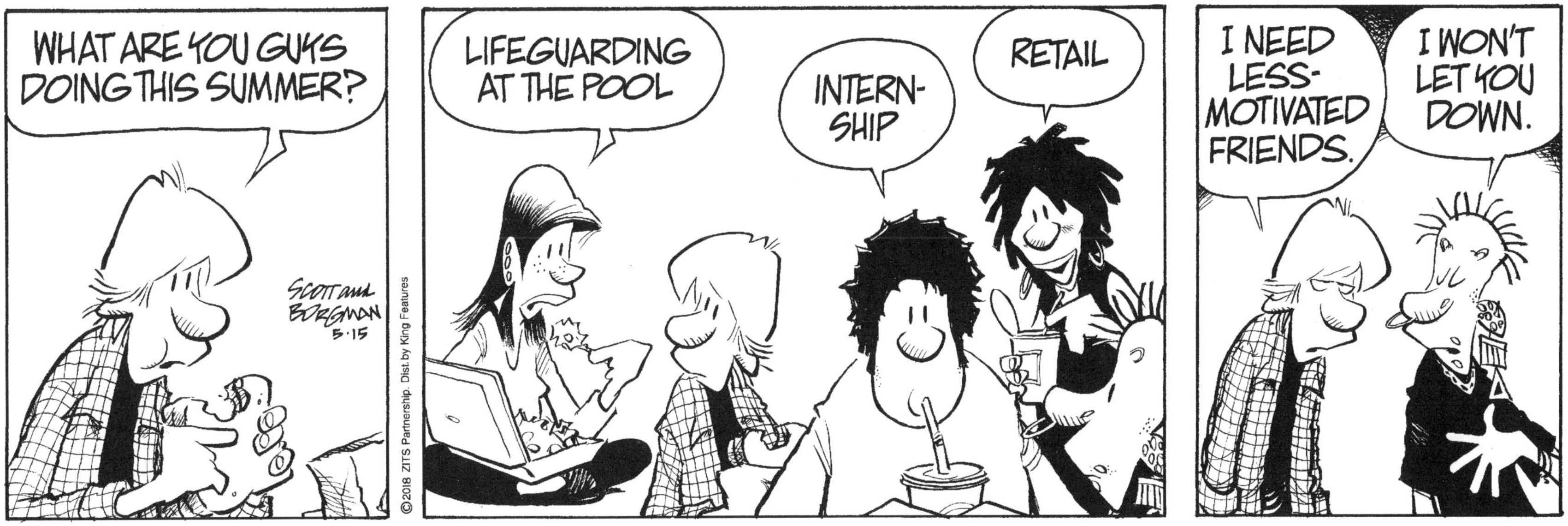
WHAT ARE YOU GUYS DOING THIS SUMMER?
SCOTT and BORGMAN 5·15
©2018 ZITS Partnership. Dist. by King Features
LIFEGUARDING AT THE POOL
INTERN-SHIP
RETAIL
I NEED LESS-MOTIVATED FRIENDS.
I WON'T LET YOU DOWN.

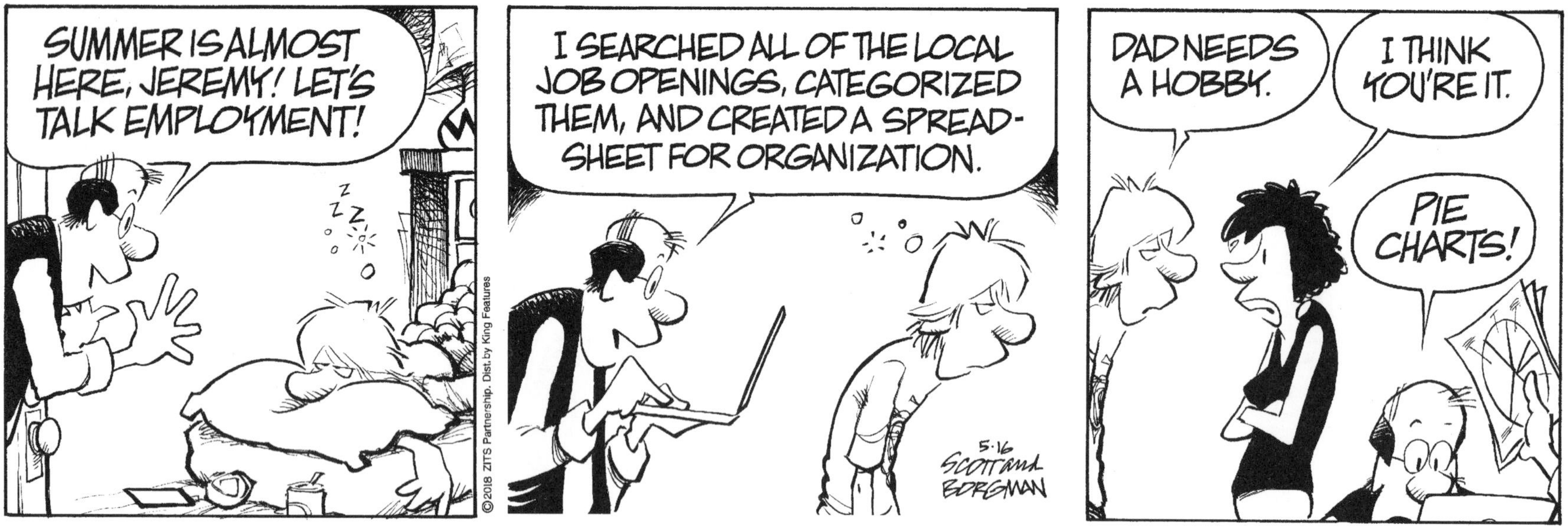
SUMMER IS ALMOST HERE, JEREMY! LET'S TALK EMPLOYMENT!
Z Z Z
I SEARCHED ALL OF THE LOCAL JOB OPENINGS, CATEGORIZED THEM, AND CREATED A SPREAD-SHEET FOR ORGANIZATION.
5·16
SCOTT AND BORGMAN
DAD NEEDS A HOBBY.
I THINK YOU'RE IT.
PIE CHARTS!
©2018 ZITS Partnership. Dist. by King Features

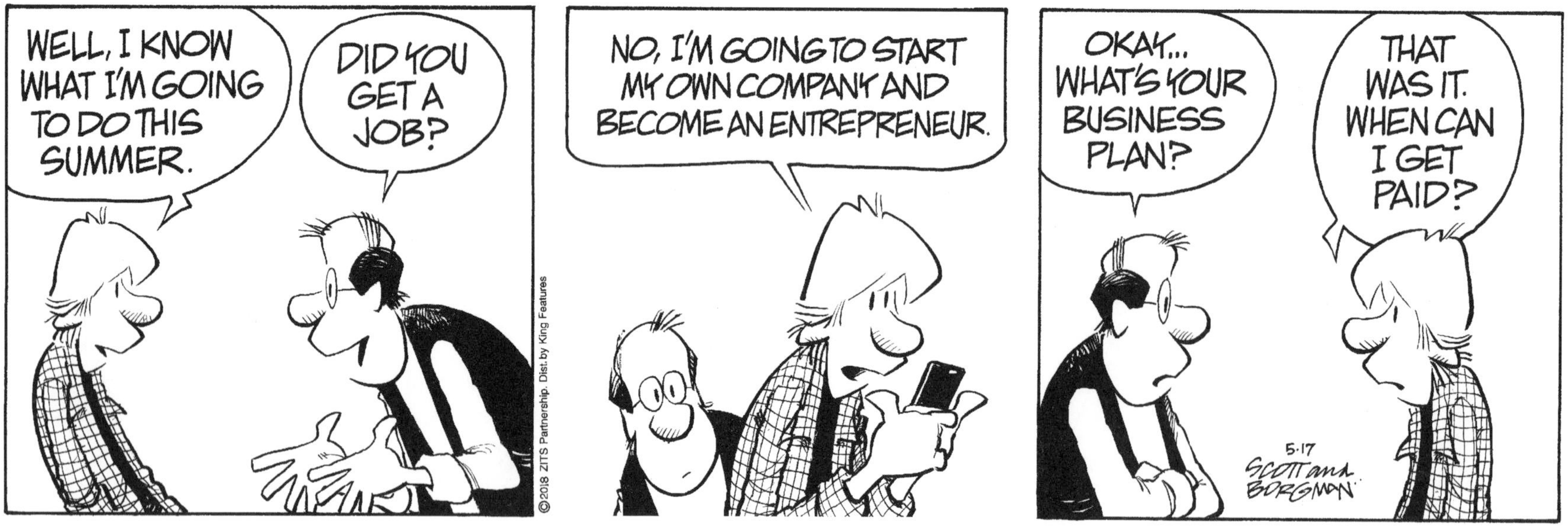
WELL, I KNOW WHAT I'M GOING TO DO THIS SUMMER.
DID YOU GET A JOB?
NO, I'M GOING TO START MY OWN COMPANY AND BECOME AN ENTREPRENEUR.
OKAY... WHAT'S YOUR BUSINESS PLAN?
THAT WAS IT. WHEN CAN I GET PAID?
5·17
SCOTT AND BORGMAN
©2018 ZITS Partnership. Dist. by King Features

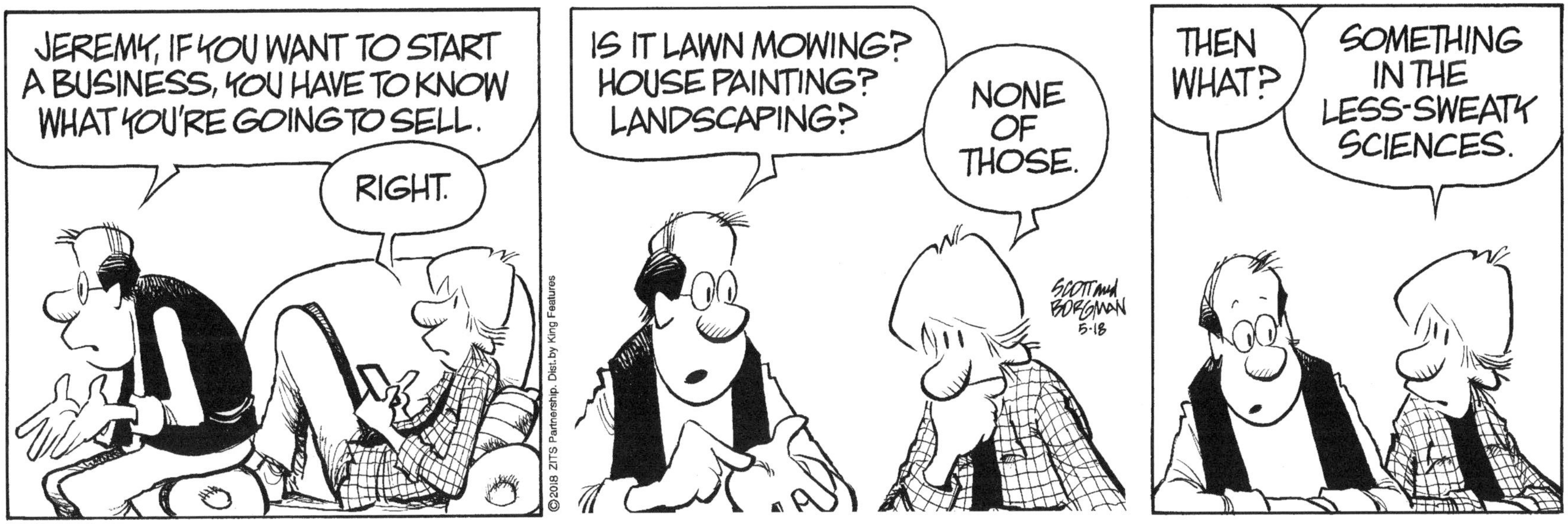
JEREMY, IF YOU WANT TO START A BUSINESS, YOU HAVE TO KNOW WHAT YOU'RE GOING TO SELL.
RIGHT.
IS IT LAWN MOWING? HOUSE PAINTING? LANDSCAPING?
NONE OF THOSE.
THEN WHAT?
SOMETHING IN THE LESS-SWEATY SCIENCES.
©2018 ZITS Partnership. Dist. by King Features
SCOTT AND BORGMAN 5-18

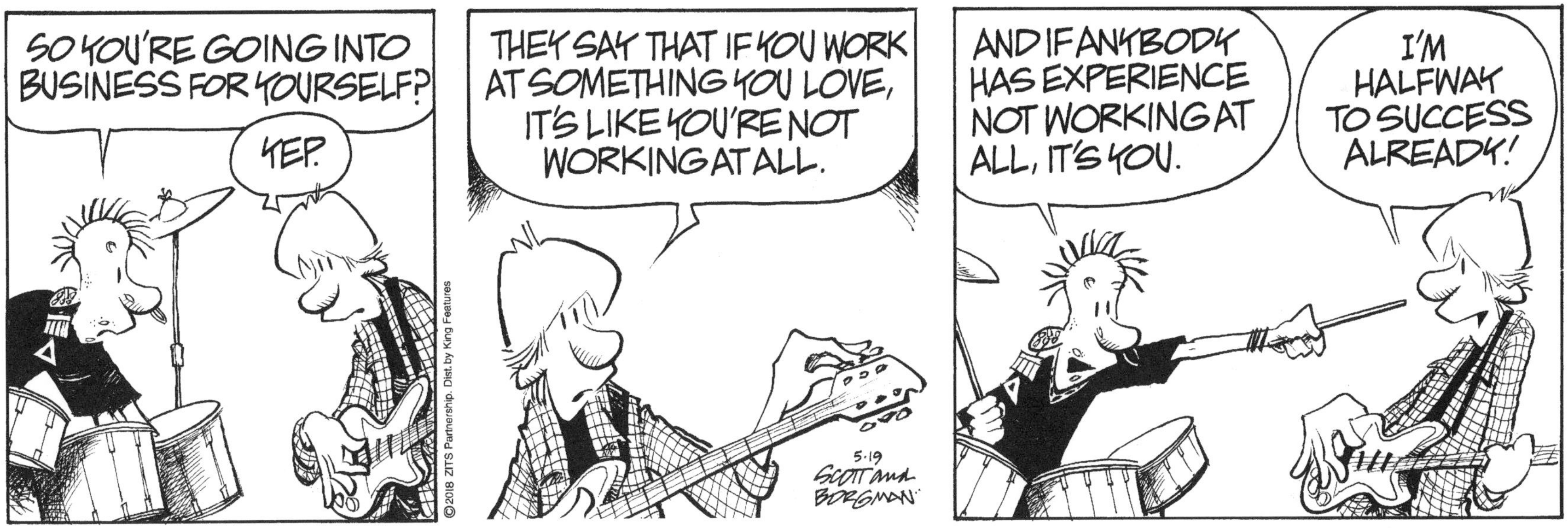
SO YOU'RE GOING INTO BUSINESS FOR YOURSELF?
YEP.
THEY SAY THAT IF YOU WORK AT SOMETHING YOU LOVE, IT'S LIKE YOU'RE NOT WORKING AT ALL.
AND IF ANYBODY HAS EXPERIENCE NOT WORKING AT ALL, IT'S YOU.
I'M HALFWAY TO SUCCESS ALREADY!
©2018 ZITS Partnership. Dist. by King Features
5-19 SCOTT AND BORGMAN

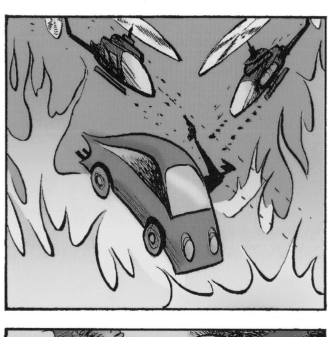

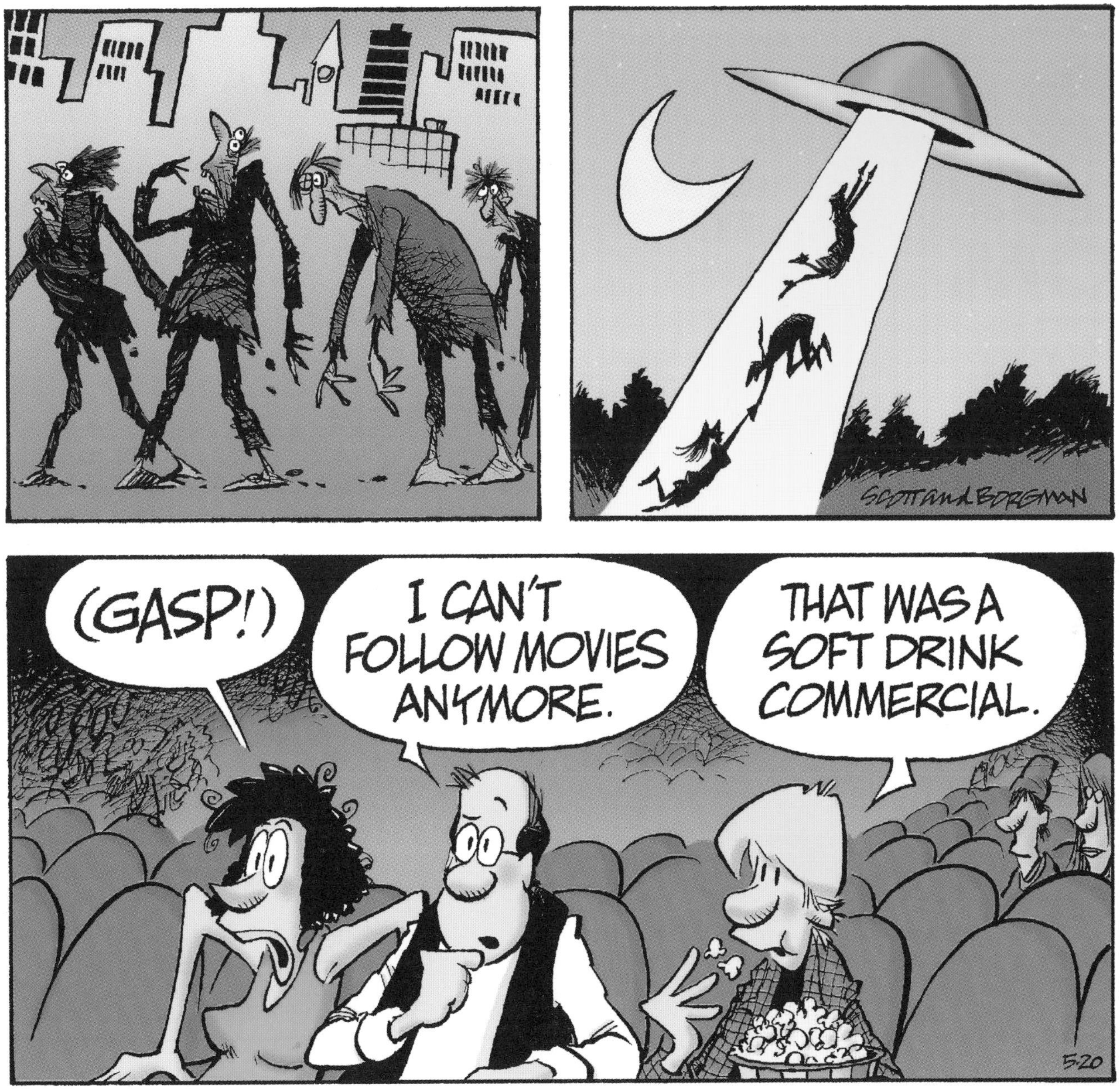
SCOTT and BORGMAN
(GASP!)
I CAN'T FOLLOW MOVIES ANYMORE.
THAT WAS A SOFT DRINK COMMERCIAL.
5-20

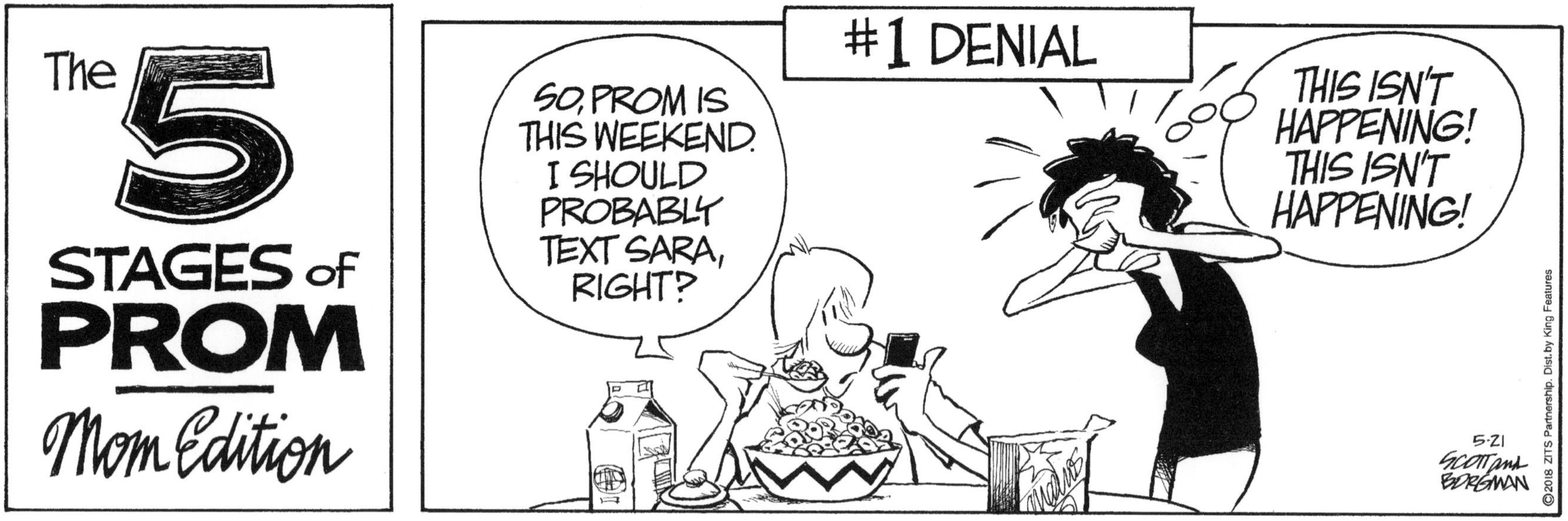
The 5 STAGES of PROM
Mom Edition
#1 DENIAL
SO, PROM IS THIS WEEKEND. I SHOULD PROBABLY TEXT SARA, RIGHT?
THIS ISN'T HAPPENING! THIS ISN'T HAPPENING!
5·21
SCOTT and BORGMAN
©2018 ZITS Partnership. Dist. by King Features

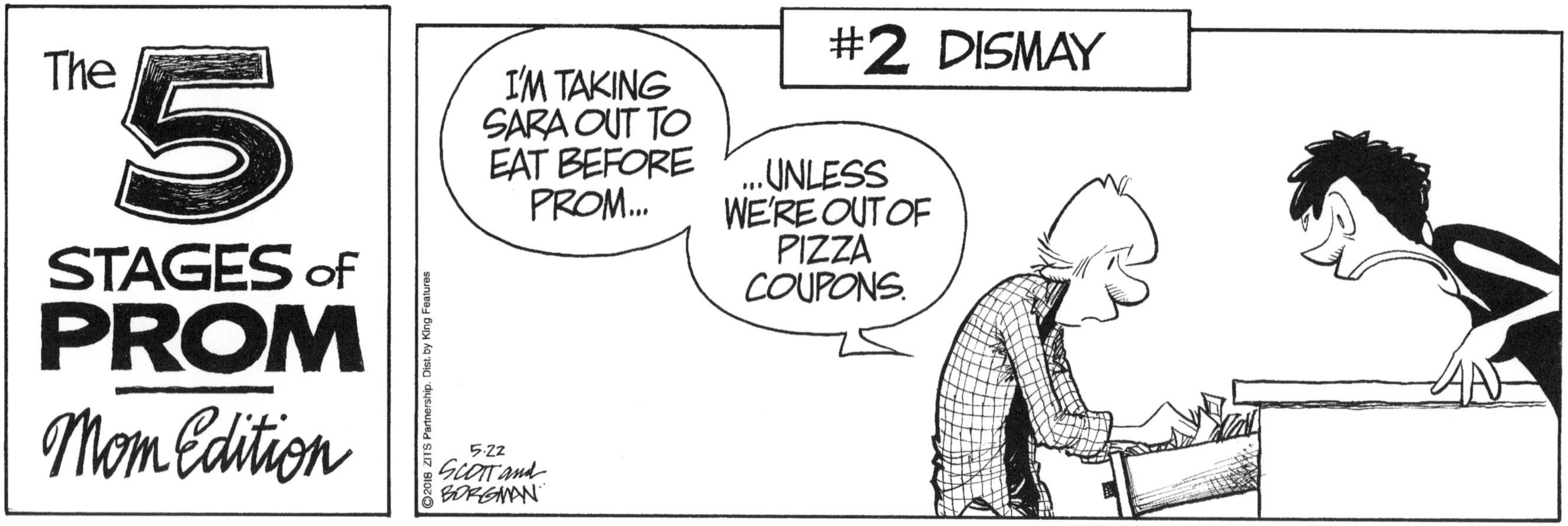
The 5 STAGES of PROM
Mom Edition
#2 DISMAY
I'M TAKING SARA OUT TO EAT BEFORE PROM...
...UNLESS WE'RE OUT OF PIZZA COUPONS.
©2018 ZITS Partnership. Dist. by King Features
5·22
SCOTT and BORGMAN

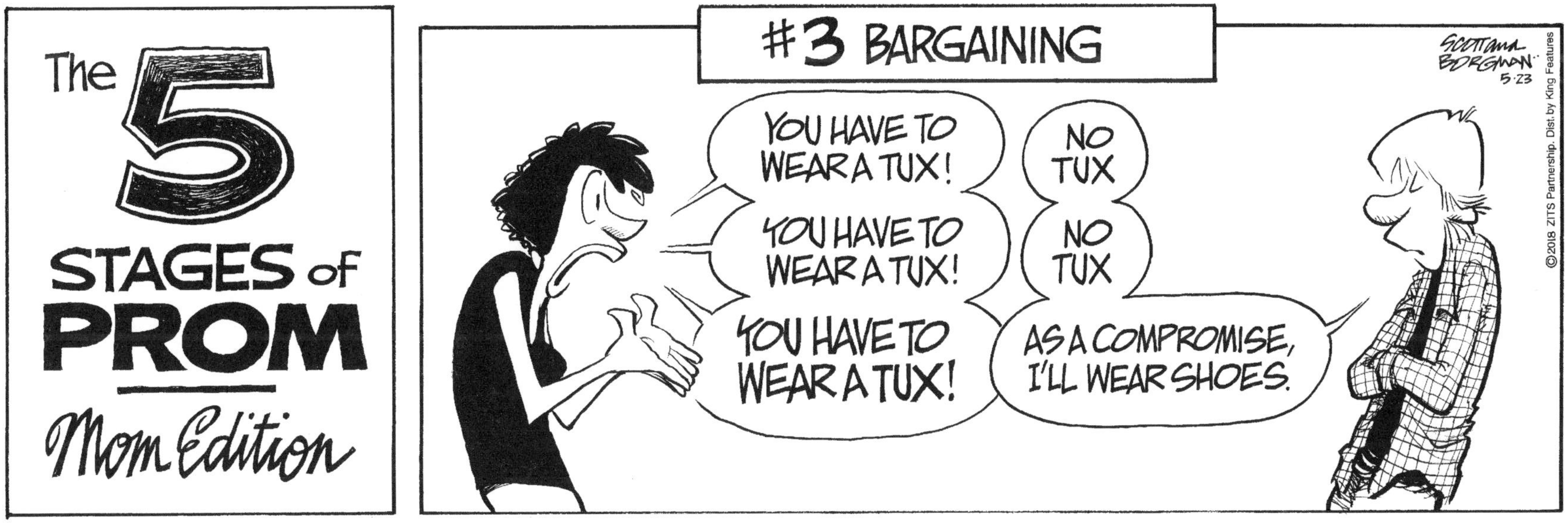
The 5 STAGES of PROM
Mom Edition
#3 BARGAINING
SCOTT and BORGMAN 5·23
©2018 ZITS Partnership. Dist. by King Features
YOU HAVE TO WEAR A TUX!
NO TUX
YOU HAVE TO WEAR A TUX!
NO TUX
YOU HAVE TO WEAR A TUX!
AS A COMPROMISE, I'LL WEAR SHOES.

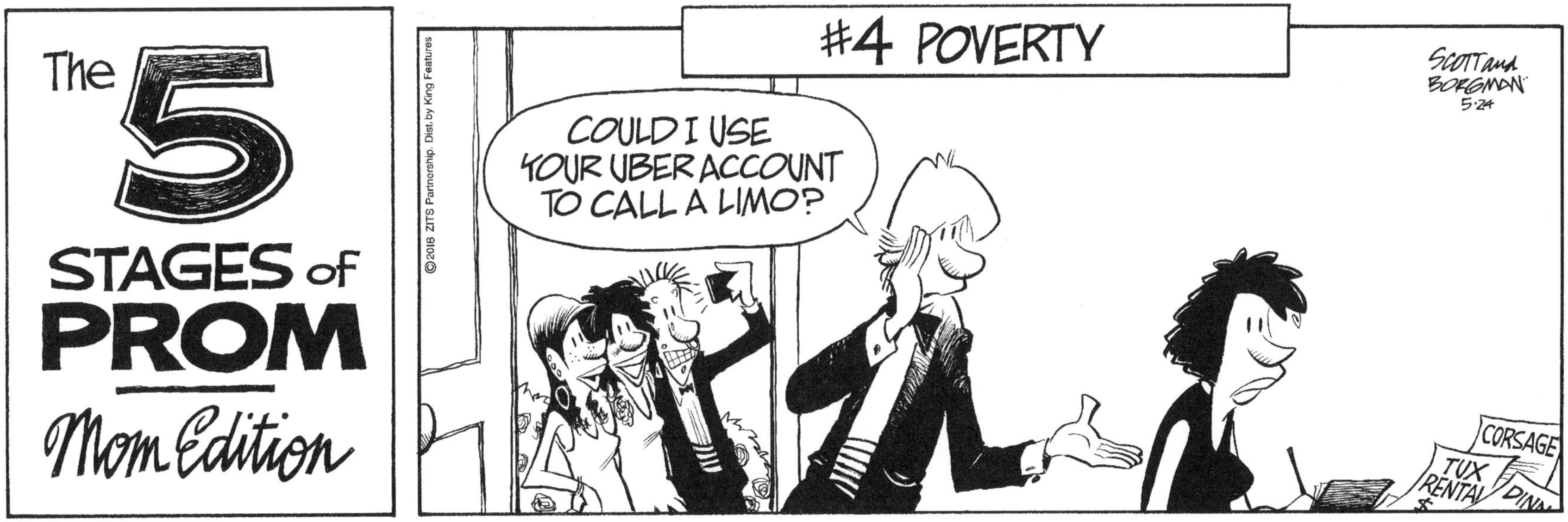
The 5 STAGES of PROM
Mom Edition
#4 POVERTY
SCOTT and BORGMAN 5·24
©2018 ZITS Partnership. Dist. by King Features
COULD I USE YOUR UBER ACCOUNT TO CALL A LIMO?
CORSAGE
TUX RENTAL
$

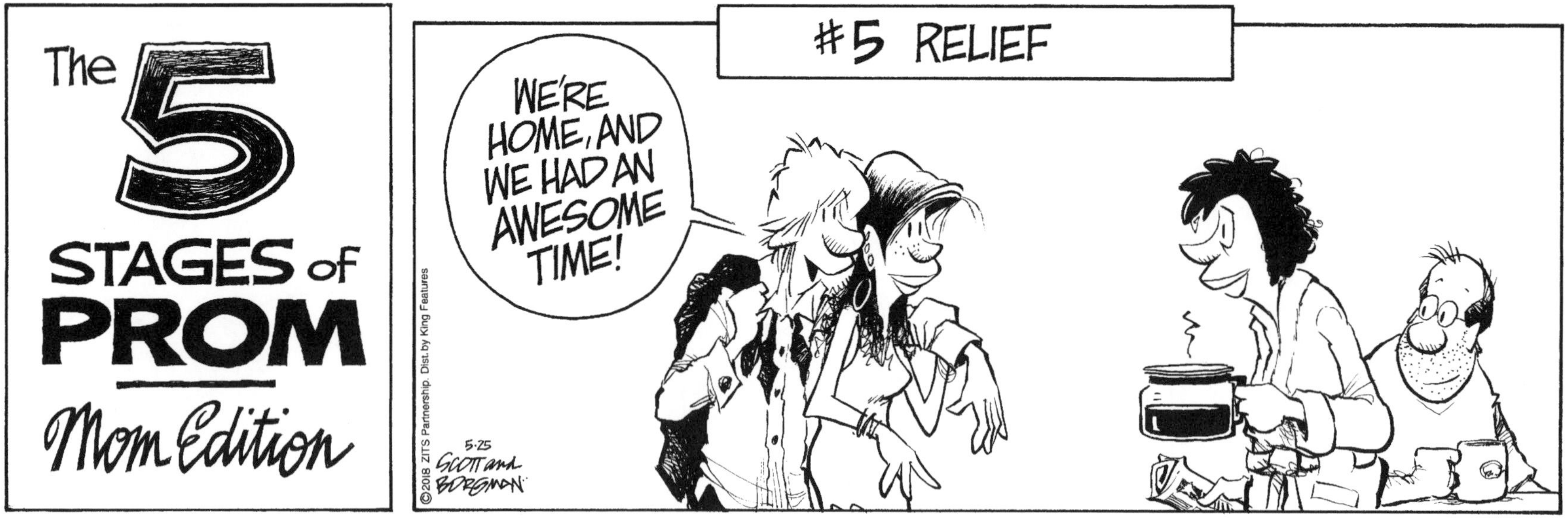
The 5 STAGES of PROM
Mom Edition
#5 RELIEF
WE'RE HOME, AND WE HAD AN AWESOME TIME!
©2018 ZITS Partnership. Dist. by King Features
5·25 SCOTT and BORGMAN

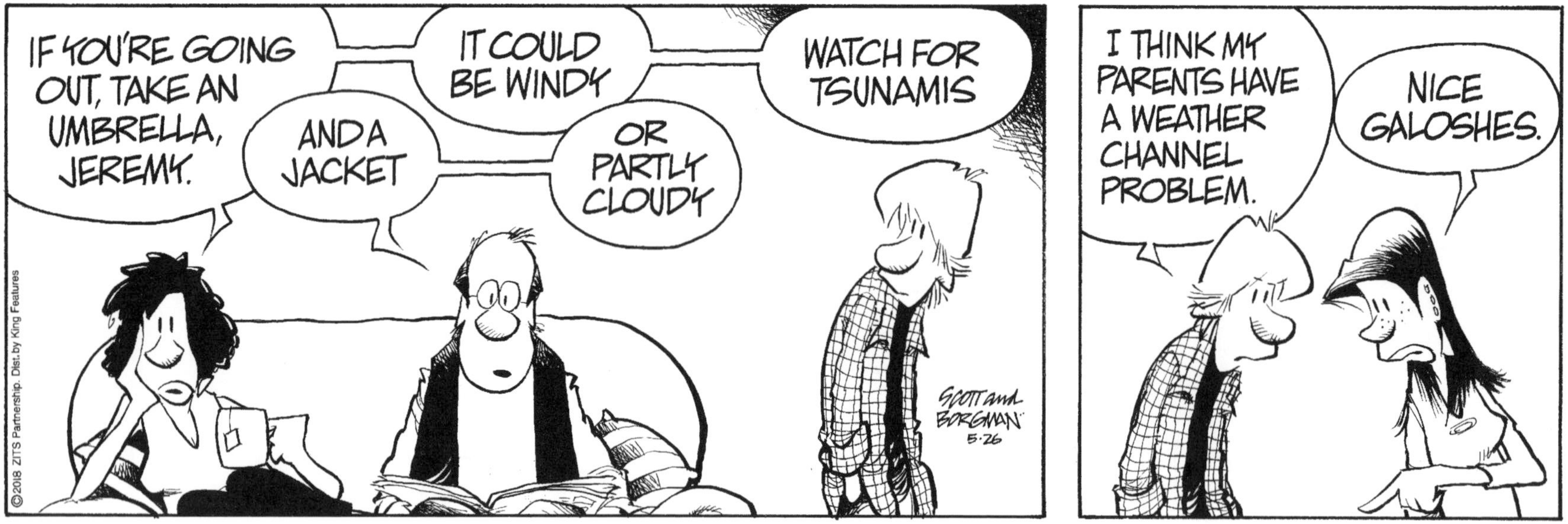
IF YOU'RE GOING OUT, TAKE AN UMBRELLA, JEREMY.
AND A JACKET
IT COULD BE WINDY
OR PARTLY CLOUDY
WATCH FOR TSUNAMIS
I THINK MY PARENTS HAVE A WEATHER CHANNEL PROBLEM.
NICE GALOSHES.
©2018 ZITS Partnership. Dist. by King Features
SCOTT and BORGMAN 5·26

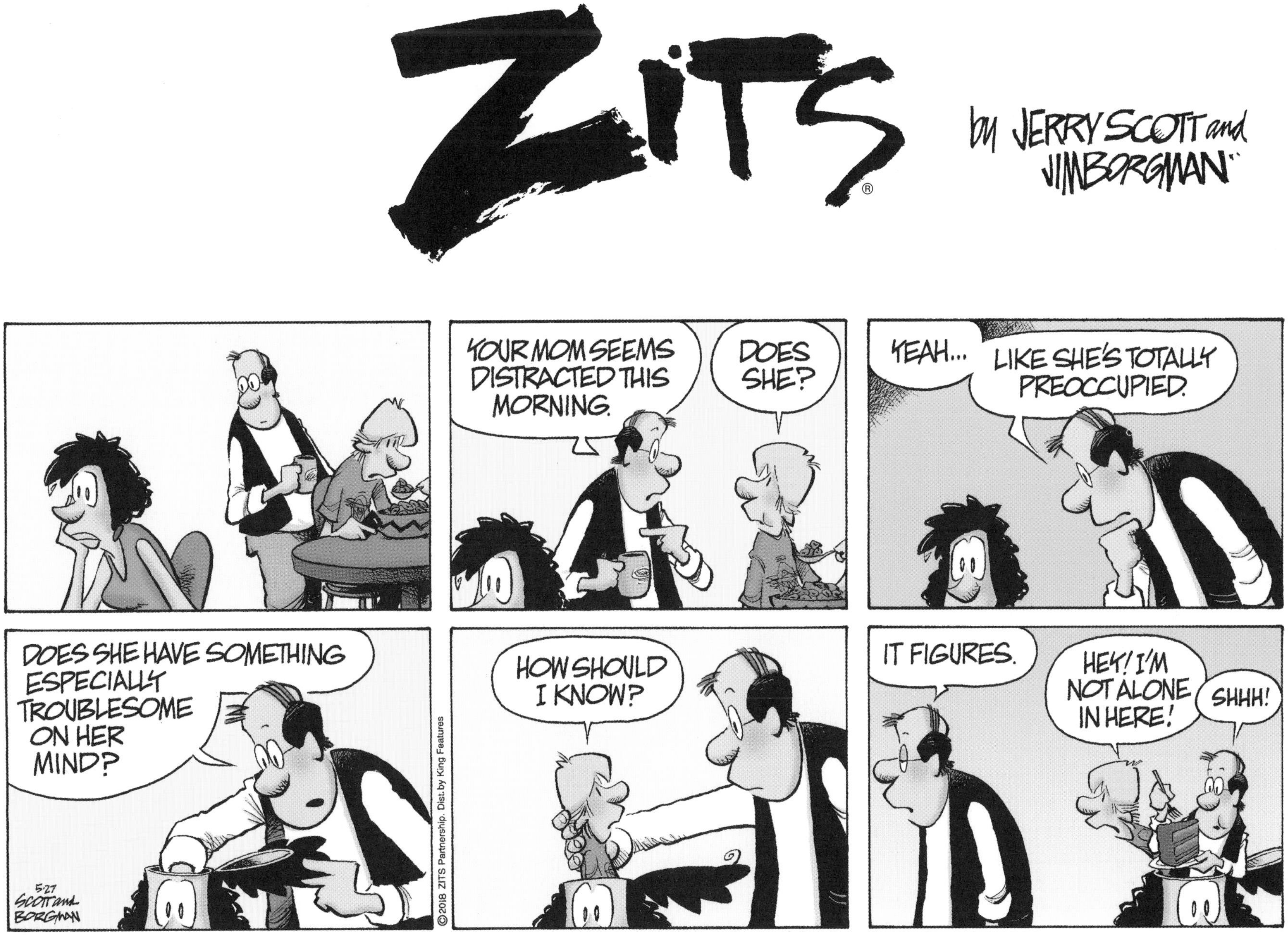
ZITS
by JERRY SCOTT and JIM BORGMAN
YOUR MOM SEEMS DISTRACTED THIS MORNING.
DOES SHE?
YEAH...
LIKE SHE'S TOTALLY PREOCCUPIED.
DOES SHE HAVE SOMETHING ESPECIALLY TROUBLESOME ON HER MIND?
5-27 SCOTT and BORGMAN
© 2018 ZITS Partnership. Dist. by King Features
HOW SHOULD I KNOW?
IT FIGURES.
HEY! I'M NOT ALONE IN HERE!
SHHH!

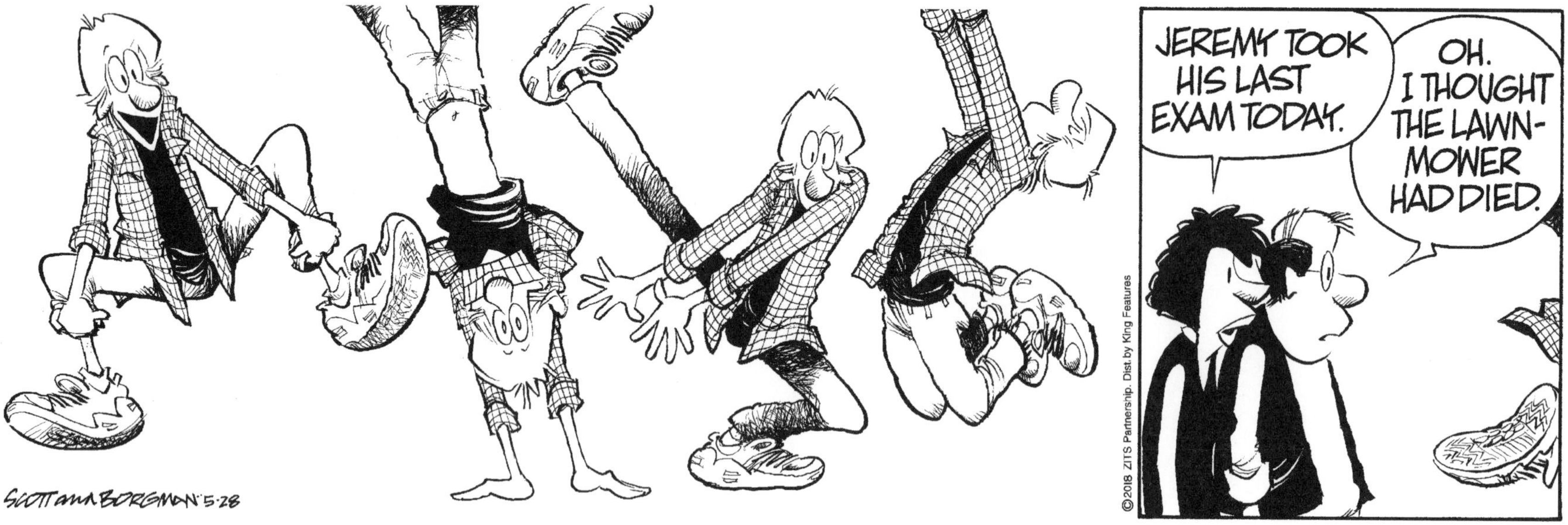

JEREMY TOOK HIS LAST EXAM TODAY.
OH. I THOUGHT THE LAWN-MOWER HAD DIED.
©2018 ZITS Partnership. Dist.by King Features

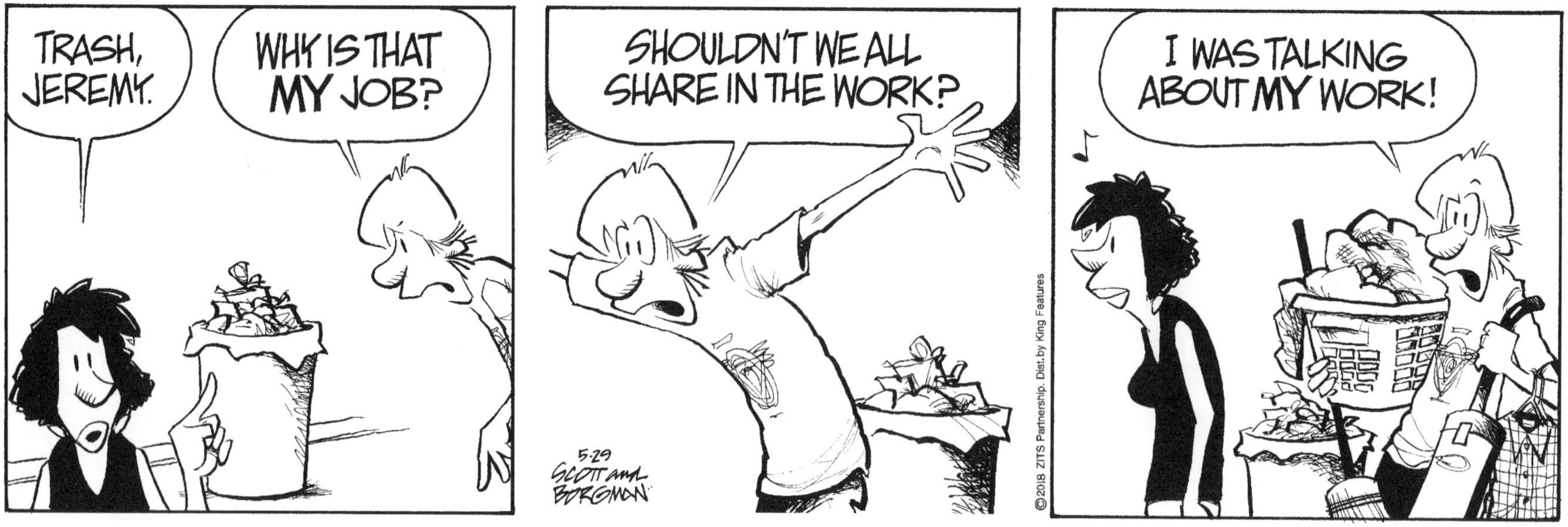

TRASH, JEREMY.
WHY IS THAT MY JOB?
SHOULDN'T WE ALL SHARE IN THE WORK?
I WAS TALKING ABOUT MY WORK!
©2018 ZITS Partnership. Dist.by King Features

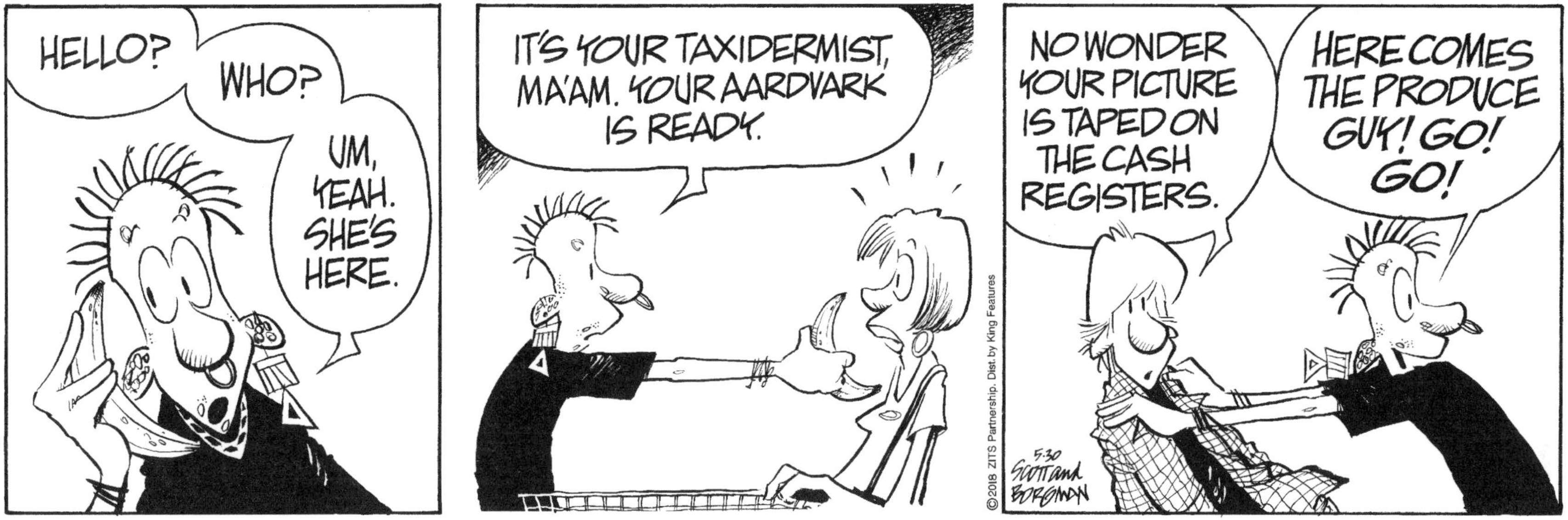
HELLO?
WHO?
UM, YEAH. SHE'S HERE.
IT'S YOUR TAXIDERMIST, MA'AM. YOUR AARDVARK IS READY.
NO WONDER YOUR PICTURE IS TAPED ON THE CASH REGISTERS.
HERE COMES THE PRODUCE GUY! GO! GO!
©2018 ZITS Partnership. Dist. by King Features
5-30 SCOTT and BORGMAN

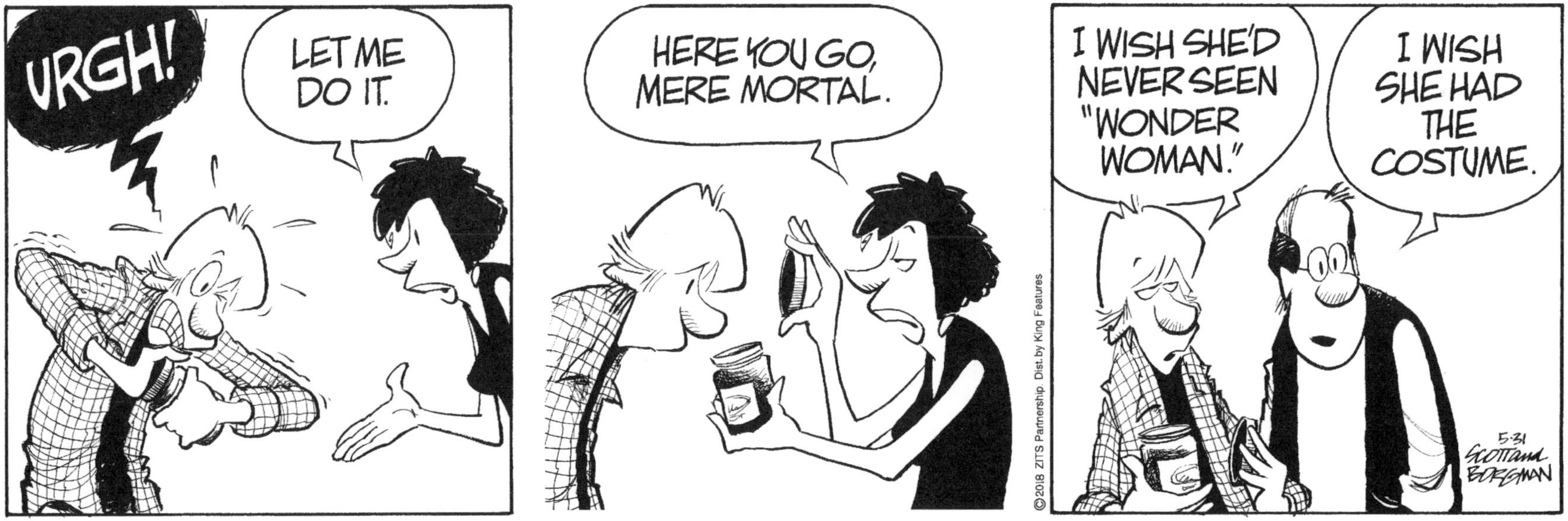
URGH!
LET ME DO IT.
HERE YOU GO, MERE MORTAL.
I WISH SHE'D NEVER SEEN "WONDER WOMAN."
I WISH SHE HAD THE COSTUME.
©2018 ZITS Partnership. Dist. by King Features
5-31 SCOTT and BORGMAN

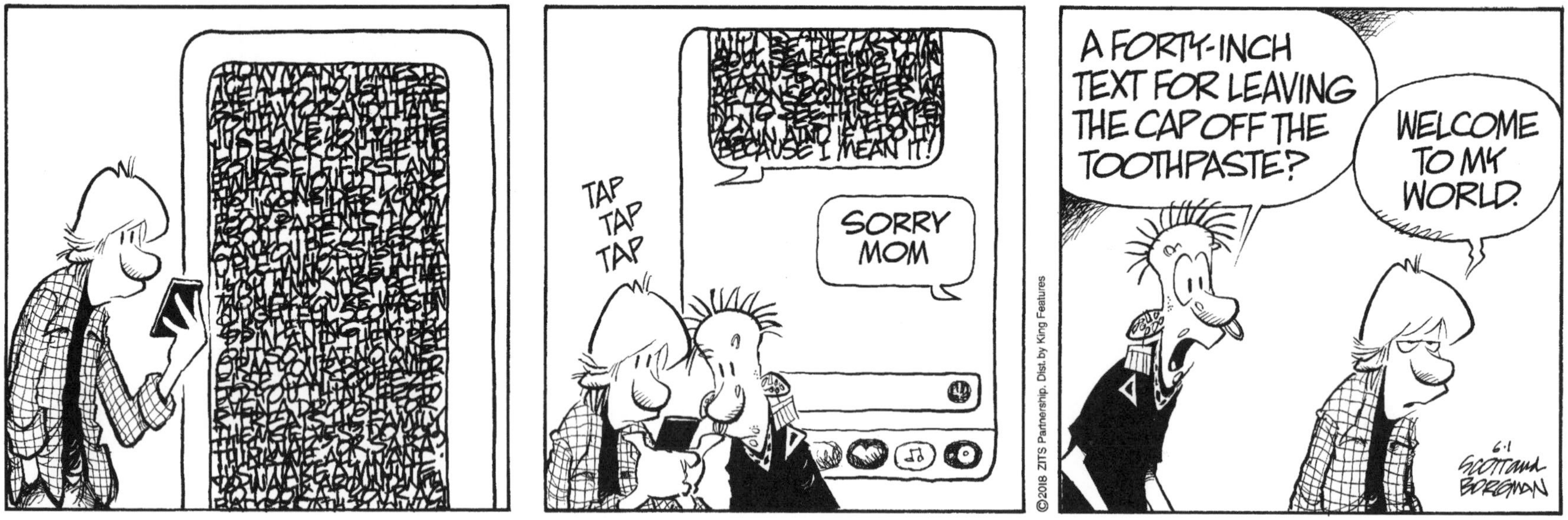
TAP
TAP
TAP
SORRY MOM
©2018 ZITS Partnership. Dist. by King Features
A FORTY-INCH TEXT FOR LEAVING THE CAP OFF THE TOOTHPASTE?
WELCOME TO MY WORLD.
6-1
SCOTT and BORGMAN

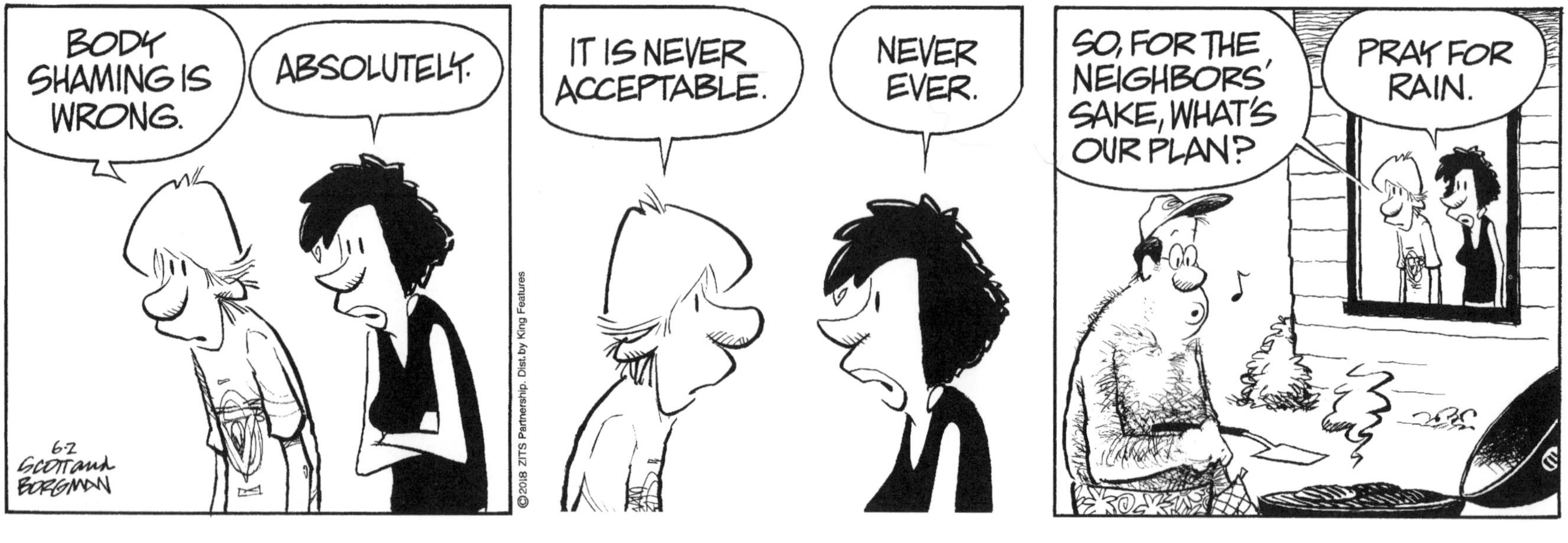
BODY SHAMING IS WRONG.
ABSOLUTELY.
6-2
SCOTT and BORGMAN
©2018 ZITS Partnership. Dist. by King Features
IT IS NEVER ACCEPTABLE.
NEVER EVER.
SO, FOR THE NEIGHBORS' SAKE, WHAT'S OUR PLAN?
PRAY FOR RAIN.

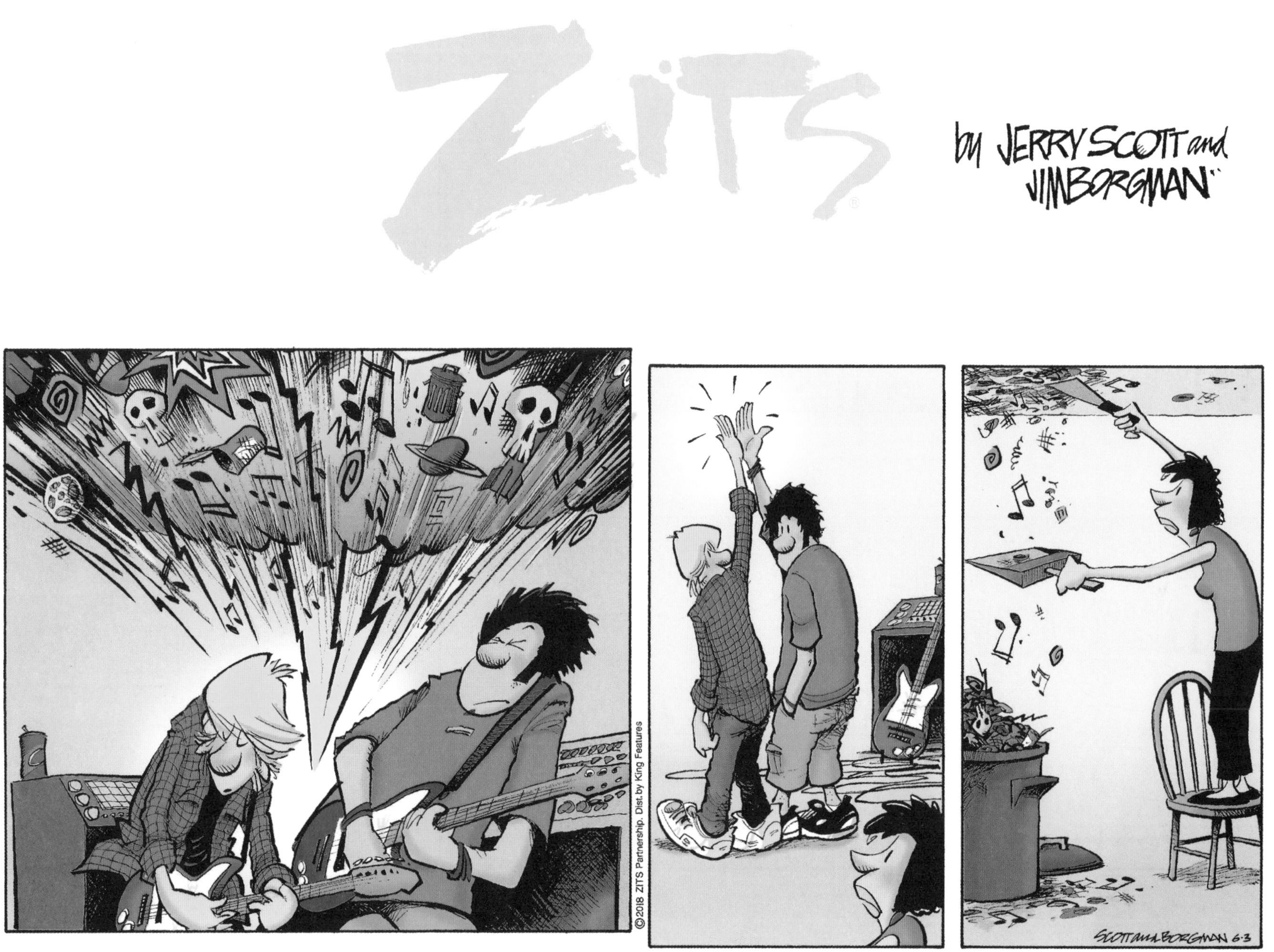
ZITS
by JERRY SCOTT and JIMBORGMAN
©2018 ZITS Partnership. Dist. by King Features
SCOTT and BORGMAN 6·3

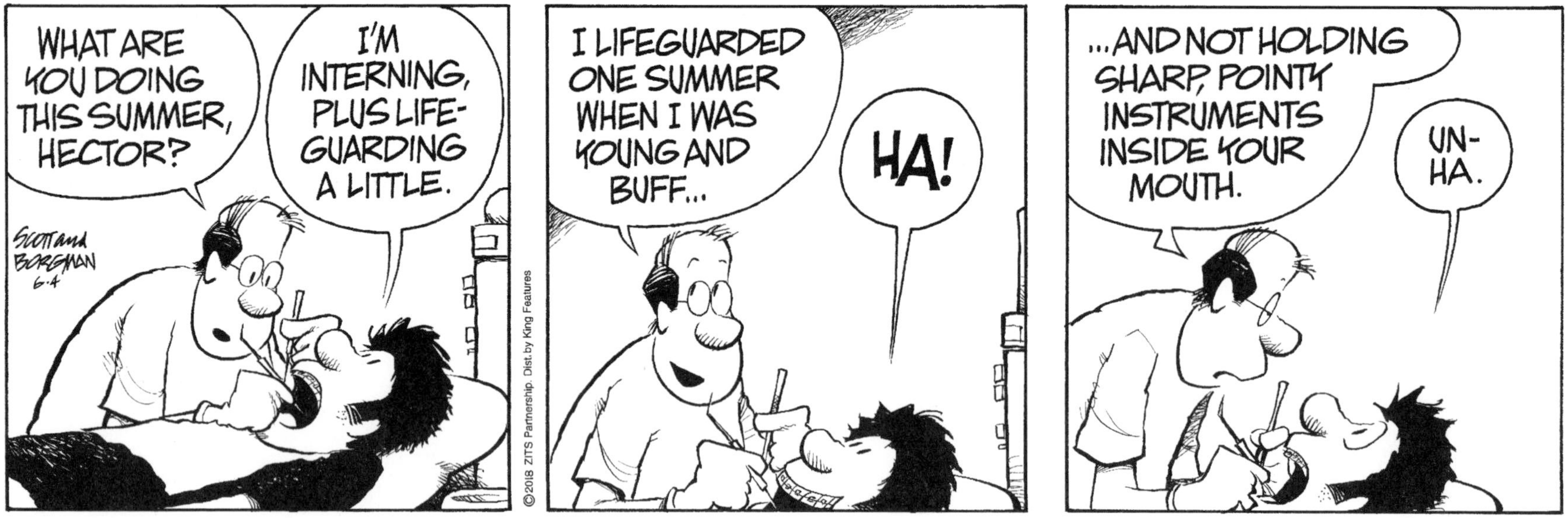
WHAT ARE YOU DOING THIS SUMMER, HECTOR?
I'M INTERNING, PLUS LIFE-GUARDING A LITTLE.
SCOTT and BORGMAN 6·4
©2018 ZITS Partnership. Dist. by King Features
I LIFEGUARDED ONE SUMMER WHEN I WAS YOUNG AND BUFF...
HA!
...AND NOT HOLDING SHARP, POINTY INSTRUMENTS INSIDE YOUR MOUTH.
UN-HA.

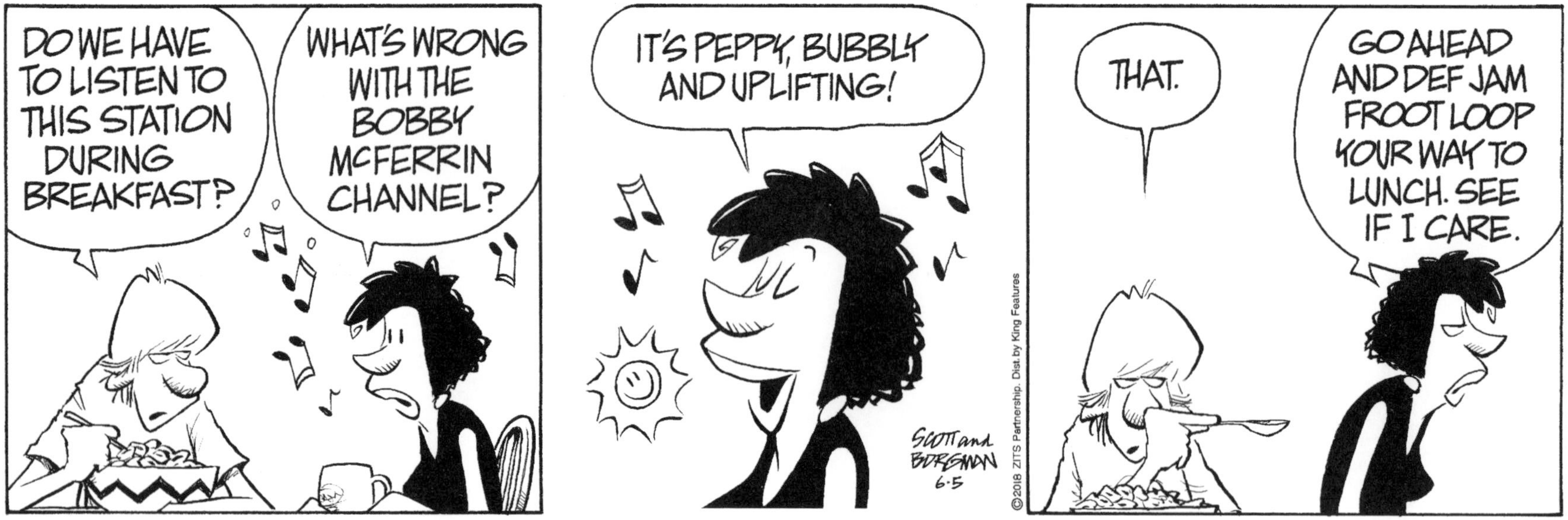
DO WE HAVE TO LISTEN TO THIS STATION DURING BREAKFAST?
WHAT'S WRONG WITH THE BOBBY McFERRIN CHANNEL?
IT'S PEPPY, BUBBLY AND UPLIFTING!
SCOTT and BORGMAN 6·5
©2018 ZITS Partnership. Dist. by King Features
THAT.
GO AHEAD AND DEF JAM FROOT LOOP YOUR WAY TO LUNCH. SEE IF I CARE.

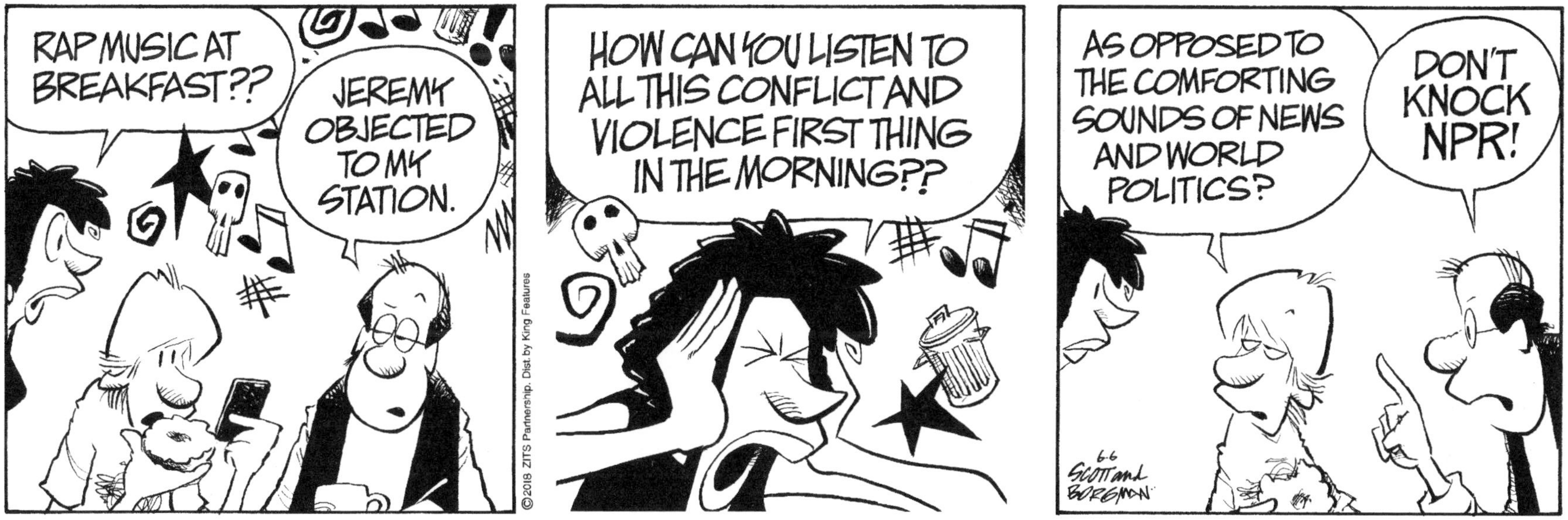
RAP MUSIC AT BREAKFAST??
JEREMY OBJECTED TO MY STATION.
©2018 ZITS Partnership. Dist. by King Features
HOW CAN YOU LISTEN TO ALL THIS CONFLICT AND VIOLENCE FIRST THING IN THE MORNING??
AS OPPOSED TO THE COMFORTING SOUNDS OF NEWS AND WORLD POLITICS?
DON'T KNOCK NPR!
6-6 SCOTT and BORGMAN

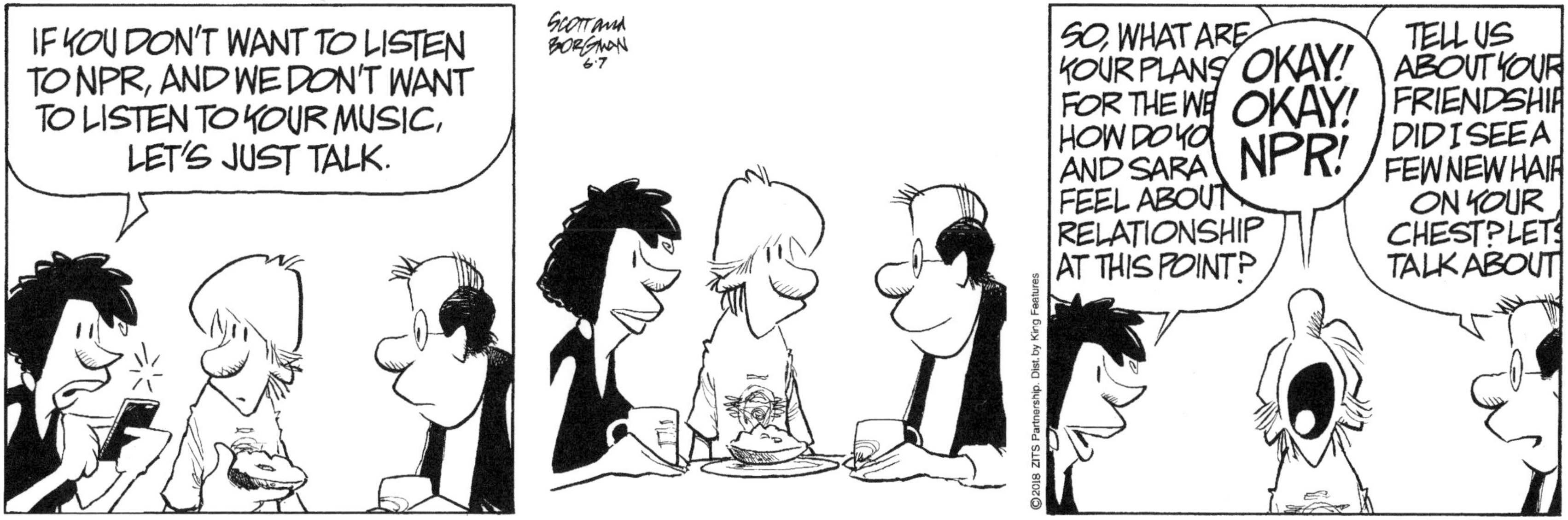
IF YOU DON'T WANT TO LISTEN TO NPR, AND WE DON'T WANT TO LISTEN TO YOUR MUSIC, LET'S JUST TALK.
SCOTT and BORGMAN 6·7
©2018 ZITS Partnership. Dist. by King Features
SO, WHAT ARE YOUR PLANS FOR THE WE HOW DO YO AND SARA FEEL ABOUT RELATIONSHIP AT THIS POINT?
OKAY! OKAY! NPR!
TELL US ABOUT YOUR FRIENDSHIP DID I SEE A FEW NEW HAIR ON YOUR CHEST? LETS TALK ABOUT

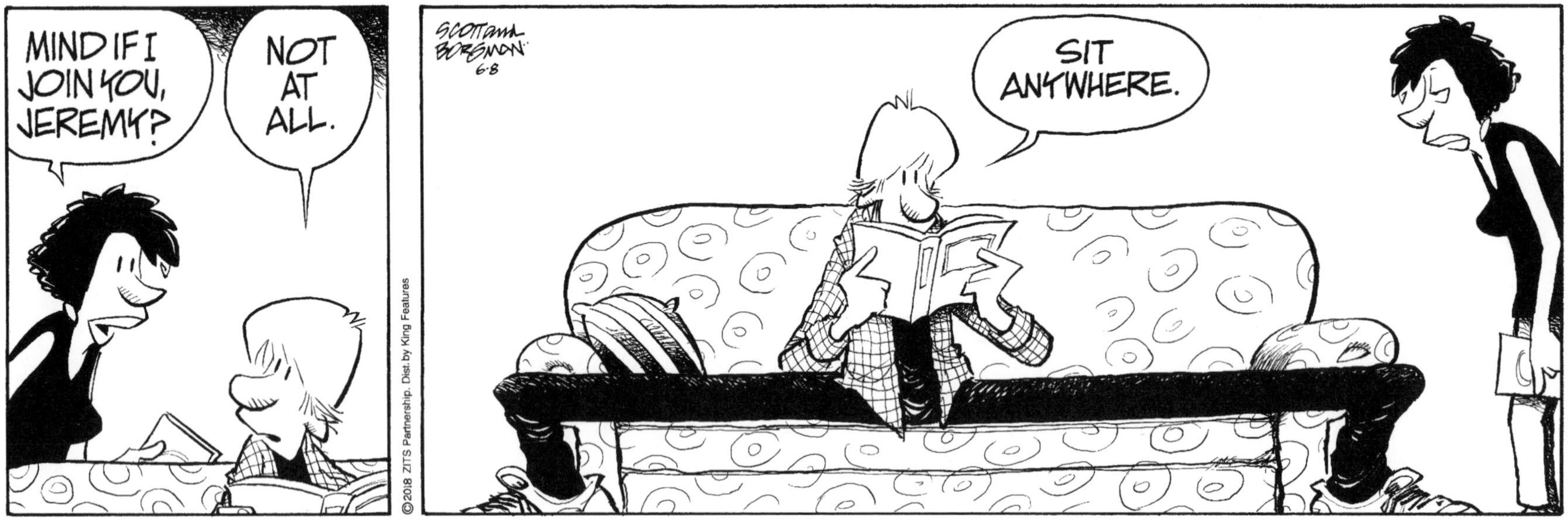
MIND IF I JOIN YOU, JEREMY?
NOT AT ALL.
©2018 ZITS Partnership. Dist. by King Features
SIT ANYWHERE.

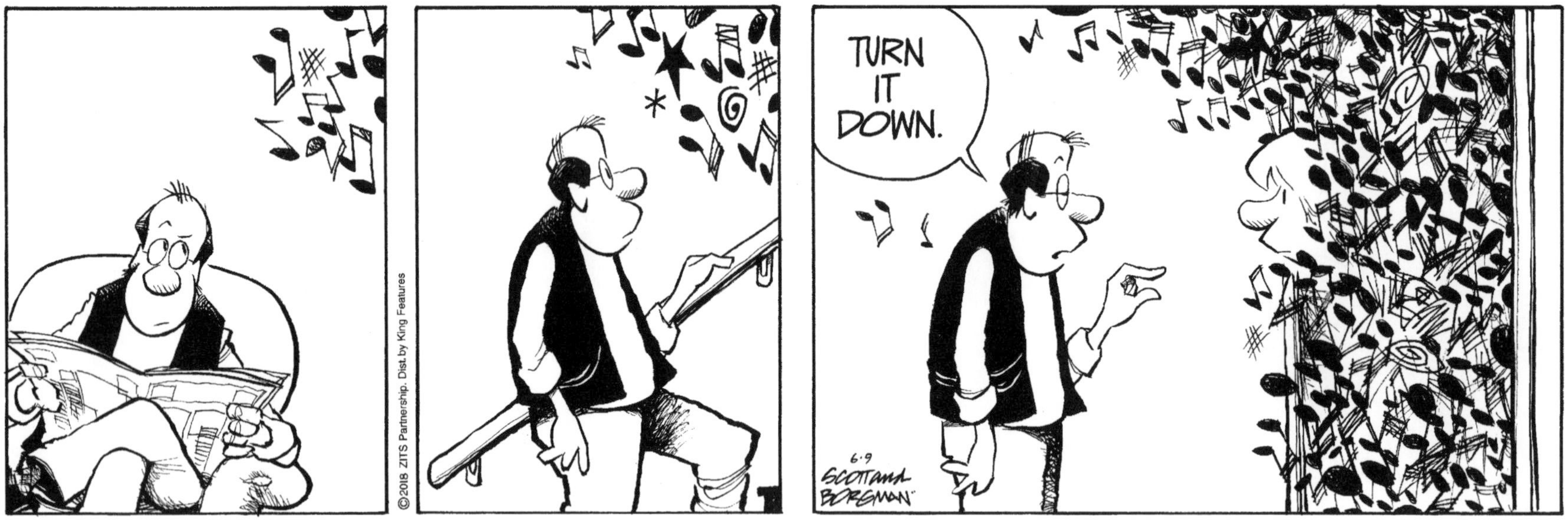
©2018 ZITS Partnership. Dist. by King Features
TURN IT DOWN.

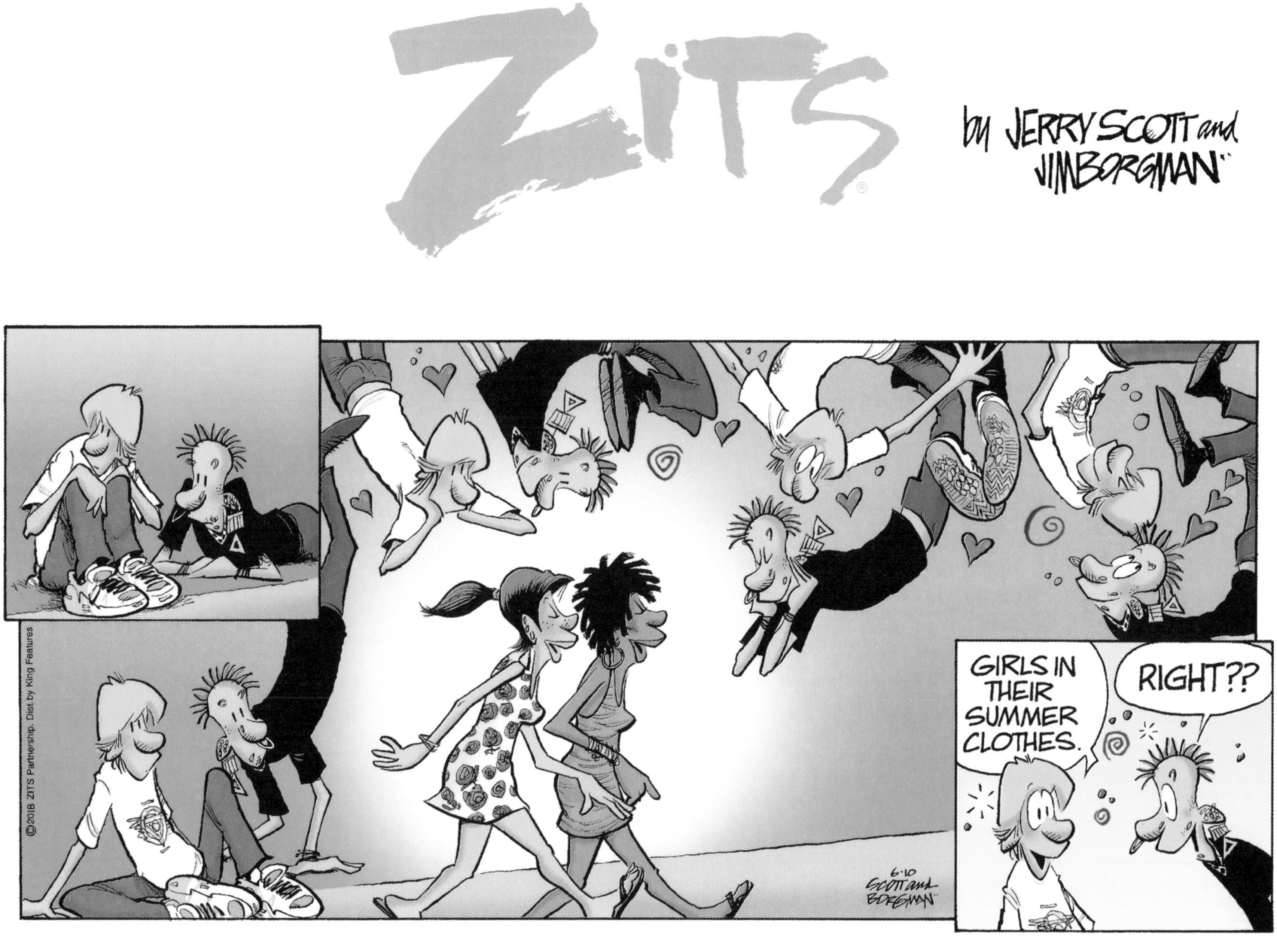
ZITS
by JERRY SCOTT and JIM BORGMAN
©2018 ZITS Partnership. Dist. by King Features
6·10 SCOTT and BORGMAN
GIRLS IN THEIR SUMMER CLOTHES.
RIGHT??

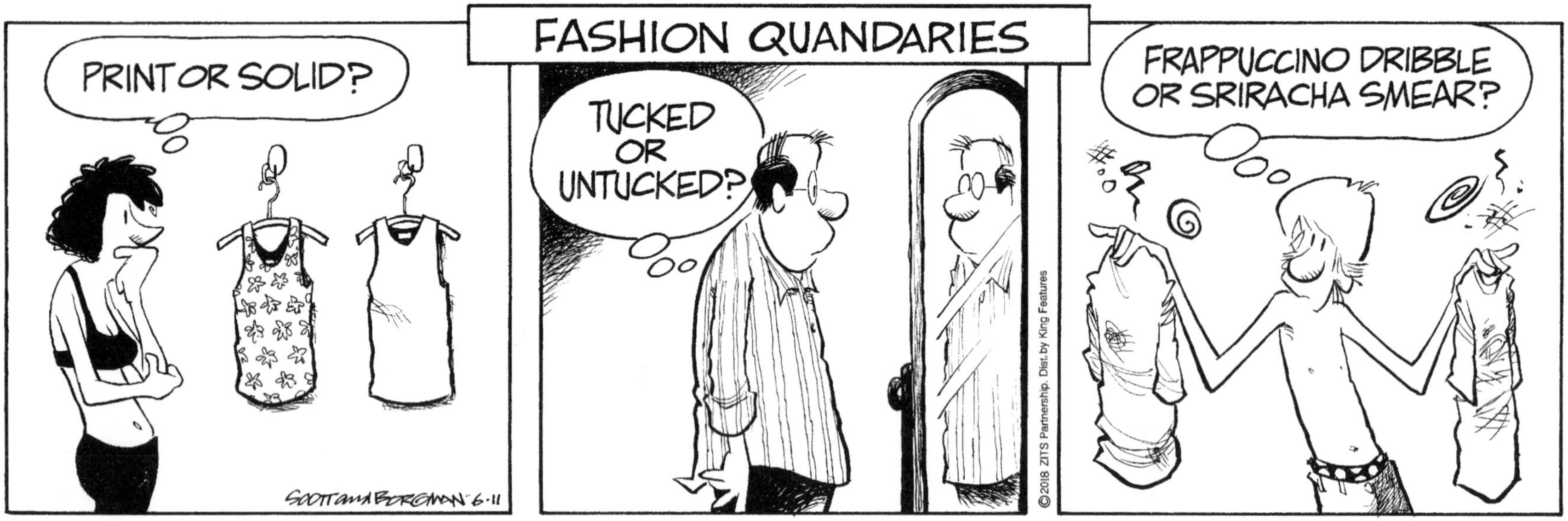
FASHION QUANDARIES
PRINT OR SOLID?
SCOTT and BORGMAN 6·11
TUCKED OR UNTUCKED?
©2018 ZITS Partnership. Dist. by King Features
FRAPPUCCINO DRIBBLE OR SRIRACHA SMEAR?

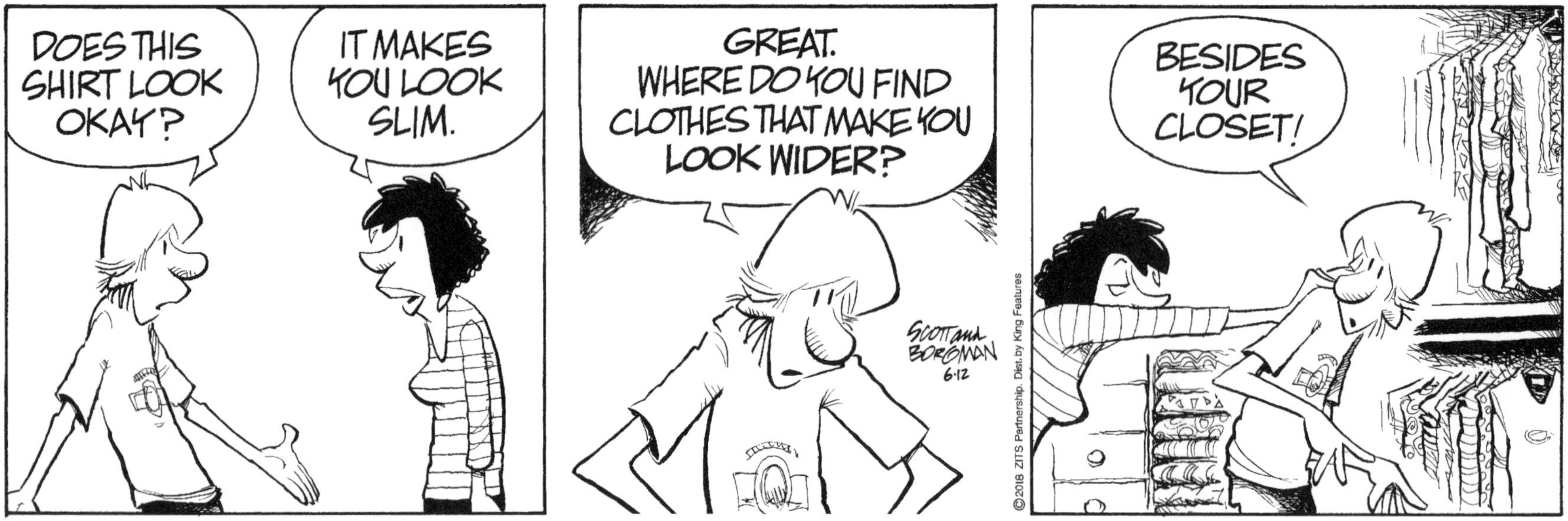
DOES THIS SHIRT LOOK OKAY?
IT MAKES YOU LOOK SLIM.
GREAT. WHERE DO YOU FIND CLOTHES THAT MAKE YOU LOOK WIDER?
SCOTT and BORGMAN 6·12
©2018 ZITS Partnership. Dist. by King Features
BESIDES YOUR CLOSET!

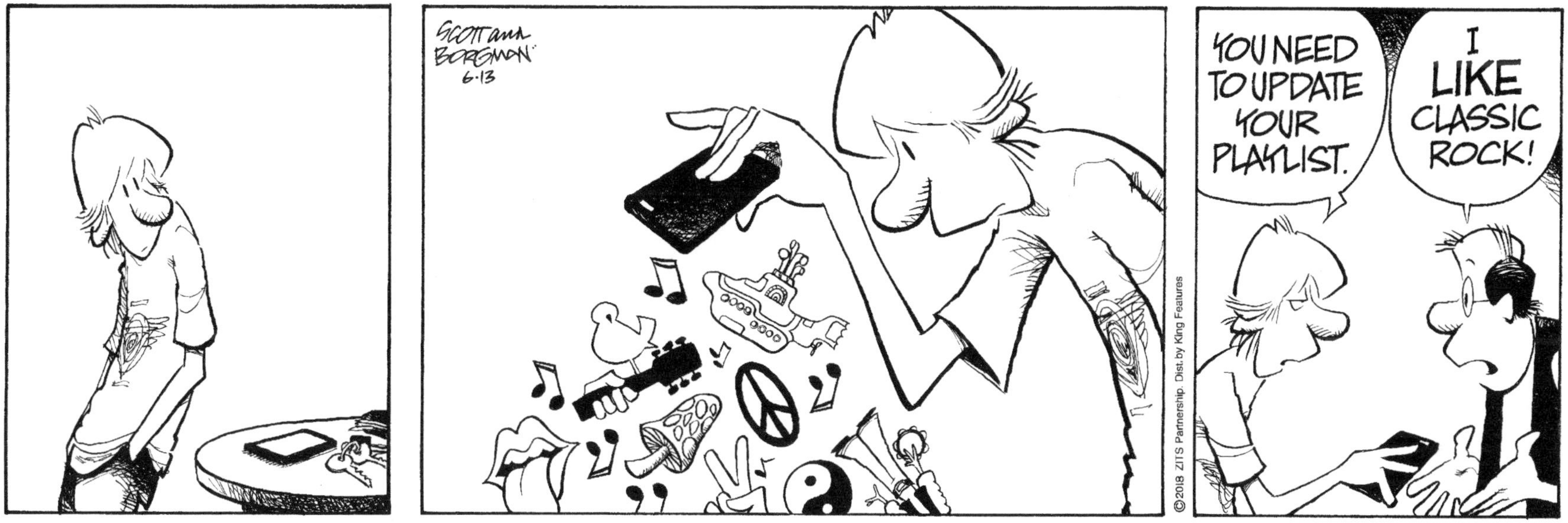
SCOTT and BORGMAN 6-13
YOU NEED TO UPDATE YOUR PLAYLIST.
I LIKE CLASSIC ROCK!
©2018 ZITS Partnership. Dist. by King Features

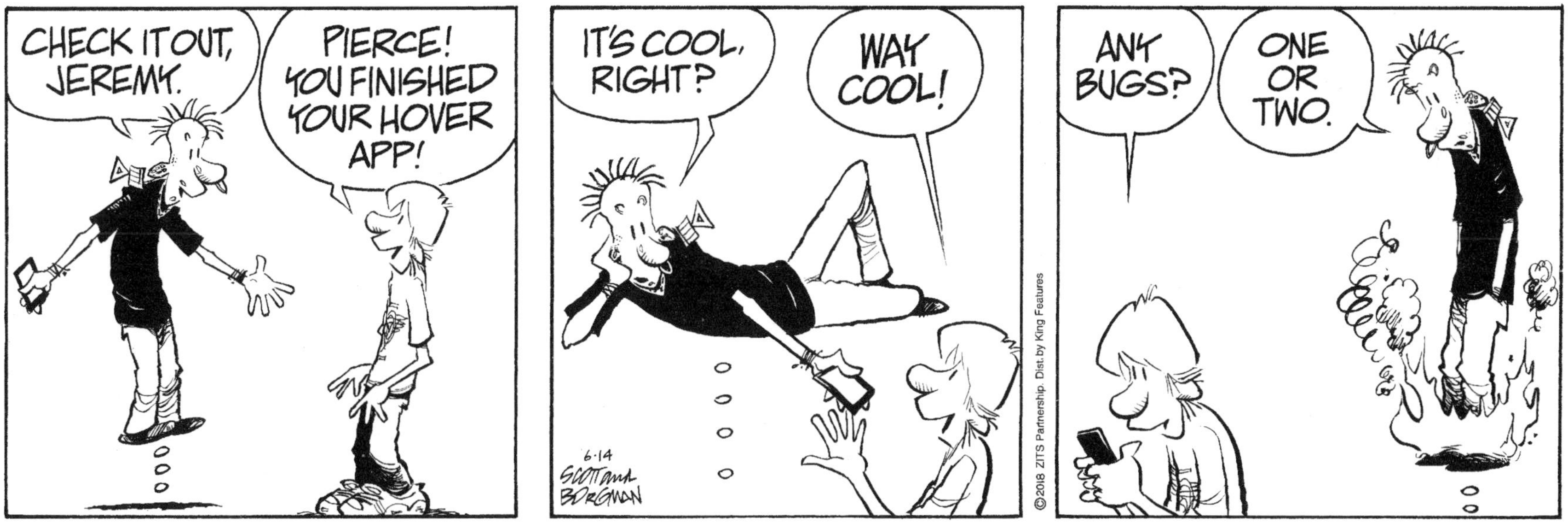
CHECK IT OUT, JEREMY.
PIERCE! YOU FINISHED YOUR HOVER APP!
IT'S COOL, RIGHT?
WAY COOL!
6-14 SCOTT and BORGMAN
©2018 ZITS Partnership. Dist. by King Features
ANY BUGS?
ONE OR TWO.

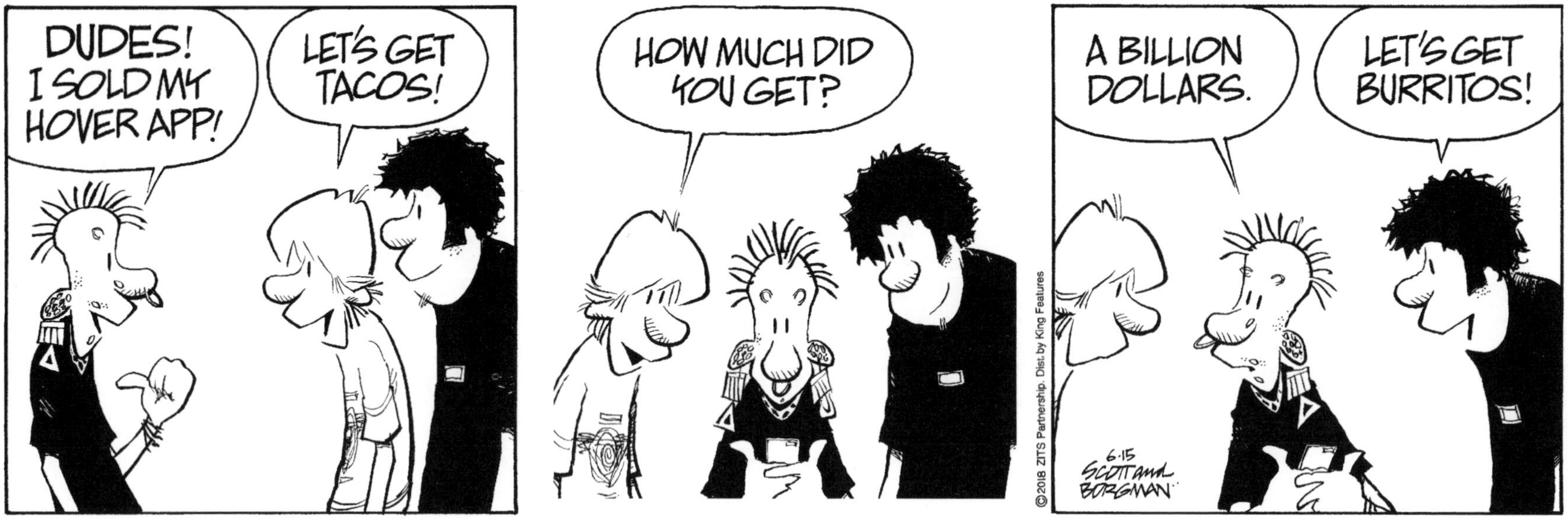
DUDES! I SOLD MY HOVER APP!
LET'S GET TACOS!
HOW MUCH DID YOU GET?
A BILLION DOLLARS.
LET'S GET BURRITOS!
©2018 ZITS Partnership. Dist. by King Features
6-15 SCOTT and BORGMAN

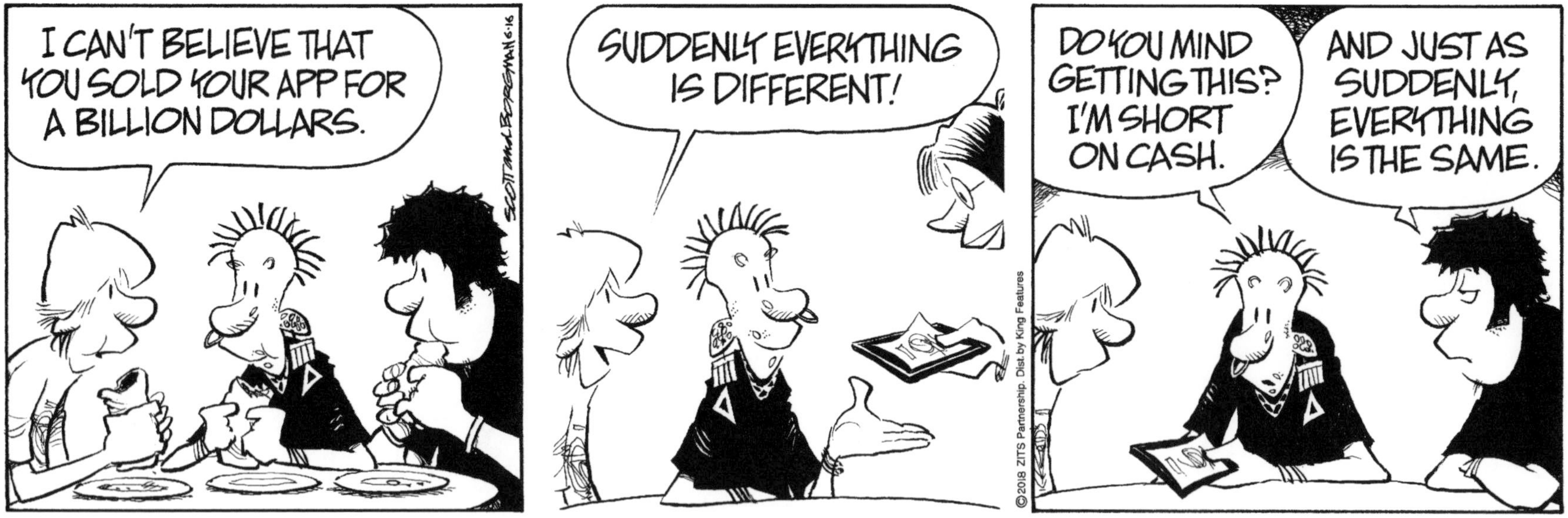
I CAN'T BELIEVE THAT YOU SOLD YOUR APP FOR A BILLION DOLLARS.
SCOTT and BORGMAN 6-16
SUDDENLY EVERYTHING IS DIFFERENT!
©2018 ZITS Partnership. Dist. by King Features
DO YOU MIND GETTING THIS? I'M SHORT ON CASH.
AND JUST AS SUDDENLY, EVERYTHING IS THE SAME.

ZITS®

by JERRY SCOTT and JIM BORGMAN

HAPPY FATHER'S DAY, DAD!
HAPPY FATHER'S DAY, DAD!
SCOTT and BORGMAN 6·17
HAPPY FATHER'S DAY, DAD!
©2018 ZITS Partnership. Dist. by King Features
HAPPY FATHER'S DAY, DAD!
GET USED TO IT.

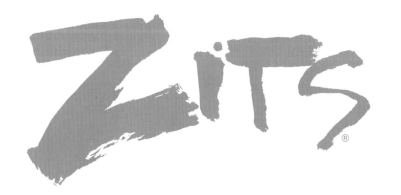

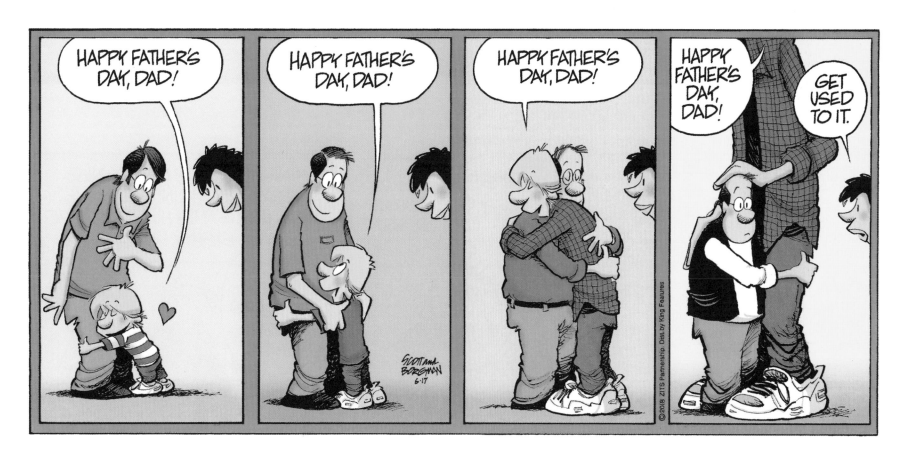

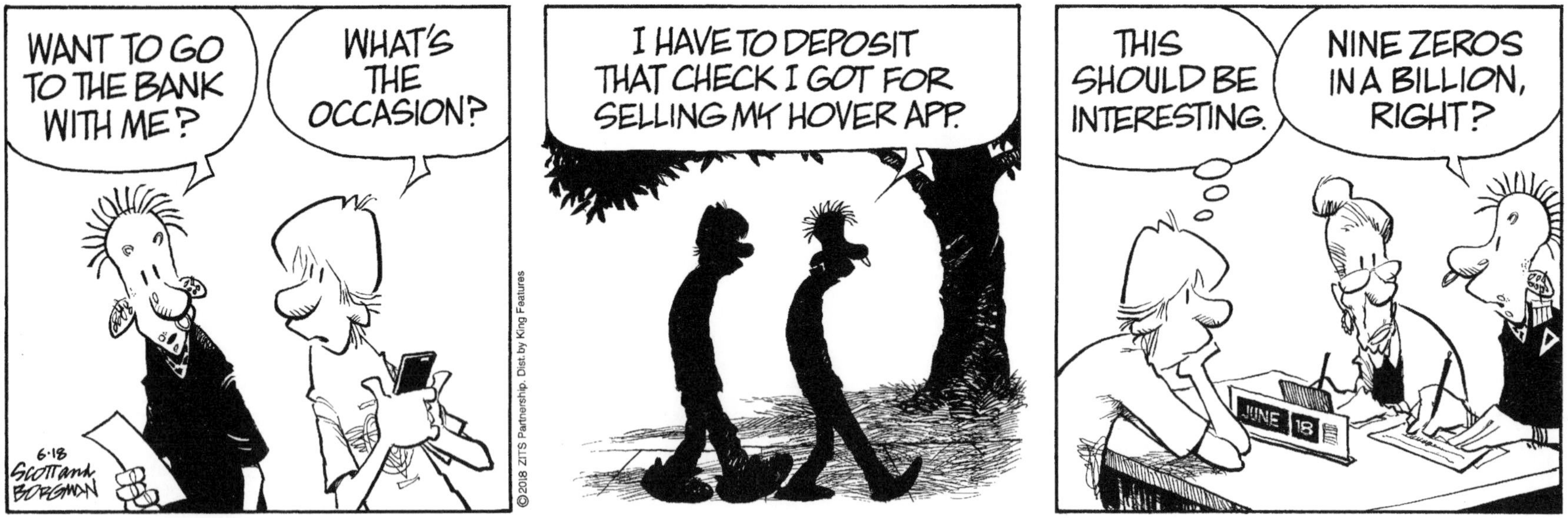
WANT TO GO TO THE BANK WITH ME?
WHAT'S THE OCCASION?
6·18 SCOTT and BORGMAN
© 2018 ZITS Partnership. Dist. by King Features
I HAVE TO DEPOSIT THAT CHECK I GOT FOR SELLING MY HOVER APP.
THIS SHOULD BE INTERESTING.
NINE ZEROS IN A BILLION, RIGHT?
JUNE 18

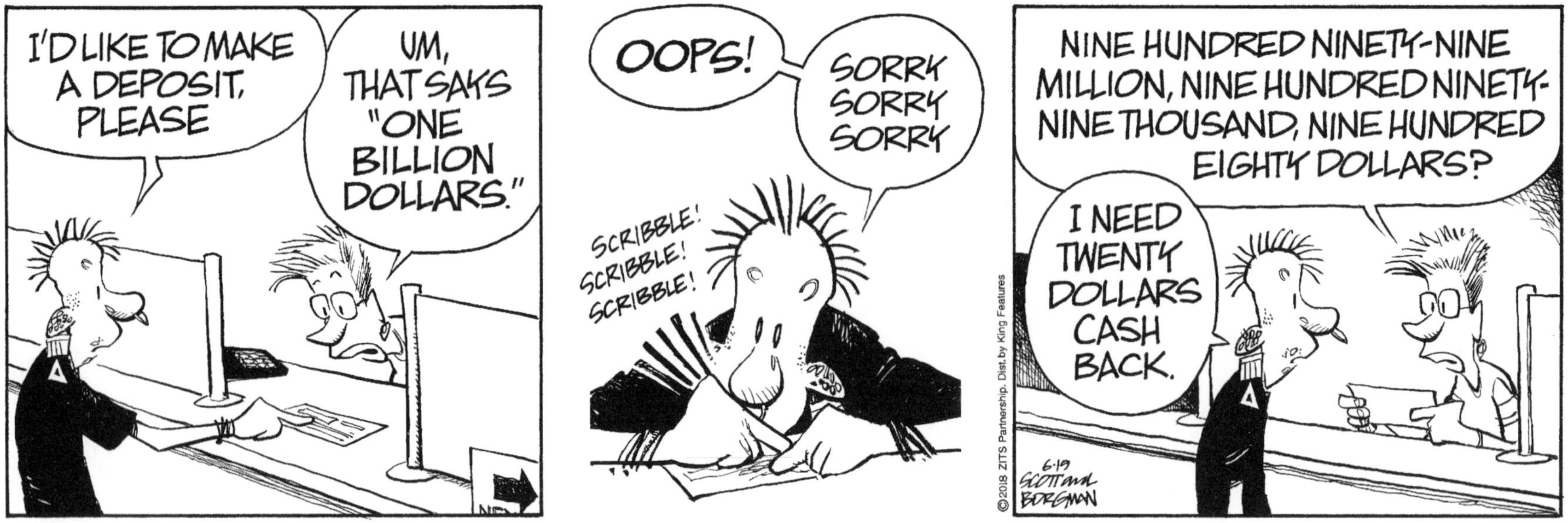
I'D LIKE TO MAKE A DEPOSIT, PLEASE
UM, THAT SAYS "ONE BILLION DOLLARS."
OOPS!
SORRY SORRY SORRY
SCRIBBLE! SCRIBBLE! SCRIBBLE!
NINE HUNDRED NINETY-NINE MILLION, NINE HUNDRED NINETY-NINE THOUSAND, NINE HUNDRED EIGHTY DOLLARS?
I NEED TWENTY DOLLARS CASH BACK.
© 2018 ZITS Partnership. Dist. by King Features
6·19 SCOTT and BORGMAN

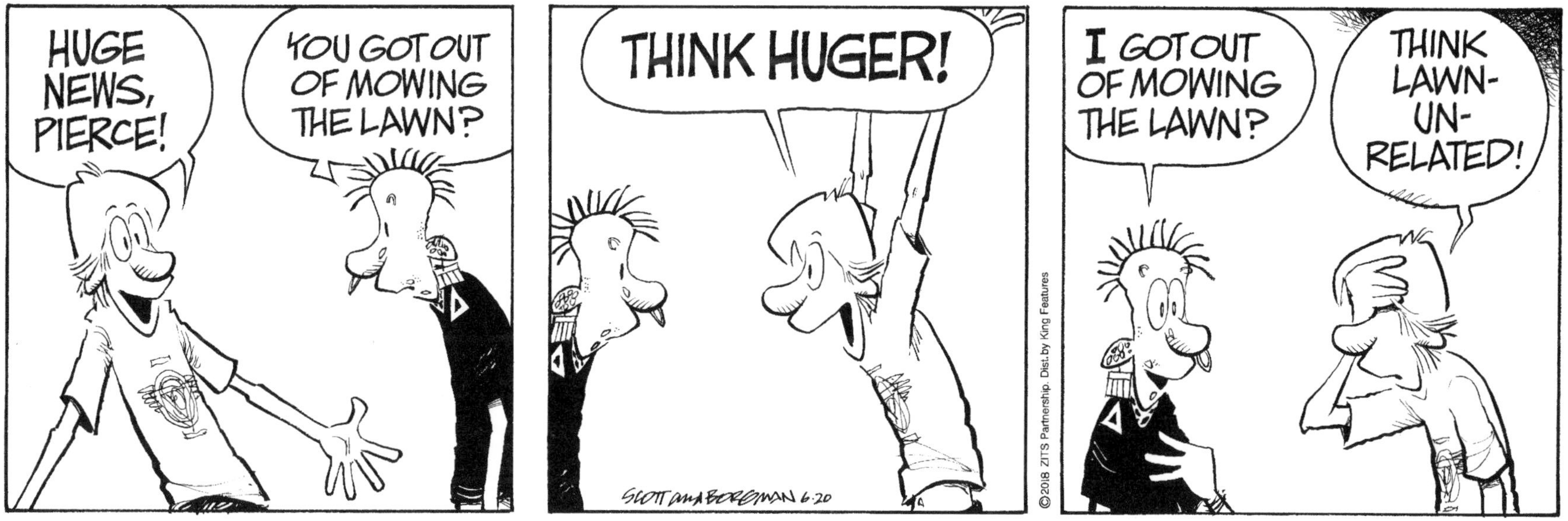
HUGE NEWS, PIERCE!
YOU GOT OUT OF MOWING THE LAWN?
THINK HUGER!
I GOT OUT OF MOWING THE LAWN?
THINK LAWN-UN-RELATED!
SCOTT and BORGMAN 6·20
©2018 ZITS Partnership. Dist.by King Features

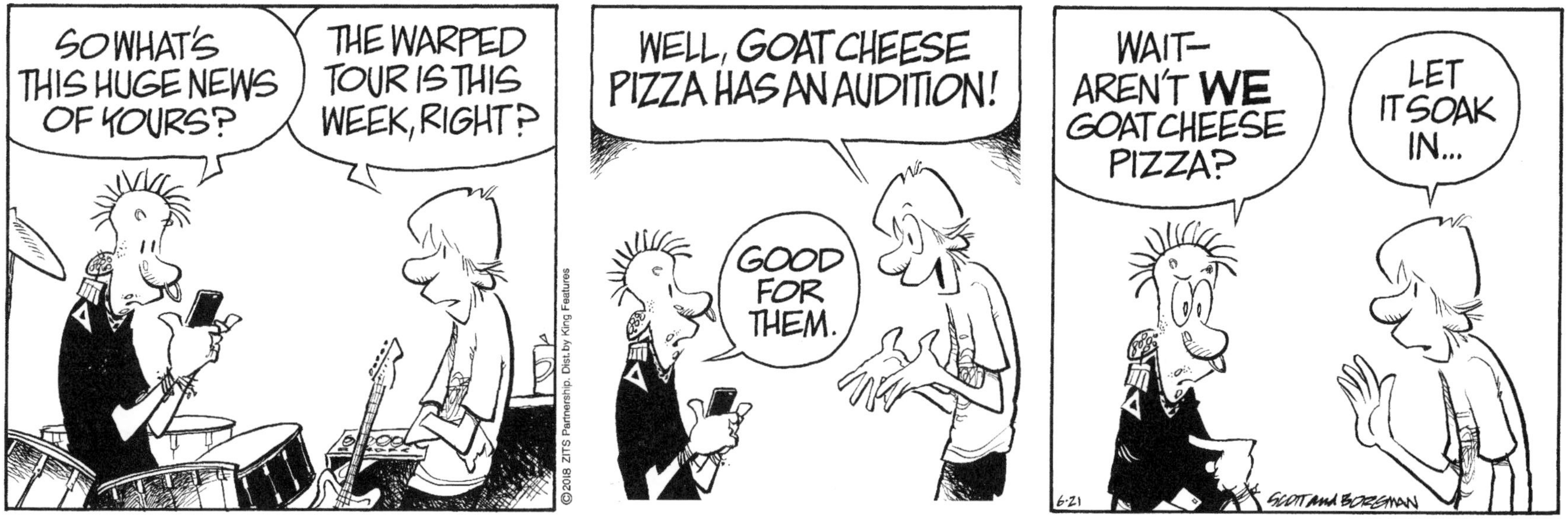
SO WHAT'S THIS HUGE NEWS OF YOURS?
THE WARPED TOUR IS THIS WEEK, RIGHT?
©2018 ZITS Partnership. Dist.by King Features
WELL, GOAT CHEESE PIZZA HAS AN AUDITION!
GOOD FOR THEM.
WAIT— AREN'T **WE** GOAT CHEESE PIZZA?
LET IT SOAK IN...
6·21
SCOTT and BORGMAN

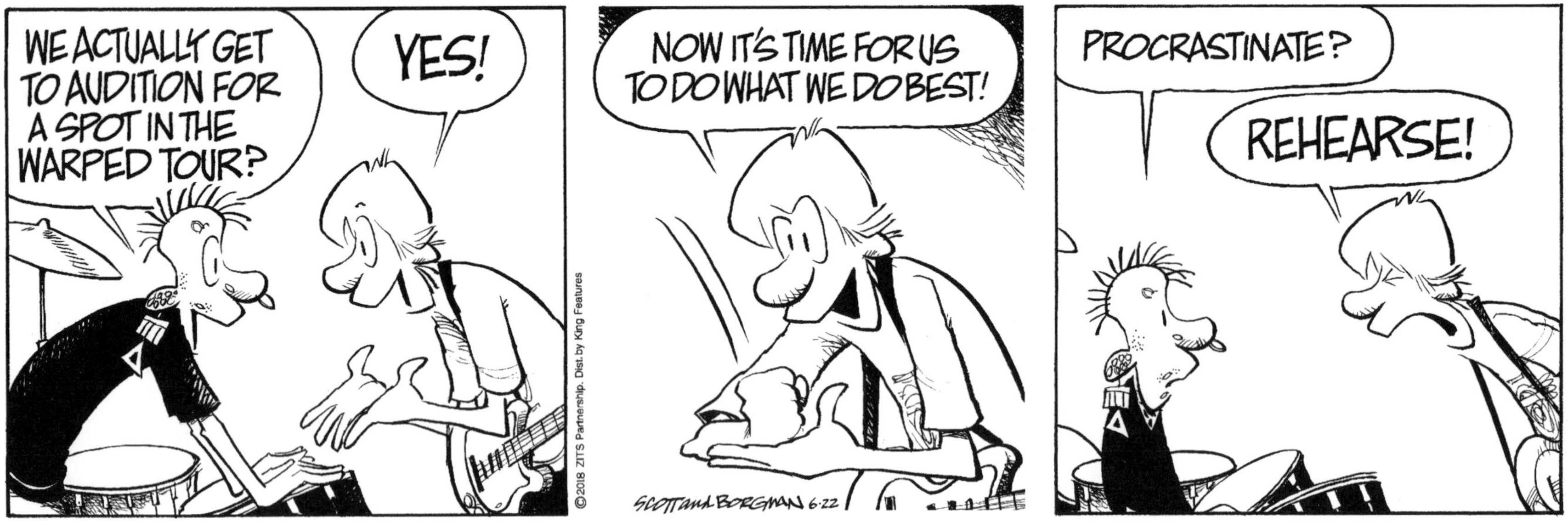
WE ACTUALLY GET TO AUDITION FOR A SPOT IN THE WARPED TOUR?
YES!
NOW IT'S TIME FOR US TO DO WHAT WE DO BEST!
PROCRASTINATE?
REHEARSE!
©2018 ZITS Partnership. Dist. by King Features
SCOTT AND BORGMAN 6-22

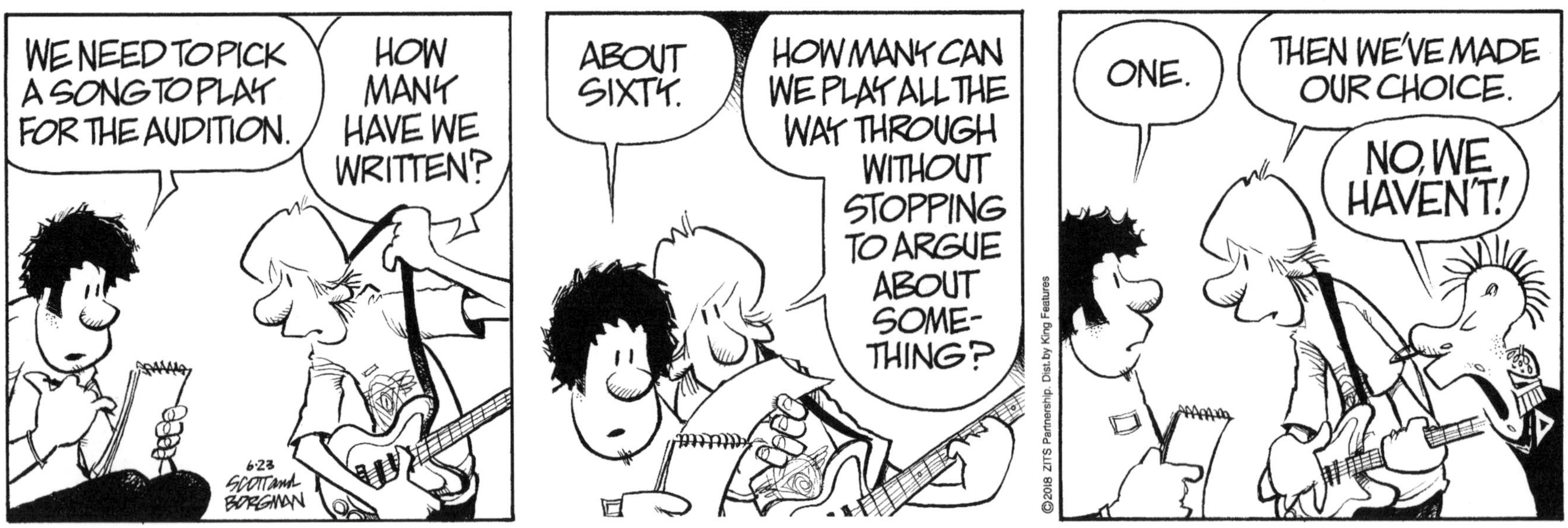
WE NEED TO PICK A SONG TO PLAY FOR THE AUDITION.
HOW MANY HAVE WE WRITTEN?
ABOUT SIXTY.
HOW MANY CAN WE PLAY ALL THE WAY THROUGH WITHOUT STOPPING TO ARGUE ABOUT SOME-THING?
ONE.
THEN WE'VE MADE OUR CHOICE.
NO, WE HAVEN'T!
6-23 SCOTT AND BORGMAN
©2018 ZITS Partnership. Dist. by King Features

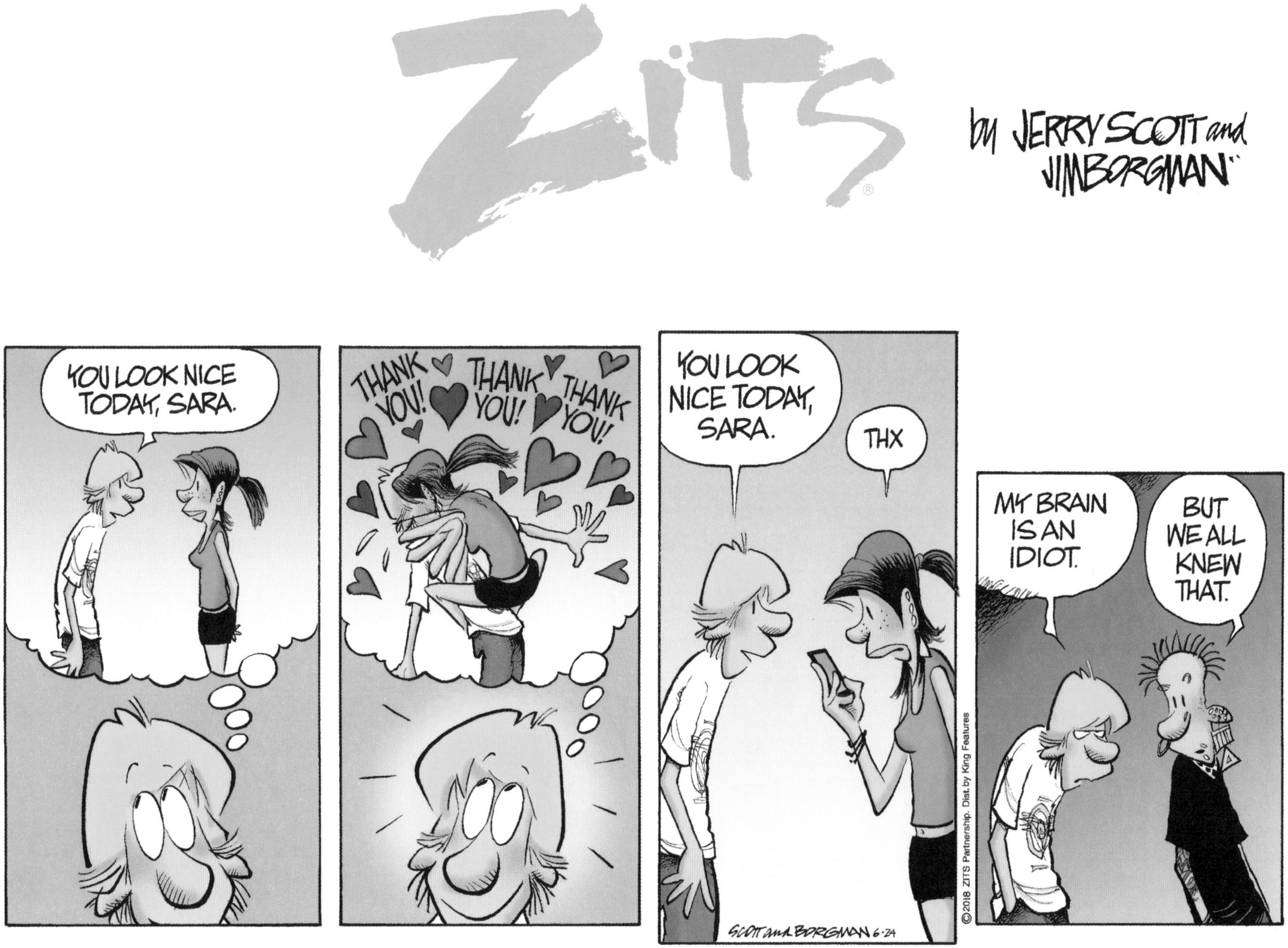

ZITS
by JERRY SCOTT and JIM BORGMAN
YOU LOOK NICE TODAY, SARA.
THANK YOU! THANK YOU! THANK YOU!
YOU LOOK NICE TODAY, SARA.
THX
SCOTT and BORGMAN 6·24
©2018 ZITS Partnership. Dist. by King Features
MY BRAIN IS AN IDIOT.
BUT WE ALL KNEW THAT.

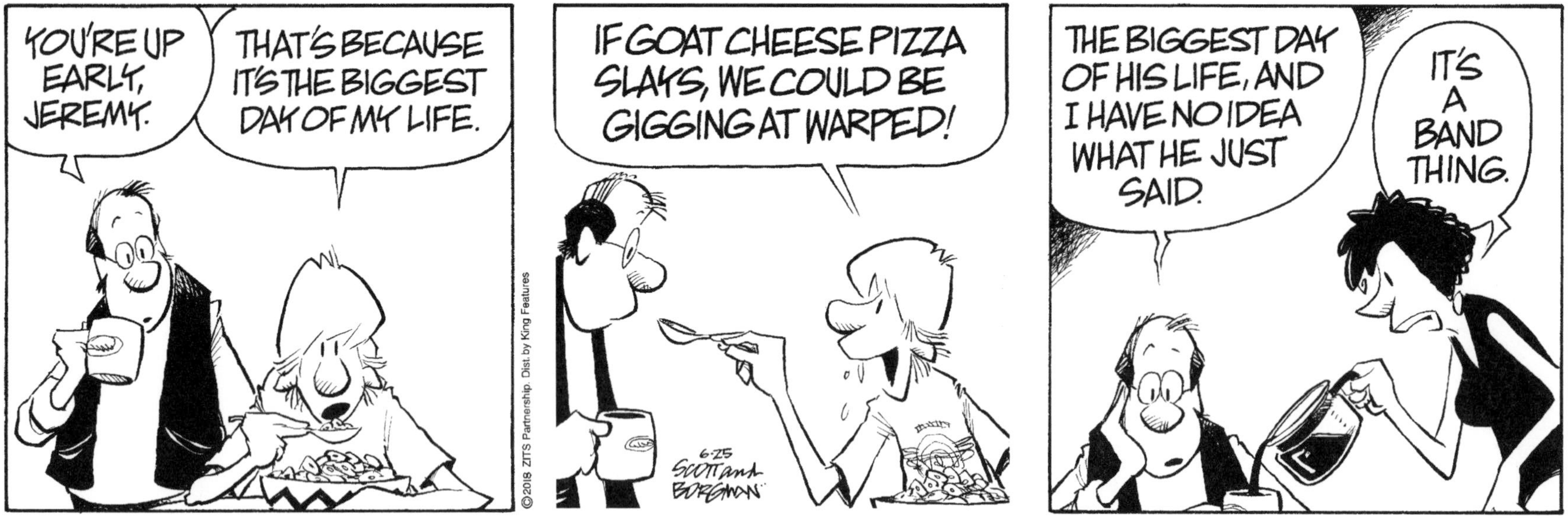
YOU'RE UP EARLY, JEREMY.
THAT'S BECAUSE IT'S THE BIGGEST DAY OF MY LIFE.
IF GOAT CHEESE PIZZA SLAYS, WE COULD BE GIGGING AT WARPED!
THE BIGGEST DAY OF HIS LIFE, AND I HAVE NO IDEA WHAT HE JUST SAID.
IT'S A BAND THING.
6·25
SCOTT and BORGMAN
© 2018 ZITS Partnership. Dist. by King Features

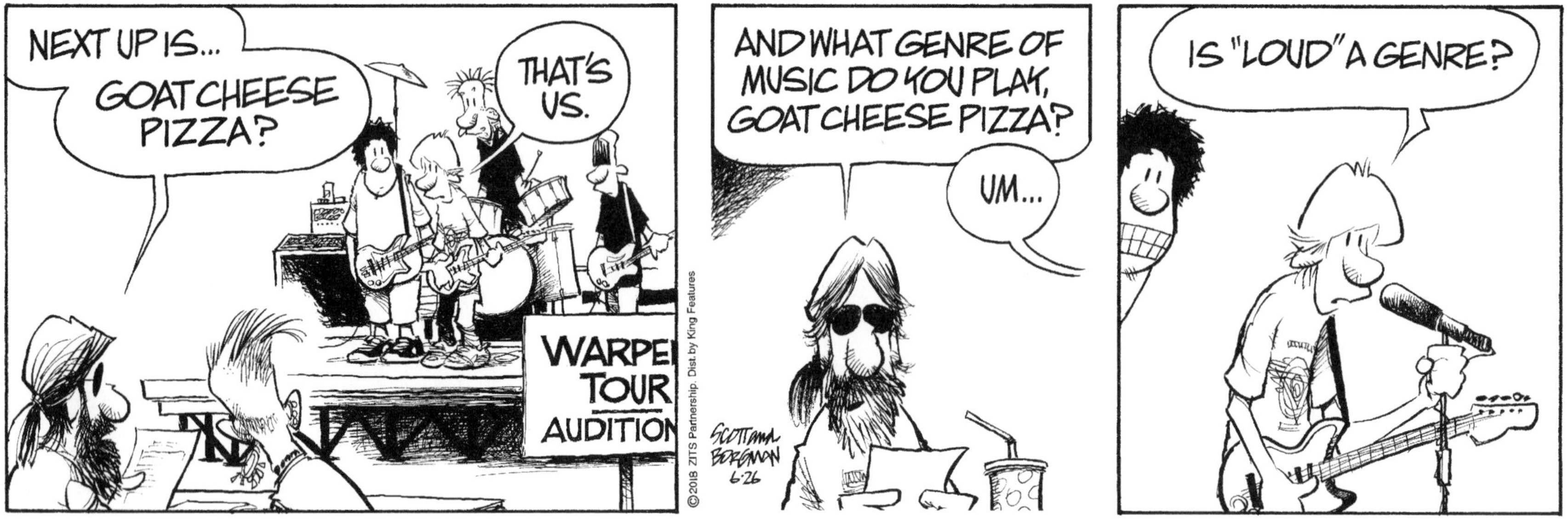
NEXT UP IS...
GOAT CHEESE PIZZA?
THAT'S US.
WARPED TOUR AUDITION
AND WHAT GENRE OF MUSIC DO YOU PLAY, GOAT CHEESE PIZZA?
UM...
IS "LOUD" A GENRE?
SCOTT and BORGMAN 6·26
© 2018 ZITS Partnership. Dist. by King Features

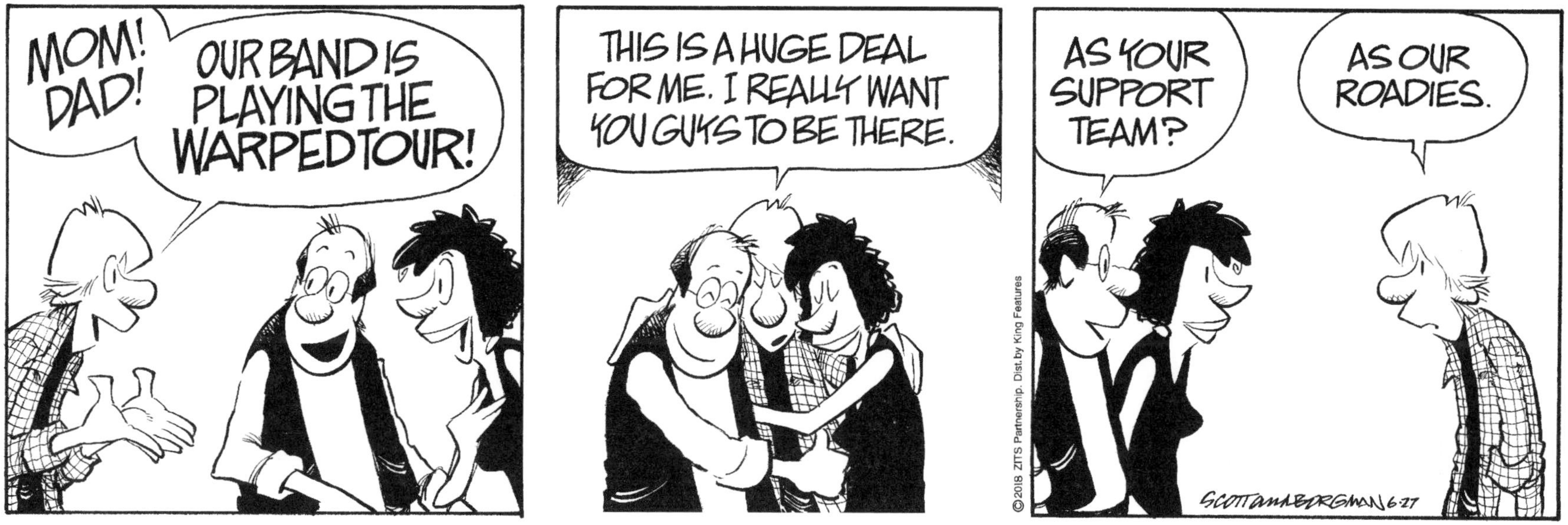
MOM! DAD!
OUR BAND IS PLAYING THE WARPED TOUR!
THIS IS A HUGE DEAL FOR ME. I REALLY WANT YOU GUYS TO BE THERE.
©2018 ZITS Partnership. Dist. by King Features
AS YOUR SUPPORT TEAM?
AS OUR ROADIES.
SCOTT and BORGMAN 6·27

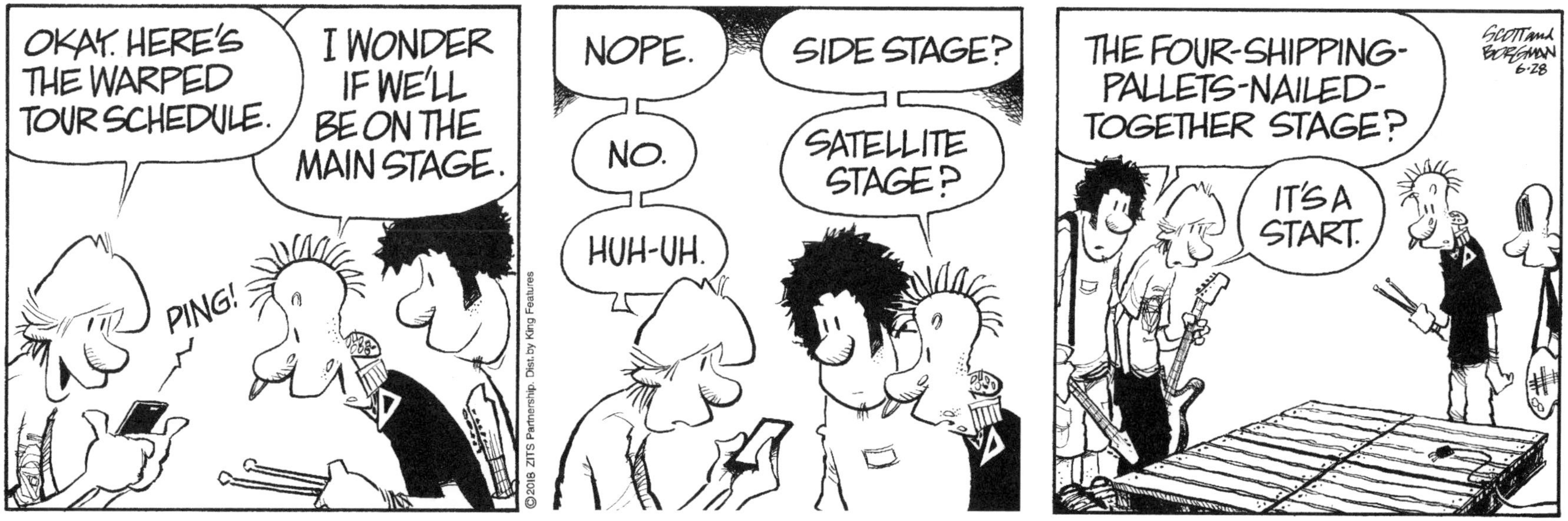
OKAY. HERE'S THE WARPED TOUR SCHEDULE.
I WONDER IF WE'LL BE ON THE MAIN STAGE.
PING!
©2018 ZITS Partnership. Dist. by King Features
NOPE.
NO.
HUH-UH.
SIDE STAGE?
SATELLITE STAGE?
THE FOUR-SHIPPING-PALLETS-NAILED-TOGETHER STAGE?
IT'S A START.
SCOTT and BORGMAN 6·28

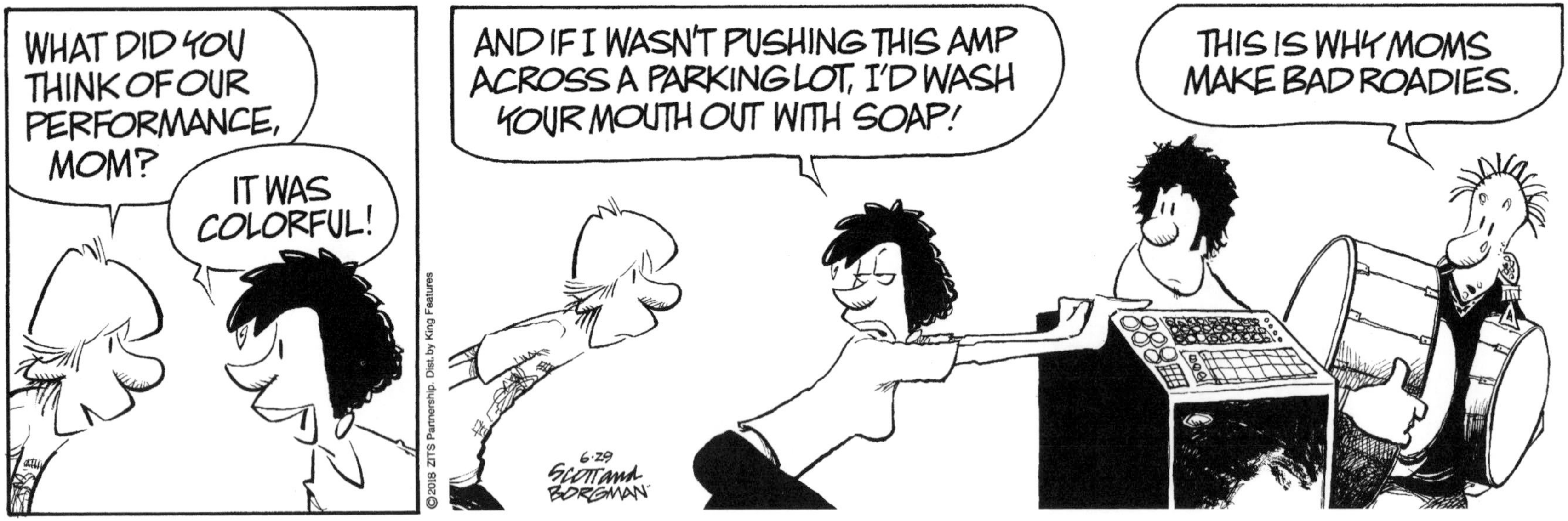
WHAT DID YOU THINK OF OUR PERFORMANCE, MOM?
IT WAS COLORFUL!
© 2018 ZITS Partnership. Dist. by King Features
AND IF I WASN'T PUSHING THIS AMP ACROSS A PARKING LOT, I'D WASH YOUR MOUTH OUT WITH SOAP!
6·29
SCOTT and BORGMAN
THIS IS WHY MOMS MAKE BAD ROADIES.

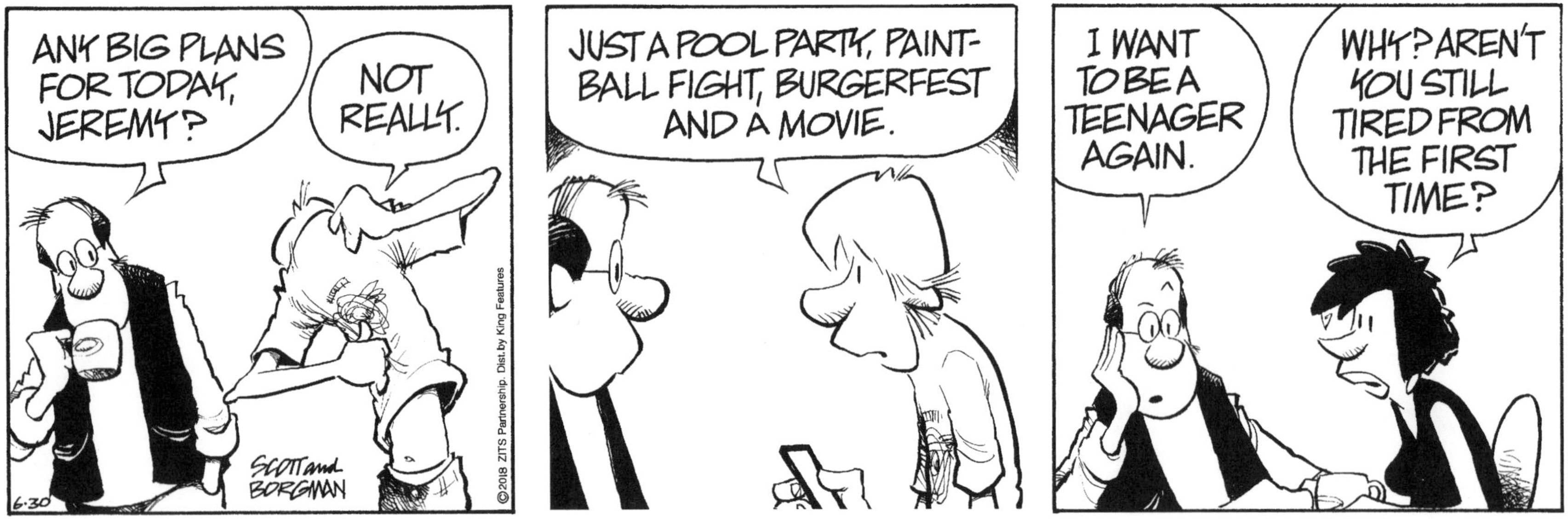
ANY BIG PLANS FOR TODAY, JEREMY?
NOT REALLY.
6·30
SCOTT and BORGMAN
© 2018 ZITS Partnership. Dist. by King Features
JUST A POOL PARTY, PAINT-BALL FIGHT, BURGERFEST AND A MOVIE.
I WANT TO BE A TEENAGER AGAIN.
WHY? AREN'T YOU STILL TIRED FROM THE FIRST TIME?

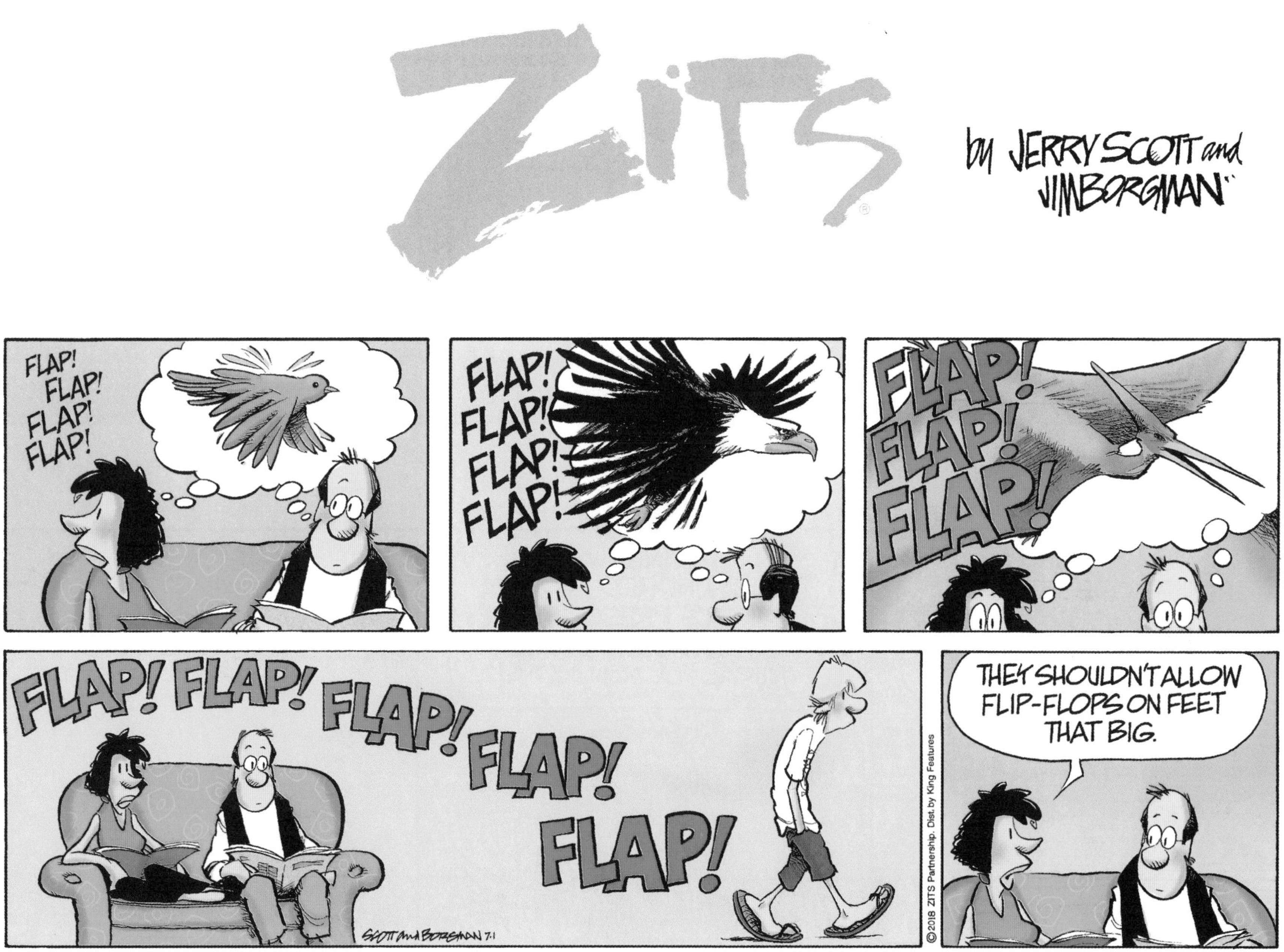
ZITS
by JERRY SCOTT and JIM BORGMAN
FLAP! FLAP! FLAP! FLAP!
FLAP! FLAP! FLAP! FLAP!
FLAP! FLAP! FLAP!
FLAP! FLAP! FLAP! FLAP! FLAP!
©2018 ZITS Partnership. Dist. by King Features
THEY SHOULDN'T ALLOW FLIP-FLOPS ON FEET THAT BIG.

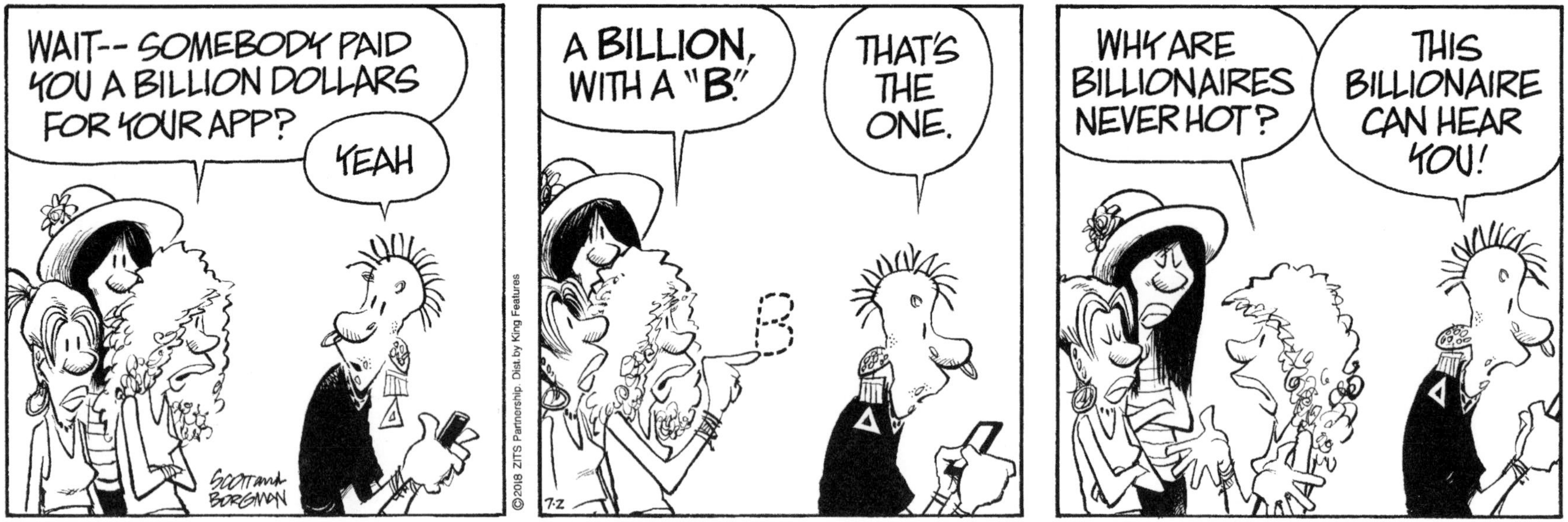
WAIT-- SOMEBODY PAID YOU A BILLION DOLLARS FOR YOUR APP?
YEAH
A **BILLION**, WITH A "**B**."
B
THAT'S THE ONE.
WHY ARE BILLIONAIRES NEVER HOT?
THIS BILLIONAIRE CAN HEAR YOU!
©2018 ZITS Partnership. Dist. by King Features
7-2

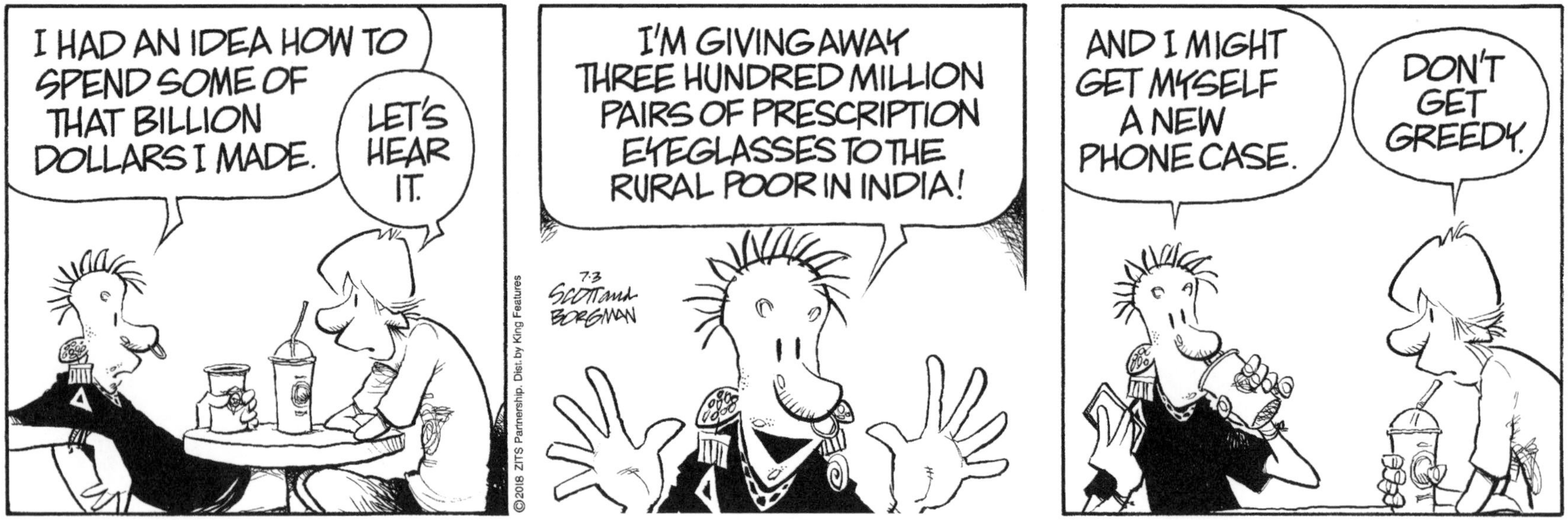
I HAD AN IDEA HOW TO SPEND SOME OF THAT BILLION DOLLARS I MADE.
LET'S HEAR IT.
I'M GIVING AWAY THREE HUNDRED MILLION PAIRS OF PRESCRIPTION EYEGLASSES TO THE RURAL POOR IN INDIA!
AND I MIGHT GET MYSELF A NEW PHONE CASE.
DON'T GET GREEDY.
©2018 ZITS Partnership. Dist. by King Features
7-3

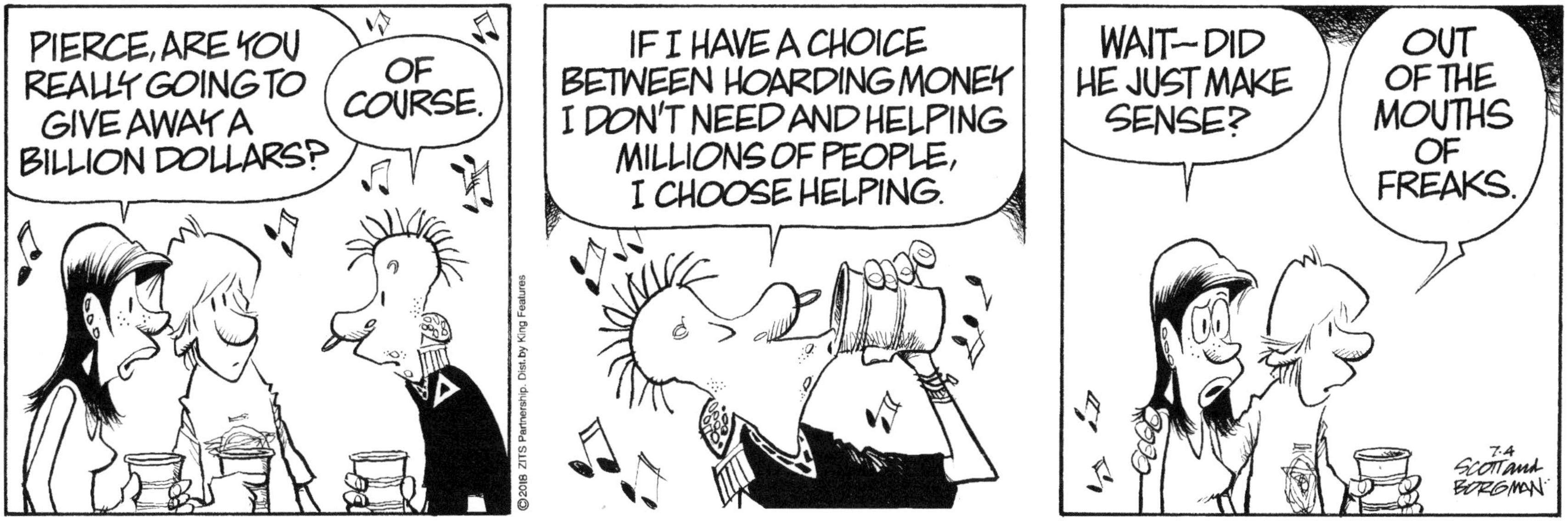
PIERCE, ARE YOU REALLY GOING TO GIVE AWAY A BILLION DOLLARS?
OF COURSE.
©2018 ZITS Partnership. Dist. by King Features
IF I HAVE A CHOICE BETWEEN HOARDING MONEY I DON'T NEED AND HELPING MILLIONS OF PEOPLE, I CHOOSE HELPING.
WAIT-- DID HE JUST MAKE SENSE?
OUT OF THE MOUTHS OF FREAKS.
7·4
SCOTT AND BORGMAN

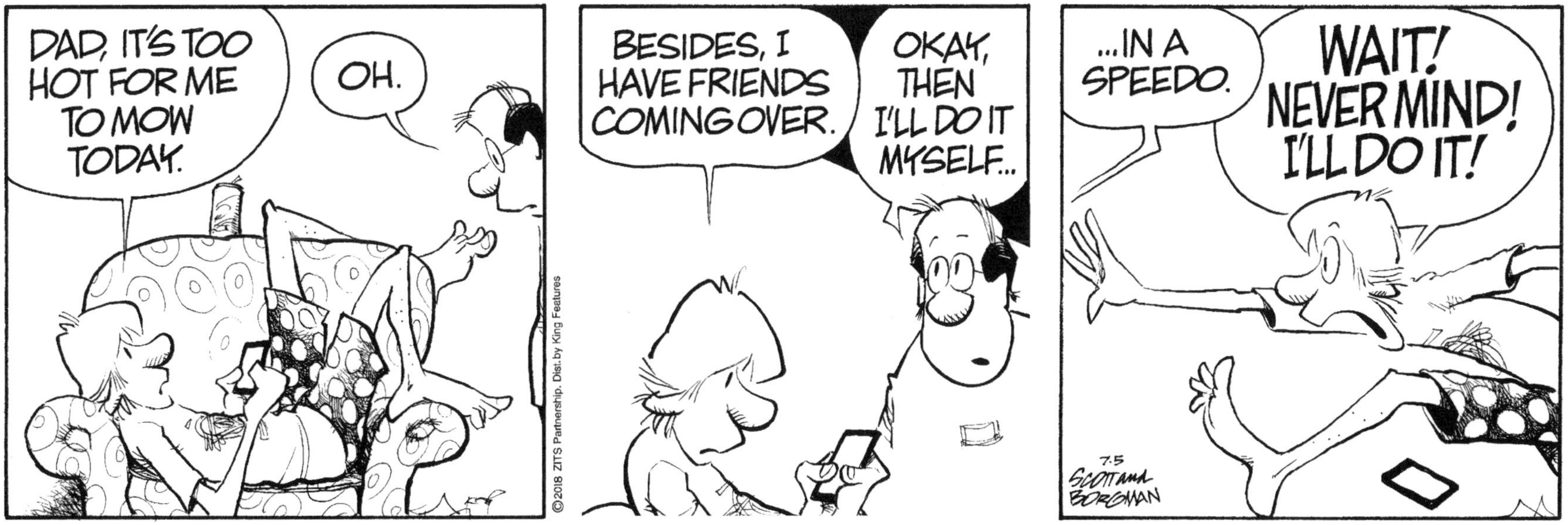
DAD, IT'S TOO HOT FOR ME TO MOW TODAY.
OH.
©2018 ZITS Partnership. Dist. by King Features
BESIDES, I HAVE FRIENDS COMING OVER.
OKAY, THEN I'LL DO IT MYSELF...
...IN A SPEEDO.
WAIT! NEVER MIND! I'LL DO IT!
7·5
SCOTT AND BORGMAN

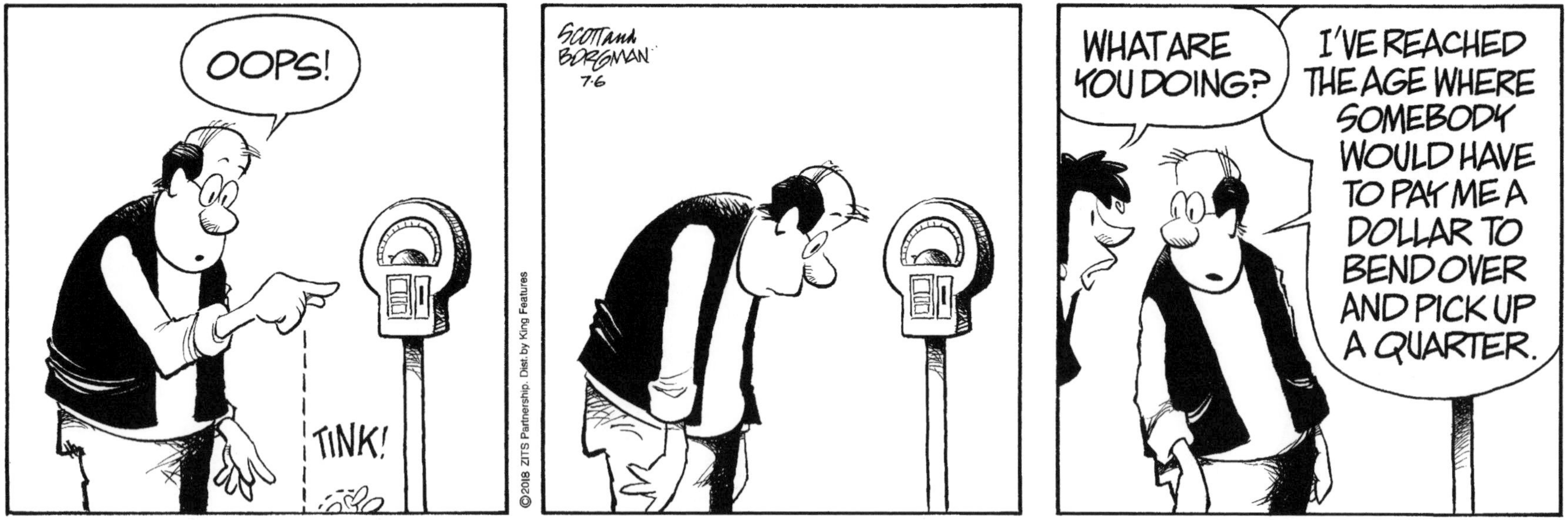
OOPS!
TINK!
SCOTT and BORGMAN 7-6
©2018 ZITS Partnership. Dist. by King Features
WHAT ARE YOU DOING?
I'VE REACHED THE AGE WHERE SOMEBODY WOULD HAVE TO PAY ME A DOLLAR TO BEND OVER AND PICK UP A QUARTER.

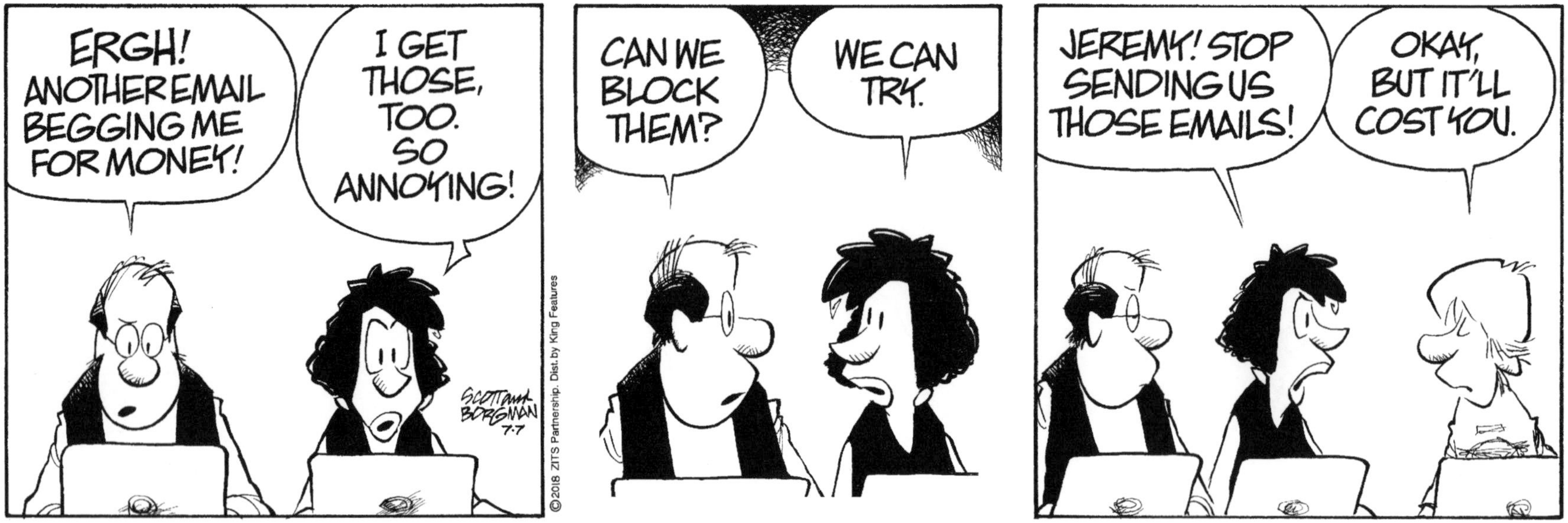
ERGH! ANOTHER EMAIL BEGGING ME FOR MONEY!
I GET THOSE, TOO. SO ANNOYING!
SCOTT and BORGMAN 7-7
©2018 ZITS Partnership. Dist. by King Features
CAN WE BLOCK THEM?
WE CAN TRY.
JEREMY! STOP SENDING US THOSE EMAILS!
OKAY, BUT IT'LL COST YOU.

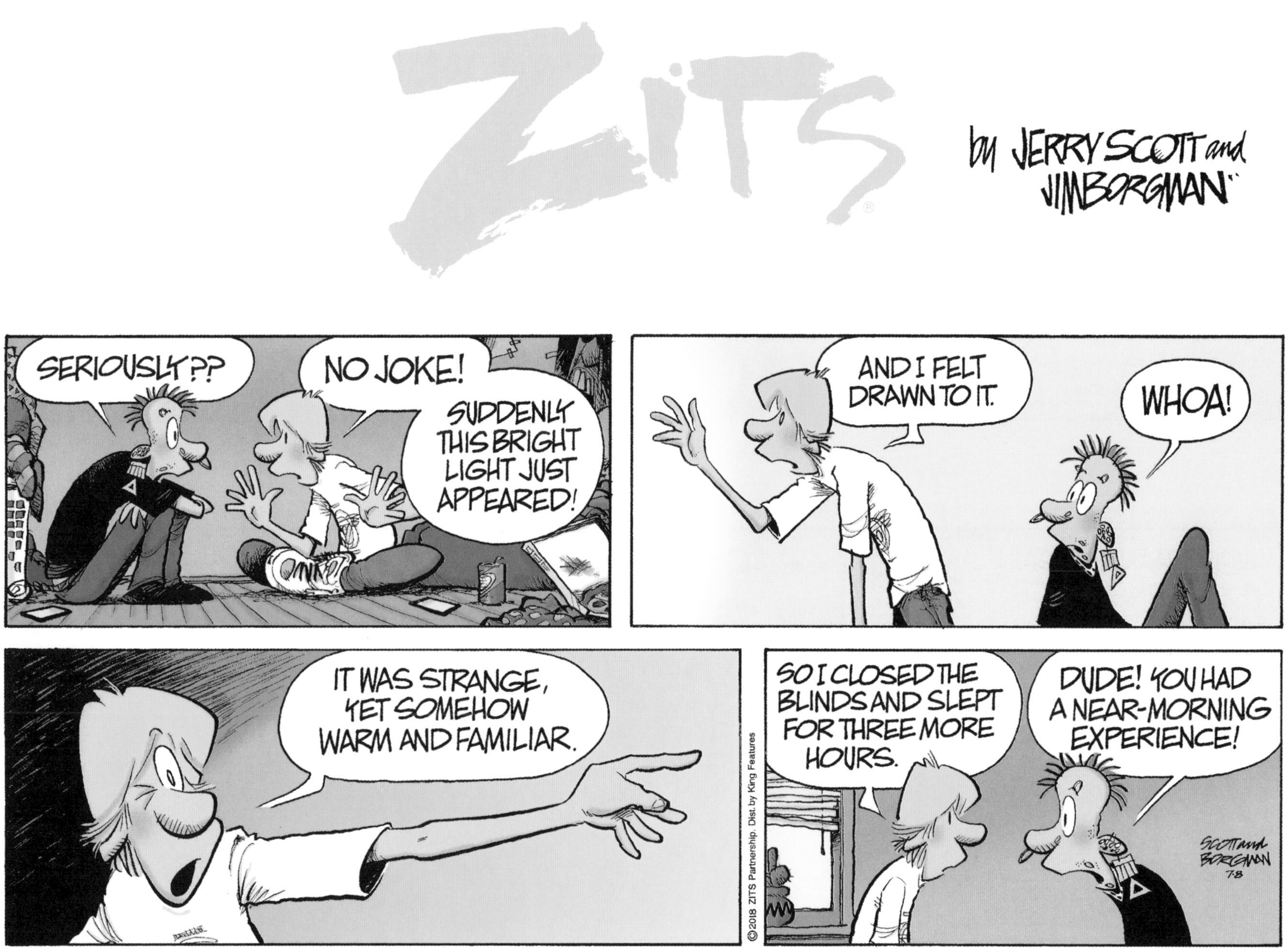

ZITS
by JERRY SCOTT and JIM BORGMAN
SERIOUSLY??
NO JOKE!
SUDDENLY THIS BRIGHT LIGHT JUST APPEARED!
AND I FELT DRAWN TO IT.
WHOA!
IT WAS STRANGE, YET SOMEHOW WARM AND FAMILIAR.
SO I CLOSED THE BLINDS AND SLEPT FOR THREE MORE HOURS.
DUDE! YOU HAD A NEAR-MORNING EXPERIENCE!
© 2018 ZITS Partnership. Dist. by King Features
SCOTT and BORGMAN 7-8

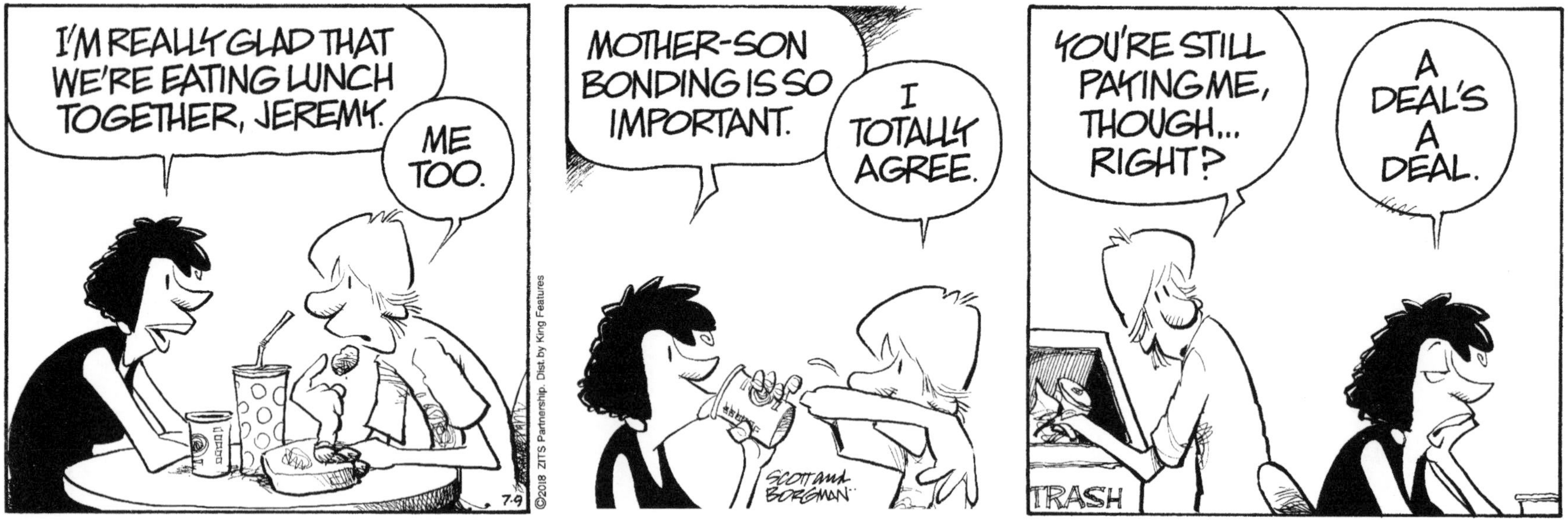
I'M REALLY GLAD THAT WE'RE EATING LUNCH TOGETHER, JEREMY.
ME TOO.
7-9
©2018 ZITS Partnership. Dist. by King Features
MOTHER-SON BONDING IS SO IMPORTANT.
I TOTALLY AGREE.
SCOTT and BORGMAN
YOU'RE STILL PAYING ME, THOUGH... RIGHT?
A DEAL'S A DEAL.
TRASH

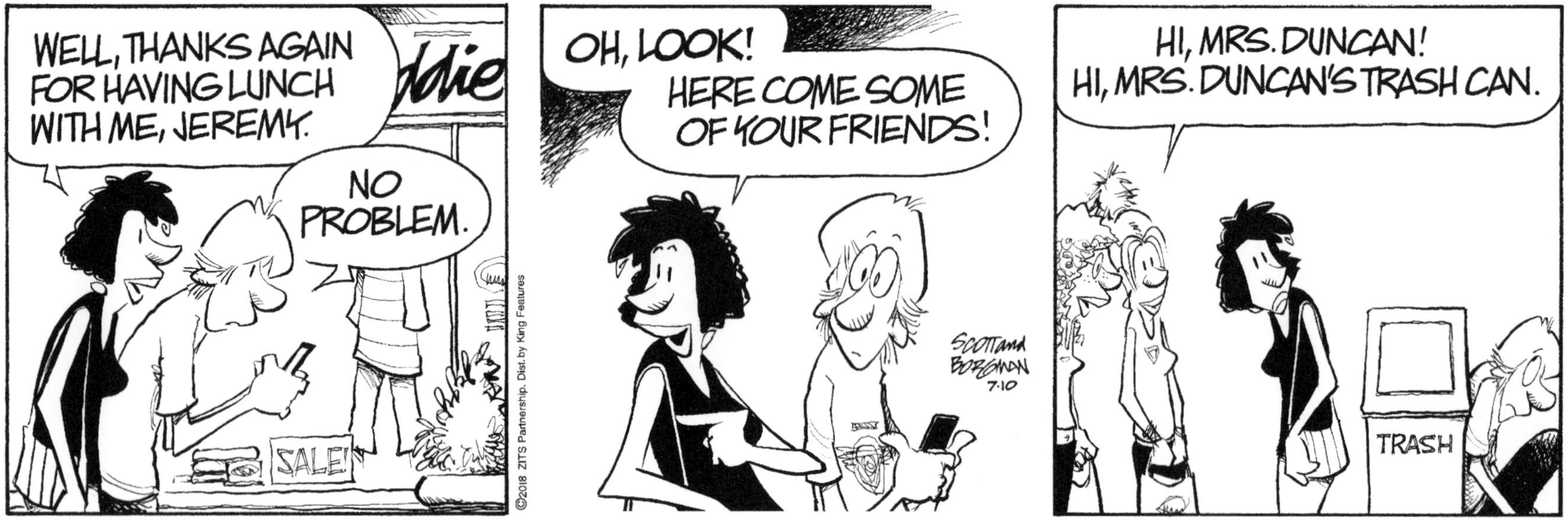
WELL, THANKS AGAIN FOR HAVING LUNCH WITH ME, JEREMY.
NO PROBLEM.
SALE!
©2018 ZITS Partnership. Dist. by King Features
OH, LOOK!
HERE COME SOME OF YOUR FRIENDS!
SCOTT and BORGMAN
7-10
HI, MRS. DUNCAN!
HI, MRS. DUNCAN'S TRASH CAN.
TRASH

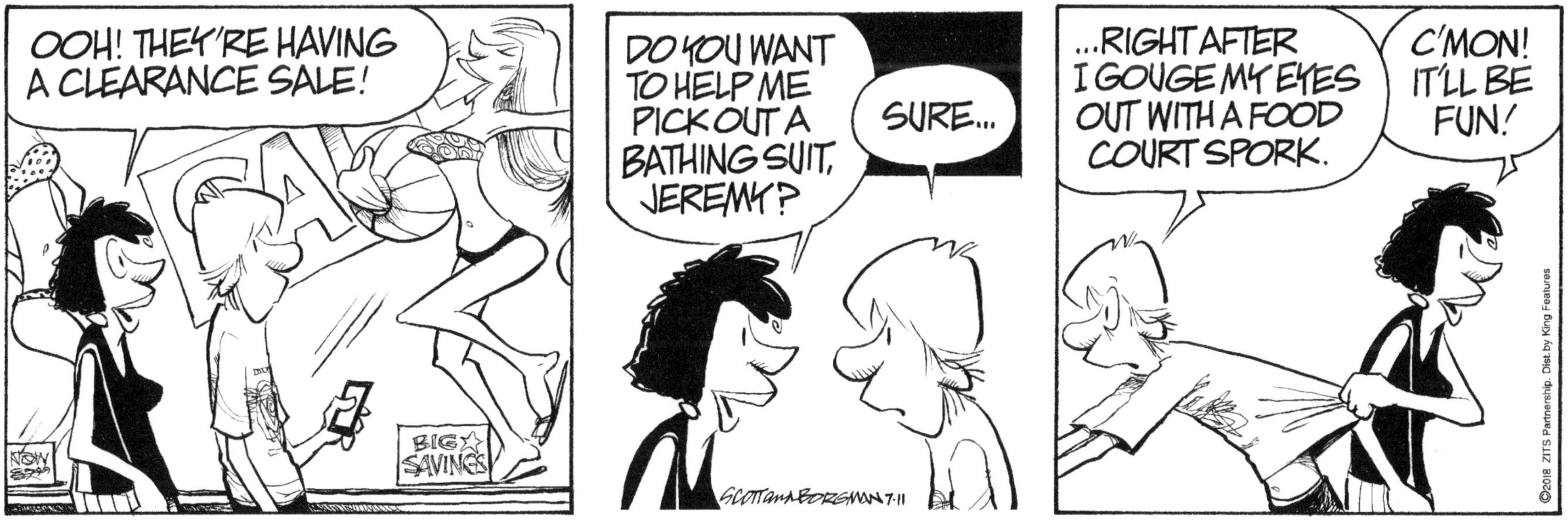
OOH! THEY'RE HAVING A CLEARANCE SALE!
BIG SAVINGS
DO YOU WANT TO HELP ME PICK OUT A BATHING SUIT, JEREMY?
SURE...
SCOTT and BORGMAN 7·11
...RIGHT AFTER I GOUGE MY EYES OUT WITH A FOOD COURT SPORK.
C'MON! IT'LL BE FUN!
©2018 ZITS Partnership. Dist. by King Features

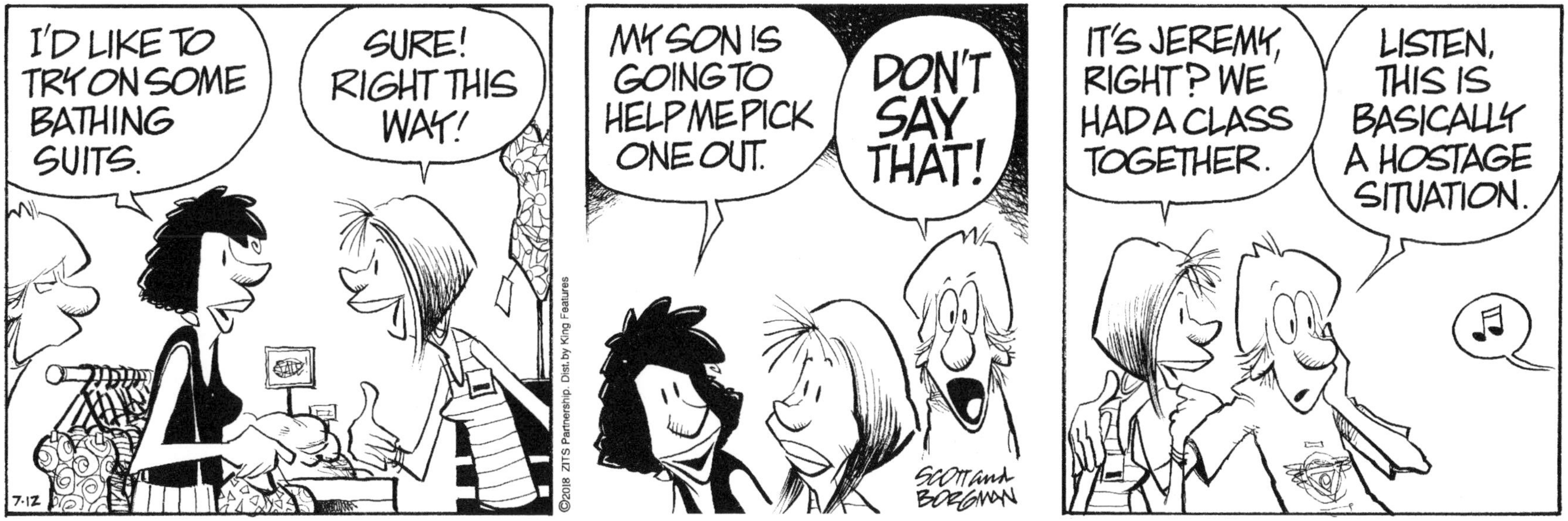
I'D LIKE TO TRY ON SOME BATHING SUITS.
SURE! RIGHT THIS WAY!
7·12
©2018 ZITS Partnership. Dist. by King Features
MY SON IS GOING TO HELP ME PICK ONE OUT.
DON'T SAY THAT!
SCOTT and BORGMAN
IT'S JEREMY, RIGHT? WE HAD A CLASS TOGETHER.
LISTEN, THIS IS BASICALLY A HOSTAGE SITUATION.

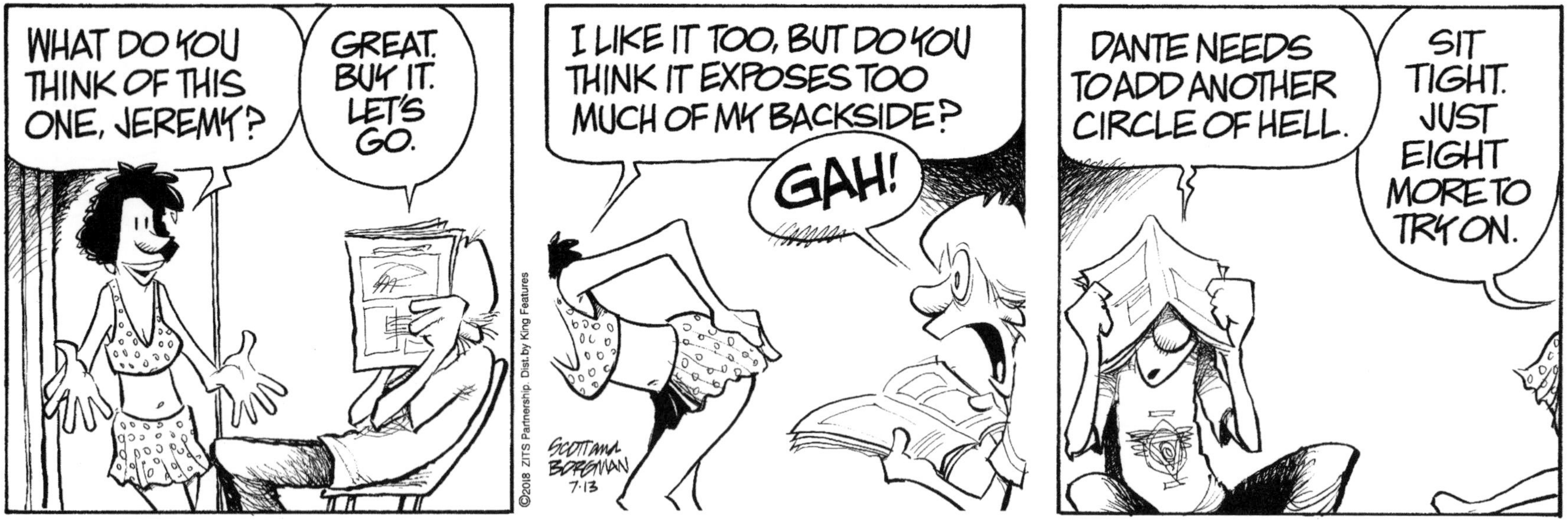
WHAT DO YOU THINK OF THIS ONE, JEREMY?
GREAT. BUY IT. LET'S GO.
I LIKE IT TOO, BUT DO YOU THINK IT EXPOSES TOO MUCH OF MY BACKSIDE?
GAH!
DANTE NEEDS TO ADD ANOTHER CIRCLE OF HELL.
SIT TIGHT. JUST EIGHT MORE TO TRY ON.
©2018 ZITS Partnership. Dist. by King Features
SCOTT AND BORGMAN 7·13

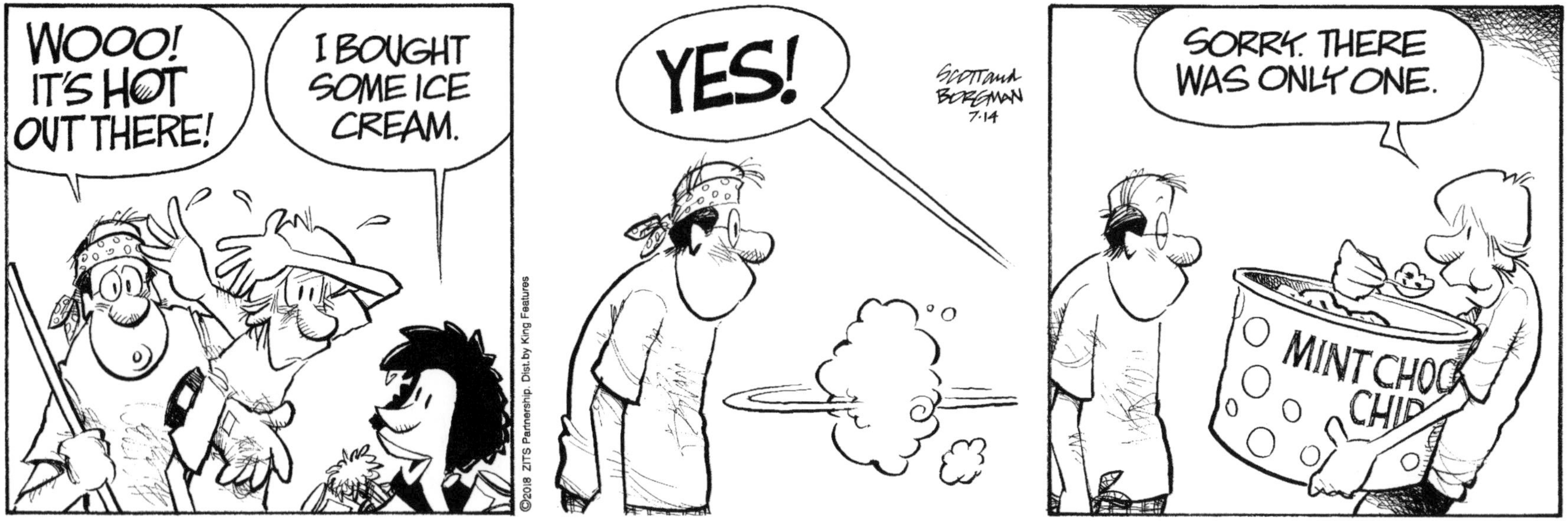
WOOO! IT'S HOT OUT THERE!
I BOUGHT SOME ICE CREAM.
YES!
SORRY. THERE WAS ONLY ONE.
MINT CHOC CHIP
©2018 ZITS Partnership. Dist. by King Features
SCOTT AND BORGMAN 7·14

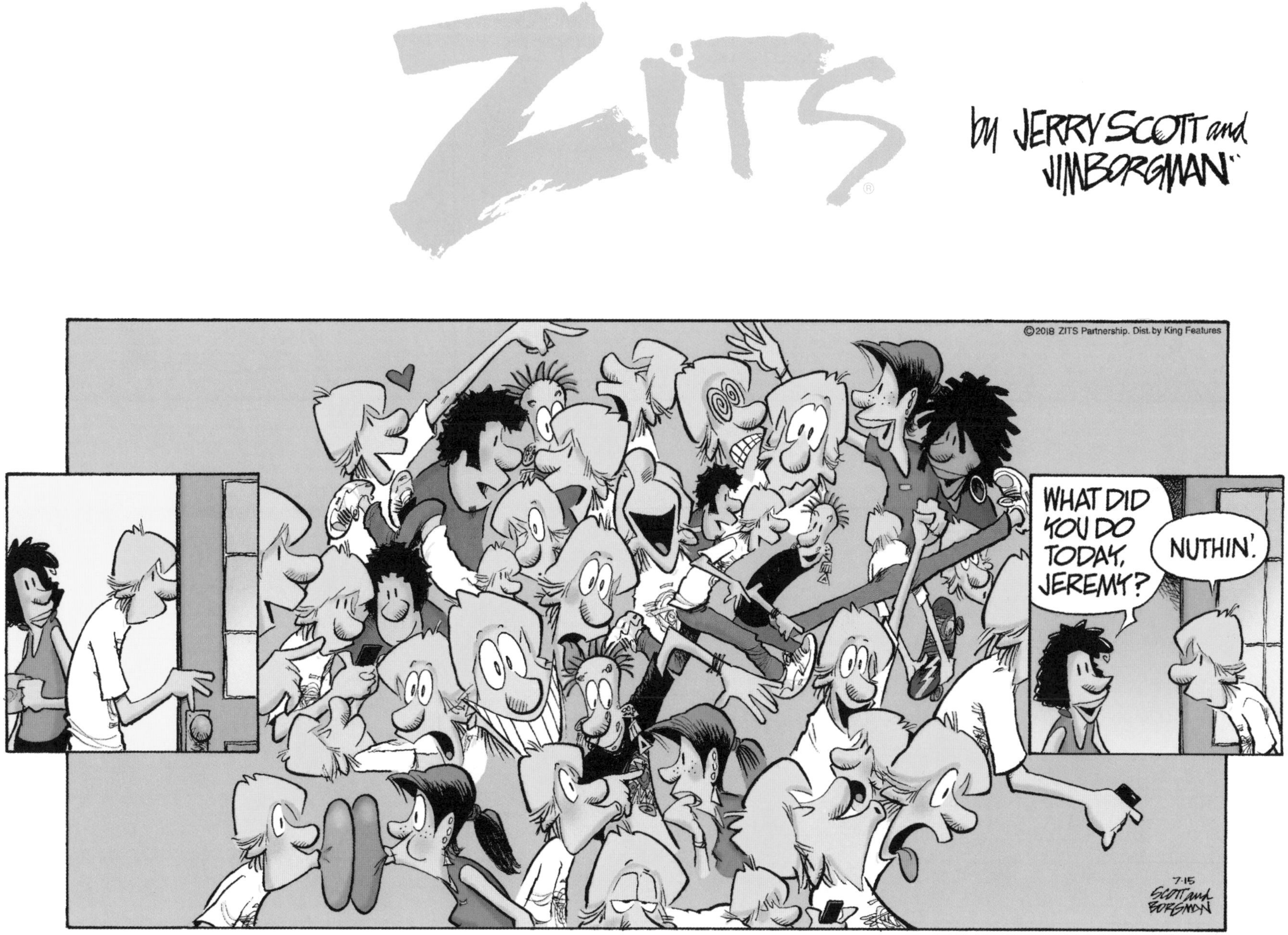
ZITS
by JERRY SCOTT and JIM BORGMAN
©2018 ZITS Partnership. Dist. by King Features
WHAT DID YOU DO TODAY, JEREMY?
NUTHIN'.
7-15
SCOTT and BORGMAN

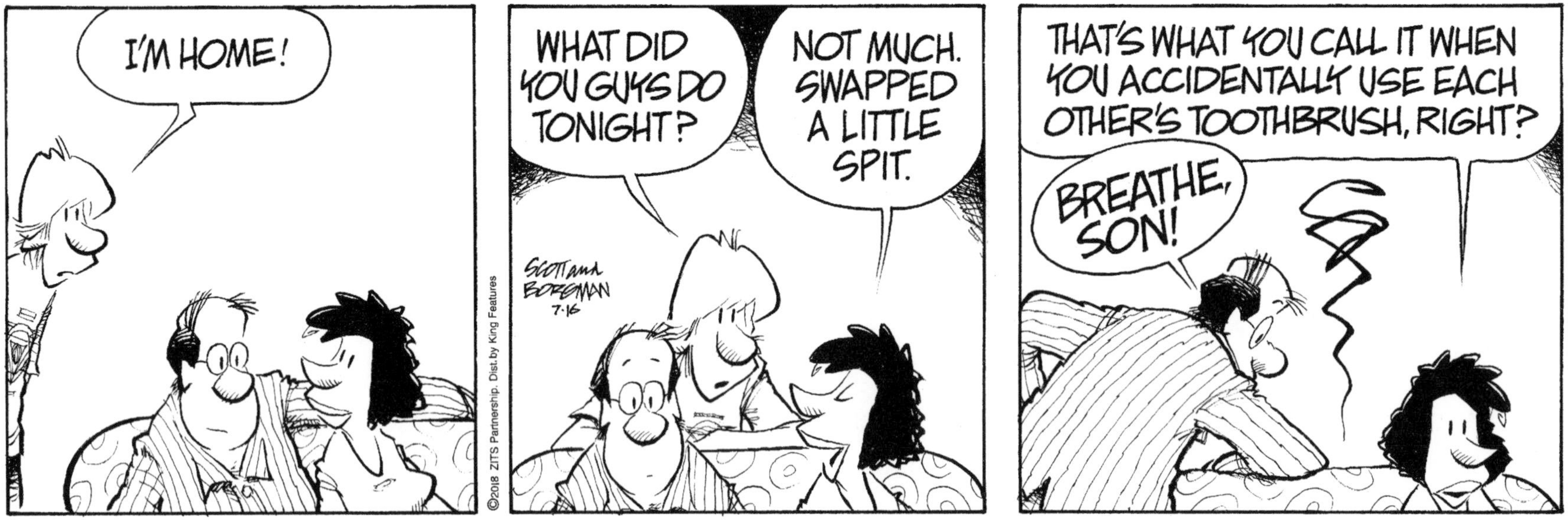
I'M HOME!
WHAT DID YOU GUYS DO TONIGHT?
NOT MUCH. SWAPPED A LITTLE SPIT.
SCOTT and BORGMAN 7·16
©2018 ZITS Partnership. Dist. by King Features
THAT'S WHAT YOU CALL IT WHEN YOU ACCIDENTALLY USE EACH OTHER'S TOOTHBRUSH, RIGHT?
BREATHE, SON!

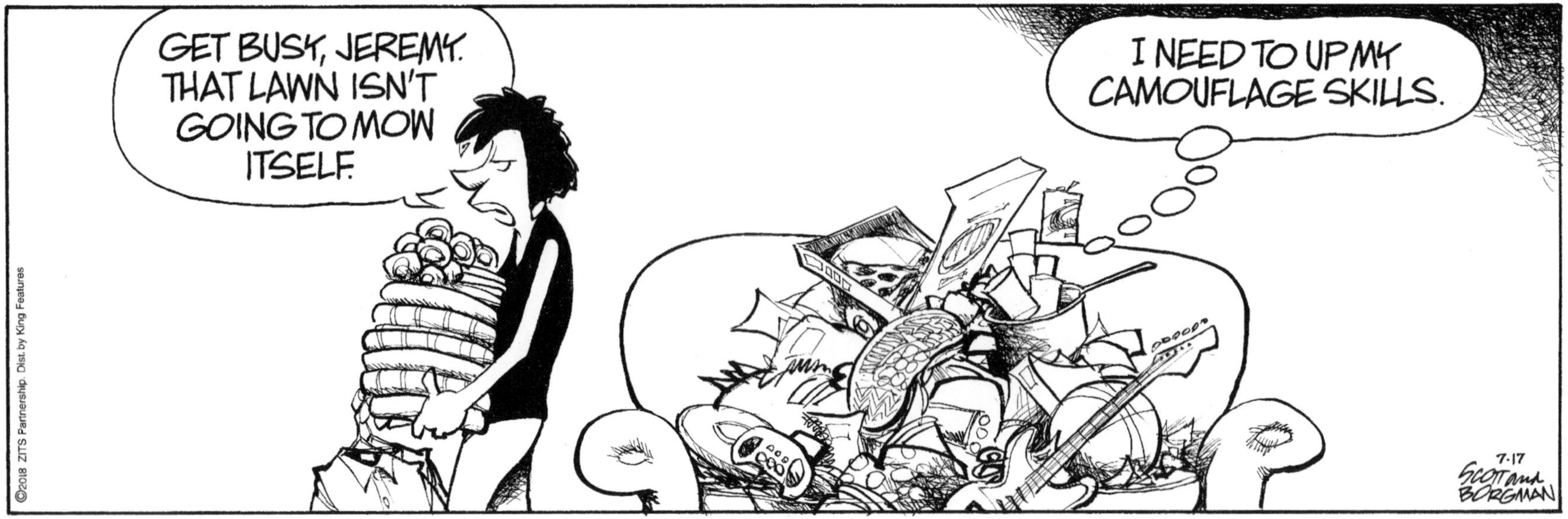
GET BUSY, JEREMY. THAT LAWN ISN'T GOING TO MOW ITSELF.
I NEED TO UP MY CAMOUFLAGE SKILLS.
7·17 SCOTT and BORGMAN
©2018 ZITS Partnership. Dist. by King Features

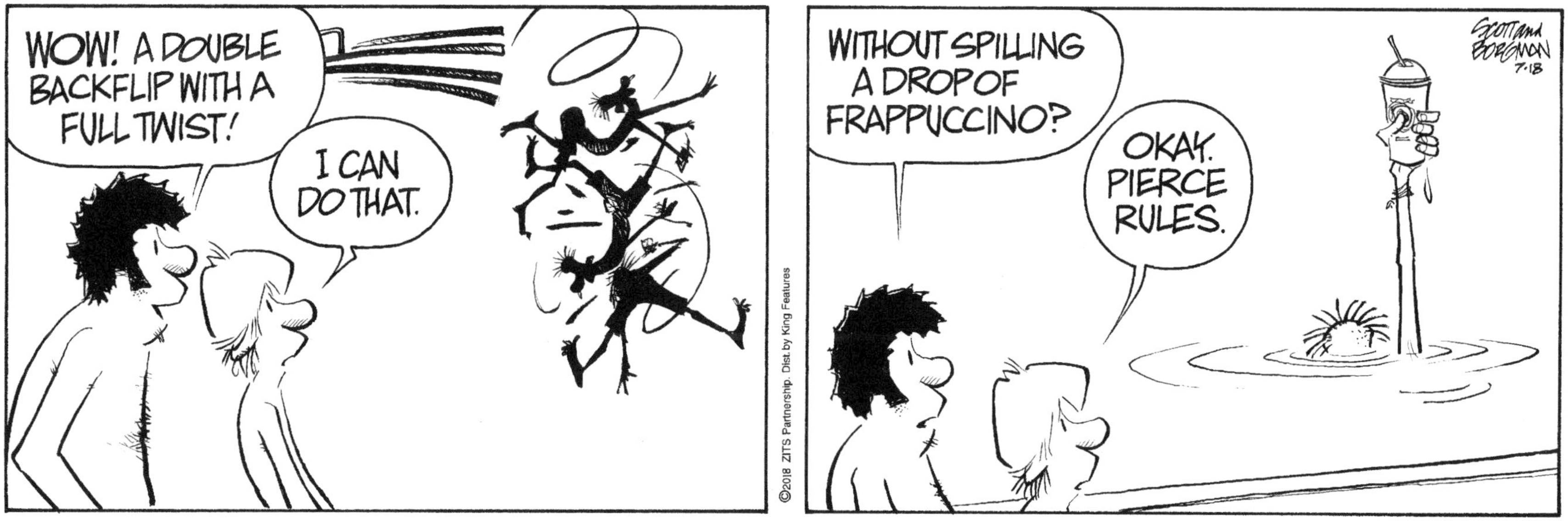
WOW! A DOUBLE BACKFLIP WITH A FULL TWIST!
I CAN DO THAT.
©2018 ZITS Partnership. Dist. by King Features
WITHOUT SPILLING A DROP OF FRAPPUCCINO?
OKAY. PIERCE RULES.
SCOTT and BORGMAN 7·18

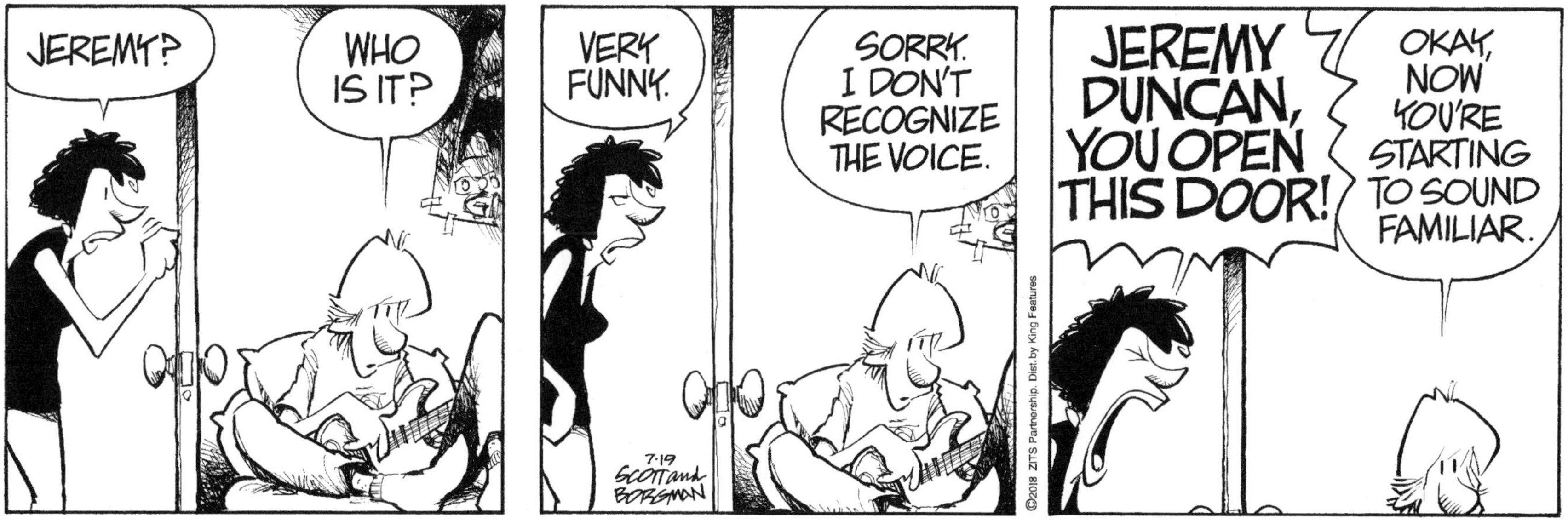
JEREMY?
WHO IS IT?
VERY FUNNY.
7·19 SCOTT and BORGMAN
SORRY. I DON'T RECOGNIZE THE VOICE.
©2018 ZITS Partnership. Dist. by King Features
JEREMY DUNCAN, YOU OPEN THIS DOOR!
OKAY, NOW YOU'RE STARTING TO SOUND FAMILIAR.

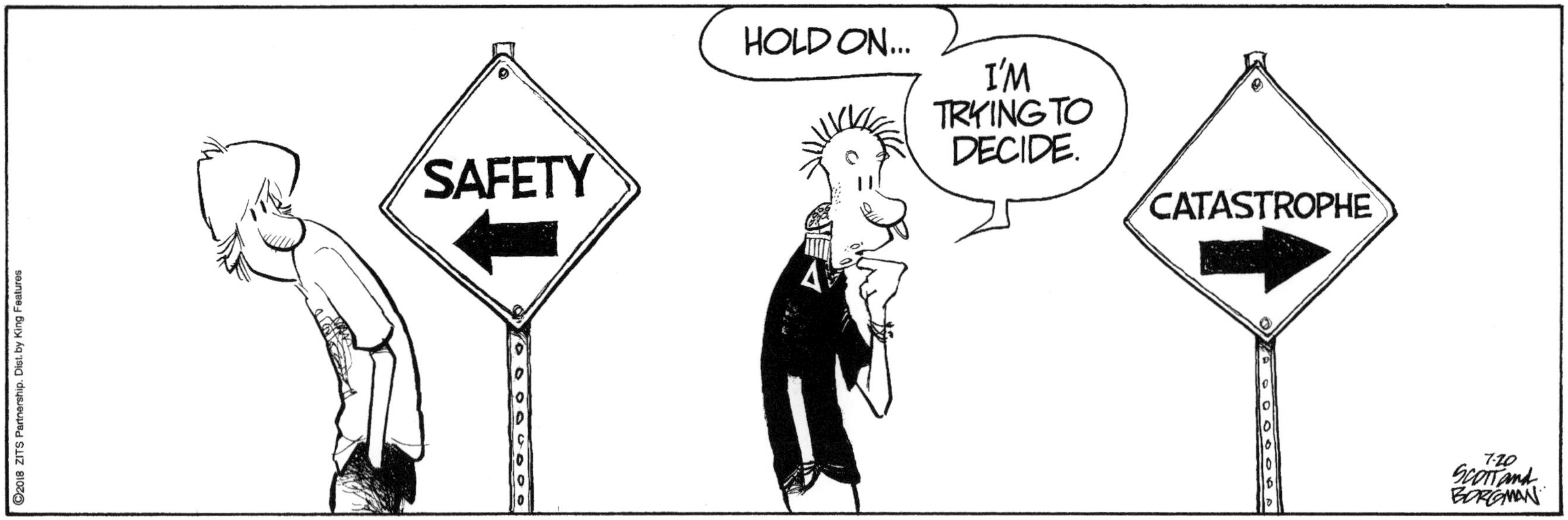
SAFETY
HOLD ON...
I'M TRYING TO DECIDE.
CATASTROPHE
7-20 SCOTT and BORGMAN
©2018 ZITS Partnership. Dist. by King Features

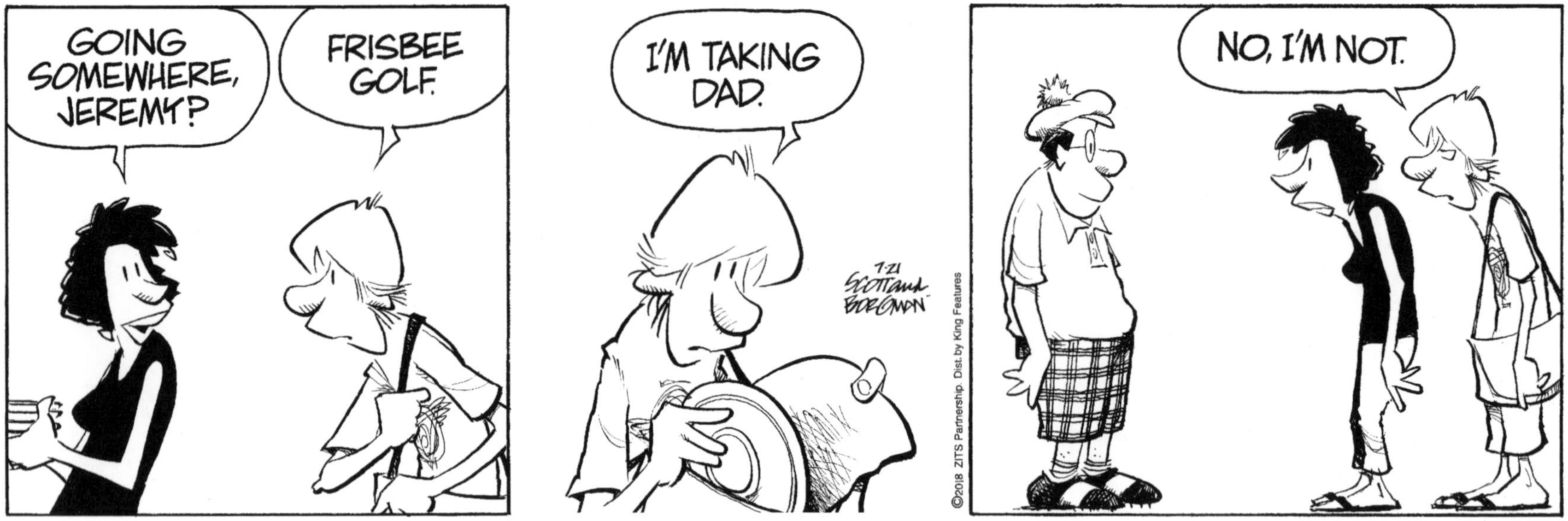
GOING SOMEWHERE, JEREMY?
FRISBEE GOLF.
I'M TAKING DAD.
7-21 SCOTT and BORGMAN
NO, I'M NOT.
©2018 ZITS Partnership. Dist. by King Features

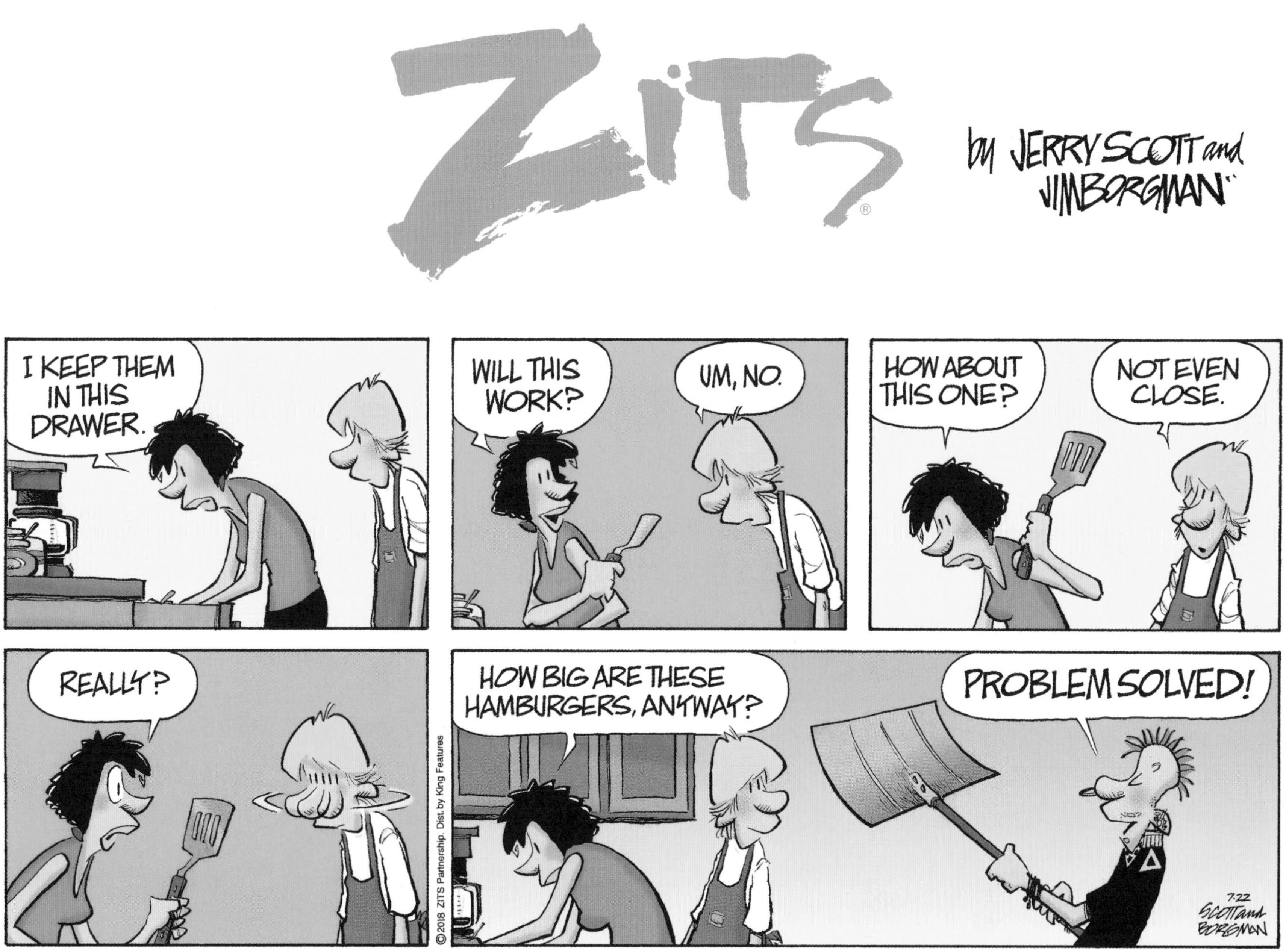
ZITS
by JERRY SCOTT and JIM BORGMAN
I KEEP THEM IN THIS DRAWER.
WILL THIS WORK?
UM, NO.
HOW ABOUT THIS ONE?
NOT EVEN CLOSE.
REALLY?
©2018 ZITS Partnership. Dist. by King Features
HOW BIG ARE THESE HAMBURGERS, ANYWAY?
PROBLEM SOLVED!
7-22
SCOTT and BORGMAN

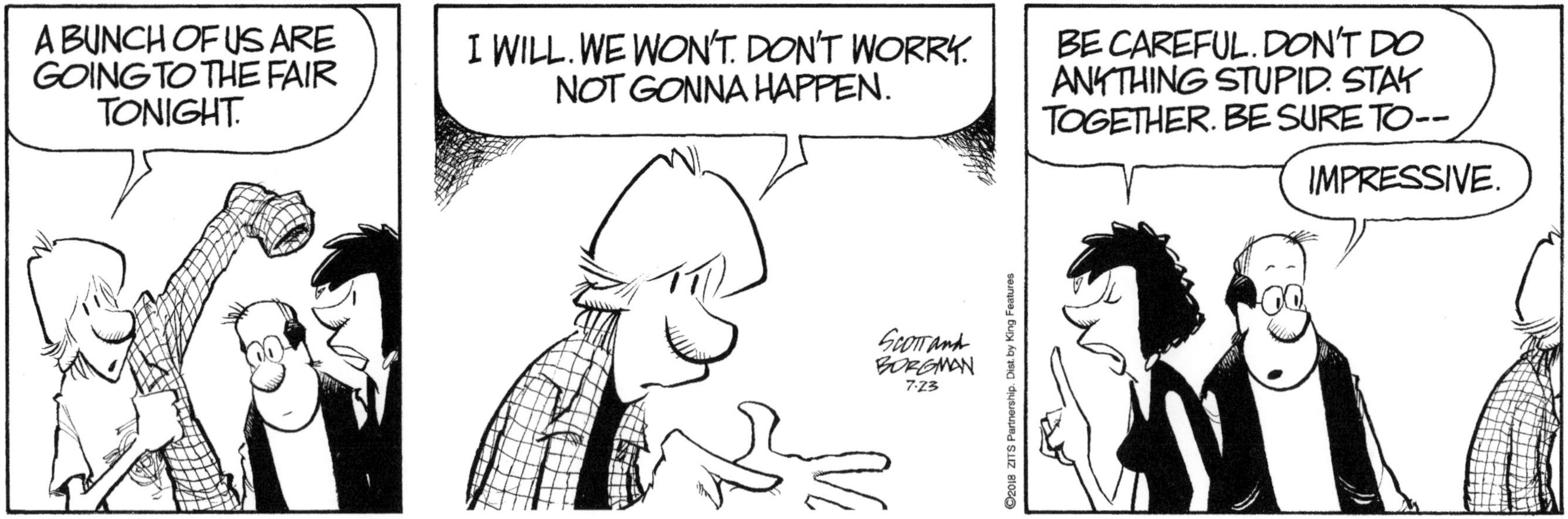
A BUNCH OF US ARE GOING TO THE FAIR TONIGHT.
I WILL. WE WON'T. DON'T WORRY. NOT GONNA HAPPEN.
SCOTT AND BORGMAN 7-23
BE CAREFUL. DON'T DO ANYTHING STUPID. STAY TOGETHER. BE SURE TO--
IMPRESSIVE.
©2018 ZITS Partnership. Dist. by King Features

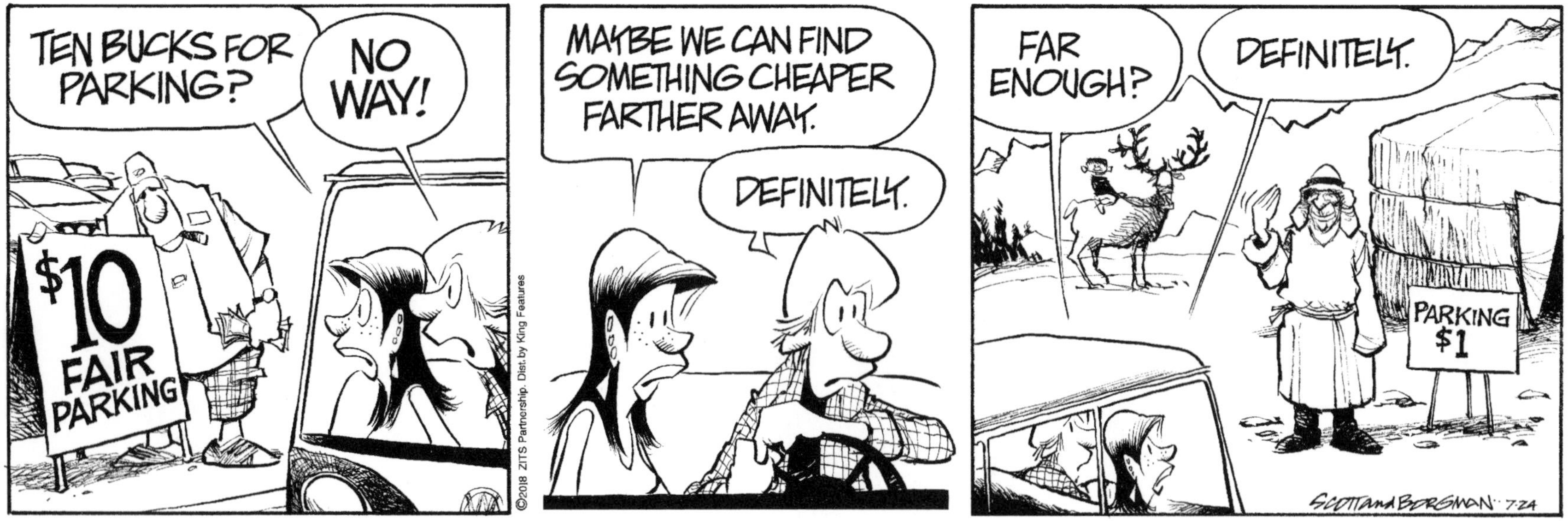
TEN BUCKS FOR PARKING?
NO WAY!
$10 FAIR PARKING
©2018 ZITS Partnership. Dist. by King Features
MAYBE WE CAN FIND SOMETHING CHEAPER FARTHER AWAY.
DEFINITELY.
FAR ENOUGH?
DEFINITELY.
PARKING $1
SCOTT AND BORGMAN 7-24

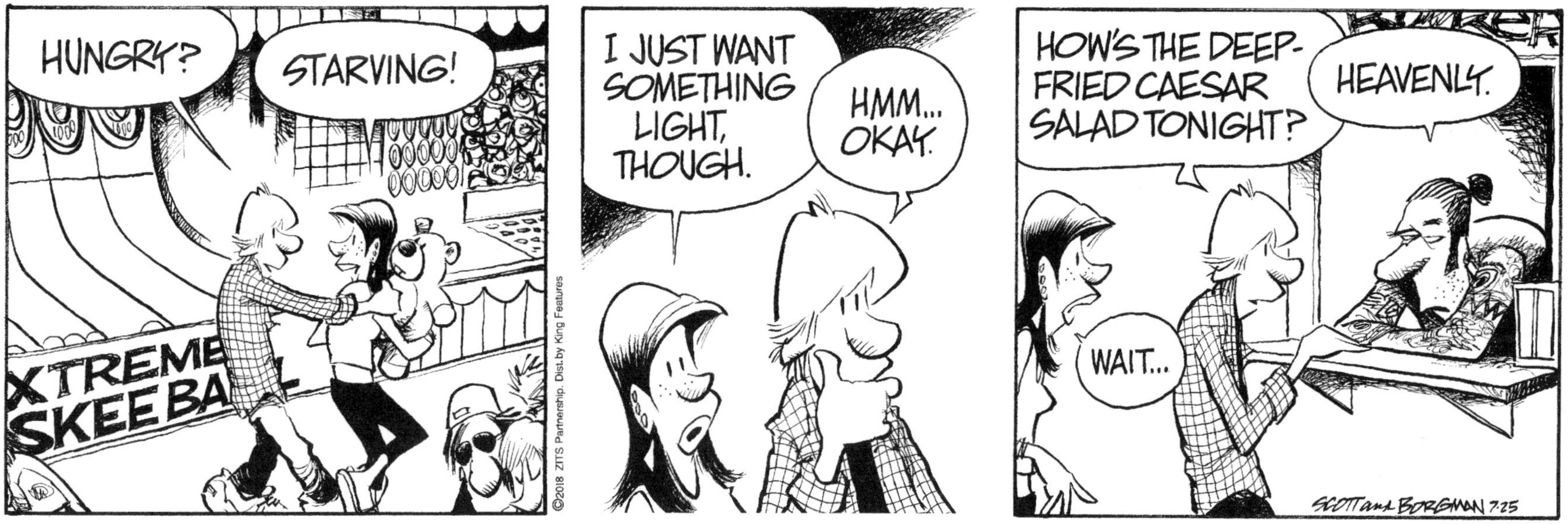
HUNGRY?
STARVING!
XTREME SKEE BA
©2018 ZITS Partnership. Dist. by King Features
I JUST WANT SOMETHING LIGHT, THOUGH.
HMM... OKAY.
HOW'S THE DEEP-FRIED CAESAR SALAD TONIGHT?
HEAVENLY.
WAIT...
SCOTT and BORGMAN 7-25

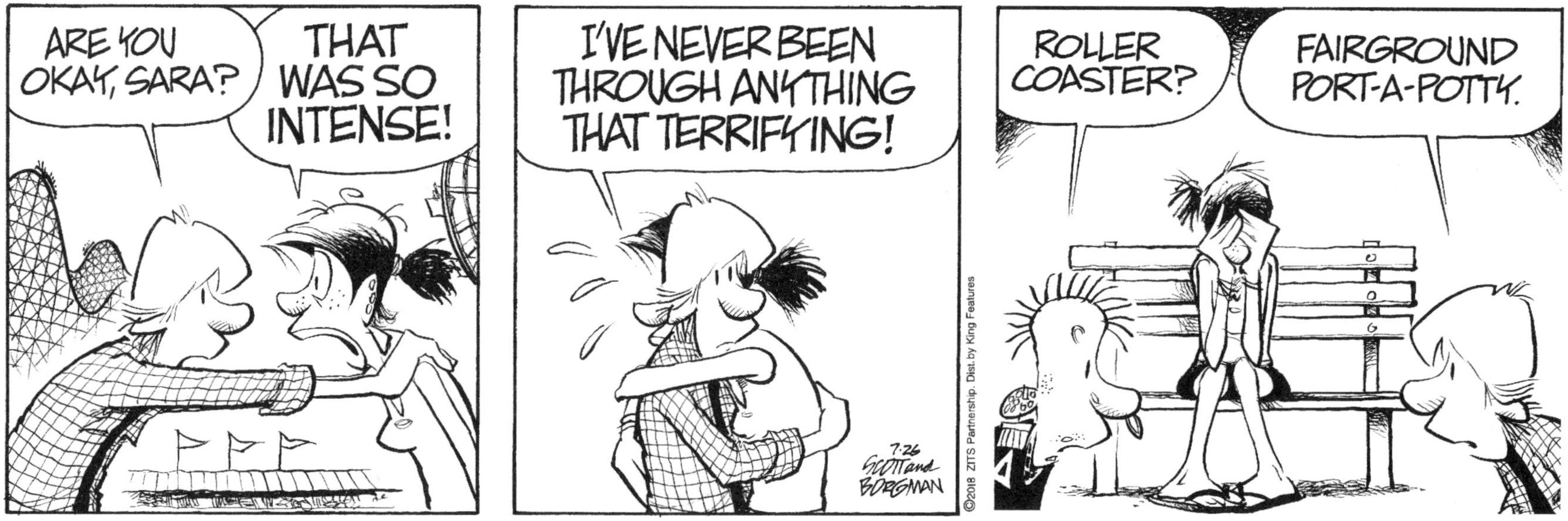
ARE YOU OKAY, SARA?
THAT WAS SO INTENSE!
I'VE NEVER BEEN THROUGH ANYTHING THAT TERRIFYING!
7-26 SCOTT and BORGMAN
©2018 ZITS Partnership. Dist. by King Features
ROLLER COASTER?
FAIRGROUND PORT-A-POTTY.

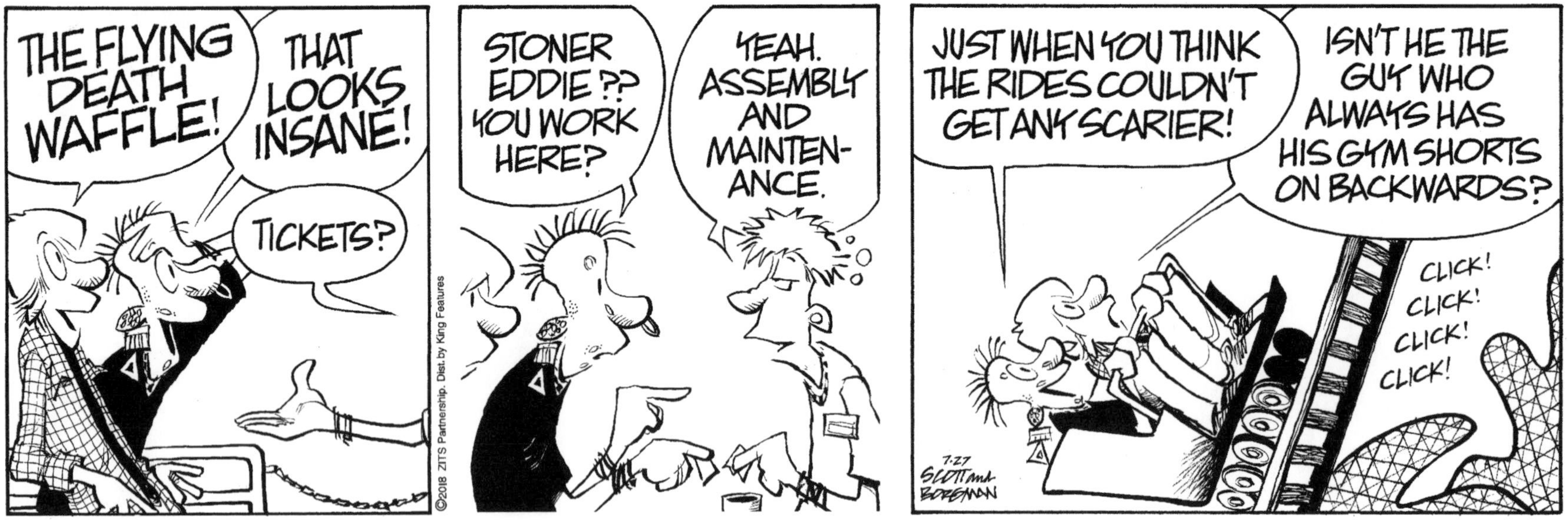
THE FLYING DEATH WAFFLE!
THAT LOOKS INSANE!
TICKETS?
STONER EDDIE?? YOU WORK HERE?
YEAH. ASSEMBLY AND MAINTEN-ANCE.
JUST WHEN YOU THINK THE RIDES COULDN'T GET ANY SCARIER!
ISN'T HE THE GUY WHO ALWAYS HAS HIS GYM SHORTS ON BACKWARDS?
CLICK!
CLICK!
CLICK!
CLICK!
7-27
SCOTT AND BORGMAN
©2018 ZITS Partnership. Dist. by King Features

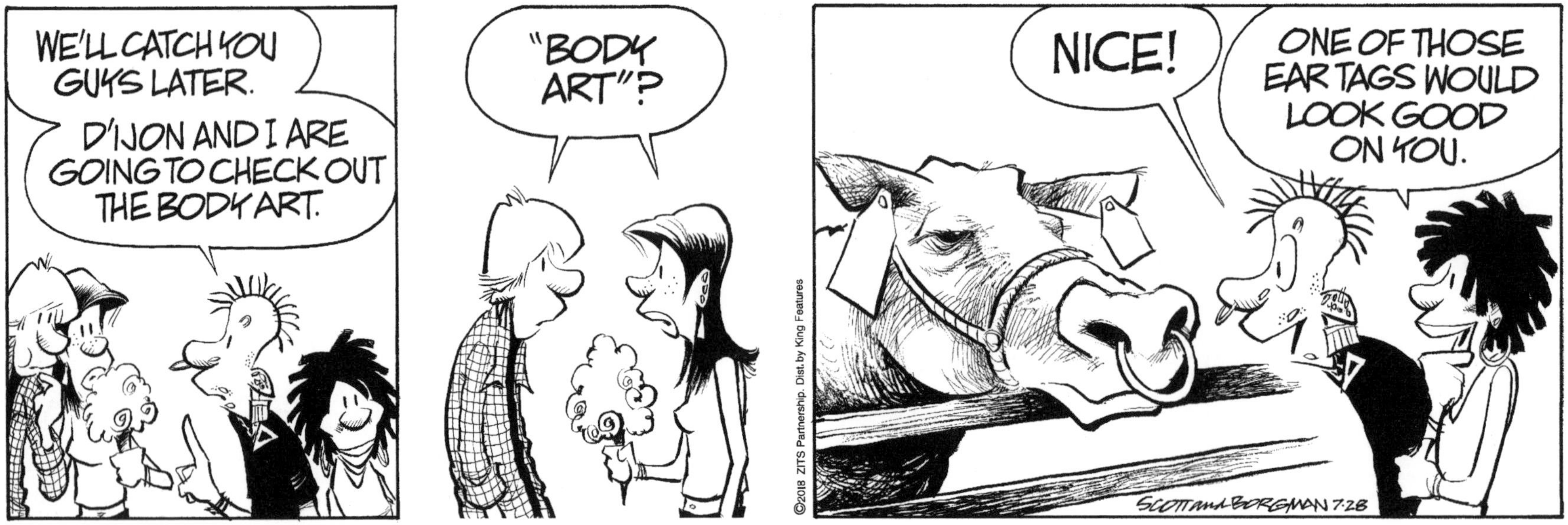
WE'LL CATCH YOU GUYS LATER.
D'IJON AND I ARE GOING TO CHECK OUT THE BODY ART.
"BODY ART"?
NICE!
ONE OF THOSE EAR TAGS WOULD LOOK GOOD ON YOU.
SCOTT AND BORGMAN 7-28
©2018 ZITS Partnership. Dist. by King Features

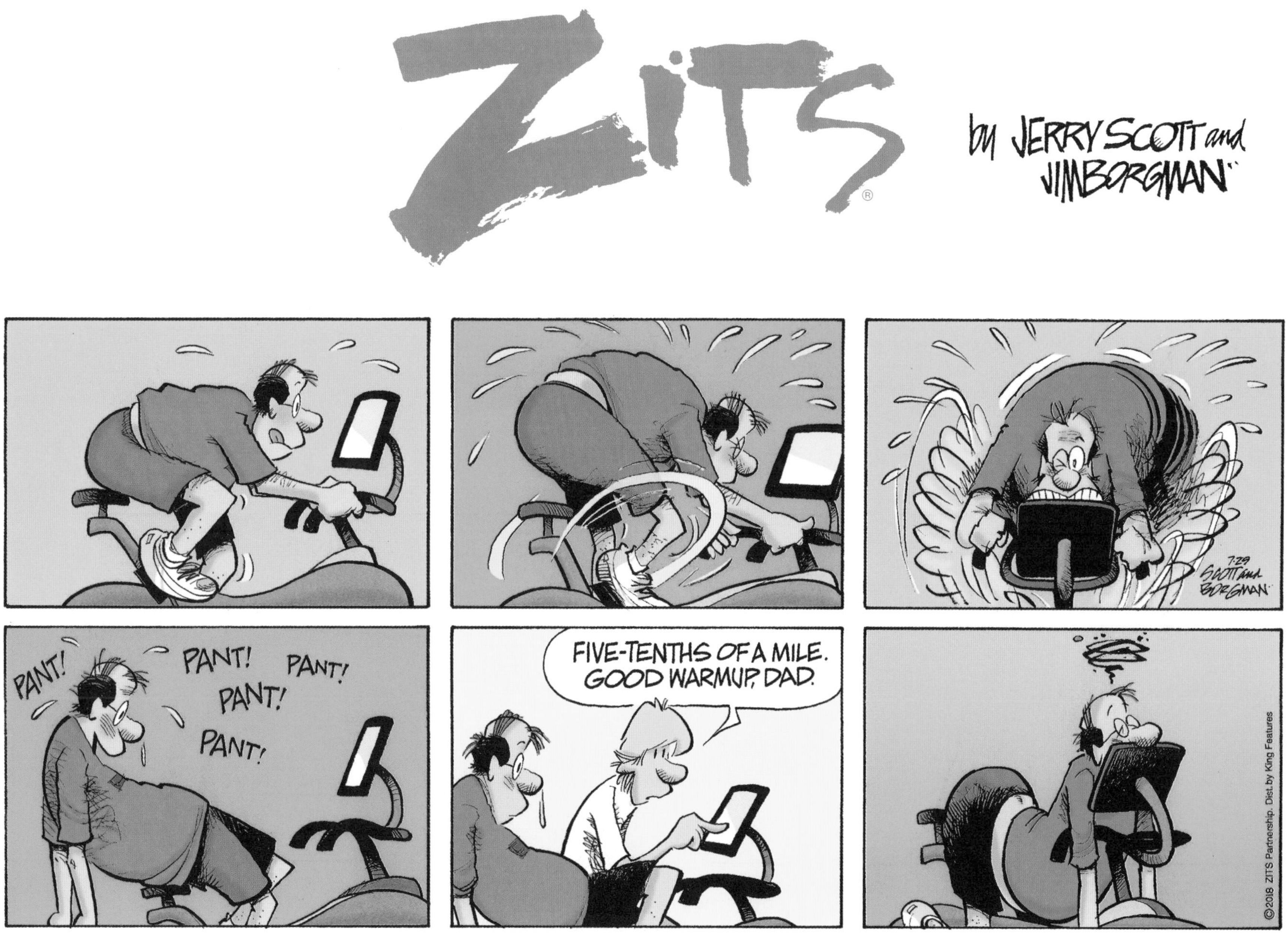
ZITS®
by JERRY SCOTT and JIM BORGMAN
7-29 SCOTT and BORGMAN
PANT! PANT! PANT! PANT! PANT!
FIVE-TENTHS OF A MILE. GOOD WARMUP, DAD.
©2018 ZITS Partnership. Dist. by King Features

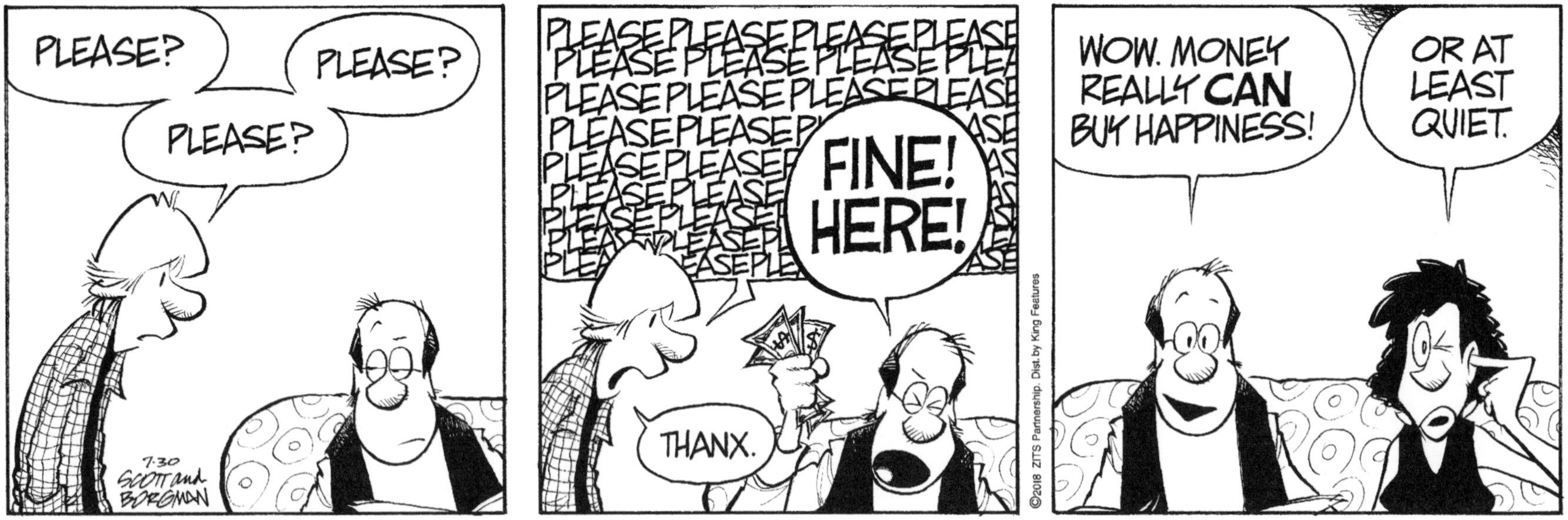
PLEASE?
PLEASE?
PLEASE?
7-30
SCOTT and BORGMAN
PLEASE PLEASE PLEASE PLEASE
FINE! HERE!
THANX.
©2018 ZITS Partnership. Dist. by King Features
WOW. MONEY REALLY **CAN** BUY HAPPINESS!
OR AT LEAST QUIET.

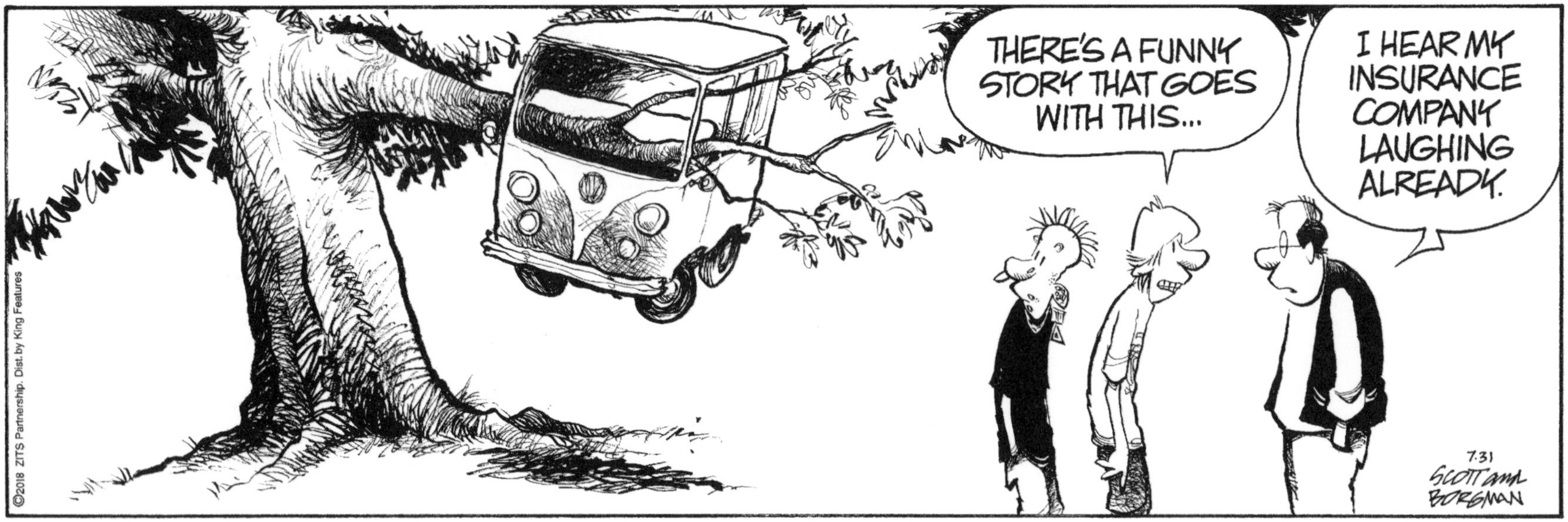
THERE'S A FUNNY STORY THAT GOES WITH THIS...
I HEAR MY INSURANCE COMPANY LAUGHING ALREADY.
©2018 ZITS Partnership. Dist. by King Features
7-31
SCOTT and BORGMAN

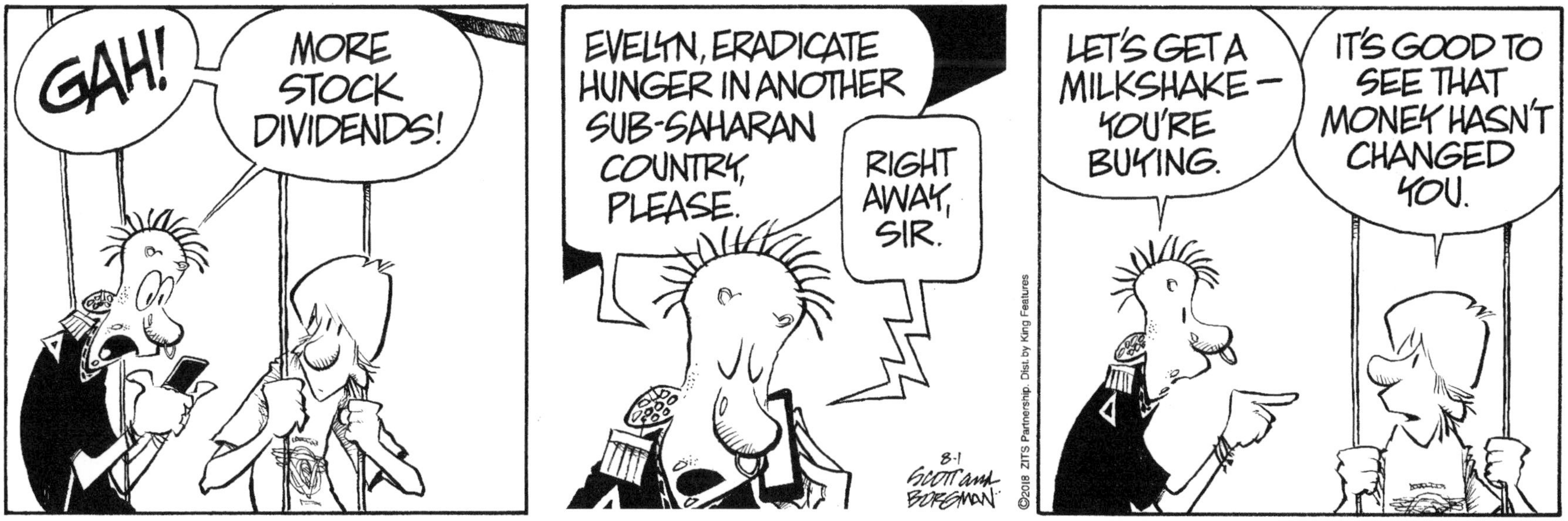
GAH!
MORE STOCK DIVIDENDS!
EVELYN, ERADICATE HUNGER IN ANOTHER SUB-SAHARAN COUNTRY, PLEASE.
RIGHT AWAY, SIR.
8-1
SCOTT and BORGMAN
©2018 ZITS Partnership. Dist. by King Features
LET'S GET A MILKSHAKE — YOU'RE BUYING.
IT'S GOOD TO SEE THAT MONEY HASN'T CHANGED YOU.

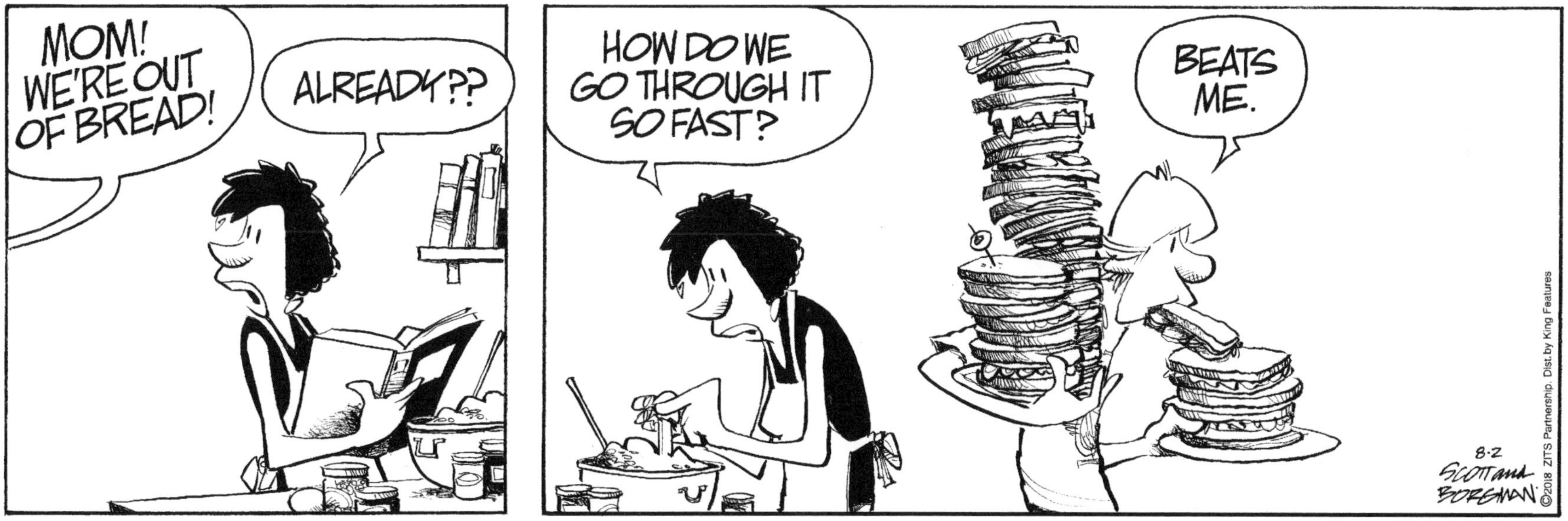
MOM! WE'RE OUT OF BREAD!
ALREADY??
HOW DO WE GO THROUGH IT SO FAST?
BEATS ME.
8-2
SCOTT and BORGMAN
©2018 ZITS Partnership. Dist. by King Features

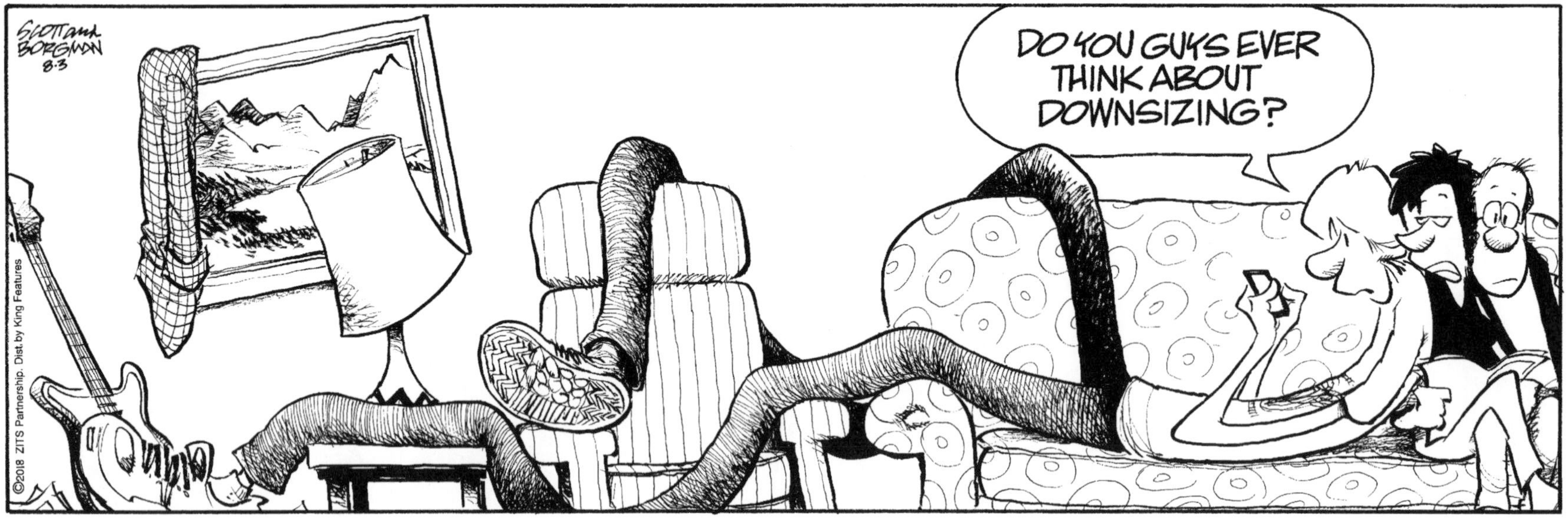
DO YOU GUYS EVER THINK ABOUT DOWNSIZING?

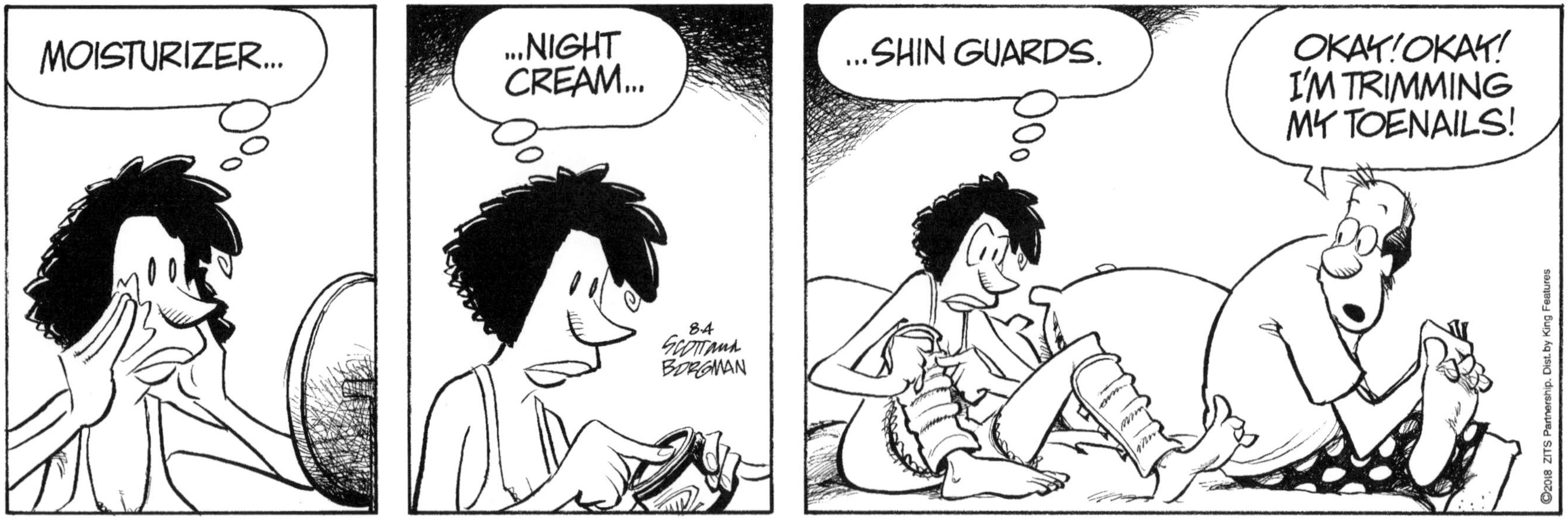
MOISTURIZER...
...NIGHT CREAM...
...SHIN GUARDS.
OKAY! OKAY! I'M TRIMMING MY TOENAILS!

ZITS

by JERRY SCOTT and JIM BORGMAN

WHOA.
IT'S SO BEAUTIFUL!
I JUST THINK--
WHAT?
NEVER MIND. IT'S STUPID.
TELL ME!
NO. IT'S STUPID.
COME ON! I WANT TO KNOW WHAT YOU WERE GOING TO SAY!
ARE YOU SURE?
I GUARANTEE THAT NOTHING YOU SAY ON A NIGHT LIKE THIS COULD BE STUPID.
I WAS JUST THINKING THAT KANGAROOS LOOK LIKE GIANT MICE.
GUARANTEE REVOKED.
SCOTT and BORGMAN 8·5
©2018 ZITS Partnership. Dist. by King Features

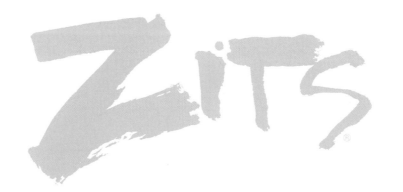

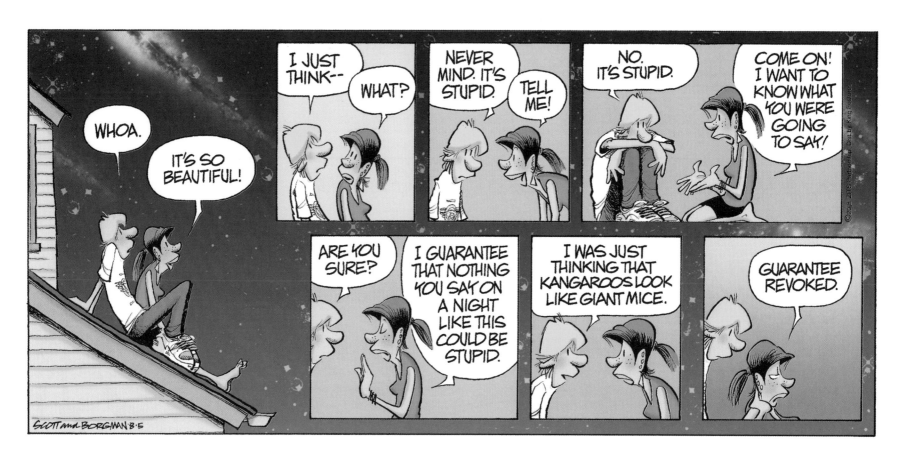

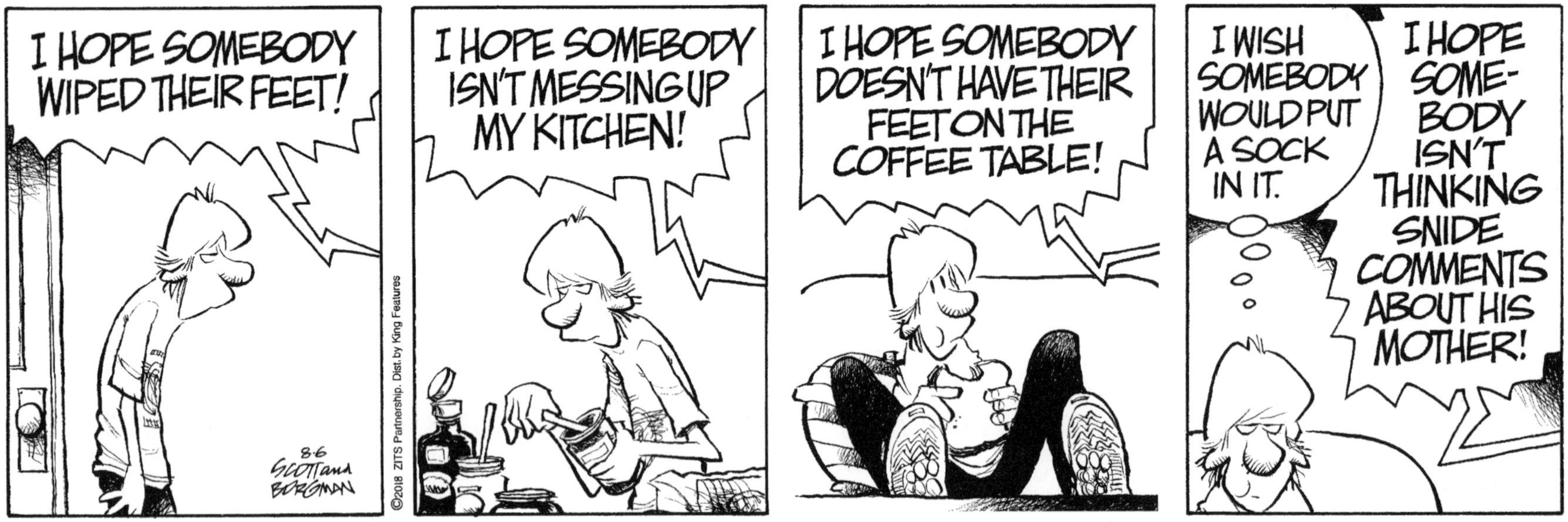
I HOPE SOMEBODY WIPED THEIR FEET!
8-6 SCOTT and BORGMAN
©2018 ZITS Partnership. Dist. by King Features
I HOPE SOMEBODY ISN'T MESSING UP MY KITCHEN!
I HOPE SOMEBODY DOESN'T HAVE THEIR FEET ON THE COFFEE TABLE!
I WISH SOMEBODY WOULD PUT A SOCK IN IT.
I HOPE SOME-BODY ISN'T THINKING SNIDE COMMENTS ABOUT HIS MOTHER!

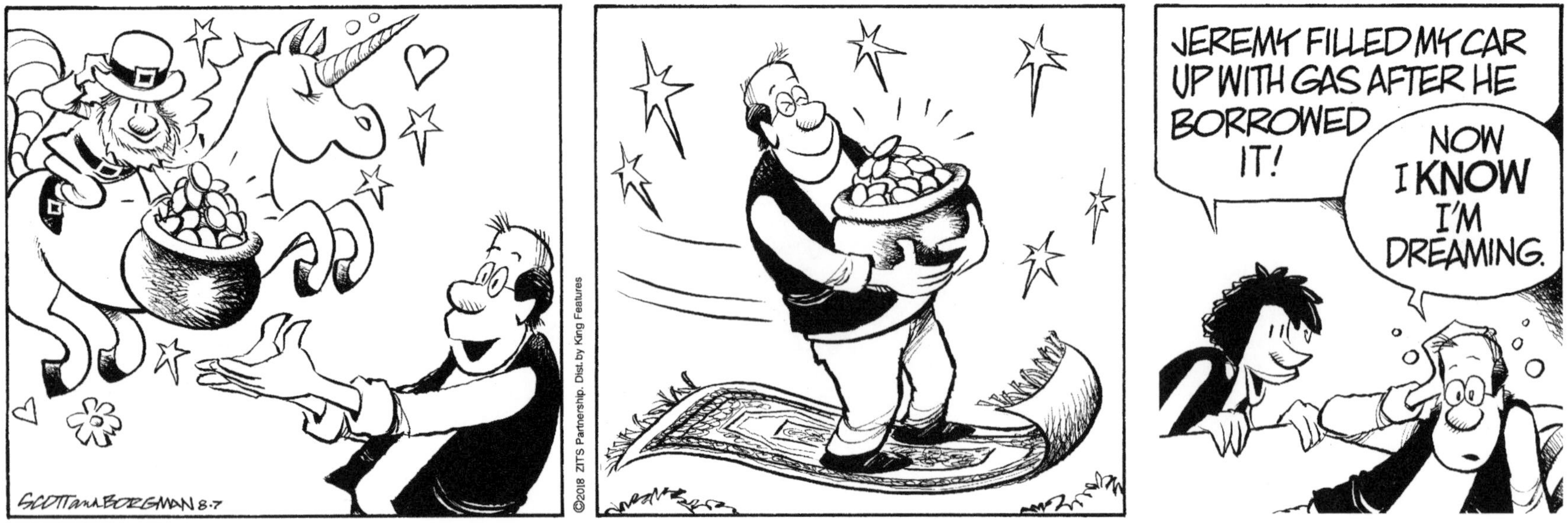
SCOTT and BORGMAN 8-7
©2018 ZITS Partnership. Dist. by King Features
JEREMY FILLED MY CAR UP WITH GAS AFTER HE BORROWED IT!
NOW I **KNOW** I'M DREAMING.

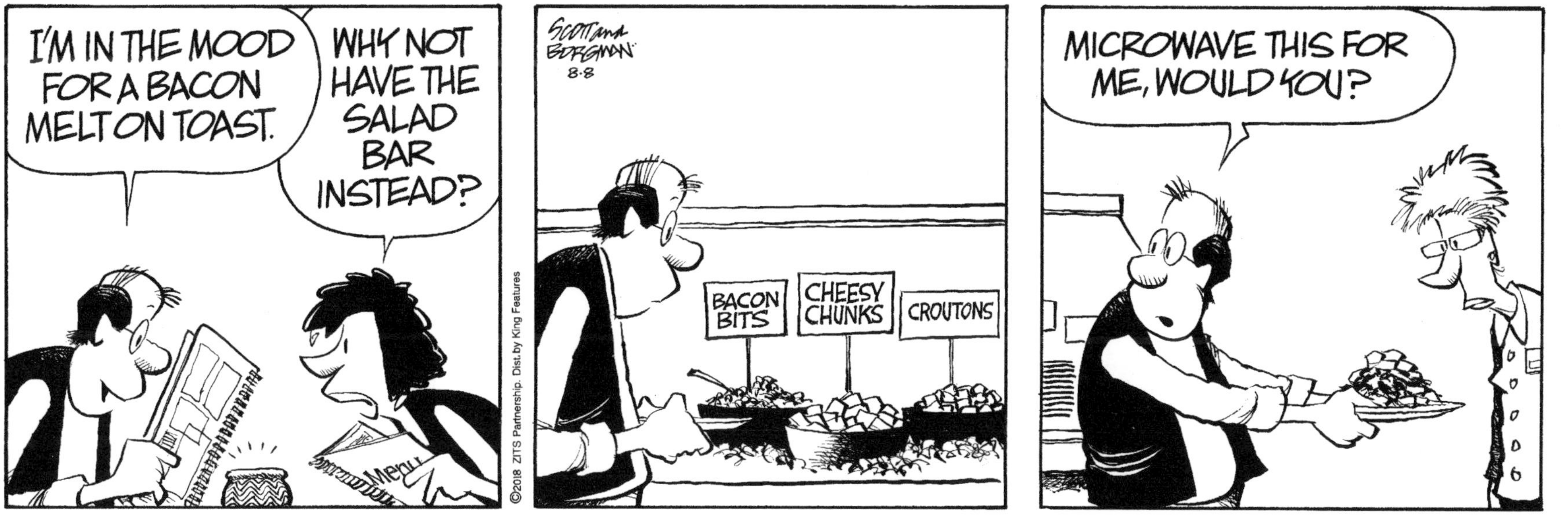
I'M IN THE MOOD FOR A BACON MELT ON TOAST.
WHY NOT HAVE THE SALAD BAR INSTEAD?
Menu
SCOTT and BORGMAN 8·8
©2018 ZITS Partnership. Dist.by King Features
BACON BITS
CHEESY CHUNKS
CROUTONS
MICROWAVE THIS FOR ME, WOULD YOU?

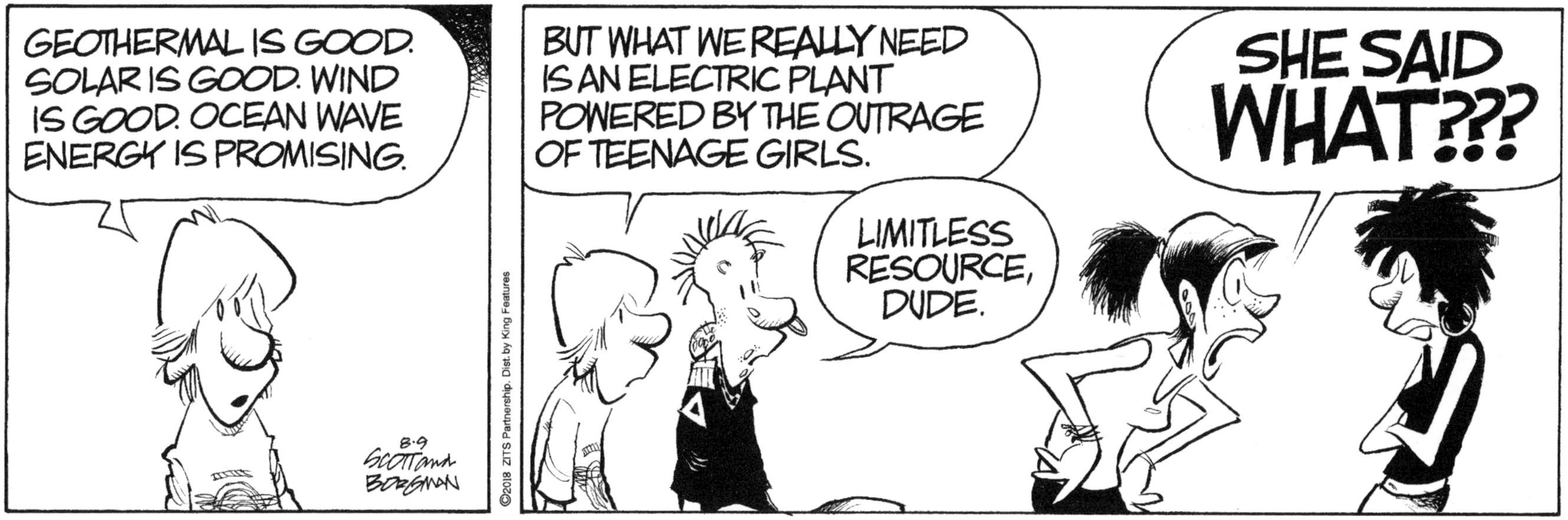
GEOTHERMAL IS GOOD. SOLAR IS GOOD. WIND IS GOOD. OCEAN WAVE ENERGY IS PROMISING.
8·9 SCOTT and BORGMAN
©2018 ZITS Partnership. Dist.by King Features
BUT WHAT WE REALLY NEED IS AN ELECTRIC PLANT POWERED BY THE OUTRAGE OF TEENAGE GIRLS.
LIMITLESS RESOURCE, DUDE.
SHE SAID WHAT???

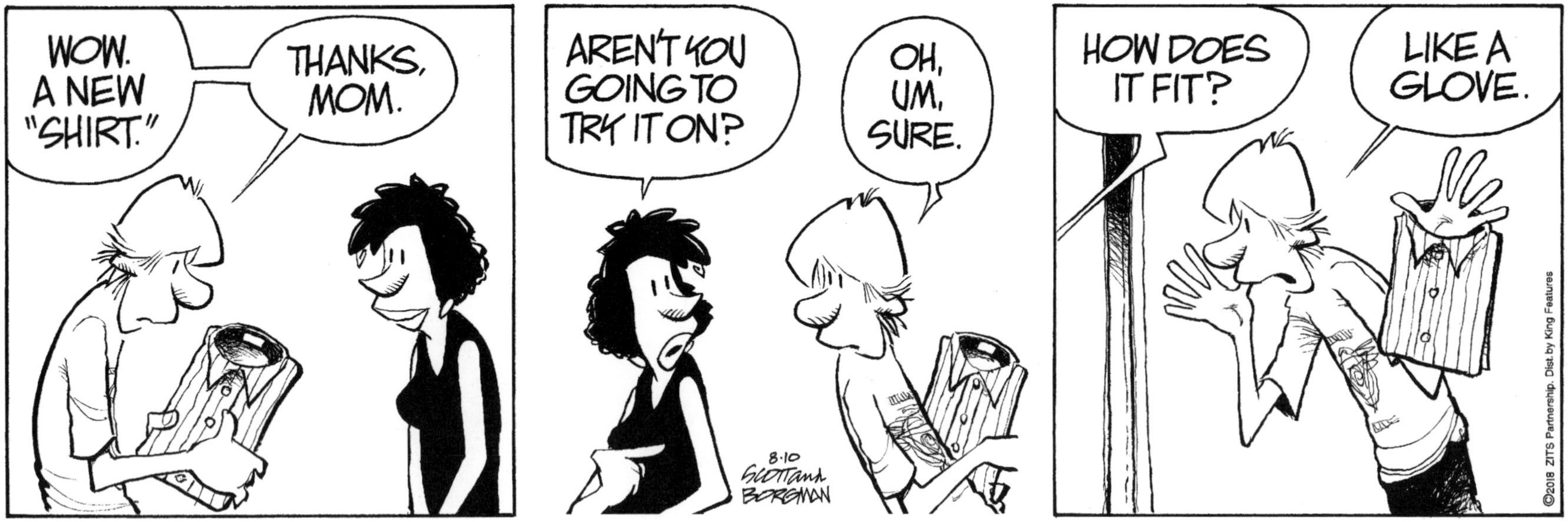
WOW. A NEW "SHIRT."
THANKS, MOM.
AREN'T YOU GOING TO TRY IT ON?
OH, UM, SURE.
HOW DOES IT FIT?
LIKE A GLOVE.
8·10 SCOTT AND BORGMAN
©2018 ZITS Partnership. Dist. by King Features

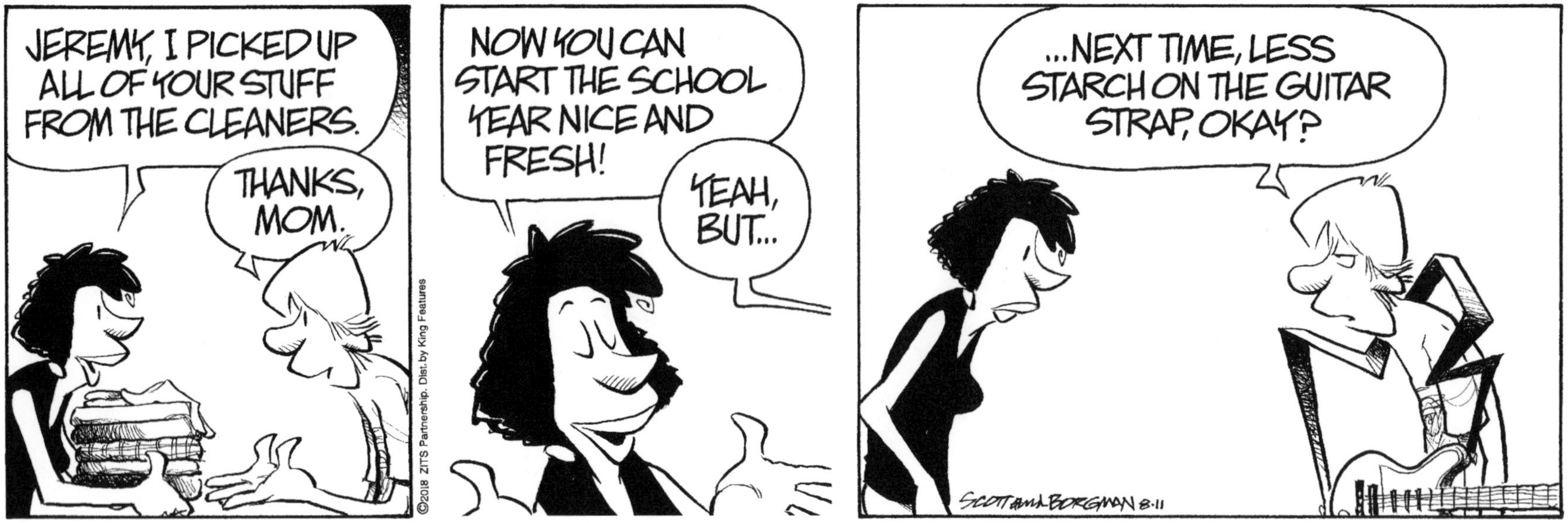
JEREMY, I PICKED UP ALL OF YOUR STUFF FROM THE CLEANERS.
THANKS, MOM.
©2018 ZITS Partnership. Dist. by King Features
NOW YOU CAN START THE SCHOOL YEAR NICE AND FRESH!
YEAH, BUT...
...NEXT TIME, LESS STARCH ON THE GUITAR STRAP, OKAY?
SCOTT AND BORGMAN 8·11

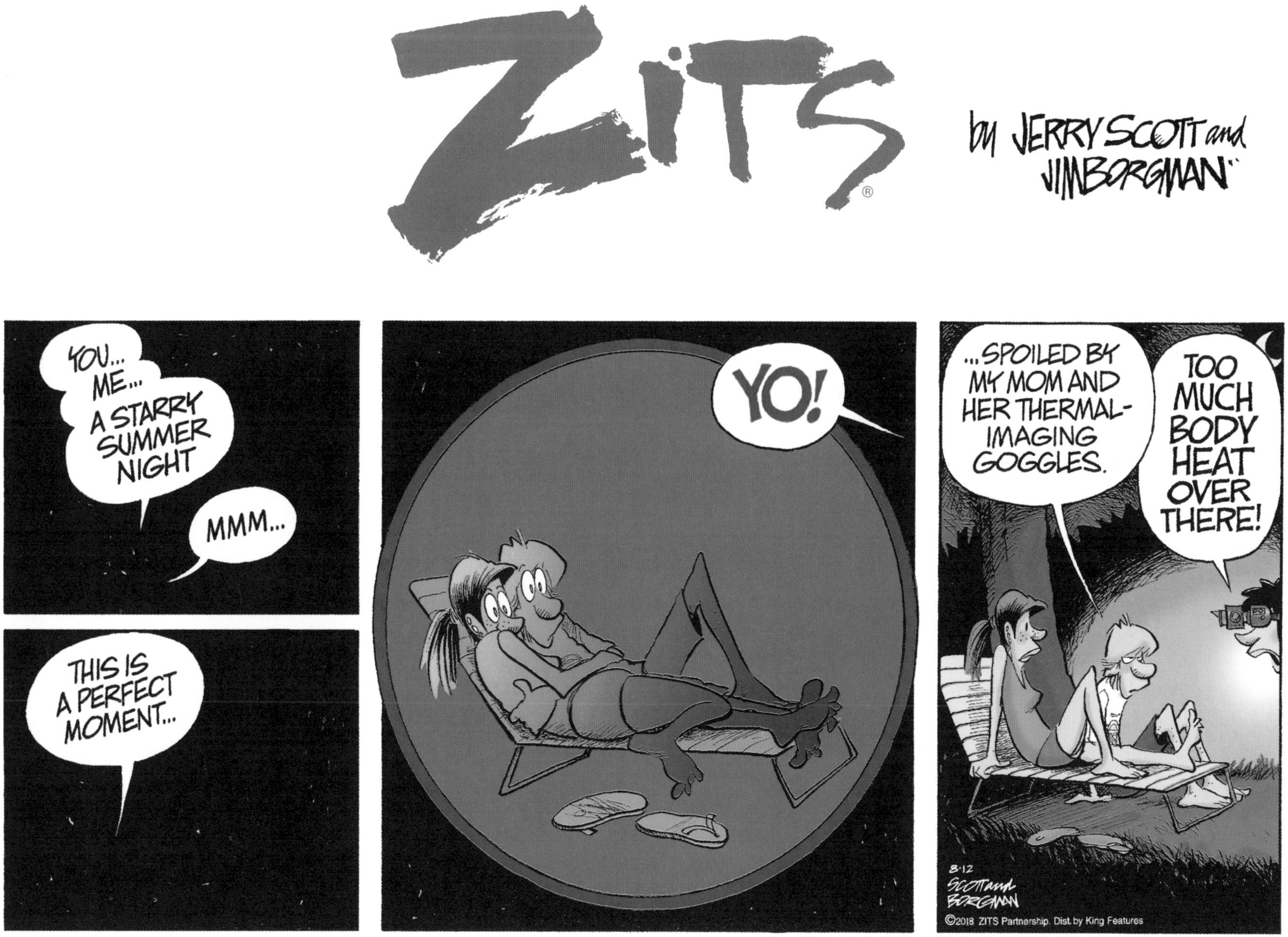
ZITS
by JERRY SCOTT and JIM BORGMAN
YOU... ME... A STARRY SUMMER NIGHT
MMM...
THIS IS A PERFECT MOMENT...
YO!
...SPOILED BY MY MOM AND HER THERMAL-IMAGING GOGGLES.
TOO MUCH BODY HEAT OVER THERE!
8·12
SCOTT and BORGMAN
©2018 ZITS Partnership. Dist. by King Features

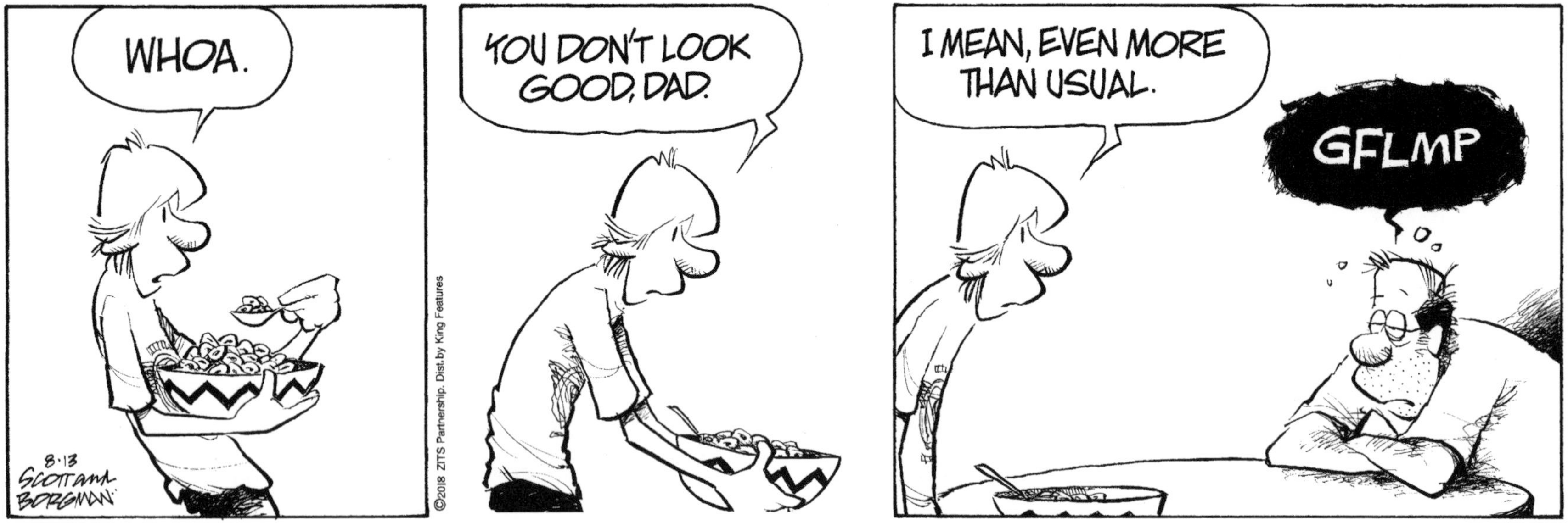
WHOA.
8·13
SCOTT and BORGMAN
YOU DON'T LOOK GOOD, DAD.
©2018 ZITS Partnership. Dist. by King Features
I MEAN, EVEN MORE THAN USUAL.
GFLMP

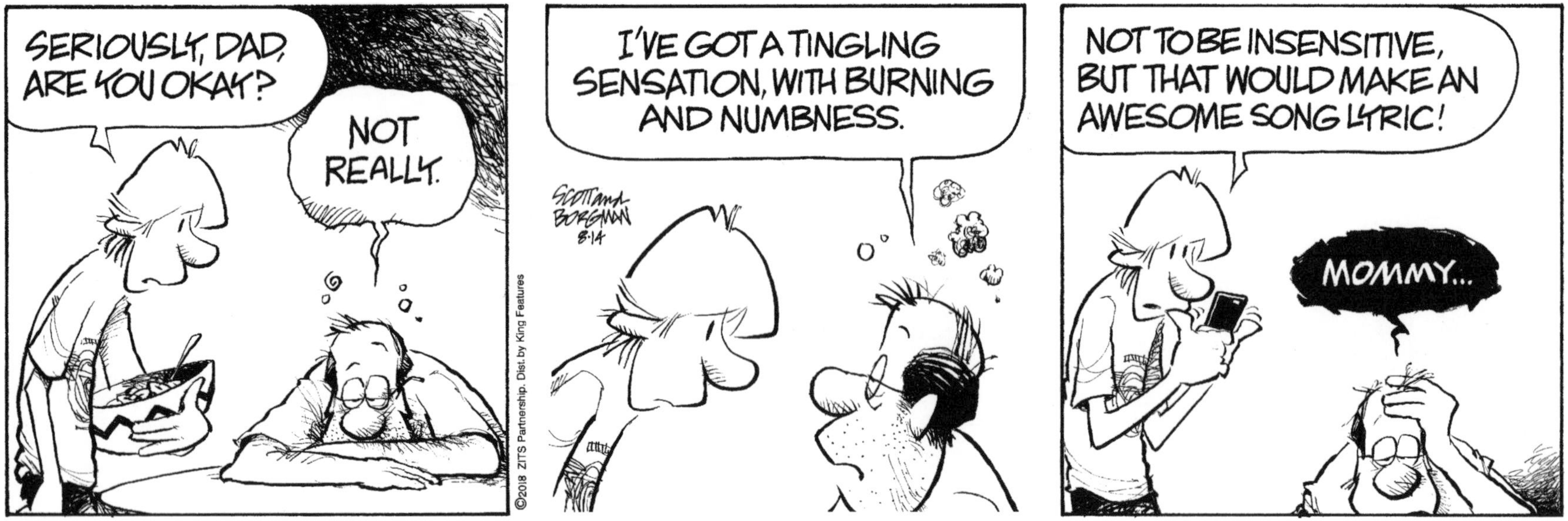
SERIOUSLY, DAD, ARE YOU OKAY?
NOT REALLY.
©2018 ZITS Partnership. Dist. by King Features
I'VE GOT A TINGLING SENSATION, WITH BURNING AND NUMBNESS.
SCOTT and BORGMAN 8·14
NOT TO BE INSENSITIVE, BUT THAT WOULD MAKE AN AWESOME SONG LYRIC!
MOMMY...

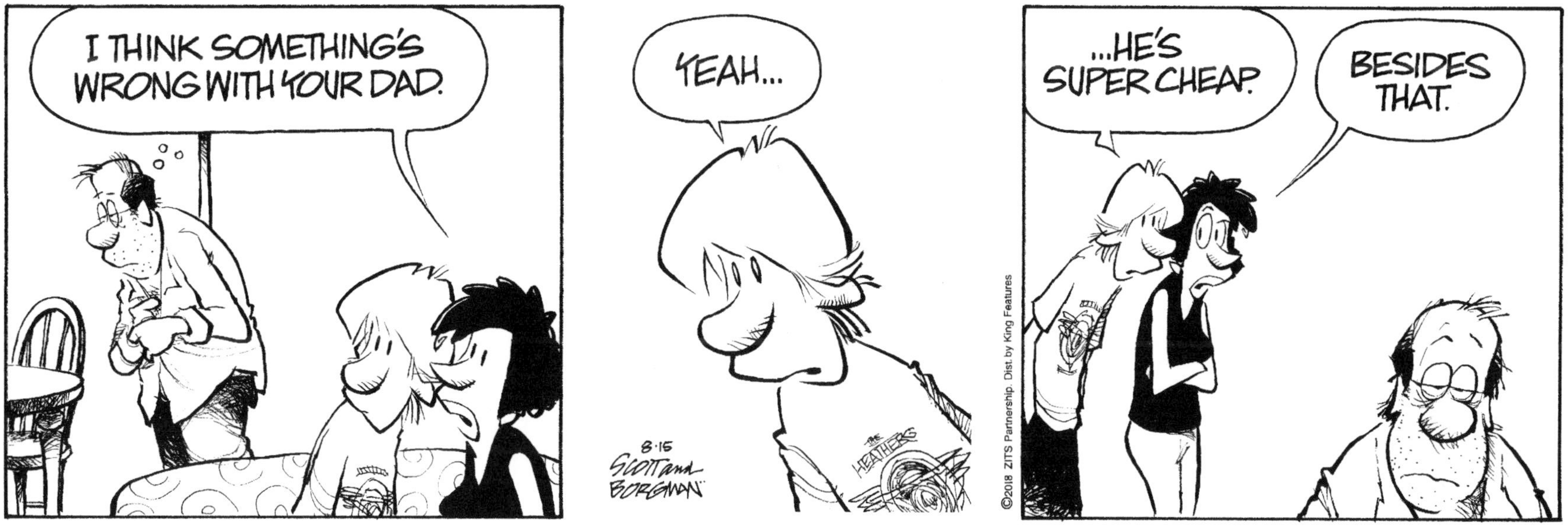
I THINK SOMETHING'S WRONG WITH YOUR DAD.
YEAH...
...HE'S SUPER CHEAP.
BESIDES THAT.
8·15 SCOTT and BORGMAN
THE HEATHERS
©2018 ZITS Partnership. Dist. by King Features

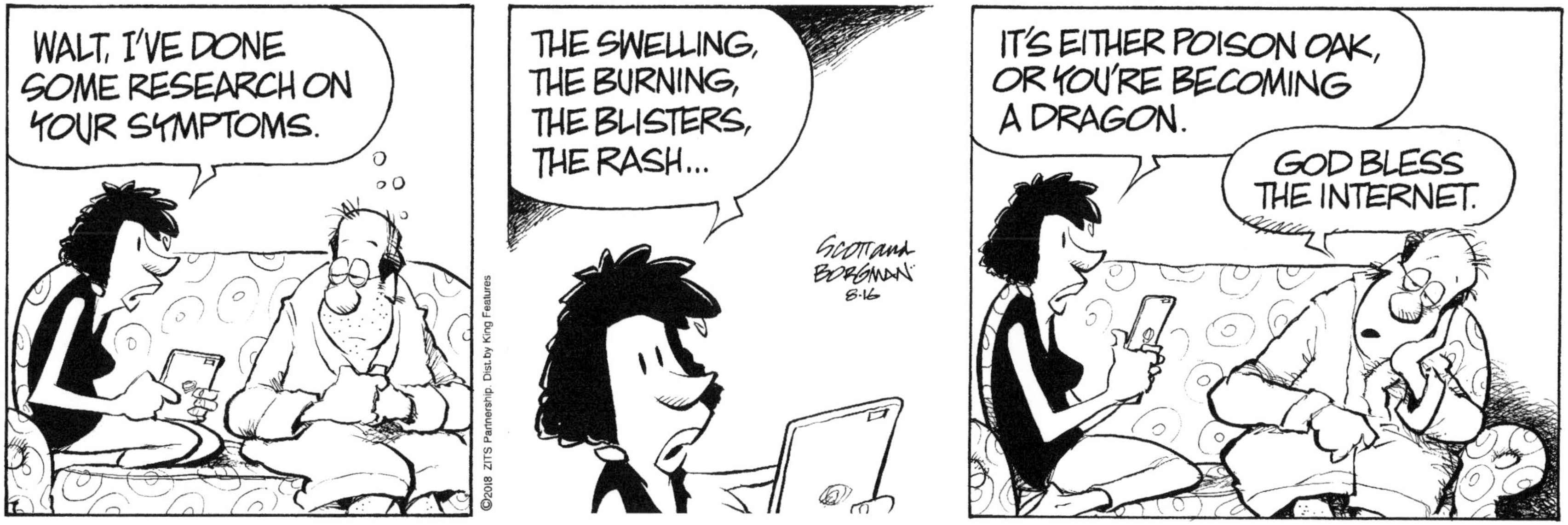
WALT, I'VE DONE SOME RESEARCH ON YOUR SYMPTOMS.
THE SWELLING, THE BURNING, THE BLISTERS, THE RASH...
IT'S EITHER POISON OAK, OR YOU'RE BECOMING A DRAGON.
GOD BLESS THE INTERNET.
SCOTT and BORGMAN 8·16
©2018 ZITS Partnership. Dist. by King Features

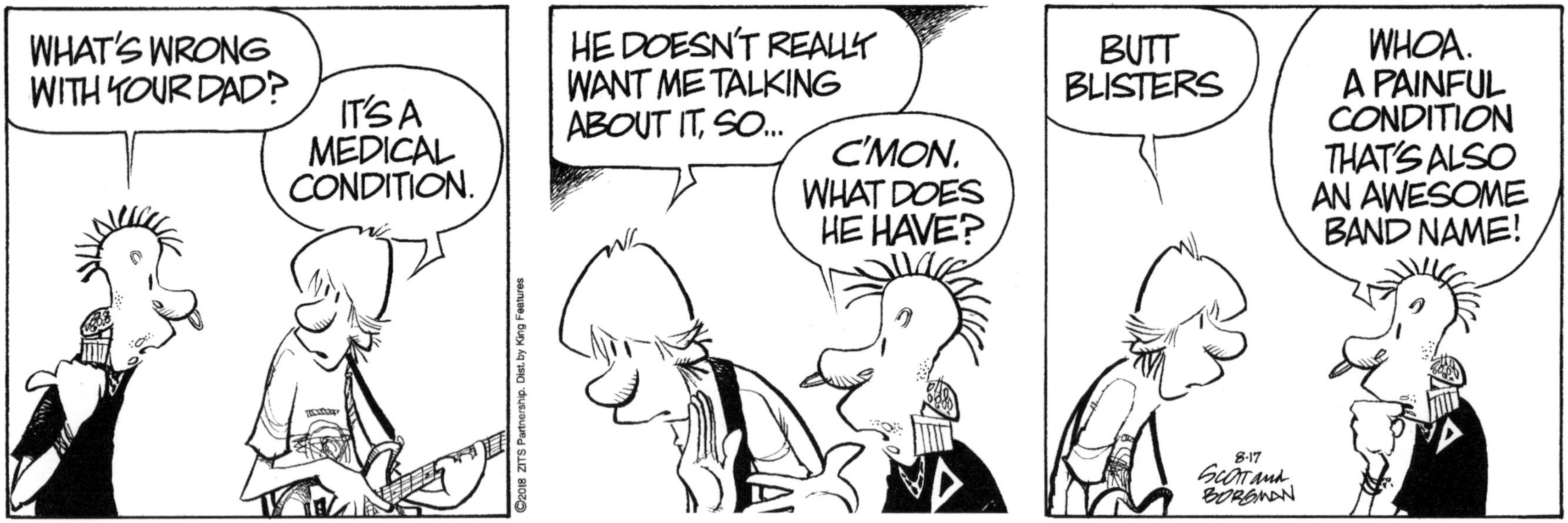
WHAT'S WRONG WITH YOUR DAD?
IT'S A MEDICAL CONDITION.
HE DOESN'T REALLY WANT ME TALKING ABOUT IT, SO...
C'MON. WHAT DOES HE HAVE?
BUTT BLISTERS
WHOA. A PAINFUL CONDITION THAT'S ALSO AN AWESOME BAND NAME!
©2018 ZITS Partnership. Dist. by King Features
8·17 SCOTT and BORGMAN

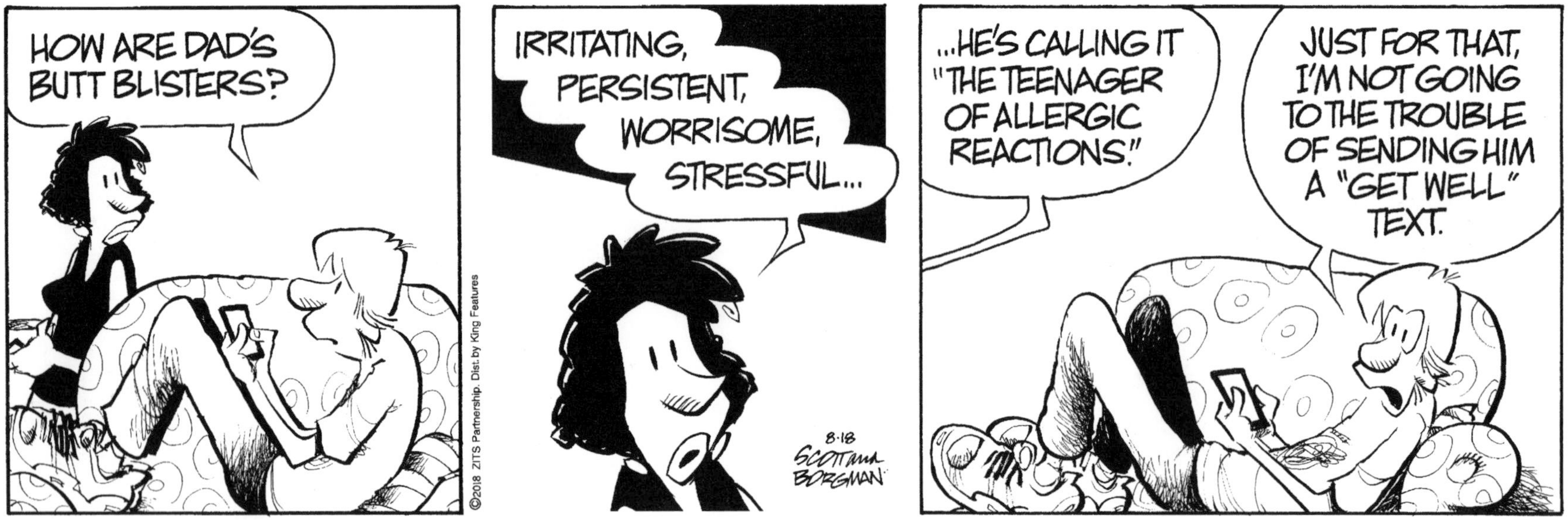
HOW ARE DAD'S BUTT BLISTERS?
IRRITATING, PERSISTENT, WORRISOME, STRESSFUL...
...HE'S CALLING IT "THE TEENAGER OF ALLERGIC REACTIONS."
JUST FOR THAT, I'M NOT GOING TO THE TROUBLE OF SENDING HIM A "GET WELL" TEXT.
©2018 ZITS Partnership. Dist. by King Features
8·18 SCOTT and BORGMAN

ZITS

by JERRY SCOTT and JIM BORGMAN

OH MY GOSH!
LOOK! RIGHT HERE IN OUR KITCHEN!
IT'S THE MYTHICAL AND ELUSIVE...
...TEENAGER UP BEFORE NOON ON A SUNDAY!
QUICK! SNAP A BLURRY PICTURE!
SCOTT and BORGMAN
8-19
©2014, ZITS Partnership. Dist. by King Features

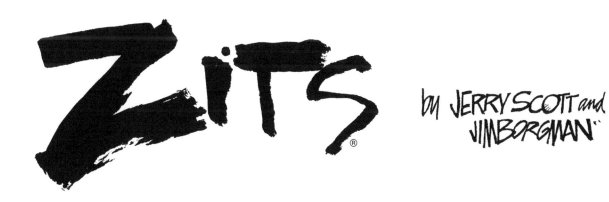

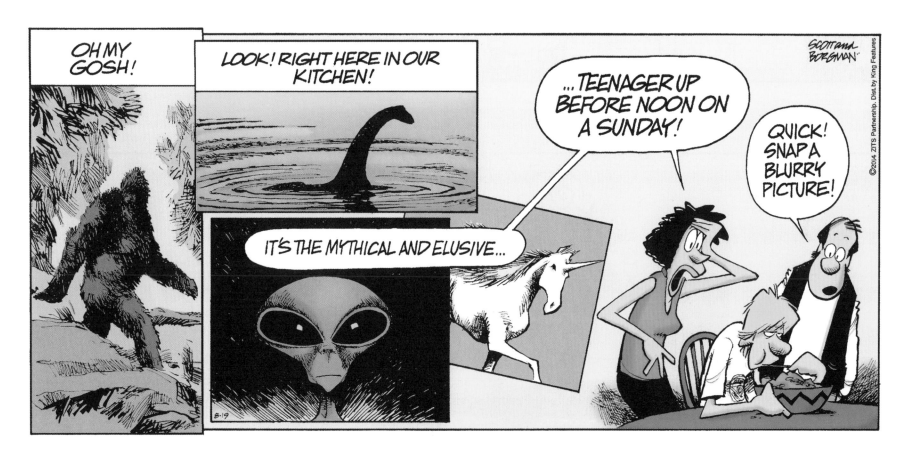

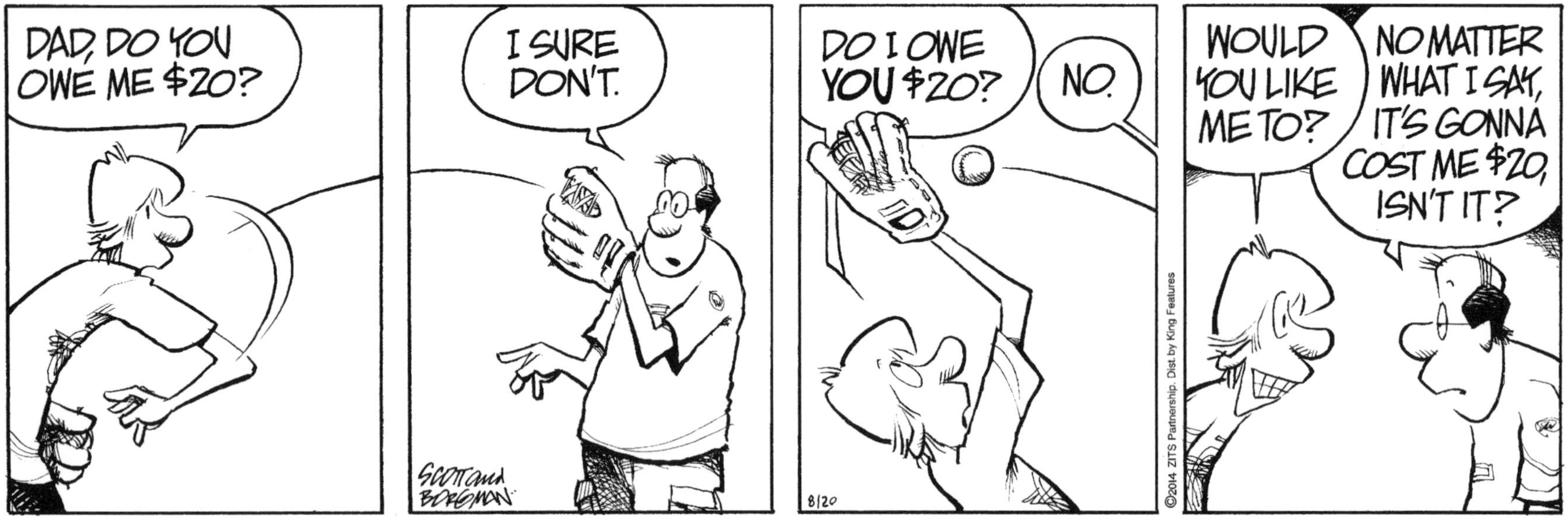
DAD, DO YOU OWE ME $20?
I SURE DON'T.
SCOTT and BORGMAN
DO I OWE YOU $20?
NO.
8/20
WOULD YOU LIKE ME TO?
NO MATTER WHAT I SAY, IT'S GONNA COST ME $20, ISN'T IT?
©2014 ZITS Partnership. Dist. by King Features

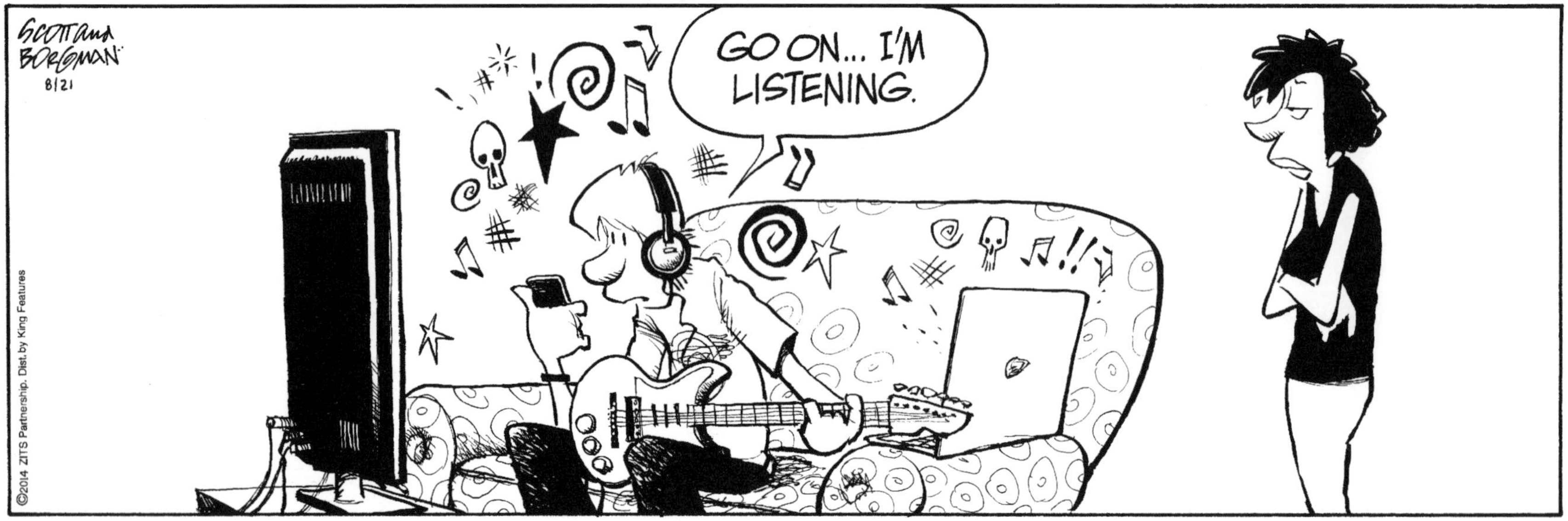
SCOTT and BORGMAN
8/21
GO ON... I'M LISTENING.
©2014 ZITS Partnership. Dist. by King Features

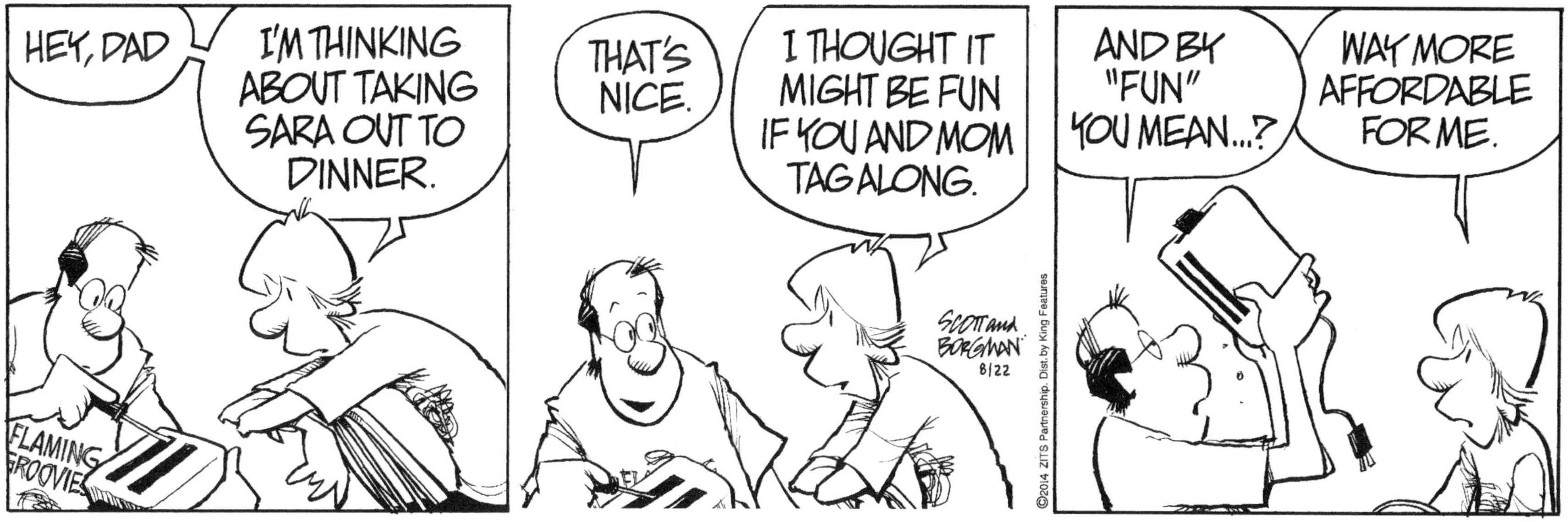
HEY, DAD
I'M THINKING ABOUT TAKING SARA OUT TO DINNER.
FLAMING GROOVIES
THAT'S NICE.
I THOUGHT IT MIGHT BE FUN IF YOU AND MOM TAG ALONG.
SCOTT and BORGMAN 8/22
©2014 ZITS Partnership. Dist. by King Features
AND BY "FUN" YOU MEAN...?
WAY MORE AFFORDABLE FOR ME.

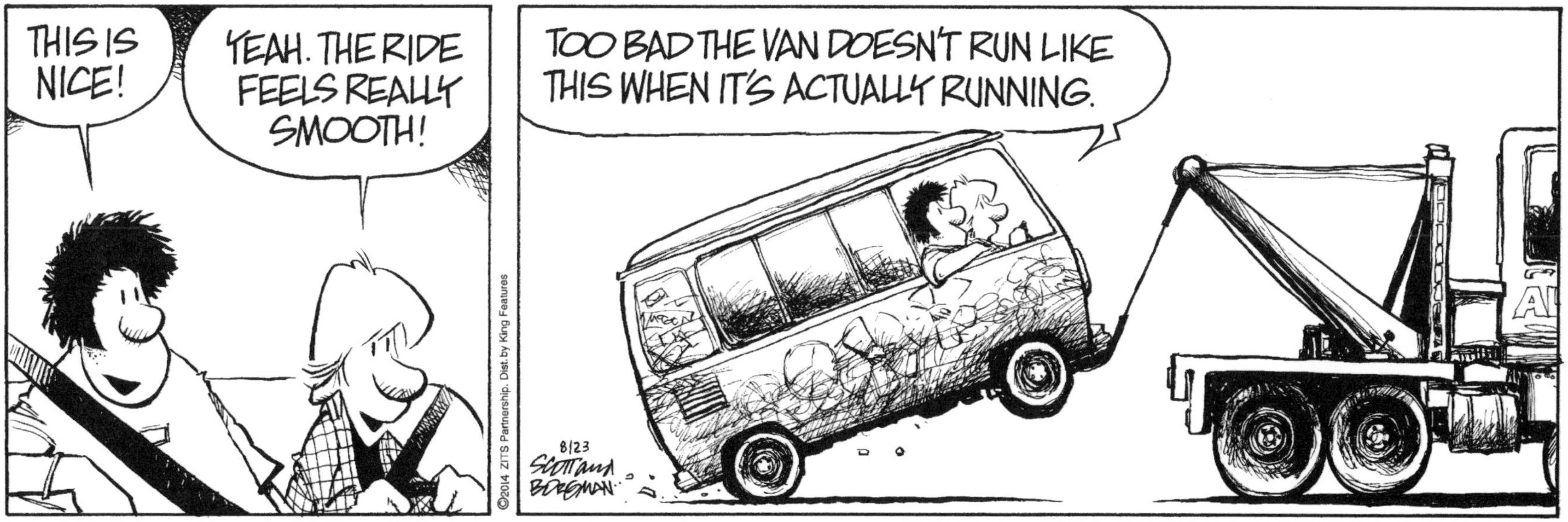
THIS IS NICE!
YEAH. THE RIDE FEELS REALLY SMOOTH!
©2014 ZITS Partnership. Dist. by King Features
TOO BAD THE VAN DOESN'T RUN LIKE THIS WHEN IT'S ACTUALLY RUNNING.
8/23 SCOTT and BORGMAN

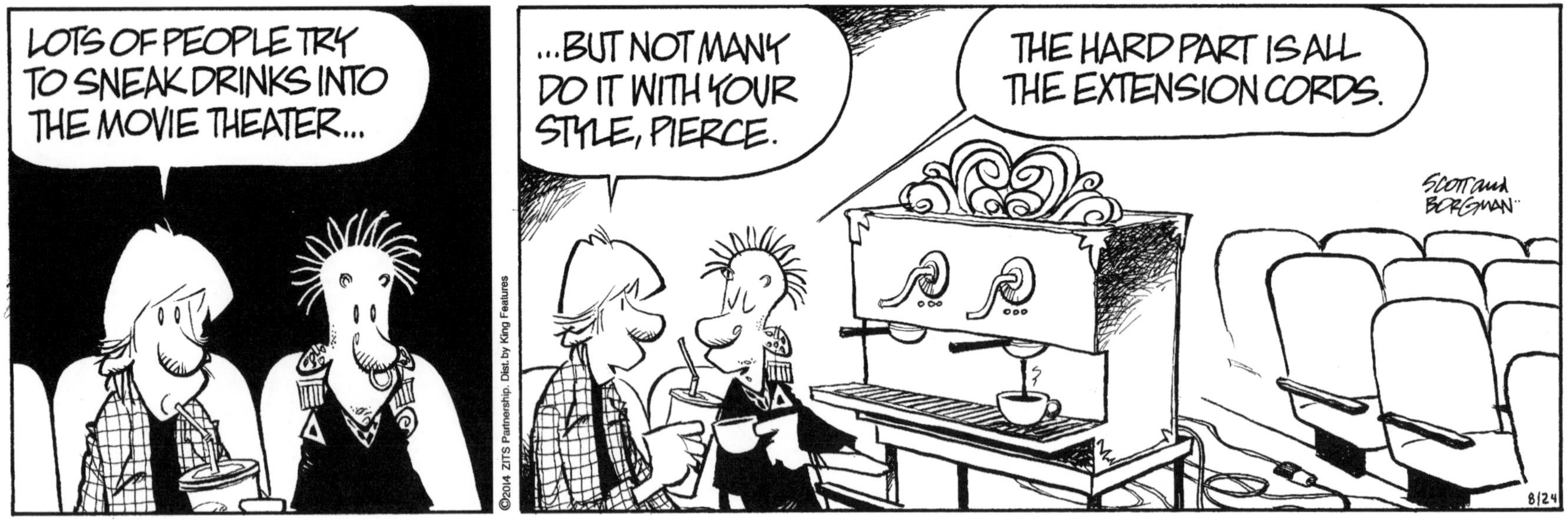
LOTS OF PEOPLE TRY TO SNEAK DRINKS INTO THE MOVIE THEATER...
©2014 ZITS Partnership. Dist. by King Features
...BUT NOT MANY DO IT WITH YOUR STYLE, PIERCE.
THE HARD PART IS ALL THE EXTENSION CORDS.
SCOTT and BORGMAN
8/24

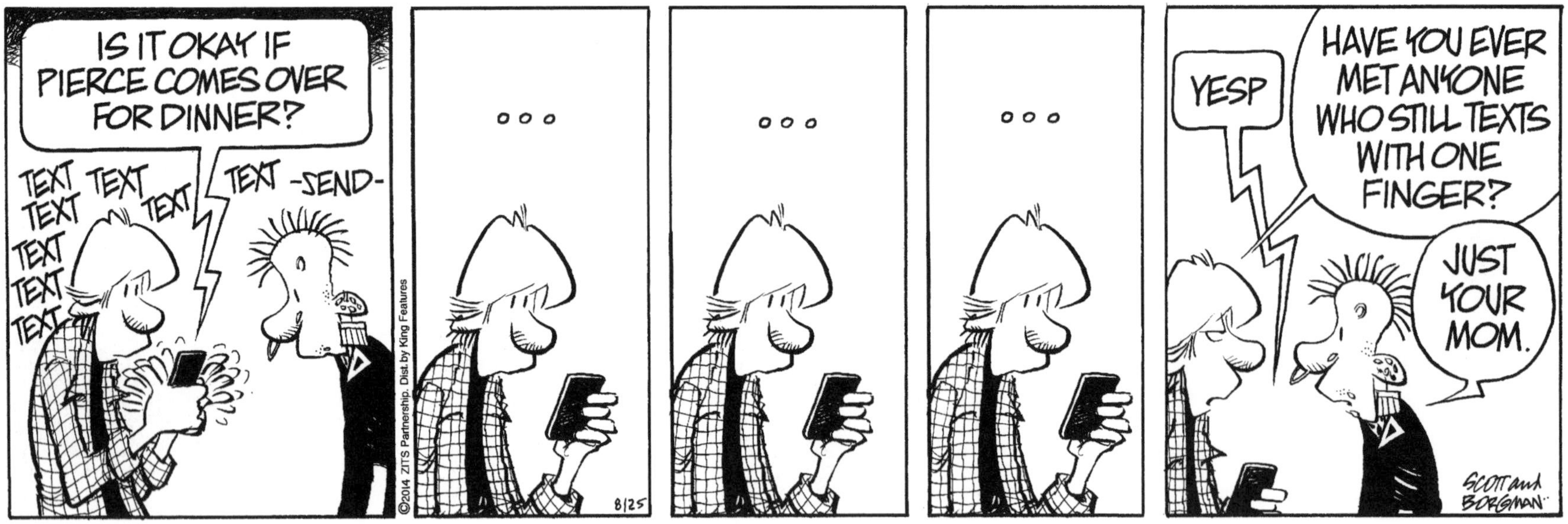
IS IT OKAY IF PIERCE COMES OVER FOR DINNER?
TEXT TEXT TEXT TEXT TEXT TEXT TEXT TEXT -SEND-
©2014 ZITS Partnership. Dist. by King Features
8/25
YESP
HAVE YOU EVER MET ANYONE WHO STILL TEXTS WITH ONE FINGER?
JUST YOUR MOM.
SCOTT and BORGMAN

ZITS®

by JERRY SCOTT and JIM BORGMAN

SCOTT and BORGMAN 9-9
DO YOU KNOW WHAT IT WOULD MEAN TO ME IF I WALKED INTO A TIDY BEDROOM FOR ONCE?
IT WOULD MEAN THAT YOU WERE IN THE WRONG HOUSE.
©2018 ZITS Partnership. Dist. by King Features

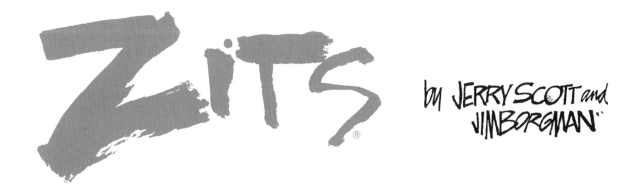

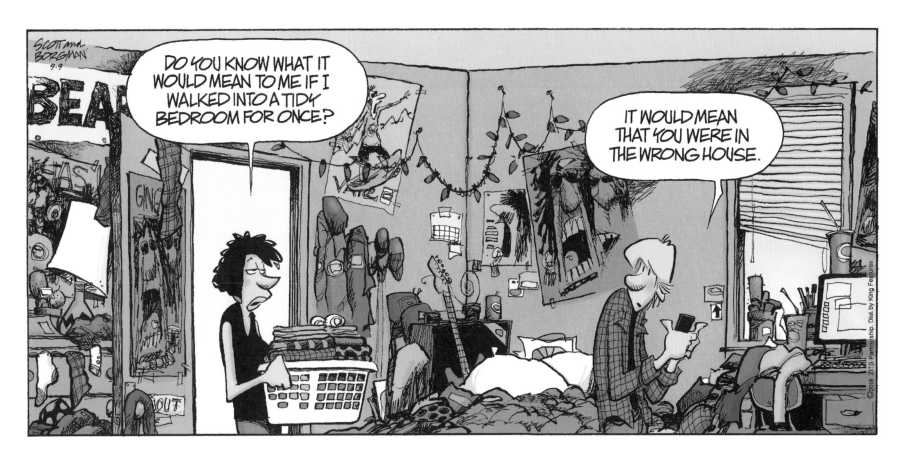

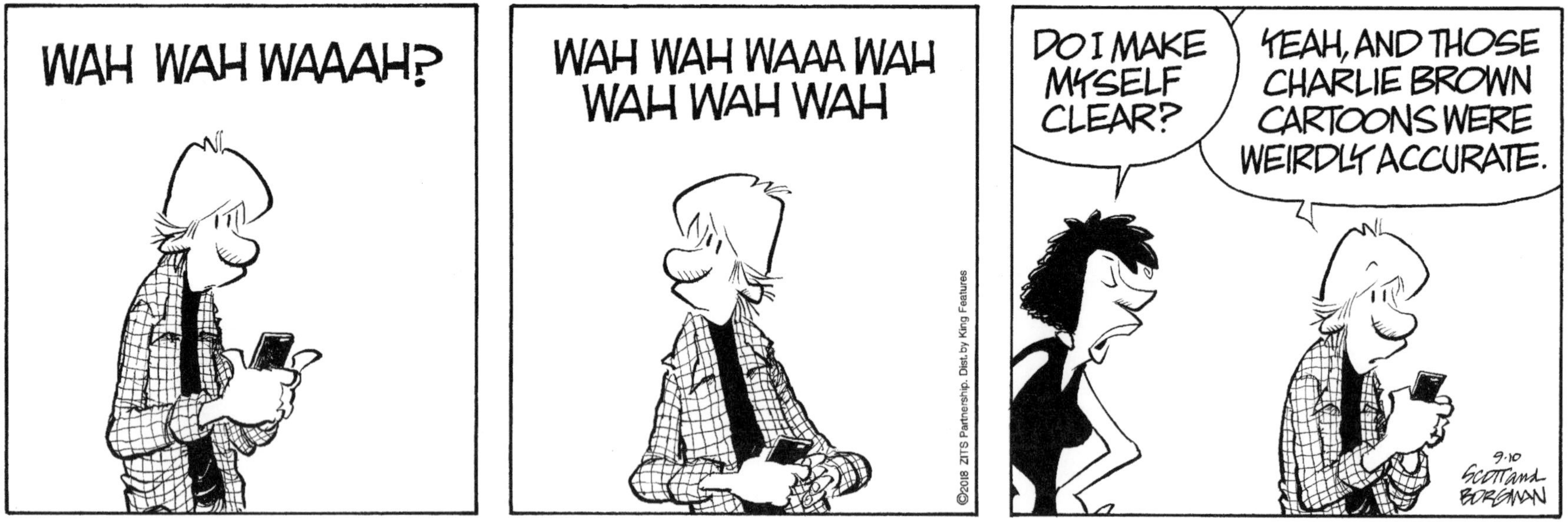
WAH WAH WAAAH?
WAH WAH WAAA WAH WAH WAH WAH
©2018 ZITS Partnership. Dist. by King Features
DO I MAKE MYSELF CLEAR?
YEAH, AND THOSE CHARLIE BROWN CARTOONS WERE WEIRDLY ACCURATE.
9.10
SCOTT and BORGMAN

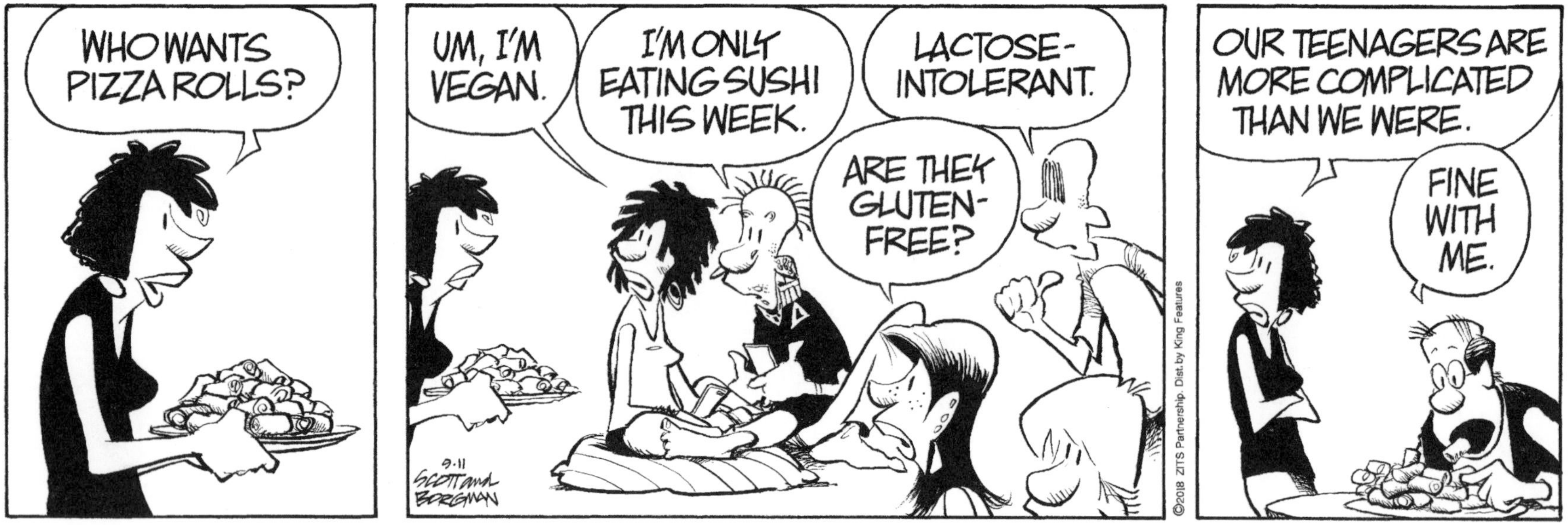
WHO WANTS PIZZA ROLLS?
UM, I'M VEGAN.
I'M ONLY EATING SUSHI THIS WEEK.
ARE THEY GLUTEN-FREE?
LACTOSE-INTOLERANT.
9.11
SCOTT and BORGMAN
©2018 ZITS Partnership. Dist. by King Features
OUR TEENAGERS ARE MORE COMPLICATED THAN WE WERE.
FINE WITH ME.

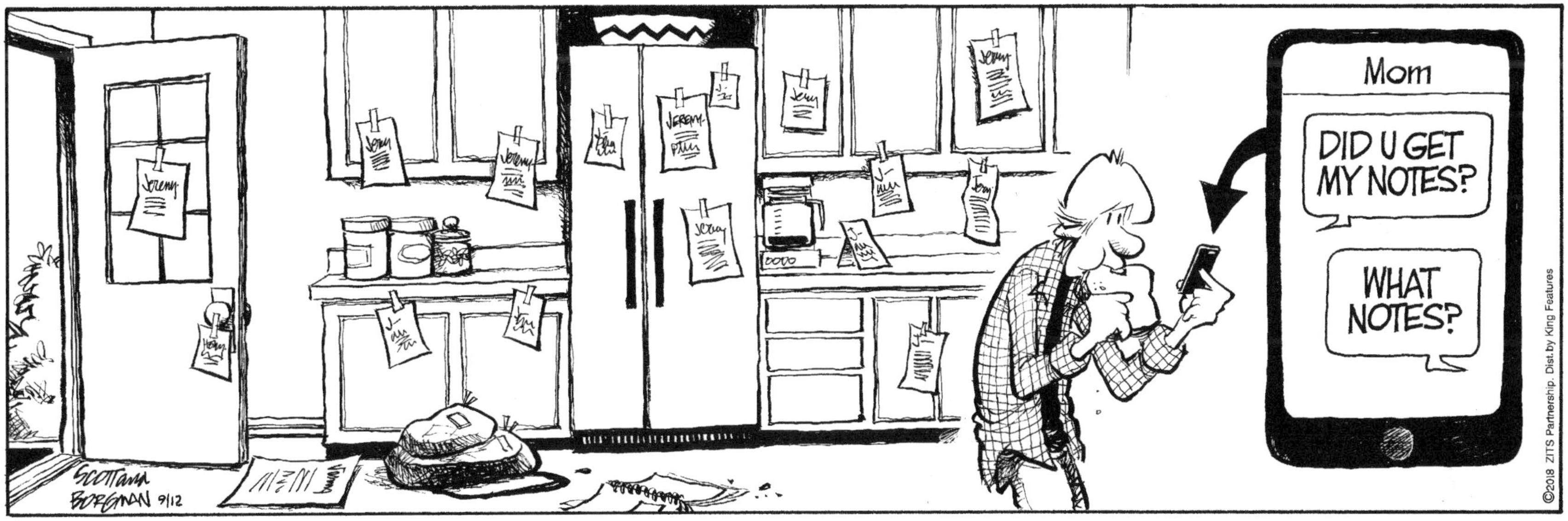
Mom
DID U GET MY NOTES?
WHAT NOTES?
SCOTT AND BORGMAN 9/12
©2018 ZITS Partnership. Dist.by King Features

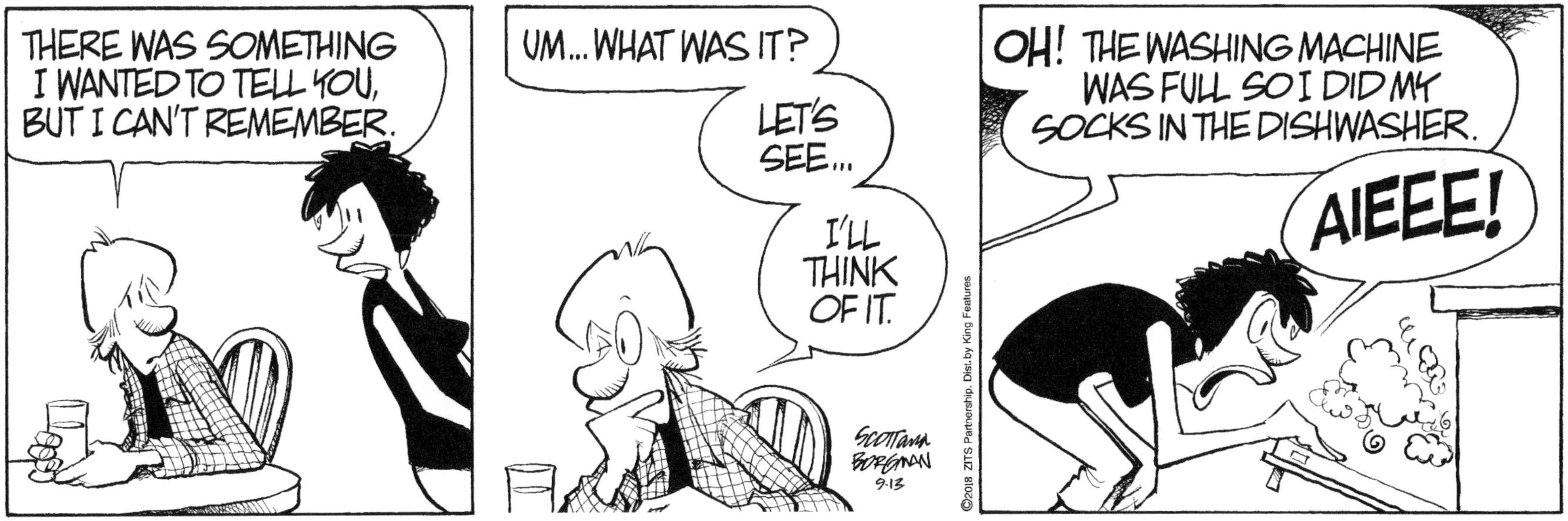
THERE WAS SOMETHING I WANTED TO TELL YOU, BUT I CAN'T REMEMBER.
UM... WHAT WAS IT?
LET'S SEE...
I'LL THINK OF IT.
SCOTT AND BORGMAN 9·13
©2018 ZITS Partnership. Dist.by King Features
OH! THE WASHING MACHINE WAS FULL SO I DID MY SOCKS IN THE DISHWASHER.
AIEEE!

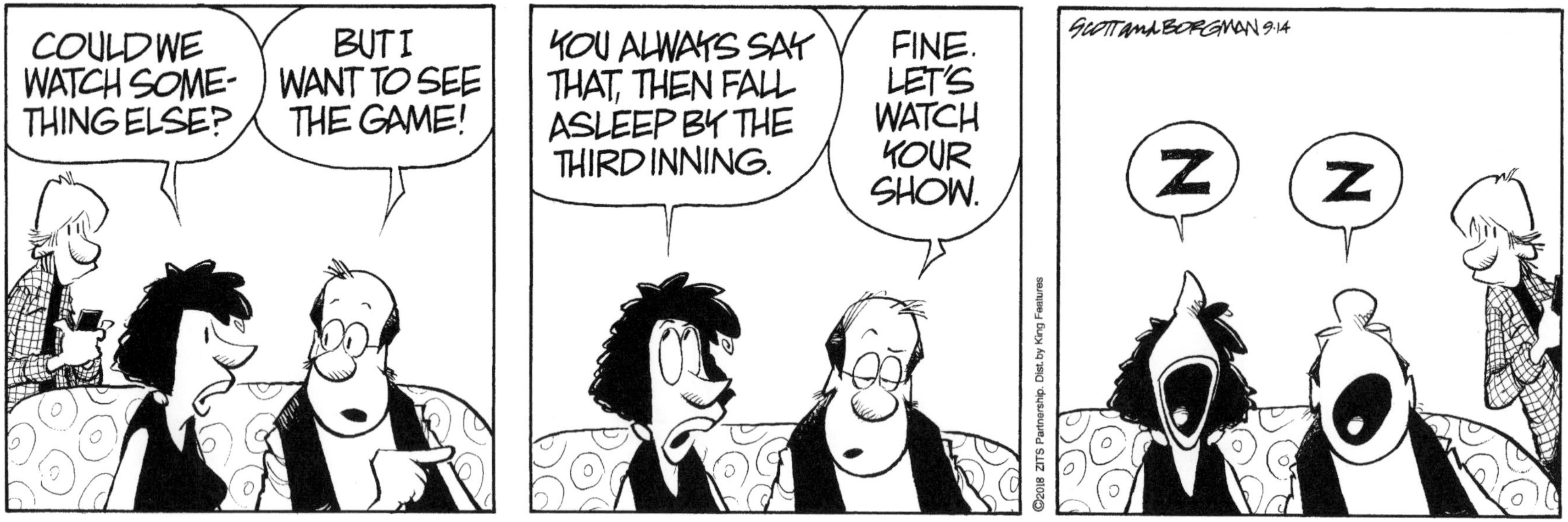
COULD WE WATCH SOME-THING ELSE?
BUT I WANT TO SEE THE GAME!
YOU ALWAYS SAY THAT, THEN FALL ASLEEP BY THE THIRD INNING.
FINE. LET'S WATCH YOUR SHOW.
SCOTT and BORGMAN 9.14
Z
Z
©2018 ZITS Partnership. Dist. by King Features

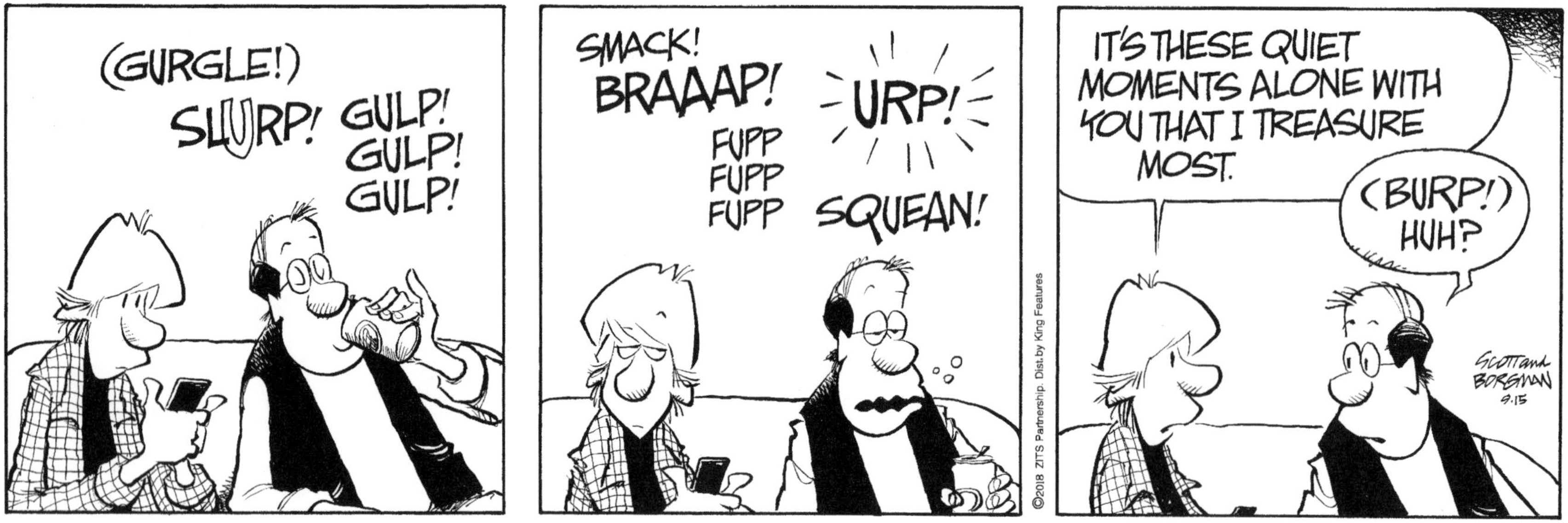
(GURGLE!)
SLURP!
GULP! GULP! GULP!
SMACK!
BRAAAP!
FUPP FUPP FUPP
URP!
SQUEAN!
IT'S THESE QUIET MOMENTS ALONE WITH YOU THAT I TREASURE MOST.
(BURP!) HUH?
SCOTT and BORGMAN 9.15
©2018 ZITS Partnership. Dist. by King Features

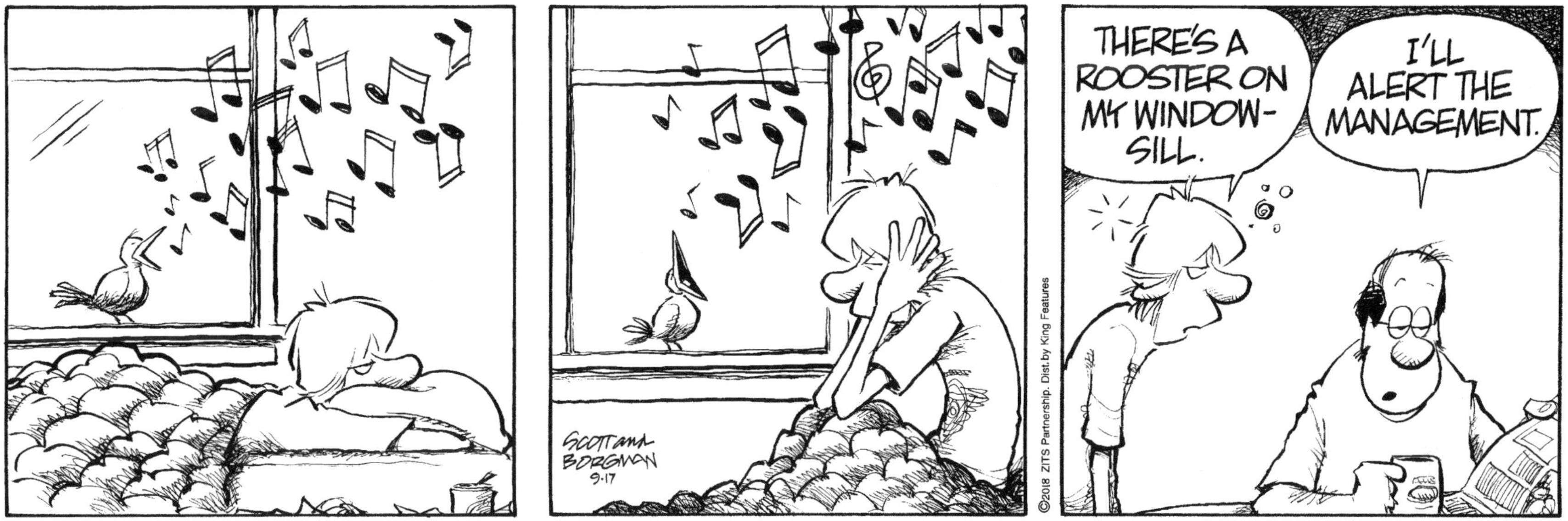
SCOTT and BORGMAN 9.17
THERE'S A ROOSTER ON MY WINDOW-SILL.
I'LL ALERT THE MANAGEMENT.
©2018 ZITS Partnership. Dist. by King Features

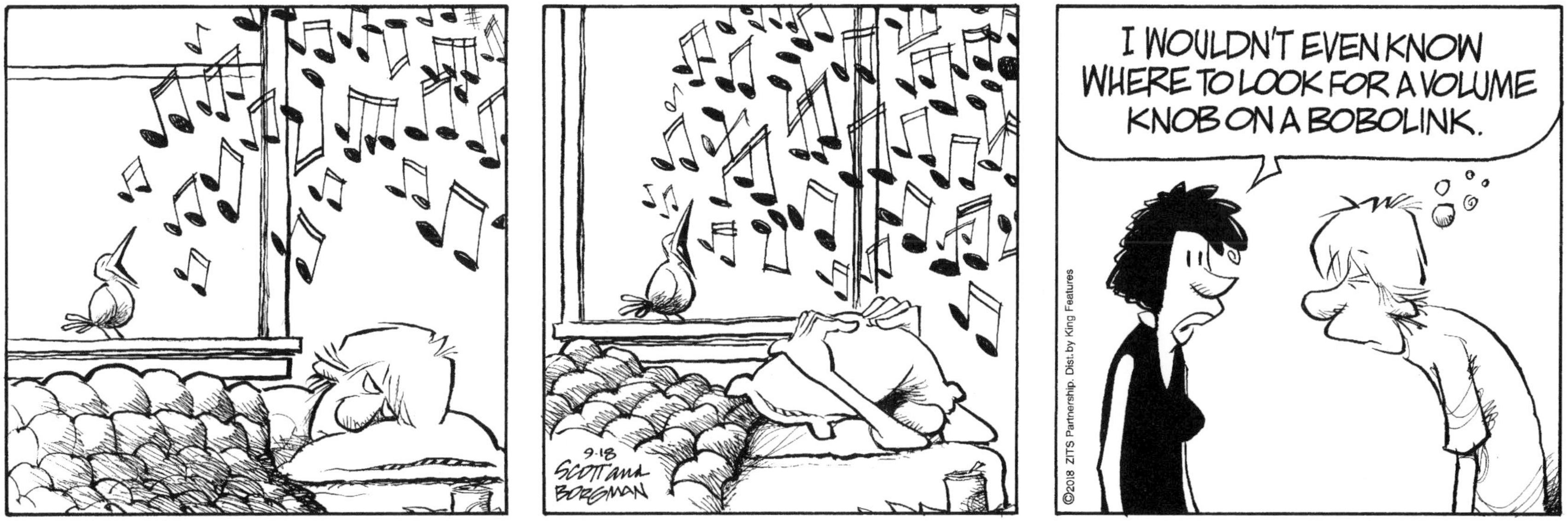
9.18 SCOTT and BORGMAN
I WOULDN'T EVEN KNOW WHERE TO LOOK FOR A VOLUME KNOB ON A BOBOLINK.
©2018 ZITS Partnership. Dist. by King Features

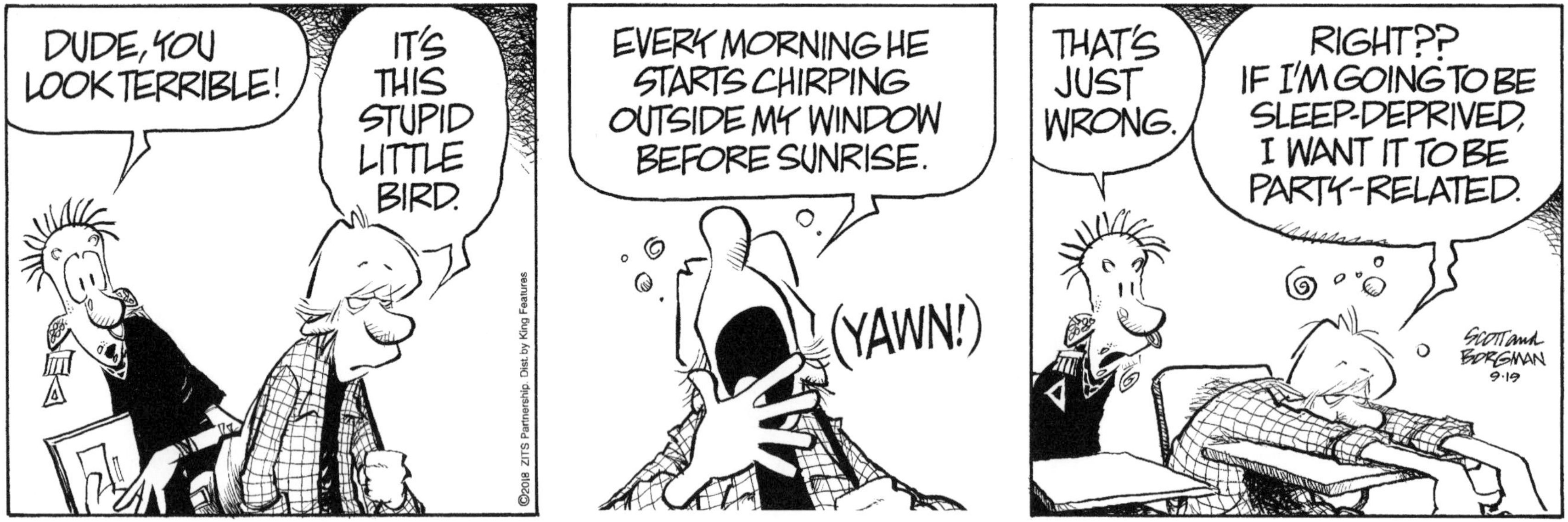
DUDE, YOU LOOK TERRIBLE!
IT'S THIS STUPID LITTLE BIRD.
©2018 ZITS Partnership. Dist. by King Features
EVERY MORNING HE STARTS CHIRPING OUTSIDE MY WINDOW BEFORE SUNRISE.
(YAWN!)
THAT'S JUST WRONG.
RIGHT?? IF I'M GOING TO BE SLEEP-DEPRIVED, I WANT IT TO BE PARTY-RELATED.
SCOTT and BORGMAN 9·19

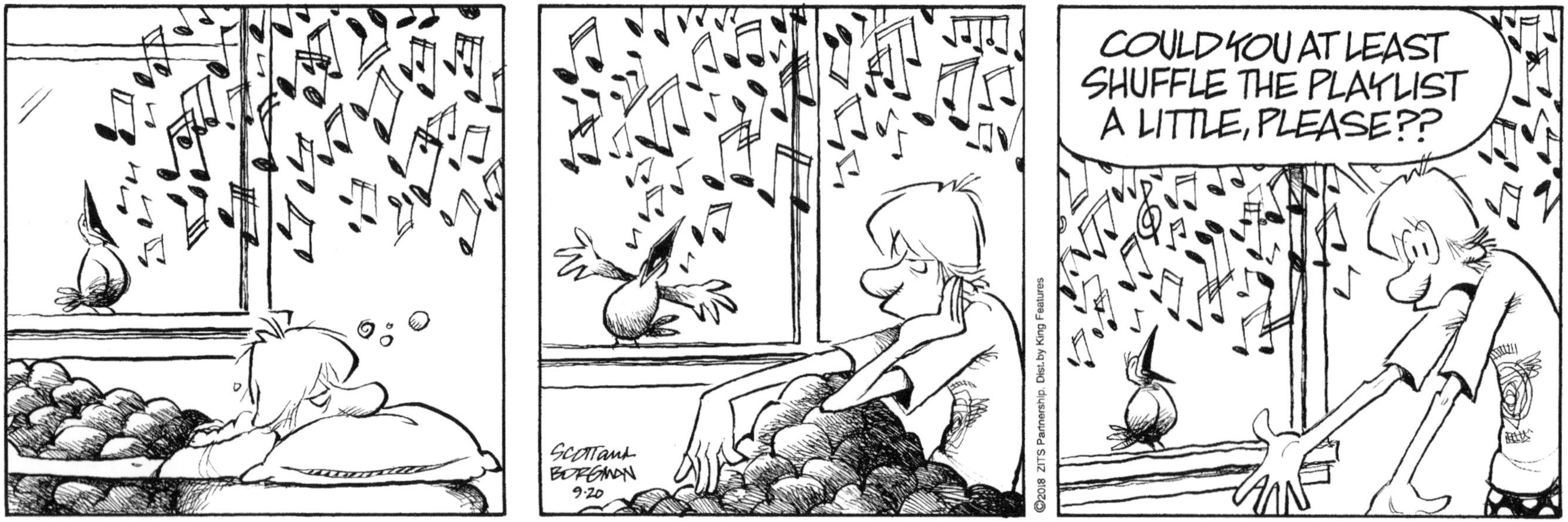
SCOTT and BORGMAN 9·20
©2018 ZITS Partnership. Dist. by King Features
COULD YOU AT LEAST SHUFFLE THE PLAYLIST A LITTLE, PLEASE??

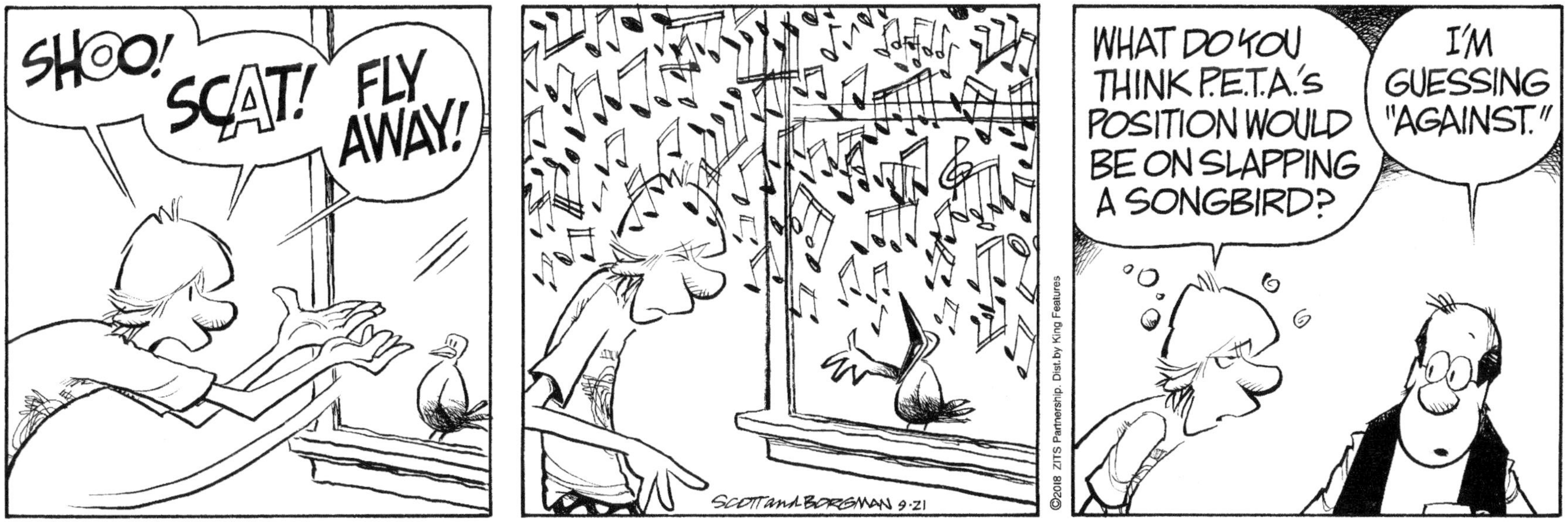
SHOO!
SCAT!
FLY AWAY!
SCOTT and BORGMAN 9·21
©2018 ZITS Partnership. Dist.by King Features
WHAT DO YOU THINK P.E.T.A.'s POSITION WOULD BE ON SLAPPING A SONGBIRD?
I'M GUESSING "AGAINST."

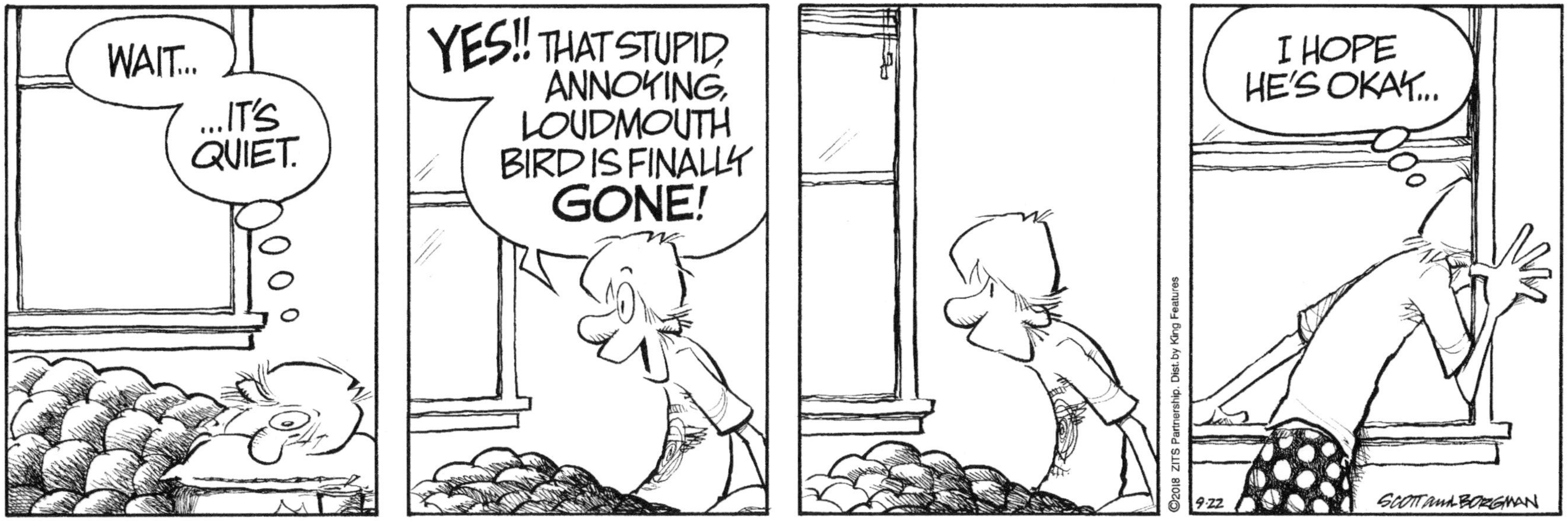
WAIT...
...IT'S QUIET.
YES!! THAT STUPID, ANNOYING, LOUDMOUTH BIRD IS FINALLY GONE!
©2018 ZITS Partnership. Dist.by King Features
I HOPE HE'S OKAY...
9·22
SCOTT and BORGMAN

ZITS®

by JERRY SCOTT and JIM BORGMAN

ALMOST DONE!
YEAH.
THIS WENT PRETTY FAST.
MAYBE TOO FAST.
YOU THINK?
©2018 ZITS Partnership. Dist. by King Features
MOM, PIERCE AND I FINISHED PAINTING THE REC ROOM.
GREAT!
9-23
SCOTT and BORGMAN
DO YOU NEED HELP MOVING THE FURNITURE BACK?
"BACK"?
I TOLD YOU!

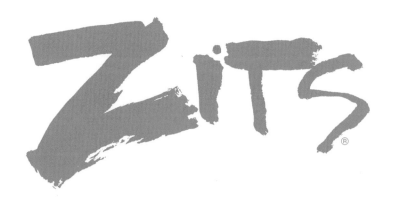

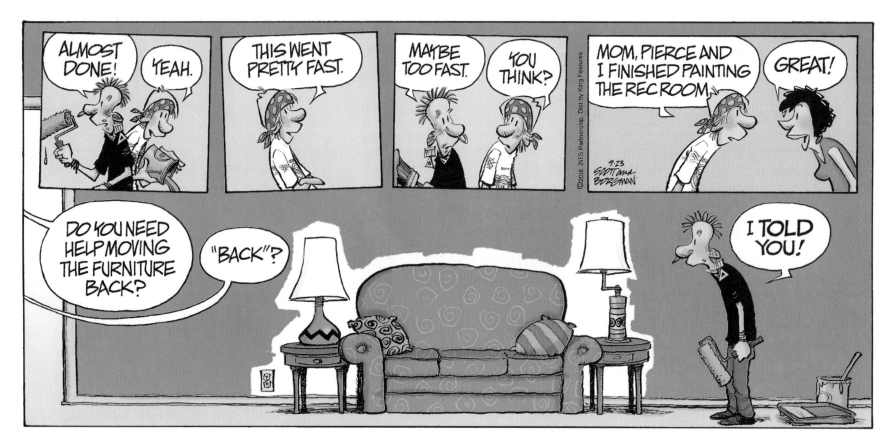

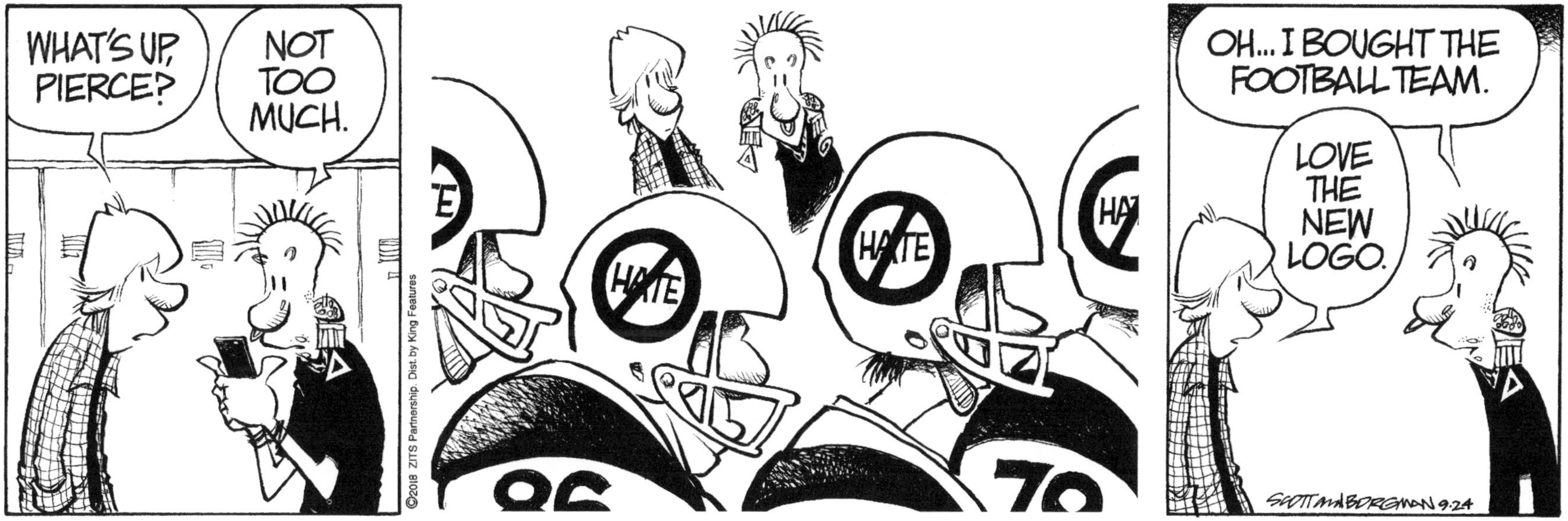
WHAT'S UP, PIERCE?
NOT TOO MUCH.
©2018 ZITS Partnership. Dist. by King Features
HATE
OH... I BOUGHT THE FOOTBALL TEAM.
LOVE THE NEW LOGO.
SCOTT and BORGMAN 9.24

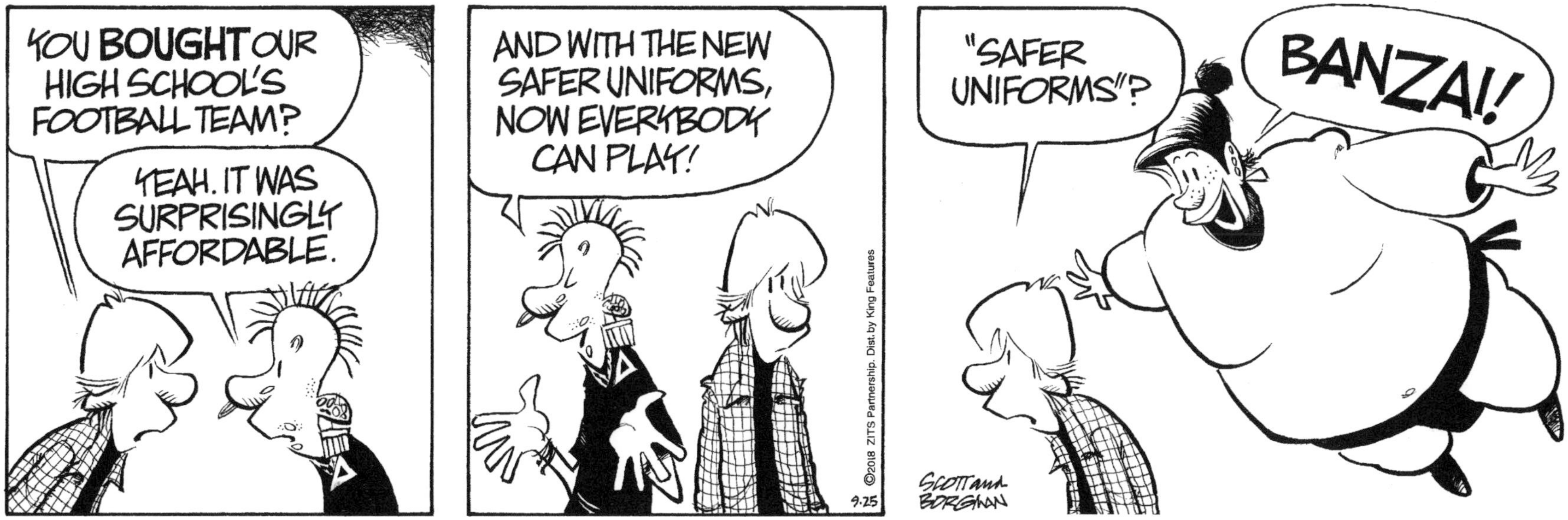
YOU BOUGHT OUR HIGH SCHOOL'S FOOTBALL TEAM?
YEAH. IT WAS SURPRISINGLY AFFORDABLE.
AND WITH THE NEW SAFER UNIFORMS, NOW EVERYBODY CAN PLAY!
©2018 ZITS Partnership. Dist. by King Features
9.25
"SAFER UNIFORMS"?
BANZAI!
SCOTT and BORGMAN

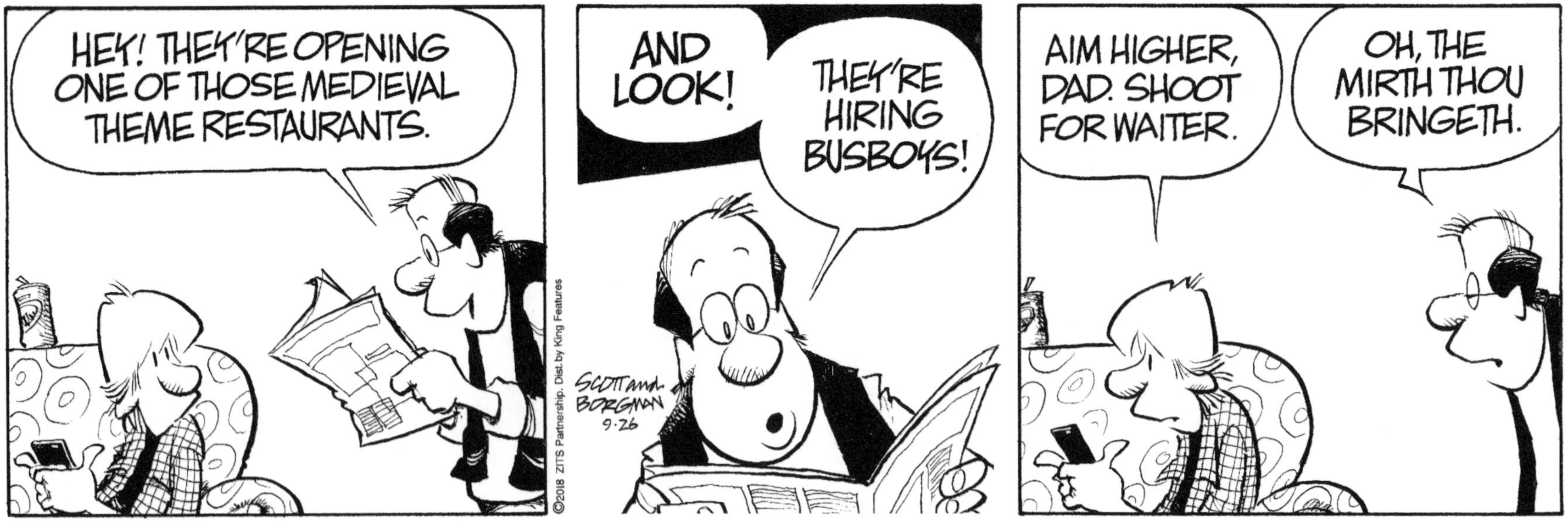
HEY! THEY'RE OPENING ONE OF THOSE MEDIEVAL THEME RESTAURANTS.
AND LOOK!
THEY'RE HIRING BUSBOYS!
AIM HIGHER, DAD. SHOOT FOR WAITER.
OH, THE MIRTH THOU BRINGETH.
SCOTT AND BORGMAN 9·26
©2018 ZITS Partnership. Dist. by King Features

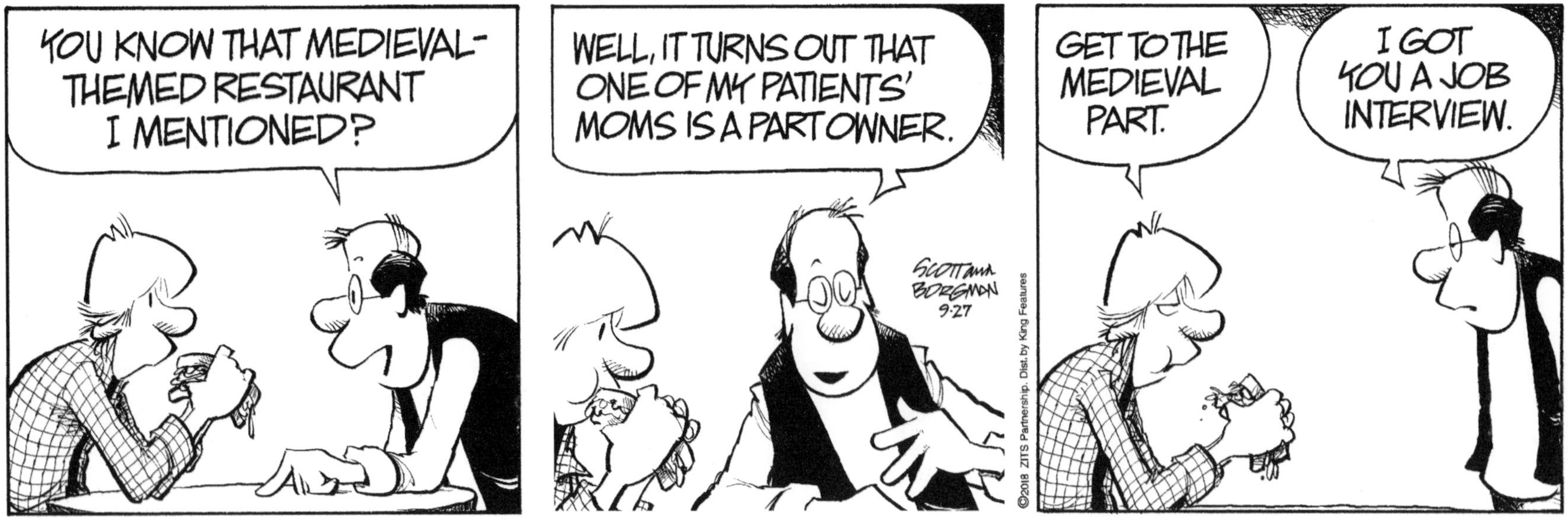
YOU KNOW THAT MEDIEVAL-THEMED RESTAURANT I MENTIONED?
WELL, IT TURNS OUT THAT ONE OF MY PATIENTS' MOMS IS A PART OWNER.
GET TO THE MEDIEVAL PART.
I GOT YOU A JOB INTERVIEW.
SCOTT AND BORGMAN 9·27
©2018 ZITS Partnership. Dist. by King Features

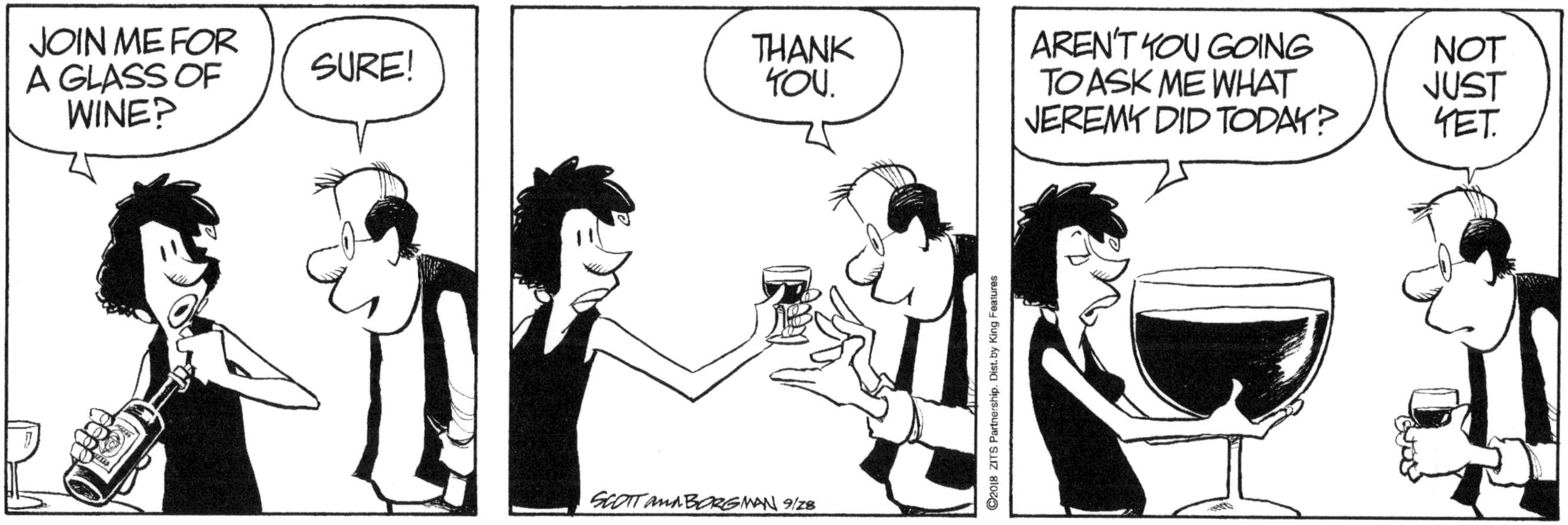
JOIN ME FOR A GLASS OF WINE?
SURE!
THANK YOU.
AREN'T YOU GOING TO ASK ME WHAT JEREMY DID TODAY?
NOT JUST YET.
SCOTT and BORGMAN 9/28
©2018 ZITS Partnership. Dist. by King Features

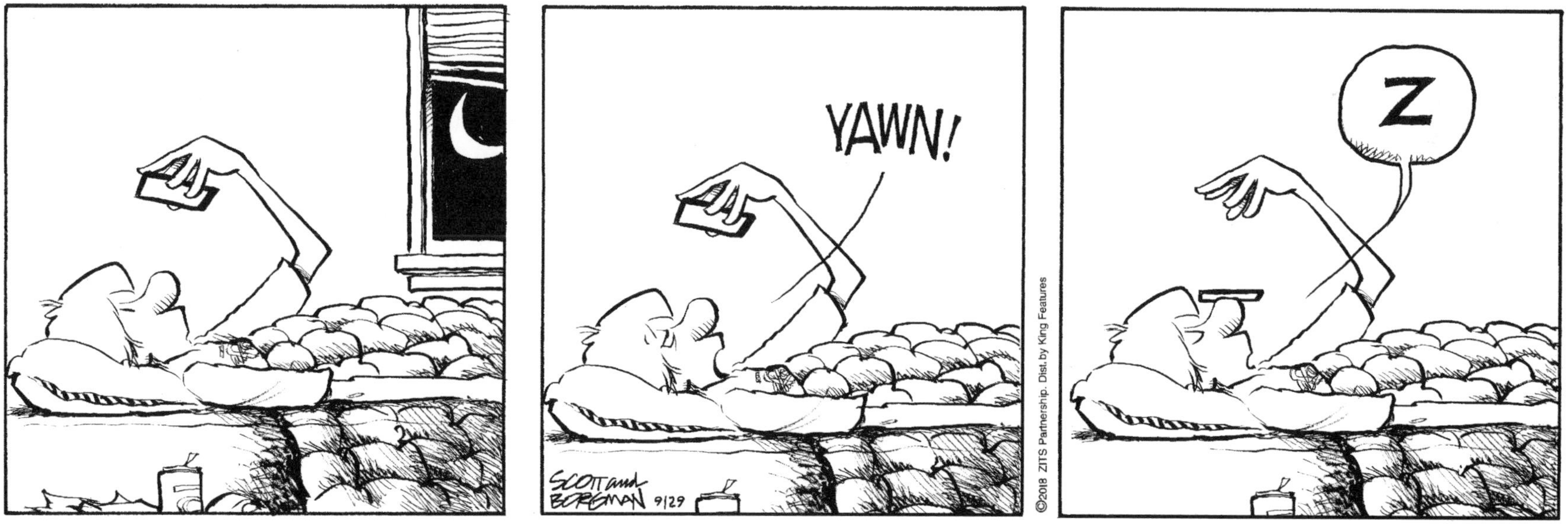
YAWN!
Z
SCOTT and BORGMAN 9/29
©2018 ZITS Partnership. Dist. by King Features

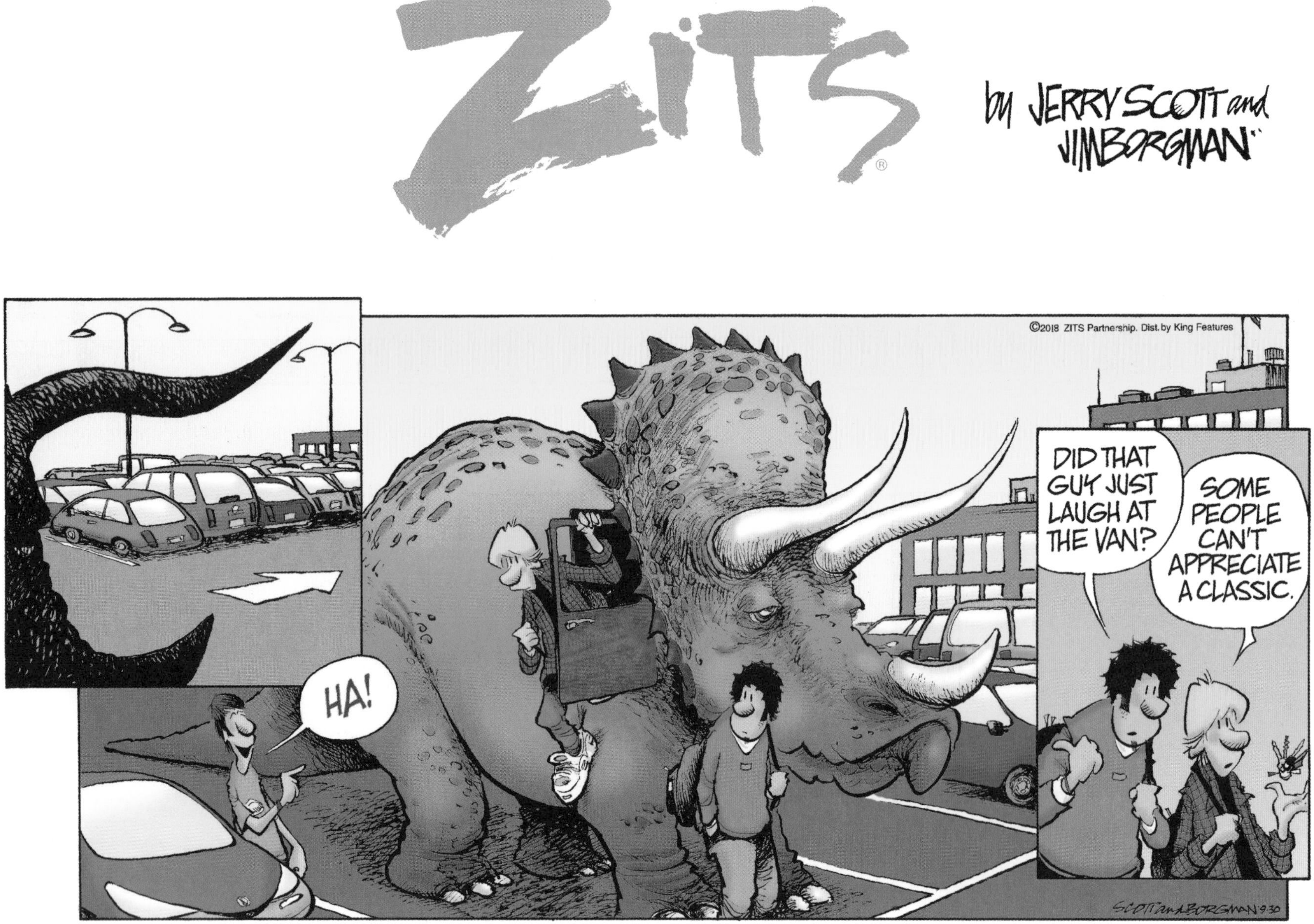
ZITS®
by JERRY SCOTT and JIM BORGMAN
©2018 ZITS Partnership. Dist. by King Features
HA!
DID THAT GUY JUST LAUGH AT THE VAN?
SOME PEOPLE CAN'T APPRECIATE A CLASSIC.
SCOTT and BORGMAN 9-30

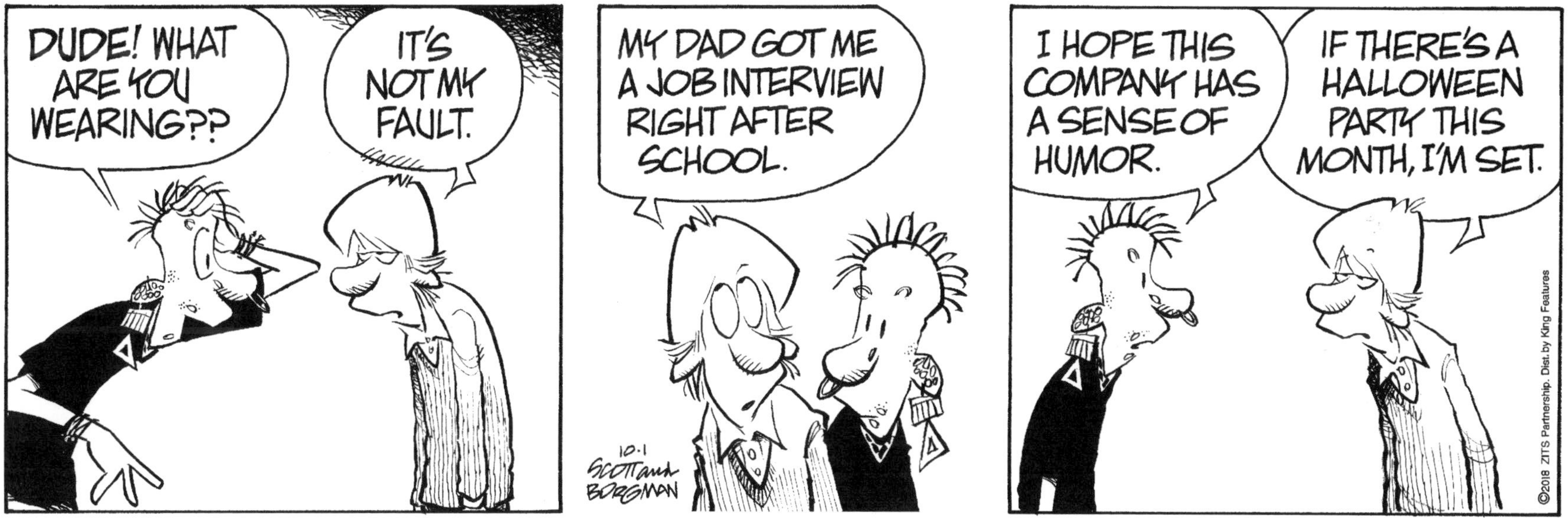
DUDE! WHAT ARE YOU WEARING??
IT'S NOT MY FAULT.
MY DAD GOT ME A JOB INTERVIEW RIGHT AFTER SCHOOL.
10·1
SCOTT and BORGMAN
I HOPE THIS COMPANY HAS A SENSE OF HUMOR.
IF THERE'S A HALLOWEEN PARTY THIS MONTH, I'M SET.
©2018 ZITS Partnership. Dist. by King Features

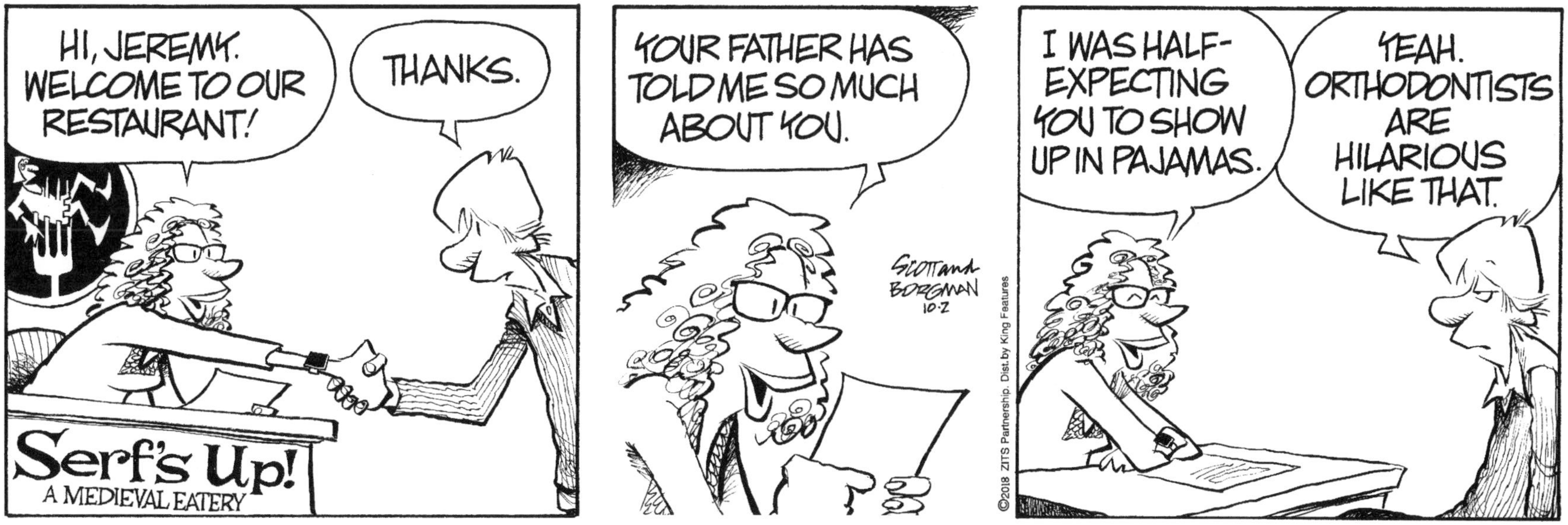
HI, JEREMY. WELCOME TO OUR RESTAURANT!
THANKS.
Serf's Up!
A MEDIEVAL EATERY
YOUR FATHER HAS TOLD ME SO MUCH ABOUT YOU.
SCOTT and BORGMAN
10·2
©2018 ZITS Partnership. Dist. by King Features
I WAS HALF-EXPECTING YOU TO SHOW UP IN PAJAMAS.
YEAH. ORTHODONTISTS ARE HILARIOUS LIKE THAT.

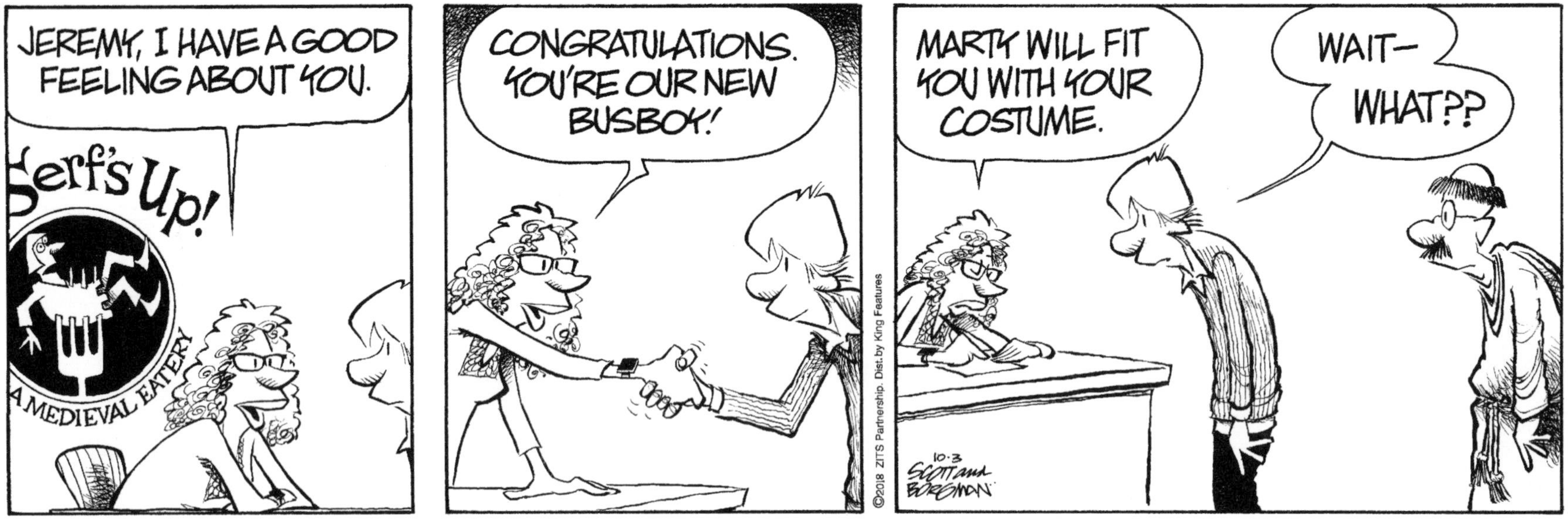
JEREMY, I HAVE A GOOD FEELING ABOUT YOU.
Serf's Up!
A MEDIEVAL EATERY
CONGRATULATIONS. YOU'RE OUR NEW BUSBOY!
©2018 ZITS Partnership. Dist. by King Features
MARTY WILL FIT YOU WITH YOUR COSTUME.
WAIT—
WHAT??
10·3
SCOTT and BORGMAN

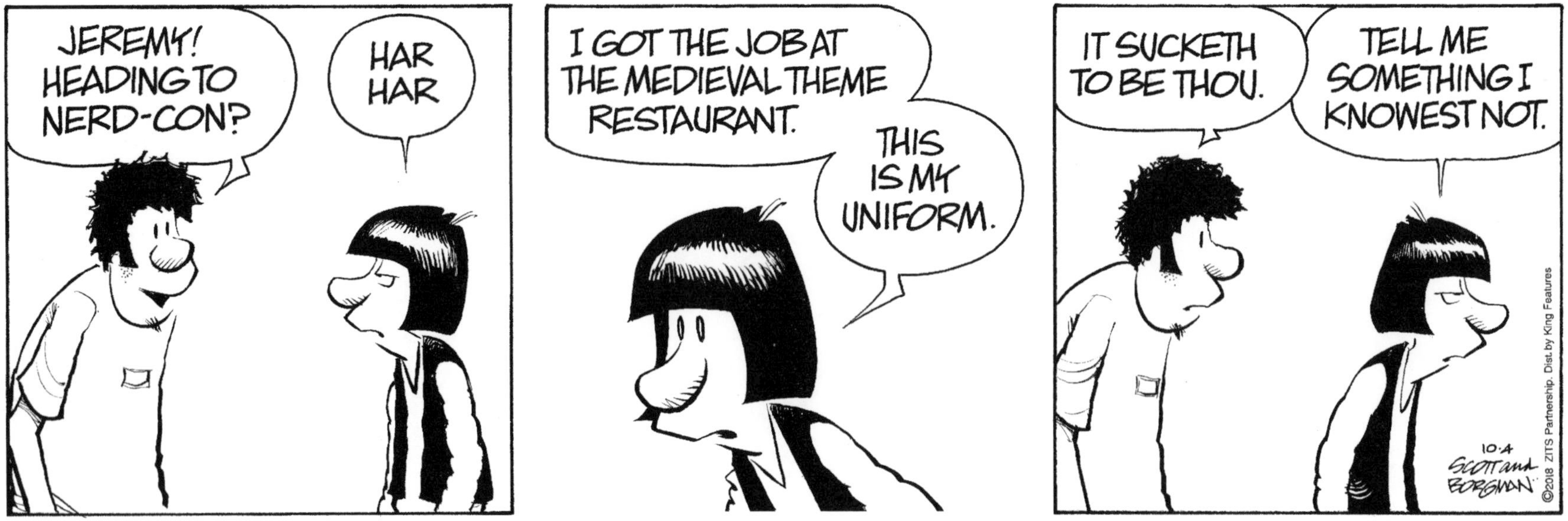
JEREMY! HEADING TO NERD-CON?
HAR HAR
I GOT THE JOB AT THE MEDIEVAL THEME RESTAURANT.
THIS IS MY UNIFORM.
IT SUCKETH TO BE THOU.
TELL ME SOMETHING I KNOWEST NOT.
10·4
SCOTT and BORGMAN
©2018 ZITS Partnership. Dist. by King Features

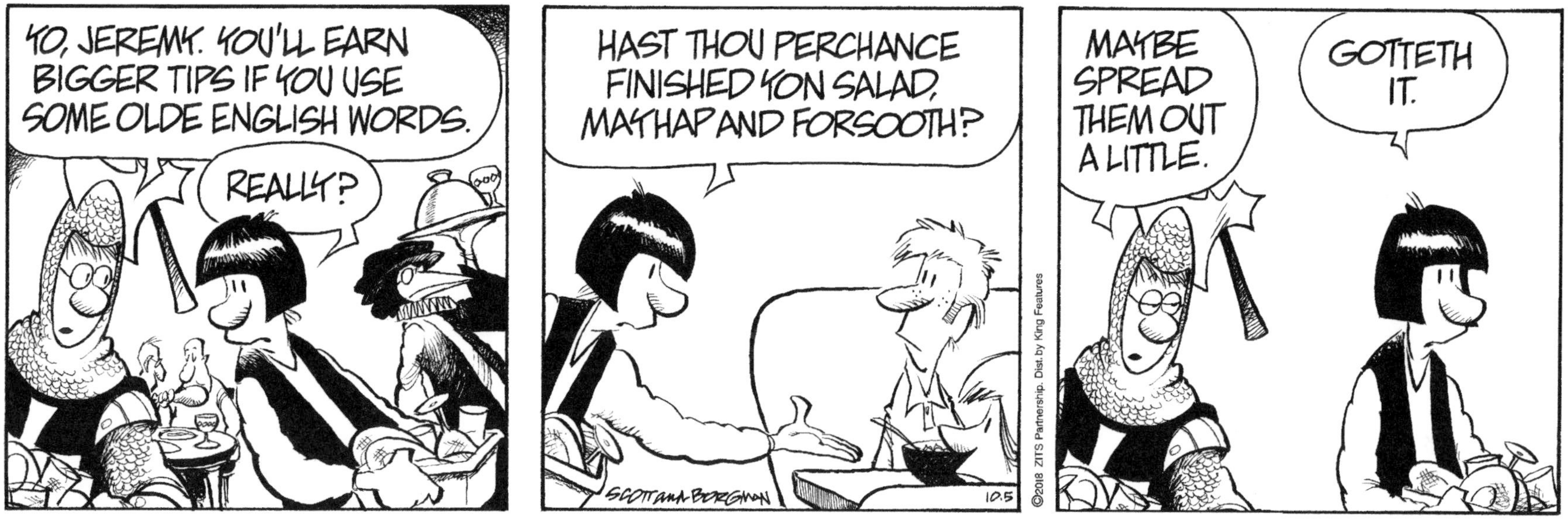
YO, JEREMY. YOU'LL EARN BIGGER TIPS IF YOU USE SOME OLDE ENGLISH WORDS.
REALLY?
HAST THOU PERCHANCE FINISHED YON SALAD, MAYHAP AND FORSOOTH?
SCOTT and BORGMAN
10.5
©2018 ZITS Partnership. Dist. by King Features
MAYBE SPREAD THEM OUT A LITTLE.
GOTTETH IT.

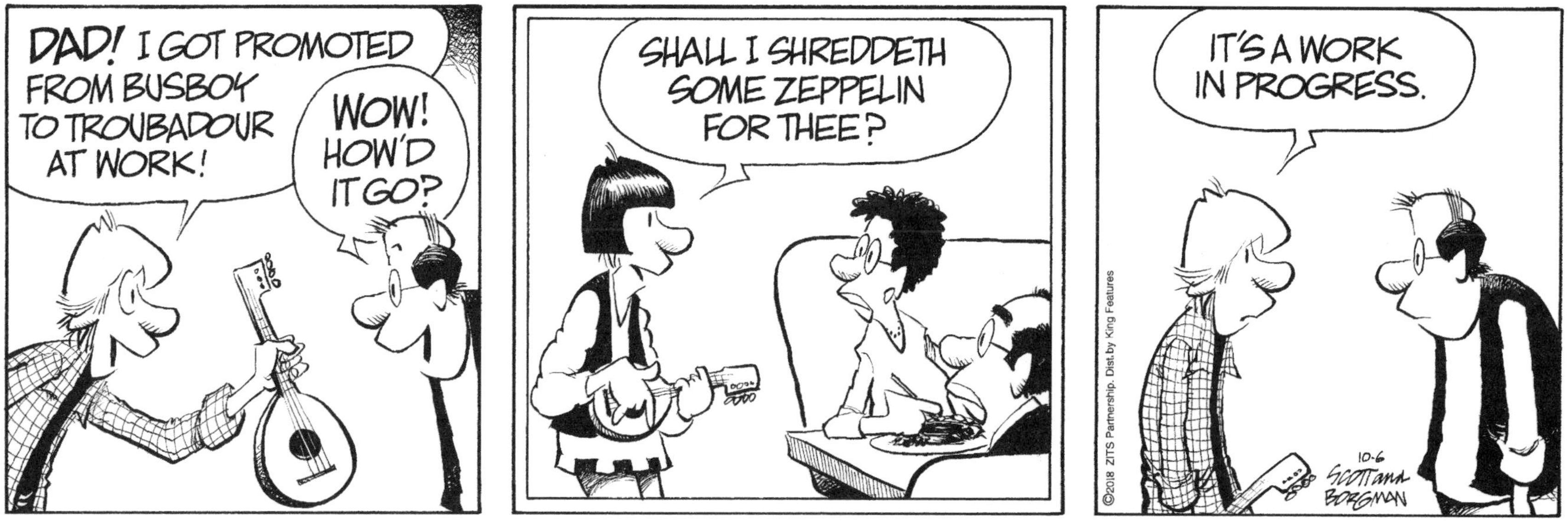
DAD! I GOT PROMOTED FROM BUSBOY TO TROUBADOUR AT WORK!
WOW! HOW'D IT GO?
SHALL I SHREDDETH SOME ZEPPELIN FOR THEE?
IT'S A WORK IN PROGRESS.
©2018 ZITS Partnership. Dist. by King Features
10.6
SCOTT and BORGMAN

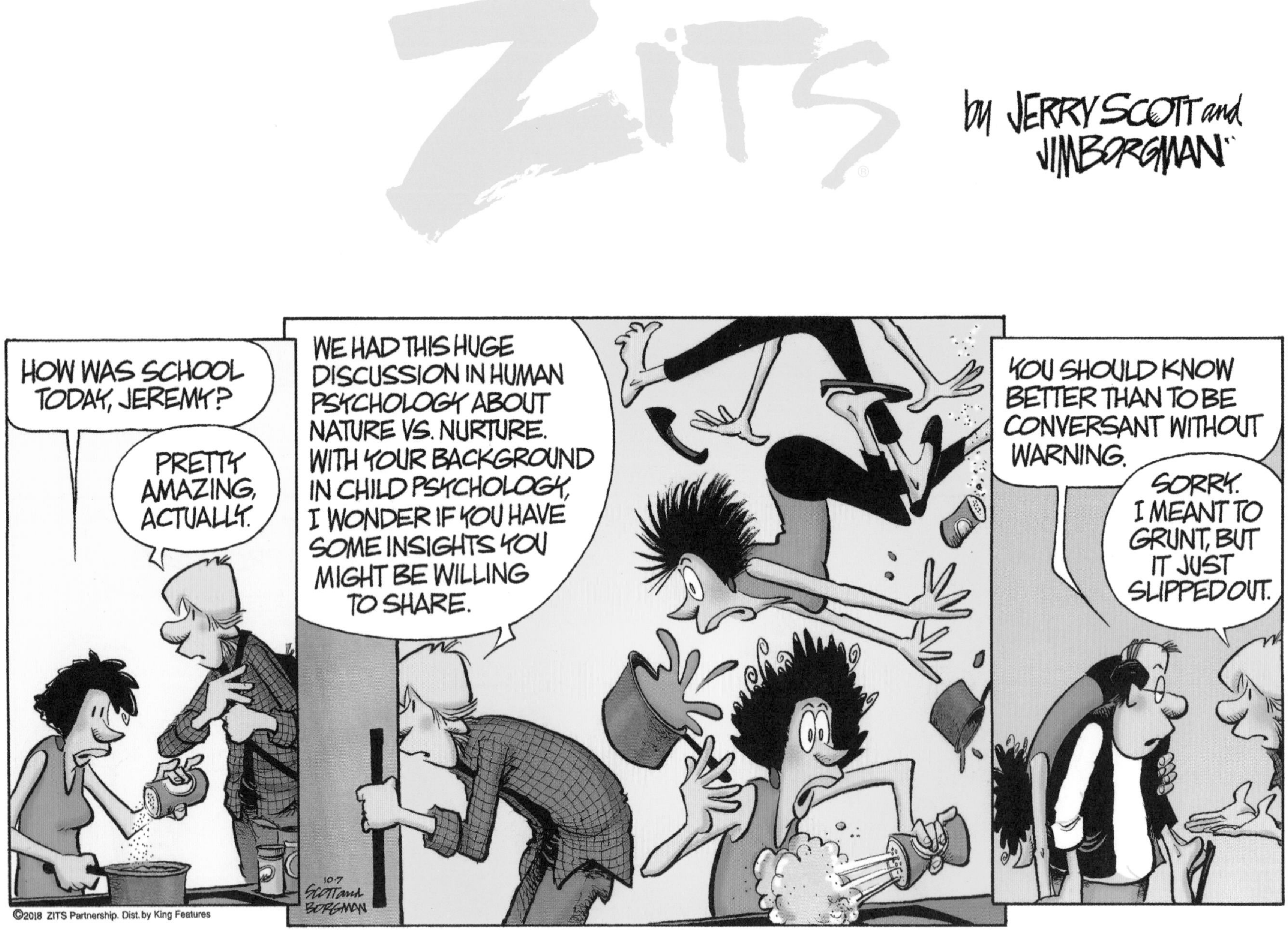
ZITS
by JERRY SCOTT and JIM BORGMAN
HOW WAS SCHOOL TODAY, JEREMY?
PRETTY AMAZING, ACTUALLY.
WE HAD THIS HUGE DISCUSSION IN HUMAN PSYCHOLOGY ABOUT NATURE VS. NURTURE. WITH YOUR BACKGROUND IN CHILD PSYCHOLOGY, I WONDER IF YOU HAVE SOME INSIGHTS YOU MIGHT BE WILLING TO SHARE.
YOU SHOULD KNOW BETTER THAN TO BE CONVERSANT WITHOUT WARNING.
SORRY. I MEANT TO GRUNT, BUT IT JUST SLIPPED OUT.
10-7 SCOTT and BORGMAN
©2018 ZITS Partnership. Dist. by King Features

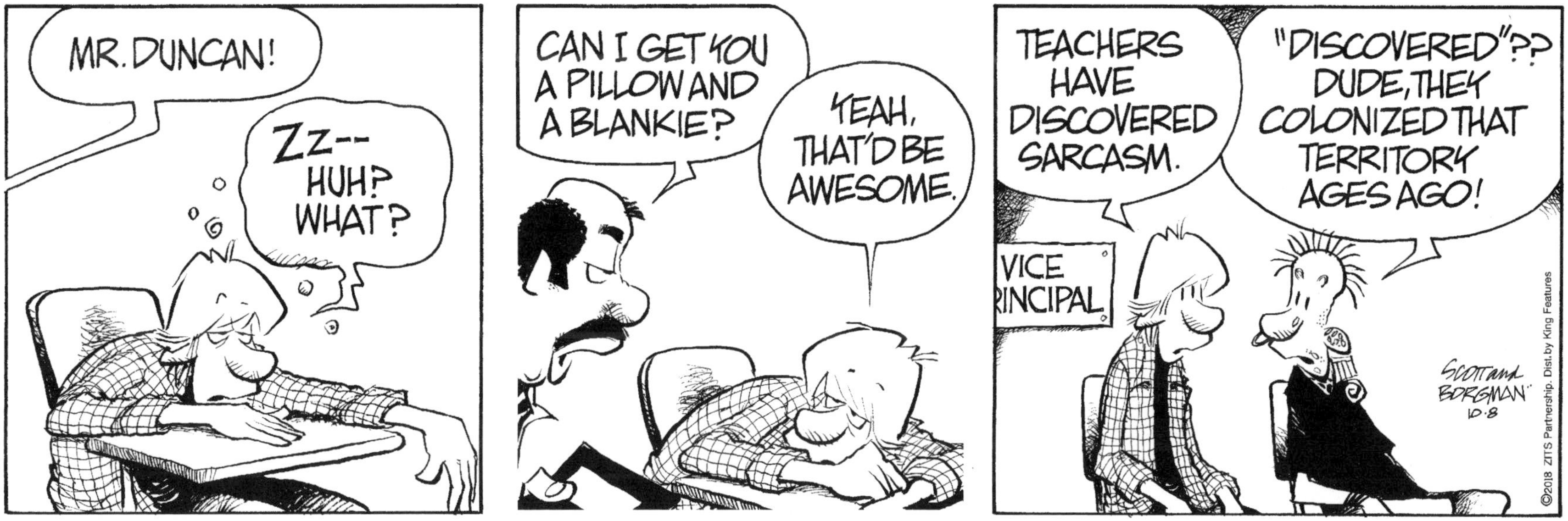
MR. DUNCAN!
ZZ-- HUH? WHAT?
CAN I GET YOU A PILLOW AND A BLANKIE?
YEAH, THAT'D BE AWESOME.
TEACHERS HAVE DISCOVERED SARCASM.
"DISCOVERED"?? DUDE, THEY COLONIZED THAT TERRITORY AGES AGO!
VICE
RINCIPAL
SCOTT and BORGMAN 10·8
©2018 ZITS Partnership. Dist. by King Features

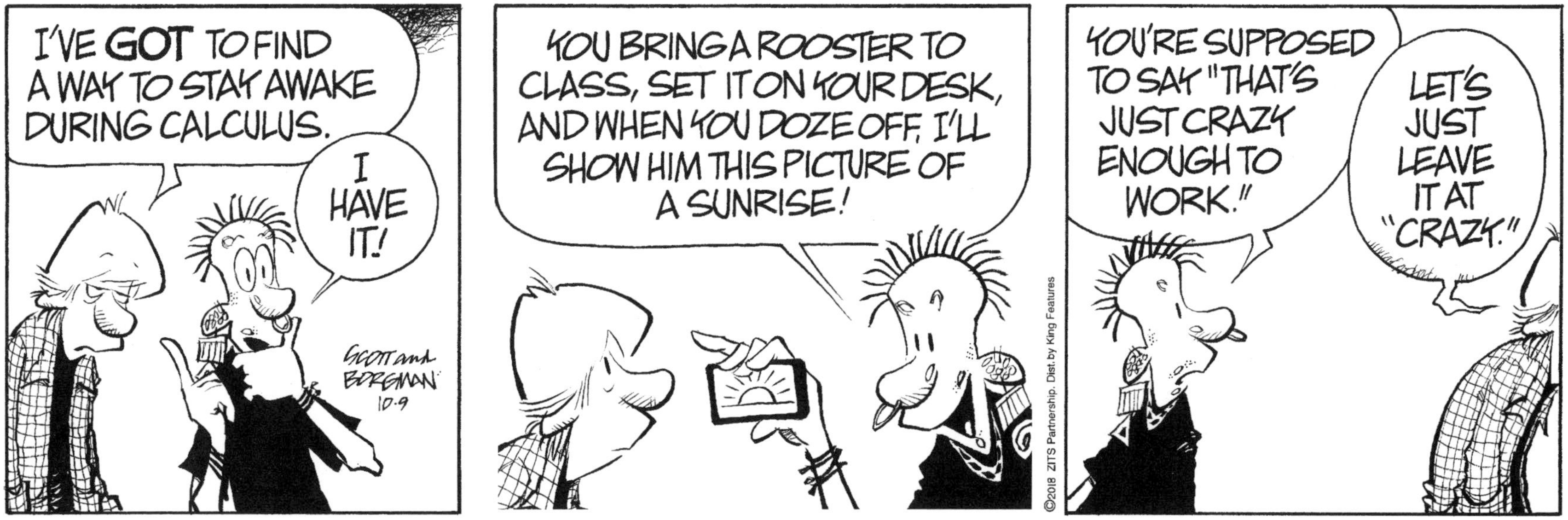
I'VE **GOT** TO FIND A WAY TO STAY AWAKE DURING CALCULUS.
I HAVE IT!
SCOTT and BORGMAN 10·9
YOU BRING A ROOSTER TO CLASS, SET IT ON YOUR DESK, AND WHEN YOU DOZE OFF, I'LL SHOW HIM THIS PICTURE OF A SUNRISE!
©2018 ZITS Partnership. Dist. by King Features
YOU'RE SUPPOSED TO SAY "THAT'S JUST CRAZY ENOUGH TO WORK."
LET'S JUST LEAVE IT AT "CRAZY."

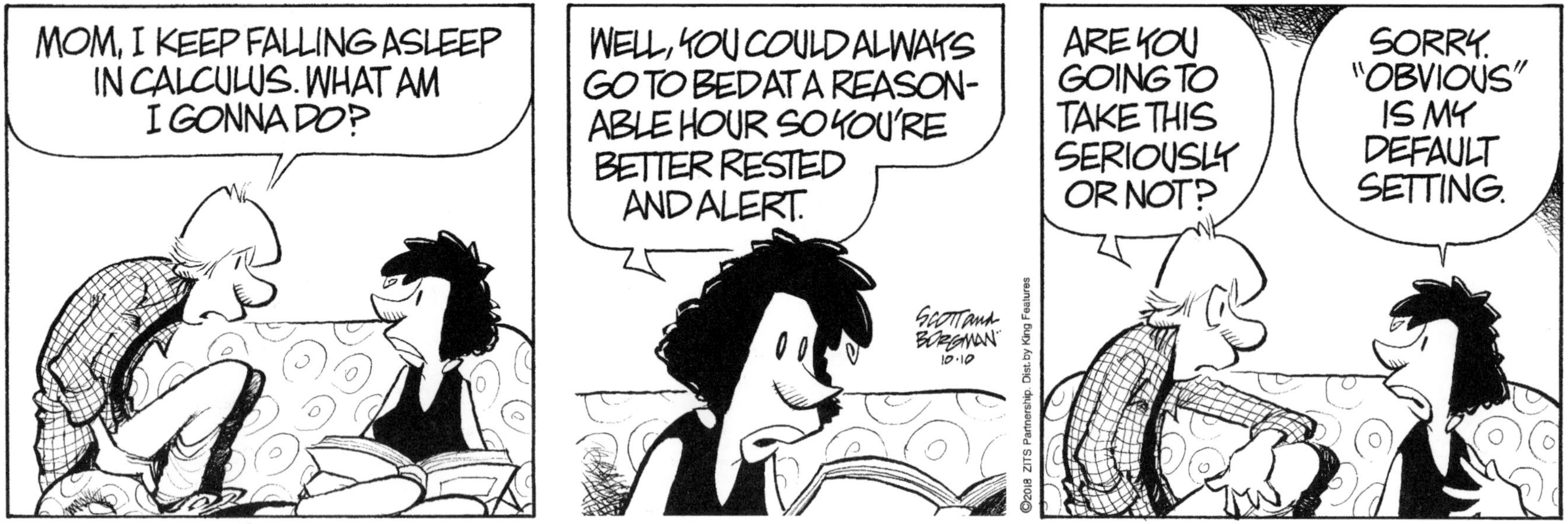
MOM, I KEEP FALLING ASLEEP IN CALCULUS. WHAT AM I GONNA DO?
WELL, YOU COULD ALWAYS GO TO BED AT A REASONABLE HOUR SO YOU'RE BETTER RESTED AND ALERT.
SCOTT and BORGMAN 10·10
©2018 ZITS Partnership. Dist. by King Features
ARE YOU GOING TO TAKE THIS SERIOUSLY OR NOT?
SORRY. "OBVIOUS" IS MY DEFAULT SETTING.

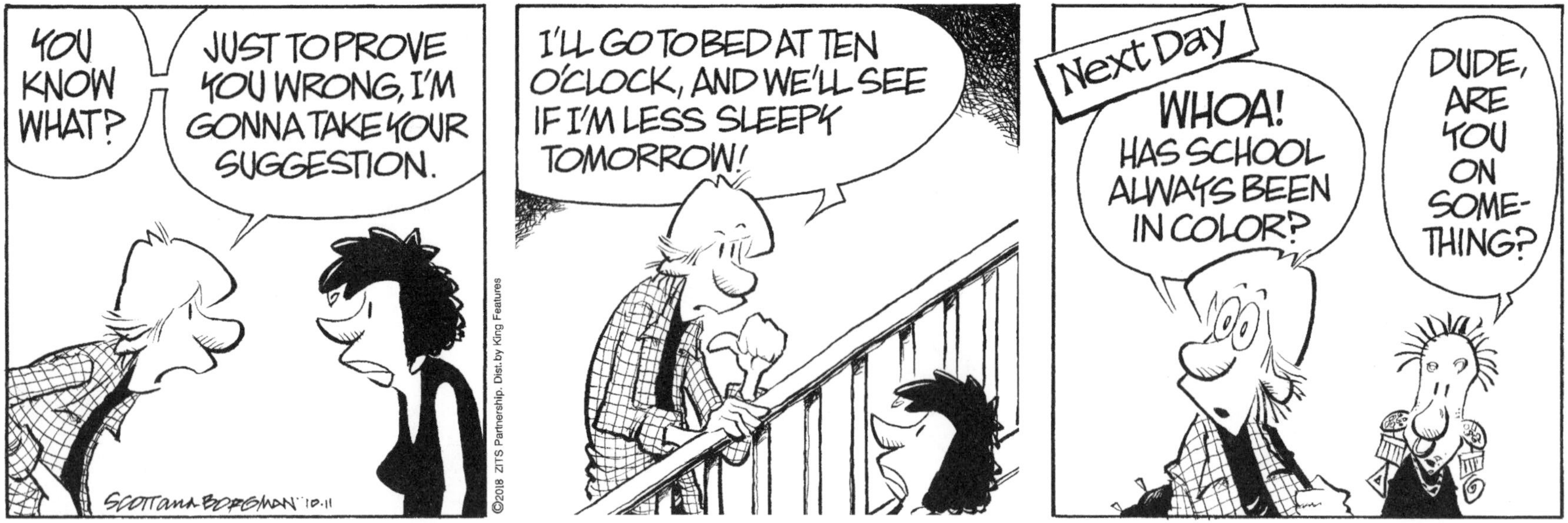
YOU KNOW WHAT?
JUST TO PROVE YOU WRONG, I'M GONNA TAKE YOUR SUGGESTION.
SCOTT and BORGMAN 10·11
©2018 ZITS Partnership. Dist. by King Features
I'LL GO TO BED AT TEN O'CLOCK, AND WE'LL SEE IF I'M LESS SLEEPY TOMORROW!
Next Day
WHOA! HAS SCHOOL ALWAYS BEEN IN COLOR?
DUDE, ARE YOU ON SOMETHING?

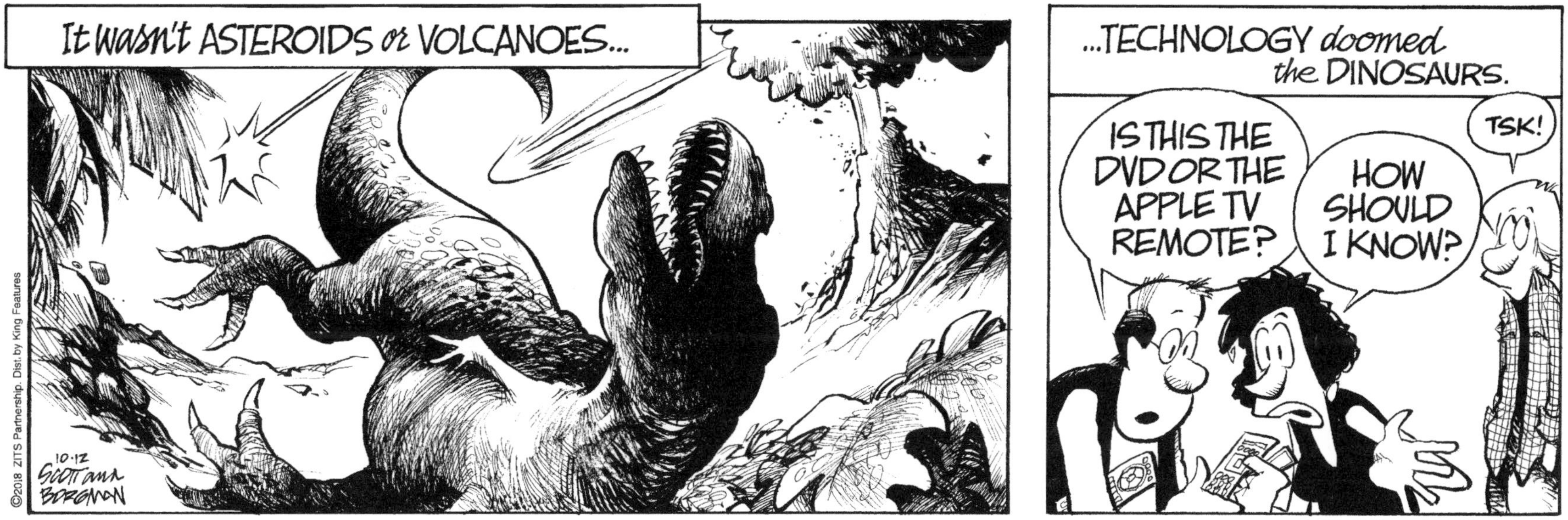
It wasn't ASTEROIDS or VOLCANOES...
©2018 ZITS Partnership. Dist. by King Features
10·12 SCOTT and BORGMAN
...TECHNOLOGY doomed the DINOSAURS.
IS THIS THE DVD OR THE APPLE TV REMOTE?
HOW SHOULD I KNOW?
TSK!

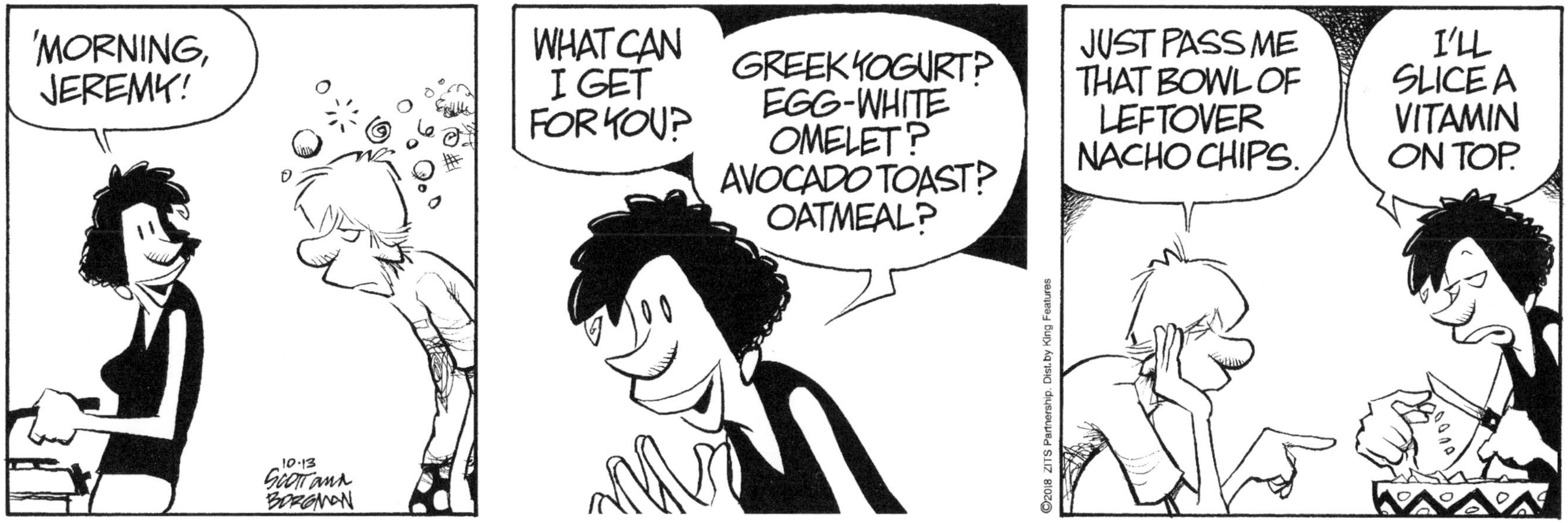
'MORNING, JEREMY!
10·13 SCOTT and BORGMAN
WHAT CAN I GET FOR YOU?
GREEK YOGURT? EGG-WHITE OMELET? AVOCADO TOAST? OATMEAL?
©2018 ZITS Partnership. Dist. by King Features
JUST PASS ME THAT BOWL OF LEFTOVER NACHO CHIPS.
I'LL SLICE A VITAMIN ON TOP.

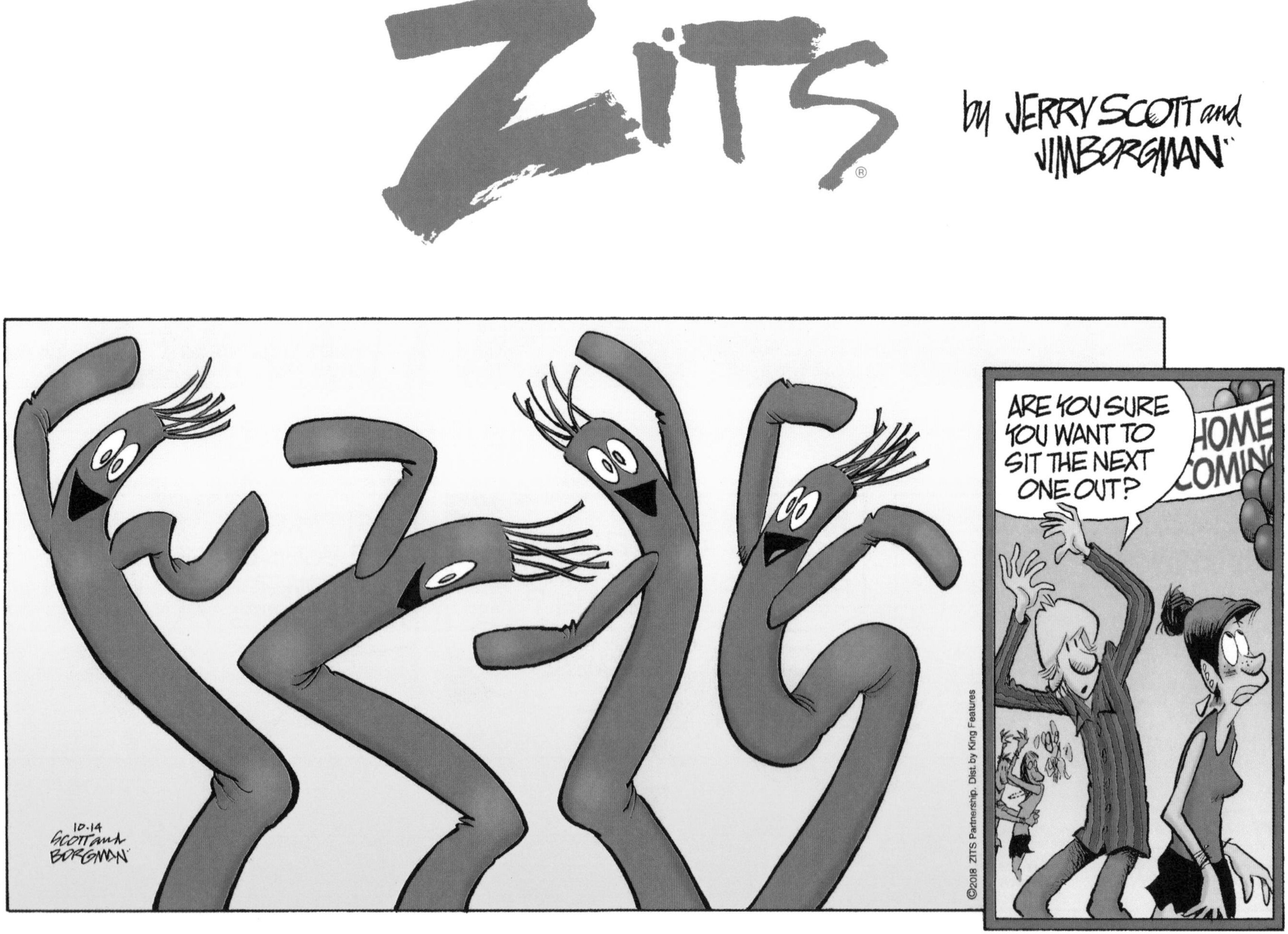
ZITS
by JERRY SCOTT and JIM BORGMAN
10.14 SCOTT and BORGMAN
©2018 ZITS Partnership. Dist. by King Features
ARE YOU SURE YOU WANT TO SIT THE NEXT ONE OUT?
HOME

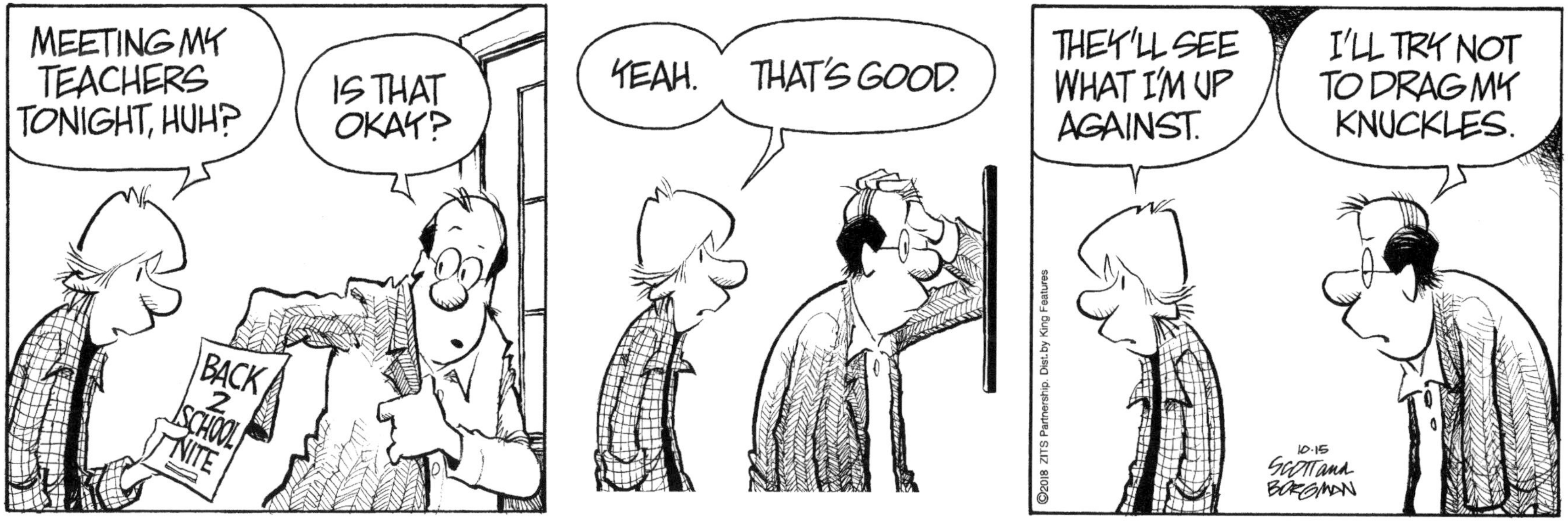
MEETING MY TEACHERS TONIGHT, HUH?
IS THAT OKAY?
BACK 2 SCHOOL NITE
YEAH.
THAT'S GOOD.
THEY'LL SEE WHAT I'M UP AGAINST.
I'LL TRY NOT TO DRAG MY KNUCKLES.
©2018 ZITS Partnership. Dist. by King Features
10·15
SCOTT and BORGMAN

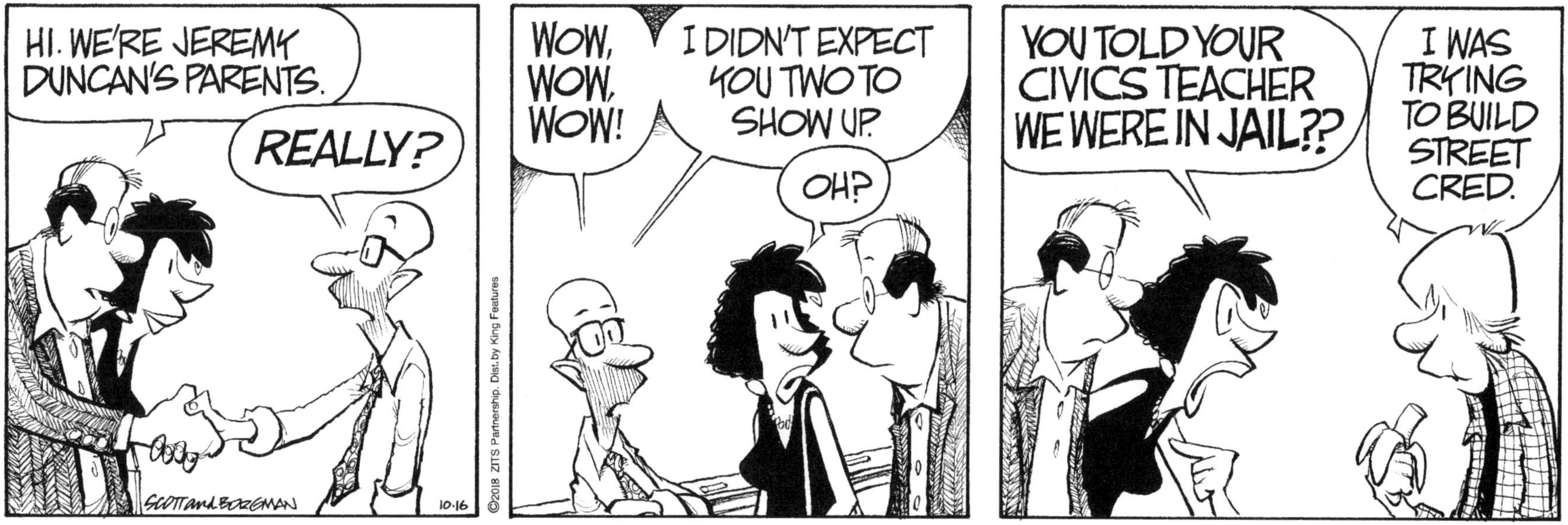
HI. WE'RE JEREMY DUNCAN'S PARENTS.
REALLY?
SCOTT and BORGMAN
10·16
©2018 ZITS Partnership. Dist. by King Features
WOW, WOW, WOW!
I DIDN'T EXPECT YOU TWO TO SHOW UP.
OH?
YOU TOLD YOUR CIVICS TEACHER WE WERE IN JAIL??
I WAS TRYING TO BUILD STREET CRED.

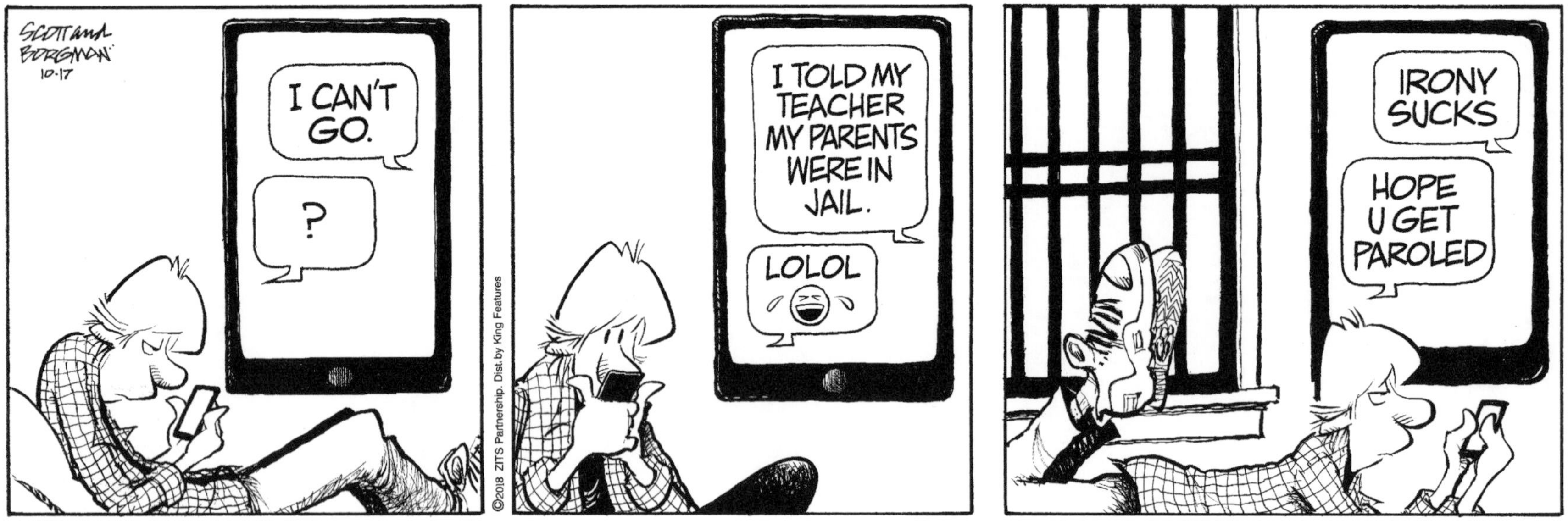
SCOTT AND BORGMAN 10-17
I CAN'T GO.
?
©2018 ZITS Partnership. Dist. by King Features
I TOLD MY TEACHER MY PARENTS WERE IN JAIL.
LOLOL
IRONY SUCKS
HOPE U GET PAROLED

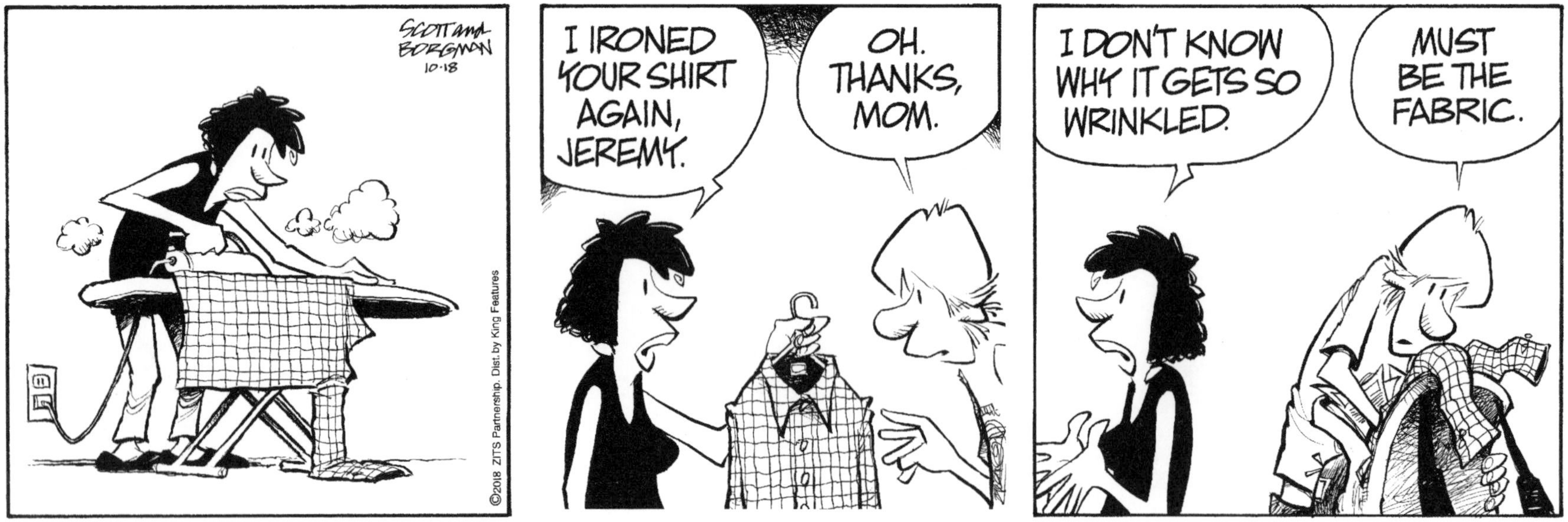
SCOTT AND BORGMAN 10-18
©2018 ZITS Partnership. Dist. by King Features
I IRONED YOUR SHIRT AGAIN, JEREMY.
OH. THANKS, MOM.
I DON'T KNOW WHY IT GETS SO WRINKLED.
MUST BE THE FABRIC.

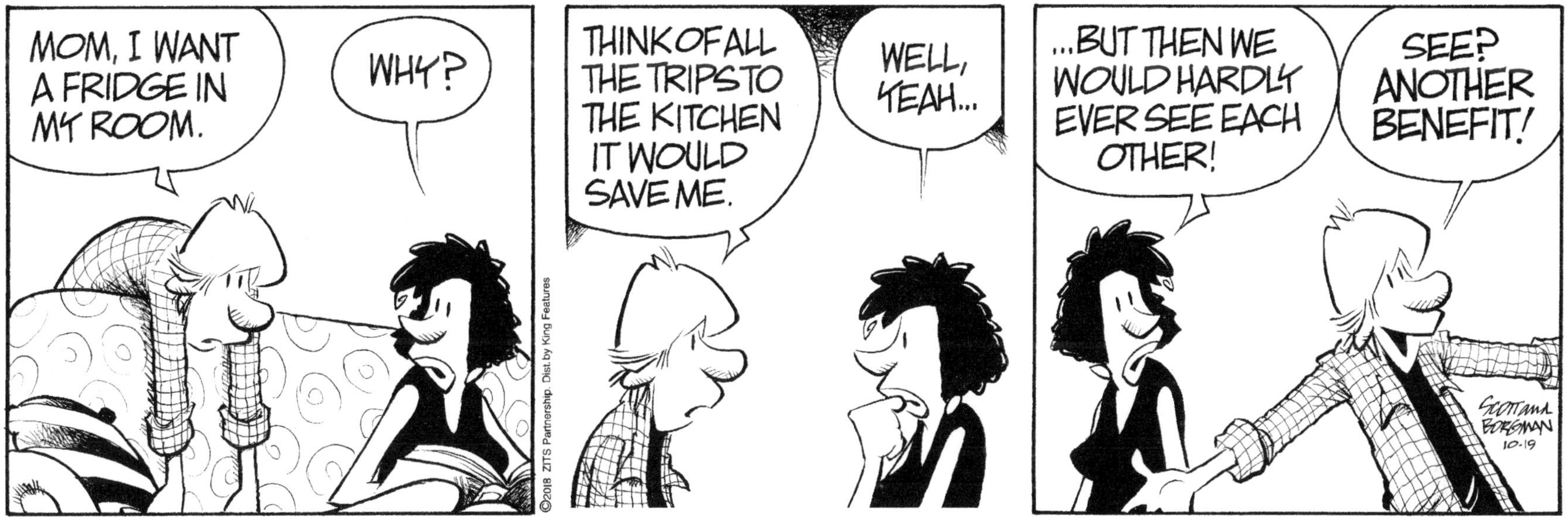
MOM, I WANT A FRIDGE IN MY ROOM.
WHY?
©2018 ZITS Partnership. Dist. by King Features
THINK OF ALL THE TRIPS TO THE KITCHEN IT WOULD SAVE ME.
WELL, YEAH...
...BUT THEN WE WOULD HARDLY EVER SEE EACH OTHER!
SEE? ANOTHER BENEFIT!
SCOTT and BORGMAN 10-19

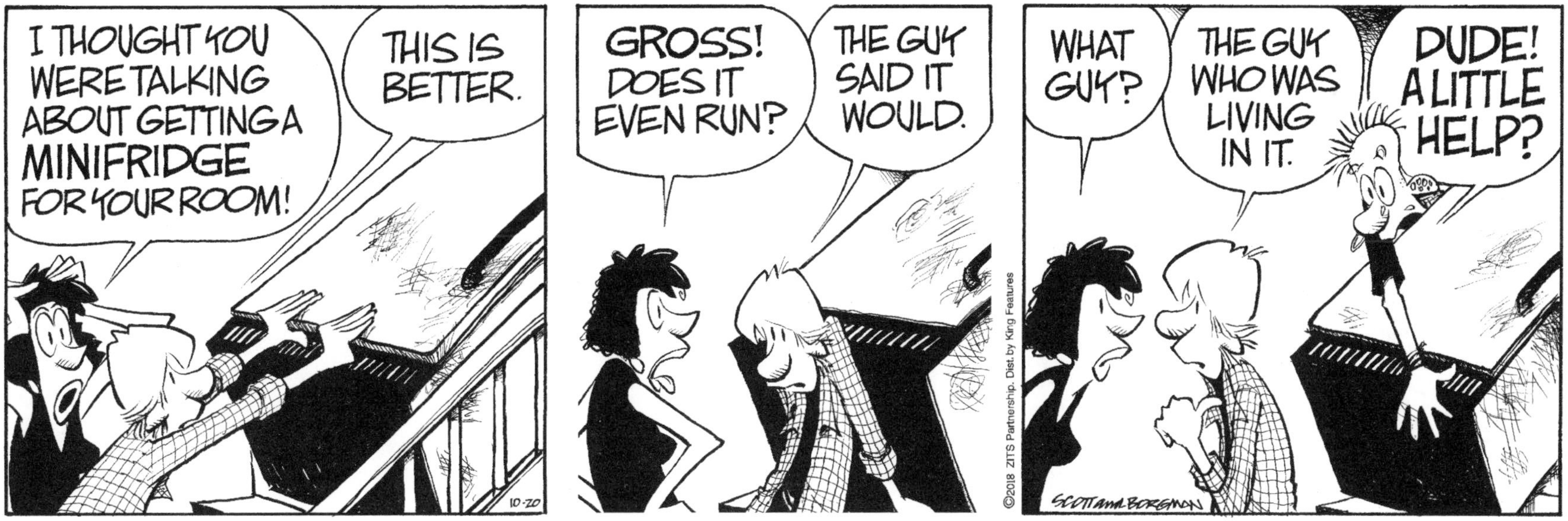
I THOUGHT YOU WERE TALKING ABOUT GETTING A **MINIFRIDGE** FOR YOUR ROOM!
THIS IS BETTER.
10-20
GROSS! DOES IT EVEN RUN?
THE GUY SAID IT WOULD.
©2018 ZITS Partnership. Dist. by King Features
WHAT GUY?
THE GUY WHO WAS LIVING IN IT.
DUDE! A LITTLE HELP?
SCOTT and BORGMAN

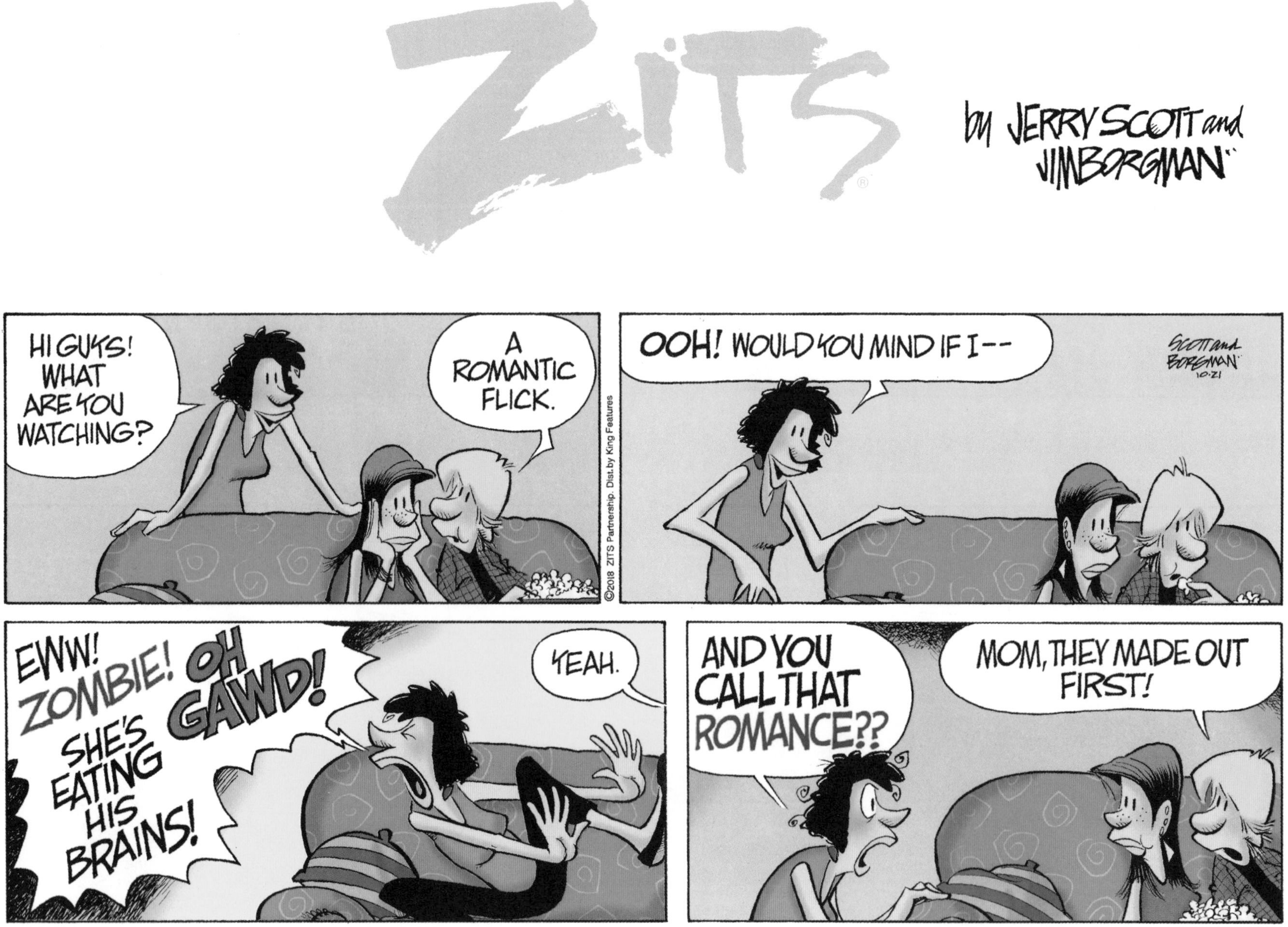
ZITS
by JERRY SCOTT and JIM BORGMAN
HI GUYS! WHAT ARE YOU WATCHING?
A ROMANTIC FLICK.
©2018 ZITS Partnership. Dist. by King Features
OOH! WOULD YOU MIND IF I--
SCOTT and BORGMAN 10·21
EWW! ZOMBIE! OH GAWD! SHE'S EATING HIS BRAINS!
YEAH.
AND YOU CALL THAT ROMANCE??
MOM, THEY MADE OUT FIRST!

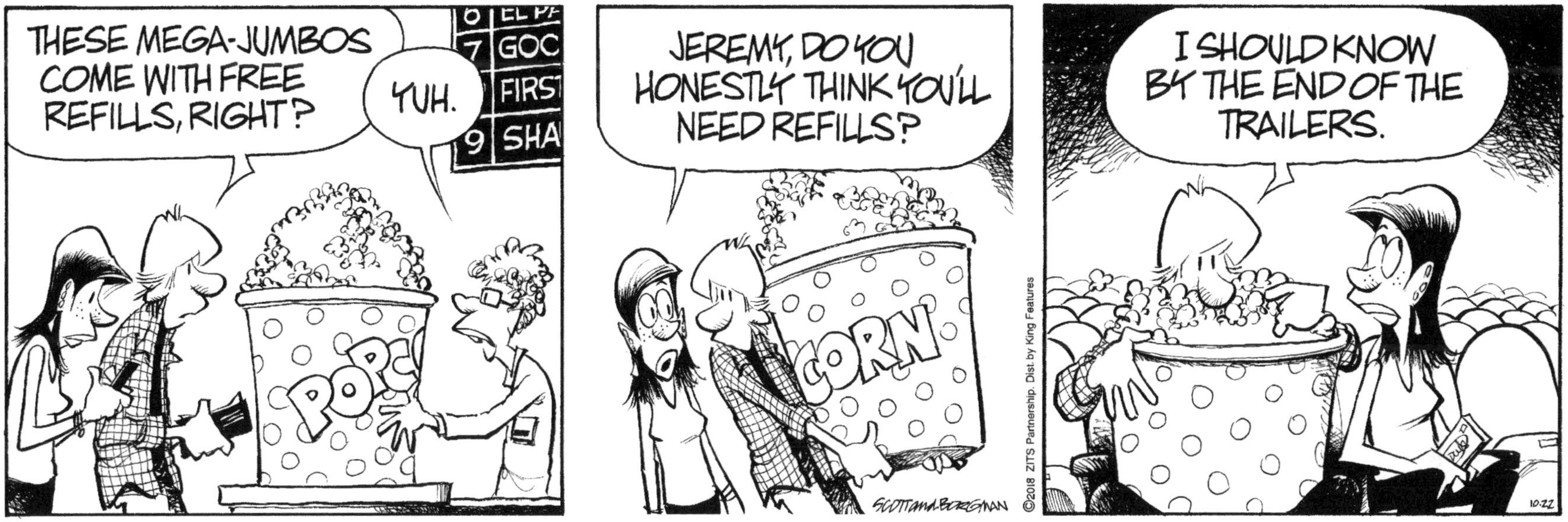
6 EL PA
7 GOC
FIRST
9 SHA
THESE MEGA-JUMBOS COME WITH FREE REFILLS, RIGHT?
YUH.
POPC
JEREMY, DO YOU HONESTLY THINK YOU'LL NEED REFILLS?
CORN
SCOTT AND BORGMAN
©2018 ZITS Partnership. Dist. by King Features
I SHOULD KNOW BY THE END OF THE TRAILERS.
10-22

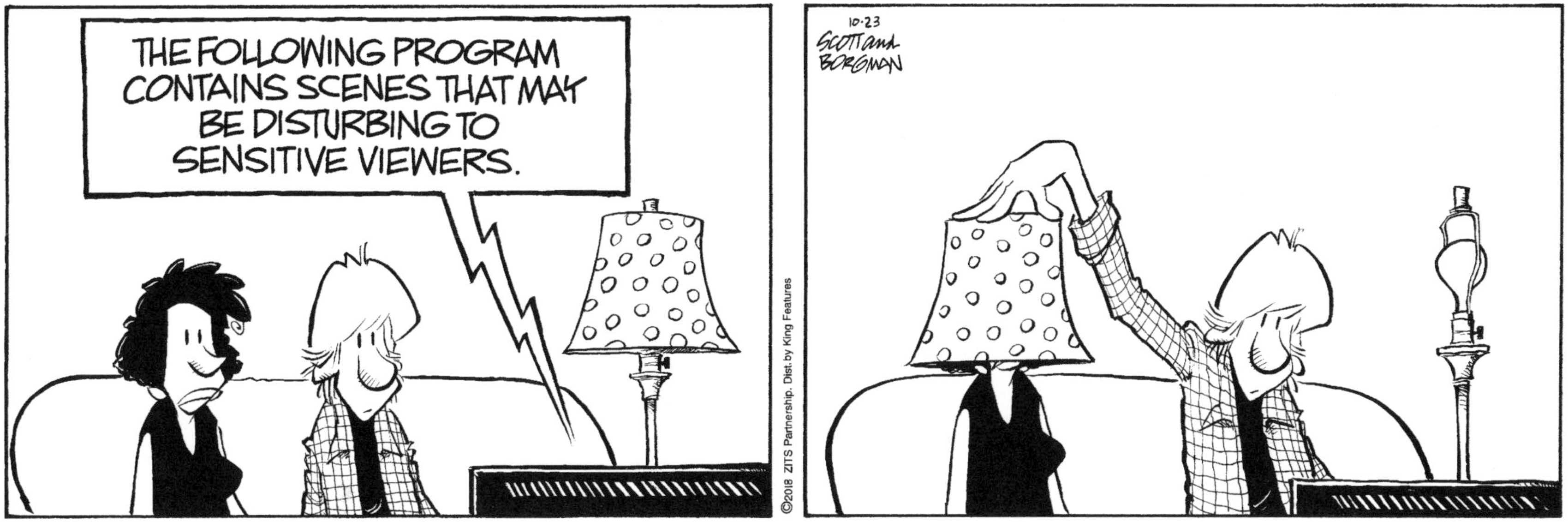
THE FOLLOWING PROGRAM CONTAINS SCENES THAT MAY BE DISTURBING TO SENSITIVE VIEWERS.
©2018 ZITS Partnership. Dist. by King Features
10-23
SCOTT AND BORGMAN

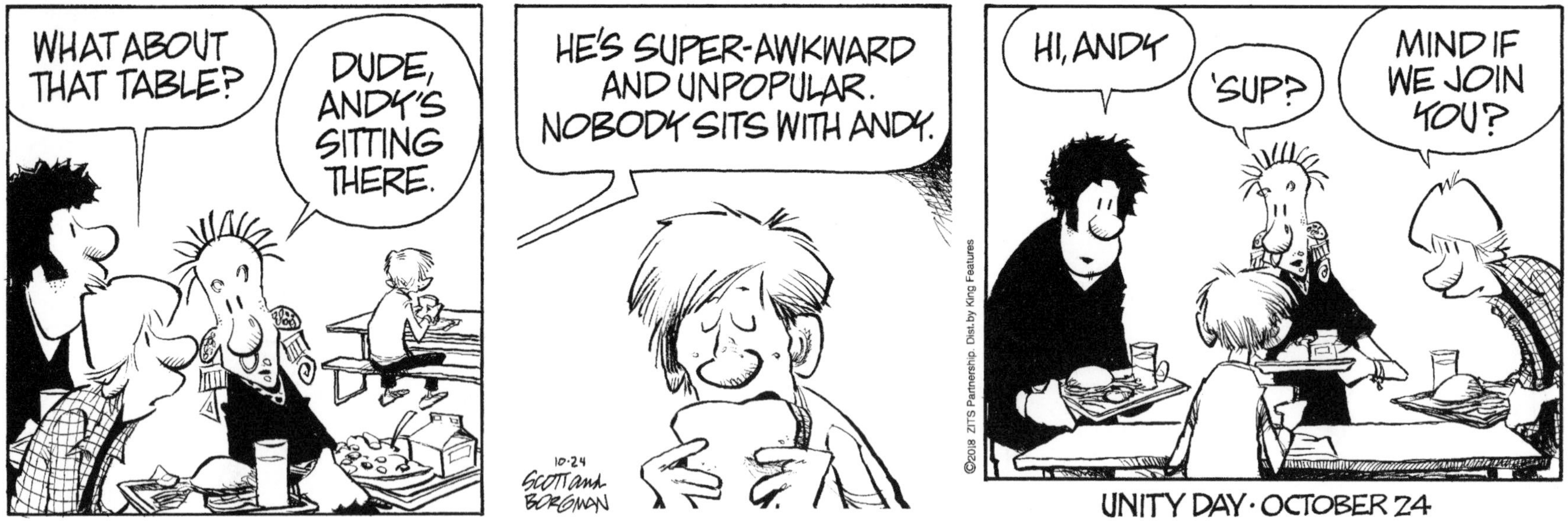
WHAT ABOUT THAT TABLE?
DUDE, ANDY'S SITTING THERE.
HE'S SUPER-AWKWARD AND UNPOPULAR. NOBODY SITS WITH ANDY.
10·24
SCOTT and BORGMAN
©2018 ZITS Partnership. Dist. by King Features
HI, ANDY
'SUP?
MIND IF WE JOIN YOU?

UNITY DAY · OCTOBER 24

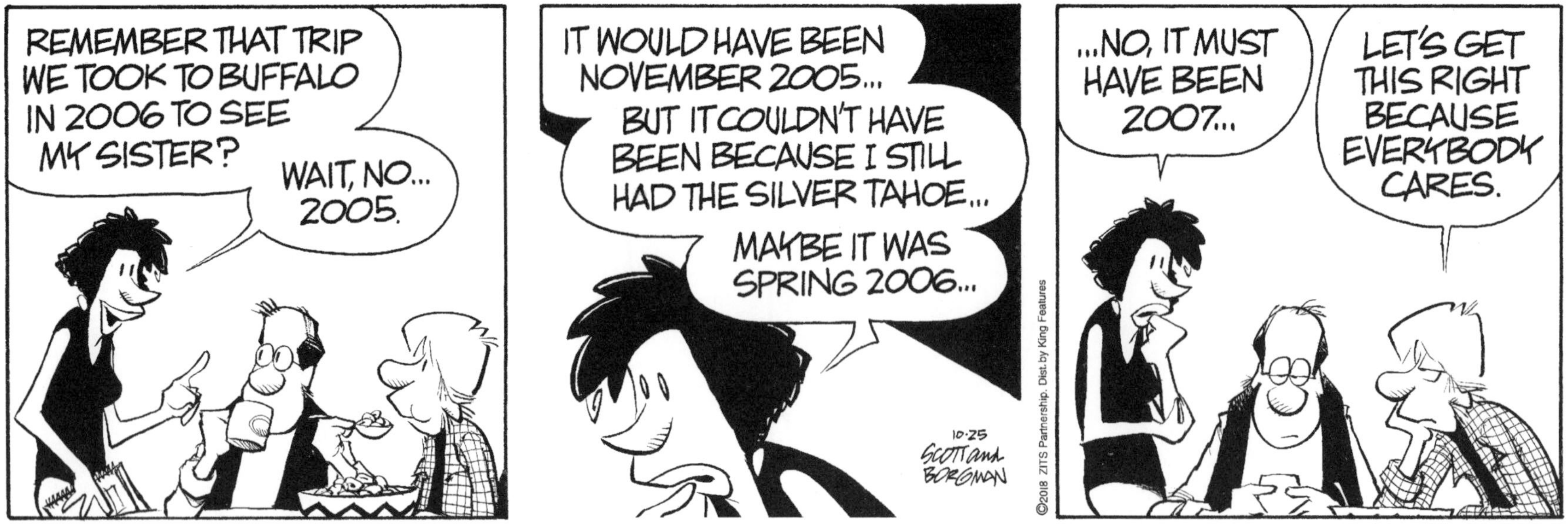
REMEMBER THAT TRIP WE TOOK TO BUFFALO IN 2006 TO SEE MY SISTER?
WAIT, NO... 2005.
IT WOULD HAVE BEEN NOVEMBER 2005...
BUT IT COULDN'T HAVE BEEN BECAUSE I STILL HAD THE SILVER TAHOE...
MAYBE IT WAS SPRING 2006...
10·25
SCOTT and BORGMAN
©2018 ZITS Partnership. Dist. by King Features
...NO, IT MUST HAVE BEEN 2007...
LET'S GET THIS RIGHT BECAUSE EVERYBODY CARES.

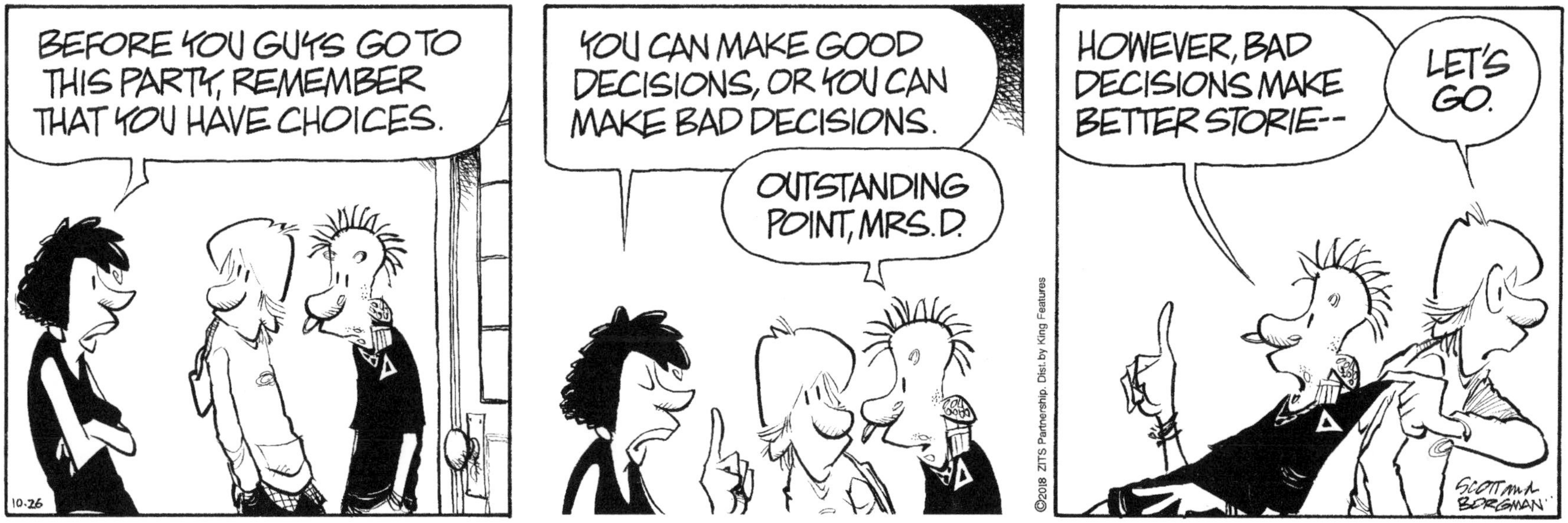
BEFORE YOU GUYS GO TO THIS PARTY, REMEMBER THAT YOU HAVE CHOICES.
10-26
YOU CAN MAKE GOOD DECISIONS, OR YOU CAN MAKE BAD DECISIONS.
OUTSTANDING POINT, MRS. D.
©2018 ZITS Partnership. Dist. by King Features
HOWEVER, BAD DECISIONS MAKE BETTER STORIE--
LET'S GO.
SCOTT and BORGMAN

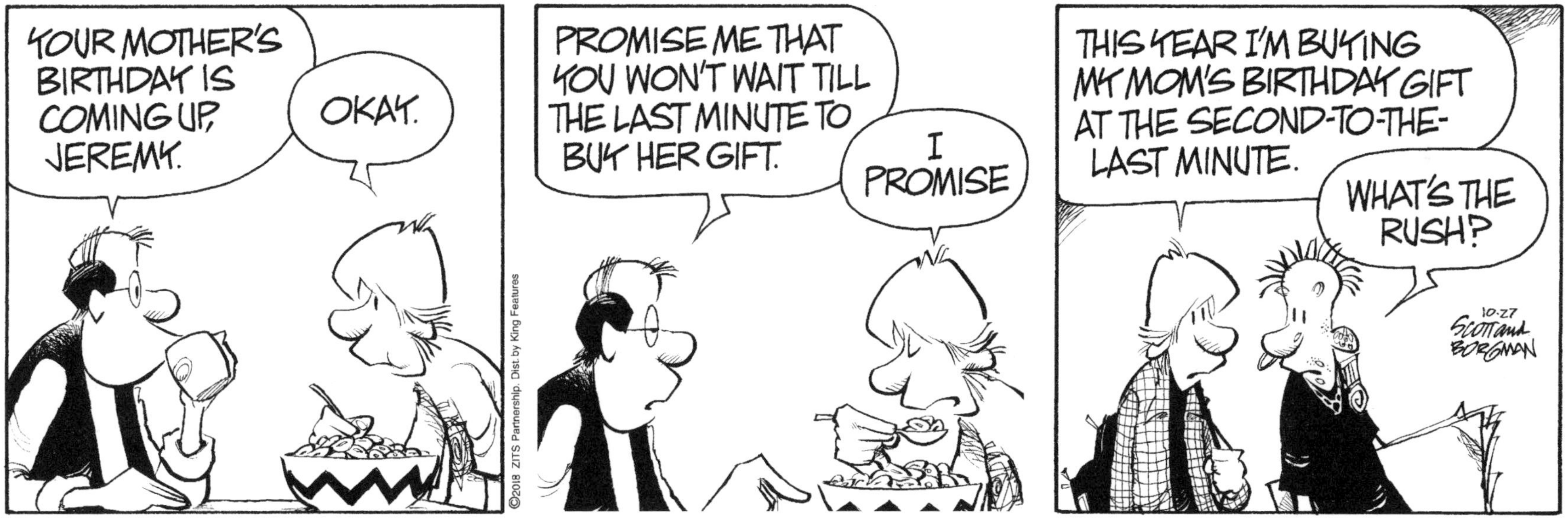
YOUR MOTHER'S BIRTHDAY IS COMING UP, JEREMY.
OKAY.
©2018 ZITS Partnership. Dist. by King Features
PROMISE ME THAT YOU WON'T WAIT TILL THE LAST MINUTE TO BUY HER GIFT.
I PROMISE
THIS YEAR I'M BUYING MY MOM'S BIRTHDAY GIFT AT THE SECOND-TO-THE-LAST MINUTE.
WHAT'S THE RUSH?
10-27
SCOTT and BORGMAN

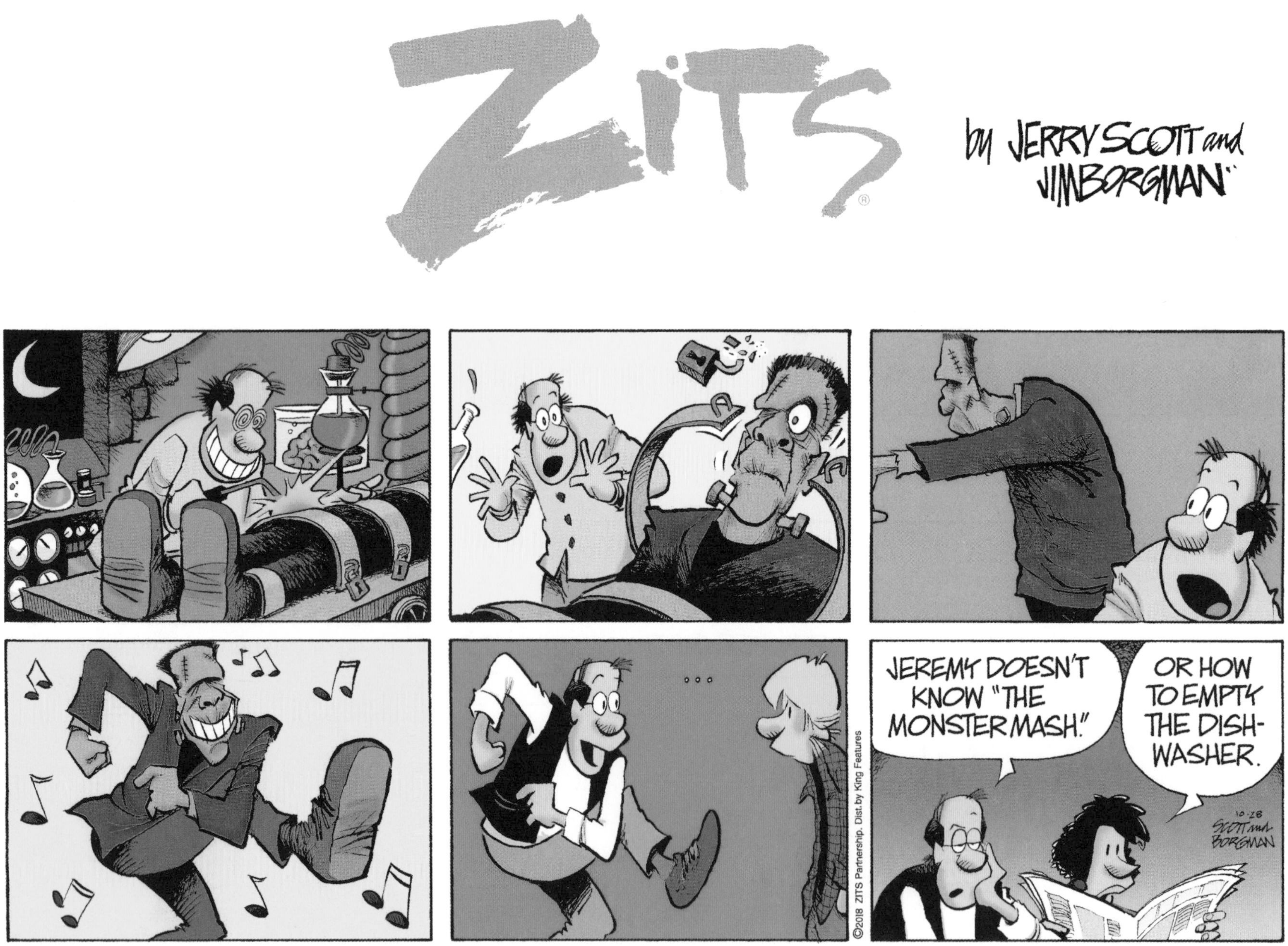
ZITS
by JERRY SCOTT and JIM BORGMAN
JEREMY DOESN'T KNOW "THE MONSTER MASH."
OR HOW TO EMPTY THE DISH-WASHER.
10-28 SCOTT and BORGMAN
©2018 ZITS Partnership. Dist. by King Features

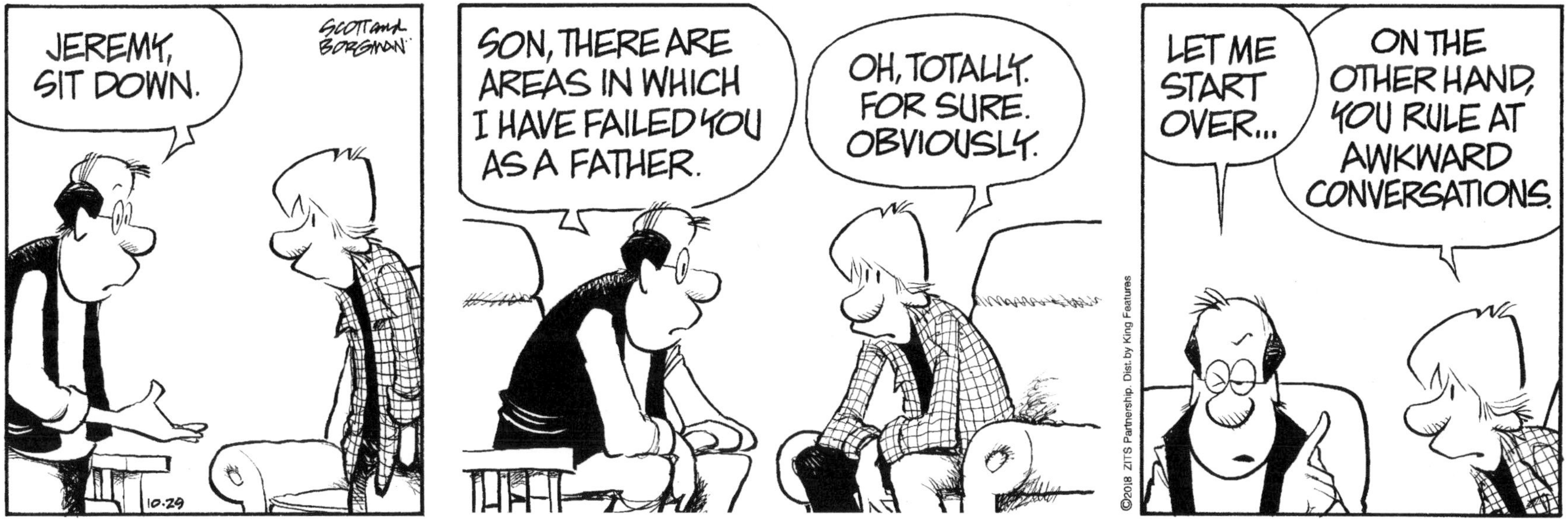
SCOTT and BORGMAN
10·29
JEREMY, SIT DOWN.
SON, THERE ARE AREAS IN WHICH I HAVE FAILED YOU AS A FATHER.
OH, TOTALLY. FOR SURE. OBVIOUSLY.
LET ME START OVER...
ON THE OTHER HAND, YOU RULE AT AWKWARD CONVERSATIONS.
©2018 ZITS Partnership. Dist. by King Features

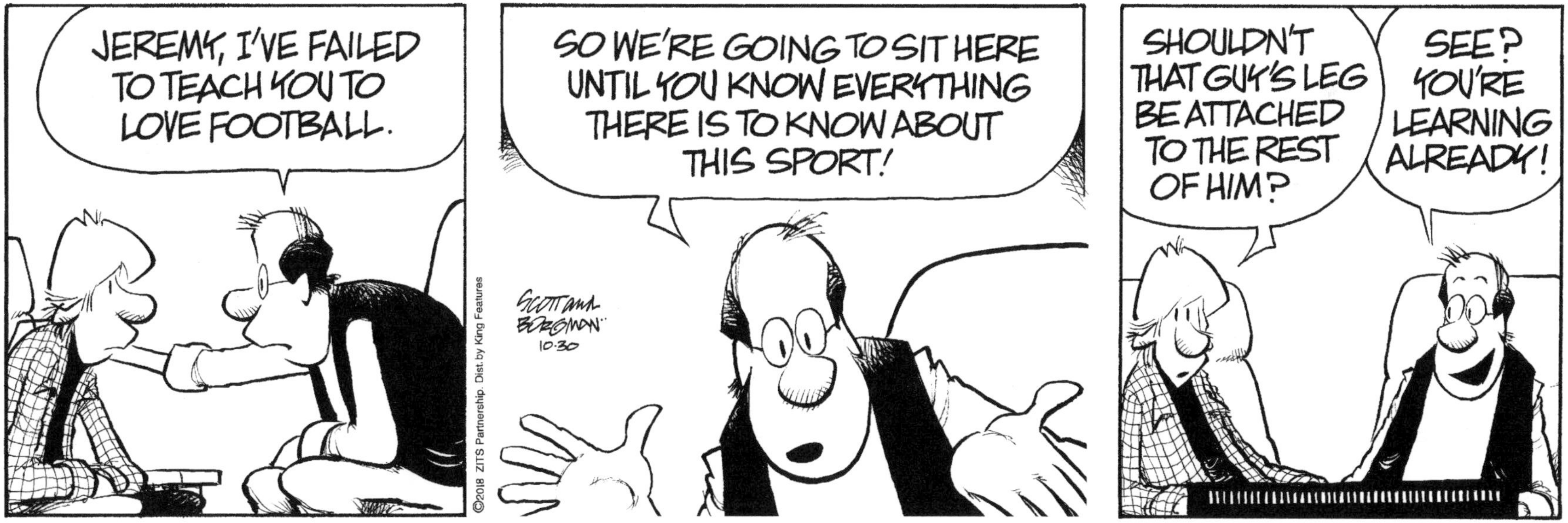
JEREMY, I'VE FAILED TO TEACH YOU TO LOVE FOOTBALL.
©2018 ZITS Partnership. Dist. by King Features
SCOTT and BORGMAN
10·30
SO WE'RE GOING TO SIT HERE UNTIL YOU KNOW EVERYTHING THERE IS TO KNOW ABOUT THIS SPORT!
SHOULDN'T THAT GUY'S LEG BE ATTACHED TO THE REST OF HIM?
SEE? YOU'RE LEARNING ALREADY!

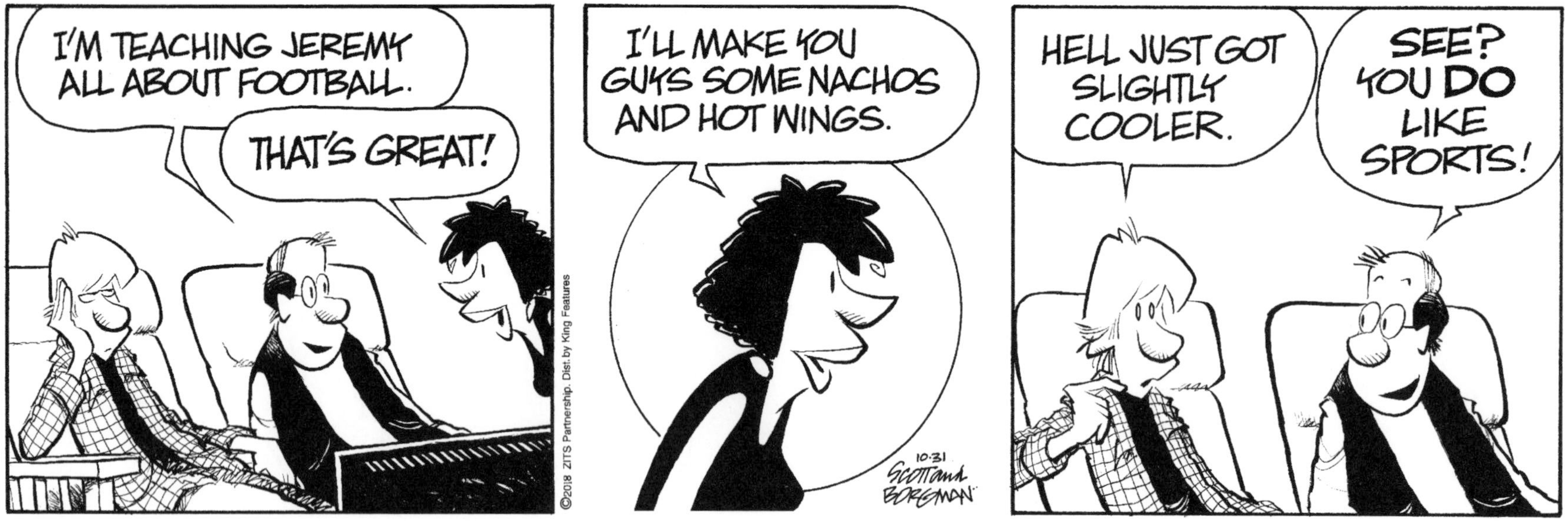
I'M TEACHING JEREMY ALL ABOUT FOOTBALL.
THAT'S GREAT!
©2018 ZITS Partnership. Dist. by King Features
I'LL MAKE YOU GUYS SOME NACHOS AND HOT WINGS.
10-31 SCOTT and BORGMAN
HELL JUST GOT SLIGHTLY COOLER.
SEE? YOU **DO** LIKE SPORTS!

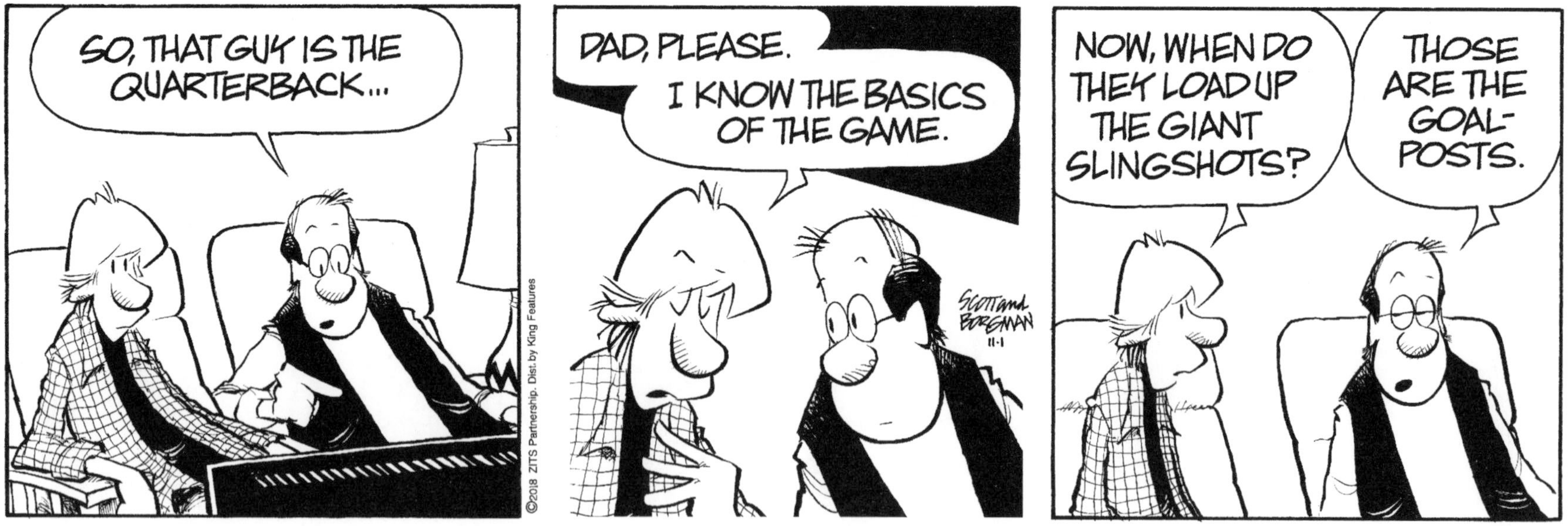
SO, THAT GUY IS THE QUARTERBACK...
©2018 ZITS Partnership. Dist. by King Features
DAD, PLEASE.
I KNOW THE BASICS OF THE GAME.
SCOTT and BORGMAN 11-1
NOW, WHEN DO THEY LOAD UP THE GIANT SLINGSHOTS?
THOSE ARE THE GOAL-POSTS.

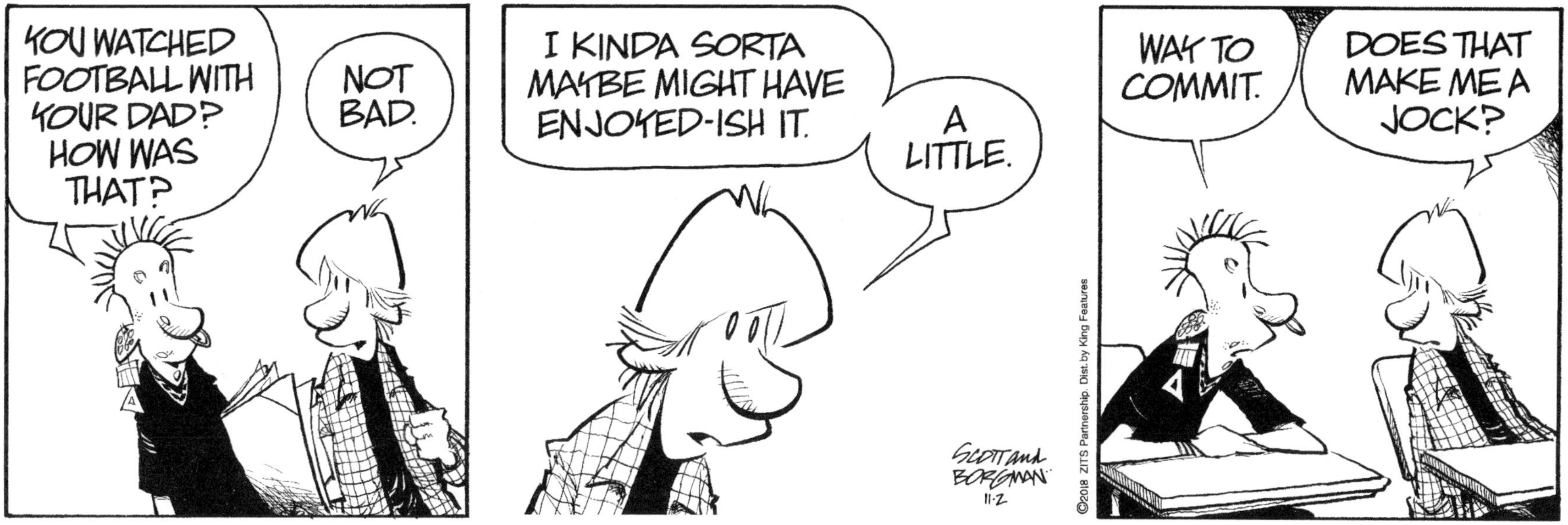
YOU WATCHED FOOTBALL WITH YOUR DAD? HOW WAS THAT?
NOT BAD.
I KINDA SORTA MAYBE MIGHT HAVE ENJOYED-ISH IT.
A LITTLE.
WAY TO COMMIT.
DOES THAT MAKE ME A JOCK?
SCOTT AND BORGMAN 11·2
©2018 ZITS Partnership. Dist. by King Features

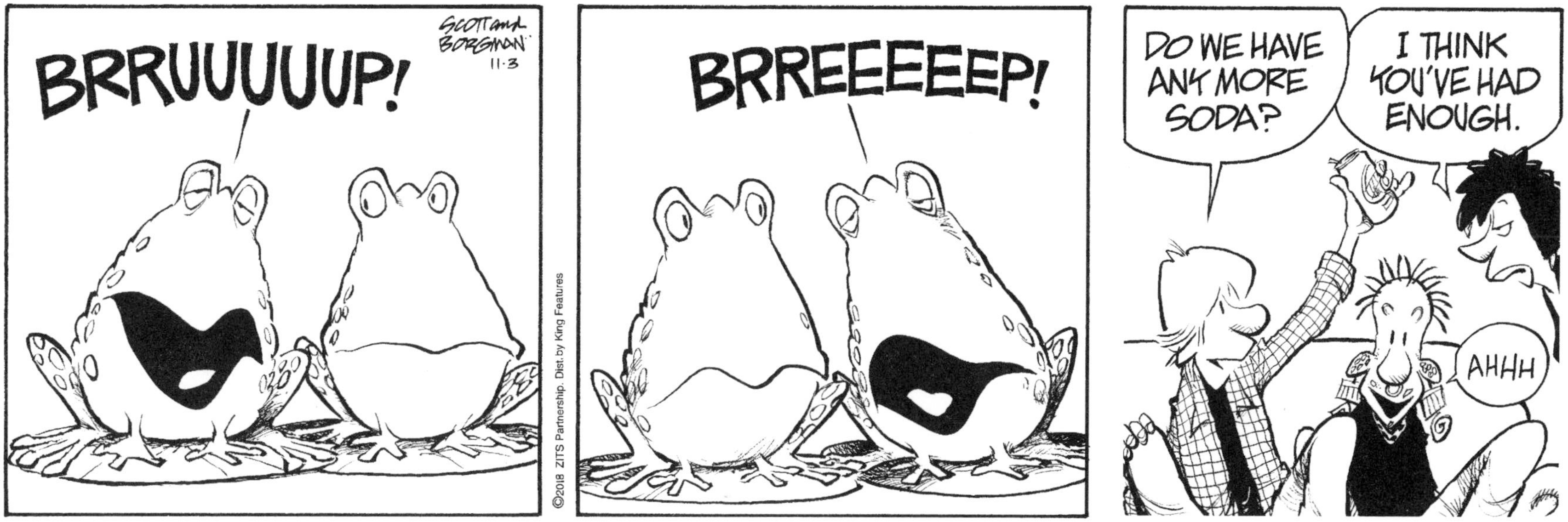
SCOTT AND BORGMAN 11·3
BRRUUUUUP!
BRREEEEEP!
DO WE HAVE ANY MORE SODA?
I THINK YOU'VE HAD ENOUGH.
AHHH
©2018 ZITS Partnership. Dist. by King Features

ZITS®

by JERRY SCOTT and JIM BORGMAN

MOM, CAN I ASK YOU A QUESTION?
SURE, JEREMY! TELL ME WHAT'S ON YOUR MIND.
THIN MINTS
THE HITCHHIKER'S GUIDE TO THE GALAXY
©2018 ZITS Partnership. Dist. by King Features
CAN I JUST ASK MY QUESTION INSTEAD?
11-4
SCOTT and BORGMAN

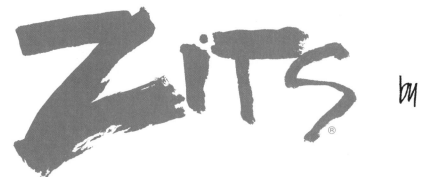

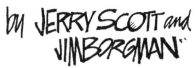

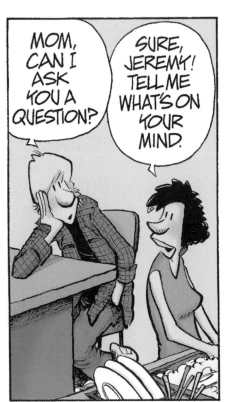

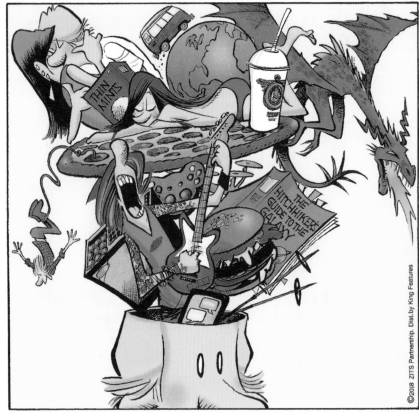

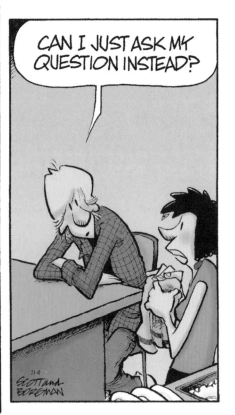

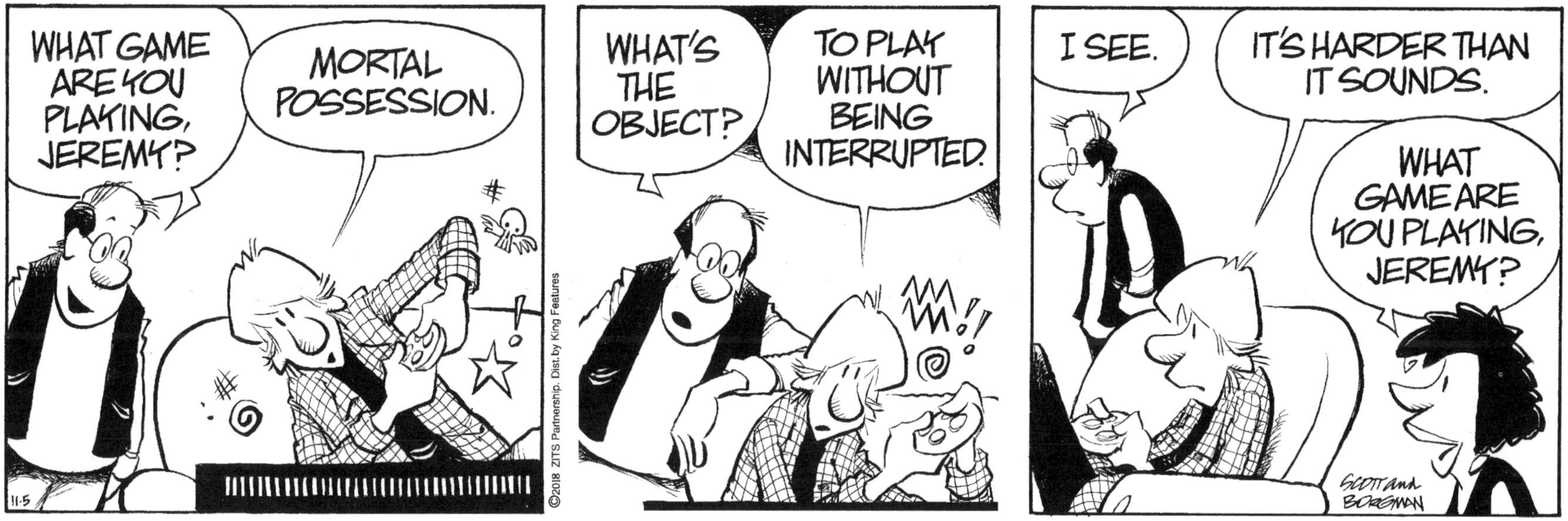
WHAT GAME ARE YOU PLAYING, JEREMY?
MORTAL POSSESSION.
©2018 ZITS Partnership. Dist. by King Features
WHAT'S THE OBJECT?
TO PLAY WITHOUT BEING INTERRUPTED.
I SEE.
IT'S HARDER THAN IT SOUNDS.
WHAT GAME ARE YOU PLAYING, JEREMY?
SCOTT and BORGMAN

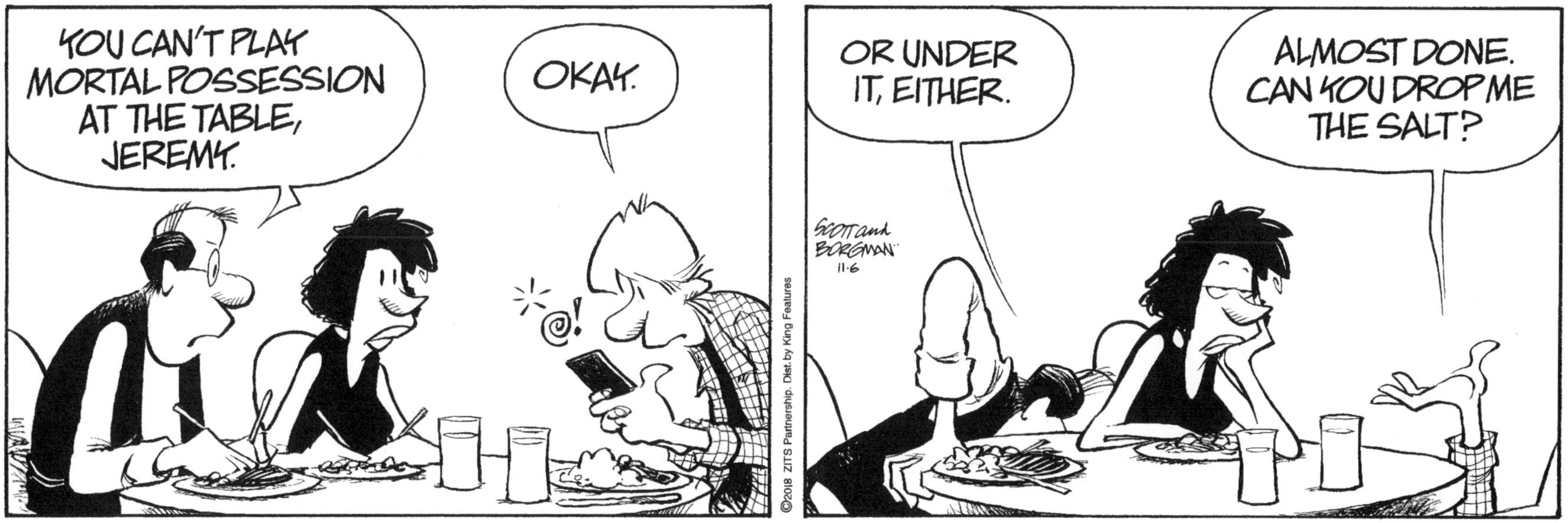
YOU CAN'T PLAY MORTAL POSSESSION AT THE TABLE, JEREMY.
OKAY.
©2018 ZITS Partnership. Dist. by King Features
SCOTT and BORGMAN
OR UNDER IT, EITHER.
ALMOST DONE. CAN YOU DROP ME THE SALT?

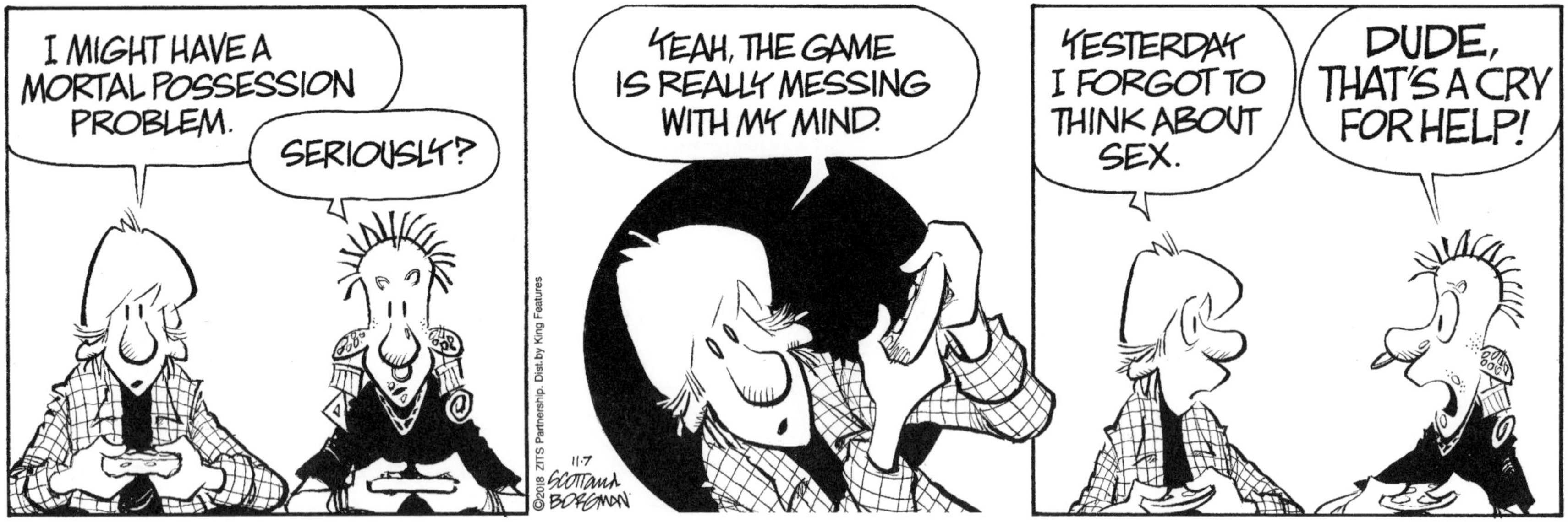
I MIGHT HAVE A MORTAL POSSESSION PROBLEM.
SERIOUSLY?
YEAH, THE GAME IS REALLY MESSING WITH MY MIND.
YESTERDAY I FORGOT TO THINK ABOUT SEX.
DUDE, THAT'S A CRY FOR HELP!
©2018 ZITS Partnership. Dist. by King Features
11·7 SCOTT and BORGMAN

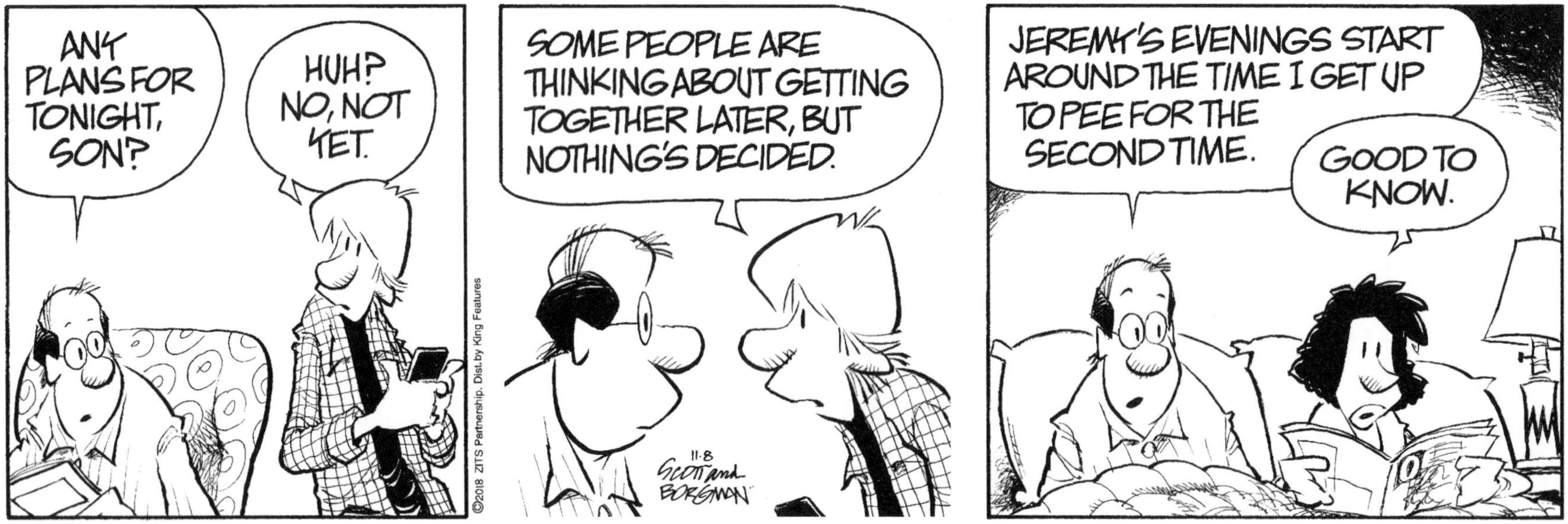
ANY PLANS FOR TONIGHT, SON?
HUH? NO, NOT YET.
SOME PEOPLE ARE THINKING ABOUT GETTING TOGETHER LATER, BUT NOTHING'S DECIDED.
JEREMY'S EVENINGS START AROUND THE TIME I GET UP TO PEE FOR THE SECOND TIME.
GOOD TO KNOW.
©2018 ZITS Partnership. Dist. by King Features
11·8 SCOTT and BORGMAN

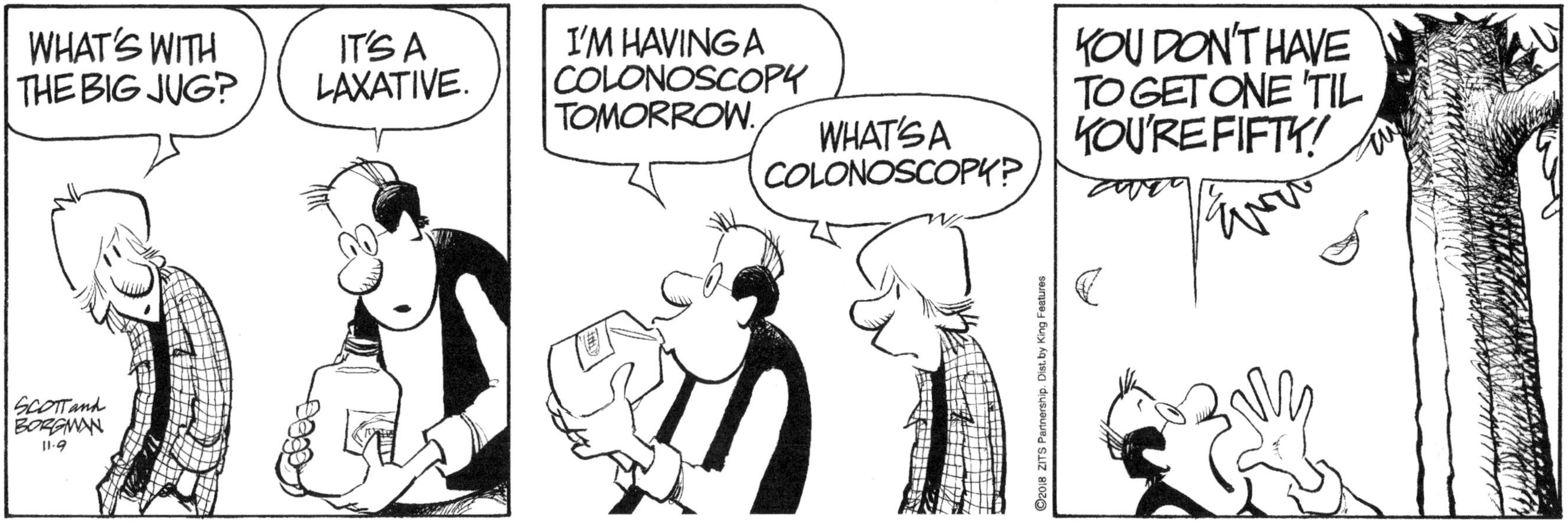
WHAT'S WITH THE BIG JUG?
IT'S A LAXATIVE.
I'M HAVING A COLONOSCOPY TOMORROW.
WHAT'S A COLONOSCOPY?
YOU DON'T HAVE TO GET ONE 'TIL YOU'RE FIFTY!
SCOTT and BORGMAN 11-9
©2018 ZITS Partnership. Dist.by King Features

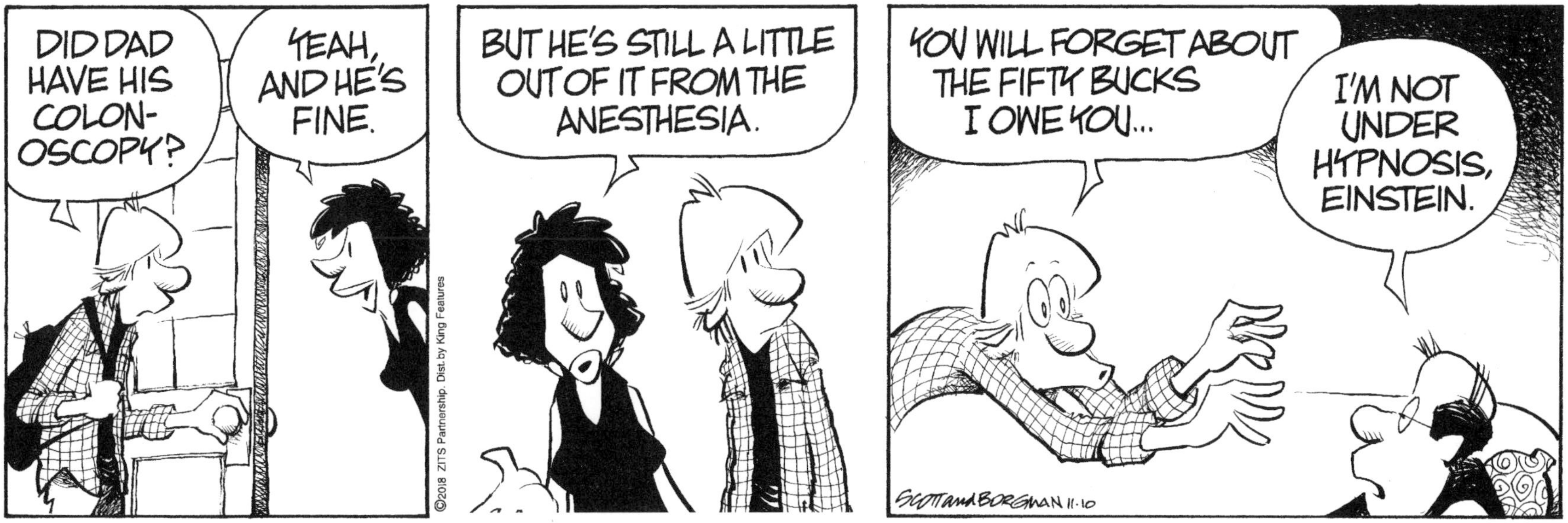
DID DAD HAVE HIS COLONOSCOPY?
YEAH, AND HE'S FINE.
BUT HE'S STILL A LITTLE OUT OF IT FROM THE ANESTHESIA.
YOU WILL FORGET ABOUT THE FIFTY BUCKS I OWE YOU...
I'M NOT UNDER HYPNOSIS, EINSTEIN.
SCOTT and BORGMAN 11-10
©2018 ZITS Partnership. Dist.by King Features

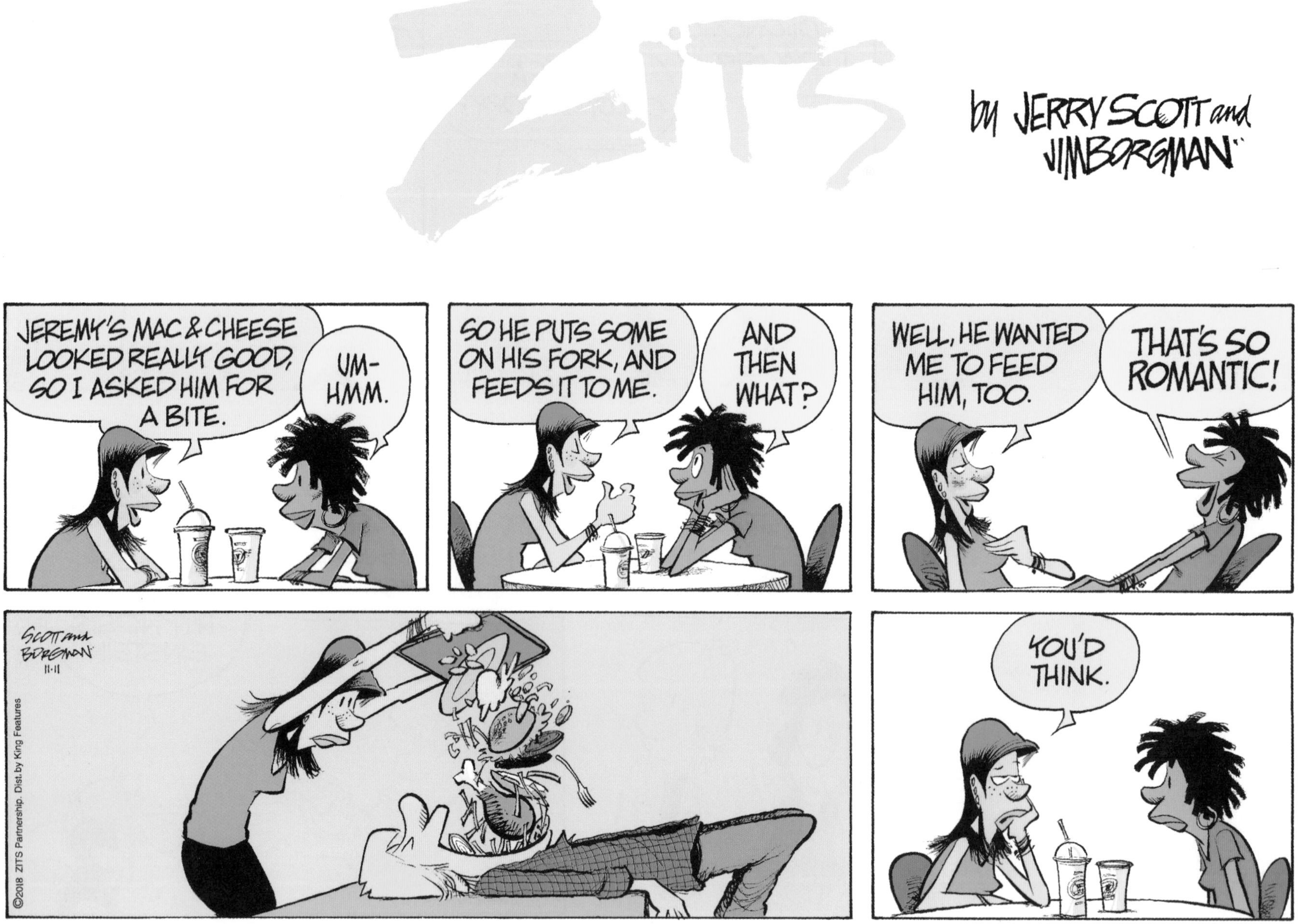
ZITS
by JERRY SCOTT and JIM BORGMAN
JEREMY'S MAC & CHEESE LOOKED REALLY GOOD, SO I ASKED HIM FOR A BITE.
UM-HMM.
SO HE PUTS SOME ON HIS FORK, AND FEEDS IT TO ME.
AND THEN WHAT?
WELL, HE WANTED ME TO FEED HIM, TOO.
THAT'S SO ROMANTIC!
SCOTT and BORGMAN 11-11
©2018 ZITS Partnership. Dist. by King Features
YOU'D THINK.

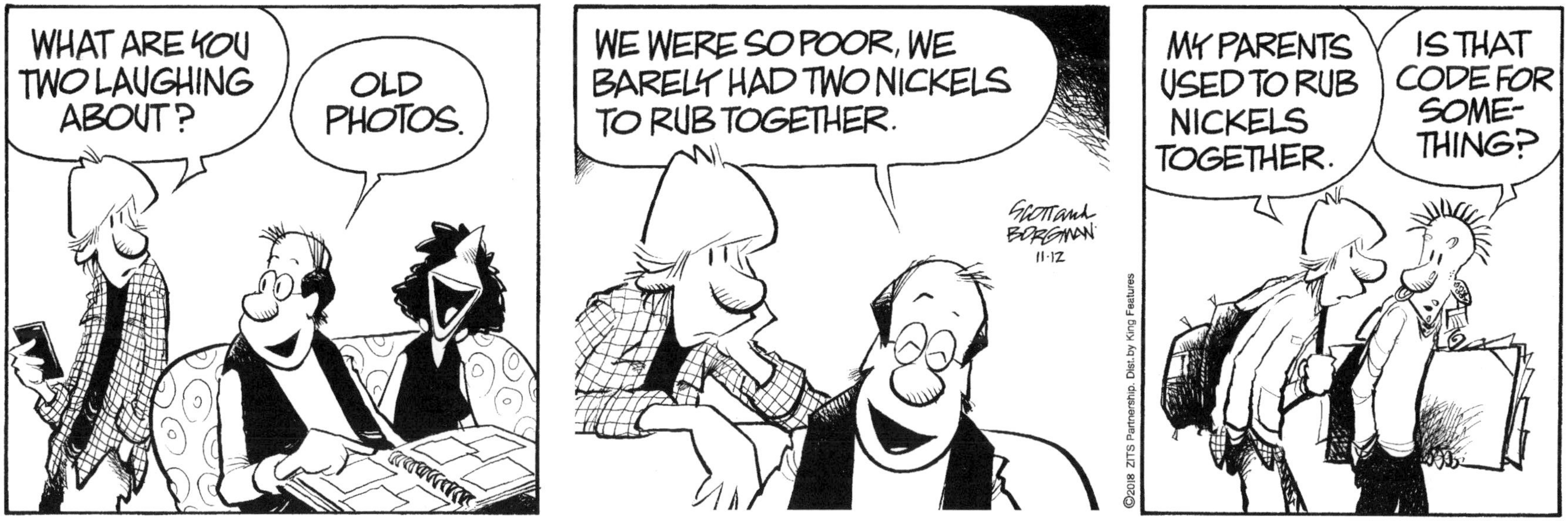
WHAT ARE YOU TWO LAUGHING ABOUT?
OLD PHOTOS.
WE WERE SO POOR, WE BARELY HAD TWO NICKELS TO RUB TOGETHER.
SCOTT and BORGMAN 11-12
MY PARENTS USED TO RUB NICKELS TOGETHER.
IS THAT CODE FOR SOMETHING?
©2018 ZITS Partnership. Dist. by King Features

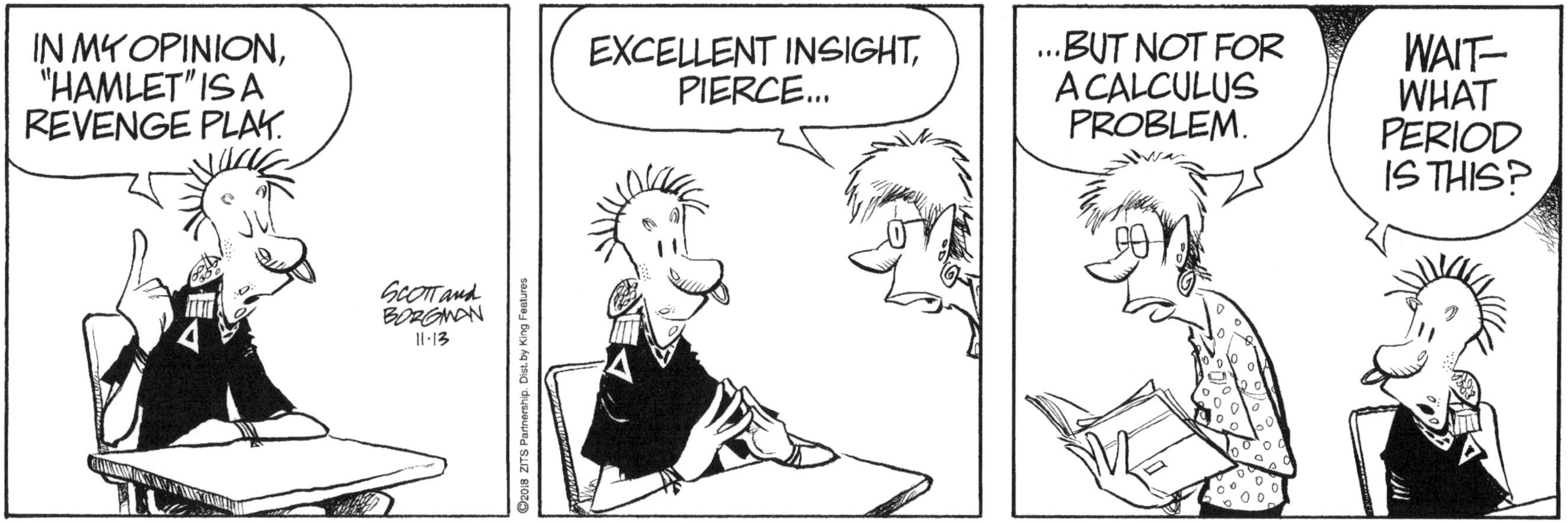
IN MY OPINION, "HAMLET" IS A REVENGE PLAY.
SCOTT and BORGMAN 11-13
©2018 ZITS Partnership. Dist. by King Features
EXCELLENT INSIGHT, PIERCE...
...BUT NOT FOR A CALCULUS PROBLEM.
WAIT— WHAT PERIOD IS THIS?

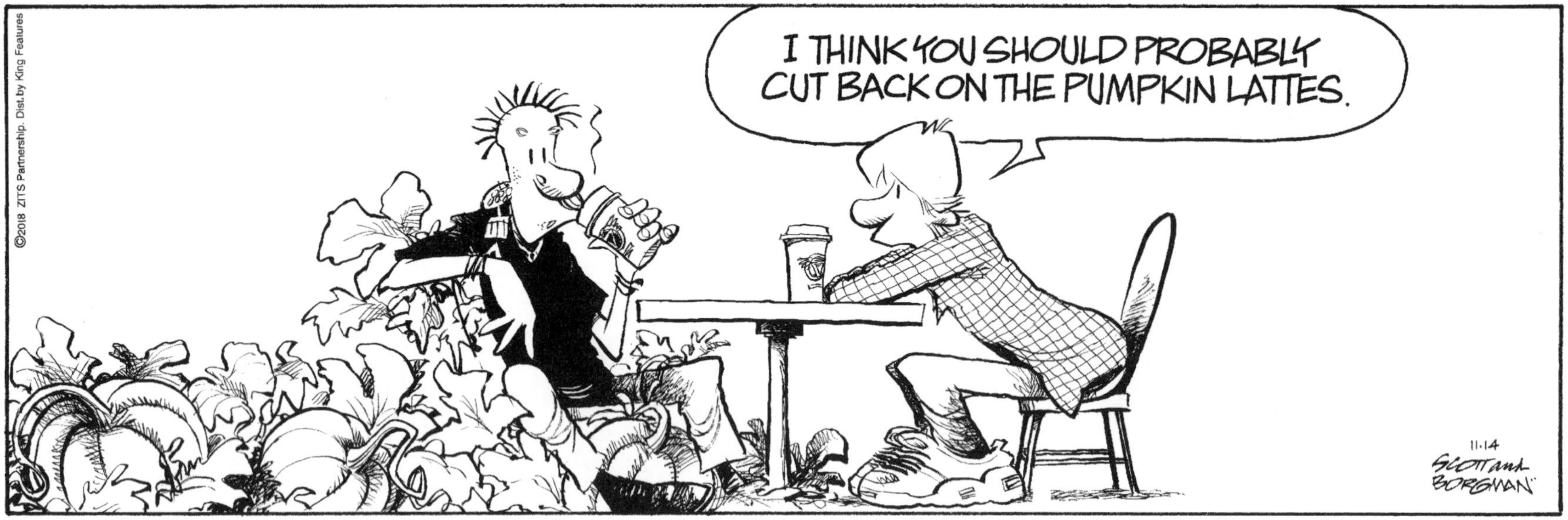
I THINK YOU SHOULD PROBABLY CUT BACK ON THE PUMPKIN LATTES.
©2018 ZITS Partnership. Dist. by King Features
11.14
SCOTT and BORGMAN

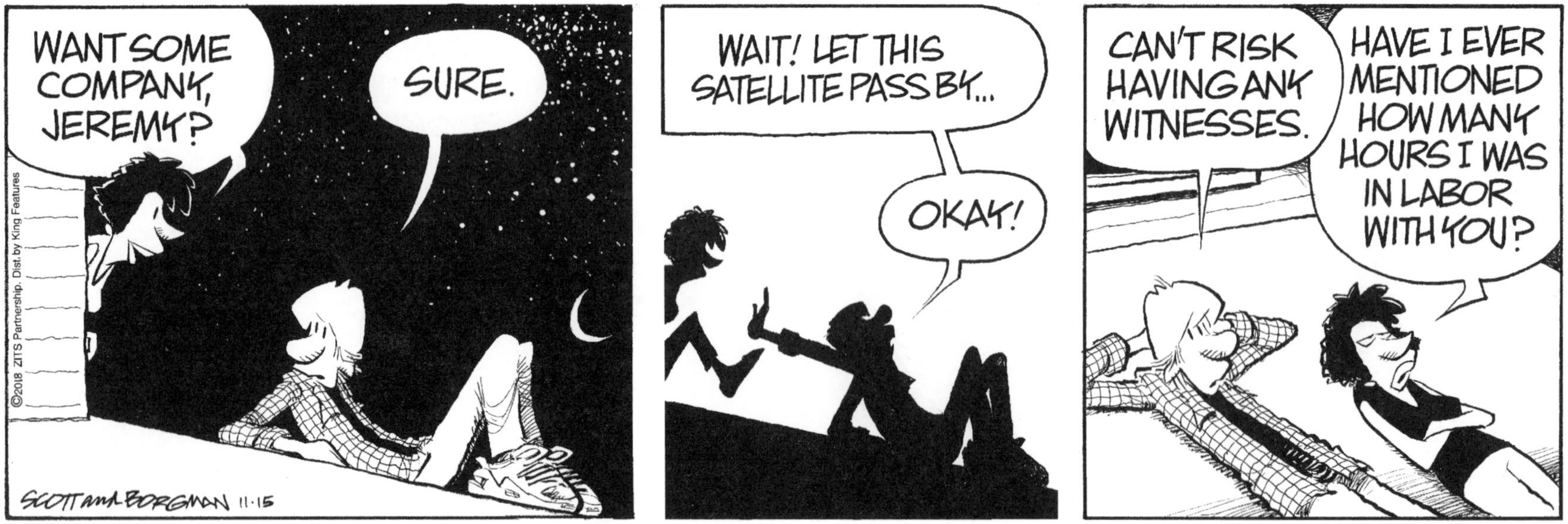
WANT SOME COMPANY, JEREMY?
SURE.
©2018 ZITS Partnership. Dist. by King Features
SCOTT and BORGMAN 11.15
WAIT! LET THIS SATELLITE PASS BY...
OKAY!
CAN'T RISK HAVING ANY WITNESSES.
HAVE I EVER MENTIONED HOW MANY HOURS I WAS IN LABOR WITH YOU?

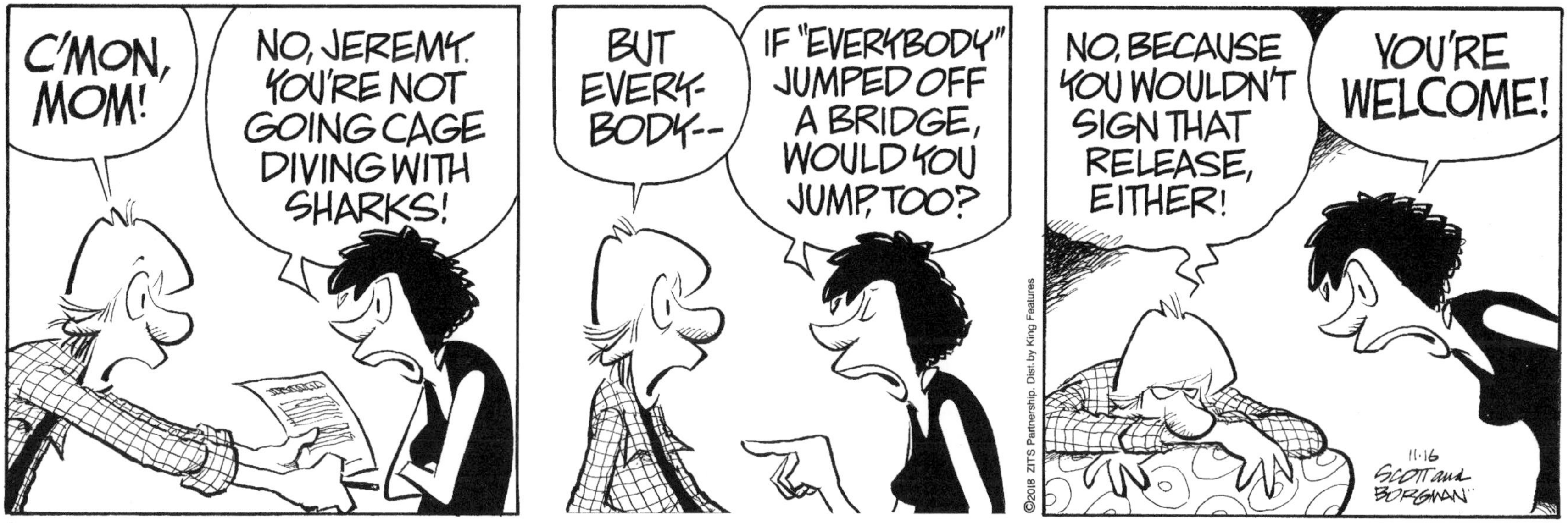
C'MON, MOM!
NO, JEREMY. YOU'RE NOT GOING CAGE DIVING WITH SHARKS!
BUT EVERY-BODY--
IF "EVERYBODY" JUMPED OFF A BRIDGE, WOULD YOU JUMP, TOO?
NO, BECAUSE YOU WOULDN'T SIGN THAT RELEASE, EITHER!
YOU'RE WELCOME!
©2018 ZITS Partnership. Dist. by King Features
11-16
SCOTT and BORGMAN

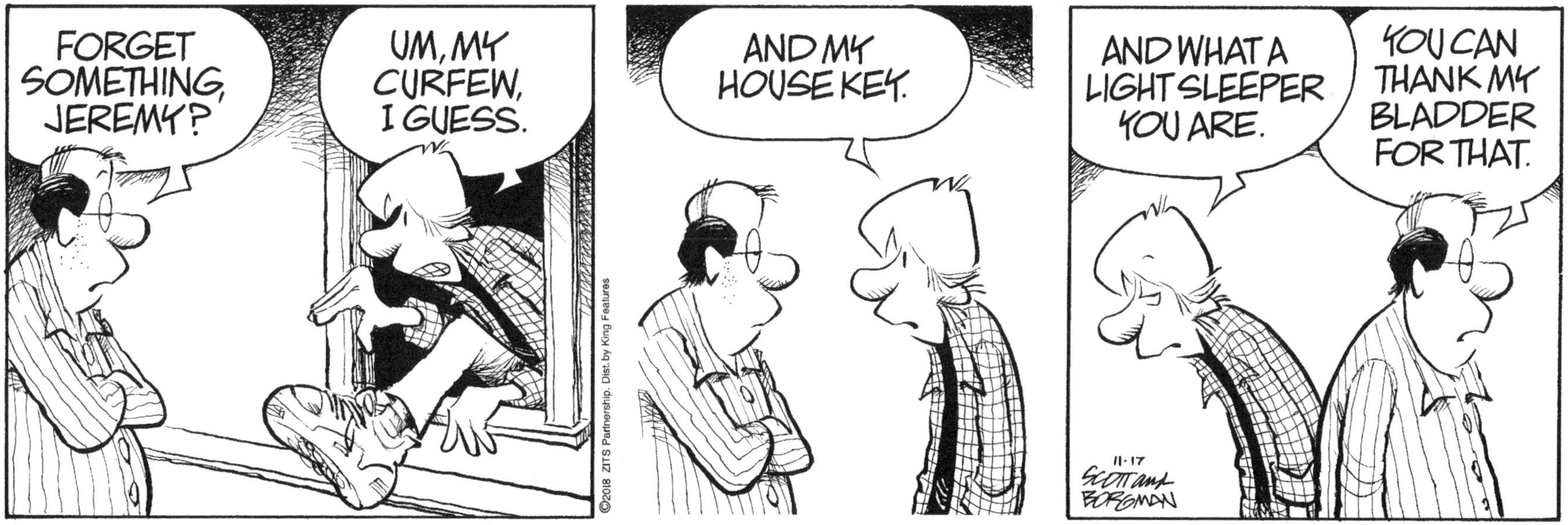
FORGET SOMETHING, JEREMY?
UM, MY CURFEW, I GUESS.
AND MY HOUSE KEY.
AND WHAT A LIGHT SLEEPER YOU ARE.
YOU CAN THANK MY BLADDER FOR THAT.
©2018 ZITS Partnership. Dist. by King Features
11-17
SCOTT and BORGMAN

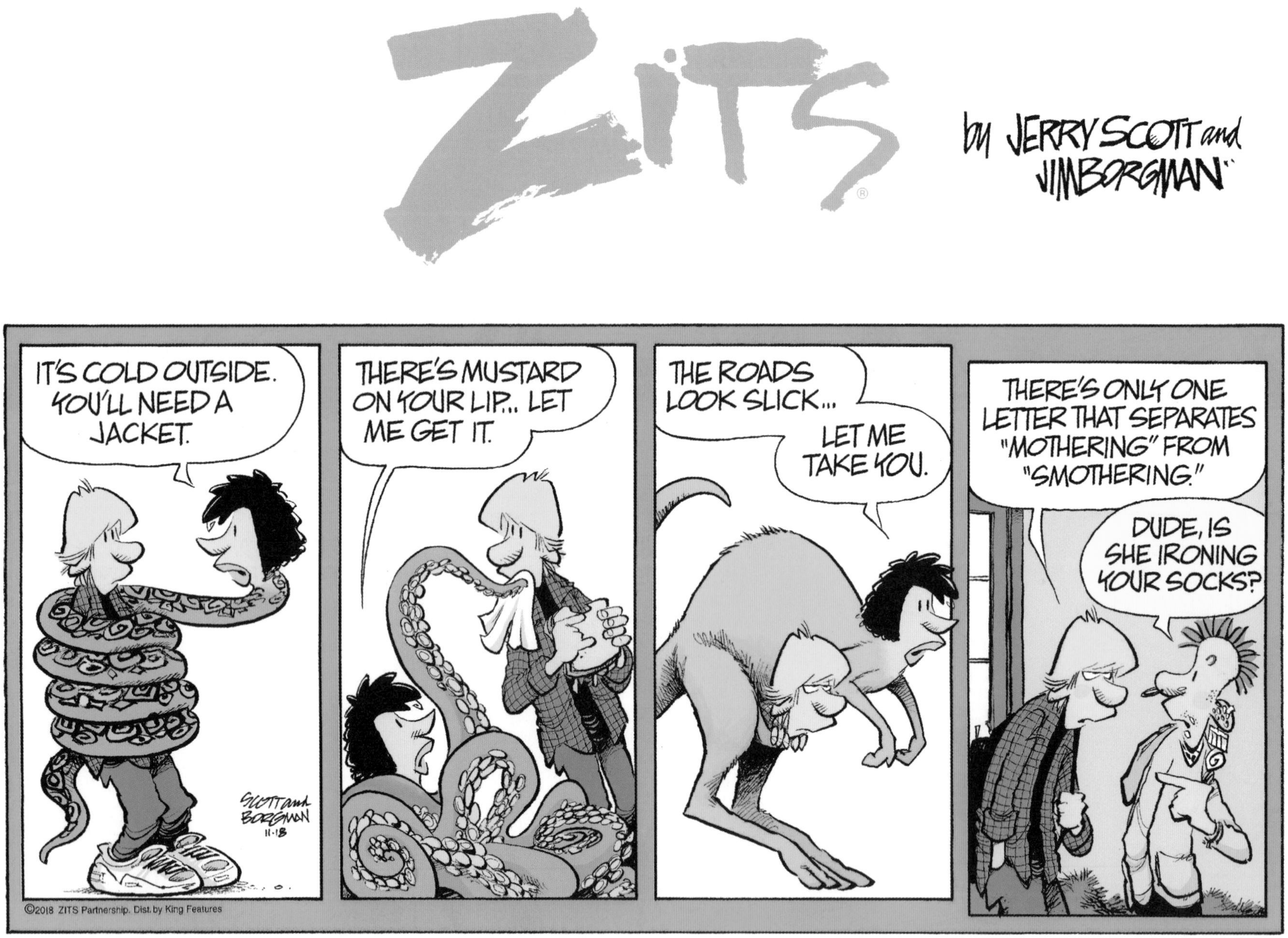
ZITS
by JERRY SCOTT and JIM BORGMAN
IT'S COLD OUTSIDE. YOU'LL NEED A JACKET.
SCOTT and BORGMAN 11-18
THERE'S MUSTARD ON YOUR LIP... LET ME GET IT.
THE ROADS LOOK SLICK...
LET ME TAKE YOU.
THERE'S ONLY ONE LETTER THAT SEPARATES "MOTHERING" FROM "SMOTHERING."
DUDE, IS SHE IRONING YOUR SOCKS?
©2018 ZITS Partnership. Dist. by King Features

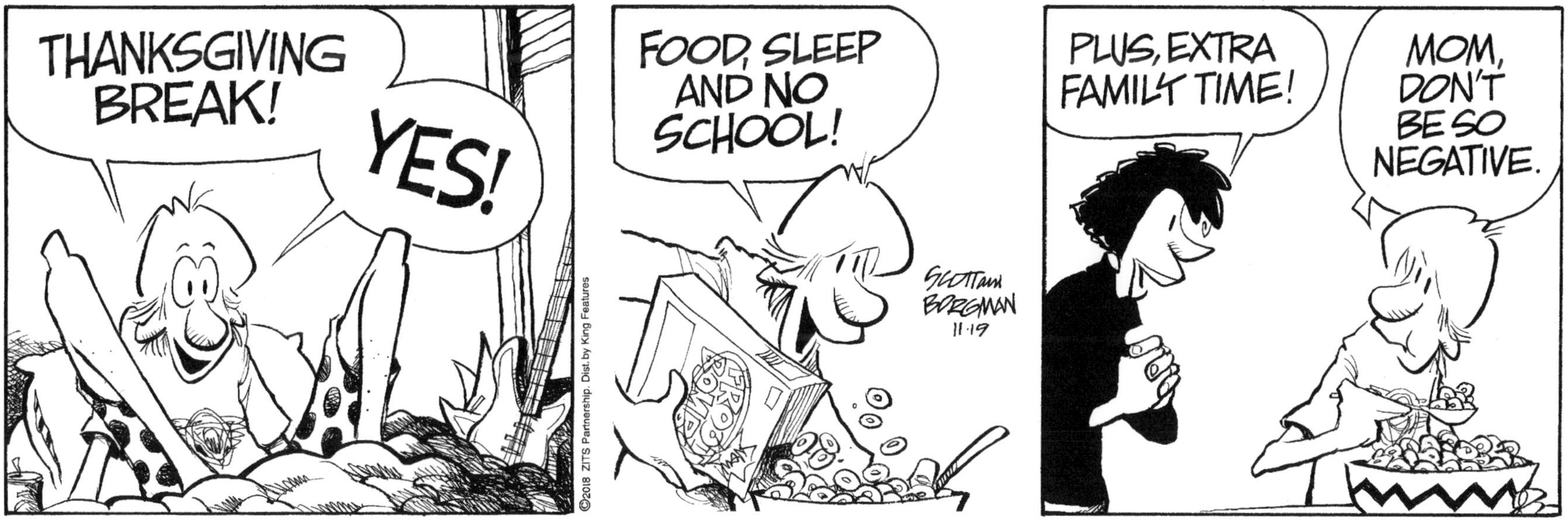

THANKSGIVING BREAK!
YES!
FOOD, SLEEP AND NO SCHOOL!
SCOTT AND BORGMAN 11·19
PLUS, EXTRA FAMILY TIME!
MOM, DON'T BE SO NEGATIVE.
©2018 ZITS Partnership. Dist. by King Features

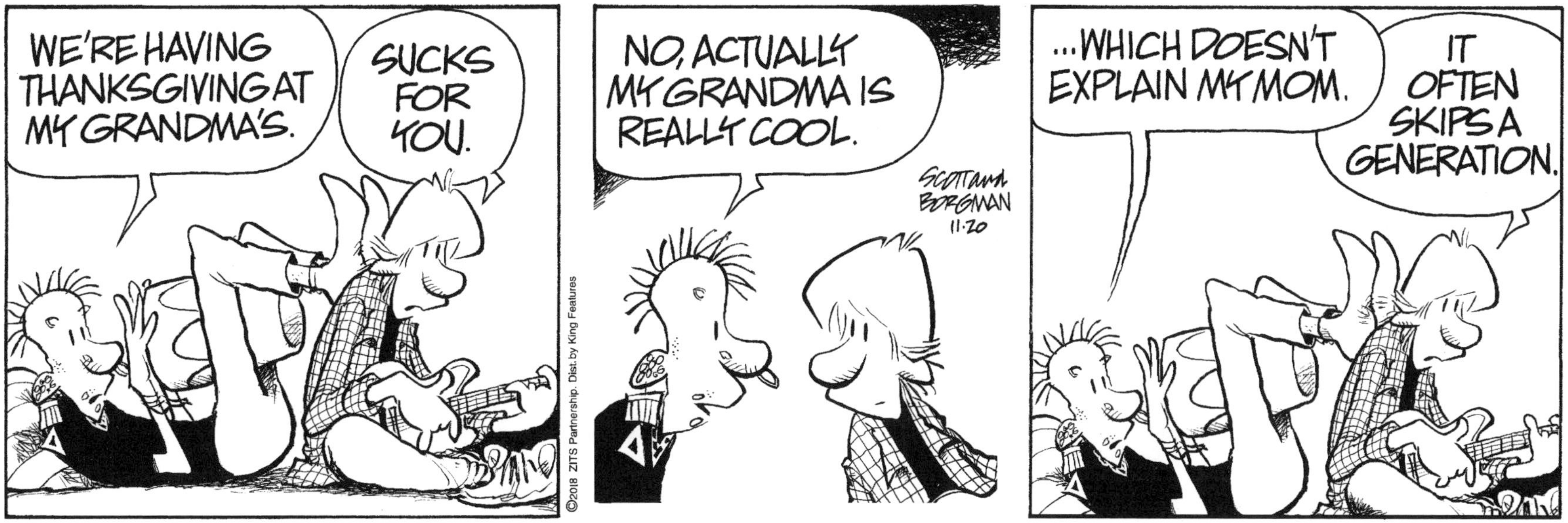

WE'RE HAVING THANKSGIVING AT MY GRANDMA'S.
SUCKS FOR YOU.
NO, ACTUALLY MY GRANDMA IS REALLY COOL.
SCOTT AND BORGMAN 11·20
...WHICH DOESN'T EXPLAIN MY MOM.
IT OFTEN SKIPS A GENERATION.
©2018 ZITS Partnership. Dist. by King Features

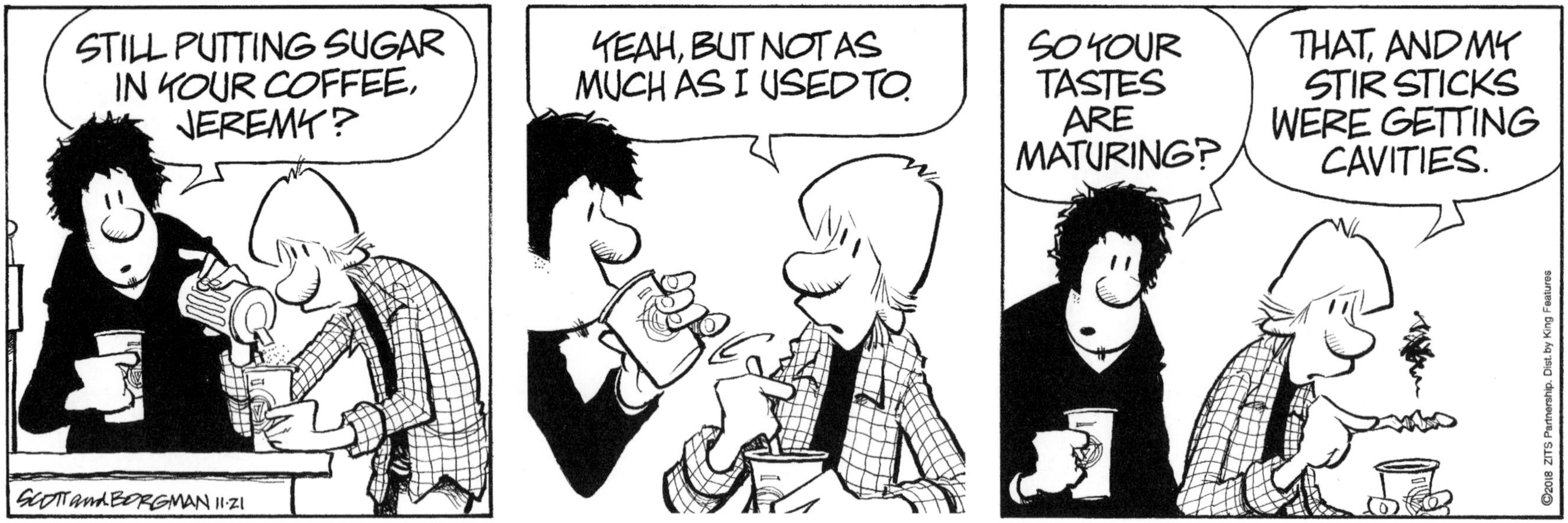
STILL PUTTING SUGAR IN YOUR COFFEE, JEREMY?
YEAH, BUT NOT AS MUCH AS I USED TO.
SO YOUR TASTES ARE MATURING?
THAT, AND MY STIR STICKS WERE GETTING CAVITIES.
SCOTT and BORGMAN 11·21
©2018 ZITS Partnership. Dist. by King Features

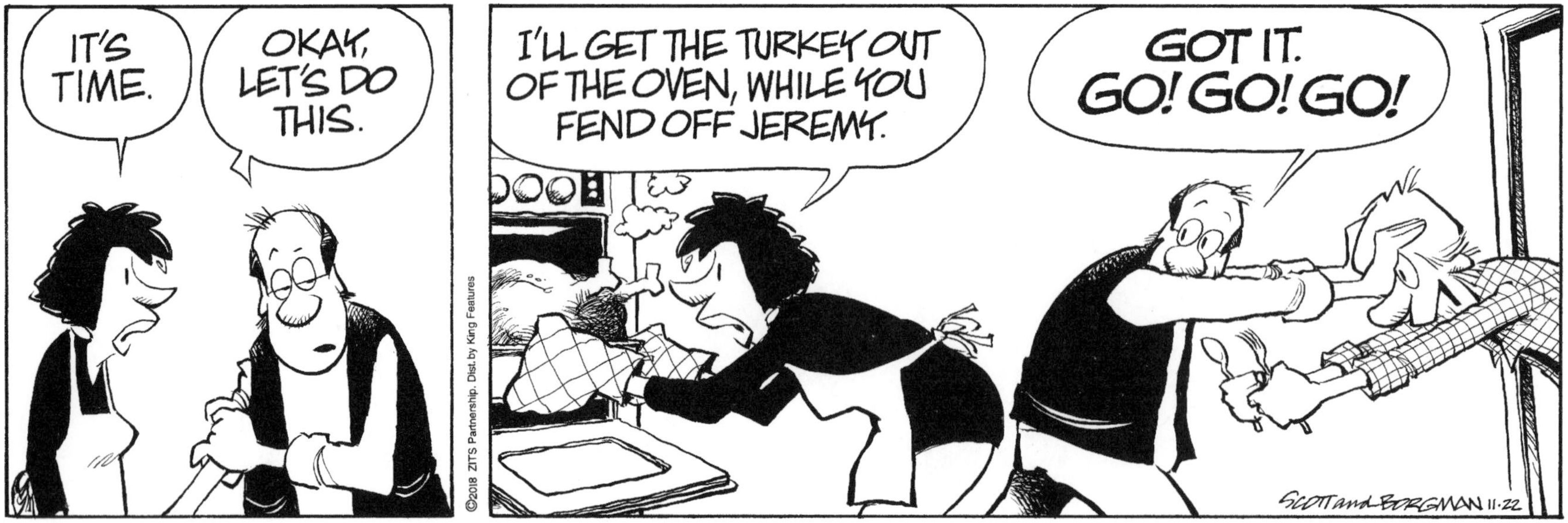
IT'S TIME.
OKAY, LET'S DO THIS.
©2018 ZITS Partnership. Dist. by King Features
I'LL GET THE TURKEY OUT OF THE OVEN, WHILE YOU FEND OFF JEREMY.
GOT IT. GO! GO! GO!
SCOTT and BORGMAN 11·22

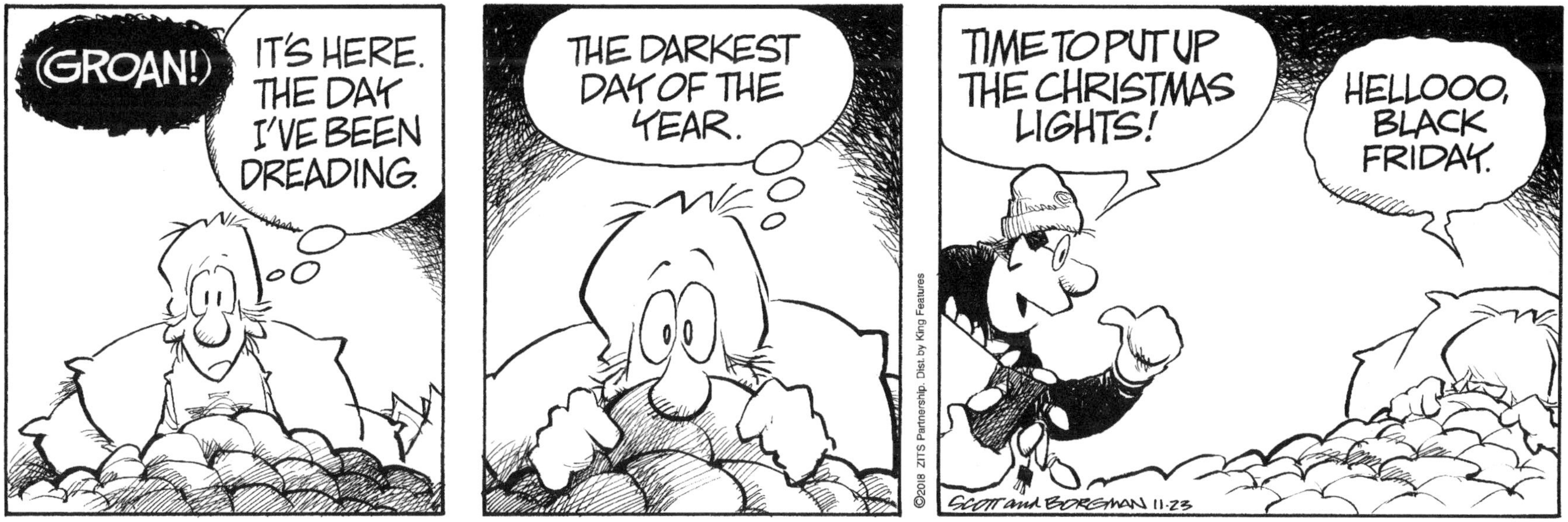
(GROAN!)
IT'S HERE. THE DAY I'VE BEEN DREADING.
THE DARKEST DAY OF THE YEAR.
TIME TO PUT UP THE CHRISTMAS LIGHTS!
HELLOOO, BLACK FRIDAY.
©2018 ZITS Partnership. Dist. by King Features
SCOTT and BORGMAN 11-23

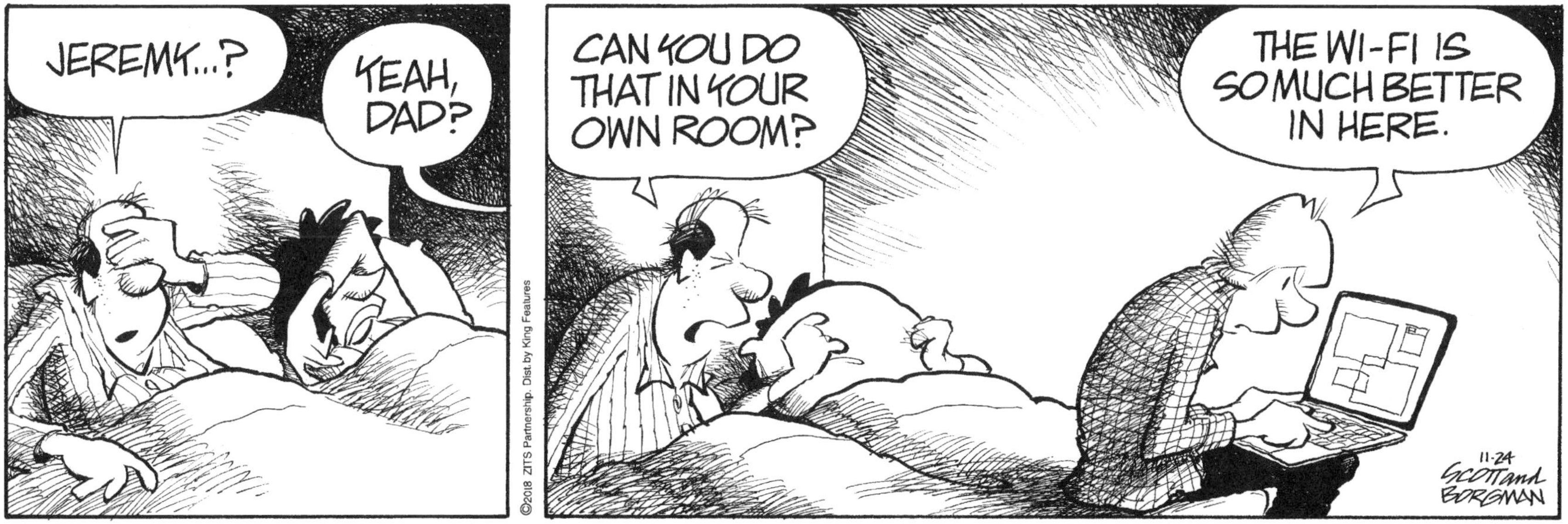
JEREMY...?
YEAH, DAD?
CAN YOU DO THAT IN YOUR OWN ROOM?
THE WI-FI IS SO MUCH BETTER IN HERE.
©2018 ZITS Partnership. Dist. by King Features
11-24 SCOTT and BORGMAN

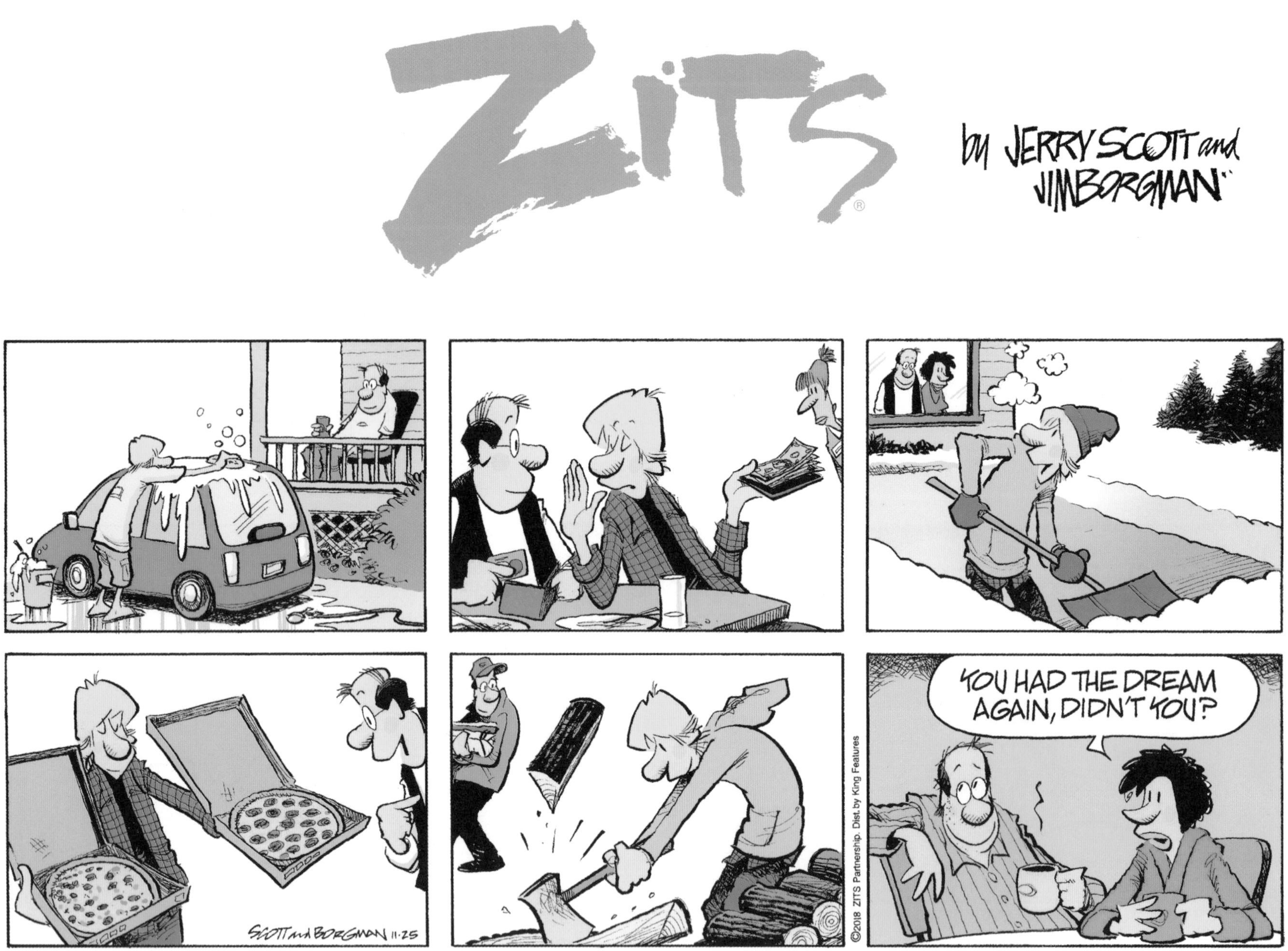
ZITS®
by JERRY SCOTT and JIM BORGMAN
SCOTT and BORGMAN 11-25
©2018 ZITS Partnership. Dist. by King Features
YOU HAD THE DREAM AGAIN, DIDN'T YOU?

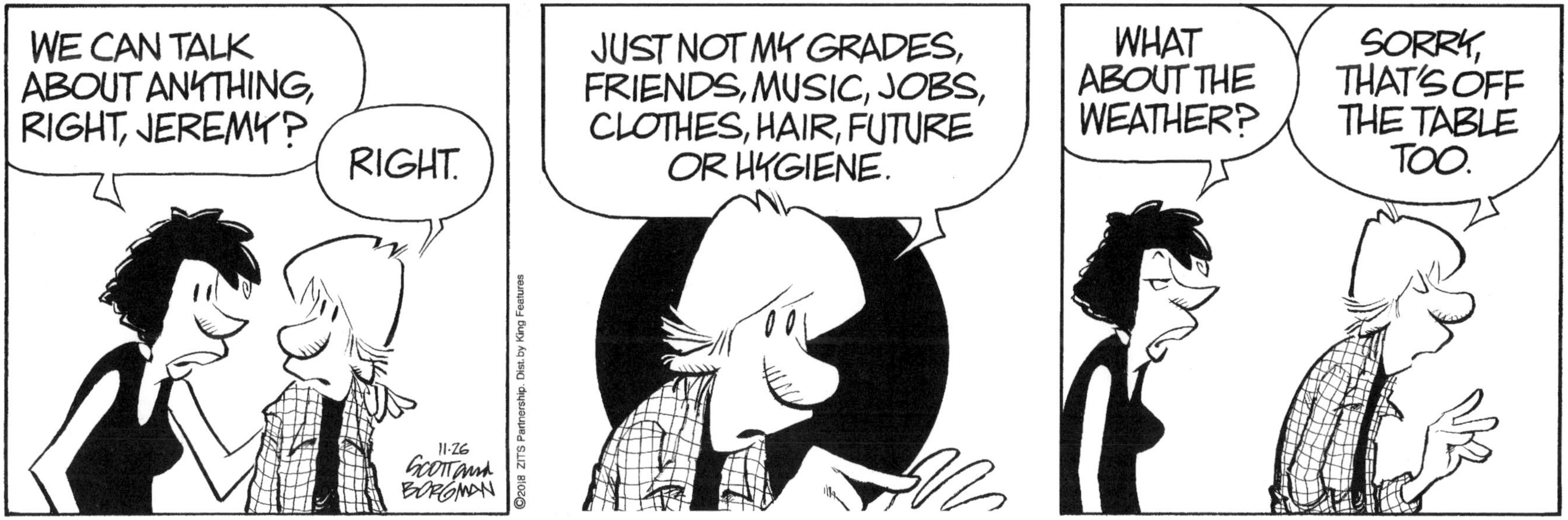
WE CAN TALK ABOUT ANYTHING, RIGHT, JEREMY?
RIGHT.
11-26 SCOTT and BORGMAN
©2018 ZITS Partnership. Dist. by King Features
JUST NOT MY GRADES, FRIENDS, MUSIC, JOBS, CLOTHES, HAIR, FUTURE OR HYGIENE.
WHAT ABOUT THE WEATHER?
SORRY, THAT'S OFF THE TABLE TOO.

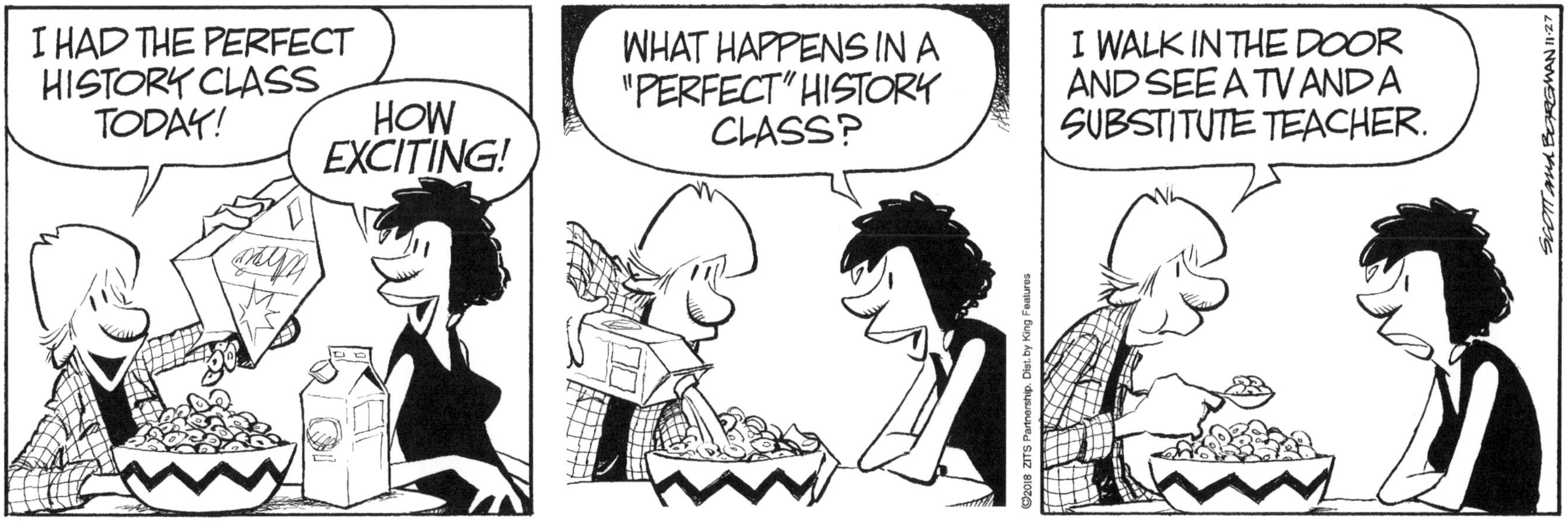
I HAD THE PERFECT HISTORY CLASS TODAY!
HOW EXCITING!
WHAT HAPPENS IN A "PERFECT" HISTORY CLASS?
©2018 ZITS Partnership. Dist. by King Features
I WALK IN THE DOOR AND SEE A TV AND A SUBSTITUTE TEACHER.
SCOTT and BORGMAN 11-27

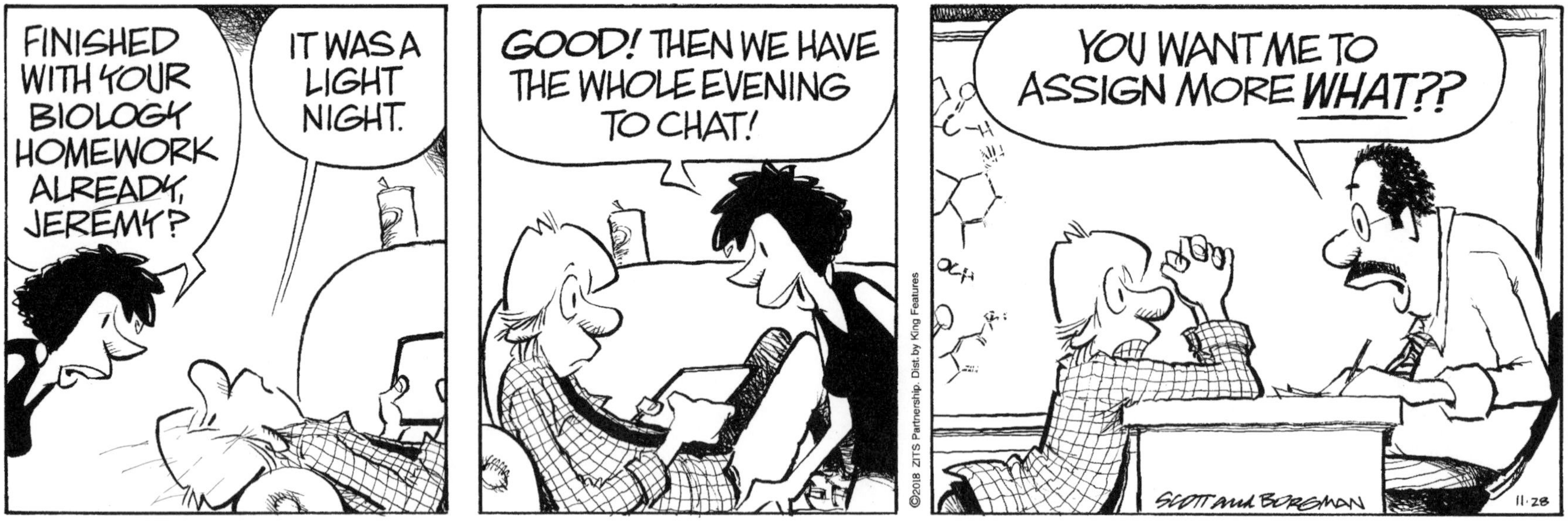
FINISHED WITH YOUR BIOLOGY HOMEWORK ALREADY, JEREMY?
IT WAS A LIGHT NIGHT.
GOOD! THEN WE HAVE THE WHOLE EVENING TO CHAT!
©2018 ZITS Partnership. Dist. by King Features
YOU WANT ME TO ASSIGN MORE WHAT??
SCOTT and BORGMAN
11·28

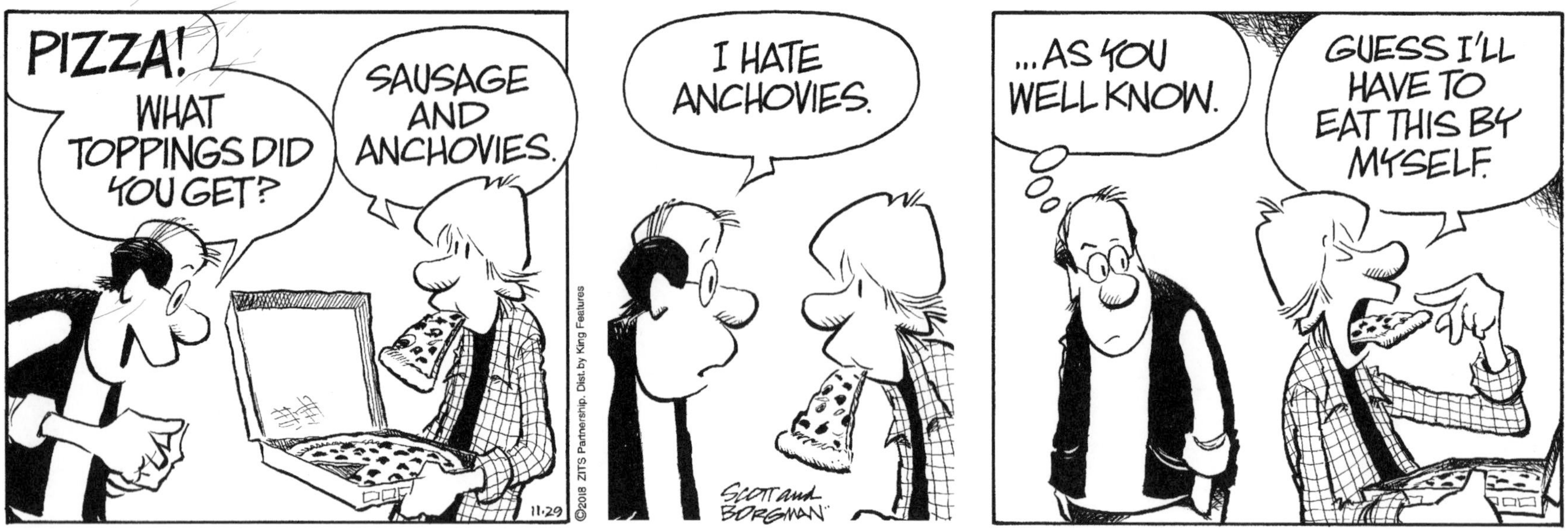
PIZZA! WHAT TOPPINGS DID YOU GET?
SAUSAGE AND ANCHOVIES.
11·29
©2018 ZITS Partnership. Dist. by King Features
I HATE ANCHOVIES.
SCOTT and BORGMAN
...AS YOU WELL KNOW.
GUESS I'LL HAVE TO EAT THIS BY MYSELF.

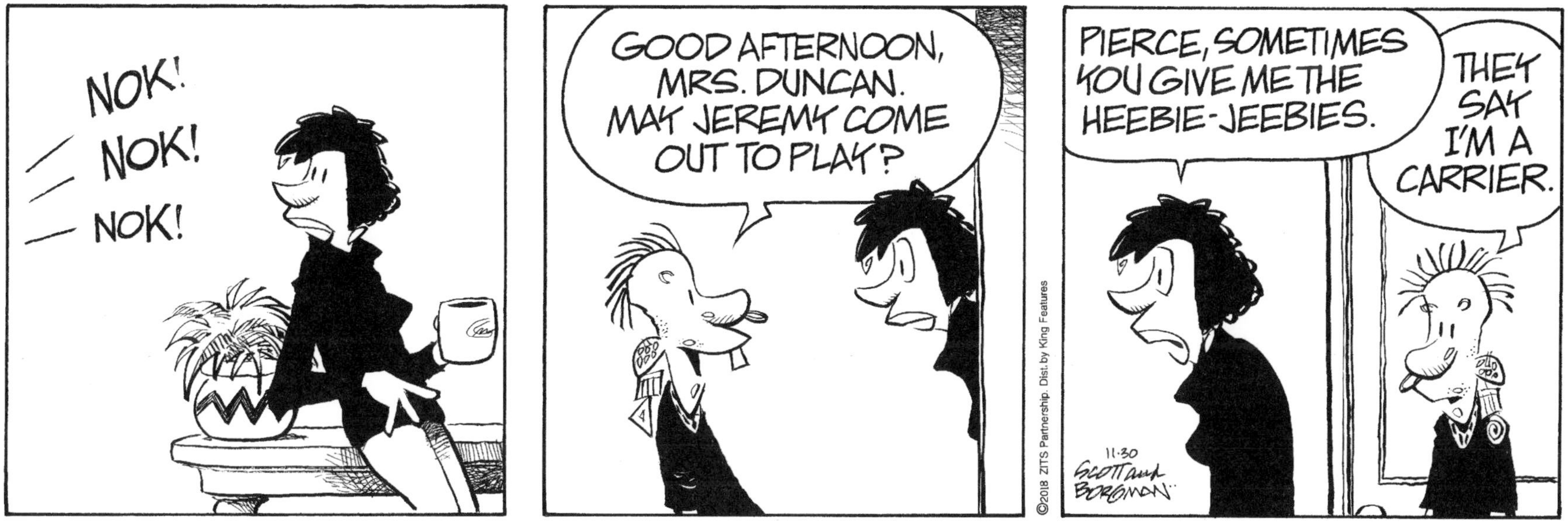
NOK!
NOK!
NOK!
GOOD AFTERNOON, MRS. DUNCAN. MAY JEREMY COME OUT TO PLAY?
PIERCE, SOMETIMES YOU GIVE ME THE HEEBIE-JEEBIES.
THEY SAY I'M A CARRIER.
11·30 SCOTT and BORGMAN
©2018 ZITS Partnership. Dist. by King Features

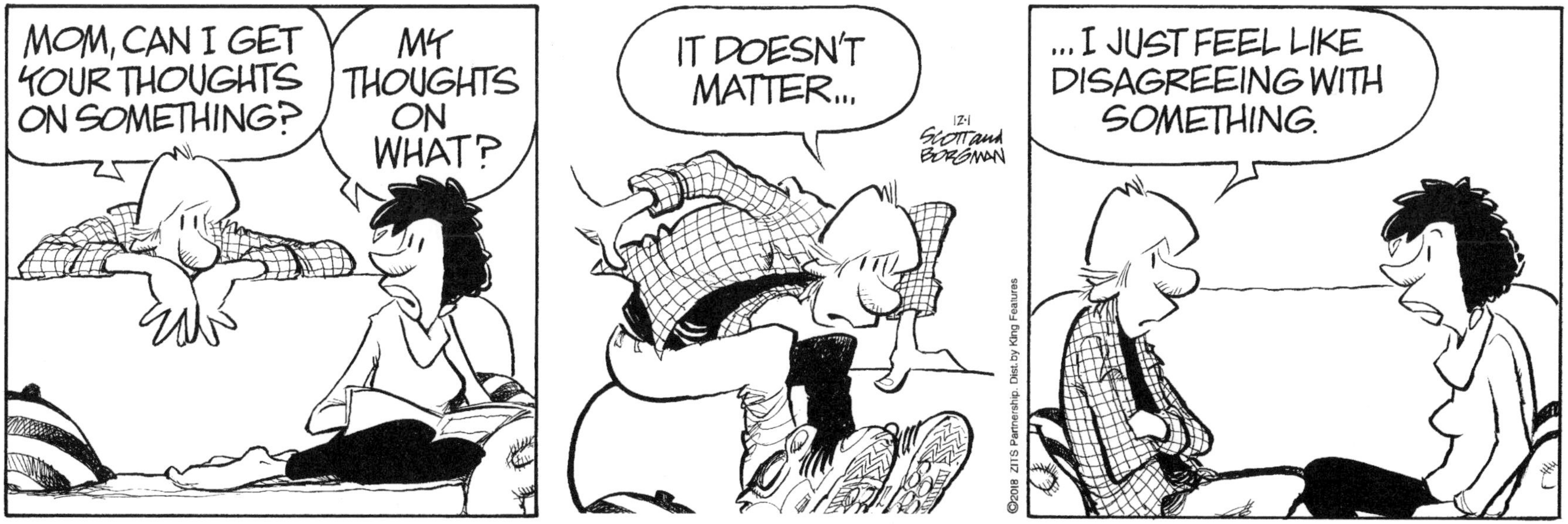
MOM, CAN I GET YOUR THOUGHTS ON SOMETHING?
MY THOUGHTS ON WHAT?
IT DOESN'T MATTER...
12·1 SCOTT and BORGMAN
©2018 ZITS Partnership. Dist. by King Features
...I JUST FEEL LIKE DISAGREEING WITH SOMETHING.

ZITS®

by JERRY SCOTT and JIM BORGMAN

SCOTT and BORGMAN
©2014 ZITS Partnership. Dist. by King Features
TAP! TAP!
ZZZ----- HUH? OH. YEAH.
8-26
MONDAY MORNINGS: SOME ASSEMBLY REQUIRED.

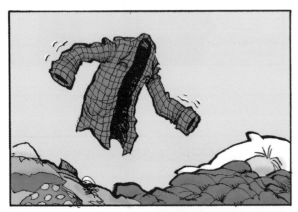

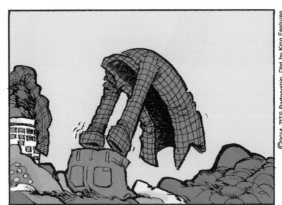

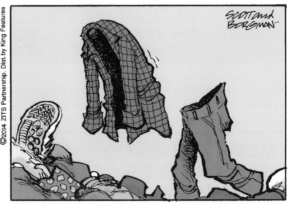

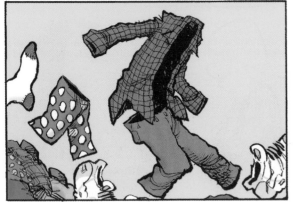

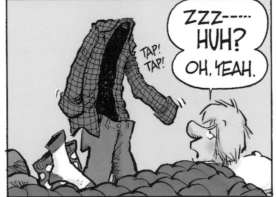

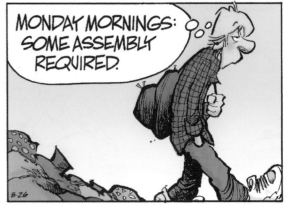

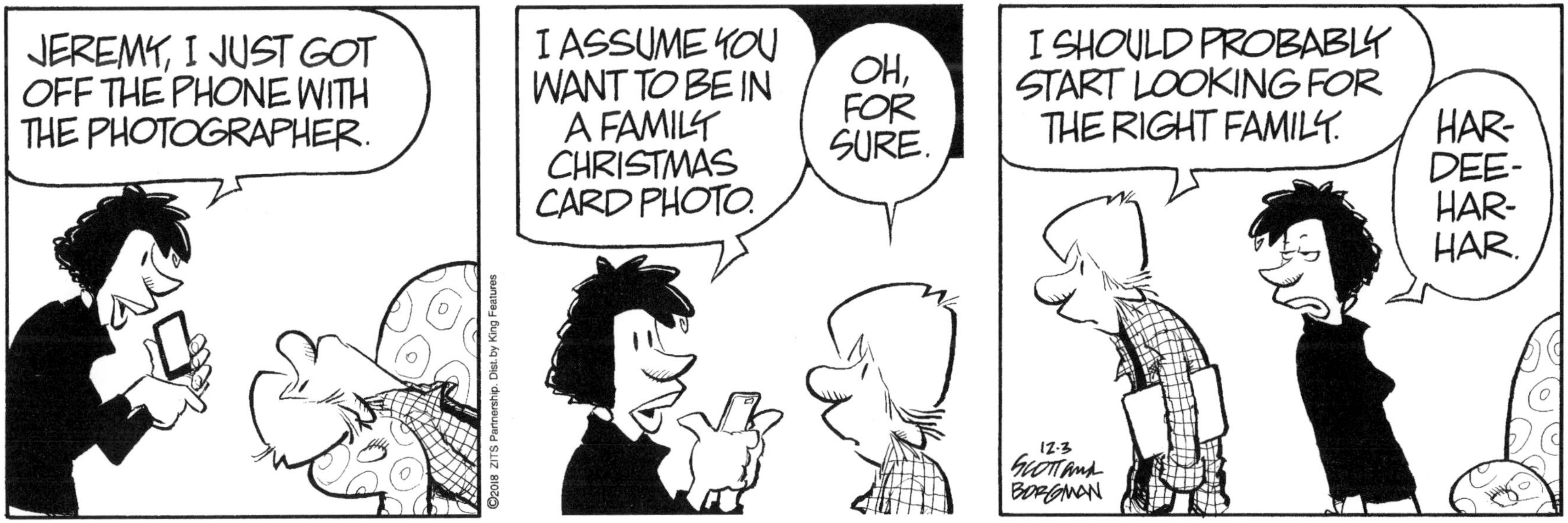
JEREMY, I JUST GOT OFF THE PHONE WITH THE PHOTOGRAPHER.
©2018 ZITS Partnership. Dist. by King Features
I ASSUME YOU WANT TO BE IN A FAMILY CHRISTMAS CARD PHOTO.
OH, FOR SURE.
I SHOULD PROBABLY START LOOKING FOR THE RIGHT FAMILY.
HAR-DEE-HAR-HAR.
12·3
SCOTT and BORGMAN

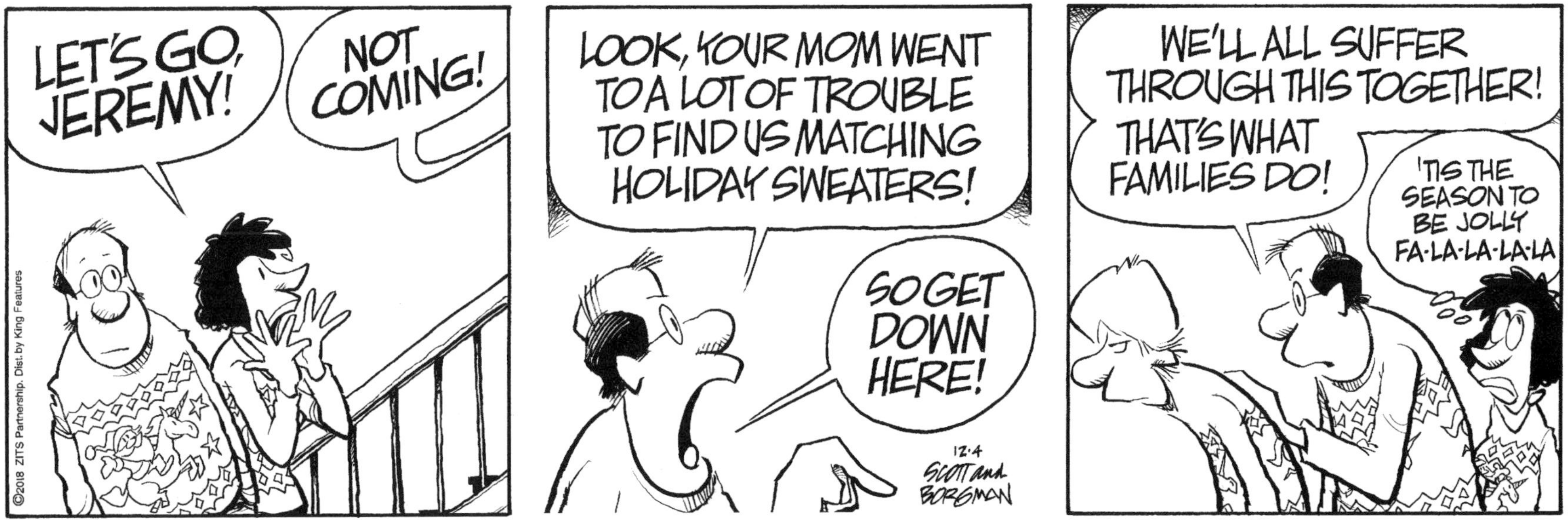
LET'S GO, JEREMY!
NOT COMING!
©2018 ZITS Partnership. Dist. by King Features
LOOK, YOUR MOM WENT TO A LOT OF TROUBLE TO FIND US MATCHING HOLIDAY SWEATERS!
SO GET DOWN HERE!
12·4
SCOTT and BORGMAN
WE'LL ALL SUFFER THROUGH THIS TOGETHER!
THAT'S WHAT FAMILIES DO!
'TIS THE SEASON TO BE JOLLY FA·LA·LA·LA·LA

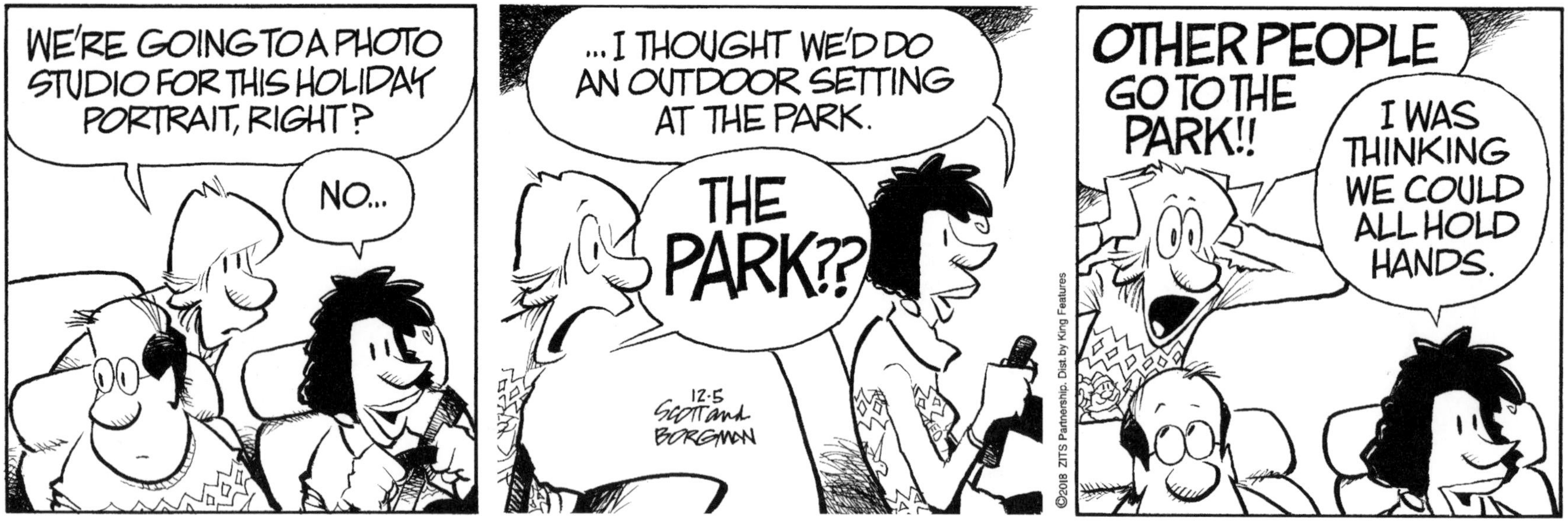
WE'RE GOING TO A PHOTO STUDIO FOR THIS HOLIDAY PORTRAIT, RIGHT?
NO...
...I THOUGHT WE'D DO AN OUTDOOR SETTING AT THE PARK.
THE PARK??
12·5 SCOTT and BORGMAN
©2018 ZITS Partnership. Dist. by King Features
OTHER PEOPLE GO TO THE PARK!!
I WAS THINKING WE COULD ALL HOLD HANDS.

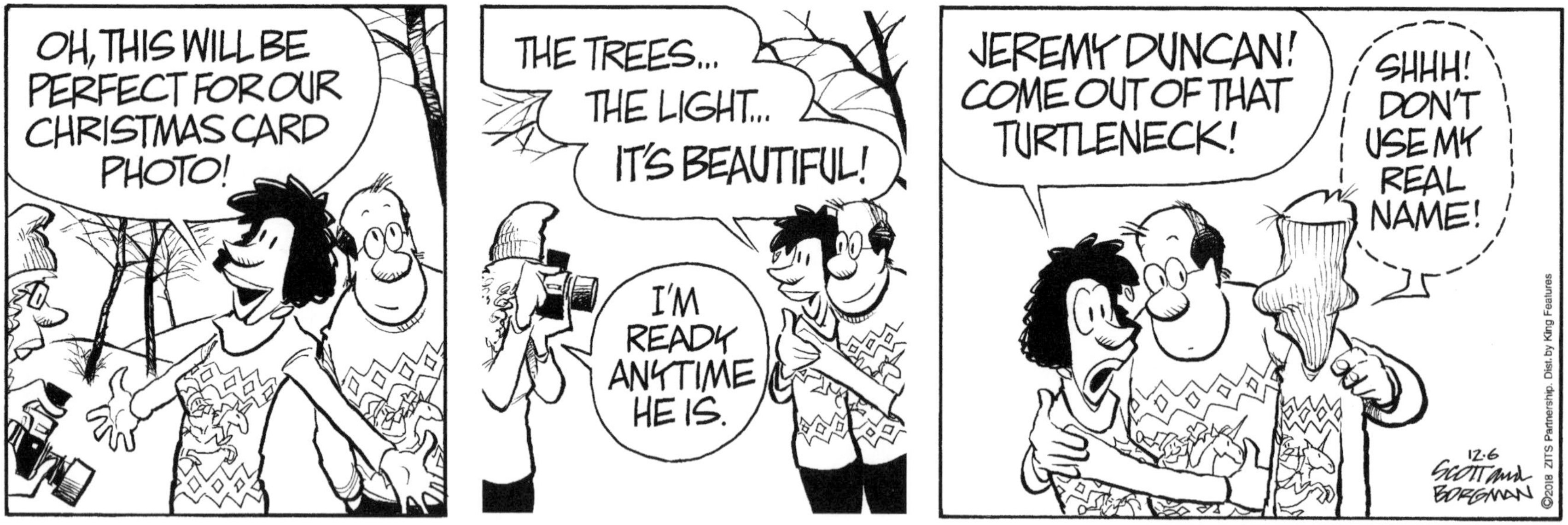
OH, THIS WILL BE PERFECT FOR OUR CHRISTMAS CARD PHOTO!
THE TREES...
THE LIGHT...
IT'S BEAUTIFUL!
I'M READY ANYTIME HE IS.
JEREMY DUNCAN! COME OUT OF THAT TURTLENECK!
SHHH! DON'T USE MY REAL NAME!
12·6 SCOTT and BORGMAN
©2018 ZITS Partnership. Dist. by King Features

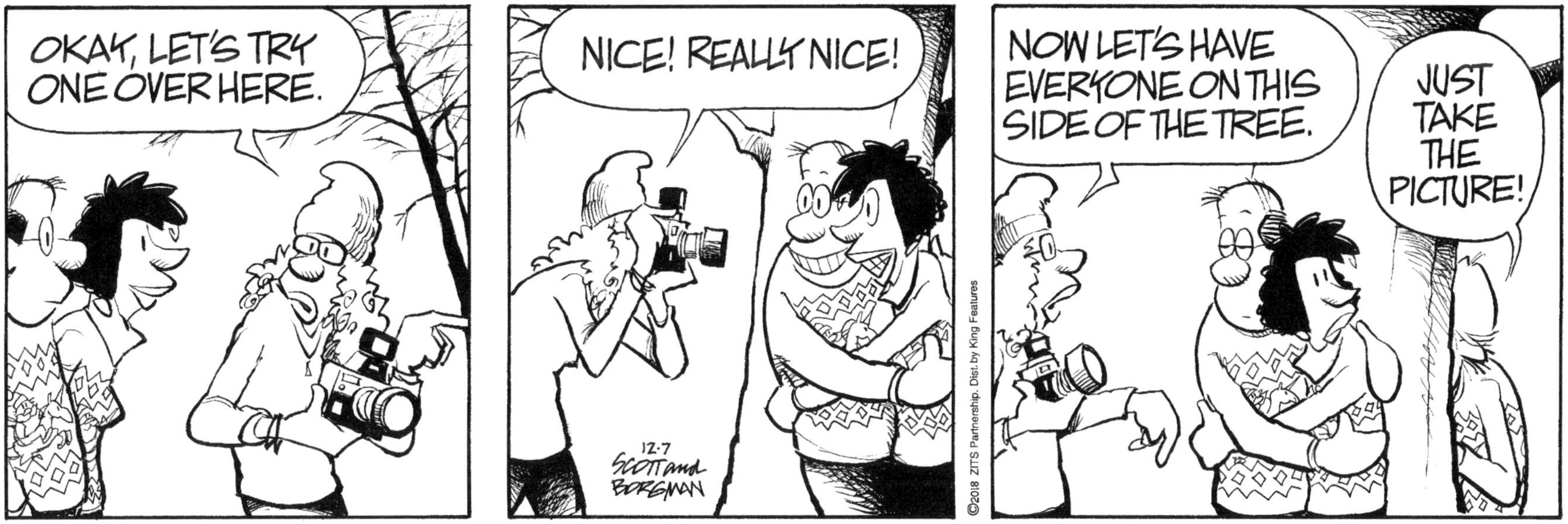
OKAY, LET'S TRY ONE OVER HERE.
NICE! REALLY NICE!
12·7 SCOTT and BORGMAN
©2018 ZITS Partnership. Dist. by King Features
NOW LET'S HAVE EVERYONE ON THIS SIDE OF THE TREE.
JUST TAKE THE PICTURE!

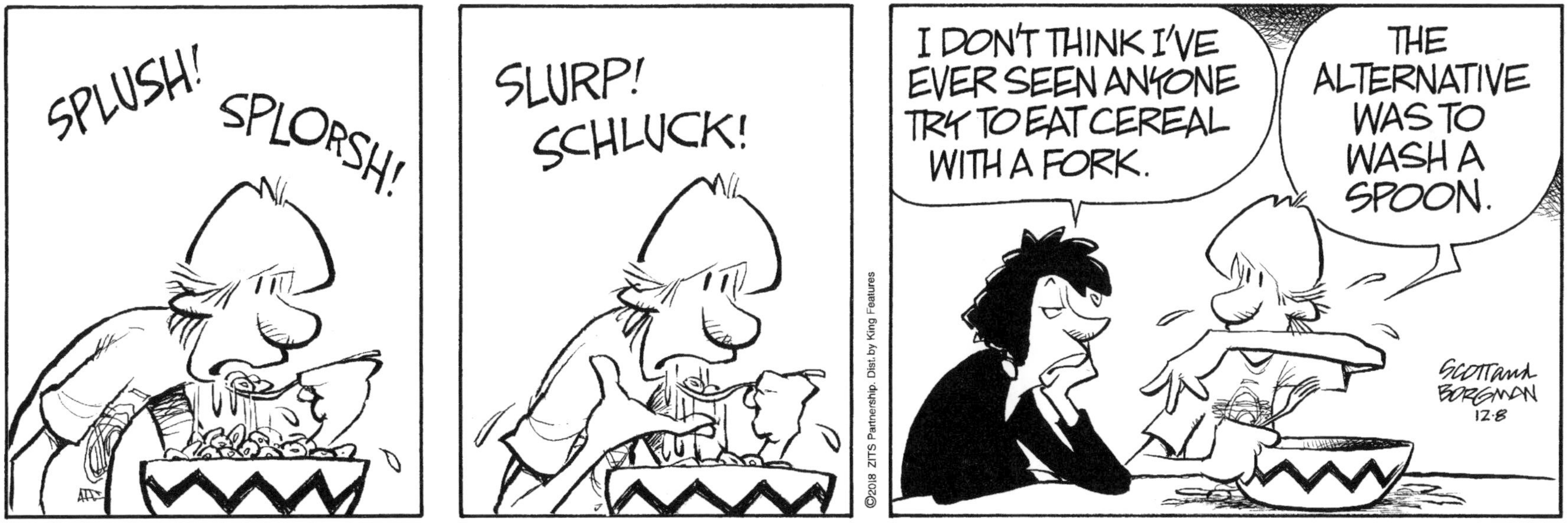
SPLUSH!
SPLORSH!
SLURP!
SCHLUCK!
©2018 ZITS Partnership. Dist. by King Features
I DON'T THINK I'VE EVER SEEN ANYONE TRY TO EAT CEREAL WITH A FORK.
THE ALTERNATIVE WAS TO WASH A SPOON.
SCOTT and BORGMAN 12·8

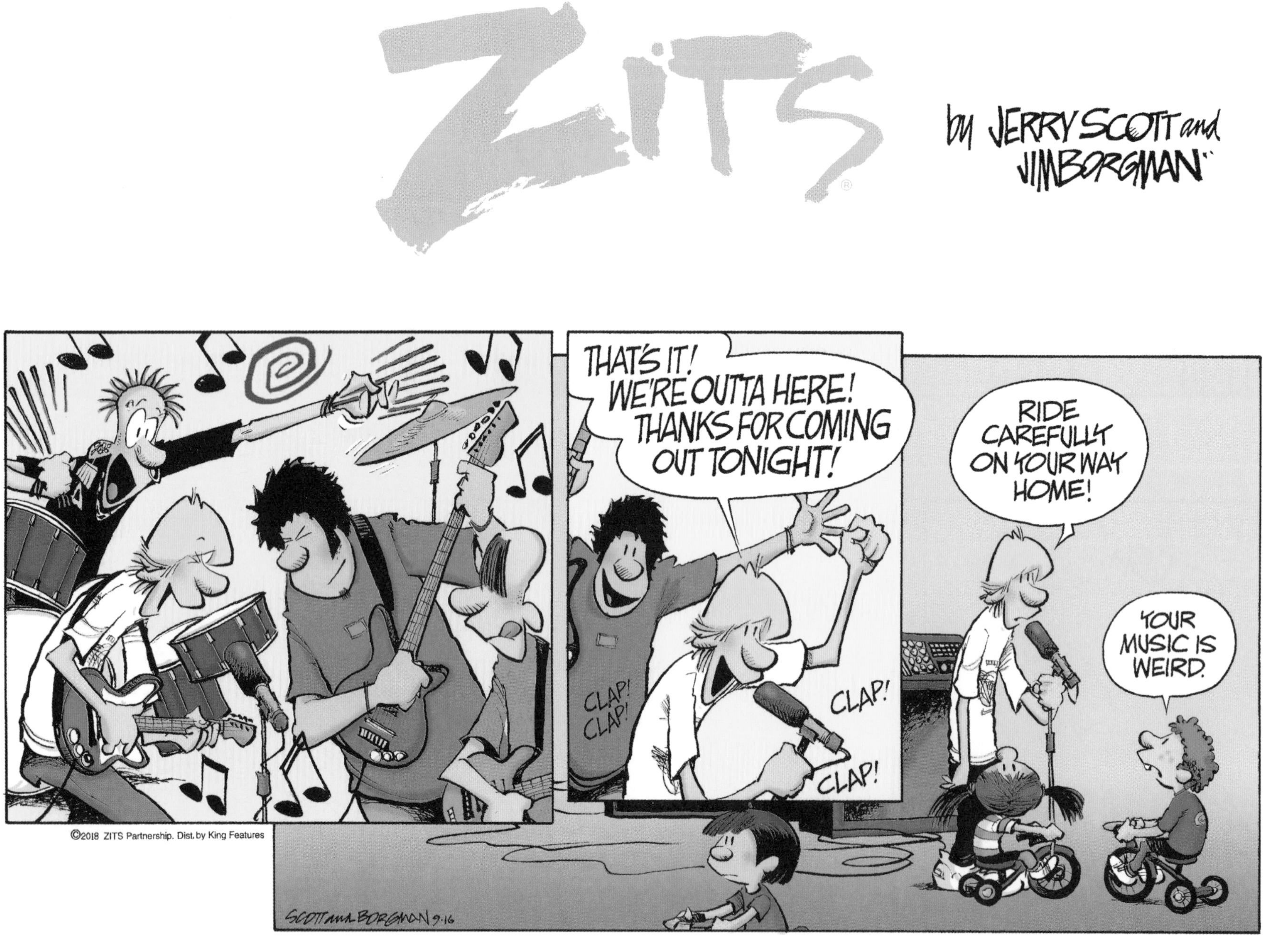
ZITS
by JERRY SCOTT and JIM BORGMAN
THAT'S IT! WE'RE OUTTA HERE! THANKS FOR COMING OUT TONIGHT!
CLAP! CLAP!
CLAP!
CLAP!
RIDE CAREFULLY ON YOUR WAY HOME!
YOUR MUSIC IS WEIRD.
SCOTT and BORGMAN 9·16

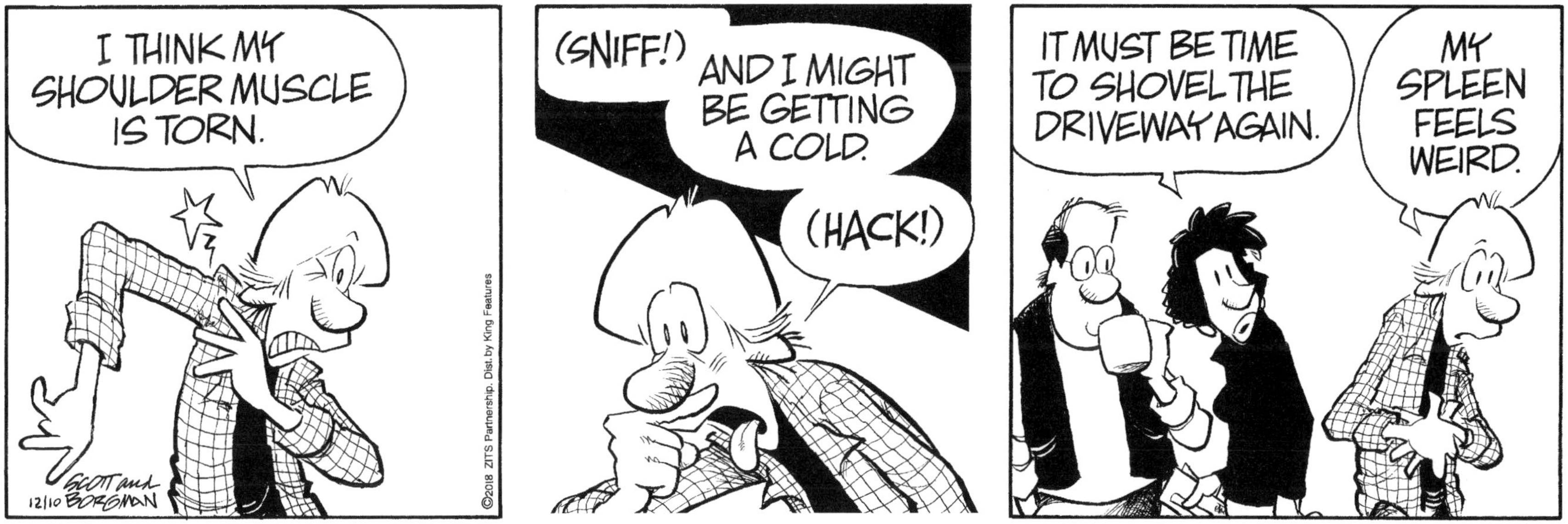
I THINK MY SHOULDER MUSCLE IS TORN.
SCOTT and BORGMAN 12/10
©2018 ZITS Partnership. Dist. by King Features
(SNIFF!)
AND I MIGHT BE GETTING A COLD.
(HACK!)
IT MUST BE TIME TO SHOVEL THE DRIVEWAY AGAIN.
MY SPLEEN FEELS WEIRD.

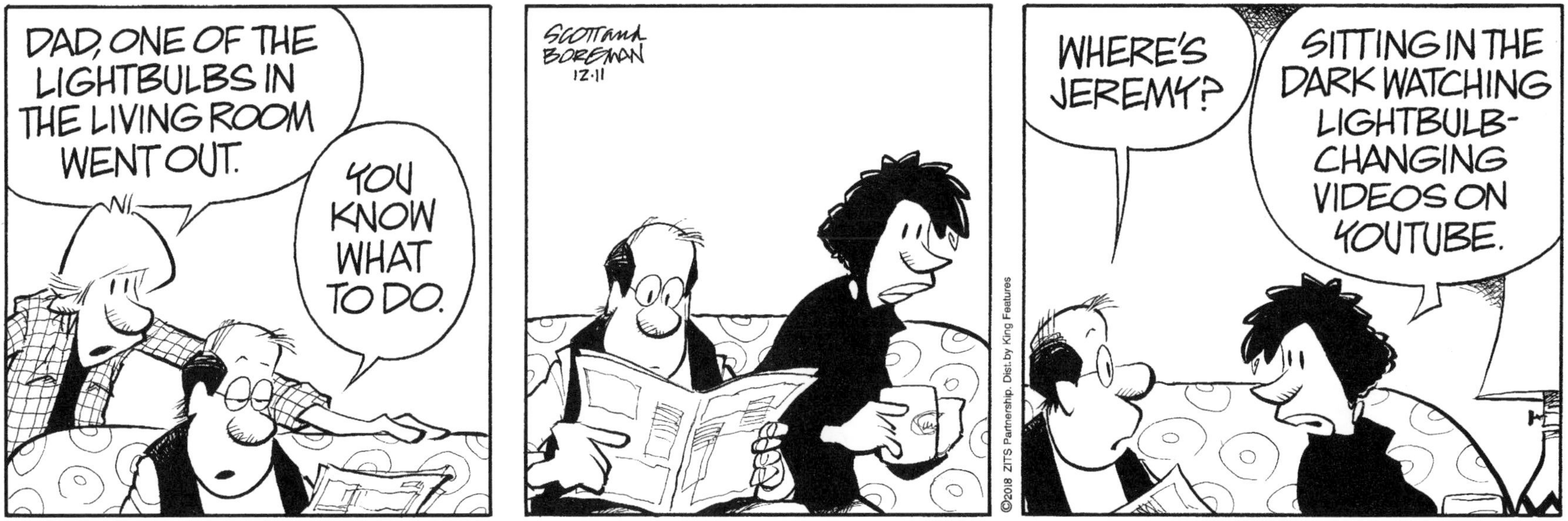
DAD, ONE OF THE LIGHTBULBS IN THE LIVING ROOM WENT OUT.
YOU KNOW WHAT TO DO.
SCOTT and BORGMAN 12·11
©2018 ZITS Partnership. Dist. by King Features
WHERE'S JEREMY?
SITTING IN THE DARK WATCHING LIGHTBULB-CHANGING VIDEOS ON YOUTUBE.

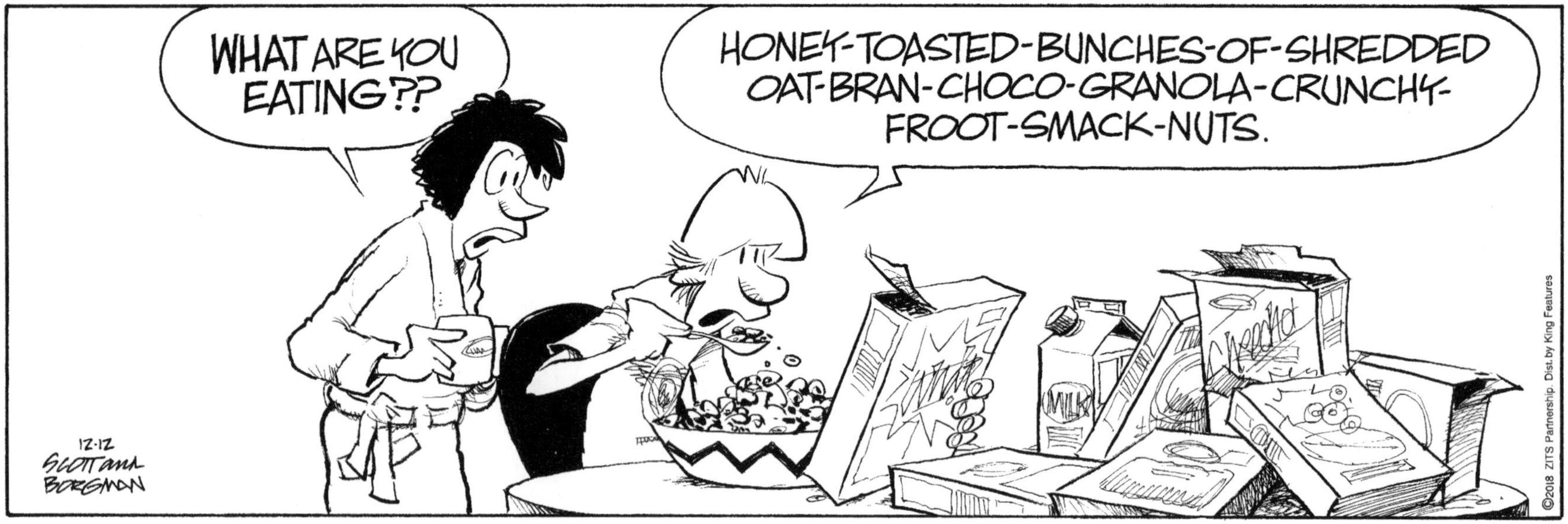
WHAT ARE YOU EATING??
HONEY-TOASTED-BUNCHES-OF-SHREDDED OAT-BRAN-CHOCO-GRANOLA-CRUNCHY-FROOT-SMACK-NUTS.
MILK
12·12 SCOTT AND BORGMAN
©2018 ZITS Partnership. Dist. by King Features

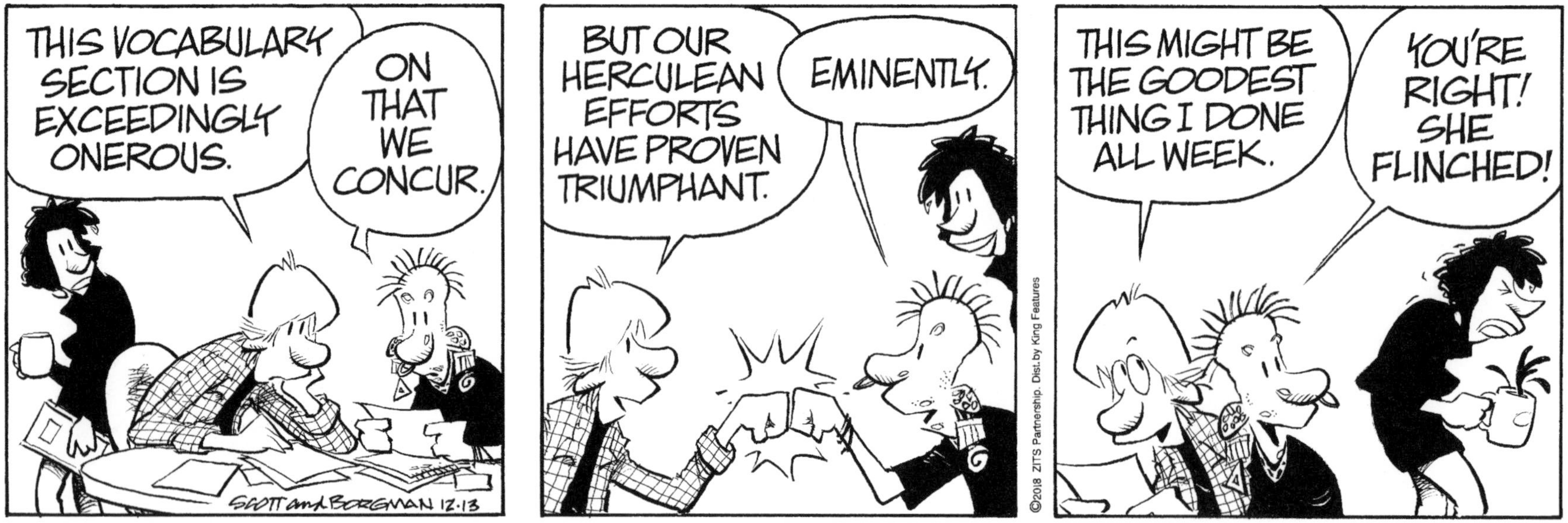
THIS VOCABULARY SECTION IS EXCEEDINGLY ONEROUS.
ON THAT WE CONCUR.
SCOTT AND BORGMAN 12·13
BUT OUR HERCULEAN EFFORTS HAVE PROVEN TRIUMPHANT.
EMINENTLY.
©2018 ZITS Partnership. Dist. by King Features
THIS MIGHT BE THE GOODEST THING I DONE ALL WEEK.
YOU'RE RIGHT! SHE FLINCHED!

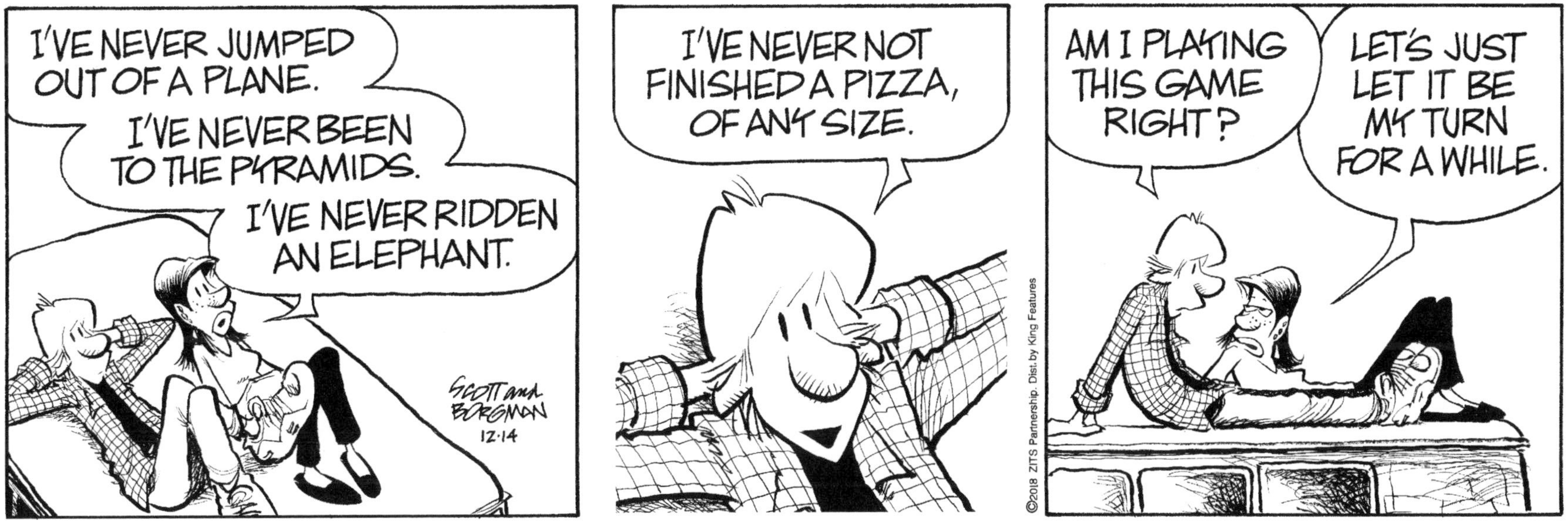
I'VE NEVER JUMPED OUT OF A PLANE.
I'VE NEVER BEEN TO THE PYRAMIDS.
I'VE NEVER RIDDEN AN ELEPHANT.
SCOTT and BORGMAN 12·14
I'VE NEVER NOT FINISHED A PIZZA, OF ANY SIZE.
©2018 ZITS Partnership. Dist. by King Features
AM I PLAYING THIS GAME RIGHT?
LET'S JUST LET IT BE MY TURN FOR A WHILE.

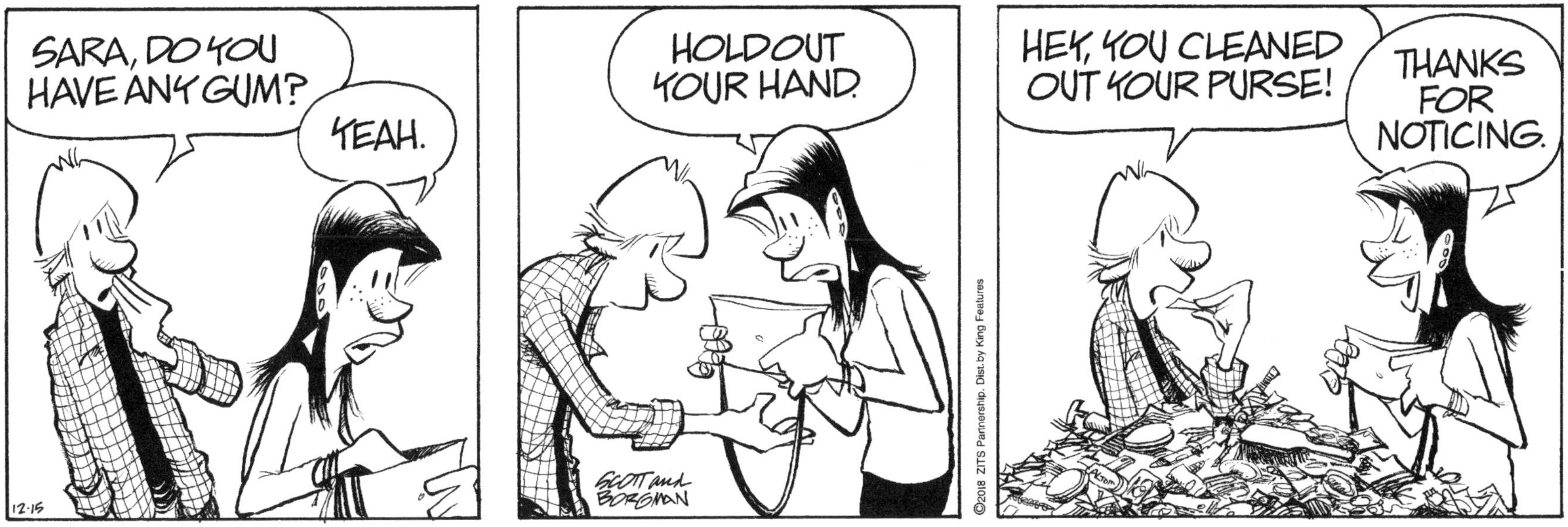
SARA, DO YOU HAVE ANY GUM?
YEAH.
12·15
HOLD OUT YOUR HAND.
SCOTT and BORGMAN
©2018 ZITS Partnership. Dist. by King Features
HEY, YOU CLEANED OUT YOUR PURSE!
THANKS FOR NOTICING.

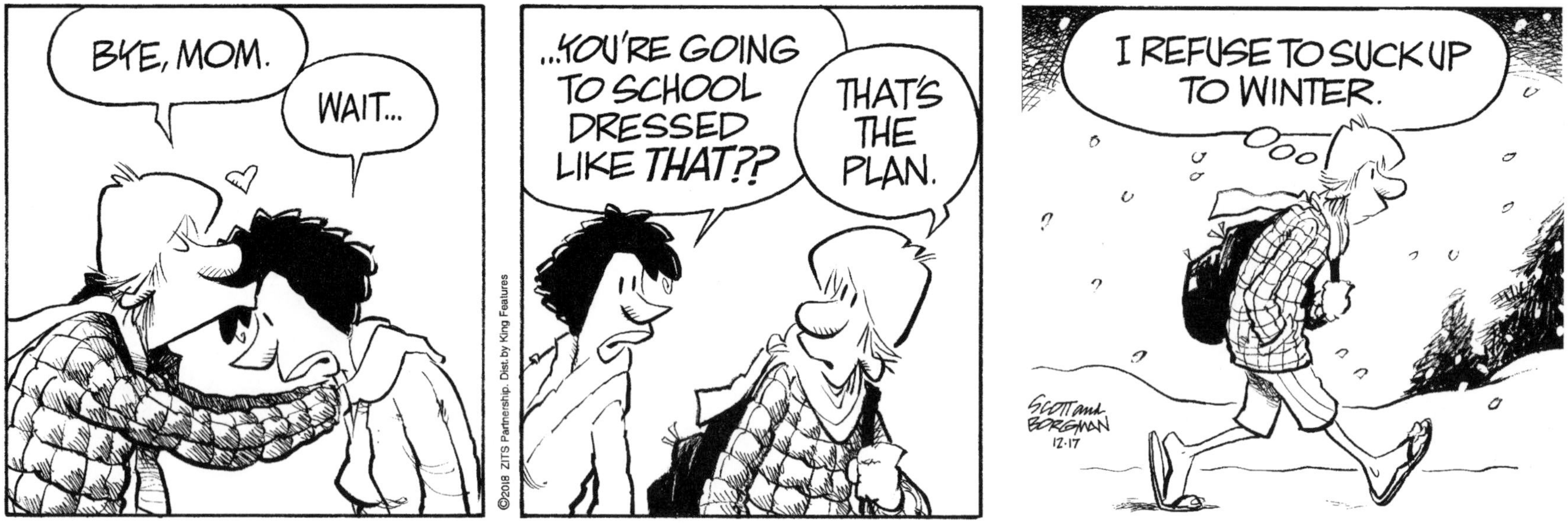
BYE, MOM.
WAIT...
...YOU'RE GOING TO SCHOOL DRESSED LIKE THAT??
THAT'S THE PLAN.
I REFUSE TO SUCK UP TO WINTER.
SCOTT and BORGMAN 12.17
©2018 ZITS Partnership. Dist. by King Features

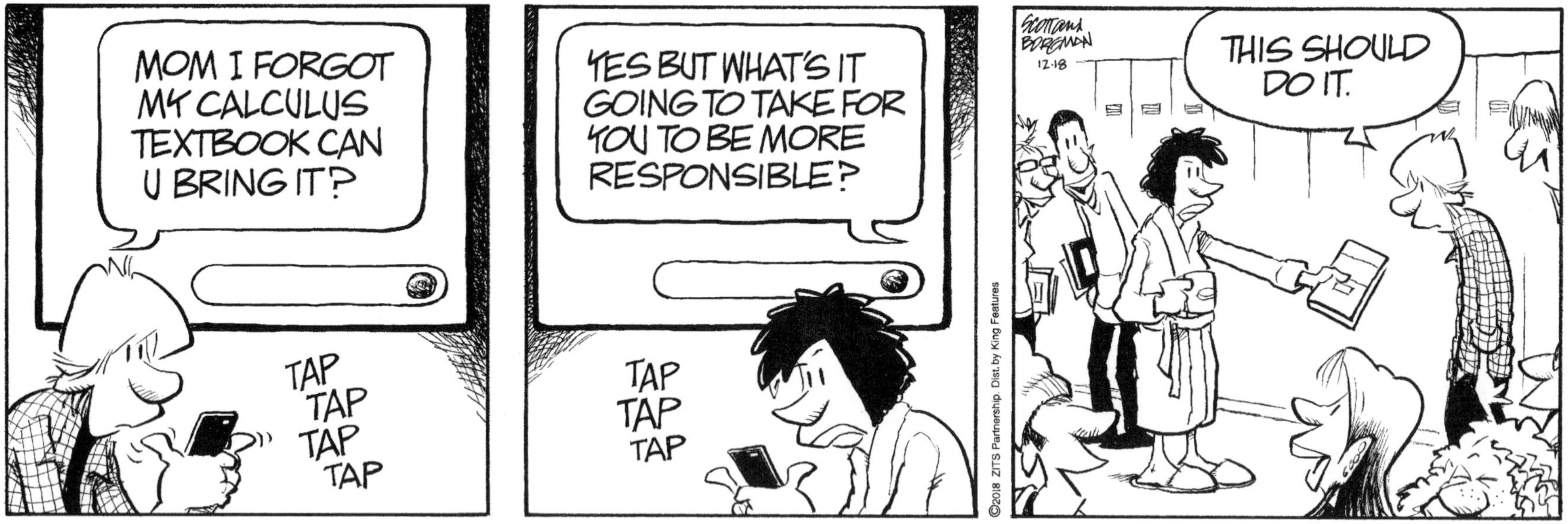
MOM I FORGOT MY CALCULUS TEXTBOOK CAN U BRING IT?
TAP TAP TAP TAP
YES BUT WHAT'S IT GOING TO TAKE FOR YOU TO BE MORE RESPONSIBLE?
TAP TAP TAP
THIS SHOULD DO IT.
SCOTT and BORGMAN 12.18
©2018 ZITS Partnership. Dist. by King Features

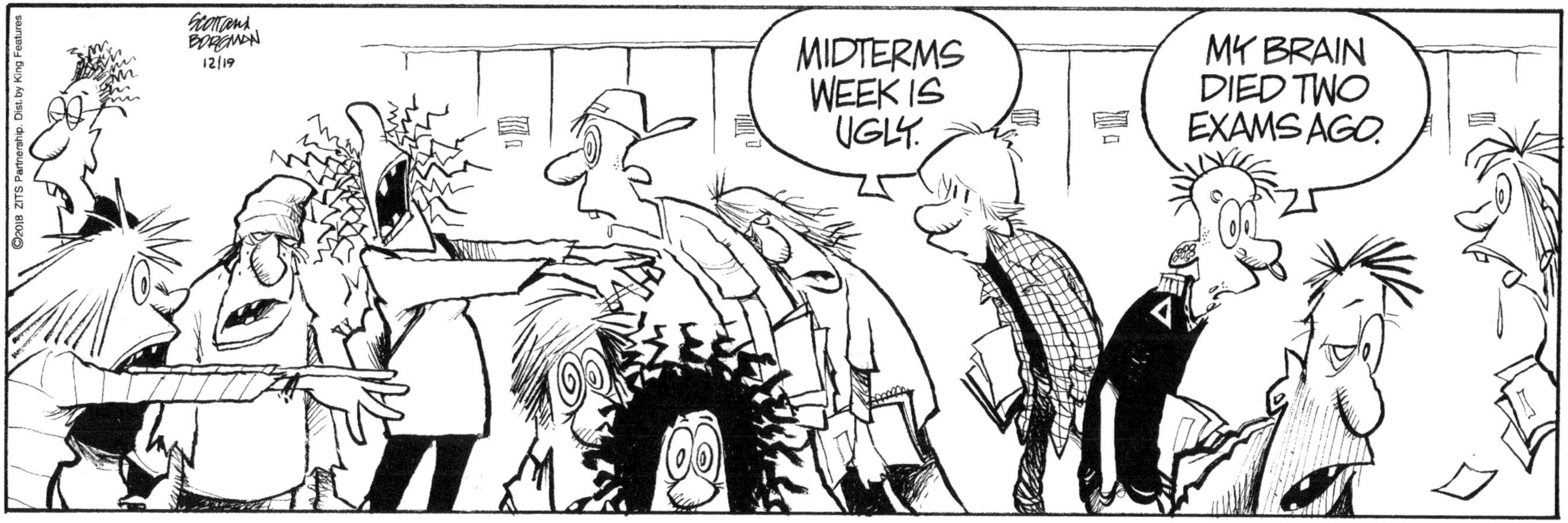
©2018 ZITS Partnership. Dist. by King Features
SCOTT and BORGMAN
12/19
MIDTERMS WEEK IS UGLY.
MY BRAIN DIED TWO EXAMS AGO.

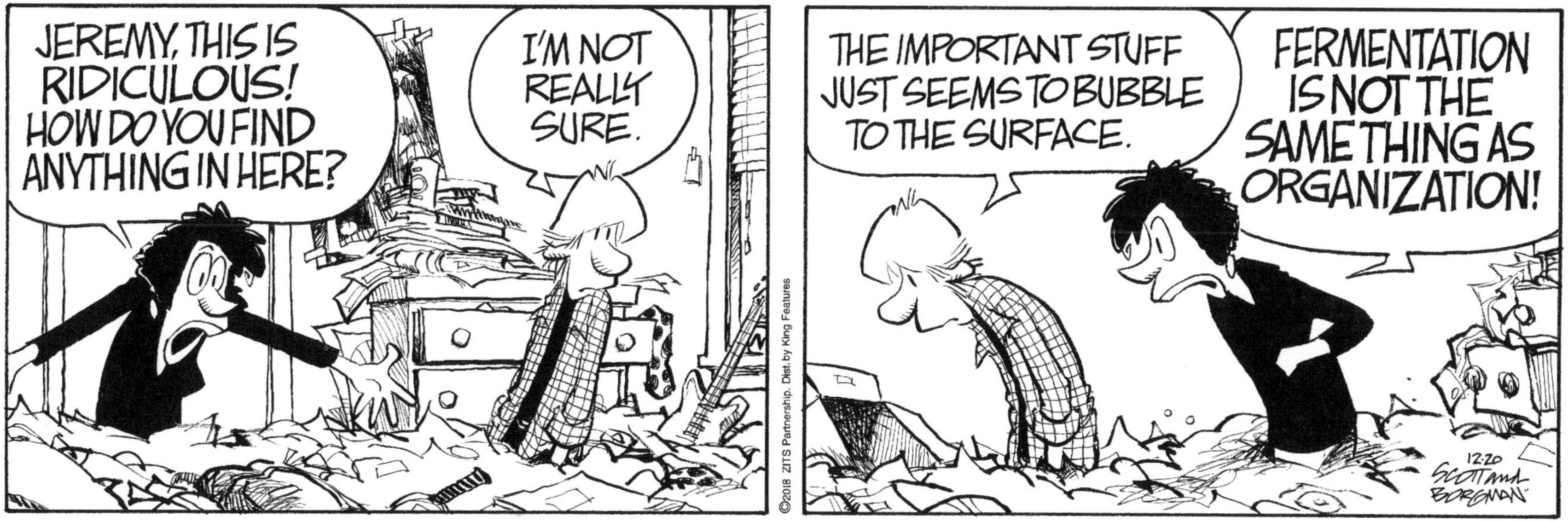
JEREMY, THIS IS RIDICULOUS! HOW DO YOU FIND ANYTHING IN HERE?
I'M NOT REALLY SURE.
©2018 ZITS Partnership. Dist. by King Features
THE IMPORTANT STUFF JUST SEEMS TO BUBBLE TO THE SURFACE.
FERMENTATION IS NOT THE SAME THING AS ORGANIZATION!
12·20
SCOTT and BORGMAN

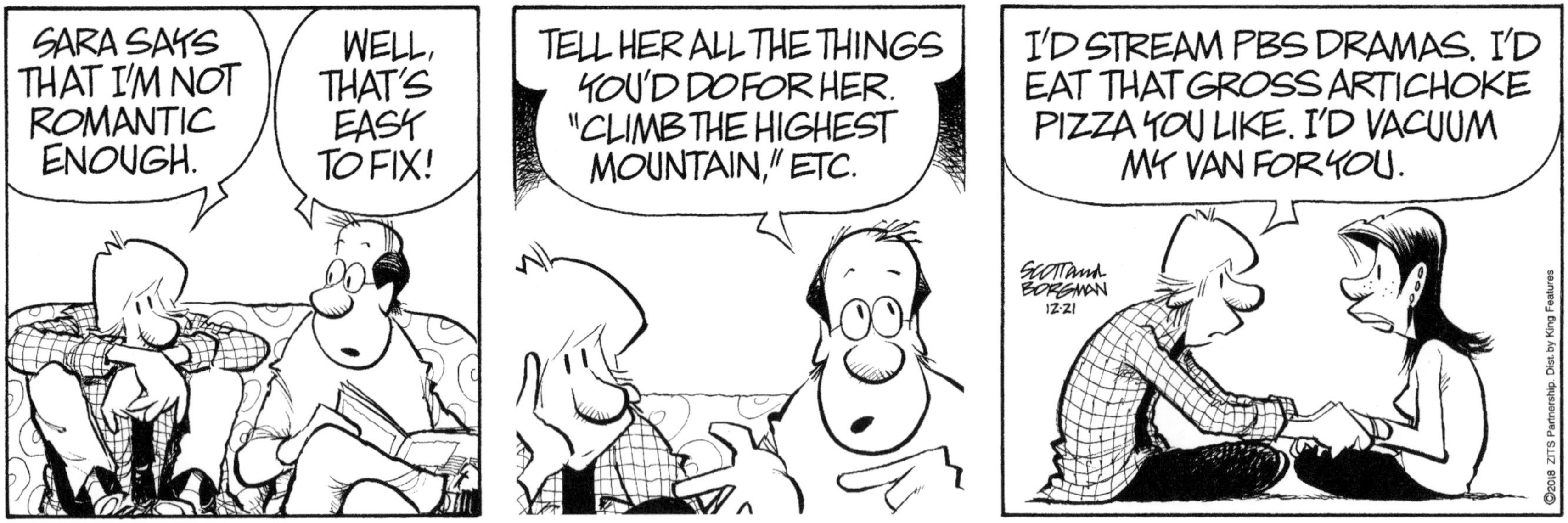
SARA SAYS THAT I'M NOT ROMANTIC ENOUGH.
WELL, THAT'S EASY TO FIX!
TELL HER ALL THE THINGS YOU'D DO FOR HER. "CLIMB THE HIGHEST MOUNTAIN," ETC.
I'D STREAM PBS DRAMAS. I'D EAT THAT GROSS ARTICHOKE PIZZA YOU LIKE. I'D VACUUM MY VAN FOR YOU.
SCOTT AND BORGMAN
12·21
©2018 ZITS Partnership. Dist. by King Features

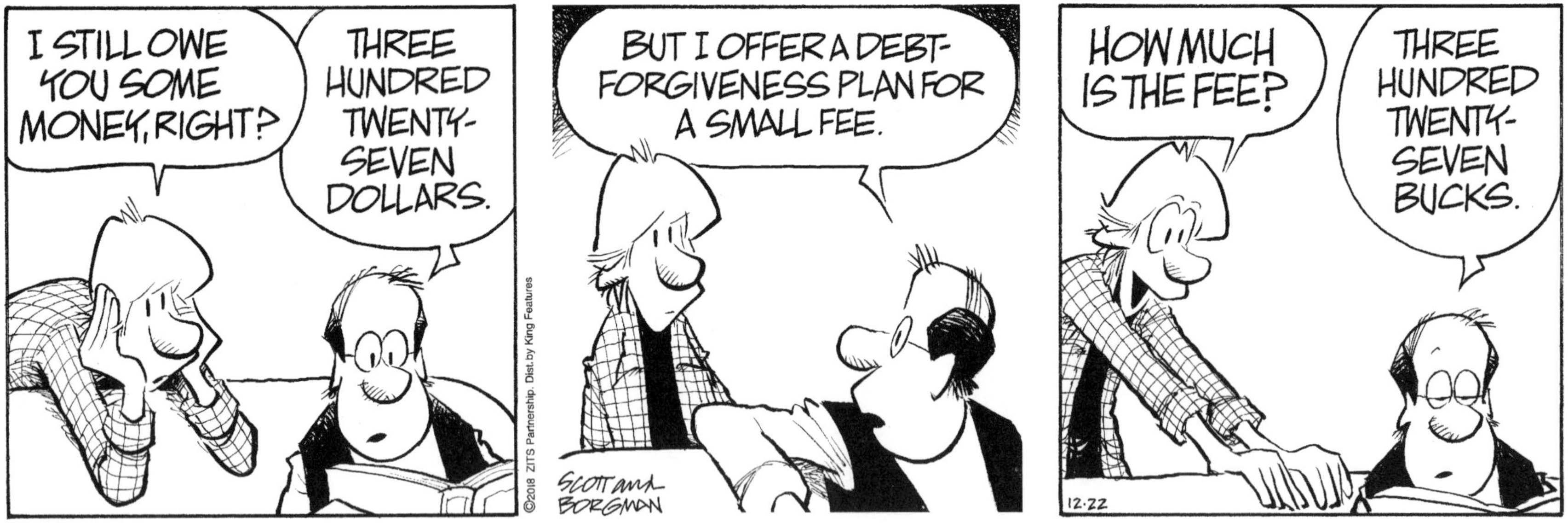
I STILL OWE YOU SOME MONEY, RIGHT?
THREE HUNDRED TWENTY-SEVEN DOLLARS.
©2018 ZITS Partnership. Dist. by King Features
BUT I OFFER A DEBT-FORGIVENESS PLAN FOR A SMALL FEE.
SCOTT AND BORGMAN
HOW MUCH IS THE FEE?
THREE HUNDRED TWENTY-SEVEN BUCKS.
12·22

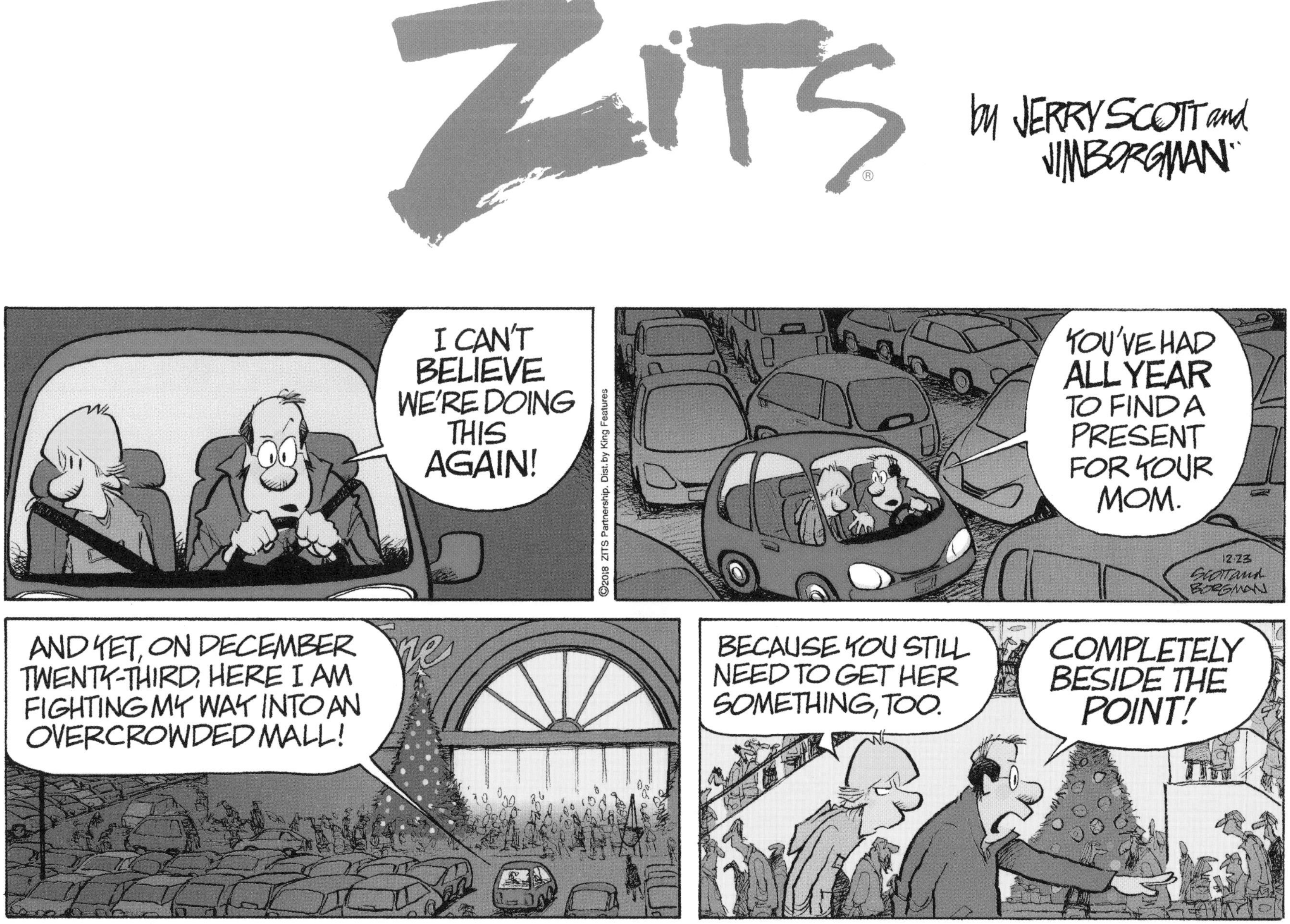
ZITS®
by JERRY SCOTT and JIM BORGMAN
I CAN'T BELIEVE WE'RE DOING THIS AGAIN!
©2018 ZITS Partnership. Dist. by King Features
YOU'VE HAD ALL YEAR TO FIND A PRESENT FOR YOUR MOM.
12-23 SCOTT and BORGMAN
AND YET, ON DECEMBER TWENTY-THIRD, HERE I AM FIGHTING MY WAY INTO AN OVERCROWDED MALL!
BECAUSE YOU STILL NEED TO GET HER SOMETHING, TOO.
COMPLETELY BESIDE THE POINT!

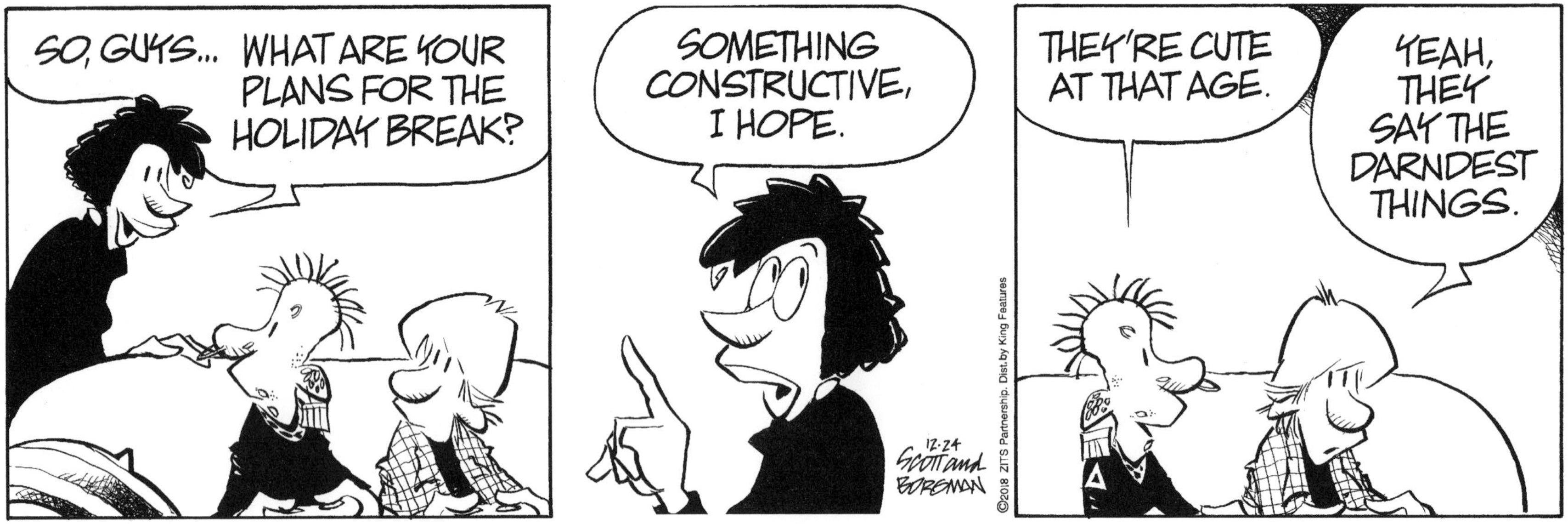
SO, GUYS... WHAT ARE YOUR PLANS FOR THE HOLIDAY BREAK?
SOMETHING CONSTRUCTIVE, I HOPE.
12·24
SCOTT and BORGMAN
©2018 ZITS Partnership. Dist. by King Features
THEY'RE CUTE AT THAT AGE.
YEAH, THEY SAY THE DARNDEST THINGS.

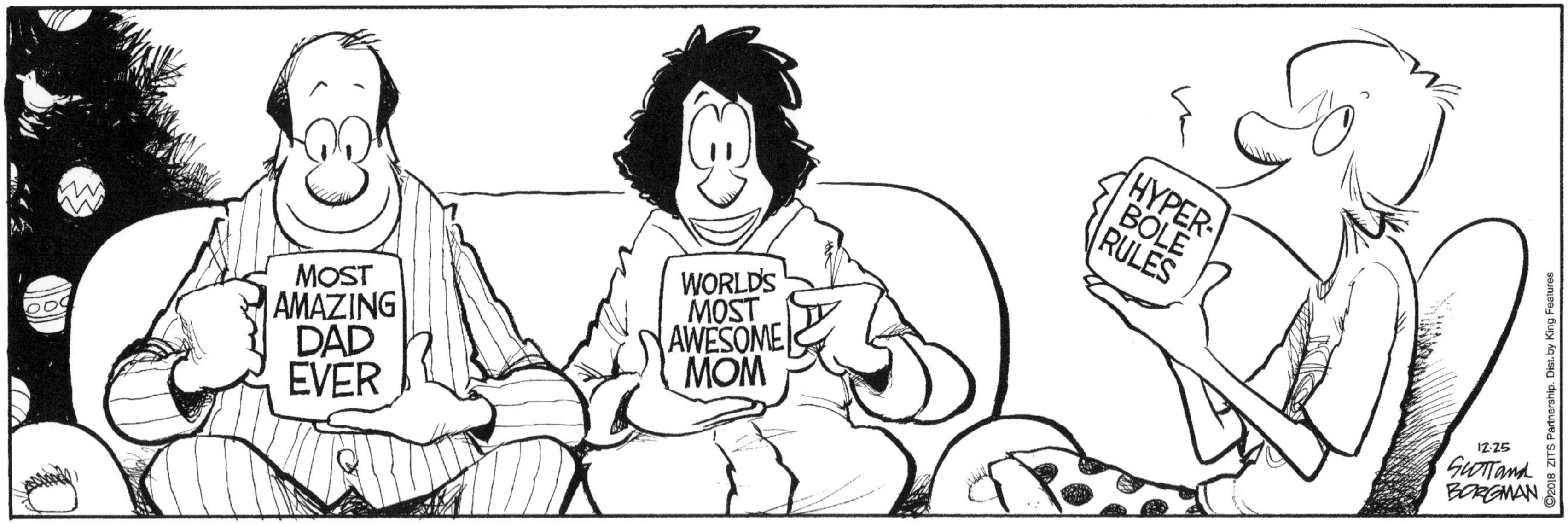
MOST AMAZING DAD EVER
WORLD'S MOST AWESOME MOM
HYPER-BOLE RULES
12·25
SCOTT and BORGMAN
©2018 ZITS Partnership. Dist. by King Features

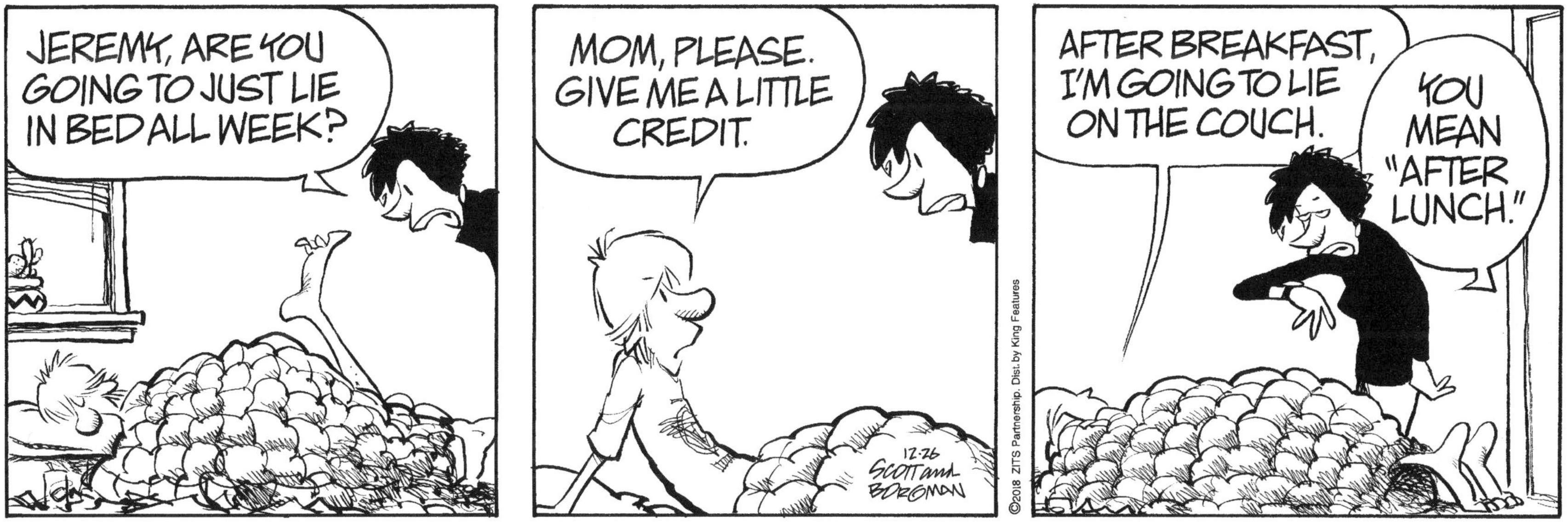
JEREMY, ARE YOU GOING TO JUST LIE IN BED ALL WEEK?
MOM, PLEASE. GIVE ME A LITTLE CREDIT.
12·26 SCOTT and BORGMAN
©2018 ZITS Partnership. Dist. by King Features
AFTER BREAKFAST, I'M GOING TO LIE ON THE COUCH.
YOU MEAN "AFTER LUNCH."

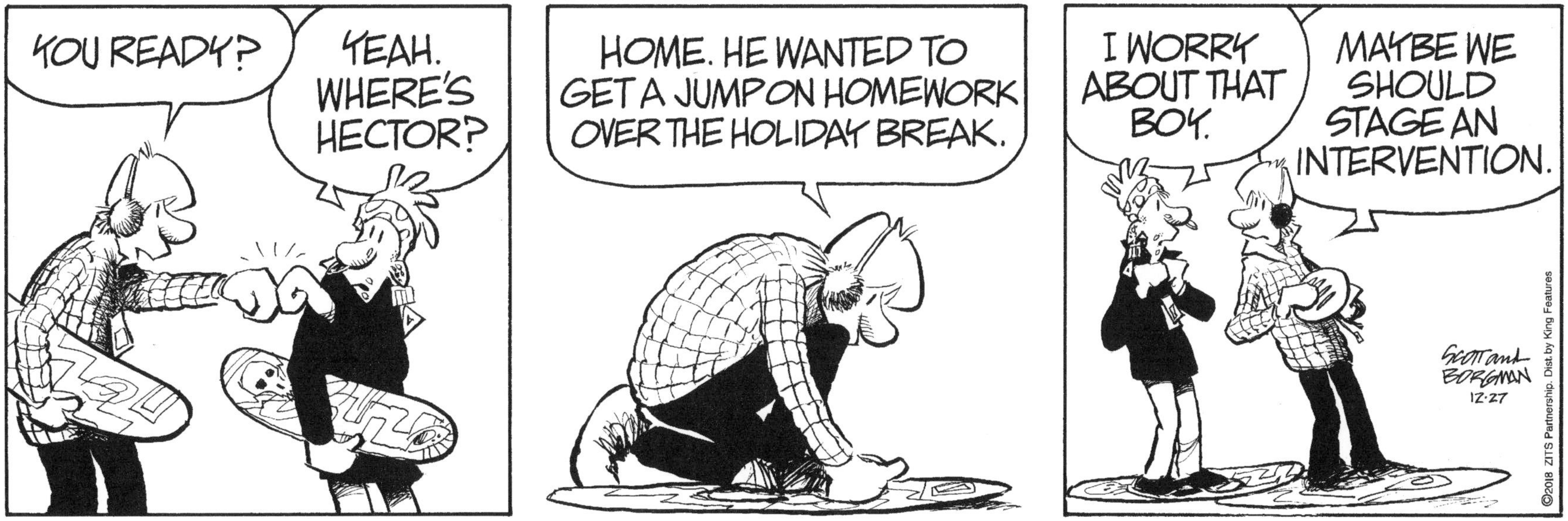
YOU READY?
YEAH. WHERE'S HECTOR?
HOME. HE WANTED TO GET A JUMP ON HOMEWORK OVER THE HOLIDAY BREAK.
I WORRY ABOUT THAT BOY.
MAYBE WE SHOULD STAGE AN INTERVENTION.
SCOTT and BORGMAN 12·27
©2018 ZITS Partnership. Dist. by King Features

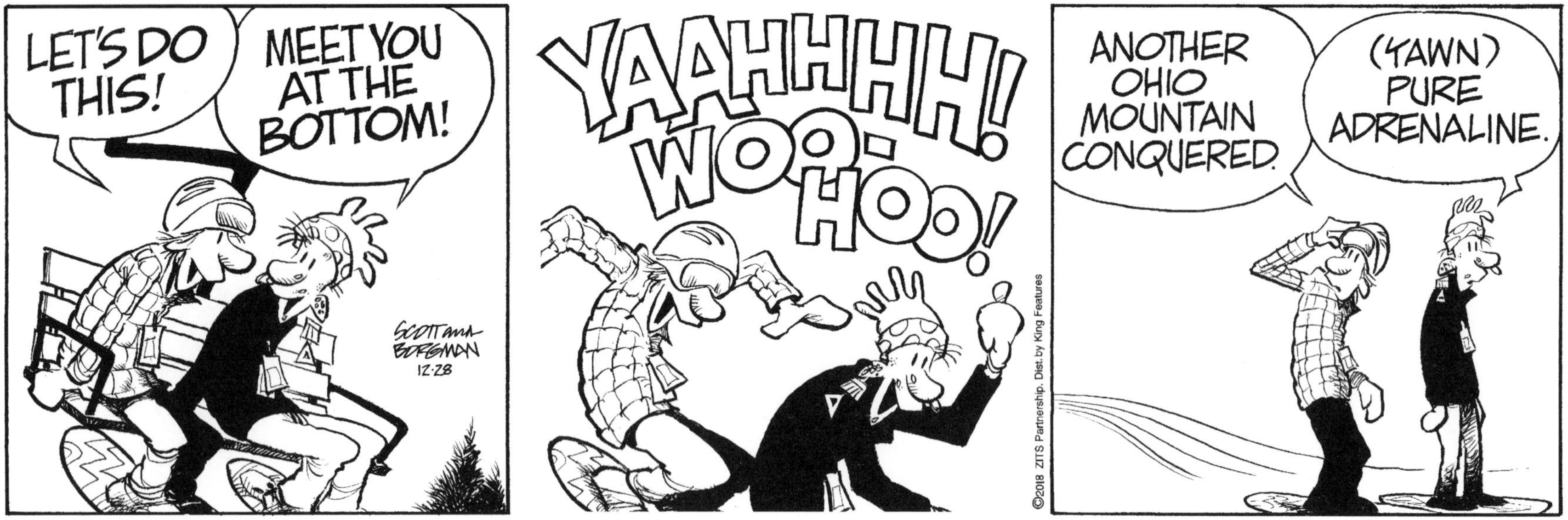
LET'S DO THIS!
MEET YOU AT THE BOTTOM!
SCOTT and BORGMAN 12·28
YAAHHHH! WOO-HOO!
©2018 ZITS Partnership. Dist. by King Features
ANOTHER OHIO MOUNTAIN CONQUERED.
(YAWN) PURE ADRENALINE.

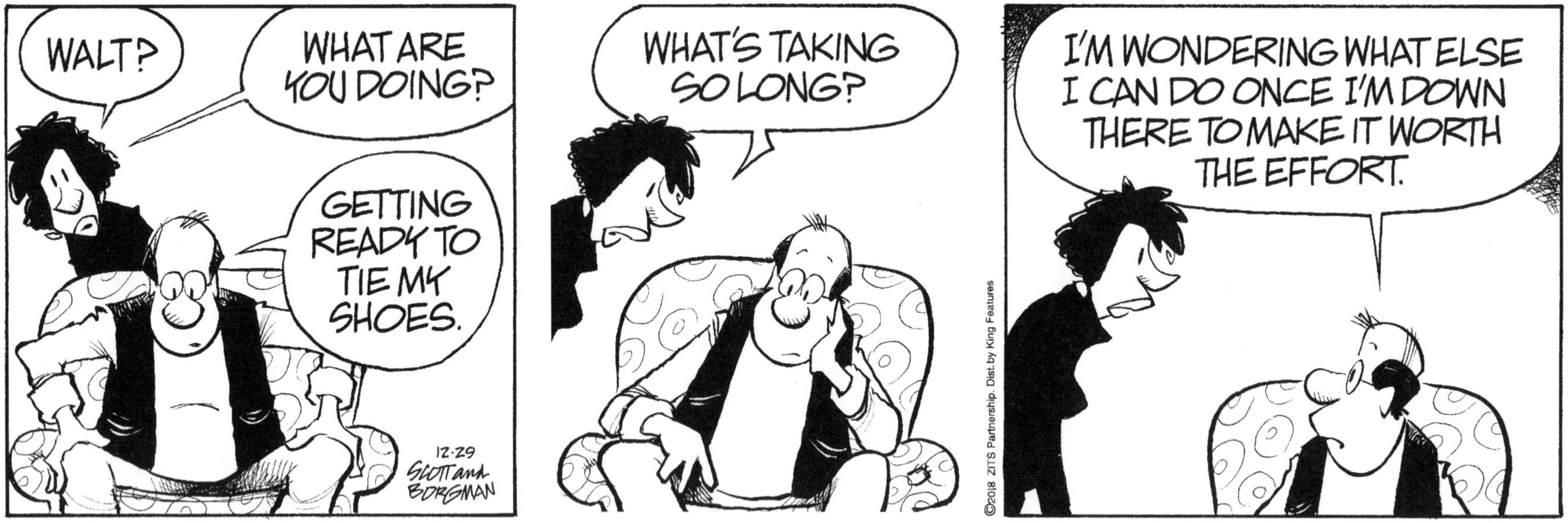
WALT?
WHAT ARE YOU DOING?
GETTING READY TO TIE MY SHOES.
12·29 SCOTT and BORGMAN
WHAT'S TAKING SO LONG?
©2018 ZITS Partnership. Dist. by King Features
I'M WONDERING WHAT ELSE I CAN DO ONCE I'M DOWN THERE TO MAKE IT WORTH THE EFFORT.

Zits

by JERRY SCOTT and JIM BORGMAN

NEW YEAR'S EVE IS TOMORROW NIGHT, BABY!
HOW DOES THIS SOUND?
FANCY DINNER... CHAMPAGNE...
©2018 ZITS Partnership. Dist. by King Features
...DANCING INTO THE WEE HOURS...
..."AULD LANG SYNE"...
2019, HERE WE COME!
Z
HE'LL BE IN BED BY 9:30.
YEAH, YOUR DAD TALKS A GOOD PARTY.
SCOTT and BORGMAN 12·30

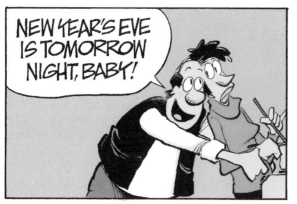

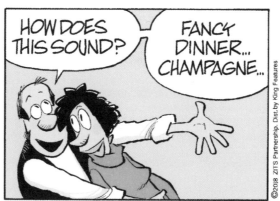

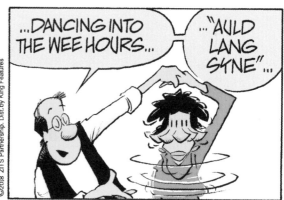

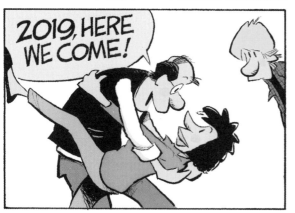

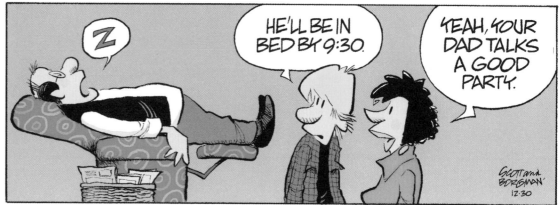

Zits® is syndicated internationally by King Features Syndicate, Inc.
For information, write King Features Syndicate, Inc., 300 West Fifty-Seventh Street, New York, New York 10019.

Andrews McMeel Publishing
a division of Andrews McMeel Universal
1130 Walnut Street, Kansas City, Missouri 64106
www.andrewsmcmeel.com

20 21 22 23 24 SDB 10 9 8 7 6 5 4 3 2 1

ISBN: 978-1-5248-5227-6

Library of Congress Control Number: 2020933206

Editor: Lucas Wetzel
Art Director: Holly Swayne
Production Manager: Chuck Harper
Production Editor: Amy Strassner

ATTENTION: SCHOOLS AND BUSINESSES

Andrews McMeel books are available at quantity discounts with bulk purchase for educational, business, or sales promotional use
For information, please e-mail the Andrews McMeel Publishing Special Sales Department: specialsales@amuniversal.com.

zitscomics.com • facebook.com/zitscomics • instagram.com/zitsguys